Educational Research

An African approach

Educational Research

An African approach

Edited by **Chinedu Okeke** • **Micheal van Wyk**

OXFORD
UNIVERSITY PRESS
SOUTHERN AFRICA

OXFORD
UNIVERSITY PRESS

Oxford University Press is a department of the University of Oxford.
It furthers the University's objective of excellence in research, scholarship,
and education by publishing worldwide. Oxford is a registered trade mark of
Oxford University Press in the UK and in certain other countries

Published in South Africa by
Oxford University Press Southern Africa (Pty) Limited

Vasco Boulevard, Goodwood, N1 City, P O Box 12119, Cape Town,
South Africa

© Oxford University Press Southern Africa (Pty) Ltd 2015

Educational Research

ISBN 978 0 19 040913 5

Typeset in Janson Text LT Std Roman 10pt on 12pt
Printed on 70 gsm woodfree paper

Acknowledgements
Publishing Manager: Alida Terblanche
Publisher: Marisa Montemarano
Development Editor: Annette de Villiers
Project Manager: Kelly Williams
Editor: Catherine Damerell
Designer: Gisela Strydom
Indexer: Michel Cozien
Typesetter: Baseline Publishing Services
Cover design: Sharna Sammy
Printed and bound by ABC Press, Cape Town
123467

Contents

Foreword

During the many years that I have taught educational research methodology and have been involved in research mentorship, I have always felt the need for a research methodology text which does two things: firstly, it situates our educational research enterprise firmly within the African context; and secondly, it can be effectively used in research methodology workshops. The publication of *Educational research: an African perspective* is a matter of real academic joy to me, because the book comprehensively answers these needs.

To fully understand and appreciate this new book's focus on the African context for educational research, readers are advised to read Chapter 1 thoroughly. Professor Micheal van Wyk eloquently sets the scene with his elucidation of Afrocentricity (as opposed to Eurocentricity) at the core of a new paradigm in research methodology. Afrocentricity expresses a perspective that "locates the African people at the centre of any investigation" (p. 6), with close reference to the African identity, cultural ideology, and history. Throughout the book, information and tasks are situated in familiar, identifiable or local settings, so that students and teachers will immediately feel 'at home' in their engagement with the text.

The book's second great merit is its interactive mode of text presentation. The text is divided into four main sections, with thematically grouped chapters covering the philosophy of research, data collection methods, fieldwork data analysis, and research report writing. Each chapter follows a pattern, starting with key concepts, learning outcomes, and a practical and thematic case study, and then moving through a interactive presentation of the main text, with many reflective and thought-provoking questions, to the closing activities which apply and consolidate learning. Throughout each chapter's text, students are appropriately challenged to reflect and think critically, to analyse their own enquiry approach and topic. This pattern of engagement enables individual students to study the book without lecturer guidance. However, the real benefit of this approach is its value in presenting workshops on any of the 30 research theory and methodology topics addressed. The book is a real asset for research orientation workshops, particularly for Master's and PhD students.

Over the years, a substantial array of meritorious research methodology textbooks has become available to local educational researchers. Some prominently used ones are also of South African origin, but this new title fills a particular outstanding need, as indicated above, and does so with distinction. I foresee its widespread use, and consequently, a strong contribution to the overall quality of educational research in South Africa and the African continent.

Gerrit D. Kamper
College of Education
University of South Africa

Preface

Educational research: an African approach brings together in one single text the basic rudiments of research in a way that will assist university postgraduate students, emerging researchers and postdoctoral fellows alike, who are engaged in the planning, designing, conducting and reporting of research findings. In addition, the many case studies, examples and critical reflective activities facilitate novice researchers' understanding of how to apply research tools in practice. This book represents an innovative approach to research in that it intends to address basic research principles and practices in a manner not yet covered by any other research textbook by African authors. Experience has shown that African research students studying in African universities are faced with many difficulties in the conducting of research and with the reporting of their research findings. African universities (including South African universities) are under pressure to increase and improve research output and the quality of African scholarship, and this book is designed to support these objectives.

The book is divided into four parts: **Part 1** prepares the way by looking at the underpinning *philosophy* of research and lays the theoretical foundations of the text. In Chapter 1 **Afrocentricity**, as a paradigm informing research methodology, is justified and the philosophical considerations of this paradigm are explored. The chapter also describes the **Afrocentric research canons** as important research principles from an African perspective which form the impetus of this book. Other important issues covered in the chapter are the role of a researcher from an African perspective, and locating Afrocentric research in the enquiry domain. If you have little or no previous knowledge of this philosophy you may find this chapter rather daunting, but you are encouraged to tackle it, just as you are urged to do when you read about other paradigms in the later chapters of this book. Chapters 2 and 3 identify the distinguishing characteristics, criteria and methodologies of **positivism** and **interpretivism**, as philosophies of research. Chapter 4 on critical research gives an exposition of what is involved in understanding and engaging in transformative action research. This chapter explains **critical theory** as a research philosophy and shows you the process and procedures of conducting action research for change, in your specific study. Chapter 5 looks at developing sensitivity towards questions of gender within disciplines through **feminist research** and indigenous knowledge systems (IKS). It unpacks the ontological and epistemological considerations from a **feminist philosophy** of research. The chapter differentiates between traditions of feminist research, discusses the issues in conversing with women towards interpreting women's own unique stories. In Chapters 6 and 7 the importance of values and **ethics** in the research process is highlighted. Chapter 6 conceptualises **objectivity** and **subjectivity** as important constructs in research. Further, this chapter discusses the challenges and demands on the researcher in conducting ethically reflexive research, while Chapter 7 explores ethics from a human sciences research perspective. Knowing about the major ethical values and issues in conducting research involving human participants can help you to understand the importance of ethical considerations in planning your own research study.

Part 2 deals with *planning, designing and conducting educational research*, in particular, doing a **literature review** (Chapter 8). Where to begin with a literature study is often a challenge for many new postgraduate students and novice researchers, but this chapter provides guidelines and components for getting started. It also shows you how to manage your references and the critical skill of detecting good and poor literature reviews, and possible gaps in existing research literature. In Chapter 9 we look at the **research process** in terms of the steps or stages involved, to inform you of the need for a rigorous approach in your study. This chapter further deals with the importance of doing a literature survey, the formulation of your hypothesis, choosing a search methodology, including research methods, design, collection of data, analysis of your data, interpretation of data and drawing conclusions. Another fundamental consideration of any research methodology is the research design. Chapter 10 describes the various research designs: quantitative, qualitative and mixed methods approaches. It discusses types of **research design** for the purposes of selecting one appropriate to your research enquiry, the benefits of various research designs, and finally, the steps in planning and implementing each design. Chapters 11 and 12 highlight crucial issues of **variables, validity, reliability, trustworthiness** and **generalisability** for all three research designs. Another important issue is the logic of **sampling** as part of the research design, which is addressed in Chapter 13. Of course, whichever research methodology you choose to use, none can be successful without sound and reliable data collection instruments and methods. In Chapter 14, we look at one of the most commonly used research instruments, the **survey research method**. The chapter unpacks the purpose of surveys, how to construct a good survey, how to design valid and reliable survey questions for collecting data. Chapter 15 then exposes you to **experimental methods and data collection**. This chapter is aligned to Chapters 10 and 11 which focus on quantitative, qualitative and mixed methods approaches. Another research method increasingly used is the **observation method** which is explored in Chapter 16. This type of data collection method is associated with qualitative research design and includes different types of instruments such as participant and non-participant observations, the benefits and disadvantages of which are discussed. In conclusion, this chapter explains how to record observation data using field notes for your qualitative research design. **Interviews** are enormously useful and widely used in research but require the researcher to acquire a wide range of specialised skills for conducting interviews, which Chapter 17 takes you through. This chapter describes different types of interviews, and gives practical advice on planning and conducting interviews, and on organising and analysing the data collected. Chapter 18 discusses the use of the **questionnaire approach** in data collection. Questionnaires gather data using sets of carefully formulated questions which may be structured in closed, open-ended instruments, or a combination of both. You are taken through the steps in designing, constructing and administering a questionnaire that might suit your research purpose. Chapter 19 explores the planning and implementing of the **focus group discussion**, as a qualitative method, currently a popular data gathering method amongst researchers. Focus group discussion, as a qualitative research instrument for data collection, is about stimulating debate and creating rich 'voices' and perspectives from participants throughout the investigation. In Chapter 20 we look at the selection, analysis and use of **secondary sources of data**. These types of data are characterised by the availability of existing data from earlier studies. It is imperative to consider ethical issues in the use of secondary data. Sometimes we use secondary sources when it is problematic to access primary sources. Chapter 21 closes Part 2, focusing on the pilot study. The chapter aims to help you understand the reasons and benefits for using a pilot study during your initial investigation. The chapter provides reasons, advantages and disadvantages for conducting a **pilot study**, while explaining how you should treat the findings of the pilot study.

Having decided on your research design and the methods for gathering data, **Part 3** now takes you through *how to analyse fieldwork data*. After collecting fieldwork data, Chapter 22 and 23 deal with doing the quantitative data analysis using either **descriptive** or

inferential statistics. These chapters explain the measurement of data and graphing quantitative data analysis. This can be a great challenge if you have not developed the appropriate analytical interpretation skills. An important tool is using Microsoft Excel to create descriptive and inferential data analysis. Chapter 24 supports you in starting to use the **statistical package for the social sciences** (SPSS) to analyse your fieldwork data. Postgraduate students and novice researchers may find the application of SPSS a challenge since you need to get to grips with a specialised software program. This chapter guides your entry to using the SPSS tool to compute your data, with a step-by-step explanation. Chapter 25 moves on to explain how to deal with a **qualitative data analysis** process. It looks at the uses of constant comparative analysis, thematic analysis, domain analysis, componential analysis, and software packages such as ATLAS.ti; MAXODA and NVIVO.

Finally, **Part 4** focuses on *reporting and disseminating research findings.* In this section, we look at how to present your data in way that enhances their credibility and effect. Chapters 26 and 27 look at different types of research reports, **quantitative** and **qualitative research reports**, respectively. These two chapters provide the basic steps in preparing your research findings for presentation. In Chapter 28, a crucial issue in academic writing, **plagiarism**, is discussed, as well as how to do proper **citations and referencing** of the research literature. This chapter explores the reasons for plagiarism, what constitutes plagiarism, and strategies to avoid plagiarism. It provides guidelines to help you identify and solve plagiarism challenges while finding your own academic voice. Chapter 29 advises on the **essentials of academic writing**, including the use of appropriate language and writing style for your intended audience, and how to coherently and cohesively structure the reporting of your research findings. Finally, Chapter 30 explores the science and art of scholarly **writing for publication**, by specifying guidelines for writing an article for particular kinds of publications. The chapter takes you through the steps in developing a title and abstract, identifying keywords, formulating the introduction, critically reflecting a complete literature review, constructing the research methodology, capturing the main findings, discussing them, and drawing conclusions.

We have collected information and designed this book so that you can use it as a research manual that explains the theoretical underpinnings of research philosophies, research design, different types of methods for gathering data, and how to disseminate your findings in an academic report for publication. It is recommended that you read through the book, focusing on the key concepts and learning objectives formulated at the beginning of each chapter. In addition, try to get a feeling about the different sections, especially regarding research philosophies, research design, different types of methods, and other important skills, attributes and issues that go to making you a competent and confident researcher. Throughout your research project, try to revisit some of the topics if you find you need further clarity. Each chapter provides a range of self-assessment and consolidation activities to further your understanding of the content of the chapter. Consult the list of further readings in the bibliography at the end of each chapter to take your understanding still further.

We hope you find this book a valuable companion throughout your research journey and that it helps you to produce excellent research outputs as a postgraduate student and emerging scholar in Africa.

Micheal van Wyk and Chinedu Okeke
Editors

Editors

PROFESSOR CHINEDU I.O. OKEKE

Chinedu Okeke is an Associate Professor and Leader of ECD research in the Faculty of Education at the University of Fort Hare, South Africa. He has also taught at universities in Swaziland and Nigeria. His interest in qualitative research culminated in a Vice Chancellor's Prize-winning doctoral thesis at the University of Nigeria, Nsukka in 2003. He also holds a Master's degree in Educational Studies and a Bachelor of Arts in Educational Foundations and History. His main research areas include the sociology of early childhood education and parental participation in the education of their children. Specifically, his research concerns how young people develop during their education studies from early childhood up until their late teens, and in particular, how their personal goals and life experiences can enable them to transcend the potential that appears to be laid out for them by their socio-economic origins. In recent years, social capital theory appears to assume a new role in his research. He is more interested in the analysis of social capital in the creation of human capital by James Coleman. Seeing that a functional ECD policy framework and programmes of action is a social capital mechanism, this particular theoretical perspective has been fundamental in his recent personal research as well as those of his postgraduate students. Professor Okeke and his postgraduate students are currently applying social capital theory to a number of different parental involvement programmes in ECD studies that try to explicate various influences on the capacity of fathers to effectively participate in the early education of their children up until the age of nine years old. He has published numerous local and international papers, books and book chapters, and has spoken at various national and international conferences on issues relating to higher education, curriculum, research methods, research supervision and sociology of education generally.

PROFESSOR MICHEAL VAN WYK

Micheal van Wyk is a Professor in the Department of Curriculum and Instructional studies in the School of Teacher Education at the College of Education, University of South Africa (UNISA). He has more than 29 years of teaching experience both at primary, secondary and higher education levels. He is a National Research Foundation rated researcher in Economics Education. He has published more than 42 research articles in accredited journals in the last seven years, reading 49 papers at educational conferences, written five academic books and 10 chapters in research books. He has delivered several keynote addresses at various teacher education conferences. He was awarded the 2013 Chancellor's Award for Excellence in Research for Education, Research and Innovation Week at UNISA. He also received an award for Outstanding Education Research Paper (International conference, Dublin, Ireland, 2010). In 2011, he received an award for the Best Researcher in the Education category at the Faculty of Education, University of the Free State. Prof van Wyk is an international reviewer for several international journals as well for South African journals. He served on several academic boards and various committees in the College of Education at UNISA. He co-edited, with Professors C.I.O. Okeke and N. Phasha, a book entitled: *Schooling, Society and Inclusive Education* published by Oxford University Press Southern Africa (OUPSA). He is a former primary and secondary school principal. He serves as an international academic board member for the *International Journal of Educational Sciences*. Prof van Wyk is the editor-in-chief for the *African Journal of Pedagogy and Curriculum*. His research interests are curriculum studies, cooperative learning, technology-integrated teaching and learning strategies, in particular, using social media in the classroom, Indigenous Knowledge (IK), social entrepreneurship and Economics education.

Notes on contributors

PROF OLADELE AROWOLO is an African Research Fellow and Chief Research Specialist: Impact Assessment, at the Human Sciences Research Council, Pretoria, South Africa. He holds a PhD. in Demography from the University of Pennsylvania, Philadelphia, USA (1973). Before joining the HSRC in March 2013, he was a Professor of Sociology and the Head of the Department of Social Sciences at Lagos State University, Lagos, Nigeria, where he also served as the Dean of the Faculty of Law and Humanities from 1984 to 1988. He also served as Senior Lecturer in the Sociology Department at the University of Ibadan, Nigeria (1973-1984). Prof Arowolo taught undergraduate and post-graduate level courses in Social Research Methods; Social Statistics; and Population Dynamics. He later joined the United Nations and worked mainly as Chief Technical Advisor in Population Planning and Development. His areas of research interest include: population dynamics and associated factors. He has published research works widely and his current research work relates to South Africa and the "Demographic Transition" possibilities.

DR FRED E.K. BAKKABULINDI is an Associate Professor of Research, Statistics and Evaluation in the East African School of Higher Education Studies and Development, College of Education and External Studies, Makerere University, Uganda. He holds a Bachelor of Statistics and Postgraduate Diploma in Computer Science from Makerere University; a Master of Science degree from Southampton University; and a PhD from Makerere University. He has taught research, statistics and related subjects since 1988 at such universities as Makerere, Uganda Management Institute, Makerere University Business School, Uganda Martyrs, Nkumba, Kisubi Brothers and Kampala International.

PROF BONGANI D. BANTWINI is a Professor of Schooling (primary and secondary) in the School of Human and Social Sciences for Education at North West University, Potchefstroom Campus. He received his Master's and PhD degrees in Science Education from the University of Illinois at Urbana-Champaign, USA. He has taught at universities both in the USA and South Africa and has also taught at various school levels, from primary to high school. He has worked for a non-governmental organization (NGO) in the capacity of a teacher trainer and as an independent consultant conducting teacher training in South Africa and the USA. He has held various positions as a researcher both in the USA and South Africa and has conducted several large scale research and evaluation studies and as well as writing successful grant proposals. His areas of research interest include: science education, trends and reforms in science education, professional development of science teachers, the role of the school district and policy implementation.

DR CHARLES CHIKUNDA is a Stakeholder Facilitator and Professional Development Trainer: Natural Resources Management, and Basin Resilience Planner at Award, an NGO based in Limpopo. His work entails project design, research design and stakeholder facilitation, professional support, skills development, and professional training in water and biodiversity management. He is a science teacher by profession and has been in teacher education since 1997, working in Zimbabwe and South Africa. At Rhodes University, he was involved in coordinating the in-service teacher development programme, as well as lecturing in Science Education and Environmental Education. His research interests include: sustainability and professional teacher development, gender and science education.

PROF GEORGE CHITIYO is an Associate Professor of Educational Research at Tennessee Technological University, Cookeville, USA. He maintains a very active scholarly agenda, working mainly in the area of the psychosocial aspects of HIV/AIDS in Southern Africa, as well as the economics of health and higher education both in the USA and Zimbabwe. He has authored and co-authored more than 20 scholarly papers published in several reputable journals. He has also presented some of his work at numerous regional and international forums.

PROF MORGAN CHITIYO is an Associate Professor and Director of the Special Education Program at Duquesne University, Pittsburgh, USA. Prof Chitiyo is also the editor of the *Journal of The International Association of Special Education* and serves on the editorial board of the *Journal of Research in Special Educational Needs*. He has authored and co-authored three books, two book chapters and over 30 refereed research manuscripts published in reputable journals. He has also presented his research at several regional, national and international conferences. His research interests include: applied behaviour analysis, positive behaviour supports, autism, and special education issues in Africa.

MR FRANCIS E. DAKWA is a Senior Lecturer in the Department of Special Needs Education at the Great Zimbabwe University, Masvingo, Southern Zimbabwe. He has written several articles on disability and special educational needs in refereed journals. He has authored two poetry books: *Poems for the young* and *Poems for couples* published in the USA. In addition, he has contributed to several book chapters and co-authored academic modules at Bachelor's and Masters' levels for the Zimbabwe Open University. He is an external examiner for special needs education courses for the Reformed Church University and the Zimbabwe Open University. Currently, he is co-authoring and editing a book entitled *Reflections on Disability* which examines disability issues from an African perspective. Mr Dakwa has spent more than 43 years in the education sector as an institutional head and principal, education officer and deputy chief education officer of special needs education in the Ministry of Education, Sports and Culture in Zimbabwe. He has over 20 years of university experience to his credit and has directed private colleges and companies.

DR MELANIE LEE DRAKE is a Lecturer and Researcher in the School of General and Continuing Education (SGCE), University of Fort Hare, East London Campus. She has taught at both public and private primary schools in South Africa, while her doctoral research explored education in rural and township communities of South Africa. She has recently moved back to South Africa after five years abroad in New Zealand, where she lectured and completed her PhD at the University of Auckland, New Zealand, as an International Commonwealth Scholar. Her areas of interest include: values education, school practice, school leadership, teacher motivation, organizational development and qualitative research methods.

DR GEORGIANNA DUARTE is a Professor in Early Childhood Education in the Department of Teaching, Learning and Innovation, College of Education, University of Texas, Brownsville, USA. Dr Duarte has been engaged in research in the areas of play, migrant education and international cultures. She has actively examined the perceptions of children and how they view their rights as defined by the Articles of the UN Rights of the Child. She has previously acted as a Head Start Teacher, Administrator, National Reviewer and Consultant. She has been involved in international work for 23 years with over 13 years of collaboration in Peru. Dr Duarte has written for international journals and, most recently, she wrote two articles about the importance of fostering outdoor play. She has co-authored and edited a book on mentoring diverse populations. She has also recently completed an edited volume on children's play as well as co-edited an international book on education diplomacy, published in June 2015.

PROF NTOMBOZUKO STUNKY DUKU is an Associate Professor in the Faculty of Education, University of Fort Hare, South Africa. She teaches pre-service, in-service and postgraduate programmes. She is also responsible for coordinating the faculty postgraduate studies (Master's and PhD). She has been involved in a number of research and capacity building projects including the Imbewu Project in which she was responsible for training SGBs and Principals, commissioned by the CEPD (Centre for Education Policy Development, Evaluation and Management) on engaging communities in educational development through the CLINGs (Community Literacy and Numeracy Groups). She participated in a comparative analysis of educational inclusion and exclusion in India as part of her doctorate, which she completed in 2006. Most recently, she was a member of a national research team that carried out a feasibility and impact study of the Advanced Certificate in Education (ACE) for school principals in South Africa. Her areas of research and publication include: policy planning, development, monitoring and evaluation, school governance, multiculturalism education, African indigenous theories in education, and issues of access and success in education.

PROF NOSISI FEZA is a Director of the Institute of Science and Technology Education, University of South Africa, Pretoria. She has obtained a PhD in Mathematics Education from the State University of New York, Buffalo, New York, as a Fulbright scholar. In 2008, she was a recipient of the inaugural Leroy and Margaret H. Callahan award for a promising researcher. Her PhD dissertation was entitled: *Being a sheep in a "cattle's kraal" does not make you a cow: Black students' thought processes in measurement activity.* This work won her an Emerging Diversity Scholar Award from the National Center for Institutional Diversity in Michigan in 2009. She turned her dissertation into a book entitled: *My culture my learning capital my tool for thought.* She initiated a collaborative mathematics education project between the University of KwaZulu-Natal and the State University of New York at Buffalo from June 2009 to December 2011. The title of the project was: *Training African female teachers for FET mathematics in South Africa* (funded by USAid). The aim of this project was to empower female teachers of UKZN. She worked for four years at the Human Sciences Research Council (HSRC) as a Senior Research Specialist conducting mathematics education research informing policies.

DR EMILY GANGA is a Psychology of Education Lecturer and Researcher within the Faculty of Education and the Department of Educational Foundations at Great Zimbabwe University. Her research interests include: child and adolescent development and learning. She has presented and published extensively on issues concerning the development and learning of children to include orphans and vulnerable children (OVC), HIV/AIDS, poverty and gender issues in education.

PROF VELISIWE GASA is an Associate Professor in the Office of Graduate Studies and Research, College of Education, University of South Africa, Pretoria. She has published a number of book chapters, conference proceedings and papers in accredited and peer-reviewed journals. She has also presented a number of academic papers in national and international conferences. She serves on the editorial boards of different academic journals and has been involved in a sustained peer review of journal articles internationally as well as nationally. She also serves on different university committees. Her research areas include: learners' aggressive behavior, education for peace, socio-economic barriers to learning, inclusive leadership and school inclusivity, youth risk behaviours, alternative parenting, and incarcerated students.

PROF MISHACK T. GUMBO is a Professor in the Department of Science and Technology Education in the College of Education, University of South Africa, Pretoria. He holds the following qualifications: PhD in Technology Education (Vista University) in which he conducted research on indigenous technologies and curriculum; MEd in Technology Education (Rand Afrikaans University); MPhil in Applied Theology (University of Pretoria); BEd (Hons) (University of South Africa); BA (Vista University); UED (Vista University); International Certificate in Technology Education Secondary School (ORT-Step Institute). His areas of interest in research include: Technology teachers' pedagogical content knowledge, indigenous technologies as part of indigenous knowledge systems, multicultural education, distance education and e-learning.

PROF MUTENDWAHOTHE WALTER LUMADI is a Professor in Curriculum Development in the Department of Curriculum and Instructional Studies, School of Teacher Education, University of South Africa, Pretoria. He has a range of experience from secondary schools to institutions of higher learning in South Africa. He lectured the following Curriculum Studies modules at the University of Venda: Principles of Curriculum Design; Curriculum Development; Curriculum Management and Implementation; and Curriculum Research and Evaluation. He also lectured at master's and doctoral levels at North West University as well as serving as the Head of the Department for Curriculum Studies; a member of the senate; School Director and member of council. He has supervised more than 40 postgraduate students. He is a reviewer for a variety of journals and has published book chapters and more than 30 articles in accredited journals.

PROF PATRICK MAFORA is a Professor and Director of Regional Services in the Department of Tuition and Facilitation of Learning, University of South Africa, Pretoria. He holds an MA in Leadership in Educational Administration (*Cum Laude*); a DEd in Educational Management; and a postgraduate certificate in Business Administration. His research interests include: democracy, transformation and social justice issues in school governance and management and Human Resource Management in Education. He has published 15 peer reviewed journal articles and presented 18 papers at international and domestic conferences. When on a Fulbright fellowship, Prof Mafora received an outstanding academic achievement from Bradley University, USA. His article published in the *International Journal of Learning* 2012, received the Journal Award for the best of the top ten articles ranked by the journal's international editorial board.

PROF MNCENDISI C. MAPHALALA is an Associate Professor in the Department of Curriculum and Instructional Studies, College of Education, University of South Africa, Pretoria. Previously, he worked at the University of the Witwatersrand as an Institutional Researcher in the Strategic Planning Division (2010-2011). He has also been a lecturer in the Faculty of Education at the University of Zululand (2005-2008) teaching Social Sciences and Curriculum Studies to Bachelor of Education (BEd) and BEd Honours students respectively as well as supervising master's and doctoral students. He was appointed as a Manager for the Centre for Cooperative Education and Experiential Learning (CEEL) at the University of Zululand between 2008 and 2010. Before he joined the University of Zululand, he had been a teacher for 10 years in two different schools serving as the Head of Department and the Deputy Principal in the Department of Education in Kwa-Zulu Natal. His research interests include: curriculum studies, assessment of learning, educational management, experiential learning, and environmental education.

MS THANDOKAZI MASETI is a Lecturer in the Family Medicine Department and Researcher at the Centre for Rural Health, University of the Witwatersrand, Johannesburg. She was previously a junior researcher in the Education Skills Development (ESD) unit at the Human Sciences Research Council (HSRC). Prior to joining the ESD unit she was a Master's DST/NRF research intern based at HSRC in the Office of the Deputy CEO of Research where she provided support for the Research Coordination function while being involved in research projects. She completed her Master's degree in Research Psychology at the University of the Western Cape (UWC). She is also currently registered as an intern research psychologist with the Health Professions Council of South Africa (HPCSA). Ms Maseti's research interests include: feminist theory, gender and development, race and identity development, cultures and traditions of patriarchy and she is also currently researching and writing within the field of gender-based violence.

PROF THENJIWE MEYIWA, a South African National Research Foundation (NRF)-rated social scientist, is a Registrar of Durban University of Technology, Durban. She holds a PhD in Feminist Oral Studies from the University of Natal and an Mcom (Organisation and Systems Management) from the University of KwaZulu-Natal. Her areas of research interest include: feminist theory, self-study, indigenous knowledge, and cultural constructions of gender, contemporary human behavioural patterns, and the impact of HIV/AIDS on parenting, women and home care givers. She is a co-author and co-editor of a number of books including: *Freedom Sown in Blood: Memories of the Impi, Yamakhanda: An Indigenous Knowledge Systems Perspective* and *Gender in Context: Transnational gender perspectives.* She has worked in South Africa and internationally with organisations and research teams ranging from government organisations, universities and human rights' NGOs.

DR. EMMA L. MILLER is Director of Academic Affairs, University of Phoenix, McAllen, Texas, USA. She has been in higher education administration in the state of Texas for nearly 19 years. She has a PhD in Applied Management and Decision Science with a concentration in Leadership and Organizational Change from Walden University. In addition, she has been an adjunct professor in the areas of Computer Science, Business Administration and Applied Business Technology and has been engaged in service learning and research in the areas of organisational behavior, organisational change, mentoring, business ethics, and leadership. She also teaches for the University of Phoenix in the areas of Business Research, Quantitative Analysis for Business, Strategic Planning and Implementation, and Research Methods, Design, and Analysis. As a researcher, she has focused on mentoring examining how it relates to student retention and attrition and its impact on the institution. She has written in international journals and presented in international conferences.

PROF MAROPENG MODIBA is a Professor and Coordinator of Curriculum Studies, Department of Education and Curriculum Studies, University of Johannesburg, Johannesburg. Prof Modiba graduated with a BA, trained as a teacher and thereafter completed a BEd degree at the University of the North. She has studied for an MEd at the University of the Witwatersrand and an MA and PhD at Keele University. She taught at the University of the Witwatersrand (1994-2006) before joining the University of Johannesburg in 2007. Her teaching and research interests include: teacher professionalism and practice, curriculum literacy captured by studying classroom instructional practices, and curriculum theory. In addition, she has published articles and book chapters in these areas as well as being a member of journal editorial boards. Since 2007, her work has begun to focus beyond her country to countries such as Zimbabwe, Kenya and Swaziland.

MR NATHAN MOYO is a PhD candidate at the University of Johannesburg and a Lecturer in Curriculum Theory, Department of Curriculum Studies, Great Zimbabwe University, Zimbabwe. He graduated with Bachelor of Education and Master of Education degrees from the University of Zimbabwe. Prior to joining Great Zimbabwe University, he taught at secondary school level for 15 years. His thesis focuses on the teaching of secondary school History and is informed by the Critical Theory paradigm. He has published several articles on History education and policy as regards social justice and epistemic access in pedagogical relationships.

PROF JOHN K.E. MUBAZI is an Associate Professor in the Department of Economic Theory and Analysis at the School of Economics, College of Business and Management Sciences, Makerere University, Uganda. He holds a Bachelor's degree in Economics from Makerere University, a Master's degree in Economics from the University of Kent at Canterbury in England, and an MPhil in Advanced Economics and Quantitative Techniques from the United Nations University through the World Institute of Development Economic Research Centre at the Bangladesh Institute of Development Studies in Dhaka, Bangladesh. His doctorate in Social and Economic Studies was obtained from the University of Economics and Business, Vienna, Austria. He has taught Research Methods at bachelor's, master's, and doctoral levels at Makerere University. He has published with Cambridge University Press, UK; Makerere University Research Journal Mawazo, Makerere University; Scientific and Academic Publishing and American Journal of Economics, USA; and Lap Lambert Academic Publishing, Germany.

MR MUZWA MUKWAMBO is a Lecturer in Science and Mathematics Education, Faculty of Education, Universtiy of Namibia, Namibia. A holder of a Licentiate degree in Physics and Astronomy obtained at Enrique Jose Varon (La Habana in Cuba), a BEd in education and an MEd in science education obtained at Rhodes University in Grahamstown in South Africa. Since 1991 he has taught Physics and Mathematics in schools and colleges of education. He has presented research papers at SACHES conferences held at Rundu and Katima Mulilo Campuses. These are entitled, "Understanding the challenges of how trainee teachers source distilled water for practical work in science in under-resourced schools" and "Novice teachers' view about incorporation of indigenous knowledge: Implication for reforms towards a broad based practical curriculum in Caprivi Region of Namibia". He has also presented a paper at a DETA conference held in Nairobi entitled "Teachers' perception on the use of situated cognition: Implications for instructional design for indigenous knowledge."

DR KENNETH M. NGCOZA is a Senior Lecturer and Deputy Head of Department in the Faculty of Education, Rhodes University, Grahamstown. He is a mathematics and science teacher by profession. In the Education Department, he is involved with science teacher education (both pre- and in-service) and is the coordinator of school experience for PGCE students. He is the chairperson of the SAARMSTE Eastern Cape Chapter and his research interests include professional development, science curriculum, cultural contexts and indigenous knowledge. He peer-reviewed the book *The Professional Knowledge base of Science Teaching*, edited by Deborah Corrigan, Justin Dillon and Richard Gunstone (2011).

DR CHRYSOGONUS C. NWAIGWE is a Lecturer at the Federal University of Technology, Owerri, Imo State, Nigeria. He obtained his BSc degree in Statistics from the University of Ibadan in 2000 and Master of Science in Statistics from the University of Nigeria in 2003. He was a part-time lecturer at the University of Nigeria (2004 to 2005) before joining the Federal University of Technology, Owerri, Nigeria as a full time lecturer in the Department of Mathematics and Computer Science in 2005. Thereafter, he moved to the Department of Statistics. He obtained his PhD in Statistics from the University of Nigeria in 2014. His area of specialisation is Probability and Stochastic Processes. He has 10 years' full-time lecturing experience as well as involvement in 12 scholarly publications both locally and internationally. Dr Nwaigwe has chaired many academic and religious committees. He is presently the Examination Officer, Department of Statistics, Federal University of Technology, Owerri.

DR KEFA L. SIMWA teaches Qualitative Research Methods and History of Education in the Department of Educational Foundations, Moi University, Kenya. He recently completed a PhD in Curriculum Studies at the University of Johannesburg, South Africa. His study focused on curriculum coherence in methods courses in History education at a Kenyan university. He also holds a Bachelor of Education and Master of Education degrees from Kenyatta and Moi, Universities respectively. His research interests include Curriculum History and Theory; Teacher Education; History Education and Pedagogy and Critical Inquiry. He has presented papers at international conferences as well as published articles on History and Government Studies on Kenya.

DR NAMHLA SOTUKU is a Senior Lecturer in the BEd Pre-service, PGCE and BEd Honour's programmes at the University of Fort Hare. She holds a PhD in Education Management and Policy. She is an experienced teacher educator and draws from a varied background as a Foundation Phase teacher, lecturer at a Teacher's college, university lecturer, researcher, curriculum trainer, author of Foundation Phase language school books and materials developer for teacher development programmes. She part of a team that designed and developed the innovative UFH Distance Education Course and produced polysemic materials that have attracted international interest and won awards locally. She mentors emerging researchers as she supervises MEd and PhD students. Dr Sotuku has led research projects including: a research project commissioned by CEPD (Centre for Education Policy Development, Evaluation and Management) on engaging communities in educational development through the CLINGS (Community Literacy and Numeracy Groups); and a research project commissioned by TESSA (Teacher Education in the Sub-Saharan Africa) on the implementation practices of TESSA Open Educational Resources for teacher education.

DR RAMODUNGOANE TABANE is a Senior Lecturer in the Department of Psychology of Education, College of Education, University of South Africa, Pretoria. He is involved in the teaching of undergraduates, training and supervision of the Masters and PhD students. His research interests include: innovative qualitative research methodologies, educational psychology, guidance and counselling, and cross-cultural psychology in the fields of child development, assessment, learning, psychological and emotional adjustment.

PROF MATSHIDISO J. TAOLE is an Associate Professor in the Department of Curriculum and Instructional Studies, School of Teacher Education, College of Education, University of South Africa, Pretoria. She holds a PhD in Curriculum Development from the University of North West. She has presented papers at local and international conferences in the field of curriculum development and implementation, and is a member of various academic associations. She is the Associate Editor for the *African Journal of Pedogy and Curriculum* (AJPC). She is presently involved in teaching practice supervision, and undergraduate and postgraduate teaching and research supervision in the field of Curriculum Studies. She has published with local and international journals.

DR SIMON G. TAUKENI is a Post-doctoral Research Fellow in the Faculty of Health Sciences, University of Fort Hare. He was a former lecturer in the Department of Educational Psychology and Inclusive Education in the Faculty of Education at the University of Namibia, Hifikepunye Pohamba Campus. He has published journal articles, book chapters and has presented at various national and international conferences on issues relating to psychosocial support, guidance and counselling, mentoring and orphan children. His main research areas include: counselling psychology, special education and research methods. Dr Taukeni has been working with Orphans and Other Vulnerable Children at AIDS Catholic Action, Tonateni centre in Oshakati town as a volunteer providing psychosocial support through sport activities and artwork.

DR ICARBORD TSHABANGU is a Lecturer at Leeds Trinity University, UK and a former Senior Lecturer and Coordinator in the Department of Educational Foundations and Management at the University of Namibia, Namibia. He is also a former Honorary Senior Lecturer in online doctoral studies at the University of Liverpool; a former Senior Lecturer at the Graduate school of the University of Arusha and also briefly at Mount Meru University both in Tanzania. He has also previously worked in other capacities as a lecturer, high school teacher and Education Consultant both in Africa and in the United Kingdom.

PROF CHARL WOLHUTER is a Professor of Comparative and International Education at North West University, Potchefstroom Campus. He has studied at the University of Johannesburg, the University of Pretoria, the University of South Africa and the University of Stellenbosch. His doctorate was awarded in Comparative Education at the University of Stellenbosch. He was a junior lecturer in History of Education at the University of Pretoria and a Senior Lecturer in History of Education and Comparative Education at the University of Zululand. He is the author of various articles and books in the fields of History of Education and Comparative and International Education. He is a fellow of the Faculty of Education, University of South Africa, and he has been guest professor at Driestar Pedagogical University, Gouda, the Netherlands; Brock University, Canada; Bowling Green State University, Ohio; University of Mount Union, Ohio, USA; the University of Canterbury, UK, and the University of Crete, Greece.

DR BRUNO L. YAWE is a Senior Lecturer and Chair of the Department of Economic Theory and Analysis, School of Economics, Makerere University, Uganda. He has taught at the School of Economics in the College of Business and Management Sciences (CoBAMS), (formerly, Faculty of Economics and Management) Makerere University since 1999. He holds a Bachelor of Science (Economics) Degree from Makerere University, Master of Arts (Economics) and Doctor of Philosophy (Economics) Degrees from the University of Dar es Salaam. At the graduate level, he teaches Gender-Aware Macroeconomics; Project Planning and Management; Quantitative Methods; Health Economics; Macroeconomics for Policy Analysis; Microeconomics; Alternative Health Systems; International Health Care Systems and Managing Health Services.

PROF ZHIDONG ZHANG is an Assistant Professor in the Department of Teaching, Learning and Innovation at the College of Education, University of Texas at Brownsville, United States of America. He received his doctoral degree in quantitative methods in educational psychology focusing on applied cognitive sciences at McGill University in Canada. He also had a post-doctoral experience in quantitative psychology in the Department of Psychology at McGill University. He has taught several research methods and data analysis courses which include qualitative research methods, practitioner research methods, quantitative research methods, intermediate statistics, univariate, multivariate analysis, categorical data analysis and multilevel analysis. Prof Zhang has published more than 15 journal articles/chapters which are in the areas of quantitative modeling and learning sciences; Bayesian networks, multivariate analysis and computing; and cognitive, behavioral and quantitative analysis. Prof Zhang's current research interests are in cognitive process modeling, applied multivariate analysis, and behavioral problems and cognitive- and neuron-scientific evidences.

PROF CONNIE B. ZULU is a Professor in the school of Educational Leadership Development in the Faculty of Education and Training at North West University, Mafikeng campus. She holds a doctoral degree in Education, as well as a Master's degree in General Linguistics. She has spent more than half of her teaching career of 36 years in higher education teaching and learning. She has taught English language and literature at high school and university undergraduate and postgraduate levels, as well as postgraduate Educational management courses. She has served as subject advisor for English at a national in-service education college, delivered papers at numerous national and international conferences, published papers in accredited local and international journals and published chapters in books. She is a reviewer for local and international journals. She has served as chairperson and as a member of various committees including the Research and publications committee and University Senate committee. Her research interests include: academic literacy and issues of gender in relation to women in educational leadership and management. She was one of two guest editors for a 2013 special edition on Learner Misconduct in public schools and co-edited peer-reviewed conference proceedings of the Southern African Society for Education. She was the recipient of the Vice chancellors' award for special achievement in 2003 and most productive senior researcher of the year in the Faculty of Education in 2009, 2011 and 2014.

Part 1

The philosophy of research

CHAPTER 1

Micheal van Wyk

Afrocentricity as a research philosophy

KEY CONCEPTS

Afrocentricity refers to an identity, cultural ideology, and worldview, particularly of black people (of African-American origin) about their African history, cultural heritage and ideological focus.

Assumptions are the specific beliefs or notions of the researcher about investigating a phenomenon.

Criteria are principles, standards, norms, yardsticks or benchmarks by which something is measured or judged (singular: criterion).

Enquiry is the formal exercise of questioning, probing or investigating a phenomenon.

Epistemology is the study of the nature and scope of knowledge production in the real world.

Introspection happens when the researcher takes a searching look at the enquiry through inward or self-examination.

Ontology is a focus on the nature of being, of becoming, existence, or reality, in the real world.

Personal philosophy is the viewpoint of an individual or group of people about their identity, beliefs, values, and attitudes.

Retrospection happens when the researcher rethinks his or her past actions in the enquiry process through critical reflection and self-questioning.

Value is the importance of something which is worth having, or is dear to you: e.g. gold is a commodity of high monetary value; or freedom of speech is valued as a democratic right.

LEARNING OUTCOMES

By the end of this chapter, you should be able to:

▶ Define Afrocentricity as an emerging research philosophy particularly in education.

▶ Conceptualise ontology and epistemology as constructs in an educational, philosophical and theoretical context.

▶ Define truth and justice in the context of an Afrocentric research methodology, as compared with the Eurocentric perspective of reliability, validity and objectivity.

▶ Explain the fundamental principles underlying the Afrocentric approach to research methodology.

▶ Critically reflect on the responsibilities of the researcher who uses an Afrocentric research paradigm to investigate cultural constructs and human behaviour.

▶ Explain briefly data collection methods in terms of ethical qualitative research design, in the context of the African perspective.

We start this chapter with a short imagined conversation between three well known Afrocentrist scholars – George J. Sefa Dei, Molefi Kete Asante and the late Joe L. Kincheloe – which expresses their particular views about the concept of Afrocentricity as a research philosophy.

Case study: What we believe about Afrocentricity

I am an African scholar. Our identity, values, and culture are based in Afrocentric philosophy. [But], because I live in North America, I am seen as an African-American. My interest was – and still is – about my values and identity as foregrounded in Afrocentricity as a phenomenon. Currently, I see African indigenous peoples in Africa, and around the world as part of this phenomenon, but now it is also good to see other African scholars promoting this philosophy. You know, to explore the African peoples and especially indigenous knowledge systems is a complex accumulation of local, context-relevant knowledge that embraces the essence of ancestral knowing, as well as the legacies of diverse cultures and values. We must as African scholars advocate and advance our cultures, identities, and histories through research. Indeed, we must promote our ideals as important virtues in becoming African scholars of excellence. This is and must be our ultimate goal.

George J. Sefa Dei

You see, African indigenous communities are the place and research site for promoting African indigenous knowledge. I agree with you, George, we as established scholars must therefore support the Afrocentric research philosophy. I see this philosophy as a means to research indigenous knowledge, as a viable tool for reclaiming our space and context through relevant ways of knowing that have deliberately been suppressed in the acquisition of Western knowledge. Indigenous knowledge should focus on systematically unravelling power relations that have entrenched the dominance of particular ways of knowing in Western academic journals, school textbooks, and other related texts. We need, in essence, to understand that keeping indigenous knowledge alive amounts to resistance, refusal, and ultimately transformation of our perspective of knowledge, here in Africa and globally.

Molefi Kete Asante

I wholeheartedly agree with you Molefi about our role as African scholars in promoting this philosophy. It is true that if Afrocentricity, as a research philosophy, can take its rightful place in the ontological and epistemological field of educational research, it will advance the knowledge of African people about themselves, and the world's knowledge of African people. This philosophy, in my view, will create a platform from which social scientists can systematically place African phenomena at the centre of their research. I have no doubt that an Afrocentric research philosophy will advance the ideals, identity, culture and values of African people because it is underpinned by the principles and requirements of the role of the researcher who takes an African perspective. If we as scholars constantly advocate this philosophy it will ultimately gain its rightful place in academic and scholarly publications concurrently with that of Western ways of knowing in academic circles.

Joe L. Kincheloe

Introduction

Already, you should have an idea of where we are going with this chapter, and what wider theoretical concepts we want you to understand and share. Throughout this chapter we hope to present a text that will equip you to use the Afrocentric paradigm in planning and conducting your own research.

One of your reasons for deciding to venture into postgraduate studies is to further your academic and chosen career; but perhaps also to gain a deeper knowledge of your chosen field. During your undergraduate studies, you would have come across such concepts as research paradigm, research design and methodology. At the same time, you would also have realised that you have to be empowered and equipped to take on the challenge postgraduate-level studies. It is not easy to make an informed decision or provide a sound motivation for your research paradigm at this stage of your research career. For this reason, we try in this text to explore with you specific philosophies of research so that you can make a qualified decision about which philosophies of research will best fit your planned investigation. Before you can make such a decision on the type of philosophy for your research paradigm and design, you will need to read about these specific elements in Chapters 1 to 5. Whether you decide to use Afrocentricity as your starting point, or to take a positivist, or interpretivist, or feminist approach as your research paradigm, will be up to you, but this book will enable you to make that choice with understanding and insight.

This chapter advocates the advancement of **Afrocentricity** as a research philosophy. This is because the Afrocentric perspective creates an avenue through which human and social scientists can systematically place African phenomena at the centre of analysis and synthesis in the research. The chapter further provides the important principles and requirements of the role of the researcher who chooses the Afrocentric perspective. Like all researchers, the Afrocentric researcher must depend on sources for useful data, and for guidance in interpreting the data and their analysis. The point of departure for the Afrocentric researcher is the *where*, *what* and *how* of these sources and data collection. This chapter presents several research designs for collecting data from an Afrocentric approach. You will be able to base your decision for choosing Afrocentricity as a philosophy of research on specific principles that best fit your research paradigm.

Now let us look at the concept of Afrocentricity as a research philosophy, in the next section.

1.1   A brief exposition of Afrocentricity as a research philosophy

As suggested by the opening case with the imagined conversation between three Afrocentrist scholars, it is essential to have a fundamental understanding of Afrocentricity as a research paradigm, compared with other philosophies, like those that will be discussed in Chapters 2, 3, and 4. To do this, we offer you with a brief exposition of Afrocentricity as a research philosophy, which should encourage you to read further on your own. The origins of the Afrocentric philosophy emerged in Molefi Kete Asante's research in the 1980s and are defined and developed in his works, *Afrocentricity* (1988), *The Afrocentric idea* (1987), and *Kemet, Afrocentricity and Knowledge* (1990). In particular, Asante (1987:1) explains Afrocentric research philosophy as, "a theory of change [that] intends to re-locate the African person as subject. [...] As a pan-African idea, Afrocentricity becomes the key to the proper education of children and the essence of an African cultural revival and, indeed, survival." From this it is clear that Afrocentricity must promote an independent identity for a scholarship of discovery, in advocating and advancing the principles of its philosophy. To advance this identity, several strategies, such as cultural heritage actions, creating platforms for critical dialogue and engagement activities as a crucial catalyst for promoting knowledge from an African perspective, are advocated (Kaphangawani & Malherbe, 1998; Letseka, 2000). Several fundamental principles emerge from Asante's texts: the principles of togetherness, equality, redress, identity, **values**, social justice, fairness, social transformation and democracy form the basis of this philosophy, which significantly locates the African people at the centre of any investigation (Asante, 1990; Appiah, 1989; Kershaw, 2003; Mazama, 2003). Steward (2011:270) also argues that the philosophy "promotes African culture and identity as an integral part of research activity and acts as the starting point of departure and of understanding the phenomenon under investigation". In addition, as an emergent philosophy of research enquiry, Afrocentrism is equal to but distinct from any other research philosophy, such as those of the positivist or interpretivist, and feminist research paradigms. Mabogo (1996) regards Afrocentric research philosophy as a strong directive for expanding and benchmarking African knowledge against other philosophies, and most importantly, as a way to improve human life. In fact, this philosophy has the potential rigour to make a meaningful contribution to educational research in Africa and globally. As already suggested, for your own understanding of the Afrocentric perspective as advocated by African scholars, you need first to study the principles that underpin this emerging philosophy of research before you can make a constructive decision about whether it will best fit your type of investigation. This paradigm embraces the idea that if research is to be Afrocentric in nature, African people must be in control of and participate in the entire research process, from beginning to end, ultimately to find solutions for their own context. From this brief exposition of the Afrocentric paradigm, you will as a researcher understand that this philosophy fundamentally requires you to investigate African people from their everyday experiences, with them and for them.

Critical thinking challenge

Before you continue with the conceptualisation of ontology and epistemology, turn back to the imagined conversation between the three African scholars.

1 Why, according to George Sefa Dei in the opening case study, is it important for African scholars to advance the ideals of an Afrocentric philosophy?

2 Why do you think it is important to understand Afrocentric research philosophy as a relevant research philosophy, as compared with Eurocentric research philosophy?

3 Return to the question you wrote down in the first *Stop and reflect* activity: how would you answer this question now?

In the following section, we explain the concepts of **ontology** and **epistemology** in relation to the Afrocentric perspective.

1.2 Conceptualising ontology and epistemology: The Afrocentric view

So far, you have been exposed to the concept of Afrocentricity and to the broad principles underpin this philosophy. As a researcher you now need to understand the meaning of **ontology** and **epistemology** as requirements for investigating any phenomenon in your field of research. Let us try briefly to explain the two concepts from an Afrocentric perspective.

1.2.1 Ontology

Ontology is concerned with the nature of what exists in the real world. In other words, in our context, ontology reflects the reality of how the African people live and work. This reality from an Afrocentric perspective is the sum of the ways in which ordinary people are live in their respective communities because of the way they understand the context of their everyday challenges. Scholars define ontology as a philosophical paradigm which studies the nature of being. Further, Carroll (2008:6) says that "ontology is the study or concern about what kinds of things exist in the world – what entities are there in the universe". Let us look at an example in which the nature of African indigenous culture is explored from an ontological point of view, but not necessarily an Afrocentric perspective. In a particular study by Hountondji (1997) we are informed that research on indigenous African culture (ontological construct) has typically addressed the concerns of the researcher (both Western researchers and African researchers trained in Western methodologies) and ignored the African point of view. We believe it is very important that as a postgraduate student you understand your subject knowledge field before you venture into the Afrocentric perspective. We suggest you read further on this idea in Chapters 2 and 3.

1.2.2 Epistemology

Epistemology is the 'theory of knowledge', in other words, what it is to know, and what knowing is. This concept focuses on how researchers construct or deconstruct facts or knowledge in their respective fields of study. The concept 'knowledge construction' is both about building or generating new knowledge in field of study, *and* about new ways of knowing. Carroll (2008) further argues that epistemology operates within the social reality of ontology. This social reality is one in which people in a particular community live and experience things like crime, unemployment and poverty. In such a context, African scholars might investigate how rural communities experience the issues and consequences of poverty and unemployment, and how they deal with these issues and find possible solutions to their problems. So finally, epistemology as a phenomenon may be understood as how African people experience reality to solve problems in their own communities. Epistemology as a construct will be further discussed in Chapter 2.

Stop and reflect

As a student researcher, how would you define and conceptualise ontology and epistemology from an Afrocentric perspective in your own field of study? Although you may not arrive at a conclusive definition at this time, it is important to start considering these concepts in terms of your own research plans.

In the next section, we discuss the **principles** for doing research, from Afrocentric perspective.

1.3 Afrocentric research canons (norms, principles or tenets)

We have dealt with the concept of Afrocentricity, and touched on the principles that underpin this philosophy, as well as ontological and epistemological requirements for conducting research from an Afrocentric perspective. However, you cannot start planning and conducting your research before you have envisaged what specific research canons (norms, tenets) form the basis of an Afrocentric perspective. Look at the diagrammatic schema of Afrocentric research canons in Figure 1.1 for your own understanding, and to inform your research activity.

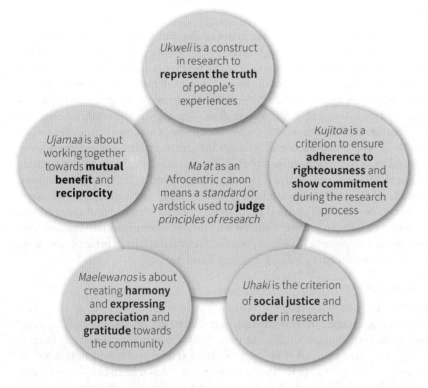

FIGURE 1.1: Ma'at as an Afrocentric canon

Before we explain the different canons, a brief overview is provided for clarity. If you take a closer look at the diagram you will realise that it forms an interrelated construct of different concepts and their interactions, to create a whole in the form of circles connected to one another. The concept 'yardstick' or canon derives from Molefi Asante's Afrocentric principle of *Ma'at*. In this case, *Ma'at* is a standard by which you can be judged on specific principles and criteria for doing your research study. *Ma'at* as a unifying Afrocentric canon is made up of the following interrelated canons or yardsticks: *ukweli, kujitoa, maelewano, ujamaa*, and *uhaki*, which will be discussed in the context of Afrocentric research criteria.

In the next section, you will learn about the Afrocentric canons of *Ma'at* as an emerging set of principles for conducting research.

1.3.1 *Ukweli*

The concept *ukweli* refers to whether a 'fact' or the 'truth' is real or genuine, or not. Fact or truth is a central standard by which your research will be judged. Suppose you conduct a study on unemployment among youth in your area, and you already know that the unemployment rate is very high. You as a researcher, notwithstanding your existing knowledge, must only report the facts or truth of your particular investigation in a 'fair and transparent' manner. You may not twist or change the evidence of the investigation to suit the purpose of the study. You have therefore to report your findings in an objective, unbiased manner. Early work by Asante (1990:12) concludes that "the standards for establishing the educational needs of the members and the individuals in that community must be determined by the real life experiences of the community". According to this statement, the researcher and community must be co-constructors of the knowledge of the enquiry process. The researched community will openly and easily support the facts or truth when reporting the findings of a study because they were participants in the enquiry process.

Research studies conducted by Reviere (2001) and Van Wyk (2014) assert that the experiences of group members should become the ultimate authority in determining "what should be taught and how it should be taught". Similarly, these authors conclude that the experiences of the community under investigation must become the ultimate authority in determining what is needed by that group. Letseka (2000:23) adds to this view, saying that in an Afrocentric research approach "one cannot ignore the real-life and historical experiences of the community". Any enquiry needs to accommodate the views of the community in the research process. For example, the whole school community must be included in the decision-making process to provide for their children's educational needs.

Overall, the principle of *ukweli* mandates the African researcher to report findings of a particular community in a fair and transparent manner, without fear or favour.

1.3.2 *Maelewanos*

Maelewanos means that the researcher jointly agrees with the researched community, to always act to serve people with dignity and gratitude. Asante (1990:23) says "this principle requires that the African scholar should actively avoid creating tensions amongst or within communities, but should instead strive to create harmonious and good relationships between and within the participating groups". The African researcher must establish a spirit of goodwill and uBuntu in his or her community. In fact, taking this canon a step further, African scholars must strive to build harmonious relationships and appreciation amongst one another to advance research. Kaphangawani and Malherbe (1998) are of the view that African scholars must strengthen relationships amongst themselves for the sake of human dignity. The researcher has to respect at all times the dignity of the community. In adhering to this call, we believe that it is imperative to build long-lasting relationships with the researched community, and indeed, the community of researchers.

1.3.3 *Akiba uhaki*

Akiba uhaki refers to promoting the spirit of human rights, dignity and social justice amongst African people. If you decide to apply this canon in your research design, you will be promoting integrity, fairness, social justice and honesty as yardsticks from an Afrocentric perspective. In fact, if you choose to apply the social justice criterion, you have an obligation to conduct your research in a fair and honest manner. The research process should be conducted with impartiality and fairness to all members of a community or group.

This informs the researcher's awareness of the manner in which research is conducted: always to apply fairness and justness when researching the community. Participants must be informed before and after the research process, and the findings must be reported in an accessible, equitable and transparent way because they involve human rights, dignity and fairness. These yardsticks align with ethical considerations in doing your research (about which you will learn more in Chapters 6 and 7), and are in the best interests and wellbeing of the community being researched and served (Letseka, 2000; Anyanwu, 1989). This urges the African researcher to be sensitive to and mindful of the interests of the community at large. It is a matter of integrity, honesty and fairness, as the central characteristics of an African scholar.

1.3.4 *Ujamaa*

The principle of *ujamaa* refers to working together with the community. As researcher, you should always work in the spirit of forming a partnership with the community. For example, you decide to plan a research project on crime, in a rural community. You would send out invitations to all stakeholders in the community to attend meetings to plan collectively how the research project will be implemented, and how results will be disseminated after the project is completed. You have first to get the community's agreement on the project before any research starts. You must establish a partnership of trust and willingness amongst all stakeholders. Reviere (2001) supports the view that the researcher at all times establishes good relationships for the betterment of the community. Van Wyk (2014) and Letseka (2000) further suggest that African scholars should work together with the community to establish partnerships as a means to uplift and develop the community.

1.3.5 *Kujitoa*

The concept of *kujitoa* requires the researcher to show commitment in conducting research in a specific community, and especially to the research process. This requirement compels the researcher to promise and pledge to uphold a code of conduct as a researcher. The researcher should adhere to the criteria of an ethics policy by acting in a professional manner at all times. Over and above this, researchers have a strict obligation to adhere to the rules stipulated in the research, and to the ethics policies of their institutions as a prerequisite to do research. These policies guide the researcher and commit him or her to the research process. Reviere (2001:709) argues that "any acceptable process requires a sufficiently comprehensive approach that addresses questions of how knowledge is being structured and used". African scholars are also compelled to reflect critically on how they design and employ research procedures, by expressing a commitment towards the community. The community, in turn, must become part of this commitment. As they work together, the researcher and participants have to realise that they are knowledge co-constructors whose aim is to advance their own community in the process. In the end, the researcher and community sign a commitment pledge for the upliftment of the community.

Stop and reflect

You decide to use the *akiba uhaki* canon in planning your research design. How and why would you use this principle in your research design for investigating, for example, poverty in a community?

1.4 The role of the researcher: An Afrocentric perspective

In this section we deal with the role, the requirements, and the qualities of a researcher in conducting research in the context of an Afrocentric perspective.

1.4.1 Contextualising the role of a researcher

In this part of the chapter, we provide a brief explanation of your role as a researcher and the required characteristics of a researcher in the research process. Sometimes students find it difficult and challenging to explain their exact role and responsibilities as a researcher. We suggest that you attend closely to the role of a researcher as described in this chapter. If you know what is expected of you in your role, it will be less of a challenge to execute all your responsibilities to best of your ability throughout your research. We take our description of the general role of the researcher and apply it in the context of the Afrocentric perspective. Akbar (2004) argues that researchers have to exercise their roles and responsibilities in a fair and transparent manner when conducting research in African communities. In following this, the researcher, for example, only reports the facts, without fear or favour, that emerge from the enquiry on the status of crime and drug abuse in the community. In relation to the contextualising role of the researcher, Kershaw (2003) advocates that African scholars in particular must play an active and constructive role in applying the canons suggested under section 1.3 when researching any community. Indeed, Asante (1987) urges that in order to support the community in solving some of these problems, such as crime, unemployment, rape, teenage pregnancy and drug abuse, the Afrocentric researcher has an ethical obligation to be the "voice of voiceless". This means the African researcher must play a critical role and assume great responsibility in researching and disseminating the findings of studies to the relevant bodies and organisations for further action, for the sake of the community (Bogdan & Biklen, 1992). Steward (2006) says that the traditional ways of doing research, which are to collect data, write up the findings and report them in a peer- reviewed journal for either monetary gain or for career advancement, is not sufficient. From an Afrocentric perspective, the researcher always seeks to know the context of the community being investigated in order to understand his or her own role and the overall importance of the enquiry. Using Afrocentric principles, the role of researcher becomes one to harmonise and set up good relationships with the diverse cultures, values and experiences of the community.

Let us now explore the important requirements that define how researchers in the context of an Afrocentric perspective become scholars of excellence.

1.4.2 Important requirements defining a researcher

In view of the importance of defining how a researcher becomes an excellent scholar, there are three distinct roles that can be applied to the Afrocentric researcher:

☑ An Afrocentric perspective compels the researcher to adhere to a particular research process and provides a rationale for conducting the research (see 1.3.5).

☑ The researcher must always acknowledge the contribution of the community. The community in an African research context will be consulted, its permission sought to conduct the research, and the finds discussed before being disseminated (see 1.3.3).

☑ The researcher may not, as far as possible, have any preconceived research bias and should never conduct the investigation, extract information, or write up the research for funding in any way that excludes the community. Scholars who advocate excellence in research will strive to build harmonious relationships and appreciation amongst community. To this end, the researcher must 'live and eat' amongst the people to understand the culture and identity of the researched community (see 1.3.1 and 1.3.2).

In striving to adhere to the described roles that define the requirements of a scholar, Walker and Greene (2006:65) take the view that researchers have to "hold themselves responsible for uncovering hidden, subtle, racist theories that may be embedded in current methodologies when researching African communities". In fact, the responsibility of the African researcher in reporting findings must be fair, non-racist, gender-sensitive, and transparent, without any 'hidden agenda', for the sake of human dignity. Mcdougal (2011:289) highlights the issue of transparency and honesty in reporting research findings, saying that the purpose of reporting findings is "to legitimise the centrality of African ideals and values as a valid frame of reference for acquiring and examining data". In almost all cases of enquiry, according to Asante (1990), the African scholar investigates the community to improve the lives of the people. More specifically, Mcdougal (2011:283) states that most researchers in the African context "believe that research findings may lead to improving African people's overall wellbeing."

Now we move on to the specific qualities that define a researcher.

1.4.3 Qualities that define a researcher

In this section, we offer a brief exposition of the important qualities that turn a researcher into a scholar of excellence:

▸ *Wisdom*: not making value judgements and providing constructive feedback, to support the community.
▸ *Humility*: being humble and not seeing oneself as above the other person, as is always expected in an African context.
▸ *Courageous*: having the ability to stand your ground without fear or favour for the sake of a just cause, in order to advance indigenous knowledge.
▸ *Integrity*: the quality of being honest and showing the moral grounds of your convictions.
▸ *Compassion*: showing sympathy through your feelings and demonstrating caring towards all people in the research community.
▸ *Intelligence*: having sufficient intellectual ability to identify problems or challenges and to research those challenges to find solutions for a specific problem in the community. Understanding that any investigation demands critical awareness, analysis, logical reasoning and innovative ways to solve the problem or answer the question.
▸ *Honesty and diligence*: being open-minded, honest in judgement and willing to consider correction and suggestions from other scholars.
▸ *Well-informed research plan*: planning thoughtfully and carefully in a systematic manner, in line with timelines, schedules and setting of priorities.
▸ *Creativity and innovation*: showing creativity and flexibility in changing plans or procedures to make things possible, and using innovative ways to solve problems encountered in the community during the research process.
▸ *Fair, objective and open-minded research reporting*: being impartial and fair in judgement, and being open to correcting or changing the analysis of data through an objective and fair-minded approach.

It is a fact that many great African scholars and leaders, in particular, Molefi Asante, Anthony Appiah and Nelson Mandela, envisage morals and ethics as the virtues which are the ultimate test of a person's character in serving his or her community, without expectation of the reward of fame or any other claim.

Before you continue with next section on the role of an African researcher in relation to ethical considerations, do the following challenge.

Critical thinking challenge

Values-based education and citizenship education for democracy

In many African countries, leaders often do not accept defeat at the voting polls, sometimes taking up arms to dispute the results of the election. If we as Africans are to be an example of people who believe in democracy and live our values according to democratic principles, we need to nurture our youth for future leadership. Citizenship education is a very important part of any country's education system which is why voter education must be included in the curriculum. All national curricula should integrate values-based content into all prescribed school textbooks and curricula, from primary to higher education. Many African schools try to teach a 'hidden curriculum' which reflects principles such as social transformation, justice, fairness, honesty, freedom of speech, inclusivity, non-racialism, freedom of expression and so forth. These principles can only enhance democracy in Africa, making it a stable and prosperous continent.

In the South African school context, it is imperative to empower teachers and learners to engage in issues relating to values, morals, ethics and democracy by creating platforms for such debates. To this end, educators must empower youth with citizenship education for a better future. Our young people are the next generation of leadership and voters in the country. We as South Africans need to build a strong democracy as the central pillar in the way in which we carry out governance, setting an example on the continent. Education is the most powerful weapon we can use to bring about social transformation, economic growth and development. Another way of looking at values education is that the wealth of a nation lies in the knowledge, skills and competence of its citizen. Through excellence in research projects we can and will succeed in educating our youth in the values to strengthen our democracy in Africa.

When you have read through this text about values-based education and citizenship education for democracy, answer the following questions:

1 In your own words, say what is meant by "values and values-based education" from an African perspective.

2 Why is it important for an African scholar to adhere to the principles of honesty and inclusivity in researching a community?

3 Why it is important to foreground values-based education in our school curricula?

In the next section, we discuss the role of the African researcher towards values and ethical considerations before, during and after the research process.

1.4.4 The role of the researcher in adhering to ethical issues

It may be useful at this point to remember what was said in section 1.3 about reporting research findings in a fair, transparent and honest manner. In this section, we discuss ethical issues as important virtues for your research. It is up to the researcher to ensure that ethical approaches are applied when conducting research. Before a researcher starts conducting his or her research in a community, the following ethical considerations must be adhered to (see also Chapter 6). We encourage you to follow and apply these ethical considerations as guidelines:

▶ To make sure that informed consent is given by the participants in the study.
▶ To give assurance of the confidentiality of any biographical information and personal experiences provided to the researcher solely for research purposes.
▶ To send a consent-seeking letter to inform each of the participants of the purpose of the study.
▶ To further assure participants of the confidentiality of all information that is given as part of the study.
▶ To secure voluntary participation by means of consent before the commencement of the research.
▶ To inform participants that they can opt out at any point if they do not feel comfortable answering questions or participating in the study.
▶ To ensure that all information solicited from participants in all data collection phases is kept safe and confidential.
▶ To ensure that data gathered are used solely for the purpose of the research and not disclosed to any other party for any reason.

In view of these ethical conditions, it is the critical responsibility of the African scholar to promote research integrity through setting values, standards, and adhering to the highest ethical principles in doing research amongst African people.

Next, we place the Afrocentric perspective in the enquiry domain by discussing criteria, techniques, and methods for collecting data for research purposes.

1.5 Locating Afrocentric research in the enquiry domain

In the following section, the applicable approaches, techniques, and data collection instruments are discussed, in locating research in the context of the African perspective.

1.5.1 Afrocentric methodological approaches to enquiry

Research is a scientific way of investigating a problem, using research methods to collect data and providing findings and recommendations from the study. According to Asante (1990), there are two main research techniques researchers can use, the approaches of **introspection** and **retrospection**. In addition, Reviere (2001) says these two techniques are used to localise the Afrocentric 'place' from which researchers conduct the enquiry. These two approaches will be discussed in terms of placing Afrocentric research methodology in the context of research.

In this approach, the Afrocentric researcher questions him- or herself about why it is important to investigate the topic for research purposes. In fact, it is useful for the researcher to write down all his or her beliefs, values and ideas in order to reflect on his or her **assumptions** about researching the topic, before the research study begins. This is to ascertain what obstacles might exist before starting the research. According to Asante (1990), the process of introspection is aimed at ensuring that any obstacles to the implementation of the Afrocentric method that exist in the researcher's own mind are unearthed. Other African scholars maintain that the retrospection approach is needed to help the researcher ascertain if any personal obstacles exist to a fair interpretation of the data collected. It is clear, then, that the techniques of introspection and retrospection are both important constructs of the Afrocentric research process.

1.5.2 Implementing the Afrocentric research techniques

With reference to research techniques, there exist several methods, techniques and instruments for scholars to use for data collection purposes. However, before the researcher considers implementing any research techniques, she should ask the following question: What is the purpose of the study, and what research techniques are most suitable for this research? In defining the purpose and techniques, researchers often define their own views in relation to the investigation topic. Van Wyk (2014:292, citing Reviere, 2001) says that "the Afrocentric paradigm allows the researcher to put people's ideas and values at the centre of the enquiry … from which he or she can analyse and criticise the rules governing hegemonic enquiries that prevent accurate explanations of the lived experiences of those being researched". This is a crucial step: to establish partnerships with the community before any research techniques and instruments can be designed and implemented for data collection purposes.

In fact, the purpose of using a specific technique is crucial to collecting and concluding findings for the study, as we will see in the next section.

1.5.3 Afrocentric method as an interactive and holistic model

Earlier work by Mkabela (2005) indicates that an Afrocentric researcher seeks to make a cross-cultural study which is directed at specific issues. Pellerin's (2012) views the use of this dual data collection approach as enabling an interactive and holistic research process for data collection. It follows then that using Afrocentric methods is both an interactive and participative approach to data collection. This process supports and enhances mutual cooperation between the researcher and the community. For example, in applying a traditional Eurocentric hypothetical-statistical model based on cause and effect, the approach is foregrounded by the principles of reliability and validity as criteria for measuring the outcomes of the study. It seems that this interventionist model of research focuses more on the researcher's biases relating to controlling the enquiry and analysing outcomes. In contrast, Pellerin (2012:152) views Afrocentric methods as an approach to research that includes "cultural and social integration as opposed to 'scientific distance'" and, as such, provides a more acceptable approach to understanding African phenomena. In fact, without cultural and social involvement, the researcher loses all ethics and cultural sensitivity.

In following section, we discuss various data collection methods.

1.6 Afrocentric research design and data collection methods

In this part of the chapter, different data collection methods such as criteria, collaboration and quantitative and qualitative research designs are explained in the context of the African perspective.

1.6.1 Collaborative and cooperative research methods

It is important for the researcher to establish a collaborative and cooperative environment with the community to be researched. The goal is to create a harmonious and balanced relationship before, during, and after the research project. Mkabela and Luthuli (1997:37) argue that "Africans are known for their strong orientation to collective values, particularly a collective sense of responsibility, which has largely been ignored, misunderstood or disregarded in the evaluation of African indigenous communities as a 'collective ethic'". Similarly, this collaborative agreement and partnership with the people being researched is an important ingredient for the success of any research project. Scholars view this process as "characterised by generosity, love, maturity, hospitality, politeness, understanding and humility" (Mkabela

& Luthuli 1997:44). Van Wyk (2014:295, citing Reviere, 2001) agrees and further argues that "collaboration and cooperation is important to re-discovering indigenous African methodological preferences and practices in research". The author emphasises that this has serious implications for African research and practice in its task and challenge of searching for, collecting and preserving knowledge to advance the lives of people on the African continent.

The next section focuses on the criteria for using a particular research methodology.

1.6.2 Criteria for establishing Afrocentric research methods

In this section, specific criteria are discussed in relation to an Afrocentric research methodology. Operating as a methodology, Afrocentricity creates an avenue through which social scientists can systematically place African phenomena at the centre of analysis and synthesis. Mazana (2003) identifies criteria for establishing an Afrocentric methodology:

☑ **It is guided and informed by enquiry** and reported in an unbiased manner.

☑ **The subject of the research is necessary**, which compels the researcher to be fair and honest in reporting.

☑ **Intuition is a valid** source of information in promoting African scholarship.

☑ **Not everything that matters is measurable**, but everything needs to be investigated through fair reporting.

☑ **The knowledge generated must be liberating** and empowering to African communities.

In addition, Banks (1992) says that Afrocentricity is an independent research methodology. It could set a benchmark for reporting research findings in a fair and just manner. In fact, Reviere (2001:709) argues that "Afrocentric methodologies are intended to be used to investigate pertinent research questions legitimately and effectively". Researchers, it appears, have an obligation to adhere to and be guided by the listed criteria for establishing an Afrocentric research methodology.

We now turn to describing specific research designs for data collection.

1.6.3 Qualitative research methods for data collection

In this section, we give only a brief description of qualitative research methods. This is because qualitative research methods will be dealt with in depth in Chapters 16, 17 and 21 which focus on qualitative methods and instruments for data collection. There are several qualitative research methods a researcher can employ for data collection purposes, namely:
▶ life histories
▶ ethnography
▶ case studies
▶ storytelling
▶ interviews
▶ questionnaires (with open-ended questions)
▶ field observations
▶ analysis of cultural documents.

All these methods can be employed in the Afrocentric approach, and are fully discussed later in Chapters 16, 17 and 21.

Conclusion

This chapter was developed to empower and equip you with the knowledge to help you make an informed decision about Afrocentricity as a research philosophy. As indicated from the outset, this chapter advocates the advancement of Afrocentricity as a research philosophy because it creates an avenue through which human and social scientists can systematically place African phenomena at the centre of analysis and synthesis in their research. To this end, we started the chapter with a brief exposition of Afrocentricity as a research philosophy (section 1.1), conceptualising ontology and epistemology (section 1.2) before proposing the canons for doing research from an Afrocentric perspective (section 1.3), as an important research paradigm in current educational enquiry. In section 1.4, we suggested the role and responsibilities, the requirements, and the qualities of the researcher for conducting research in the context of an Afrocentric perspective. We concluded with approaches, techniques, and data collection instruments as tools in locating research in the context of the African perspective, in sections 1.5 and 1.6.

In brief, in this chapter we have exposed you to the concept of Afrocentricity as a research philosophy to help you to make a decision about your own research direction, and how you might use it in your research endeavours. You should now be in a position to make a logical and informed decision on whether you support Afrocentricity as a philosophy of research which may be both applicable and best suited to your research.

Before you move on to the next chapter, complete the closing activities to consolidate your understanding of the Afrocentric perspective.

Closing activities

Reflection questions

1 Define the term Afrocentricity in your own words. (You may want to revisit the notes you made in answer to your first question about Afrocentricity that you would have posed to the Afrocentric scholars.)
2 Why is the Afrocentric paradigm an emerging philosophy in the research arena, compared with Eurocentric paradigms?
3 In line with Afrocentric canons, you decide to employ the new Afrocentric perspectives in your research design. Briefly explain how you will plan and use the principles in your own academic research.

Practical applications

4 After studying the text on page 13 on the values that drive our democracy, and the imagined conversation between three well known Afrocentrist scholars that started this chapter, you are selected to make a presentation to your fellow postgraduate students on emerging Afrocentric research methodology. What will be your main points of departure? What applied examples would you use to illustrate your ideas? How would you prepare yourself to answer specific concerns and uncertainties that might arise? Write up your detailed plan for this presentation.
5 Write an essay on the qualities and responsibilities of the researcher who uses an Afrocentric research paradigm to investigate cultures.

Analysis and consolidation

6 Analyse what you see as the scholarly value and relevance of an Afrocentric research methodology for the purpose of publication.

Bibliography

Akbar, N. 2004. Paradigms in African American research. In R. Jones (Ed). *Black psychology*. Hampton: Cobb & Henry Publishers.

Anyanwu, K.C. 1989. The Problem of Method in African Philosophy. In C.S. Momoh (Ed). *The Substance of African Philosophy*. Washington DC: Brookings Institute.

Appiah K.A. 1989. *Necessary Questions: An Introduction to Philosophy*. Englewood Cliffs: Prentice-Hall.

Asante, M.K. 1980. *Afrocentricity: the theory of social change*. Buffalo, NY: Amulefi Publishing.

Asante, M.K. 1987. *The Afrocentric idea*. Philadelphia: Temple University Press.

Asante, M.K. 1988. *Afrocentricity*. Trenton, NJ: Africa World Press.

Banks, W.C. 1992. The theoretical and methodological crisis of the Afrocentric conception. *Journal of Negro Education*, 61(3):262–272.

Bogdan, R.C. Biklen, S.K. 1992. *Qualitative Research for Education: An Introduction to Theory and Methods*. Boston, MA: Allyn & Bacon.

Carroll, K.K. 2008. Africana Studies and Research Methodology: Revisiting the Centrality of the Afrikan Worldview. *The Journal of Pan African Studies*, 2 (2):4–25.

Hountondji, P.J. 1997. *Endogenous knowledge: Research trails*. Oxford, UK: CODESRIA.

Kaphangawani, D.N. & Malherbe, J.G.1998. African Epistemology. In P.H. Coetzee & A.P.J. Roux (Eds). *Philosophy from Africa*. Johannesburg: Thompson Publishers.

Kershaw, T. 2003. The black studies paradigm: The making of scholar activists. In J.L. Conyers (Ed). *Afrocentricity and the academy: Essays on theory and practice*. Jefferson: McFarland & Co.

Letseka, M. 2000. African Philosophy and Educational Discourse. In P. Higgs, N.C.G. Vakalisa, T.V. Mda & N.T. Assie-Lumumba (Eds). *African Voices in Education*. Cape Town: Juta.

Mabogo, J.S. 1996. African Philosophy Revisited. *Alternation* 3(1):109–129.

Mazama, A. 2003. *The Afrocentric Paradigm*. Trenton, New Jersey: Africa World Press, Inc.

Mcdougal III, S. 2011. The Future of Research Methods in Africana Studies Graduate Curriculum *Journal of African American Studies* 15(3):279–289.

Mkabela, Q. 2005. Using the Afrocentric method in researching indigenous African culture. *The Qualitative Report*, 10(1):178–189. Accessed 12 October 2013 from http://www.nova.edu/ssss/QR/QR10-1/mkabela.pdf

Mkabela, N.Q. & Luthuli, P.C. 1997. *Towards an African philosophy of education*. Pretoria: Kagiso Tertiary Press.

Pellerin, R. 2012. Benefits of Afrocentricity in Exploring Social Phenomena: Understanding Afrocentricity as a Social Science Methodology. *The Journal of Pan African Studies*, 5(4):149–160.

Reviere, R. 2001. Toward an Afrocentric research methodology. *Journal of Black Studies*, 31(6):709–728.

Steward, R.E. 2011. Exploring Afrocentricity: An Analysis of the Discourse of Barack Obama. *Journal of African American Studies*, 15(3):269–278.

Tillman, L. 2006. Researching and writing from an African-American perspective: reflective notes on three research studies. *International Journal of Qualitative Studies in Education*, 9(3):265-287. Special Issue: Research on the Color Line: Perspectives on Race, Culture and Qualitative Research. Accessed 12 January 2014 DOI: 10.1080/09518390600696513

Van Wyk, M.M. 2014. Towards an Afrocentric-indigenous pedagogy. In C. Okeke, M. van Wyk & N. Phasha. *Schooling, Society and Inclusive Education: An Afrocentric perspective*. Cape Town: Oxford University Press.

Van Wyk, M.M. 2014. Conceptualizing an Afrocentric-Indigenous Pedagogy for an inclusive classroom environment. *Mediterranean Journal of Social Sciences*, 5(4):292–299.

Walker, F.R. & Greene, D.M. 2006. Exploring Afrocentricity: an analysis of the discourse of Jesse Jackson. *Journal of African American Studies*, 9(4):61–71.

CHAPTER 2

Fred Bakkabulindi

Positivism and interpretivism: Distinguishing characteristics, criteria and methodology

KEY CONCEPTS

Empiricism is a methodological standpoint that holds that in order for any claim about the world to be meaningful, it has to be verified through direct observation.

Grounded theory is an interpretive/qualitative research design, whereby a researcher intends to build a theory, that is grounded within the data collected. In other words, it is interpretive/qualitative research that is used to construct a theory.

Natural sciences are sciences that deal with physical and material phenomena such as animal life (zoology) or plant life (botany), or chemical properties of matter (chemistry). They may also be called the pure, basic, hard or physical sciences.

Paradigm is a worldview that underpins the theories and methodology of a subject or phenomenon, to which one belongs or subscribes (Greek: *paradeigma* = to show side by side). When someone changes sides in their thinking, that person is said to have undergone a paradigm shift.

Philosophy is the study of the nature of knowledge and knowing; philosophical means taking a rational and logical approach to knowledge. Its derivation is the love for wisdom (Greek: *philos* = love; *sophia* = wisdom).

Sociology is the study of human beings living together as companions (Latin: *socius* = companion).

LEARNING OUTCOMES

By the end of this chapter, you should be able to:

▶ Define both the positivist and interpretive research paradigms in a way that distinguishes the two.

▶ Discuss five philosophical characteristics distinguishing positivism from interpretivism.

▶ Discuss in detail the methodological characteristics distinguishing positivism from interpretivism.

▶ Discuss five criteria to use in deciding between positivism or interpretivism as the main approach in a study.

▶ Outline the hypothetico-deductive methodology of positivist research.

▶ Outline the inductive methodology of interpretive research.

Case study

Consider the following conversation between two university students, Abaca and Diefu, who have just finished the coursework part of their degree and are now starting the research phase. Both are grappling with what type of research to undertake:

Abaca: Congratulations on finishing the coursework part of our degree.

Diefu: Congratulations too.

Abaca: You know, I always thought the research phase would be a walkover.

Diefu: I still think it will be. Why not?

Abaca: This morning, I went to my potential supervisor for advice on what kind of research to undertake, but I was in for a shock!

Diefu: What kind of shock?

Abaca: Instead of the supervisor giving me a research topic as I expected, he asked me first to assure him that I am a posi…, posi…, I think 'positivist', as he is. Or else I should go to his colleagues, who are …

Diefu: Negativists?

Abaca: No, no, no! I don't think there are any 'negativists'. He said they are 'interpretivists'.

Diefu: What is that?

Abaca: I am just as confused by the term. He told me to be sure of what each category of researchers subscribes to, and to convince him with reasons, about which camp (or did he say '**paradigm**'?), I want to belong to

Diefu: Then you are in trouble!

Abaca: And you? You are surely in the same boat as I am!

Diefu: Then we had better get acquainted to what those terms mean.

Introduction

Having looked at a general introduction to research in Chapter 1, this chapter is intended to help researchers – such as the students cited in our opening case study – who are grappling with what type of research to undertake. As the case study suggests, often the fact that students have done research methodology as part of their coursework does not mean that they are fully ready for every question on research that may arise later. For this reason, we will try in this chapter to equip you with the knowledge to help you to properly decide on whether and when to undertake research that belongs to the positivist or interpretive paradigm. We do this because often students impulsively decide to do positivist or interpretive research without a firm basis for doing so. Indeed, we venture to say that sometimes a student chooses a research paradigm just because others have done so. We hope that at the end of the chapter you will be in position to clearly and rationally decide whether the positivist or interpretive paradigm is more suitable for your research.

   You will also be in a better position to appreciate many of the following chapters in this book which expand on the positivist and interpretive paradigms respectively. Chapters 10, 13, 15, 18, 22, 23, 24 and 26 will discuss the positivist paradigm, while Chapters 3, 4, 5, 6, 10, 12, 13, 14, 16, 17, 19, 20, 25 and 27 are developed around intrepretivism. In helping you to appreciate the two research paradigms and their related issues, in the next section of this chapter, we introduce the concept of a research paradigm, and its significance in research. We then discuss positivism and interpretivism as the two major contrasting research paradigms. We give five philosophical characteristics distinguishing positivism from interpretivism in section 2.2, with more details on the methodological differences in section 2.3. Five criteria are suggested for you to use in deciding whether to use positivism or interpretivism as the main approach for your own study in section 2.4. Then in section 2.5, you will read about the methodology or steps of positivist research, and those of interpretivism in section 2.6, before the conclusion to the chapter draws together the main ideas that have been covered.

Let us now start with the concept of a research paradigm, in the next section.

2.1 Research paradigms

Guba and Lincoln (1994:107) give a comprehensive definition of the term paradigm, thus:

> A paradigm may be viewed as a set of basic beliefs [...] that deals with [...] first principles. It represents a worldview that defines, for its holder, the nature of the "world," the individual's place in it, and the range of possible relationships to that world and its parts [...]. The beliefs are basic in the sense that that they must be accepted simply on faith [...]; there is no way to establish their ultimate truthfulness

So in simple terms, we can define a research paradigm as a sort of 'camp', to which a researcher belongs in terms of assumptions, propositions, thinking and approach to research. Research paradigms are therefore important because they are the philosophical bases for us as researchers, that inform our choices about which research questions to address, and what methodology to employ. Two research paradigms are discussed widely in the literature, namely, the positivist and the interpretive. A positivist study is one whose implementer takes a position which is underpinned by the positive belief or assumption that most phenomena in the world are observable and measurable. In particular, Gay and Airasian (2003:8) observe that positivists have

> the belief or assumption that we inhabit a relatively stable, uniform, and coherent world that we can measure, understand and generalise about. This view adopted from the **natural sciences** implies that the world, and the laws that govern it, are relatively stable and predictable, and can be understood by scientific research [...]. In this quantitative – also called positivist – perspective, claims about the world are not considered meaningful unless they can be verified through direct observation.

Thinking about paradigms

The concept of a paradigm was introduced by the philosopher Thomas Kuhn in *The Structure of Scientific Revolutions* (Kuhn, 1962/2012), which first appeared in 1962, (and recently republished in commemoration of 50 years of the work (Kuhn, 2012)). In particular, Kuhn devoted Chapter V of the book to "the priority of paradigms". Ironically, however, in this publication, Kuhn does not directly define a paradigm, let alone a research paradigm.

Noting that the positivist research paradigm is also termed the quantitative, the traditional, the experimental, or the **empiricist** paradigm, we can define a quantitative or positivist study as one based on testing a theory, where the theory relates to variables, which variables are measured with numbers, and analysed with statistical procedures. Positivist thinking in the social sciences comes from an empiricist tradition established by such authorities as the Frenchman who founded **sociology**, Auguste Comte (1798–1857), British philosopher John Stuart Mill (1806–1873), and the classical French sociologist Emile Durkheim (1858–1917).

In contrast, an interpretive study is one whose implementer takes an anti-positivist or post-positivist position, which stipulates that interpretive research is based on beliefs and purposes that are very different from those of positivism. In particular, Gay and Airasian (2003:9) assert that

> qualitative [or positivist] researchers do not accept the view of a stable, coherent, uniform world. They argue that all meaning is situated in a particular perspective or context, and, since different people and groups have different perspectives and contexts, there are many different meanings in the world, none of which is necessarily more valid or true than another.

It follows then that in interpretive research, a researcher must be ready to understand what the participants are thinking and feeling, in addition to how they communicate, both verbally and non-verbally. Having noted that the interpretive research paradigm is also termed the qualitative, constructivist, naturalistic, post-positivist or postmodern perspective, we can define a qualitative or interpretive study as one that is based on building a holistic picture, formed with words, and reporting detailed views of the respondents or study subjects. Interpretive social science can be traced back to German sociologist, Max Weber (1864–1920) and the German philosopher Wilhem Dilthey (1833–1911); it began as a counter-movement to the dominant positivist tradition.

With this background on research paradigms, we will now deal philosophically with five characteristics distinguishing positivism from interpretivism. Before moving on, test your understanding of the concepts we have covered so far, by doing the foliong activity.

Stop and reflect

1 Earlier, we defined a research paradigm, and suggested other names, that is, synonyms, for the term. Which ones? By searching the internet, get more such synonyms and note how each is defined.
2 Now search for the term positivism, its synonyms, and again note the definitions.
3 Repeat the search for synonyms and definitions, but this time, for the term interpretivism.

2.2 Characteristics distinguishing positivism from interpretivism

As suggested by the opening case study, it is important to know the distinction between positivism and interpretivism as research paradigms. In this section, then, we discuss five differences between the positivist and interpretive research paradigms, based on the philosophical concepts, ontology, epistemology, axiology, rhetoric and methodology. This is drawn from Creswell (2003:6), who observes that "philosophically researchers make claims about what is knowledge (ontology), how we know it (epistemology), what values go into it (axiology), how we write about it (rhetoric), and the process for studying it (methodology)". Why are we concerned with **philosophy** here? Our approach is in answer to Kezar's (2004:44) call to the effect that "it is our responsibility as teachers to have students read the philosophical texts", because, "students who do not read philosophy have a much harder time with [...] fundamental aspects of the research process" (Kezar, 2004:46).

So in this section we will expand on these five philosophical differences, starting with ontological ones.

2.2.1 Ontological differences

"Ontologists study what we mean when we say [that] something exists" (Mack, 2010:5). Ontology or metaphysics is therefore the science of being; the science dealing with matters of existence or reality. It also deals with questions of whether reality is objective or subjective. Objective reality is that which exists independent of the beholder, such as the researcher; while subjective reality is that reality that is created in the beholder's mind. On the ontological or metaphysical issue of what is real, the positivist or quantitative researcher views reality as objective, 'out there', and independent of the researcher. Positivists believe that reality is separate from the individual who observes it. They consider the subject (the researcher) and the object (the phenomenon being researched) to be separate, independent things. In short, positivist ontology is dualistic in nature. For positivist researchers, something can be measured objectively by using an instrument (e.g. a questionnaire).

In contrast, interpretivists believe that reality and the individual who observes it cannot be separated. Put slightly differently, "reality is not waiting to be discovered. Instead, the social world is largely what people perceive it to be. Social life exists as people experience it and give it meaning" (Neuman, 2000:72). Thus for the qualitative or interpretive researcher, the only reality is that construed by the individuals involved in the research situation. In the interpretive paradigm, multiple realities exist in any given situation. So the qualitative researcher must be ready to report holistically from the perspective of those individuals being researched, his or her own perspective, and even to anticipate the readers or audience who will interpret the study findings from their own perspective.

Ontology aside, another question is about how someone comes to know, and what constitutes knowledge, leading to the issue of epistemology in the next section.

2.2.2 Epistemological differences

Epistemology relates to how a researcher comes to know and what constitutes that knowledge. In other words, epistemology is the science of truth, that is, the reliability of claims about knowledge. In a view that rather differs from those we have covered earlier, Creswell (1994:5) defines epistemology as relating to the "relationship of the researcher to the researched". With positivism, the relationship of the researcher to that being researched, "the researcher should remain distant and independent of that being researched" (Creswell, 1994:6). Thus in positivist or quantitative studies, the researcher attempts to control for bias, to select a representative sample, and be 'objective' in assessing a situation.

Weber (2004:vi) observes that "interpretivists recognise that the knowledge they build reflects their particular goals, culture, experience, history, and so on …". Interpretive or qualitative researchers interact with those they study. This interaction may take the form of the interpretivist living with and/or observing the study subjects for a considerable length of time. In short, we are saying that the while the positivist researcher tries to maximise the distance between the researcher and those being researched, the interpretive researcher tries to minimise the distance.

In addition to epistemology, there is also the issue of what values go into the research process (axiology), as discussed in the next section.

2.2.3 Axiological differences

Axiology relates to the study of such issues as values, value judgements and ethics. Mahoney and Goertz (2006:227) observe that the positivist and interpretive research traditions are alternative cultures, each with "its own values, beliefs and norms". Positivist axiology stipulates that observable facts are distinct from personal ideas and values. Thus a positivist researcher is enjoined by axiology to keep personal values out of the study. This the positivist will accomplish by entirely omitting statements about values from a written report, using impersonal language, and reporting the facts, arguing closely from the evidence gathered in the study.

On the other hand, interpretivists consider it ambitious to claim that a researcher can be impartial, objective, and neutral. In other words, interpretivism allows a researcher to give meaning to whatever phenomenon they are researching in a partial, subjective, and biased way. Hence, the interpretive or qualitative researcher admits to the value-laden nature of the study and actively reports own values and biases, as well as the value nature of information gathered from the field. With the interpretive or qualitative paradigm, the language of the study may well be first person and personal.

Apart from ontological, epistemological and axiological differences, positivist and interpretive researchers also differ in terms of rhetoric; that is, the way they write about research, as will be elaborated in the next section.

2.2.4 Rhetorical differences

Rhetoric is one's ability to shape one's discourse in writing or speaking, aware of one's ideological stance and that of the audience. As we have said, positivist and interpretive researchers differ in terms of rhetoric, that is, in the way they write about research. For example, when writing say, a proposal or report, the language should be impersonal and formal, and based on accepted forms such as those which demonstrate relationship and comparison. Readers will see such phrases as "data were collected" and "the researcher established that ...", language that is intended to remove the subjective personality of the researcher or author. In contrast, the language of interpretive or qualitative studies can be personal, informal and based on definitions that evolve during the study. The readers will see such expressions as "I collected data" and "I established that ...", which reflect the subjective personality of the researcher or author. From these four differences emerges a methodology – the entire process of a study – that differs too.

The methodological differences between the two paradigms are discussed next.

2.2.5 Methodological differences

Methodology refers to the best strategy for gaining knowledge. The research paradigm you choose for a given study – whether positivist or interpretive – has a great impact on your choice of strategies for data collection, analysis and interpretation. If you choose the positivist paradigm, you will have decided to use a deductive form of logic wherein theories and hypotheses are tested in a cause-and-effect sequence; whereby concepts, variables, and hypotheses are chosen before the study begins, and remain fixed throughout the study – in other words, a static design. Sekaran (2003:27) officially defines deduction as the "process by which we arrive at a reasoned conclusion by logical generalisation of a known fact". On the other hand, in an interpretive study, inductive logic prevails, in which induction is the process where a researcher observes certain phenomena and, on this basis, arrives at conclusions. In other words, in induction the researcher logically establishes a general proposition (or **grounded theory**), based on the observed facts. Thus with interpretive or qualitative research, the categories emerge from the respondents, rather than being identified in advance by the researcher.

In the next section you will learn about these methodological differences in detail, but try the activity that follows to consolidate your understanding of what has been covered.

Stop and reflect

In the last section, we presented five philosophical differences between positivism and interpretivism. With a colleague or peer who has read the same section, discuss these differences with a view to understanding them in your own words.

2.3 Methodological differences in detail

So far, we have dealt with the differences between positivism and interpretivism as research paradigms under five headings. However, are all those differences really fundamental? According to Weber (2004), apart from the methodological ones, the other differences are not fundamental; rather, he asserts:

> I believe the differences lie more in the choice of research methods rather than any substantive differences at… [another] level. In this regard, researchers who are labelled as positivists tend to use certain kinds of research methods in their work – experiments, surveys, and field studies. Interpretivists, on the other hand, tend to use other kinds of research methods in their work – case studies, ethnographic studies, phenomenographic studies, and ethnomethodological studies. (Weber, 2004:x).

In this section we deal with the details implied in Weber's (2004) assertion that the methodological differences are more fundamental than the other differences. We will start with how positivist research is more deductive, while interpretivists in contrast tend to emphasise induction.

2.3.1 Deduction for positivists versus induction for interpretivists

Positivist, or quantitative, research is said to be deductive because the research starts from a general theory about the specific study context. This implies that positivist research is theory-driven. That is, for positivist research, the problem under study, as reflected in the research title or topic, is usually a follow-up of a theory. And since many theories are co-relational, that is, they relate to at least two variables, positivist research topics will also usually be co-relational. In other words, these topics relate at least two variables, with at least one independent variable (IV), and at least one dependent variable (DV).

Interpretive or qualitative research is the opposite in that it is usually inductive, that is, it usually moves from specific study contexts to a general (grounded) theory. In other words, while positivist research is usually theory-driven, that is, it tests a theory, interpretive research is usually aimed at theory-building.

Further, because of the theory-driven nature of positivist research, theories may feature more prominently in research proposals and reports for positivist research than in those of interpretive research. For example, a proposal or report for positivist research may feature a so-called theoretical perspective of the background, which may not feature in a proposal for interpretive research. The proposal or report for positivist research may feature a theoretical review, while such a section may be irrelevant in a proposal or report for interpretive research. We will develop this issue of positivist and interpretive research being deductive and inductive respectively, in sections 2.5 and 2.6 of this chapter.

Next, let us look at how the positivist and interpretive research paradigms put emphasis on numbers and words respectively.

2.3.2 Numbers for positivists versus words for interpretivists

When positivist and interpretive researches are perceived as quantitative and qualitative respectively, several differences can be deduced between the two research paradigms. For example, while quantitative research emphasises the numbers or statistical quantities, qualitative research stresses the power of words or qualitative descriptions. While quantitative research is more interested in what can be quantified, qualitative research is holistic or interested in details. Indeed, in Latin, the question *quantum*? from which the adjective quantitative originates, translates as 'how much or how many?', which usually calls for either one answer involving numbers or quantities. On the other hand, the Latin question *qualis*? from which the adjective qualitative is derived, means 'what sort of?' which calls for either multiple answers or one answer that is layered and detailed. In a number of other chapters in this book, you will see the issue of positivist and interpretive research being either quantitative or qualitative respectively, taken further. For example, Chapter 10 on research design will distinguish between quantitative or positivist and qualitative or interpretive research designs.

In Chapter 13 on the logic of sampling, you will see the distinction between the random sampling strategies preferred by quantitative or positivist researchers, and non-random sampling techniques being of more relevance to the interpretive or qualitative paradigm. Chapter 15 on experimental methods of data collection and Chapter 18 on the questionnaire approach to data collection, are of more relevance to positivism, while Chapters 16, 17, 19 and 20 on the observation method, the interview method, the focus group discussion method, and secondary sources of data, are key methods of data collection for interpretivists. Further, while Chapters 22 and 23 on descriptive statistics and inferential statistics respectively are of more relevance to positivists or quantitative researchers, Chapter 25 on qualitative data analysis is a key chapter for interpretivists or qualitative researchers. While Chapter 26 is on the presentation of quantitative research reports, Chapter 27 is on the presentation of qualitative research findings.

Let us now see how positivists claim to be more objective, while interpretivists allow subjectivity.

2.3.3 Objectivity for positivists versus subjectivity for interpretivists: Implications for data collection

While positivist research is ontologically objective, interpretive research is ontologically subjective. Positivist research, being ontologically objective, assumes the existence of only one reality, and hence it usually relies on only one category of respondents (e.g. lecturers in a university; students following a particular course; teachers of mathematics), and one method of data collection. This is usually the survey method, involving only one instrument, which is often the self-administered questionnaire (SAQ). In contrast, the interpretive approach is ontologically subjective, which means it allows for multiple realities, implying that interpretive researchers are interested in triangulation (i.e. using several sources of data and/or respondents), and they use several methods and/or instruments of data collection. In Chapters 14 and 18 of this book respectively, you will read more about survey research and the questionnaire approach to data collection.

To maintain its epistemologically objective nature, the positivist research paradigm calls for maximising the distance between the researcher and researchee, This involves the use of the less interactive methods of data collection, such as the survey method, through the use of self-administered questionnaires (SAQs). Interpretive research, on the other hand, being epistemologically subjective, calls for minimising the distance between the researcher and researchee. This, then, involves the use of such subjective/interactive methods of data collection as observation and interviewing. In Chapter 6, you will read more about the issue of objectivity versus subjectivity in research. Positivists and interpretivists also differ on how they choose subjects (samples) to study.

We discuss these differences in sampling methods next.

2.3.4 Sampling: Large and random for positivists vs small and non-random samples for interpretivists

Since positivist research is deductive (section 2.3.1), that is, interested in testing theories, to determine whether the predictive generalisations of a given theory of interest hold true, positivist researchers deal with relatively large samples. These large samples are more likely to be representative of their parent populations. Interpretive researchers, on the other hand, usually deal with small samples that are often not representative of their parent populations, but which they study holistically, that is, from all angles, to bring out the many realities. Also, because of the need to generalise, positivist researchers are stricter about the way their samples are chosen, insisting on objective or random sampling methods, such as simple random, systematic random, and stratified random. In contrast, interpretive researchers usually make do with subjective or non-random sampling methods, such as accidental, judgmental, quota, and snowball sampling. Chapter 13 on the logic of sampling will expand on these sampling methods for you.

How does positivism differ from interpretivism as far as data analysis is concerned? An answer is suggested in the next section.

2.3.5 Data analysis: Statistical methods for positivists vs non-statistical methods for interpretivists

In the data analysis step, researchers derive meaning from the data they have gathered. While data analysis can take several forms and consequently use different names, data analysis techniques can be generally categorised as either positivist or interpretive, depending on the research approach or paradigm. Chapters 22, 23 and 24 of this book are devoted to positivist or quantitative data analysis, while Chapter 25 deals with interpretive or qualitative data analysis. While positivist data analysis involves statistical procedures, interpretivists analyse their data interpretively by "synthesising, categorising, and organising data into patterns that produce a descriptive narrative synthesis" (Gay & Airasian, 2003:9).

In the next section you will read about some criteria to use when choosing between positivism and interpretivism. Before moving on, try the challenge that follows to help think through the different paradigms and what they entail. It may be useful at this point to think about what has been covered in section 2.3 and to try and summarise the arguments about or differences between paradigms.

Summarising what we understand

The discussed differences between the paradigms are numerous and sometimes raise suspicion, antagonism and enmity between the followers of the respective research paradigms. Differences notwithstanding, there are several authorities who either say that those differences are non-existent or, if they do exist, they are not fundamental. For example, Gay and Airasian (2003:9) note that, "despite the differences between them, you should not consider quantitative [or positivist] and qualitative [or interpretive] research to be oppositional," They advise that the two paradigms should be considered as complementary because, when taken together, they represent the full range of research methods. Some authorities even advise that, "the terms 'quantitative' [or positivist] and 'qualitative' [or interpretive] should be avoided [… because] the quant–qual distinction distracts us from consideration of more important issues, and tends to constrain opportunities for innovation" (Wood & Welch, 2010:57). In other words, no good research is purely positivist or purely interpretive, hence the new research paradigm of "mixed research methods" (DeLisle, 2011:89) or "critical social science" (Neuman, 2000:75). You will read more on the issue of critical research in Chapter 4.

Critical thinking challenge

In this chapter, we have introduced the positivist research paradigm, contrasting it with the interpretive paradigm. To which of the two paradigms do you feel you belong now? In other words, assess your position on the discussion in sections 2.1 through 2.3 in this chapter.

2.4 Criteria for choice between positivist and interpretive research

As suggested by the opening case study, it is important to have a basis for choosing between positivism and interpretivism as research paradigms. In this section we suggest five criteria that you as a researcher can use when choosing which of the positivist and interpretive approaches to employ in a given study. These criteria are: the researcher's worldview, training or experiences, psychological attributes, the nature of the problem in his or her study, and the audience.

We start with how the researcher's worldview is important.

2.4.1 The researcher's worldview

A researcher brings to a given study a worldview, an outlook, that favours a set of qualitative or quantitative ontological, epistemological, axiological, rhetorical, and methodological assumptions. For example, some individuals see reality as subjective and want a close interaction with informants. These individuals are more likely to opt for interpretive research. Others may be more comfortable with an objective stance, using survey or experimental instruments. These people are more inclined towards positivist research.

Next, let us consider how important the researcher's training or experience is.

2.4.2 The researcher's training or experience

If an individual is trained or experienced in technical, scientific writing, statistics, or computer statistical programs, and is familiar with quantitative journals in the library, that individual would most likely choose the quantitative paradigm. The qualitative approach incorporates much more of a literary form of writing than the quantitative approach. Library experience with qualitative journals and texts is important in providing illustrations of good writing. With the advent of qualitative computer software programs, experience in using these, too, is in asset in choosing the qualitative approach.

The psychology of the researcher also matters, as elaborated in the next section.

2.4.3 The researcher's psychological attributes

When it comes to psychological attributes, it is important to note that because quantitative studies are the traditional mode of research, carefully worked-out procedures and rules exist for the research. In addition, collecting and analysing data usually involves a shorter period than that of qualitative designs. So if a researcher engages in a quantitative study, he or she is choosing a paradigm that offers a low-risk, fixed method without ambiguities and frustrations. Alternatively, qualitative design is one in which the rules and procedures are not fixed, but rather, they are open and emerge with the research process. The design calls for an individual who is willing to take the risks that are inherent in an ambiguous procedure. This person, too, needs to have the time and patience for a lengthy study.

Another important issue is the nature of the problem in the study.

2.4.4 Nature of 'the problem' in research

A research problem is a concern or anomaly that needs to be addressed; it is a puzzle or question that begs an answer (e.g. why more than half of all students who enrol for a doctoral degree do not complete it). Whether certain problems are better suited to qualitative or quantitative studies is open to debate. However, the nature of the problem is an important factor. For quantitative or positivist studies, the problem evolves from the literature. The relevant variables are known, and theories may exist that need to be tested and verified. For example, if the problem in your study is identifying factors that influence an outcome, the utility of an intervention, or understanding the best predictors of outcomes, then a quantitative approach is better for you. It is also the better approach to use to test a theory or an explanation. For a qualitative study, on the other hand, the problem needs to be explored because little information exists on the topic. The relevant variables are largely unknown, and the researcher wants to focus on the context that may shape the understanding of the phenomenon being studied. In many qualitative studies, a theoretical base may not guide the study because those available theories may be inadequate, incomplete, or simply missing.

What about the researcher's audience? Is it important? We try to answer such questions now.

2.4.5 The researcher's audience

A researcher's choice of research paradigm must be sensitive to his or her audience, whether this audience consists of journal editors, journal readers, graduate committees, or colleagues in the field. The paradigm of choice must be one that the audience understands, or at least supports as a viable, legitimate methodology. This implies that as a student, even if you are interested in positivist research, if your potential mentors insist otherwise, you are better off reconsidering because the mentors are part of your research audience. Therefore as a student you are advised to study your teachers (your potential supervisors), your department, school, research group, and the like, to see the research paradigm they typically support, and then to try to adjust accordingly.

In the next section, you will read about the methodology you will follow if you choose to do positivist research. Before moving on, try the following challenge to focus your own ideas about approaches.

In section 2.4, we suggested five criteria that you as a researcher can use when choosing which of the positivist and interpretive approaches to employ in a given study.

1 Assuming you are a positivist, assess yourself on how ready you are to undertake the research implied by the paradigm. In other words, convince yourself that you satisfy the criteria of positivist research, as suggested in section 2.4 of this chapter.

2 Repeat the self-assessment process, but this time for interpretive research.

2.5 Methodology of positivist research: the hypothetical-deductive process

Chapter 9 in this book is specifically devoted to the research process, that is, the steps a researcher will follow when doing research, whether the research is positivist or interpretive. However, in this section, we want to stress the deductive nature of positivist research, which we have alluded to earlier (sections 2.2.5 and 2.3.1). In other words, we want to look at the steps involved in deduction as a tool for positivist research. Several authors outline the deductive process, some (for example, Sekaran, 2003:29) preferring to term it the hypothetico-deductive method of doing research. The etymology of the word can be traced in Wood and Welch (2010:62), who observe that in the process, "hypothesis testing involves proposing a hypothesis and then deducing its consequences". We will use the seven steps of Sekaran's hypothetico-deductive method as our basic framework of discussion. The seven steps are 1) Observation; 2) Preliminary information gathering; 3) Theory formulation; 4) Hypothesising; 5) Further scientific data collection; 6) Data analysis; and 7) Deduction. Let us examine these in detail next.

2.5.1 Observation

Also known as 'scouting' (Bordens & Abbott, 2008:20), observation is the first step in the hypothetico-deductive process, in which some problematic behavior or event catches the researcher's attention. A potential researcher may sense changes in behaviour, attitude, and feelings of say, workers in a given organisation. Students' lack of interest in their studies, and the like, could easily attract the attention of the teacher or lecturer, though why these changes occur may be unclear.

Next, is the need for preliminary information gathering.

2.5.2 Preliminary information gathering

It is through preliminary information gathering that a potential researcher gets an idea or a feel for what is transpiring in the situation. For example, by doing library research or a literature review, the investigator would identify how such issues have been tackled in other situations. This information will give additional insights into the possible factors that could be operating in the particular situation. It is worth noting that Chapter 8 of this book deals with literature review, which, as we are suggesting here, is an important tool during the preliminary information gathering step of the hypothetico-deductive methodology of positivist research.

Once the researcher has increased his or her level of awareness as to what is happening, she or he can then focus on the problem and the associated factors, through theory formulation.

2.5.3 Theory formulation

Theory formulation is an attempt by a researcher to integrate all the information so far gathered, in a logical manner, so that the factors or independent variables (IVs) responsible for the problem on the dependent variable (DV), can be conceptualised and tested. In formulating the theoretical framework, a researcher is often guided by experience and intuition. In this step, the researcher examines the critical variables (CVs), what their contribution or influence is in explaining why the problem (on the DV) occurs, and how it can be solved. The research will theoretically weave the network of associations identified among the variables with a justification as to why they might influence the problem.

Why is it that a researcher has to formulate a theoretical framework every time he or she investigates a problem? Why can the researcher not act on the information obtained in previously published research findings, as he or she surveys the literature? There are reasons for this. One is that different studies may have identified different variables, some of which may not be relevant to the current researcher's study situation. Also, in the previous studies, some of the hypotheses may have been substantiated and others not, thus presenting to the current researcher with a puzzling situation. So, when solving any given research problem, a researcher has to formulate and test an applicable theoretical framework relevant to that particular situation.

Having looked at theory formulation, we now turn to hypothesising.

2.5.4 Hypothesising

Also known as "formulating tentative explanations" (Bordens & Abbott, 2008:20), hypothesising is the next logical in the hypothetico-deductive process, after theory formulation. From the theorised network of associations among the variables, a researcher can generate testable hypotheses or educated conjectures. As just suggested, a hypothesis is a statement that is verifiable or testable by a researcher; it is an educated guess by a researcher.

Hypotheses have to be subjected to testing, which is preceded by further scientific data collection.

2.5.5 Further scientific data collection

After the development of hypotheses, a researcher needs to obtain data with respect to each variable in the hypotheses. In other words, the researcher needs to undertake further scientific data collection in order to test the hypotheses that he/she has generated in the study. The data collected by the researcher now forms the basis for his or her further data analysis. But before the data collection, the researcher has to design and/or adapt instruments to measure the respective variables in the study. While the researcher can design the instruments from scratch, it is usually advisable to look for and adapt ready-made instruments whose psychometric properties (validity and reliability) can be cited.

You will read more about the design of (positivist) research instruments or tools in Chapters 11 and 21 of this book. In particular, Chapter 11 is dedicated to defining and measuring variables which is an important step when one is designing one's research instruments. Chapter 21 will deal with how to carry out a pilot study aimed at, among other aims, testing whether the research instruments are valid, and have reliability. Validity refers to whether a given instrument is correctly measuring the variables that it is intended to measure. Reliability refers to whether the respondents will potentially answer a given instrument consistently, that is, without guessing. During the actual research or data collection stage, a researcher has two general approaches (to data collection), namely, primary and secondary. Primary, first-hand or field research is that which aims to collect new data by contacting or observing respondents directly in the field; while secondary, second-hand or desk research, uses existing data, by consulting secondary sources, such as books in a library.

A researcher can choose from at least three methods of primary data collection, namely observation, interviewing, and survey/questionnaire methods. However, while the issue of data collection cannot for now be examined in full detail in this limited section, we should note that positivist or quantitative researchers usually opt for the survey method of primary research. This usually involves the use of questionnaires because of the large samples needed in quantitative research. With this background note in mind, you will read further on the issue of data collection in positivist research in Chapter 14 (survey research); Chapter 15 (experimental methods of data collection); and Chapter 18 (the questionnaire approach to data collection).

As illustrated in the next section, the data collected have to be analysed.

2.5.6 Data analysis

In the data analysis step, researchers statistically analyse the data they have gathered to see if the hypotheses they initially generated are supported. For instance, to see if remuneration influences the job commitment of an employee, a researcher might want to do a correlational analysis and determine the relationship between the two factors. Similarly, the researcher can test other hypotheses through appropriate statistical analyses. It is worth noting, however, that data analysis is only a component of data management. During data management, two major activities take place, namely, data processing and analysis. Data processing is the preparation of data for analysis, and involves such activities as editing data for errors; coding the data; entering the data into a computer program; and presenting the data in such forms as tables and graphs.

You will find the issue of data processing examined briefly in Chapter 22 of this book. Data analysis is an attempt by a researcher to make sense of, or interpret, data, which is to get what the data mean. In Part Three (Chapters 22 to 25), it will become more apparent to you that while data analysis can take several forms and hence names, data analysis techniques can be categorised as either positivist or interpretive, depending on the research approach or paradigm. While Chapters 22 to 24 are devoted to positivist or quantitative data analysis, Chapter 25 deals with interpretive or qualitative data analysis. In particular, it will be made clearer that positivist data analysis has two major branches, namely, the descriptive and inferential components.

Descriptive data analysis, which uses tools which are collectively known as descriptive statistics (Chapter 22) deals with the description of data that have been collected on a sample; while inferential data analysis, which uses tools which are collectively known as inferential statistics (Chapter 23) deals with the use of descriptive statistics, that is the data collected from a sample, to draw inferences or to make deductions or genaralisations on the whole population from which the sample was chosen. You will also learn that data analysis can be done either manually or with the help of a computer program. In Chapters 22, 23 and 25, you will deal with manual data analysis, while in Chapter 24 you will examine data analysis that is facilitated by a computer.

From the data analysis, the researcher is now in position to make deductions.

2.5.7 Deduction

Deduction is the process of arriving at conclusions or inferences, by interpreting the meaning of the results of data analysis. For instance, if a researcher finds from data analysis, that increasing remuneration is positively correlated with the job commitment of employees, the researcher can deduce that if the job commitment of the employees is to be increased, the remuneration of the employees has also to be increased. Based on such deductions, the researcher would make recommendations on how the job commitment problem of say, lecturers in Uganda, could be solved. In Chapter 23, you will read about inferential statistics and how to use different statistical techniques in order to come up with such deductions or inferences.

Critical thinking challenge

In section 2.5, we outlined the research process for positivist research. Now assume that you have been commissioned to carry out positivist research to establish why the use of information and communication technology (ICT) by the students in your university is not as high as would be expected.

1 Outline how you envisage going through the hypothetico-deductive process to suggest the way forward.

2 At each stage of the process, what problems do you anticipate, and how will you deal with them?

2.6 Methodology of interpretive research

Having outlined the methodology of a positivist research process, let us now look at its counterpart – the methodology of an interpretive research process. We should note, however, that while interpretive researchers follow certain steps, these steps are less rigid than those in positivist research. This implies that in interpretive research there is more flexibility than in positivist research in so far as following the 'rules' is concerned. We will use the six steps of the interpretive qualitative research process defined by Gay and Airasian (2003) as our framework for discussion. The six steps are: 1) Selecting the research topic or issue; 2) Reviewing the literature; 3) Selecting the research participants; 4) Data collection; 5) Analysing the data; and 6) Writing the report.

2.6.1 Selecting the research topic or issue

The first step in interpretive research is to select a topic or issue to study. There is an unlimited number of useful and viable research topics worth considering by an educational researcher. The following are a few examples: The quality of university education in an African country; The academic life of students in an African university; or Pedagogical practices in an African university. Gay and Airasian (2003:171) point out that a "new domain of qualitative research topics derives from the inequity and needs of lower socio-economic-status persons, ethnically diverse groups, persons with disabilities, and other advocacy groups".

The interpretive researcher has to begin with an open-ended, broad research topic that will narrow in focus and emerge as the researcher learns more about his or her research participants, their thoughts and ideas, and their settings. In other words, an interpretive researcher "might explore the many factors included in the general research topic to understand them and then select some feature to investigate" (Gay & Airasian, 2003:172). In summary, an interpretive researcher does not restrictively predefine his or her research topic before the study begins. This means that in interpretive research, there is not likely to be a well-defined problem statement until the research is well under way.

Next, we look at the need for reviewing the literature.

2.6.2 Reviewing the literature

Should an interpretive researcher spend a great deal of time examining the literature on their topic at the outset of a study? According to Gay and Airasian (2003), interpretive researchers differ in their opinions on the issue, with some interpretive researchers opting not to delve deeply into their literature until their topic has emerged, while others engage deeply with the literature initially. Those who do not go deeply into their literature initially, believe that too much emphasis on the literature at the start can prematurely narrow the focus of the intended topic prior to interaction with participants. Those interpretive researchers who engage with the literature upfront, assume that familiarity with literature gives the researcher a particular mind set or frame of reference for beginning his or her exploration.

In summary, because interpretive studies are open-ended in their enquiry, and plans and procedures emerge during the study, the interpretive research process follows the lead of the participants. This implies that different interpretive studies can have varied approaches to dealing with the literature, with some dealing with many literature sources, especially at the beginning, while others may use fewer literature sources, sometimes later in the study. The purpose and process of doing a literature review is dealt with in Chapter 8. Also, Chapter 28 guides you on how to cite and reference sources used in the literature review.

Having looked at the review of the literature, we now turn to the selection of research participants.

2.6.3 Selecting the research participants

After getting approval from perhaps the graduate school, or other relevant authority of their university to conduct the study, the interpretive researcher should identify the potential participants for the study. Chapter 13 on the logic of sampling deals with this issue in more detail. Here we present an abbreviated version of what you will find later. Gay and Airasian (2003:173) advise that the researcher "should do this [identification of the potential participants] first-hand, because the initial communication with potential participants is the start of the relationship with them throughout the study". They suggest that the interpretive researcher establishes a day and time when they can meet the potential participants in their natural setting to discuss the study.

This initial, face-to-face meeting with the potential participants has several benefits. For example, it gives the interpretive researcher a chance to view the participants' setting or settings. It also shows the potential participants that the interpretive researcher is willing to make an independent contract with them to discuss the study, showing his or her personal interest in them as participants. It allows the interpretive researcher to explain his or her expectations of the participants and to find out if they are interested in participating.

Tip

Resolving ethical issues

Some ethical issues to consider when selecting the research participants include protecting the interests of potentially vulnerable participants. In this respect, the researcher has to be clear about issues of confidentiality or anonymity. You will find out more about managing such issues in Chapters 6 and 7.

Once participants have been selected, the interpretive researcher has to obtain the formal and informed consent of the participants for being part of the study. This essential consent ensures that both the participants and the researcher know the rights and expectations of either party. Again, you will learn more about dealing with ethical issues in Chapter 7. When selecting the research participants, all interpretive researchers face the question of how many participants are enough, that is, the question of sample size". While Chapter 13 elucidates such issues, we quote Gay and Airasian (2003:195) who, in answer to the question of how many participants, observe that:

> The answer is, "it depends." There are no hard and fast numbers that represent the "correct" number of participants in a study. [However,] it is usually true that sample sizes in quantitative research are larger than [those in] qualitative [research]. Qualitative studies can be carried out with a single participant or, when studying multiple contexts, may have as many as 60 or 70 participants. However, rarely will qualitative studies have more than 20 or so participants [...]. The qualitative researcher's time, money, participant availability, participant interest and other factors will influence the number of participants engaged in a research sample.

Next, we look at the phase of data collection.

2.6.4   Data collection

Gay and Airasian (2003) observe that while there is a multiplicity of sources of interpretive data including observation, interviews, phone calls, personal and official documents and photographs, the most commonly used sources of interpretive data are observation and interviews. It is worth noting that Chapters 16 and 17 of this book are devoted to these two respective methods of data collection. The data collection methods used in interpretive research share one commonality: the researcher is the primary source of data. The researcher's ability to integrate data and analyse them is crucial because the data collected are typically narrative, and rich in both length and detail. It is also worth noting that interpretive researchers employ more than one data collection method. Indeed for them, any data collection method that is ethical and feasible, and that contributes to the understanding of the phenomenon being studied, can be used as necessity demands.

What about analysis of the data collected? We try to map an answer for you in the following section.

2.6.5   Analysing the data

The analysis of data collected in an interpretive research is quite lengthy and time consuming because of the large quantities of data, which are not usually organised in a manner that facilitates analysis. So, unlike in positivist research, the analysis of data in interpretive research is not left until all the data have been collected. Gay and Airasian (2003:228) assert that:

> The qualitative researcher begins data analysis from the initial interaction with participants and continues [...] throughout the [...] study. During the study, the qualitative researcher tries to progressively narrow and focus in on, the key aspects of the participants' data. Thus, the qualitative researcher goes through a series of steps and iterations: gathering data, examining data, comparing prior data to newer data, and developing new data to gather. There is simultaneous interaction of data collection and analysis, so that the researcher's emerging hunches or thoughts become the focus for the next data collection period.

Gay and Airasian (2003:229) also propose five steps in analysing interpretive data, namely: 1) Data managing; 2) Reading/memoing; 3) Describing the context and participants; 4) Classifying; and 5) Interpreting the data. Data managing, they explain, "involves creating and organising the data collected during the study" (p. 230), and before an interpretive researcher begins managing his or her data, he or she must put them in a form that will facilitate analysis. For example, the researcher might have to make sure that they have dated, organised and sequenced all their notes, transcripts, observer's comments, memos and reflections. This data managing serves not only to organise and check the data for completeness, but also to start the process of analysing and interpreting the data.

Reading/memoing will involve reading and writing memos about all the field notes, transcripts, and observer comments to help the analyst get an initial sense of the data. In the reading/memoing phase, it is important that the interpretive data analyst writes notes in the margins or highlights sections of importance. 'Describing' addresses what is going on in the setting of, and among, the participants, and is based on the researcher's collected observations and field notes. It is intended to provide a true picture of the setting and events that take place in it, so that the interpretive analyst understands his or her study context fully. Classifying, the fourth step in analysing interpretive data, entails breaking down the interpretive data through the process of coding or classifying.

> When concepts in the data are examined and compared to one another and connections are made, categories are formed. Categories are used to organize similar concepts into distinct groups [...]. Without data that are classified and grouped, there is no reasonable way for a researcher to analyse qualitative studies. The categories provide the basis for structuring analysis and interpretation (Gay & Airasian, 2003:232).

Interpretation of the data is the last step in the analysis of interpretive data, and is the reflective, integrative, and explanatory aspect of dealing with a study's data. During data interpretation, the issue is to answer three questions, namely: What is important in the data? Why is it important? What can be learned from it? The interpretive analyst's task, then, is to determine how one identifies what is important, why it is important, and what it indicates about the participants and the study context. For a fuller discussion of the analysis of qualitative data, please refer to Chapter 25.

Next, we move on to the phase of report writing.

2.6.6 Writing the report

The final stage in interpretive research, according to Gay and Airasian (2003), is the writing of a report which describes the study and its findings. The characteristics and length of the report will depend on the type of report that one is writing. If the researcher is writing a dissertation or thesis, the report will be lengthy and structured as per the format of the institution. If he or she is preparing a conference paper, it will be relatively shorter, limited by the number of pages available to the editor of the book to originate from the conference. If the researcher is writing a journal article, it will even be much shorter than a dissertation and or conference paper, limited by the number of pages available to the journal's editor. As a general rule, "the shorter the report, the harder it is to write because of the large amounts of data obtained in qualitative studies" (Gay & Airasian, 2003:247).

Usefully, Chapter 27 is devoted to the presentation of qualitative research findings. Chapter 29 describes the essentials of academic writing; while Chapter 30 is about writing for publication. These chapters will make it clear that the writing process not only helps the researcher to produce the research report, but it also compels researchers to re-examine their data interpretation:

> The concrete process of writing your thoughts in a logical and explanatory manner inevitably identifies flaws in your thinking, missing links in your descriptions, and new interpretations of your concepts and understandings [...]. That is [...], writing is also a test of your thoughts and interpretations (Gay & Airasian, 2003:247).

It is now time for another critical thinking challenge.

Critical thinking challenge

In section 2.6, we outlined the research process for interpretive research. Now, assume that you have been commissioned to carry out interpretive research to establish why the use of information and communication technology (ICT) by the students in your university is not as high as might be expected.
1 Outline how you envisage going through the inductive process to suggest the way forward.
2 At each stage of the process, what problems do you anticipate, and how will you deal with them?

Conclusion

This chapter is intended to equip you with the knowledge to help you to properly decide on whether and when to undertake positivist or interpretive research. We did this so that you can avoid the tendency that students often have, of impulsively deciding to do positivist or interpretive research without a firm basis for choosing to do so. We started the chapter by defining a research paradigm, before proposing the positivist and interpretive research paradigms (section 2.1) as the major research paradigms in current practice. Then we looked philosophically at several characteristics distinguishing the positivist from the interpretive paradigm (section 2.2). Noting that the methodological differences between the two paradigms were more fundamental than the other differences, we gave them (the methodological differences) more emphasis in their own section (section 2.3).

In section 2.4, we suggested the criteria for you as a researcher to use when choosing between the two research paradigms, before we focused on the methodology or steps of positivist and interpretive research respectively in sections 2.5 and 2.6. In short, in this chapter we have progressively taken you through the fundamentals of positivism and interpretivism, fulfilling we hope the learning objectives we set ourselves at the beginning of the chapter. You should now be in a position to informedly and logically decide under which circumstances the positivist or interpretive paradigm is more suitable for your research. You are also in a better position to appreciate many of the following chapters in this book (e.g. Chapters 10, 13, 15, 18, 22–24 and 26), which are built around the positivist paradigm. Similarly with Chapters 3–6, 10, 12–14, 16–17, 19–20, 25 and 27, which are built around intrepretivism.

Now, after completing the final activities, you can confidently move to the next chapter which is devoted solely to the interpretive paradigm.

Closing activities

Analysis and consolidation questions

Question 1
The positivist versus interpretive debate has raged for decades and is bound to continue the world over for years to come. Contribute to the debate by:

a Discussing the philosophical differences between the two research paradigms in terms of (i) ontology; (ii) epistemology; (iii) axiology; (iv) rhetoric; and (v) methodology.

b Suggesting the criteria to base one's research process on when deciding on which paradigm to adopt.

c Suggesting which paradigm is more suitable for a contemporary social sciences research student.

Question 2
We dealt with the positivist and interpretive research paradigms respectively in this chapter. The similarities and differences between the two were given in detail. Comment on the meaning and implications of the following differences between the two research paradigms:

a While interpretive research allows subjectivity, positivist research tries to be as objective as possible.

b While interpretive research tries to minimise the distance between the researcher and the researchee, positivist research tries to maximise the distance.

Bibliography

Bordens, K.S. & Abbott, B.B. 2008. *Research design methods: A process approach* (7th ed.). Boston, US: McGraw-Hill.

Creswell, J.W. 1994. *Research design: Qualitative and quantitative approaches.* London, UK: Sage.

Creswell, J.W. 2003. *Research design: Qualitative, quantitative and mixed methods approaches* (2nd ed.). London, UK: Sage.

DeLisle, J. 2011. The benefits and challenges of mixing methods and methodologies: Lessons learnt from implementing qualitatively led mixed methods research designs in Trinidad and Tobago. *Caribbean Curriculum,* 18(10):87–120.

Gay, L.R. & Airasian, P. 2003. *Educational research: Competencies for analysis and applications* (7th ed.). New Jersey, US: Merrill/ Prentice-Hall. Printed and electronically reproduced by permission of Pearson Education Inc., New York, New York.

Guba, E.G. & Lincoln, Y. S. 1994. Competing paradigms in qualitative research. In N. K. Denzin & Y. S. Lincoln (Eds). *Handbook of qualitative research.* Thousand Oaks, CA: Sage (pp. 105–177).

Kezar, A. 2004. Wrestling with philosophy: Improving scholarship in higher education. *The Journal of Higher Education,* 75(1):42–55. Available: http://www.questia.com/library/journal/1g1-1113056620/wrestling-with-philosophy-improving-scholarship-in.

Kuhn, T.S. 1962/2012. *The Structure of Scientific Revolutions* (1st/ 4th eds.). Chicago, US: University of Chicago Press.

Mack, L. 2010. The philosophical underpinnings of educational research. *Polyglossia,* October, 19:5–11. Available: www.apu.ac.jp/rcaps/uploads/fckeditor/publications/polyglossia_v19_lindsay.pdf.

Mahoney, J. & Goertz, G. 2006. A tale of two cultures: Contrasting quantitative and qualitative research. *Political Analysis,* 14:227–249. doi: 10.1093/ pan/ mpj017.

Neuman, W.L. 2000. *Social research methods: Qualitative and quantitative approaches* (4th ed.). Boston, US: Allyn & Bacon.

Sekaran, U. 2003. *Research methods for business* (4th ed.). New York, US: Wiley & Sons.

Weber, R. 2004. The rhetoric of positivism versus interpretivism: A personal view (Editorial). *MIS Quarterly,* 28(1):iii–xii. Available: http://misq.org/downloads/download/editorial/25/weber2004positivism.

Wood, M. & Welch, C. 2010. Are "quantitative" and "qualitative" useful terms for describing research? *Methodological Innovations Online,* 5(1):56–71. doi: 10.4256/ mio.2010.0010

CHAPTER 3

Icarbord Tshabangu

Interpretive research: Construction of meanings

KEY CONCEPTS

Demographics quantifiable data on population trends such as gender, ethnicity, political, social, and economic descriptors.

Empiricist a view that knowledge only comes from sensory experience.

Epistemological relates to the theory of knowledge, its construction, and what it is to know.

Methodological relates to procedures and acceptable practices and rules in a particular discipline or enquiry.

Ontological relates to the nature of being, or existence of phenomena.

Phenomena a representation of something/things under study.

Philosophical describes something dedicated to the study of knowledge, existence, and the reality of things.

LEARNING OUTCOMES

By the end of this chapter, you should be able to:

▶ Construct a research study design that is solidly underpinned by the interpretive paradigm.

▶ Demonstrate the use of an appropriate and clear rationale at every level of the design.

▶ Engage in appropriate research activities, being mindful of and guided by the philosophical assumptions embedded in interpretive research.

▶ Differentiate interpretive research from positivist approaches.

▶ Develop knowledge of interpretive research's strengths and limitations, where a researcher may want to use mixed methods.

Case study

John, a PhD student at the University of Johannesburg, travels from Durban one afternoon to meet with his thesis supervisor, as planned. He believes his appointment is scheduled for 3:30pm as discussed with his supervisor the previous evening. To John's surprise, when he arrives on campus at 3:20pm, he is informed by the administrative staff that his supervisor had gone to conduct a lecture and is only due to finish at 4:30pm. Puzzled, John reaches for his diary to check what he has jotted down the previous day, to discover that he had written in bold, capital letters: **WEDNESDAY APPOINTMENT 2:30PM**. In his mind, somehow 3:30pm was retained, instead of 2:30. He then decides to wait until 4:30pm, after the lecture, to apologise to his supervisor and possibly get another appointment although this would incur further travelling costs and absence from work. After meeting with his supervisor and apologising for the mix-up, he is relieved when the supervisor offers to see him immediately, from 4:30pm to 5:30pm. The supervisor expresses sympathy with John having come all the way from Durban.

Introduction

The case study shows how easy it is to misunderstand or misinterpret what a person says, despite your best efforts. So, too, what you see and hear can also be interpreted in different ways by various people, or by yourself, at different times. A clear universal example is where, despite reading from a sacred text, there is varied interpretation of scriptures, leading to the emergence of many different churches or religious sects. The critical task in interpretive research is therefore that of thorough interpretation of what you see or hear. Otherwise, the meaning in a conversation becomes lost. It is further noted that to be an effective observer/listener, you may need to involve others, or use different tools (e.g. the diary in John's case) to establish understanding.

The interpretive paradigm emerged from among other qualitative approaches as a challenge to positivist approaches, as discussed in Chapter 2. It advances a view that data never speak for themselves, as in some quantitative research, but that the researcher assesses and interprets data to construct meanings so as to establish understanding (Collins, 2010). In this chapter we discuss the **epistemological** and **ontological** foundations of interpretive research, noting its origins, **philosophical** underpinnings and criticisms. The following sections will seek to provide you with a philosophical grounding for use in research design.

3.1   What is interpretive research?

In this section we briefly consider what interpretive research means. The interpretive paradigm assumes that people construct and merge their own subjective and intersubjective meanings as they interact with the world around them (Packer, 2011). Interpretive researchers tend to "look upon human life as chiefly a vast interpretive process" (Blumer, 1959:686), where people, individually or collectively, describe and define their social worlds. The interpretive researcher therefore seeks to understand studied people through accessing the meanings that participants attach to those social worlds. It concerns itself not about whether facts exist in a given context, but how facts are interpreted.

What if ...?   e.g.

If we look at the sky we would tend to agree that it is blue, that snow is white, blood is red, and that a white flag in battle means peace or surrender. But how sure are we, for example, that the sky is blue?

Remember that arriving at an understanding that the sky is blue, snow is white and blood is red, is part of a negotiated construction of meanings that people assign to a whole range of issues.

Motorists in southern Africa and elsewhere in the world would normally stop at a red traffic light. The meaning they attach to the colour red in this traffic control activity is 'stop'. The meaning they attach to the colour green is 'go'. You may notice that these constructions may just as reasonably be the reverse, i.e. green = stop; and red = go. Red as a colour therefore does not necessarily mean stop, but it is a collectively negotiated construction that motorists attach to a traffic control activity, its significance, and what it means in a certain context.

The negotiated meanings as shown in the example are therefore not an objective fact, but a subjective one. In interpretive research, we assert that there is no objective reality to be discovered by researchers, and replicated by others. Interpretive researchers tend to avoid the notion of reliability in research because, as a rule, interpretive researchers do not manipulate the field or data collection instruments. This follows the understanding that the study of human beings is made complex by their perceptions, emotions, motivations, interactions and dynamic circumstances, that are ongoing and changing in the social world.

What is meaning?

When you conduct an enquiry as an interpretive researcher you are engaged in a process of constructing meanings, where there is some convergence of interpretations between participants and yourself as the researcher. The interpretive researcher's tools for data collection, such as interviews or observations, are designed around the understanding that our knowledge of reality and our social world is always a social construct by human actors.

Some university students may enter courses in qualitative research thinking that the search for truth and knowledge about the world through observation and conversation, is not adequate for rigorous academic study. For them, facts about life and experience must include 'number crunching' and a belief that scientific knowledge can only be obtained through positivist procedures and statistical manipulation, where credibility is achieved through large samples, standardised instruments, and measures of reliability and validity. Based on this background and assumptions, some students may perceive that qualitative research is somehow of a lesser status than quantitative research, yet the opposite may be true. Students with such perceptions may be assisted to change their views if teaching in qualitative methodologies immerses them in challenging class exercises. This would help them to appreciate the philosophical foundations of qualitative research, and the rigour applied in the practical activities of data collection in the field.

Using the activity that follows, pause and reflect on what you have learned so far before we turn to the key factors in interpretive research.

Stop and reflect

1 What aspects of the chapter are you finding interesting and how do these further your understanding of interpretive research?
2 From what you have learned so far in this chapter, reflect on interpretive philosophical underpinnings in contrast to positivist assumptions, about which you read in Chapter 2. What are your ideas at this point?

3.2 Key factors in interpretive research

Critical to establishing meaning and understanding in an enquiry is exploring participants' social world, their utterances and their interactions with the immediate environment, without which the interpretive act may lack validity. The social act of engaging participants in meaning construction goes beyond the mere stating of facts that may exist, but provides for a negotiated understanding of what is going on in their social world.

As stated earlier, facts don't speak for themselves, implying that, on their own, facts are meaningless. Much will depend on who is interpreting the facts, how, and what motivation they may have. Knowing about a country's population figures, for example, is a mere statistical fact, limited in scope and sometimes meaningless compared with when there is interpretation attached. Interpretation helps you understand what the facts mean in the present and in forecasting into the future, which may include demographic trends and how these further impact the socio-economic and the political domains.

Example

Study the table that depicts the population growth of Southern African Development Community (SADC) countries. On its own, the table is just a listing of facts and statistical data which may not be of any value. Anyone studying the table will need to embark on an interpretive journey which seeks to establish deeper meanings and understanding about the factors that cause population growth rates in southern Africa.

TABLE 5.1: Population growth rate in SADC, (%) 2001 – 2011

Country/year	2001	2002	2003	2004	2005	2006	2007	2008	2009	2010	2011
Angola	3.11	3.23	2.80	3.10	1.96	2.93	2.93	2.93	3.00	3.20	3.22
Botswana	2.40	1.17	1.17	1.17	1.17	1.27	1.27	1.27	1.27	1.27	1.27
D R of Congo	3.58	3.40	3.40	3.40	3.40	3.41	3.39	3.40	3.40	3.40	3.40
Lesotho	0.11	0.11	0.05	0.11	0.11	0.08	0.14	0.19	0.22	0.24	0.29
Madagascar	2.94	2.91	2.88	2.84	10.26	2.77	2.74	2.70	2.67	2.57	2.75
Malawi	3.20	3.26	3.29	3.31	3.32	3.32	3.31	2.80	3.14	3.11	3.11
Mauritius	1.02	0.92	0.93	0.81	0.85	0.66	0.65	0.56	0.46	0.44	0.41
Mozambique	2.37	2.38	2.39	2.39	2.39	2.39	2.75	2.77	2.78	2.79	2.79
Namibia	0.77	1.64	1.67	1.69	1.77	1.74	1.86	1.82	1.84	1.90	−1.77
Seychelles	0.1	3.1	−1.1	−0.4	0.5	2.1	0.5	2.2	0.4	2.80	2.40
South Africa	1.42	1.33	1.30	1.28	1.25	1.23	1.20	1.18	1.15	1.12	1.10
Swaziland	2.69	2.52	2.37	2.22	−8.51	0.40	0.30	1.38	1.16	1.05	1.16
Tanzania	3.08	2.90	2.90	3.00	3.00	3.00	3.00	3.00	2.90	2.90	2.90
Zambia	2.05	3.17	3.22	3.22	3.17	3.13	3.06	3.01	2.96	2.80	2.80
Zimbabwe	−0.26	−0.27	1.10	1.86	−1.27	1.52	0.25	0.68	0.97	0.86	
SADC Total	3.25	2.48	2.60	2.42	2.47	2.57	2.46	2.40	2.62	2.67	2.68

(**Source:** Courtesy of SADC, 2012 online)

To engage your mind in an interpretive exercise as you view this data, you may want to explore, for example, why Zimbabwe along with Seychelles, have recorded lower population growth rates on average; and why the Democratic Republic of Congo and Malawi on the other hand, have maintained a higher population growth rate on average. Exploring the points below about each country's population growth rate will help bring to life what might otherwise be seen as lifeless or meaningless facts in table form.

The points to consider and explore for your deeper understanding may include, but are not limited to, the following issues:

▸ Family planning programmes, women empowerment and education.
▸ Infant mortality rates, birth and death rate, life expectancy and health facilities.
▸ Conflict and war; politics and government policies.
▸ Emigration of citizens due to poor economic climate and opportunities.
▸ Immigration due to increased economic growth and employment prospects.

Once meaning and understanding has been established around the issues raised by these points, and how these affect each of the countries, policymakers can then embark on long-term plans that address the needs of citizens.

Finally, the percentages in Table 5.1 may be accurate and factual but they are seen as of little value in interpretive research. On their own they don't tell us the real stories behind the figures and as such they are deemed meaningless. The interpretive researcher therefore believes that what we do with facts is more important than just being in possession of them.

Critical thinking challenge

1 From what you have learned in this chapter so far, discuss in pairs the value of interpretive research in establishing meanings and better understanding.
2 Select two countries from the SADC table and give an interpretive analysis of the population growth rates and trends between 2001–2011. (Use some of the points in the issues list on page 42 to help you.)

In the next section we explore the origins of interpretivism, which initially made its indelible mark in Europe before spreading its influence to the rest of the world.

3.3 Origins and developments in interpretive approaches

3.3.1 Arguments

For as long as we know, there has been a controversy raging among social scientists (or their earlier predecessors, philosophers). This has been twofold: firstly, it is about people's understanding of their own actions; and secondly, it is about the purpose of social sciences. Those who argue that social sciences should follow a positivist approach maintain that such an approach should only constitute a starting point in the search for testable hypotheses and theories, as part of explaining the social world. However, there are others who argue that since social life is a product of everyday complex experiences, the aim of social sciences should be 'interpretation', and not mere scientific 'explanation' of the social world.

3.3.2 Developments

In the seventeenth century, the interpretive view of the nature of social sciences took prominence among Protestant theologians who sought to develop a method for how the meaning of the Bible could be understood through the reading of the written text without explanations from the clergy. This interpretation of the meaning of the Bible was called 'hermeneutics'.

In the seventeenth century, hermeneutics emerged as a favoured science of interpretation of written texts, not just in the theological world but also in art, literature, music and philosophy. In the nineteenth century crossing over to the twentieth century, the hermeneutic method had become a central feature in key **methodological** arguments which in some ways led to a stronger foundation of interpretivism. In the early twentieth century, German sociologists such as Max Weber and Georg Simmel among others, rejected the doctrine of positivism in sociological studies, leading to the founding of anti-positivism, also known as interpretivism. Werner Heisenberg, a German theoretical physicist, who later in his career distanced himself from positivism, noted that:

The positivists have a simple solution: the world must be divided into that which we can say clearly and the rest, which we had better pass over in silence. But can anyone conceive of a more pointless philosophy, seeing that what we can say clearly amounts next to nothing? (Dahneke, 2006:52).

These developments in post-positivist approaches led to the establishment of methodological branches such as phenomenological, critical, and interpretive research, among others. Post-positivism emerged founded on a philosophy that questions our ability to know and to interpret knowledge with certainty. It advances a view that the goal of science is not to uncover the truth, but to establish meanings and understanding, since all measurement and observation is fallible and subject to researcher bias and error. To argue that knowledge can only be obtained through what we can measure and observe overlooks a huge body of knowledge that exists in our social world, which we may never fully observe or measure.

What if ...?   e.g.

The fact that we cannot see the stars during the day when the sun is shining does not necessarily mean the stars are not there. Furthermore, our spiritual world which is closely linked to our social world cannot be clearly explained by natural sciences, yet it influences some people's lives regularly. It may therefore be folly to argue that we should pass over this influential body of knowledge and existence, simply because we can't explain it scientifically.

It may also interest you to note that the writing of colonial history from an **empiricist** worldview was heavily influenced by positivist philosophy. That is why in history lessons we are sometimes confronted by assertions such as that the explorer David Livingstone 'discovered' the Victoria Falls (when in fact the waterfall had long been known to the indigenous people as *Mosi oya tunya*, meaning the 'smoke that thunders'); or that Vasco da Gama 'discovered' the sea route to India.

In contrast to this approach of dubious discoveries, interpretive researchers concern themselves rather with 'self-discovery', and not the discovery of something out there, because these phenomena already exist even before the 'discoverer' seeks to make a claim to them. To be clear, consider the example that follows before we turn to the philosophical assumptions about constructing meaning.

What if ...?   e.g.

In present-day Africa, if you have never been to Johannesburg you do not arrive there and claim to have 'discovered' the city. From an interpretive standpoint your first encounter with the city would be seen as a starting point in 'self-discovery,' in light of a new social world you now find yourself in.

3.3.3 Constructing meaning

Rooted in its philosophical underpinnings, interpretive research is founded on the belief that reality is personally constructed (Myers, 2008), and as such, uses qualitative methods to explore in depth each individual's experience of a phenomenon, artefact or social world. As noted earlier, the interpretive researcher does not necessarily believe that truth and/or objectivity can be discovered, but that achieving truth is more like consensus building – seeking to construct meanings rather than uncovering an objective fact. Hence there is often a need for a multidisciplinary approach in apprehending phenomena, as will be discussed later. It can be argued that in this way the interpretive researcher becomes more critical in his or her worldview than perhaps the positivist researcher.

Leading to the emergence of post-positivism, the question often paramount in the methodological debates had been about what constitutes a legitimate enquiry; and what should be the ultimate values in an enquiry: realism or idealism, objectivity or subjectivity? From an interpretivist philosophical standpoint there are many who have strongly believed that objectivity is dead (Eisner & Peshkin, 1990), and some who question whose validity counts in an enquiry. In all these methodological debates, we note that whether one pronounces objectivity dead or alive, that on its own, remains essentially a subjective judgement. Following this line of thought, and in tandem with interpretivism, all forms of enquiry whether positivist or naturalistic can hardly be said to be objective, or value-neutral and 'innocent'. As Wolcott (1995:162) observes "even the most scientific of research procedures, regardless of how systematic and objective, can be neither perfectly systematic nor ultimately objective". The desire for objectivity often traps some researchers into portraying a neat, linear, logical sequence of what is actually a dialectical process, where all critical judgements are made by fallible humans, and fraught with bias and error.

Although the positivist paradigm to research may have influenced our earlier constructions and notions of knowledge in research, an interpretive researcher (or those using mixed approaches) may study the social world much better if they avoid following a mechanistic approach to research. This would be one which largely seeks to show that some orthodox requirements have been followed, as opposed to a rigorous multidisciplinary approach that seeks to establish deeper meaning and understanding in a research conversation.

Stop and reflect

1 Consider how influential philosophy is to all forms of research, giving some examples of your own.
2 How would you justify the interpretive approach to those who perceive it as a weaker methodology?

In the next section we discuss the foundations and philosophical links to interpretivism

3.4   Foundations of interpretive research

Interpretivism is seen as a philosophy strongly associated with and heavily influenced by phenomenology, ethnomethodology, critical approaches, and hermeneutics.

3.4.1   Phenomenology

Phenomenology is the study of consciousness as experienced by an individual, based on their own point of view. It identifies concepts by the way they are perceived by the participants in a given context. When studying humans, this allows for data gathering that goes into depth by employing qualitative methods such as interviews, discourse analysis and observation accounts.

Max Weber advanced a view that the key difference between the subject matter of sociology and that of natural sciences, stems from the realisation that studied people are actively conscious beings, constantly making choices and assigning meanings to the event they are involved in. In contrast, natural sciences phenomena, such as clouds or rocks, are not actively conscious and they do not assign meanings to the event, or for those involved.

Max Weber therefore argued that if we are to interpret or explain an event in the social world, we have to take into account what those involved feel and think about it. The phenomenological approach to research has over the years influenced our approaches in education, promoting participatory strategies in teaching which have given rise to student- or learner-centred learning. This is where phenomenological perceptions of students and their needs matter in the teacher's planning and delivery processes. The banking concept of education, as described by Paulo Freire (1970), which turns students into receiving objects, and where teachers are regarded as 'the haves' and students 'the have-nots', has over the years been diminished even in schools set largely in conservative communities such as in Africa's rural regions.

3.4.2 Ethnomethodology

The ethnomethodology approach is founded on a sociological notion which focuses on how people make sense of their social world and everyday experiences. People are seen as capable, rational participants, employing practical reasoning rather than depending on existing forms of logic to make sense of their social world and their roles in society. Their own methods and sense-making abilities are seen as an avenue by which people achieve and demonstrate their understanding of phenomena. This kind of approach to interpretivism originates from Max Weber's *verstehen* sociology. Researchers in sociological studies have over the years gradually moved away from referring to studied people as subjects, now more appropriately acknowledging them as participants.

Ethnomethodologist researchers believe that participants bring order to a social event or setting by observing or following various methods that help the activity to become sensible.

What if ...?   e.g.

In a court of law, for example, there are methods and procedures that the judge and the lawyers will have to observe and follow for a trial to be procedural, credible, and to make sense. Lawyers will use certain methods and procedures in handling and presenting evidence in court, failing which even useful evidence may be discarded by the judge as inadmissible, tainted or prejudicial. In the same vein, the judge pursues certain methods that allow everyone involved to perceive him or her as fair, impartial and operating transparently. Some of the methods or principles are: that the judge should not have vested interests in the case – if this is so, he or she may need to recuse him- or herself; that the judge promotes natural justice methods or principles such as 'the right to be heard' and to 'hear the other side'. Added to this, law officers are expected to address one another in a particular, formal way, such as 'your worship', 'my lord', 'my lady', 'my learned colleague', etc., rather than by name. Can you think why they do this?

In the ethnomethodological approach the participants are therefore seen as critical actors in making the activity formal through shared methods and practices enacted in a given context. When interpretive researchers conduct an enquiry, they are mindful of these ordered, formal constructions, and their implications in our understanding of meanings and phenomena.

3.4.3 Critical approaches

Critical approaches in social science are heavily associated with Marxism, and they help to increase the awareness of the social actors of contradictions, distortions or hidden meanings in people's everyday understanding. They are founded on principles of equality where all people, regardless of gender, race, religion or creed, are seen as potential active participants in their social world, and not mere objects for abuse and neglect in the historical process.

The standpoint of the critical approach views research from a political perspective, where research output can help liberate social actors from the false ideologies that enslave them. It seeks to illuminate the self-consciousness of social actors, by transforming how they construct meanings and understanding in ways that address social inequalities and power differentials.

What if ...? Education for transformation **e.g.**

A good example of transforming social consciousness comes from education: owing to long-standing global inequalities, most contemporary governments, through the efforts of the United Nations, have adopted and implemented the 'Education for All' agenda. This has led to improved social lives and opportunities, particularly for economically marginalised people in the world. Critical approaches have also aided feminist methodologies, leading to the advancement of women's rights. Do you think all education is transformative?

3.4.4 Hermeneutics

As noted earlier, hermeneutics initially applied to the interpretation of biblical scriptures in the seventeenth century and later gained prominence as a key theory of human understanding in studied phenomena. It is now a much broader discipline that involves the interpretation of written texts, as well as verbal and non-verbal forms of communication. This will be discussed in depth later as it is closely and fundamentally linked to interpretive research.

We now discuss a collection of philosophical foundations in interpretive research characterising its fundamental pillars and clearly separating it from positivist approaches.

3.4.5 Foundational characteristics of interpretive research

The key philosophical points in interpretive research are as follows:
▶ Knowledge does not exist 'out there', separate from the human consciousness.
▶ Human beings as participants in a research activity are capable of examining their own experiences and accurately describing them.
▶ The individual and his or her world are seen as interwoven. A person has no existence separate from the world, and the world has no existence apart from the person.
▶ All measurement is seen as fallible and prone to error and bias, hence the advocacy for multiple measures and observations to achieve credibility in a study.
▶ The interpretive study seeks to reach the depth of participants' perceptions and their lived world, through a multicultural conversation.
▶ The data produced during research are a collection of the researcher's own constructions of other people's constructions, and of what participants and their associates have constructed, to establish understanding.
▶ Interpretive methods such as interviews allow for deep descriptions of participants' social worlds, with sufficient detail so as to convey exact meanings.
▶ Data or facts never speak for themselves. On their own, facts are seen as meaningless and requiring interpretation.
▶ The researcher is seen as a key instrument. The researcher can never assume a value-neutral position, and is always an integral factor in the phenomena being studied.

- Interpretive research is inductive in nature: Conclusions or theories are drawn from specific observations and patterns.
- Conclusions based on findings are considered tentative, and explanations are open to change when or if new evidence emerges.
- The research findings aim at describing multiple realities; establishing meanings; understanding of phenomena; social constructions; and contextual relevance to studied phenomena.
- Research design is flexible and unstructured, and this approach may evolve over the course of the research.
- Research studies often involve a small number of participants who are purposively sampled because of specific characteristics that are of interest to the researcher.
- Research reports often use narrative data (i.e. text) which is typically collected over a period of time from observations, interviews, analysis of documents and artefacts.

Using the critical thinking challenge activity that follows to consider how you could design your research before moving to next section on hermeneutics.

Critical thinking challenge

As part of designing an interpretive study, what considerations would you make about the following:
- methodology
- sampling strategy
- research instruments
- your role as researcher
- analysis and reporting
- conclusions?

3.5 Hermeneutics as underpinning interpretive research

We have now established that within interpretivism, the social process and the social world cannot be captured in hypothetical deductions and statistical outputs. Understanding the social world involves getting inside the world of the people being studied. Conversing, listening and multicultural understanding, as noted by Kimball & Garrison (1996), are some of the key elements of getting inside participants' social world. Although this may not be achieved completely, the above elements help the interpretive researcher aim at 'getting inside a person' so as to understand from within (Grinnell, 2000), or to empathise and identify with the people studied.

According to Gadamer (1993:385), "conversation is a process of coming to an understanding. Thus it belongs to every true conversation that each person opens and transposes himself into the other." Engaging in a conversation to understand the social world of participants through the use of interviews and observations is therefore to undergo change. It involves critical reflection on self and self-discovery in the light of new, emerging information. A 'true' conversation between the researcher and participants is seen as fruitful to both parties and brings a varied and emergent understanding to multiculturalism.

The multicultural worldview is significant because it is sensitive to diversity, where no person can or ought to speak for another, or think on their behalf, but each participant

If you have conducted interpretive research in the past, you will be readily aware of the greater effort one has to engage in when unlocking the cultural codes of a community or group, and breaking down social barriers before any fruitful interaction can occur. The interpretive approach to research is like engaging in a conversation, by scaffolding and constructing meanings so as to better understand the researched participants and their social worlds. It is a process of unlocking the cultural codes that divide individual social worlds and communities, to bring about that desired understanding.

actively contributes to the construction of meanings in their social world. The notions of hermeneutics as stated earlier largely came into force as a challenge to positivist traditions thus rejecting the positivist's overarching methodological dominance in social science research. Now we turn to the notion of listening in hermeneutics.

3.5.1 Hermeneutic listening

As stated earlier, listening is one of the critical elements in interpretive research and should also occupy much of the researcher's time, and that of the participants. Hermeneutic listening does not mean you should be passive and submissive, that is, not actively engaged, since such passivity could be disempowering, leading one to being assimilated by the dominant culture or allowing oneself to be defined in someone else's terms.

Earlier we alluded to the fact that the objective of the interpretive researcher is to empathise and identify with the studied participants. While such a desire and effort is commendable, it may pose a problem because it is often difficult to achieve. Frequently, we listen to and interpret the experience not according to the lived experiences of the one telling it, but according to the one listening. When this happens, as it sometimes does, the understanding of the studied phenomenon may be seen in dissimilar ways from various participants' perceptions. In turn, this may create a misunderstanding in the researcher's constructions and interpretation. Without necessarily seeking to be objectivist, the hermeneutic philosophy of Gadamer challenges social actors to confront their lived experiences as they fuse them with those of others. After all, everyone has his or her own story to tell, and through research we endeavour to bring to life a fraction of many lived experiences.

Since interpretive researchers seek to understand meanings in their search for the 'truth', the role of understanding what a person says will often prove critical, as opposed to merely understanding a person. The search for truth in this sense is not to be seen in an objectivist way – as a 'discovery', but should be seen profoundly as search for 'truthfulness' in the conversation. The interpretive methodological approach to research has been found suitable for subject matter where the aim is deeper exploration of ideas and participants' social experiences. Such subject matter may include sociological studies such as organisational culture, democracy, leadership, education, health practices, and many more.

One sees therefore that in hermeneutic listening, engaging in a conversation with researched participants may bring out that different 'voice' (Gilligan, 1982), where there is a fusion of narrow horizons to create broader horizons of understanding (Gadamer, 1993). This is where the teacher-researcher for example, has engaged in the conversation and challenged his or her earlier judgements so as to increase the range of his or her vision.

The need to establish understanding should be paramount in the researcher's mind, and in all encounters. Listening intently and processing some views against other constructions can be one of the best approaches when interacting with participants through interviews. In these interactions, what participants say and how they say it will often impact on the researcher's understanding in many ways. In a cyclical way, for example, it will also keep the study (conversation) going thus opening up new and broader understandings.

In the next section we briefly discuss how to apply interpretive research.

3.6   Applying interpretive research

Since the participants and their social world are seen as co-constituted, the researcher, through the use of methods such as the interview, explores in depth the participants' social world, providing access to what is 'inside' a person's head. The interpretive researcher proceeds without letting preconceived notions influence data collection, letting participants talk and lead the way. The words and actions of participants determine meanings and interpretations constructed in the research which lead to in-depth understanding of their social world. Because of the often intimate and deep nature of the descriptions, the research results are much more likely to be vivid and real. Interpretive methodologies position the meaning-making practices of human participants at the centre of scientific explanation by using their authentic experiences and perceptions. The researcher does not start explanations from theoretical models already determined, but draws out theories from empirical evidence.

3.6.1   The researcher

Interpretive researchers are characterised as participant observers. They observe and report data that reflects the subjective perspectives of participants (Rowlands, 2005). To achieve this, in some cases they must develop a long-term, close, trusting relationship with the participants.

As the major instrument in arts or social sciences research, the researcher faces significant implications in terms of reflexivity in how she or he approaches the research process and how she or he behaves towards participants. The researcher should not be content with solely using their reflective accounts and social world experiences as these may unfairly dominate the research process. For it is said that as individuals, based on our personal experiences we tend to have attitudes towards situations, issues and phenomena and that these attitudes play a significant role in our understanding of phenomena. One may therefore limit prejudices arising out of this subjectivity, but may not eliminate them completely.

The interpretive researcher operates between multiple worlds when engaged in research, that is, the social world of participants and the world of his or her own sociological perspective. The merging of these worldviews may sometimes give rise to interpretations that might not be completely understood by the people studied. At times, even if comprehended, they may not agree with the interpretations and meaning constructed. It is common in business mergers that when you bring two entities together, each of them loses part of its previous identity or meaning. If, for example, you were studying say, marijuana users or sex workers, the constructed meanings within their subcultures may be at variance with your sociological perspective as a researcher, or with another existing body of knowledge. It is noted therefore that while the researcher should endeavour to engage in hermeneutic listening during data gathering, his or her earlier preconceived constructions will in some way influence the ultimate constructions and interpretations in the research output.

As part of developing further understanding, pause and reflect on the questions raised in the activity that follows before we look at the influential role of politics in research.

Stop and reflect

Consider that conducting research is like entering into a conversation.
1 Why do you think listening is an important element in the interpretive research process?
2 How relevant is interpretive research in studying educational organisations and contexts?

3.7 Politics, research and social worlds

In parts of Africa where democracies fluctuate and conflicts often arise, conducting research in such environments can become very complex. This tends to suggest that research phenomena can best be apprehended through an interpretive and multidisciplinary approach.

Hammersley (1995) has noted that most research is seen as political. It is not uncommon that educational research becomes tainted with politics. Conservative political parties would tend to commission research that is sympathetic to their values, while liberal and labour parties would tend to utilise research output that is socialist, liberal and 'left of centre'. Although the natural sciences may claim objectivity, they are also not immune from political interference and manipulation, particularly in controversial studies such as stem cell research or genetic modification, for example.

Head and Sutton (1981) note that the need to make sense of the world is essentially an emotional need. This implies that though rationality is often held in high esteem, it may sometimes play a subordinate role to political influences in a social sciences research enquiry. Often this is because some enquiries not only involve knowing about others, but also self-knowledge and discovery. It is therefore not surprising that some research enterprises become too personal and sometimes emotional since most research conversations are individual stories rooted in deep personal experiences: they may only be understood through a 'true' conversation that is non-patronising, non-judgemental.

In conflict-ridden communities, the politicisation of research work, especially on issues of religion, democracy, race, citizenship, and so on, may be magnified, raising the stakes even higher and thus negatively contributing to an already emotive environment. Some researchers have been subjected to arrest and imprisonment in some cases, or temporary detention in some countries, thus curtailing the effectiveness of an enquiry. Researching in Kosovo during the late 1990s conflict, Moore (2003) observed that in politicised communities there is a division of people into groups of 'us' and 'them'. Doing research under these forces of conflict and political strife often poses an enormous challenge and impediment to the research process, hence the need for interpretive research that allows for multidisciplinary approaches.

3.8 Multidisciplinary approach as a strategy in interpretive research

It has been argued by some interpretive researchers that "the field of education in particular needs to avoid methodological monism" (Eisner, 1985:198). Methodological monism, which suggests viewing reality in one-dimensional ways, can be seen as existing in two forms. The first may have to do with a preoccupation or obsession with doing all research in a positivist way; the second is a failure to appreciate that a diverse methodology complements and enriches an enquiry. We are living in a very complex and rapidly changing world, and social sciences and research should not exist in a vacuum (Smith, 1998).

Critical in the interpretive researcher's skills set is applying multidisciplinary methods with a view to apprehending the complex social world of studied people, so that we might understand where their constructions originate. The multidimensional approach, where there is use of varied data sources and instruments, is pivotal in an interpretive study since it provides access to intricate layers of meaning construction from different perspectives. It is owing to such an undertaking that it becomes possible for the researcher to produce rich and deep descriptions in a study which, in turn, enhances plausibility, validity and trustworthiness.

The primary aim of exploring many data sources when studying a school for example, is to provide a broad-based wealth of information, which should then be analysed and discussed. You will often find that students' or learners' interpretation and comments are of great interest, but the data they provide may not necessarily constitute 'the whole truth, and nothing but the truth'. The same can be said of teachers' original interpretations and comments. The researcher's direct observations have the benefit of bringing a fresh, impartial view, but have limitations too. The triangulation of sources of data as portrayed will always help enhance levels of validity in educational research. Validity in interpretive research may manifest in "honesty, depth, richness and scope of the data achieved, the participants approached, and the extent of triangulation" (Cohen, Manion & Morrison, 2000:105). Validity is seen as important as long as systematic methods are not used to validate claims in a study.

For research that is located within an interpretive paradigm, the earlier definition of validity is a summation of efforts that an interpretive enquirer should seek to make. Based on triangulation as expanded upon by Kirk and Miller (1986, cited in Cohen, et al., 2000), you should engage in the following triangulation to enhance rigour in your study.

The interpretive researcher's use of triangulation should not be seen as an effort to prove research reliability and perhaps achieve some validity. On the contrary, these are applied primarily to show the extent of rigour that has gone into the research activities through a multiplicity of methods. The triangulation exercise is an elaborate expression and a desire to achieve a 'good enough' enquiry amid complexities in the participants' social world. Let us now consider how the interpretive approach can be evaluated and judged.

3.9 Judging interpretive research

Key in its identity, interpretive research is opposed to permanence of knowledge and criterion validity. The correspondence criterion of truth rule holds that "facts are out there to which our ideas and constructs, measuring tools, and theories must correspond" (Salner, 1989:47). While this may be acceptable in positivist research, the interpretive researcher rejects this notion of the permanence of knowledge and discovery of 'truth'. In fact, the use of correspondence criterion of truth is in opposition to interpretive research. Such rejection of truth criteria by the interpretive researcher does not necessarily seek to undermine the possibility that some methods are more effective than others in producing valid knowledge, but is against the notion of certainty in our understanding of an otherwise complex social world. Key characteristics in judging an interpretive enquiry may therefore be determined by the following:

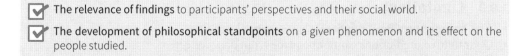

☑ **The relevance of findings** to participants' perspectives and their social world.

☑ **The development of philosophical standpoints** on a given phenomenon and its effect on the people studied.

In the next section we focus on the advantages of using interpretive approaches.

3.9.1 Advantages of interpretive research

While truth is seen as good and necessary, the respect for human dignity is given priority. By its nature, the interpretive paradigm is considerate of ethical issues, treating its participants with respect since they are perceived as key social actors in meaning construction. The researcher empathises with participants so as to effectively apprehend and faithfully answer questions about what is going on in their social world. Below are some of the advantages of using interpretive research.

- ☑ **Interpretive data is based on the participants' own constructions** of meaning and therefore highly relevant in problem solutions.
- ☑ **It is effective and relevant for studying small numbers** of participants, or cases in depth, in answer to the how and why questions.
- ☑ **It is efficient for describing the complex social worlds** of participants.
- ☑ **It allows for deeper exploration of individual cases**, as opposed to relying only on what can be observed from the majority of respondents.
- ☑ **It is highly suitable for cross comparisons** and analysis of studied cases.
- ☑ **It can produce rich and detailed information** as it exists in given contexts.
- ☑ **It allows the researcher to study dynamic processes** with flexibility, allowing for the development of patterns and themes.
- ☑ **It is responsive to local contexts**, conditions and participants' needs.

Like any other philosophical approach, there are criticisms of and limitations to interpretive research sometimes raised by opponents and seldom acknowledged by proponents. Below are some of the criticisms of interpretive research.

3.9.2 Criticisms of interpretive research

- ▸ The critics of interpretive research have argued that it is unscientific, too value-laden and subjective.
- ▸ Critics also claim that there is a greater challenge in arriving at the truth because of the need to negotiate meanings among social participants.
- ▸ The varied interpretive research approaches have given rise to new possible spaces or meanings, which has also led to a form of crisis of interpretation.
- ▸ The growing popularity of interpretive research methodologies particularly among higher education students has led to concern that there is not sufficient understanding of the rigour necessary to ethically utilise them.

Now we turn to some observed limitations in interpretive research

3.9.3 Limitations

- ▸ The findings produced might not have external validity.
- ▸ Quantitative predictions cannot be made from data collected.
- ▸ Data collection often takes more time when compared to quantitative research.
- ▸ Analysis of data is often time-consuming.
- ▸ The findings are seen as prone to be influenced by the researcher's personal agenda.

Despite these limitations, interpretive research continues to be seen as a suitable approach where studies seek to go into depth. It is now important that you pause for critical reflection.

Critical thinking challenge

Think about a time when you were confronted with the need to carry out a study or conduct research:

1 What fears did you have? If not, why not?
2 What is your idea of good research?
3 What do you think or feel about conducting interviews or spending time observing phenomena in a remote location, such as a village or rural school?
4 How important to you is the need to consider what people feel and think in a research study?
5 Do you find these words relevant and important in a research activity: truthfulness, empathy, fairness and respect? Why or why not?
6 In your view, is interpretive research really necessary when positivist research is adequate, or do we need both? Explain why.
7 What did you find interesting in this chapter in relation to expanding your knowledge in educational research?

Conclusion

We noted from the case study at the beginning of this chapter how easy it is to misunderstand or misinterpret what you see or hear. This chapter has sought to bring understanding of why this is so, from a philosophical standpoint. But it has also gone further to show how misunderstanding could be minimised through the use of phenomenological, critical and hermeneutic approaches in your research conversation with research participants.

This chapter has therefore introduced you to key concepts that underpin interpretive research, which go towards designing studies in educational research. In the process of developing these concepts, we have highlighted the interpretivist origins, philosophical assumptions and criticisms, separating interpretive research from the positivist approaches discussed in Chapter 2. It was noted how interpretive approaches to research have grown and gained prominence in their use in the academic world, particularly in education, humanities and the social sciences. The critical reflective activities drawing on your own learning in this chapter sought to advance and reinforce your knowledge in educational research. We believe that the foundational characteristics of interpretive research learned in this chapter, will equip you to exploit further its advantages, as well as to navigate its few limitations, as you seek to conduct rigorous research enquiries iso as to better understand your participants' social worlds.

As part of evaluating your learning in this chapter, try the following closing activities now.

Closing activities

Practical application activities

Choose A or B.

 A As a small group or an individual, design an interpretive research study and give a rationale at every level for why the interpretive paradigm would be the best approach to follow.

B Conduct a short study on a human activity or an organisation. This might be an activity you are currently involved in or have observed in the past (e.g. an initiation ceremony, or an event in the school environment). Address the following questions in your brief study:

1 What is the activity or organisation? Give a name or title and brief description.

2 Who are the participants? (NB. you may also be a participant observer.)

3 What are the perceptions of participants about the activity or organisation?

4 What are the observed interactions/relationships in the activity or organisation?

5 What triangulation approaches can be used to understand this activity or organisation in depth?

6 Evaluate your observations paying attention to the construction of meaning and understanding.

Bibliography

Blumer, H. 1959. Collective Behavior. In J.B. Gittler (Ed). *Review of Sociology: Analysis of a Decade.* New York: John Wiley and Sons. (pp. 833–876.)

Cohen, L., Manion, L. & Morrison, R. 2000. *Research Methods in Education.* London: RoutledgeFalmer.

Collins, H. 2010. *Creative Research: The Theory and Practice of Research for the Creative Industries.* New York: AVA Publications.

Dahneke, B.E. 2006. *Define Universe and Give Two Examples: A Comparison of Scientific and Christian Beliefs.* New York: BDS Publications.

Eisner, E. 1985. *The Art of Educational Evaluation.* Lewes: Falmer.

Eisner, E.W. & Peshkin, A. (Eds). 1990. *Qualitative inquiry in education: The continuing debate.* London: Teachers College Press.

Freire, P. 1970. *Pedagogy of the Oppressed.* London: Penguin.

Gadamer, H.G. 1976. *Philosophical hermeneutics.* Los Angeles: University of California Press.

Grinnell, R.M. 2000. *Social Work Research and Evaluation: Quantitative and Qualitative Approaches* (6th ed.). Belmont, CA: Wadsworth.

Gilligan, C. 1982. *In a different voice: psychological theory and women's development.* New York: Harvard University Press.

Hammersley, M. 1995. *The Politics of Social Research.* London: Sage.

Head, J. & Sutton, C. 1981. *Structures of Understanding and the Ontogenesis of Commitment.* London: Macmillan.

Heisenberg, W. 1971. *Physics and Beyond: Encounters and Conversations.* New York: Harper & Row.

Kimball, S. & Garrison, J. 1996. Hermeneutic listening: An approach to understanding in multicultural conversations. *Studies in Philosophy and Education,* 15(1&2):51–59.

Moore, C. 2003. Researching Ethnic Conflict in Kosovo and Macedonia. Available at: http://www.bisa.ac.uk/bisanews/0207/Field%20Research.pdf. Accessed 25 June 2009.

Myers, M.D. 2008. *Qualitative Research in Business & Management.* London: Sage.

Packer, M.J. 2011. *The Science of Qualitative Research.* Cambridge: Cambridge University Press.

Rowlands, B.H. 2005. Grounded in Practice: Using Interpretive Research to Build Theory. *Electronic Journal of Business Research Methods,* 3(1):81–92.

SADC, 2012. Population Growth Rate in SADC, 2001 – 2011. [online], Available at: http://www.sadc.int/index.php/download_file/view/1416/681/. Accessed 15 January 2013.

Salner, M. 1989. Validity in human science research. In S. Kvale (Ed). *Issues of validity in qualitative research.* Lund, Sweden: Studentlitteratur. (pp. 47–72.)

Smith, M.J. 1998. *Social Sciences in Question: Towards a Post-disciplinary Framework.* London: Sage.

Wolcott, H.F. 1995. *The art of fieldwork.* London: Sage.

CHAPTER 4

Nathan Moyo, Maropeng Modiba and Kefa Simwa

Critical research: Understanding material constraints and engaging in transformative action research

KEY CONCEPTS

Action research is a form of research that is practitioner-based and focuses on generating both knowledge and change on the issues that affect people directly.

Afrocentric paradigm is an example of critical research that draws from indigenous ways of knowing. This paradigm argues that African ways of knowing are valid ways of knowing alongside Western ways of knowing.

Critical research refers to one of the major research paradigms in educational research. It is distinguished by its explicit desire to transform existing situations by rejecting taken-for-granted assumptions that define the world.

Indigenous knowledge systems refer to ways of knowing and doing things that are culturally rooted in African experiences. Such knowledge makes use of cultural aspects that are uniquely African.

Material constraints refer to the challenges that researchers are likely to encounter as they carry out research because of the different paradigmatic assumptions that action research makes.

Methodological eclecticism refers to the use of multiple methods in a research study.

Praxis is associated with the ideas of Paulo Freire (1921—1997) who rejected the separation of what is known from the knower. Praxis emphasises the unity of theory and action as the basis of a critical consciousness that can change the world.

LEARNING OUTCOMES

By the end of this chapter, you should be able to:

▶ Discuss the characteristics of critical research.

▶ Explain the differences between critical research and other paradigms.

▶ Outline the key tenets of an Afrocentric research paradigm.

▶ Explain the transformative nature of participatory action research.

▶ Explain the importance of the stages in the action research cycle.

▶ Develop and implement an action research cycle in your context.

▶ Discuss material constraints in carrying out action research in your context.

Case study: Understanding critical research

Ms Tennyson, a Life Orientation teacher at a high school in a South African township has become increasingly worried by the behaviour of some of her learners. It seems that a good number are engaging in delinquent activities, notably drug abuse and petty crime. This is affecting their performance at school. She is determined to change this trend but realises that, first, she has to understand why learners are behaving in the way they are, and second, that this is a complex societal problem whose causes go far beyond her class and the school. For these reasons she needs a plan that would bring together the major stakeholders in ways that would enable them to take control of their lives. Ms Tennyson discusses her concerns with the school principal who supports her desire to get to the root of the problem. In short, she needs to do research – not just for the sake of gathering information but to bring about change among the learners, as well as in the community at large. Such research has to be critical and transformative. She soon finds that she needs to engage in critical action research. But first, she has to understand critical research and its methodologies.

Introduction

This chapter looks at one of the major research paradigms in educational research, the critical research paradigm. It is important that all research students read this chapter very carefully as it introduces a research paradigm that one needs to be aware of before undertaking any research. The critical research paradigm is markedly different from the other research paradigms that you have been introduced to in the preceding two chapters, namely the positivist and interpretivist paradigms. Critical research, as discussed in this chapter, draws from two schools of thought: critical theory and Afrocentrism. The two schools are concerned with promoting a different view of reality and ways of knowing that can help change society for the better. As the case study illustrates, many teachers who seek to change their communities are attracted to the critical research paradigm for reasons that will become clearer as you read this chapter. The chapter explains the basic theories of critical research and Afrocentrism. In addition, action research is discussed as a research method. We invite you to read this chapter whether your intended research will follow this paradigm or not, as doing so is certain to broaden your understanding of all the other research paradigms, thus making you an effective researcher.

4.1   What is critical research?

The opening case study is typical of the range of problems that many teachers face in classrooms across southern Africa. It also demonstrates the commitment of many teachers who continually seek to improve the ways in which they teach in order to transform existing situations and thereby enhance the performance of the learners they teach. We believe that you, too, are such a committed teacher who is always seeking ways of improving what to teach and how to teach, as well as the circumstances in which we all work and live. This concern is at the heart of what has come to be known as **critical research**. Three major points clearly distinguish critical research from both the positivist and interpretivist paradigms, as follows:

▶ Critical research is broadly concerned with not only understanding the world, but also changing it.

- Critical research assumes that knowledge does not merely exist for its own sake, but is aligned to particular groups or interests in society.
- Knowledge is never neutral but always serves particular groups, while denying other groups their right to knowledge.

Before reading any further, let us pause here and reflect on the case study by answering questions in the following activity. We suggest that you re-read the case before attempting the questions.

Stop and reflect

Read the case study again and answer these questions:
1 What problem does the teacher face?
2 Why do you think this is a problem that is worthy to research?
3 What issues stand out as being characteristic of critical research?
4 Do you find any similarities between the story narrated above and your own work experiences?

The case study gives an example of a teacher who is drawn to the critical research paradigm because of its potential to bring change and transformation in society. We can deduce four major points from the case study to help us understand what critical research involves:

☑ **Critical research** arises from a lack of satisfaction with the existing situation.

☑ **The concern** is with the real-life experiences of real people that we can easily identify with.

☑ **Action is involved** as the teacher realises that she has to act in order to change the circumstances she lives and works in.

☑ **The underlying implication** is that people have to become involved because of what they do know and do, and this cannot be separated from their lives.

A concern with transformation makes it particularly suitable for use in African contexts, as well as educational settings, where we face many problems inherited from the past.

4.2 Overview of paradigms in research

All research is guided by assumptions or beliefs about the world, and what is perceived as real or the truth. These assumptions are important because they influence the conduct of research, and what may be considered as evidence, as well as the relative importance of evidence. Simply put, a paradigm is a way of looking at the world, or a worldview, that shapes what we hold to be true.

A paradigm establishes particular ways of engaging in research as it provides what we may call lenses through which an investigation is carried out and its findings presented. The concept is defined in detail in Thomas Kuhn's (1962) work, *The Structure of Scientific Revolutions*.

In order to understand what paradigms are concerned with, we need to be aware of two terms that are often used in research. The terms are epistemology and ontology.

4.2.1 Epistemology

Epistemology is concerned with the question: What is knowledge? Through this notion we find that different paradigms tend to hold different views of what is considered knowledge.

4.2.2 Ontology

Ontology is concerned with questions such as, What is truth? and What is real? Similar to epistemology, the concept ontology makes us aware that different paradigms hold different views of what truth is. This is best illustrated in the case of each paradigm, as discussed in the following sections.

There are at least four major paradigms in research that this chapter deals with, namely:

4.2.3 Positivist paradigm

This is the oldest of the major paradigms. It has its origins in the scientific world of what has come to be known as the 'hard' sciences, e.g. physics, chemistry, biology. It is usually associated with quantitative research methods. Positivism views the truth as empirical, that is, it is subject to testing through the laws of natural science, and hence it also called the empiricist paradigm. It is an evidence-based approach to research that focuses on a single reality in which results are neutral and value-free, owing to the supposed objectivity of the researcher and the methods used. It rejects as invalid anything that cannot be tested through the laws of science. More recently, this paradigm has been undergoing revisions, resulting in what is called post-positivism. Positivism is also described as foundationalist because it presupposes that there are certain universal laws that define what truth is. For a detailed understanding of these issues, revisit Chapter 2.

4.2.4 Interpretive paradigm

This paradigm arose partly as a reaction to the positivist views that argued that there was an objective reality that existed independently of people's ideas and perceptions. It draws on what are called qualitative research methods, as opposed to quantitative methods. In contrast to positivism, interpretivism tries to interpret and understand social reality in its own terms. As a naturalistic and interpretivist paradigm it uses different ways to find out about and understand reality or the social world. This is reality as a social construction which individuals experience and construct. To interpret, understand and represent perceptions of this reality, the researcher has to be positioned in it as in a natural setting, and to use a variety of methods to uncover it in the least disruptive way. The objective is to develop a shared understanding of this reality that is together created by the researcher and participants. The researcher makes sense of the meanings that participants attribute to their world. It is called the interpretive paradigm because it argues that facts do not make sense on their own, but need to be interpreted in the context of people's lives. In other words, the interpretive paradigm states that there is no objective reality that exists on its own 'out there'. Rather it sees all knowledge as socially constructed by people and hence subject to change. It is sometimes called the hermeneutic, phenomenological or symbolic paradigm. For a detailed understanding of these issues, revisit Chapter 3.

4.2.5 Critical paradigm

The critical paradigm began as a paradigm that was opposed to the establishment of 'grand narratives', especially the narrative of positivism. In other words, it was opposed to the view that the world could be interpreted though a single truth. For this reason, it is also described as anti-foundationalist in that it argues that there can be no one basis on which the truth or the world is founded. Instead, it sees the world as founded on many truths that are all influenced by human interests. The rest of this chapter explains this concern and the implications for research in detail.

4.2.6 Afrocentric paradigm

This is a relatively new branch of research which we view as an extension of the critical research paradigm. The Afrocentric paradigm is closely associated with **indigenous knowledge systems** and has developed explicitly as a way of challenging Western ways of knowing. One of its key assumptions is that traditional African ways of viewing the world are useful in helping us interpret the world we live in today. Like the critical paradigm, the Afrocentric paradigm is committed to changing society by empowering people to take control of their lives.

4.3   Aims of critical research

As its name suggests, critical research aims to be critical in that it seeks to find out what cannot be accepted as socially or politically responsible in our world and what we can do to change it. The word 'critical' has its origins in the Greek word, *krinein* which means to discern, reflect and judge. Used in research, it means taking a set of ideas and questioning them, making them problematic by subjecting them to analysis, in order to identify ways of changing them without distorting their essence or meaning. We can therefore see that research carried out under this paradigm does not just seek to describe or understand social phenomena but also to change them.

The aim of critical research is to critique and transform the dominant structures within society. Critical research is also concerned with the broad social and historical context in which phenomena are interrelated. As the case study shows, problems experienced at school can be seen to extend beyond the boundaries of the school. In this way, critical research focuses on the important societal issues with a view to finding solutions that result in improvement. The critical thinking challenge will help you focus on the important characteristics of critical research.

Critical thinking challenge

The major characteristics of critical research include the following:
▶ The desire to achieve **transformation** of society
▶ The desire for **emancipation** as an envisaged outcome
▶ **Advocacy** and **activism** are identified as characteristics of the researcher
▶ Advocacy and activism imply **political commitment** on the part of the researcher
▶ The researcher has a clear idea of the transformations that are needed.

Pay special attention to the terms in **bold** above and reflect on what they mean. Now try to answer the questions that follow, and again later when you have read through the whole chapter.
1 Explain the meanings of the terms that are in bold in the above section. Use other sources to first get a literal meaning of the word.
2 Explain what the terms imply in the context of critical research.
3 Compare the implications of these terms with the goals of research, as given in the positivist and interpretive paradigm. (Refer to Table 4.1 for more information, as well as the earlier chapters in this book.)

Most of the highlighted terms that you have just discussed in the critical thinking challenge are drawn from critical theory. Now that we have a sense of what critical research is about, let us find more about the role of critical theory in guiding this type of research.

4.4   Critical theory and research

The aims of critical research are best understood by looking at critical theory whose key assumptions help us in defining critical research. It is important to bear in mind that critical research, like the other paradigms, is defined by what it views as the nature of knowledge and what knowledge is valid. For example, positivism draws its notions of knowledge from logical empiricism while interpretivism draws from hermeneutics. To remind yourself of these important concepts we suggest that you re-read Chapters 2 and 3 when you finish reading this chapter.

Critical research draws its key concepts from a school of thought known as critical theory. This school of thought developed at the Frankfurt Institute of Social Science Research in Germany in the 1930s and became known as the Frankfurt School. Its leading members included Max Horkheimer, Theodor Adorno and Herbert Marcuse. As founder member and one of the early directors of the School in 1931, Horkheimer believed strongly that the purpose of the Frankfurt School was to pursue social philosophy "as the source of important questions to be investigated", and to critique 'positivism' or 'empiricism', which he associated with the logical positivism of the Vienna Circle (see Bottomore, 2002). In his 1937 milestone paper, 'Traditional and Critical Theory', Horkheimer (1937:222) writes that "critical theory is in contradiction to the formalistic concept of mind which underlies such an idea of the intelligentsia". He argues that "the concept of necessity in the critical theory is itself a critical concept; it presupposes freedom, even if a not yet existent freedom" (Horkheimer, 1937:230). He argues too that "the transmission of the critical theory in its strictest possible form is, of course, a condition of its historical success", and that "critical theory is incompatible with the idealist belief that any theory is independent of men and even has a growth of its own" (see also Rush, 2004, on contemporary critical theorists). Amongst these theorists, more recently Jürgen Habermas has emerged as the leading thinker in critical theory, with what he calls "knowledge-constitutive interests".

Habermas uses the term knowledge-constitutive interests to illustrate that knowledge is not neutral but is determined by the historical and social conditions in which it is produced. As a result, knowledge tends to serve particular interests because it is particular people who determine what knowledge is, in order to defend their interests Knowledge-constitutive interests thus explains the mode or science of discovering knowledge and whether the knowledge claims that they make are warranted or not. There are three major knowledge-constitutive interests that correspond to ways of knowing paradigmatically. These fall within:

▶ the empirical-analytical sciences, which are concerned with the cognitive aspects of an individual
▶ the historical-hermeneutic sciences, which are guided by a practical cognitive interest
▶ critically oriented sciences, which are informed by an emancipatory cognitive interest.

The information box summarises these key points of critical theory, as developed by both the Frankfurt School theorists and Habermas. We recommend that you read it carefully as it helps us to establish what are considered valid forms of research in the critical paradigm.

Key points of critical theory

- Critical theory does not only describe, but seeks to promote social change by providing insights about power relations in society.

- Critical theorists aspire to a more just and democratic society.

- Critical theorists view reality as a product of differing social and economic forces, political, ethnic and gender values.

- Critical theorists argue that reality cannot be separated from those who know.

- Critical theorists argue that there is no one truth but many truths. For this reason, the critical paradigm is sometimes described as anti-foundationalist because it rejects grand narratives on which all knowing can be based.

- Critical researchers therefore believe that social reality is historically constituted and that it is produced and reproduced by people.

- From the critical theory perspective, knowledge always reflects interests of one kind or another.

Now let us pause to think for a moment about the key points of critical theory. As we carry out research within the critical paradigm, it is important for us always to bear in mind that there is no one truth, but multiple ones. This means that in the process of doing research, there is a need to use data-gathering instruments that can capture different forms of data. This concept is further developed in later chapters.

It is also important to note that knowledge is not neutral, but is linked to interests and power. Therefore, research within the critical paradigm is aimed at shattering the taken-for-granted assumptions that often define what we believe, see and do. In educational research, shattering the taken-for-granted assumptions means asking questions about the content we teach and the methods we use to teach. In short, it requires that we pose questions such as:

- What counts as knowledge?
- Whose knowledge matters in education?
- How is knowledge determined?
- Whose interests are best served by the knowledges we teach?
- How do we engage in more democratic ways of teaching?

These questions are the major concerns of critical research in that they aim at transforming existing practices. The questions also point out the major differences between the positivist and interpretivist paradigms. When applied to research, these terms denote a form of political action, which aims at self-reflective understanding that enlightens people by explaining why the conditions under which they operate are the way they are, oppressive or emancipatory; and suggesting the sort of action that is required if transformation is to occur. In this case, the overriding concern of critical theory is to emancipate people from the domination of their own understandings and actions. The major epistemological and ontological assumptions of critical theory are summarised in the information box. We suggest that you read this information carefully as it prepares you for understanding the use of critical theory in educational research that follows.

Stop and reflect

Summarise the main tenets of the critical research paradigm using your own words, by answering the following questions:

1 In what ways can you say the critical research paradigm differs from the other research paradigms presented in this book?

2 What aspects of critical research do you find most suitable for investigating an educational problem of your choice?

What are the major assumptions of critical theory?

The major epistemological and ontological assumptions of critical theory are:

- Existing ideas are influenced by power as whoever has power determines the knowledge that is considered useful.
- Ideas do not exist 'out there' on their own but are closely linked with human interests and the powers that they serve.
- There is no fixed reality out there that exists independently of the people who know it.
- Reality is continuously shaped and made by people as they interact in their day-to-day lives
- Language is the medium through which meaning is made and remade.

4.5 Critical research and education research

Now that we have discussed the theories that guide critical research, we can move on to see how it can be applied to educational contexts. In this context, critical research focuses on diverse areas that may include some of the following:

- Examining and interrogating the relationships between school and society;
- Interrogating how schools perpetuate or reduce inequality;
- Examining the social construction of knowledge and curricula;
- Examining who defines worthwhile knowledge, and what ideological interests this serves;
- Examining how power is produced and reproduced in society;
- Examining whose interests are served by education and how legitimate these are.

Let us pause for a moment here, and reflect on these issues as critical research focuses on them. We are likely to make the following pertinent observations:

- The issues that critical research focuses on are political in the sense that they have to do with contested issues in society; for example, the relationship between school and society is never a simple and straightforward matter.
- The issues have to do with power and control; for example, questions about who defines knowledge and whose interests are served by such control or influence.
- These issues do not lead to definite and conclusive answers as is usually the case particularly in the positivist paradigm, and to a lesser extent in the interpretivist paradigm.
- These issues, as subsumed in the questions, present notions of knowledge and truth that are quite different from those of other paradigms; for example, the reference to the social construction of knowledge is a marked departure from the assumptions of an objective truth that exists out there in the world, as we saw in Chapter 2.
- Concerns with ideology, vested interests, and unmasking whose interests are served, is what makes critical research potentially dangerous since it challenges the status quo and seeks to empower people to emancipate themselves from coercive structures.

The following section introduces the second purpose of this chapter which is to explain the Afrocentric paradigm as a methodological approach in critical research. Methodology in this case refers to a strategy or plan of action which informs the nature of the investigation that one intends to do. For example, it answers questions such as why, what, from where, when and how data are collected and analysed. Guba and Lincoln (1994:108) explain that methodology asks the question: how can the inquirer go about finding out whatever they believe can be found?

4.6 Critical research paradigm and Afrocentric paradigm as an approach in critical research

The **Afrocentric paradigm** is an important example of critical research in that it challenges the dominance of the traditional Eurocentric research paradigms. We are particularly interested in this paradigm because both its major theories, post-colonialism and indigenous knowledge systems, are relevant to understanding and improving African conditions. Both these theories emphasise that Western ways of knowing are not the only valid ways of knowing. Instead, they remind us that African experiences ought to operate alongside Western scholarship. When applied to educational research the aim of the Afrocentric paradigm is to change, enlighten within the classroom and facilitate overall improvement through democratic practice

The major difference between critical research in general and research from an Afrocentric perspective is that the Afrocentric perspective requires that we interrogate events from the standpoint of Africans as actors in their own destiny and not passive victims of outside forces, especially European colonialism.

Afrocentricity, as a paradigm has gained recognition mainly through the works of Molefi Kete Asante (1992), Ama Mazama (2001), Marquita Pellerin (2012), and Micheal van Wyk (2014), among others. Its main thrust is that Africans have the right to define what are worthwhile ways of knowing in their context. In short, the paradigm seeks to promote African ways of knowing, thinking and of viewing the world. In this way, indigenous knowledge systems become an important basis for challenging and interrogating Western ways of thinking and seeing the world.

Some of the key tenets of the Afrocentric research paradigm are that:
▸ it focuses on local phenomena with an interest in understanding how this impacts on the local and not the global;
▸ it makes use of locally relevant constructs, methods and theories, derived from local experiences and indigenous knowledge;
▸ it is not opposed to Western ways of knowing as it is integrative, that is, combining Western and indigenous theories;
▸ knowledge is seen as relational, that is, truth is informed by the set of multiple relations that one has within a context.

At this point let us stop for a moment to reflect on the factors that make the Afrocentric paradigm a critical research paradigm. The following issues stand out:
▸ The African paradigm is concerned with social and cultural factors that influence the ways in which knowledge is produced, for example, what we teach in schools and universities
▸ The Afrocentric paradigm is concerned with critical inquiry to emancipate and liberate people from all forms of oppression.

In order to get a better understanding of the Afrocentric paradigm, we invite you to do this activity now.

In the next section we explore the ways in which transformative research, such as action research, provides answers to these questions.

4.7   Action research

The origins of action research are to be found in the work of Kurt Lewin (1890–1947) who developed the term **action research** in 1946. Lewin was concerned with the social problems of his day, especially the social conflicts and crises brought about by immigration in the United States of America. He was concerned with bringing about change within organisations and thus saw action research as an attempt to find specific solutions to societal problems. His view was that society needed to be improved through a systematic process whose first step would be to find out the source of the problem and then imagine possible ways of solving the problems.

To illustrate the principle of action research, Lewin used a simple example of a dog owner who is not happy with the behaviour of his pet. To address the problem, the dog owner realises that something has to be done to change the behaviour of the pet. The dog owner then formulates a plan from several options that are available to him. One of these options includes sending the dog for expert training after which the behaviour of the dog will be observed. Further action would be based on the observations made about the dog's behaviour, leading to further plans. Lewin called this stage the reflection stage, as decisions are made as to what further action may be required in order to achieve a long-term solution to the problem. This process of identifying a problem, formulating a plan, and then observing the outcome as a basis for further action, became the foundation of what has come to be known as action research.

Lewin was interested in applying this theory to investigate conditions in organisations that would lead to a change of social action. In order to do so, he envisaged a cyclical process comprising steps of planning, action and fact-finding about the result of the action, as illustrated in Figure 4.1. The steps would unfold in a spiral way while also allowing for backwards and forwards movement in the research process.

This process is what we know as action research and is now acknowledged as a research method that is aimed at addressing real problems in people's lives. It has been employed in education at the level of the classroom for individual teachers who are interested in improving the ways in which they teach. As you read more about how action research operates we suggest that you began to think of how you could possibly apply the method to the problems that you face as a teacher.

Lewin established two key components of action research. These are:
▸ generating knowledge, and
▸ changing systems.

According to Lewin, the cyclical process of action research must begin with a general idea which could also be a problem that requires action and intervention for desired improvements to occur. At this stage, we recommend that you read Lewin's example of the dog owner again and answer the questions in the activity that follows. After doing this, you should be ready for the next section which explains the stages of action research in an educational context.

Stop and reflect

Read the dog owner example (p. 66) again carefully and then answer these questions:.
1 What is the problem or idea?
2 What action or planning is envisaged?
3 Are the goals or outcomes of the research clearly stated?
4 How are the two notions of research and action envisaged in this example?

4.7.1 Stages in action research

Action research is a systematic way of finding solutions to problems in which the researcher may be involved. The problem is often localised and possible solutions usually do not require massive resources. For this reason, action research can be used in a classroom or school context to address pertinent problems as teachers continually seek to improve the ways in which they teach. The major stages of action research are outlined in Figure 4.1.

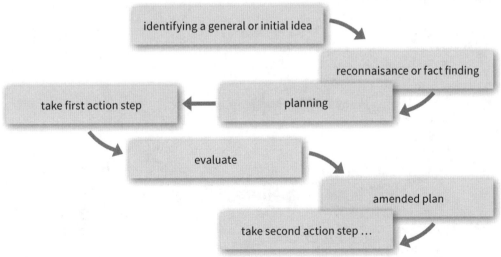

FIGURE 4.1: Lewin's stages of action research
(**Source:** Kurt Lewin, 1946:36).

The stages outlined in the figure need to be understood in the context of what more recent scholars view as action research. It is important to note that there is no single definition for action research. Instead, what is common are the key features of doing action research that have established it as a distinct method of research. The following critical thinking challenge contains some recent definitions of action research from scholars which relate directly to the stages illustrated in Figure 4.1.

Critical thinking challenge

Take a few minutes to reflect on each of the following definitions of action research and then answer the questions that follow.

A   Carr and Kemmis (1986:162) define action research as
simply a form of self-reflective enquiry undertaken by participants in social situations in order to improve the rationality and justice of their own practices, their understanding of these practices, and the situations in which the practices are carried out.

B   Reason and Bradbury (2008:4) define action research as
a participatory process concerned with developing practical knowing in the pursuit of worthwhile human purposes. It seeks to bring together action and reflection, theory and practice, in participation with others, in the pursuit of practical solutions to issues of pressing concern to people, and more generally the flourishing of individual persons and their communities.

1 State the goals of action research as given in each definition, in your own words.
2 State the different stages of action research as given in each definition.
3 Explain the significance of each of the stages of the action research cycle.
4 How do the different stages connect to one another?
5 What reasons make reflection an important stage of the action research process?

The key concepts captured in the definitions are carried out in practice in the form of a model presented in Figure 4.2

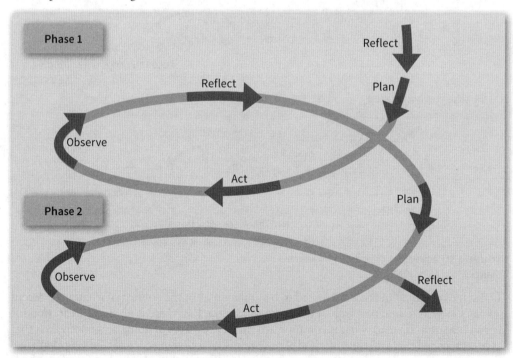

FIGURE 4.2: Carr and Kemmis's Action Research Model
(**Source:** Carr and Kemmis, 1986:166).

We can use Kemmis and McTaggart's (2010:277) descriptor of a "spiral of self-reflective cycles" to explain the cyclic stages of action research. In their view, the cycle comprises the following stages:

- ☑ Planning a change.
- ☑ Acting and observing the process and consequences of the change.
- ☑ Reflecting on these processes and consequences and then re-planning.
- ☑ Acting and observing.
- ☑ Reflecting (often, from this point of rethinking the research activity, one may begin another cycle of action research in order to further improve the situation or activity concerned).

It is important that we bear in mind that the described processes are not linear (one way) but spiral (cyclic). In other words, the processes are iterative (repeating steps). This means that when doing research it may be necessary to revisit some steps several times in no particular order as the research may take twists and turns not foreseen at the beginning of the study.

If you can recall, the teacher in the opening story to this chapter demonstrates the repetitive nature of the processes involved in action research. Often, an action researcher will realise that the data gathered during the reconnaissance stage may lead to more questions.

In turn, this will require the gathering of still more data. For this reason, action research has been described as a dynamic method of carrying out research. The advantage of its spiral nature is that it provides us with opportunities to revisit the problem at a higher level each time, resulting in better perception of the key issues involved in the problem.

Although in this chapter we have presented a single model of action research, it is important to note that there are many other models. For example, models have been developed by Elliot (2003) and Kemmis & McTaggart (2010). Nevertheless, our focus in this chapter is on the key features that distinguish action research from other types of research.

From these broad features of action research, as a researcher you are guided in framing your own action research. Therefore, we strongly advise that you study them carefully and make sure you understand their implications.

In addition, as you will find out in the later chapters of this is book, data gathering can be undertaken with the researcher playing different roles, and by using many different techniques such as questionnaires, interviews, focus groups, interviews, and participant observation.

4.8 Transformative action research

Transformative action research, also known as participatory action research, is associated with the ideas of Brazilian educator Paulo Freire. Freire popularised the notion of **praxis** as a means through which people come to understand their own oppression and take action to liberate themselves. The term 'praxis' is thus used to refer to action that results from an individual's or a group's own reflection (considerable and deep thinking) about an aspect or condition/situation/circumstance that poses a challenge and from that reflection, make a decision(s) for action that is worthwhile and beneficial, and ultimately empowering or transformative.

Freire worked with peasants in Brazil. From this experience, he saw the direct involvement of people as instrumental to empowering them to become agents of their own liberation. He was clearly guided by an intention to liberate, and empower people so that they could develop the agency to reform their own situations (Freire, 1990). This explains the transformative aim of this research.

In order to ensure that this process of emancipating people is not imposed on them but is carried out by the people themselves, the researcher acts as facilitator of an inquiry involving as many stakeholders in the situation as they wish to be involved (Bentz & Shapiro, 1998:128). Therefore, action research involves a collaborative effort by participants (as stakeholders). Collectively, stakeholders not only continually reflect on the issue at hand but also participate in data generation and their interpretation and analysis. In this way, participants are assisted to develop deeper understanding of what they do, and how each one of them affects and is also influenced by the activity at hand.

Since Freire was interested in the liberation of people from what he saw as oppressive structures of society, such liberation required that they first understand the nature of their problems before beginning to take action. This understanding Freire called theory. It had to be combined with action which he called practice. In Freire's view, action alone without theory could not result in desired transformation; it has to be combined with theory. This link between theory and practice Freire called praxis.

In order to gain a clearer conception of the notion of praxis, it is necessary that we examine it as it was introduced in the work of Freire.

4.8.1 What is praxis?

The concept of praxis implies that any social action communicates its conception and practice. It is the medium that carries its own message. Carr (2006) views such action as having a historical and cultural context within which practical reasoning is embedded. It has to be understood as part of the historical consciousness that is integral to, or part of, the transformation of behaviour that has to occur. It is in this sense that praxis is both practical and emancipatory, as described by Carr and Kemmis (1986). While it exposes subjective understanding, it is also associated with the adoption of a reflexive stance towards a context in which understanding/conception and action/practice were developed to liberate the person from such a context (Carr, 2006; Carr & Kemmis, 1986; Elliott, 1991).

Praxis involves doing research *with* people and not *on* people. In practical terms this means people become involved in research not as objects of the research but as the subjects of the research. It builds on people's understanding of their experiences and actions and empowers them to take control. In doing so, they become critical thinkers in that they actively engage in understanding the circumstances in which they exist. This leads to transformation as people attempt to change their world.

Now that we have a clear idea of what praxis involves, we need to understand its relevance to critical action research which is research that seeks to change people's lives through participation as actors and not passive objects. In Figure 4.3 we illustrate the stages of action research that make use of the notion of praxis as explained.

Stop and reflect

Before you study the figure, reflect on these questions in order to enhance your understanding of praxis:
1 Explain in your own words the meaning of praxis.
2 What do you understand by the term 'transformation' as the goal of praxis?
3 Why must theory and action work together for praxis to occur?
4 In your view, what gives praxis the potential to transform situations?
5 What are the similarities between critical theory and praxis?

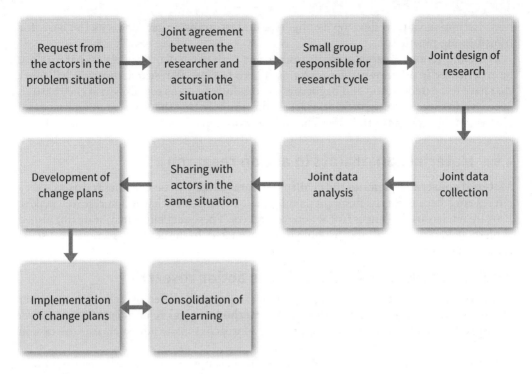

FIGURE 4.3: Steps in 'ideal' participatory research approach
(**Source:** Adapted from Cohen, et al., 2011:38)

At this point in the discussion, after looking at what action research and praxis entail, we move on to learn about the stages of participatory action research.

Participatory action research (PAR) as an approach enables the researcher to collect data in a non-threatening way. Being situated in the research context allows him or her to establish a rapport, a relationship, with participants so that they feel comfortable interacting and being understood as individuals with their own values, beliefs and ways of knowing. In practical terms, participation provides natural entry into the research to encourage self-expression and reflection on behaviour (as theory and practice) while suspending judgement to examine the assumptions on which it is based. Communicating in a democratic and respectful way makes the participants feel comfortable engaging with the researcher especially when encouraged to be involved in a process of self-reflection and explain things from their own perspective. At this stage, the researcher can use these views to build explanations together with the research participants in way that takes into account their context, emotions and relationships, or the interactions s/he has with them. What is important in PAR is the adoption of a critical stance towards what is taken for granted when encouraging participants to look beyond their present and past, and give attention to what would be possibilities for the future. They have to use their understanding to diagnose and disrupt the theory/ knowledge and practices that have become taken-for-granted in the present. This is so as to understand the role played by the past on them, and effect change on the present with the help of the researcher.

Epistemologically, PAR involves placing taken-for-granted assumptions at the centre of the research process, to make sense of them collaboratively with the researcher. Ontologically, PAR exposes the origins of these assumptions in a systematic and non-threatening or non-disruptive way, to develop a collective understanding that serves as the basis for transforming practice.

Therefore action research presents researchers with particular difficulties that may not be experienced in other research paradigms. This is because all research involves challenges that have to be understood and negotiated successfully by us as researchers if the research process is to succeed. Such difficulties act as constraints in that they present unique material challenges that constrain the researcher in the processes of research.

4.9   Material constraints in action research

Material constraints refer to the challenges that are likely to be encountered as we carry out research because of the different paradigmatic assumptions that action research makes. Broadly, numerous challenges face action researchers. These challenges may be distinguished as methodological, ethical, and dissemination-orientated. In the next sub-section, we discuss these challenges.

4.9.1   Methodological eclecticism in action research

As we have already seen earlier, action research can use many different techniques to gather and analyse data. This at times is referred to as **methodological eclecticism**. Simply stated, it means the use of a combination of different approaches in a study, such as is the case in action research.

The use of a combination of different approaches in action research may be seen as both its strength as well as its weakness. In terms of strength, this allows for a high degree of flexibility in approaches so that you, as the researcher, are at liberty to select the method(s) that best suit the problem under study. However, as a weakness, eclecticism leads to apparent confusion and lack of specificity as to which particular approaches are unique to action research.

The combination of different methodological approaches may present for inexperienced researchers as follows:

▶ The use of many different methods may tend to blur rather than clarify the intended uses/purpose of gathering data. The researcher would thus have to be familiar with techniques of analysing the data obtained using different techniques.
▶ The use of multiple methods may create problems for practitioners especially when their competencies are varied. The researcher may not have adequate expertise to handle the often conflicting demands of each approach.

These challenges notwithstanding, as a researcher, you need to bear in mind that a combination of multiple methodological practices, empirical materials, perspectives, and observers in a single study ought to be understood as a strategy that allows rigour, breadth, complexity, richness and depth.

4.9.2   Free flow of information

Another challenge in action research may be the free flow of information. For example, the success of participatory action research depends very much on the free flow of information between and among researchers and participants. Therefore, this challenge requires that there be opportunities for extensive and open communication. Communication among participants should not be dependent on one's position in the research. It is for this reason that action research is described as an exercise that is not only dialogical but also dialectical in terms of communication among all those engaged in it.

4.9.3 Time constraints

The availability of time is always a constraint in any research undertaking. Time constraints are likely to be particularly pronounced in action research as the researcher is very often in full-time employment while also undertaking the research. The challenge, therefore, as Zuber-Skerrit (1996:17) puts it is:

> How can we formulate a method of work which is sufficiently economical as regards the amount of data gathering and data processing for a practitioner to undertake it alongside a normal workload, over a limited timescale?

4.9.4 Audiences in action research

The involvement of participants in action research as subjects and not just objects of the research requires that the findings of the research be communicated to the different stakeholders. These stakeholders are what we call audiences in action research. Audiences are often varied and hold different expectations of what the research findings should provide.

In an educational research project, the various audiences include: colleagues who may be engaged as collaborative researchers; colleagues from other institutions who are interested in the findings of the research because of similarities to their own situations; and finally, the action researchers themselves for whom the findings must transform their practices.

4.9.5 Different orientations

Action research brings together practitioners from different professional bodies into one study, for example, a collaborative project undertaken jointly between professionals based at a school and those at a university. Each group in such a case is likely to hold its own objectives and value assumptions. Thus, while the group as a whole may be interested in finding solutions to a common educational problem, they bring to the problem their different orientations. Their different and even contesting orientations are likely to be problematic and require handling with sensitivity on the part of all participants in the project.

4.9.6 Resistance

Since the aim of critical action research is to change some of the existing practices, this is likely to appear threatening to those who are used to the old ways of doing things. In an educational setting, resistance may come from the leadership that is interested in maintaining the status quo, as it finds change to be both threatening and unsettling. Also, teachers may resist the action researchers' desire to scrutinise their work and viewpoints since they may feel that this is intended to perhaps expose their incompetence.

As an action researcher, you will need to be sensitive to the feelings of colleagues and participants. These ethical considerations are closely related to issues of validity and reliability as discussed in the section that follows.

4.9.7 Validity and reliability in critical action research

Action research is concerned with the issue of quality and rigour just as are all other forms of research. This is because through keenness on the validity and reliability of the instruments of data collection and analysis dependable findings are obtained. Specifically, the criteria for worthwhile action research focus on qualities such as the level of participation and activity by practitioners; the practical ('do-able', realistic, authentic) outcome; the multiple ways of learning and knowing (discerning) by participants; the significance of the effort by participants); and whether the effort leads to a new and enduring structure (Reason & Bradbury, 2008). In short, a concern for validity and reliability in action research compels a researcher to examine closely the nature of his or her research processes and outcomes so as to realise the goal of such an undertaking – the transformation or empowerment of participants.

In addition to the challenge of validity and reliability, ethical considerations may also pose constraints to an action researcher as discussed in the following subsection.

4.9.8 Ethical issues in action research

In research, especially any that involves human beings, ethical concerns relate to participants' consent and confidentiality. Participants ought to involve themselves in a study willingly. Findings have to be presented in ways that reflect what was witnessed, and honour and accord privacy to individuals. For example, participants should not be coerced into participating in research and should retain the right to withdraw at any stage of the research. In research involving children, the consent of their parents/guardians has to be sought and obtained.

Conclusion

The discussion in this chapter focused on critical action research as a distinct paradigm from among the more traditional paradigms. This type of research aims at achieving transformation in the lives of people. It employs methodological approaches that include critical action research. In this approach, research findings will emerge as action develops, but these are not conclusive or absolute. The basic tenet of critical action research is that it is both practical and collaborative. This is a characteristic that presents critical action research as not only necessary but also an appropriate practitioner-oriented undertaking with potential for initiating collaborative and transformative practices in Africa, and the developing world as a whole. It is a research endeavour that may have significant influence in the transformation of the education sector on the African continent and beyond. The major theories that have been identified as helpful in this regard are critical theory and the Afrocentricism. We hope especially that the chapter has made clear the ways in which the critical paradigm differs from the other paradigms.

Closing activities

Analysis and consolidation

1 State at least three distinguishing characteristics of the critical research paradigm.

2 In what ways does critical research differ from the other research paradigms that you have studied?

3 Explain the importance of the Afrocentric paradigm as a key aspect of the critical research paradigm?

4 Explain why you would consider action research to be an example of critical research.

5 Discuss a possible educational problem that you think can best be investigated through action research.

6 State six major constraints that one is likely to experience when undertaking action research in your particular context.

7 Suggest ways of negotiating your way in action research in order to minimise the effects of these constraints.

Practical application activity

8 Teachers should be encouraged to undertake action research in their schools. Discuss this in the context of what you have learned in this chapter, using your own experience as a teacher.

Bibliography

Asante, M.K. 1988. *Afrocentricity*. Trenton, New Jersey: Africa World Press.

Asante, M.K. 1992. *Afrocentricity and Knowledge*. Trenton, New Jersey: Africa World Press.

Bentz, V.M. & Shapiro, J.J. 1998. *Mindful inquiry in social research*. Thousand Oaks, CA: Sage.

Bottomore, T. 2002. *The Frankfurt School and its Critics: Key Sociologists*. London: Routledge.

Burns, A. 1999. *Collaborative Action Research for English Language Teachers*. Cambridge: Cambridge University Press.

Carr, W. & Kemmis, S. 1986. *Becoming Critical: Education, Knowledge and Action Research*. Lewes: Falmer Press.

Carr, W. 2006. Philosophy, methodology and action research. *Journal of Philosophy of Education*, 40(4):421–435.

Chilisa, B. 2012. *Indigenous Research Methodologies*. Thousand Oaks, California: SAGE.

Cohen, L., Manion, L. & Morrison, K. 2011. *Research Methods in Education*. London: Routledge.

Elliot, J. 2003. Collecting, analyzing, and reporting data in action research: Some methods and techniques used in assessment for teaching and learning project at HKIEd. *Asia-Pacific Journal of Teacher Education & Development*, 6(1):181–219.

Elliott, J. 1991. *Action Research for Educational Change*. Milton Keynes: Open University Press.

Freire, P. 1970. *Pedagogy of the Oppressed*. Harmondsworth: Penguin Books.

Guba, E.G. & Lincoln, Y.S. 1994. Competing paradigms in qualitative research. In N.K. Denzin & Y.S. Lincoln (Eds). *Handbook of qualitative research* Thousand Oaks, CA: Sage (pp. 105–117).

Habermas, J. 1974. The public sphere: An encyclopedia article. *New German Critique*, 3:49–55.

Hart, E. & Bond, M. 1995. *Action research for Health and Social Care*. Thousand Oaks, CA: SAGE Publications.

Horkheimer, M. 1937. Traditional and Critical Theory. In P. Connerton (Ed). *Critical Sociology: Selected readings*. New York: Continuum (pp. 206–224).

Jove, G. 2011. How do I improve what I am doing as a teacher, teacher educator and action-researcher through reflection? A learning walk from Lleida to Winchester and back again. *Educational Action Research*, 19(3):261-278.

Kellner, D. 2004. Critical Theory and Education: Historical and meta-theoretical perspectives. In I. Gur-Ze'ev (Ed). *Critical Theory and Critical Pedagogy Today: Towards a new critical language in education*. Haifa: University of Haifa Studies in Education (pp. 49–69).

Kemmis, S. & McTaggart, R. 2010. Participatory Action Research: Communicative Action and the Public Sphere. In N.K. Denzin & Y.S. Lincoln (Eds). *The SAGE Handbook of Qualitative Research* (4th ed.). Thousand Oaks, CA: Sage (pp. 559–604).

Kemmis, S., McTaggart, R. & Nixon, R. 2013. *The action research planner: Doing critical participatory action research*. Singapore: Springer.

Kemmis, S., McTaggart, R. & Nixon, R. 2014. The Action Research Planner. DOI 10.1007/978-981-4560-67-2_2. [online] Retrieved from http://www.springer.com/education+&+language/learning+&+instruction/book/978-981-4560-66-5. Accessed 15 February 2014.

Kincheloe, J.L., McLaren, P. & Steinberg, R. 2011. Critical Pedagogy and Qualitative Research: Moving to the Bricolage. In N.K. Denzin & Y.S. Lincoln (Eds). *The SAGE Handbook of Qualitative Research*. Thousand Oaks, CA: Sage (pp.163–177).

Kuhn, T.S. 1962. *The Structure of Scientific Revolutions* (1st ed.). Chicago: University of Chicago Press.

Lewin, G.W. 1948. *Resolving social conflicts: Selected papers on group dynamics*. New York: Harper & Row.

Lewin, K. 1946. Action research and minority problems. *Journal of Social Issues*, 2:34–46. 14 April 2010. DOI: 10.1111/j.1540-4560.1946.tb02295.x.

Mazama, A. 2001. The Afrocentric Paradigm: Contours and Definitions. *Journal of Black Studies*, 31(4):387–405 From http://www.jstor.org/page/info/about/policies/terms.jsp.

McNiff, J. 2013. *Action Research: Principles and Practice* (3rd ed.). Abingdon: Routledge.

Noffle, S. & Somekh, B. 2005. Action Research. In B. Somekh & C. Lewin (Eds). *Research Methods in the Social Sciences*. London: SAGE (pp. 89–96).

Pellerin, M. 2012. Benefits of Afrocentricity in exploring social phenomena: Understanding Afrocentricity as a social science methodology. *The Journal of Pan African Studies*, 5(4):149–160.

Reason, P. & Bradbury, H. 2008. Introduction. In P. Reason & H. Bradbury (Eds). *The SAGE Handbook of Action Research*. London: SAGE Publications Ltd (pp. 1–10).

Reason, P. & Bradbury-Huan, H. 2013. *The SAGE Handbook of Action Research: Participative Inquiry and Practice*. London: SAGE Publications.

Reviere, R. 2001. Towards an Afrocentric Research Methodology. *Journal of Black Studies*, 31(6):709–728.

Rush, F. 2004. Conceptual foundations of early critical theory. In F. Rush (Ed). *The Cambridge Companion to Critical Theory*. Cambridge: Cambridge University Press (pp. 6–39).

Van Wyk, M.M. 2014. Conceptualizing Afrocentric-Indigenous Pedagogy for an Inclusive Classroom Environment. *Mediterranean Journal of Social Sciences*, 5(4):292–299.

Winter, R. 1989. *Learning from Experience: Principles and practice in action research*. Philadelphia: Falmer Press.

Zuber-Skerritt, O. 1996. *New Directions in Action Research*. London: Falmer Press.

CHAPTER 5

Thenjiwe Meyiwa and Thandokazi Maseti

Developing sensitivity in questions of gender, using feminist research and IKS principles

KEY CONCEPTS

Epistemology is the theory of knowledge. It refers to claims made about the ways in which knowledge can be gained, and involves investigating the origin of human knowledge, the nature of knowledge, and what can be regarded as knowledge rather than beliefs and opinions.

Feminism is a school of thought that places women at the centre of its enquiry. It seeks to confront systematic injustices that are based on gender, as well as oppression in gendered relationships.

Feminist epistemologies simply put, refer to what we regard as the theory of knowledge, i.e. how we come to know, and who possesses that knowledge. Feminist epistemologies allow for the production of knowledge by those who are being represented. The process, then, of producing knowledge is centred on the participants rather than only the researcher.

Feminist ontology is based on multiple and dynamic realities that are context-dependent. A feminist ontology assumes the participant's own interpretation of reality as being of value.

Feminist research is research grounded in feminist principles in terms of the production of knowledge, and is constantly being redefined by the concerns of women. Feminist research is grounded in feminist theory, its types of questions, the methods it employs during the research process, and the knowledge produced, makes feminist research unique.

Liberal feminism is a type of feminism that challenges prescribed gender roles which perpetuate discrimination towards women. Liberal feminists believe that men and women have the same capabilities and should assume the same positions in society.

Marxist feminism is a type of feminism that seeks to represent working-class women, citing the structural oppression and the disadvantaged position of women in the workplace.

LEARNING OUTCOMES

By the end of this chapter, you should be able to:

▶ Gain a general understanding of feminist research practice.
▶ List the various traditions of feminist research.
▶ Building on the understandings of feminist research, delineate the meaning and characteristics of feminist research alongside IKS principles.
▶ Present the contexts and rationale of feminist and IKS research.
▶ Elaborate on how feminist research can be undertaken.

Case study: Women of Cofimvaba

In a project funded by the National Research Foundation we sought to investigate how identities were constituted among women in Cofimvaba (one of two main towns in the Chris Hani municipality in the Eastern Cape), in support of an indigenous way of life. The women of Cofimvaba live in abject poverty, but somehow they manage to provide for their families. As with many rural women, Cofimvaba women are primarily responsible for caring for the elderly and the young, for household food security, for gathering firewood, as well as for earning an income.

During the first phase of the project, 76 people were interviewed. From this number, we conducted 2–4-hour intensive interviews with 38 individuals (17 men and 21 women). Almost all the women we interviewed opted to concentrate on different topics rather than follow the main focus of the researchers, with many significantly focusing on their personal lives and relationships. The women were found to be the primary brokers of indigenous knowledge systems (IKS). Most respondents who participated in the study made reference to them as "sources of information" for the indigenous knowledge (IK) data they shared with us.

Introduction

The subject and practice of feminist research from an African point of view has been relatively neglected in standard research methods works. In this chapter we invite students to explore the range of feminist perspectives and postmodern perspectives. The purpose is to bridge the divide between theory and research methods. We provide a 'hands-on' approach to feminist research by offering activities that demonstrate feminist researchers at work. The objective therefore is to challenge 'silences' in mainstream research – in relation to studies involving African indigenous women, the manner in which they are studied, as well as formats in which they are presented. In this introductory feminist research discussion, we seek to understand the meaning of feminist research and to outline what is entailed in doing feminist research, both from an indigenous knowledge systems (IKS) theoretical social sciences, and a practical perspective.

Central in our discussion is the fact that the difference between the conduct of feminist and IKS research, and conventional social science research, is embedded in the method of enquiry; namely, the mode of conducting research and epistemology, and not simply the methods related to data collection. We also explore what makes a feminist methodology particularly African 'feminist' – which will enable you to distinguish feminist research from non-feminist work.

Hence, broadly, in this chapter we pose these questions:
▶ How do we conduct a feminist kind of research and engage with local knowledge from an African perspective?
▶ What underpins feminist methodologies in 'reading' research projects and case studies?
▶ How does one, as an African man or woman, interpret research projects and case studies?
▶ What is the relationship between feminist and gender-sensitive analysis?
▶ What are the features of a gender-sensitive text?

5.1 What is feminist research?

Feminist research is a 'continuation of feminism', having developed from this larger movement. It has grown rapidly and evolved in different fields and can be understood as a multidisciplinary voice that seeks to advocate for social change. Feminism places women at the core of its enquiry and seeks to confront systematic injustices that are based on gender. For an African feminist researcher it becomes essential to locate the questions we list in the introduction within matters that concern people in Africa.

Some people provide narrow definitions of feminism. They associate feminism solely with women's rights and fail to understand it as a critical ideology in its own right. So at this point it is essential that we provide a rigorous critique of both feminist theory and research. **Feminism** concerns itself with confronting the oppression rooted in gendered relationships, i.e. how men and women, and boys and girls, treat one another. Feminism provides a lens through which to view individuals, groups, and organisations in their social, political, economic and cultural contexts. It is essential that these facets are studied, taking into account the experiences and realities that African people confront.

In this chapter we provide a discussion related to these facets. In addition, we demonstrate how feminism as an ideology and a movement for socio-political change, based on a critical analysis, could be employed in research processes to critique systems that propagate the subordination of women and other marginalised groups within society. The discussion will further demonstrate how feminist research – drawing on feminist theory – seeks to re-balance social, political, economic and political power between men and women. Feminism, as theory and research practice, is thus action- and politically-oriented as it is committed to social activism and justice. We draw from various feminist scholars and related theoretical underpinnings that reflect the origins of feminist research methodology. Read the next section carefully and begin to reflect on how different feminist research is, relative to the research approaches discussed in the previous chapters of this book.

5.1.1 Differences between feminist research and other research approaches

Feminist research with an African bias should seek to examine the experiences of women across cultures and traditions, and to examine gender equality with a sensitivity to specific African cultural contexts. It should aim at producing results to inform policies that may strengthen efforts towards challenging the subordination of women and other marginalised groups.

Feminist research is an emancipatory type of enquiry (Sarantakos, 2005); it is aimed at transforming the position of women and minorities, and ultimately contributes toward social change and reconstruction. In its emancipatory nature, feminist research does not merely document aspects of reality but takes a personal, political and engaging stance in the world. It is based on the idea that the world is socially constructed, and rejects empirical positivistic methodology. (Please see Chapter 2 of this book to learn more about positivism.)

In this chapter we address questions around **feminist ontology** and epistemology – and show that feminist researchers possess particular characteristics in their work, such as their dedication not merely to conducting research about women but being equally concerned about working for women and with them. Feminist researchers are concerned with understanding ways in which gender affects how we come to know, and how practices of knowledge acquisition disadvantage women and other subordinated groups.

There is an ongoing debate about whether a feminist methodology exists. Some argue that a feminist methodology will mark the uniqueness of this approach. Others are of the view that feminists are diverse and use different methodological principles belonging to other paradigms. Feminist researchers have collectively challenged conventional ways of collecting, analysing and presenting data. Until recently, quantitative methods were especially challenged for their inability to adequately capture women's experiences, which are at the core of feminist research.

Feminist methodologies are characterised by their determination to produce unbiased knowledge through the methods that are used, while acknowledging the standpoint of the researcher during the research process. In the next section we turn to the values and underlying knowledge that has given rise to feminist research.

5.2 Feminist ontology and epistemological questions

Epistemological positions and epistemologies inform us about how we make sense of acquired knowledge. The term **epistemology** refers to the claims made about the ways in which knowledge of the reality can be gained; what can be regarded as knowledge; and the criteria that it meets in order for it to be regarded as knowledge instead of mere opinions and beliefs. Crotty (1998) distinguishes only three epistemologies, namely, objectivism, constructionism and subjectivism, as follows:

▶ Objectivist epistemology: there is an absolute truth waiting for us to discover, even if we are not aware of its existence.
▶ Constructionist epistemology: when meaning is found in our interactions with the world. We construct meaning and our own realities; different meanings can thus be found about a single phenomenon.
▶ Subjectivist epistemology: when meaning is imposed on the object by the subject, there is no interchange between the object and the subject. While the subject is responsible for making meaning, the object makes no contribution in the making of meaning, and we can generate meaning from anything but the object, and impose it on the individual.

Feminist researchers are concerned with the tensions around how what is to be known is represented. This plays out in power displays in the research process. Issues of power, masculinity and authority in knowledge creation have become critical in the discussions of feminist epistemologies and ontologies.

Feminist epistemologies answer questions related to who can possess knowledge, and what knowledge is legitimate. Can women be knowers? Can we write knowledge from the point of view of a woman; and have women as agents of knowledge?

Now that we have distinguished three different epistemologies, we can see that epistemological positions inform the way in which we make sense of the knowledge we acquire: they represent the nature of the relationship between the researcher (knower) and what can be known. We turn next to looking at what we mean by a feminist ontology.

Ontology refers to the basic assumptions of the nature of reality that is to be studied, and what can be known about it: it is the assumptions we make about the nature of reality. Epistemologies specify the relationship between the knower and what can be known, and focus on how we come to derive knowledge. The knowledge of the researcher is said to have a role that it plays within the research process. Hence the importance of the topic on ontological assumptions in feminist research.

Traditional epistemologies, it has been argued, exclude the possibilities of having women as agents of knowledge, therefore excluding women's point of view and producing knowledge with a masculine bias. Conversely, feminist researchers place at the centre subordinated groups and attempt to work for and with them in producing knowledge; they are careful about how they represent their realities. Thus feminist research allows for knowledge to be produced in the voice of those being presented and thereby empowers them. Feminist ontologies and epistemologies therefore allow for the understanding of human behaviour in the context that it is presented, in order to acquire an unprejudiced view of these experiences. This is crucial for feminist research conducted in Africa as the continent and its people have a unique interpretation of their reality, with expressions that often vary from one context to another.

Having established the epistemologies and ontologies used by feminist researchers in making sense of acquired knowledge, we will now learn about different traditions of feminist research.

Stop and reflect

Now that you have read this brief background, think about an assignment you have done in the recent past and how, if you were to do it again, you might approach it differently to ensure that all the people are represented in an equal manner.

5.3 The different traditions of feminist research

Feminist research is influenced by different contexts, such as social, political, and cultural contexts. It is therefore highly contextual. When feminists are dissatisfied with older feminisms, a new feminism is developed which will seek to address the problems of that new time and context adequately. Hence, there is no one common feminism. There are many approaches in feminism which are all multi-faceted.

However, central to feminist theory is the analysis and nature of women's oppression. Such oppression may be a lack of education, inequality in political rights, and economic dependence. Feminist researchers therefore aim to question and address oppression produced in these contexts in order to provide strategies that can better women's lives.

The variations in feminism to be discussed are: liberal, radical, socialist/Marxist, and postmodern feminism, as alignments that have significantly influenced the wider feminist movement.

5.3.1 Liberal feminism

Liberal feminists place women's rights at the centre, and challenge gender roles that rationalise discrimination on the basis of sex. It follows that liberal feminist researchers would concern themselves with proving the insignificance of differences between men and women except for basic biological differences. These differences are said to perpetuate discrimination and oppression, so liberal feminists question these gender roles and advocate that men and women have equal capabilities. Women and men are said to deserve equal opportunities in accessing education, economic independence and citizenship, as their differences are merely biological. Liberal feminists assert that challenging these prescribed gender roles and promoting equality between men and women will essentially lead to the reduction and elimination of inequalities and discrimination towards women (Lay & Daley, 2007).

5.3.2 Radical feminism

Like liberal feminists, radical feminists advocate equality between men and women. However, unlike liberal feminism, radical feminism maintains that inequalities and discrimination on the basis of sex are attributed to patriarchy and gender hierarchy rather than prescribed gender roles (Lay & Daley, 2007). Radical feminist researchers explore issues related to male power, and attributes the oppression of women to men. Patriarchy as a system that disadvantages women and maintains male domination and violence towards women is said to be a result of women's oppression. Gender- and racially-motivated division of labour is questioned and rejected by radical feminist research, where only men are supposed to belong in the public (work) sphere, while women remain at home and dependent on men.

5.3.3   Socialist and Marxist feminism

Both socialist and **Marxist feminists** promote the assumption that women's oppression is perpetuated by social class and capitalism. Socialist and Marxist feminist researchers are concerned with representing working-class women, and assert that structural oppression and the disadvantaged position of women in the workplace is due to their roles as caregivers and their involvement in reproduction (Charles, 1995). Capitalism is believed to perpetuate oppression as it only benefits men, as it is they who work and control the means of production, while women remain in the private sphere (Bowden & Mummery, 2009). In Marxist critique, it follows that the disadvantage of women and their oppression would be done away with by dismantling the capitalist system.

5.3.4   Postmodern feminism

Postmodern feminists assert that there is no universal feminism that can adequately address the problems facing all women in the world. Women are seen as different within and across groups. This feminism rejects the dominant order and all theories of knowledge that rest on justified belief and a secure foundation of certainty. Explanations of the condition of women and their oppression supplied to date are rejected by postmodern researchers and theorists. Women, in their thinking, are to be left alone and given the opportunity to just be themselves. Postmodern feminism also challenges binary thinking and questions the narrow use of terms in opposition to each other, e.g. white and black; thin and fat; rich and poor.

The following table is a summary of the different types of feminisms discussed so far in this chapter. Read through the analysis and discussion presented in the table and earlier in the chapter before responding in the next activity.

TABLE 5.1: A summary of traditions in feminist theory

	Liberal feminism	Radical feminism	Marxist and socialist feminism	Postmodern feminism
Origin	Roots are in traditional liberalism. Social and political demands and developments of the time shaped feminist politics. Traditional liberal theory ascribed rights to all people on the basis of their capacity to reason.	Radical sociology and Marxism's attempts to analyse women's position in patriarchal society.	Dismisses women's oppression, considering it less important than the struggle against working class oppression. Rejects liberal and radical feminism.	Simone de Beauvoir has influenced much thinking on postmodern feminism. Dissents itself away from mainstream feminism. Attempts to move away from giving explanations for why women are oppressed.

	Liberal feminism	Radical feminism	Marxist and socialist feminism	Postmodern feminism
Discourse	Stresses women's rights as individuals, irrespective of their sex. Main concern is autonomy and freedom of women. Believes in the reform of society for change to occur. Domestic work is devalued and needs to be revalued. De-emphasises men's power over women.	Argues that liberal or Marxist debates have not gone far enough in addressing the subordination of women. The patriarchal system is responsible for the oppression of women. Male power is at the root of the social construction of gender.	Focus is on working-class women and women's work-related concerns. There is a need for women to understand the manner in which oppression occurs in the 'private' as well as 'public' domain. Men are secondary oppressors of women – it is capitalism that is the main oppressor.	Women should not be 'given' the explanation for why they are oppressed. Women need to be left alone to have an opportunity to be themselves. Feminist discourse, e.g. feminist, lesbian, etc., says such terms divide women and should instead use words that do not view 'feminists' or 'lesbians' as people who deviate from the norm.
Analysis and critique	Has made enormous strides in improving legal and economic conditions for women in the public sphere. Does not have much resonance for working-class women.	Radical feminists are criticised for their claims about the goodness of women's nature and evilness of men's nature.	In its adoption of Marxist class explanations, Marxist feminists have been questioned about whether women constitute a class, or share similar problems, given that some are wives, friends, lovers, and daughters of the bourgeoisie. Marxist feminism has been blamed for being non-feminist as it fails to hold men responsible and focuses only on issues that are work- and class-related.	Its refusal to construct one explanatory theory may threaten the unity of the feminist movement, a refusal that adds fuel to feminist multiplicity and difference. Criticised for trying to create a feminine language and a female society outside masculine language and male society.

Stop and reflect

Look back at the discussion we have just had on the different origins and perspectives of feminist research. Do you understand the different variations of feminist research? Can you distinguish one tradition of feminist research from another? Think of your neighbourhood, family and relatives, and social community. Can you draw any connections between what you have learned and what happens within your community, neighbourhood, and family?

5.4 The importance of researching women

At the high point of the apartheid era in South Africa, black people's opinions were either thinly represented or misrepresented, and black women's opinions were hardly ever covered. This situation was worse for women within societal systems with a strong patriarchal base. Feminist writers emphasise the need for women to find an opportunity to make their own history. This call is crucial given that marginal people are often not able to choose or influence the structures within which they live, much less the structures that report their stories.

Tip

Many oral history researchers and authors, despite doing a significant job of recording and disseminating people's stories, use their own words and style of writing. These are often not the actual words of the research participants. This is something to consider in your own research: how to render the true voice of research participants.

Although most of Africa's black indigenous people are a wounded group, it is compared with men that the status of most of the continent's women has always been the lowest. Women's stories and experiences have not been vigorously sought, despite common knowledge of the existence of women's forums. Their meeting places are accorded minimal respect.

Women's stories need to be asserted. Owing to a scarred past, one might argue that foregrounding their stories may be regarded as a healing project earmarked to address long-neglected and silent voices. Publishing more women's stories that use their direct words, in different kinds of publications and media, may help in dealing with this concern. What compound women's state of affairs are circumstances within the home. Incidentally, as far as research and literature is concerned, this points to the realities that reflect fewer women respondents than men.

In the past decade there has been intense consciousness among researchers about the need to investigate women's lives and eventually tell their stories. Since women's stories have been largely told by a male figure: father, brother, or son, it is common for contemporary researchers to now inundate women with requests for their testimonies. Women have found this interest both overwhelming and also an unwelcome irritation. At worst as research participants, they are reported as a difficult group to work with. Part of this problem can be attributed to the fact that they regard themselves 'unsuitable' information providers (You will notice that two summaries of case studies

Why don't women's groups matter?

Although *manyano* (a generic term for women's church movement), and places where water or firewood is gathered, are forums dubbed 'safe places' in which women express themselves, people who do not participate in these forums do not take them seriously. Instead, they are often perceived as convenient places for women to gossip.

that appear later in this chapter make reference to this fact and provide more details). Some scholars who research women term this attitude a "consciousness of the self" (Bozzoli, 1991:166), i.e. being fully aware of one's identities in different contexts. This means that women are aware of how the patriarchal structures within which they live limits their capabilities as women.

In addition to having been mostly left out of many historical stories, in particular, South African women as a group have had a lot to contend with, also operating within forces and structures that do not work for them. Reference here is made to the South African socio-cultural and apartheid systems both of which are patriarchal in nature.

Tip

As a powerless group, women, however, are not simply passive recipients of the dominant structures. To a certain extent women do express scorn or even fight back at oppressive ideologies and practices. James Scott (1990), an oral history writer is of the view that the powerless are not just unreflecting subordinates, but have a tendency to resist and question their domination 'offstage'. Researchers working in Africa ought to be aware of this tendency and consciously investigate such opinions and strategies among women.

In the interests of redress, more conscientious efforts should be made to accommodate stories of both men and women – otherwise the whole story is not told, or gets compromised. Coupled with this effort must be an eagerness amongst researchers to bring out the role of women in their own stories, thereby employing research processes that aim at women's self-affirmation. Women's stories and identities need to be reclaimed beyond the so-called 'safe places' and be afforded a platform that can be accessed by many people. This is no mean task.

In the following sections we discuss two theories that inform most of our research related to women.

5.5   Developing sensitive research principles

Feminist and indigenous knowledge systems (IKS), research principles and approaches complement one another. In our research we use them as a unit, which we find useful in investigating women's stories. Although these two approaches have different histories (see section 5.2 earlier, and 5.6 later) and are hardly viewed as one continuum, they are strikingly similar. In our research work we often blend them. We have found that they share a number of commonalities. As more multidisciplinary research studies are conducted in Africa, there are greater possibilities for blending such methodological approaches.

Both the feminist and IKS approaches regard the marginalised as their subject of study. They also vie for a greater recognition of personal experiences, maintaining that personal testimonies are crucial in getting a comprehensive understanding of the stories of the marginalised.

For the purposes of the discussion of this chapter we use the term, the *sensitive approach* to refer to the practice of feminist and IKS research practices. This term has been adapted from the grounded theory's research principle of always intending to discover the research participants' main concern. The theory was developed by sociologist Barney Glaser, who maintains that the research focus should be on the participants' main problems and the manner in which they try to solve them, rather than on pre-formed hypotheses. At the centre of this approach is the act of 'being sensitive', that is, being acutely aware of the lives and presence of the interviewees. Sensitivity implies taking care in the manner in which interview questions are constructed and posed. Later, data derived from the interactions ought to be interpreted with careful consultation and presented in modes that reflect sensitivity. Let us turn to how you could apply these principles in practice.

Critical thinking challenge

As students based and studying in Africa, pair up with a fellow student. Each of you should share your thinking related to this question: What do researchers need to think about and do in their research practices when they interview and analyse women's stories?

5.6 Feminist research principles

Unlike its counterpart the IKS approach, the feminist approach's distinct focus is on girls and women. The use of this approach allows for learning and understanding women's lives and experiences better. Feminist writers strongly advise on the importance of incorporating lived experiences within research projects, and they emphasise the need to understand issues that are beyond raw research data.

Indeed, everyone has a story to tell. Stories that people tell have always varied in format, purpose and presentation. It is unfortunate, however, that many researchers have largely adopted a linear approach to relaying the stories of ordinary women and men. People's stories have been and are still largely told from the researcher's point of view. This approach mainly considers the aspects which the researcher deems fit to tell. This has led to a scarcity of literature based on data produced by marginal people. This state of affairs has long been one of the greatest concerns of feminist researchers. Equally, IKS researchers have raised the same concern, as we see in the next section.

5.7 Indigenous knowledge systems research principles

With most of Africa achieving independence and the advent of democracies, with governments composed largely of indigenous Africans, there has been a move towards 'resuscitating' the dignity and the heritage of Africa's indigenous peoples. Within South Africa, along with other countries on the continent, the IKS research approach has been strengthened by a strong renaissance agenda. Taking lessons from the past in order for individuals and communities to live a meaningful and beneficial life, forms one of the approaches of the discipline. Emanating from this principle, researchers are advised to investigate and draw attention to continuing practices from the past amongst indigenous peoples.

The IKS research paradigm maintains that, with such a conscious research approach, researchers can contribute towards the excavation, preservation, and knowledge generation of indigenous people. It also argues for a research practice that allows for storytelling strategies, and new modes of investigation of the oral tradition and indigenous knowledge.

A number of scholars have made a bold contribution towards the development of indigenous knowledge systems as an academic site of enquiry. However, most publications are in a range limited to ethnographic and anthropological literature. Varied perspectives and approaches on indigenous knowledge research – signifying the interdisciplinary nature of IKS – are expressed in our work.

Indigenous knowledge has served as a fundamental basis upon which the historical experiences of ordinary local people can be built. Even in circumstances where IKS have adapted to social, economic, environmental, spiritual and political changes, personal and group narratives are essential as a resource for an evidence-based understanding of a people's culture.

For IKS scholars, foregrounding indigenous languages is of major importance, with the claim that the interviewees' actual vernacular words should appear in the research report or publication. This practice will assist in the preservation of the languages that are slowly dying out; in particular, the Khoe and San languages of southern Africa.

Tip

Given an often long history of disregard or misrepresentation of the indigenous peoples, researchers are urged to treat interviewees as partners both in the processes of investigation and in knowledge generation. IKS scholars take this principle further by contending that the researchers ought to acknowledge the interviewees not only as sources of data but as co-authors, and that, as a result, their names should be put on research publications. Our research work demonstrates that the IKS research approach is based on principles and values that resonates feminist research.

5.8   Commonalities between feminist and IKS principles

In this brief commentary we look at the crossing points between the research principles of feminist and indigenous knowledge systems. Both approaches are concerned with highlighting the profile of individuals and groups that has been pushed to the periphery of dominating structures and systems. These may be: faith institutions, schools, government, places of work, and even the family. One of the underlying principles of both research approaches is to pose the question: How will the excavated data, findings and recommendations effectively change marginal people's lives?

Feminist and IKS approaches consciously advance research that:

- ☑ Seeks to bring about change;
- ☑ Gets marginal people actively involved in the production and publication of knowledge;
- ☑ Ensures that marginal people participate as equal partners in research projects; and
- ☑ Commits to preserving, producing and disseminating local knowledge and stories of marginal people.

Tip

The two research approaches discussed here acknowledge the researched community as a producer of knowledge, and aim to raise the profile of the knowledge that is collected. How would you consider making this an aim in your research?

This approach is based on the principle that although the knowledge and the stories of ordinary people are significant, for the purposes of redress, it is first and foremost the marginalised that should be prioritised. This is what being sensitive to the next person or community is all about; hence we regard these two principles as the *sensitive approach*.

5.8.1 The view of the sensitive approach

The sensitive approach calls on researchers to examine power relations that may be at play in a research process.

Pitfall warning

Research participants may feel overwhelmed and give in to the demands of researchers. The sensitive approach cautions researchers to be aware of their role and the manner in which they may be perceived by most interviewees, that is, as an elite group looking for 'correct' information. There may be instances in which the information that is provided by the research participants is intentionally altered. Changing information could be out of the innocent intention of trying hard to present facts that the participants think will not clash with what the researcher wants to hear.

Case study: Telling different stories

In a meeting of a group of researchers who studied the Ngome women of KwaZulu-Natal, it emerged that two members of the group had spoken to the same person on the same day. They had been talking about the character of Bambatha (Chief Bambatha kaMancinza of the amaZondi, who led the Bambatha Uprising against British rule and poll taxes in 1907) and how people nowadays seem to come up with not only totally different information, but make opposing statements. To the isiZulu-speaking member of the team, he was defined as a hero who made his mark and is highly revered by the amaZondi; while to the non-isiZulu-speaking white member of the team he was painted as an insurgent who caused a lot of trouble for everyone.

Drawing from this experience, and noting that research participants may give conflicting information in different contexts, it is for such reasons that both feminist and IKS writers urge researchers to reflect on how the interview process impacts on the collection of data. Analysis of interview interactions allows us to consider how interests and assumptions hinder or encourage the respondent's narration.

Respect and sensitivity for the interviewee forms a crucial part of the sensitive approach. Practically, respect and sensitivity mean accommodating the wishes of the interviewee without putting upfront the research objectives. For example, prior to drawing up the written version of the report on the Shembe women (see later), we ascertained that the report would be in a format that all four women would be happy with.

Although pseudonyms were used, the women preferred an interactive format reflecting the manner in which the information had been relayed. Alongside this principle is the use of the actual words that interviewees employ in an interaction. Both feminist and IKS schools of thought hold that this approach should prioritise the language and expression of the indigenous people, thereby preserving knowledge in the manner in which it was conveyed.

The manner in which the data are interpreted is a pressing question for both schools of thought. Feminist and IKS proponents alike maintain that all stories have more than one side, and that one needs to listen to all sides as various perspectives and interpretations may assist in completing the research puzzle. This does not, however, mean that research processes incorporating rigorous validation of data are overlooked.

Both feminist and IKS thinking share a concern for the contextualising of interviews.

There is a strong notion that data ought to be interpreted in the presence of the sources. In practice, this means requesting meanings or any symbolic significance that may be inferred by the collected data. Although this can be a challenging task, efforts should be made towards achieving this ideal.

Often researchers with all good intentions take away the collected data to analyse in the comfort and privacy of their homes or offices, and this usually happens some time later. The sensitive approach calls for a large amount of data to be analysed at research sites while it is being collected from research participants. Adhering to this call would minimise the instances where research respondents strongly dispute the researchers' consolidated interpretations. It is thus crucial to follow this approach when conducting interviews, as evidenced in the following discussion in 5.9.

5.9 Conversing with women and the importance of context

Case study: Women of the Shembe church

A group of women of the Shembe church served as participants in one of our studies. It was found that even though women feature in substantial numbers in church activities, they are 'absent' from all church positions and decision-making structures. We set out to interview 10 women and get their opinions on this matter. The women were all professionals – ranging from an accountant to a human resources manager – and all were married. Some were in polygamous marriages. The study found that the Shembe women have internalised or accepted patriarchy. Judging from the conversations, there is no doubt that the church matters to women: they find spirituality a source of strength in the face of personal challenges and sufferings.

Although we term most of our interactions with study participants 'interviews', the word falls short of capturing what actually happens during the various research sessions, hence the regard for these interactions as conversations. This term better fits the interactions we had with the women. The interactions involved formal interviews, deliberate non-verbal messages, and casual chats while the women are busy with their domestic or church duties, and not particularly concentrating on the conversations. Such kinds of interaction contribute to creating contexts that assist in gaining better insights into the personal lives of the research participants, as well as information about their cultural and social lives.

When conversing with women, we should bear in mind that they are not only the narrators of their stories but the subjects of that narration. Hence the need to focus on the aspects and situations that they find themselves in. In the opening case study, it appears that in Cofimvaba, poverty has a greater impact on women than on men; and that in the Shembe church the women's managerial skills are disregarded on the grounds of their gender. So if we are to make memory itself the subject of study, "our interviews must be carefully contextualised, with attention to who is speaking, what their personal and social agenda is, and what kind of event they are describing" (Sangster, 1998:88).

It is important to take into account the context in which stories are told in order for the collected stories to give us a full picture of the reality of a narrative. This may include other stories that women make reference to, which at face value may seem unrelated to the main subject of the research or the current political or social situation. Against this background, it is common for women to repeatedly think back, and explain from distant experiences how a political or social event affected their lives. It is essential that researchers search out these references, as they will contribute to a better understanding of the women's responses.

Citing the importance of the context in an education structure, both feminist and IKS writers suggest the need for a strong relationship between policymakers and people who put into practice the policies. One of the ways being proposed to bridge the gap between researchers, teachers, administrators, and policymakers is to try to get a fuller, more detailed, more human view of what is going on in the education process through ecological approaches.

One cannot overemphasise the importance of providing a context for a chosen study. Doing so prevents making blanket statements about factors that otherwise are only applicable to a limited sample. However, the context must be considered with sensitivity. In order for women's stories to find their way to a text, it is essential that when we are in exchanges with them, we become fully aware of the past and current wounding experiences of these women. Unless there is this kind of cognisance and consciousness, exchanges with and among women may produce stories that only respond to the researcher's agenda.

Respect for their personal accounts and how they are presented should form part of an investigation. This will allow researchers the confidence and eagerness to participate in the process of 'giving back collected data' to their sources. In this way, researchers become mindful that individuals and the community are at the centre of an investigation, as well as the authors of their own narratives. These are the people that most African research projects examine.

Also, because of the limited coverage given to ordinary people in the various media, their ideologies and values are a closed book that is not easily and readily understood. Women, unlike men, are even more difficult to interview. It is therefore essential for researchers to understand this challenge with women. Besides expecting, understanding and accepting this difficulty with women, we have found that planning ahead is necessary. It is more common for women than men to be reticent, to opt to say nothing, or to get angry or impatient at the questions posed to them.

Case study: Some challenges in interviewing women

In our initial attempts to interview women, the following and similar responses have cropped up over and over again.

▸ *Kungani nje ngempela ufuna ukukhuluma nami ngane yami abantu bebaningi kangaka. Dlula!* (My child, I am puzzled by your insistence on talking to me when there are so many people you could talk to. Pass on!)

▸ *Leyo ndaba yaziwa ngamadoda, futhi kangcono yaziwa ngabantu basebukhosini. Ngingubani kodwa bantu ngingaqetheka lezo zindaba?* (Men know that story well and the royal house even better. Who am I to talk about these matters?)

These responses were found to be peculiar to women. We also found that even when men refuse to talk, they are not as blunt as the women in the case study examples. In their refusal to talk to you, men mostly, unlike women, refer you to other people you could talk to. Our conclusion is that because African culture recognises men as spokespeople, they consciously regard it as their 'natural' duty to speak.

A behaviour also found in women was their preference for talking about relationships and aspects of events that have an emotional effect on their lives. Women have little concern themselves for the minute details of events. They would rather share the emotions triggered by events. Further, there is intense concentration on the practical effects of these events. This may result in naming practices with children, and homesteads named after events that carry significant memories. So it is essential to carefully listen and accurately interpret your respondents' stories. This is exemplified in the next section.

Pitfall warning

Dismissive or reluctant behaviours can be easily mistaken by a young, inexperienced researcher as a sign of failure. Instead, these observations should be seen as rich accounts that, on their own, can create a historical record and assist in achieving a better understanding of the studied group.

5.10 Listening to and interpreting women's stories

As researchers, we set out to interview research participants with the hope that they do most of the talking, right? In our experience we have found this to be wrong. Most women we have interacted with challenge this expectation. You may have received permission to talk to some women and think "let the interview start", but brace yourself for a real interview with – and by – the intended interviewees.

This process requires that the researcher gets upfront, not only about her or his research mission, but about her or his identity. It may not be enough to your research participants to have you state what you are about, what you know, have heard, etc. The sensitive approach necessitates divulging the researcher's identity at both the data gathering and reporting stages. One should acknowledge the presence and the effects that one's identity as an interviewer may have on the research process.

Tip

Unlike men, we found most women to have a special interest in the people who come to interview them. They want to know about you as much as you want to learn more about their lives. Some participants may want to know about you at length, well before they tell you anything about their lives and experiences. Some of the details they require may seem intrusive, but remember, so is your intervention as a researcher. They desire only to allow researchers into their world on condition that they too can get personal – it works both ways.

Toolbox Essential information for researchers

It is essential for the researcher to place her or his class, race, culture, and gender assumptions, beliefs and behaviours within the frame of the picture that she or he is trying to paint. In case you are required to give them, plan in advance which aspects of your own life you may be prepared to share without feeling vulnerable. The need to plan in advance cannot be overstated. Planning and thinking ahead should not only apply before arriving in the community, but also as the research process progresses, and with every follow-up visit. It is advised that the following checkpoints go into any list of field researchers who aim to interview women; and, in turn, plans be adjusted accordingly:

(continued)

✓ **Ways of communicating with women** of a particular group within a community

✓ **Authority structures**, levels and individuals that exist in particular importance for women

✓ **Necessity of understanding identified women**, besides the cultural matters discussed elsewhere in this chapter

✓ **Painful experiences** the identified women may have been through because of their gender

✓ **Sensitive aspects** related to the realities and challenges that women have faced from their socio-political history

✓ **Expectations from an outsider** and behavioural patterns, as a male or female researcher

✓ **Events that have taken place in the area**, including ones as recent as the day of your visit

✓ **The expected dress code** as a man or woman, in relation to your age and race.

Once you have been allowed to conduct an interview, you may find that the women prefer to talk about people other than themselves. Family and relationships take centre stage thus shifting the spotlight from themselves; this has been found to be common with women respondents. This also explains the subjective focus that feminist researchers encourage and reference in the expression, 'the person is political'. Essentially, this calls for the need to unpack the stories that at face value seem too personal and probably not related to the objectives of the research.

Feminist scholars argue that a closer look into such personal stories will reveal interconnections between subjective accounts and the wider context in which the stories are told. For instance, a woman may choose to concentrate on the lives of her children because her own life perhaps has many painful memories of the abuse she has suffered. Her children may be the only good thing that has happened in her domestic life. Her own absence from the family story could be a resonant story in itself, indicating aspects of her life that she desires to shut out. It is therefore crucial for researchers, as the sensitive approach advises, to make all attempts to probe further, check why women choose to tell the stories they tell and, more importantly, interpret with them the significance, the meaning, the weight, of their stories. It is fascinating that, unlike men, women are keen to interpret their stories. One of the reasons why women tell stories differently could be their inevitable acceptance of the reality that men are often in positions of leadership and power. Thus the thinking is that men would be sooner listened to, and taken seriously, compared with women.

With careful planning, appropriate probing and good listening, the researcher can facilitate the interaction so that a research participant, while telling her story, can simultaneously provide its significance. It would be a pity to miss the opportunity of getting women to interpret their stories themselves on the research site.

We have found that the practice of accommodating interpretation at the research site contributes to making women feel valued. Eliciting comments on the significance of a story shows that this story is important and is worthy of being told. Considering that most stories in women's lives and experience have largely concentrated on men, not surprisingly women downplay the importance of their own stories. Therefore, they need to be reassured that their stories are unique, that they are valuable, and that they constitute a contribution to history.

uBuntu as a factor in research

uBuntu is a philosophy that is largely based on respect for other people and, in particular, strangers and visitors. Interviewees may feel the need to go to great lengths to provide the 'right' information to the researcher, out of politeness or empathy.

On the other hand, the reluctance to tell one's story can indicate an African value system that propagates modesty. As most African interviewees subscribe to the ideals of uBuntu, they may concentrate on being of service to their 'visitor', to an extent that the data they provide are tainted. It is essential to understand the worldview of the African interviewee, and the philosophy from which she operates, to get a full grasp of her utterances in an interview context. This understanding is vital; it means possessing some knowledge about what should and should not be asked, and by whom. The researcher therefore ought to familiarise herself in advance with the intended participants' worldview.

Toolbox Some strategies for researching women

Researching women is not very different from researching any other group. There are, however, a few aspects that researchers have to be aware of. Here are some pointers that ought to be taken into consideration when researching women. We should add that most of these pointers may in fact be applicable to any human group that is studied.

The following generic pointers should be treated as examples that are based on certain research experiences. They should not be treated as the absolute truth, nor are they exhaustive.

Always

☑ **Allow women first and foremost to interpret their own stories**. The best practice is to encourage narrators to reflect and interpret the events they describe.

☑ **Check if there are any middle- and low-level authority structures** that ought to be consulted before securing interview appointments with identified participants. It should be noted whether the said structures are male or elderly.

☑ **Acknowledge your full identity** and, in advance, think about certain parts of your life that you may be willing to share with research participants.

Work towards

☑ **Recording and presenting** some of the shared stories verbatim, taking into account the tone and mood of the interviewees. Such a strategy affirms the women's actual experiences since it allows the reader an opportunity to 'directly listen to and engage with' research participants

☑ **Reporting the collected information** as soon as possible after the event, as women's lives and interests change rapidly. You may want to revisit the interviewees and find out whether attitudes have changed, resulting in behaviours different from the ones to which the researcher was initially exposed.

☑ **Appreciating and recognising** that the researched community's life choices and behaviours are rooted in their culture. The produced research reports should express awareness that these cultures in Africa serve as reference frameworks.

☑ **Showing women that their stories are important** and worth being told and listened to.

☑ **Understanding, accepting and allowing** the women's authentic forms of expression.

(continued)

☑ **Acknowledging and reflecting on the processes** that did not work well. This important practice, which is strongly advocated by feminist researchers, should form part of your report. It is an opportunity for future researchers to draw lessons from your study.

☑ **Allowing collected information** to emanate from an enabling range of open-ended probing questions that largely draws from the women's personal memory and experience.

Look closer into

☑ **Narratives** that are told by people about themselves, their environments.

☑ **Special ways** of telling stories and stories that differ from the rest, which certain participants may prefer to use.

☑ **Direct experiences** of people who were involved in a researched event, or those who were able to listen to and engage with direct participants. Go to the primary sources to gather the data, wherever possible.

☑ **Emotional points** of a story. It is essential to try to get as close as possible to the original person who had the experience. Then go beyond this task and look for emotions, responses and the effects of an experience. This requires that both the 'how' and 'why' questions are posed to participants.

☑ **Women's special role** and understanding of the events they have been involved in.

☑ **Check on how distinct those roles** and understandings are, as well as to what extent they have affected or arisen from the researched events, or aspects.

Avoid the following

☑ **Interpreting women's stories** on your own, and coming to a final conclusion without having consulted participants first.

☑ **Claiming and providing information** that is suggestive of representing everyone or all women, even within a single community, be specific.

Conclusion

This chapter has noted issues and practices that researchers ought to be cognisant of when interviewing women. Despite the complications entailed in investigating and telling women's stories, it should be noted that no two women will behave in the same way. There is a variety of social strands which affect the women's responses, including their geographical location, class, level of education, as well as cultural expectations of women. It is critical to caution against neglecting to recognise the dynamic and layered nature of women's lives.

For the purpose of recording and publishing, stories need to take the form in which the women typically communicate, or for which they express a preference. This requires that before the end of the stage of collecting data, the researcher checks with his or her interviewees on the manner in which collected data could be presented

The use of IKS and feminist principles, presented in this chapter as the sensitive approach in conducting research, need not only be confined to researchers who fully subscribe to the ideals contained in these schools of thought. Complementing research approaches with the sensitive approach would afford women from all communities maximum opportunity to express their views on a wide range of issues. In turn we would succeed in putting a human face on the lives of all people.

Closing activities

Reflection questions and activities

1 Find a partner for this activity. It should *not* be your friend or someone you often interact with. Talk to each other about your values, i.e. things that matter to you most. Each list at least three such values and provide reasons why they matter, drawing links between your values and any human rights aspects discussed in this chapter.

2 Working in pairs, identify an organisation that you both know, e.g. religious organisation, government department, non-governmental organisation, etc. Discuss the organisation's values, interrogating them by answering the following questions:

   a What is the name and purpose of the organisation?

   b Who is its membership?

   c Does the organisation value African perspectives? (How can you tell?)

   d From the organisation's general practice, and the manner in which it relates to people not belonging to the organisation:

   i Does it come across as an organisation that values and upholds human rights?

   ii How are the men and women who belong to the organisation treated?

   iii How are people external to the organisation treated?

   iv From your observation, is the organisation sensitive to the elderly, people with disabilities, and children?

   e If you were to join this organisation, what changes would you want to see, and why?

Bibliography

Babbie, E. & Mouton, J. 2010. *The practice of social research*. Cape Town: Oxford University Press.

Blaikie, N. 2007. *Approaches to social enquiry*. Cambridge: Polity Press.

Bowden, P. & Mummery, J. 2009. *Understanding feminism*. Stocksfield: Acumen Publishing Limited.

Bozzoli, B. 1991. *Women of Phokeng*. Johannesburg: Ravan Press.

Charles, N. 1996. Feminist practices: Identity, difference, power. In N. Charles & F. Hughes-Freeland (Eds). *Practising Feminism*. Taylor & Francis.

Chase, S.E. & Bell, C.S. 1994. Interpreting the complexity of women's subjectivity. In E.M. McMahan & K.M. Rogers (Eds). *Interactive oral history interviewing*. New Jersey: Lawrence Erlbaum. (pp. 63–81)

Crotty, M. 1998. *The Foundations of Social Research: Meanings and Perspectives in the Research Process*. London: Sage.

Conolly, J. & Sienaert, E. 2006. The oral tradition and research: Principles, perspectives and practices. In T. Magwaza, et al. (Eds). *Freedom sown in blood: Memories of the impi yamakhanda*. Thohoyandou: Ditlou Publishers.

Feast, L. & Melles, G. 2010. *Epistemological positions in design research: A brief review of the literature*. Melbourne, Victoria, Australia: Swinburne University of Technology.

Glaser, B.G. 1978. *Advances in the Methodology of Grounded Theory: Theoretical Sensitivity*. Mill Valley, California: Sociology Press.

Harding, S. 1987. *Feminism and Methodology*. Bloomington: Indiana University Press.

Hesse-Biber, S.N. 2014. *Feminist Research Practice: A Primer* (2nd ed.). London: Sage Publications.

Lay, K. & Daley, J.G. 2007. A critique of feminist theory. *Advances in Social Work*, 8(1):49–61. Retrieved from http://journals.iupui.edu/index.php/advancesinsocialwork/article/view/131/122

Magwaza (Meyiwa), T. 2004. Conversations with women of the Shembe Church. *Agenda*, 60:34–41.

Magwaza (Meyiwa), T. 2006. IKS methodological pilgrimage: Processes and procedures. In T. Magwaza, Y. Seleti & M.P. Sithole (Eds). *Freedom sown in blood: Memories of the impi yamakhanda*. Thohoyandou: Ditlou Publishers.

Sangster, J. 1998. Telling our stories: Feminist debates and the use of oral history. In R. Perks & A. Thompson (Eds). *The oral history reader*. London: Routledge.

Sarantakos, S. 2005. *Social research* (3rd ed.). Basingstoke: Palgrave Macmillan.

Scott, J.C. 1990. *Domination and the arts of resistance: Hidden transcripts*. New Haven: Yale University Press.

CHAPTER 6

Melanie Drake

Objectivity, values and subjectivity: Issues of values and ethics in the research process

KEY CONCEPTS

Disconfirmation This term acknowledges that researchers often have a tendency to give more weight to data and data sources that confirm rather than disconfirm their prior assumptions and hypothesis. Reviewing evidence obtained to make sure appropriate weight has been given to both confirming and disconfirming evidence, helps to address disconfirmation while in the field.

External value constraints These are the external implications of the research – for example, the findings and their impact on the surrounding social environment.

Internal value constraints These are the plans on how to conduct the research with the research participants. It is a research process consideration that should be undertaken by all researchers.

Member-checks means getting participants to check their transcripts and to check for consensus among participants on events, incidents and behaviours.

Objectivism This complex term refers to reflecting on the researcher's beliefs, opinions, values and/or the context when planning and embarking on research; this includes trying to acknowledge these and prevent them from influencing how the researcher approaches, conducts and reports on the research.

Reflexivity is about challenging and questioning your own assumptions and thoughts as researchers, and how they impact on the research process.

Subjectivism Another complex term that almost serves as the opposite of objectivism (see section notes in chapter for list of opposing terms). This term acknowledges that researchers approach research with agendas and with opinions, beliefs and values that can impact on how they conduct the research, and on all other aspects of the research process.

Value freedom refers, in a general sense, to eliminating, or attempting to eliminate, the researcher's judgements on data collected in the field and in research findings.

LEARNING OUTCOMES

By the end of this chapter, you should be able to:

▶ Determine what ethics is and why ethical practice is important in education research.

▶ Understand objectivism and realise why it is an important feature in the ethical considerations of your research.

▶ Discuss historical studies that shaped the ethical procedures and considerations that we make today.

▶ Approach your research as ethically reflexive researchers.

▶ Reflect on, discuss and think about value judgements through reflecting on experiences from researchers in the field.

Thandi is an education student doing research at a rural school in Limpopo province, South Africa. Her research investigates teachers' practice, and the impact this practice has on learners' development in the classroom. Although she received consent from her educational institution for the research process, she is now faced with unexpected ethical dilemmas. After a period of three months of observation at the rural school, she interviews her participants. Her two sets of evidence –observation notes and interviews – do not match. Her participants say things they do not do. For example, teachers say that they run after-school, extra-curricular activities to help learners develop social and teamwork skills, but after the first few months, she notices that the teachers always leave school at midday. She is confused about how to continue. At the same time, her car is broken into and her digital audio recordings are stolen. Furthermore, although parents of children at the school were intended to be among her research participants, no parents offer to volunteer their time. Teachers say that parents are involved, yet she never observes any parents at the school. She also notices that a teacher is 'selling' goods during class, aggressively persuading his learners to purchase things from his stock. None of Thandi's ethical planning and application to an ethics committee prepares her for these situations in her fieldwork. She decides to do the following:

▶ She ignores her observation evidence and chooses to report only on her interview transcripts from the teachers. After all, if they say it, it must be true, right?

▶ When her vehicle was broken into, transcripts from a learner who spoke of being subjected to corporal punishment were stolen. She decides to ignore this issue. Besides, that is not what she is researching, so why should it matter?

▶ A parent offers up time to be interviewed, but only if Thandi pays him in cash. She decides to pay up as she cannot get any other parents to agree to be interviewed.

▶ She feels too intimidated by the aggressive nature of the teacher who forces his learners to purchase goods during his class. She deletes these data from her observation field notes.

Do *you* think Thandi's decisions are ethical?

Introduction

Navigating ethics in research is a difficult task, even for the most experienced researchers. The case study highlights the difficult decisions and complications that can emerge during research. Thandi completed her ethics approval process through her educational institution. She had prepared a satisfactory research proposal that was presented and passed by her faculty and supervisors. But nothing prepared her for the actual research context, where so many unplanned circumstances shifted her thinking and caused her to question her ethical responsibilities in her research. Thandi was surprised, but perhaps should have been forewarned by Strauss (1987:7–8), who states:

> Researchers need to be alive not only to the constraints and challenges of research settings and research aims, but to the nature of their data. They must be alert to the temporal aspects or phasing of the researches, the open-ended character of the "best research" in any discipline, the immense significance of their own experiences as researchers, and the local contexts in which the research is conducted [...] Methods, after all, are developed and changed in response to changing work contexts.

This chapter explores an introduction to ethics in research for novice researchers. Within this text, you will come to understand key philosophical and methodological considerations that come to the fore when embarking on research that is ethically sound. We will unpack ethics in research, focusing particularly on the notion of objectivism, value judgements, and how one becomes an ethically reflexive education researcher. We will also analyse reflections from the field which highlight issues that could potentially arise in your own research. This chapter aims to equip you with the knowledge of how to approach ethics in your research design.

6.1   What is ethics?

In many disciplines, research has become an issue of ethics. Understanding how to protect the interests of those who are ready and willing to take part in research, has repeatedly drawn research ethics to the foreground (Flick, 2006).

Resolving ethical issues

Codes of ethics, and ethics committees have been established all around the world in an attempt to ensure the protection of people who participate in the research process. Yet, formal codes of ethics are not always the best way of addressing ethical issues arising in educational research. Research ethics is not only about the welfare of research participants. It also extends to areas of scientific misconduct and plagiarism. In South Africa, most leading universities require that research involving human participants be reviewed by an independent research ethics committee (REC) before data collection can commence.

Research ethics should be a fundamental concern for education researchers when planning, designing, implementing and reporting research with human participants. Individual researchers have a fundamental obligation to treat research participants ethically, and not as "a simple means to researchers' end" (Wassenaar, 2006:61). Yet ethics is often difficult to generalise about. When we consider the demands of day-to-day practices in the field, and the challenging processes of undertaking research, we understand how navigating ethics can easily become tricky. Ethics is frequently difficult to put into clear-cut, transparent clarifications. "However, all aspects of the research process, from deciding upon the topic, through to identifying a sample, conducting the research and disseminating the findings, have ethical implications" (Norway, as cited in Flick, 2006:49).

Researchers need to protect their research participants, develop a trust with them, promote the integrity of the research, guard against misconduct and impropriety that may reflect on themselves and their institutions, and cope with challenging and surprising problems. Issues such as personal disclosure, authenticity, credibility, the role of the researcher in cross-cultural contexts, and the issues of personal privacy all create a mirage of complexities.

As Thandi encountered during her fieldwork (see case study), and as you prepare your research topic and processes, there will be ethical issues to consider at every stage of the research process (see Table 6.1 for a summary of ethical issues in educational research (adapted from Creswell, 2014:93)).

Table 6.1 outlines the specific thinking that you should do when embarking on ethically sound research. This chapter, through a more philosophical lens, will unpack why and how we do these things when researching. Let's begin by analysing what it means to remain objective as a novice researcher embarking on the research process.

TABLE 6.1: Potential ethical issues in education research

Research process	Ethical issues	Suggestions for resolving issues
Before conducting study	1 Find out all relevant information about institutional approval. 2 Seek local permission from site and participants. Often the Department of Education (DoE) and/or principal can give site access. 3 Select a site that is without vested interest in the outcome of the study. 4 Negotiate authorship for publication.	1 Discuss ethical considerations with your supervisor from the outset of your research design. It is not something to be 'added on' at the end. 2 Apply for ethical clearance from your university prior to planning the fieldwork. 3 Identify and go through local approval, like district offices and government departments. 4 Contemplate potential 'power relations' issues with different sites and address this adequately in your proposal and findings.
Beginning the study	1 Identify a research problem that will benefit participants. 2 Disclose purpose of the study. 3 Do not pressure participants into signing consent forms. 4 Respect norms and values of different cultures. 5 Be sensitive to needs of vulnerable groups, like children, disabled people.	1 Have an informal discussion with participants about their needs. 2 Contact participants and share the general purpose of the study. 3 Tell participants that they do not have to sign the form unless they want to. 4 Find out more about cultural, gender, religious, socio-economic, and other differences that need to be respected. 5 Obtain appropriate consent, like that of parents of children.
Collecting data	1 Disrupt the site as little as possible. 2 Make sure all participants receive the same treatment. 3 Do not deceive participants 4 Respect potential power imbalances (like researcher/participants during interviews). 5 Do not just 'use' participants by gathering data and leaving the site immediately. 6 Avoid collecting harmful information. 7 Stay safe. Should unsafe environments present themselves to you, remove yourself from the site.	1 Build trust and anticipate disruptions in gaining access. 2 Discuss purpose of the study and how data will be used with participants. 3 Avoid leading questions. Withhold sharing personal impressions. Avoid disclosing sensitive information. Treat participants as collaborators. 4 Provide necessary resources to make participants comfortable during interviews. 5 Stick to questions stated in the interview sheet.
Analysing data	1 Avoid siding with the participants. 2 Avoid disclosing only positive results. 3 Respect the privacy and anonymity of participants.	1 Report multiple perspectives. 2 Report contrary findings. 3 Assign fictitious names or aliases.

Research process	Ethical issues		Suggestions for resolving issues	
Reporting, sharing and storing data	1	Avoid falsifying authorship, findings, evidence and/or conclusions.	1	Report honestly.
	2	Never plagiarise.	2	Gain appropriate permissions to reprint or adapt work.
	3	Do not disclose information that would harm participants.	3	Use composite stories so that participants cannot be identified.
	4	Communicate clearly and straightforwardly.	4	Use unbiased language.
	5	Disseminate findings.	5	Provide copies of reports to participants and stakeholders.
	6	Raw evidence should be stored securely.	6	Store raw evidence for five years.
	7	Provide complete proof of compliance with ethical issues.	7	Disclose funders and other support structures in the research; all who will profit from the research.
	8	State who owns the data from a study.		

(**Source:** Adapted from Creswell, 2014:93)

6.2 Objectivism and subjectivism in research

One of the primary considerations for you as young researchers when thinking about the ethical considerations of research, is the notion of remaining objective. Objectivity is a word, like 'truth' and 'reality' that creates a lot of scepticism in the research world, and is often interpreted in different ways by researchers and scientists. In the simplest of explanations, **objectivism** in research can be understood as the researcher trying to approach elements in the research for exactly what they are (in a scientific sense), and not allowing their beliefs, opinions, experience, and the context to influence how they approach, conduct and report on the research. Over time, objectivity together with subjectivity, have been interpreted in different ways, by different people. Hammersley (2011) suggests the relationship between objectivity and subjectivity is intended to highlight contrasts, such as:

▸ Mental versus physical
▸ Internal as against external
▸ Private rather than public
▸ Implicit rather than explicit
▸ Judgement as against mechanical procedure
▸ Idiosyncratic rather than shared or inter-subjective
▸ Variable versus stable or fixed
▸ Particular rather than universal
▸ Dependent as against independent
▸ Relative rather than absolute
▸ Erroneous versus true.

These contrasts are important as they help us view research in multiple perspectives, instead of relying on one framework or lens through which to explore research and fieldwork. Objectivism is used to combine these different meanings, and refers to a particular conception of the nature of scientific enquiry, how it should be looked at, and what it produces (Hammersley, 2011b). For you as beginner researchers, it is important to think deeply and often about your understanding of objectivism in your research.

Objectivism begins by acknowledging that we are often led into error by false or misinterpreted preconceptions and preferences: these result in us seeing things or finding things that we expect or wish to see and find, rather than what is true. If you go back to the case study on Thandi's research, you will find that many of her ethical dilemmas stem from misinterpreted or false preconceptions on her part. Perhaps Thandi thought that corporal punishment no longer happened in schools. Maybe she didn't think that extra-curricular activities were important for learners' development. Hence, when she was faced with these realities, her personal opinions and feelings may have distorted her 'objective' desire to report accurate and trustworthy findings. It is our subjective factors that can redirect or deviate us from the truth.

Subjectivity is believed to bias enquiry, deflecting or distracting us from the truth that we would discover. Research must be unaffected by our personal and social characteristics. **Subjectivism** acknowledges that researchers are people, and it is sometimes difficult for people to be unhindered by the beliefs, ideas, opinions and values when conducting research. Subjective characteristics include our prior beliefs, values, preferences, attitudes, history, personality traits, and culture. It is very important that you unpack your personal views, opinions, beliefs and values about your research topic before you embark on the research process. When you do not consciously thinking about these important aspects of yourself as a researcher, you run the risk of planning an unethical study. This chapter will help you to achieve a deep understanding of what you think and believe, and how these beliefs could impact on what you do in the research context. Let us now review the original studies that occurred, which contributed to ethical considerations in research as we know it today.

Critical thinking challenge

With your current understanding of objectivism, go back to the resolutions Thandi made during her research fieldwork, and think again about what she should have done in these circumstances. Put yourself in her shoes, and discuss with a class partner what you would do and how you would proceed with the research.

How did we start thinking about ethics in research?

Ethics in research is said to have originated in the aftermath of the atrocities committed by Nazi medical researchers in Germany during World War II. As in medicine, increased awareness of the need for ethical considerations in the social sciences was caused by the outraged reactions to specific studies that took place. Read more about the studies that have informed our thinking in 6.3 now.

6.3 Studies that contributed to understanding ethics in research

Perhaps you are asking yourself, 'Where did ethical considerations in research originate from'? Let us take a moment to analyse a few of the important research studies that contributed to ethics as we know it today. This will deepen your understanding of ethics and allow you to reflect on your research more deeply.

6.3.1 Milgram's obedience study

This controversial study by Yale psychologist Stanley Milgram in the 1960s required participants to believe that they were administering a lethal electric shock on other people. In reality, the shocks were not really being delivered, but if they were, they would have certainly been lethal. The participants themselves and the research community at large were distressed when they learnt that participants were deceived, as well as, that participants were encouraged to administer fatal shocks if they had been real.

6.3.2 The 'Tearoom Trade'

In the 1970s, sociologist Laud Humphreys became interested in the study of homosexuality. His research focused on casual and fleeting homosexual acts that were performed between strangers that met in public restrooms in parks, called 'tearooms'. Humphreys began showing up at public restrooms, offering to be the 'lookout', and in that way he was able to conduct field observations. But Humphreys needed to know more about the participants, so he would record the car and licence details of the participants. He was then able to gain personal information, such as addresses and names from the police department. He would then visit men at their homes, disguising himself, while seek further information. This study provoked considerable controversy. Some critics accused Humphreys of gross invasion of privacy – what men did in public restrooms was their own business. Others were concerned over the deceit that was caused with Humphreys offering to be a lookout, and not disclosing his research intentions. Others said it was all fair game, that these participants were performing these acts in public facilities. Some felt that it was unethical for Humphreys to follow them to their houses to interview them. Humphreys himself felt that the study could not have been conducted any other way (Babbie & Mouton, 2011). These ethical debates have not been resolved and this study stirs many emotions due to these ethical issues.

6.3.3 The Tuskegee syphilis study

This study took place in 1932 when there was no effective treatment for syphilis. The study enrolled over 300 male syphilis sufferers from an impoverished area where syphilis prevalence was high. A control group of 200 uninfected males were matched. It is uncertain whether the men knew they were participating in a study, as there were no clear records of informed consent. They were subjected to various examinations and medical procedures. During the course of this study, penicillin, an effective treatment for syphilis, became available. However, the men in this study were not informed of this new treatment, nor were they given the medication as it would have undermined the scientific purpose of the study. Many men died as a result of their untreated condition. The study was eventually stopped and survivors and families of the deceased were awarded compensation many years later.

To you as novice research students, these studies provide an opportunity to look at research in a different light. It is your responsibility to think about how the research will impact on the participants involved, and how you can go about ensuring that the greatest care is taken with those who are involved. Let us now unpack ways in which to approach our research with ethics at the forefront of our thinking, beginning with value freedom.

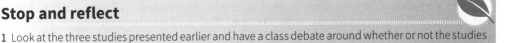
1 Look at the three studies presented earlier and have a class debate around whether or not the studies were ethically directed. What is acceptable and unacceptable in research?

2 Consider the recent developments in medical research and how these have possibly advanced human life. What are your feelings about this, and why?

6.4   Value freedom and the conduct of research

Research ethics strongly emphasises that the ends of research do not justify the means. Research participants' dignity and welfare should always transcend the interest of the research (or researcher). These considerations leads to questions such as: How solid is the evidence base upon which claims have been made? Are the interpretations plausible? Have alternative interpretations been overlooked?

We cannot deny that social science researchers are also involved in making evaluative and political judgements and choices during the research process. Researchers decide what questions to ask, what evidence to record and collect, how to interpret the evidence, what findings to report or present. Value judgements are unavoidable in the research process. Although we strive for an objective approach to research, it becomes difficult to draw a distinctive line between social researchers trying to maintain a separation between facts and values, and to prevent their values from distorting the facts (objectivism), with social researchers allowing their values to shape their research (Gewirtz & Cribb, 2006). **Value freedom** in research refers to attempting to eliminate the researcher's judgements on research findings, and data that are collected in the field.

There is a need for researchers to be self-conscious about the way in which their value judgements shape their research. Researchers need to be especially wary of their value judgements preventing them from actively seeking out and taking account of evidence that might challenge their prior beliefs and values. For example, when Thandi witnessed corporal punishment in the classroom, her belief that corporal punishment had been abolished may have influenced her decision to not report this finding in her evidence. She may have allowed her judgement to believe what teachers told her to influence her ultimate neglect of the evidence about the lack of extra-curricular activities at the school. Researchers need to be prepared to defend and articulate the evaluative stances that inform their work.

Furthermore, it is argued that researchers are part of the world they are researching, and the work of research is inevitably bound up with countless ethical and political choices. Within social research, such as in education, practical implications lie at the heart of the knowledge that is generated from it (Gewirtz & Cribb, 2006). So it is that the role of researchers becomes an even more crucial factor in the research process. In the next section, we look at how researchers can approach value freedom in the field.

6.5   Ethical reflexivity

Reflexivity is, in basic terms, thinking critically about what you are doing and why, confronting and often challenging your own assumptions, and recognising the extent to which your thoughts, actions and decision-making processes shape what you see and how you research. Being reflexive adds to the responsibility and complexity of what researchers do, and what research is about.

Researchers should be constantly engaging in self-questioning activities, "reflexive acts, that constitute a way of doing research" (Mason, 2002:5). Reflexive acts should be focused on the research itself. Researchers should resist the temptation to use research for egocentric purposes, or for confessional tales that tell very little about the research practice and problem.

Pitfall warning

When conducting research, it is difficult to resist sharing confidential information with others, be they your friends, family, or colleagues. However, it is important for you to understand the impact your research data can have on the lives of the participants. Always try to remain professional researchers when conducting research and keep transcripts and recordings safely stored away. It is your responsibility!

Tip

How do we become ethically reflexive in our approach to our research? Gerwirtz and Cribb (2006) offer a few crucial elements:

- ☑ **Be explicit**, as far as possible, about the value assumptions and evaluative judgements that inform, or are embedded in, every stage of the research.
- ☑ **Be prepared** to offer a defence of your assumptions and judgements to the extent that either they ought to be shared by others, or, conversely, that they are not sufficiently problematised by others.
- ☑ **Acknowledge**, and where possible, **respond to tensions** between various values that are embedded in the research.
- ☑ **Take seriously** the practical judgements and dilemmas of the participants you are researching.
- ☑ **Take responsibility** for the political and ethical implications of the research.

These tips allow us to prepare for research fieldwork to the very best of our abilities. The next section continues to unpack the difficulties and challenges that the research field can present to researchers.

6.5.1   Challenges for ethically reflexive research

With the statements posed earlier, and the discussions this chapter has raised about objectivity, subjectivity, value freedom and reflexivity, you may be feeling overwhelmed by these ethical dilemmas. Research students often suggest that ethics is all about informed consent and confidentiality. To be truly ethically sensitive and confident in research, we have to acknowledge the difficulties that come with these terms.

We cannot deny that reflexivity can seem boundless. How far do we go in attempting to be ethically reflexive researchers? Questions, analyses, questioning and reflecting can be neverending, particularly in education research. The suggestion is to focus on the nature of the research being undertaken, and the social, political and organisational contexts in which the researcher is working. Within any research community there will be controversial and contentious values. Towards the end of this chapter, we will analyse actual 'tales' from the field that highlight these contentious and controversial issues. The three steps described next allow us to think about and prepare ourselves for how best to become ethically reflexive researchers.

☑ *Firstly,* it is important that we strive to make explicit those values that form part of the taken-for-granted worldview, particularly in the field of education. For example, education is often referred to as a basic human right. It is almost a taken-for-granted view that everyone has a right to basic education. Have you ever taken the time to interrogate that assumption? How differently would our world look, if education was not seen as a basic human right?

☑ *Secondly,* we cannot combine reflexivity about values and value tensions in the abstract, without thinking about the practical realisation of values. Making your values visible in your beliefs and opinions is not only an abstract matter. It has practical implications for what we do in the context in which we are working. Social researchers have to be prepared to develop their value judgements in a way that is responsive to, and learns from, the practical challenges when working and researching in social contexts, like schools and communities. There will be times when you will get your hands dirty responding to the social environment in which you are researching, and abandon abstract ideals.

☑ *Thirdly,* we have a practical responsibility when reporting on findings and research evidence that lends itself to falsification claims and alternative readings of the evidence. This responsibility is the "intractability of the problem of values in social research" (Gewirtz & Cribb, 2006:150). A disjunction is caused between social researchers value commitments that fuel their research, and at the same time they are being careful about not simply 'discovering' what it is that they would like to investigate. This tension involves an understanding about knowledge production and knowledge use. We would like to know that what we are studying has some type of impact on the practical use of the knowledge. However, this assumption is discussed with great caution by academics in the field. Let us examine an example to understand this difficult point.

What if ...?   e.g.

Imagine your research topic involves investigating academic outcomes of learners from impoverished schools. You suppose that the academic outcomes would be weak. You believe (your value judgements) that without appropriate resources and infrastructural support, learners could not possibly do well in school. You have read many newspaper articles about schools that have no textbooks, toilets, computers, laboratories, libraries, and so forth. So inevitably you look for this type of evidence when you are in the field: evidence that supports your value judgements and beliefs. You believe that your findings will add to the body of knowledge that supports impoverished schools being unsuccessful. You are not critically evaluating or disconfirming the evidence that presents to you.

There is a real problem if the researcher carelessly or deliberately approaches evidence collection and analysis to selectively support what he or she thinks prior to the investigation.

> If we are concerned to explicate the way in which our values help to shape fieldwork practices and analysis in the production of knowledge, then as part of that, we need to be self-conscious about the way our interests in, or concerns about, potential applications or readings of our research influence the process and products of our research (Gewirtz & Cribb, 2006:51).

Rigour is best served by incorporating reflexivity about research into the approach and process taken by the researcher.

We need to say something about **disconfirmation** at this point: "Researchers often have a tendency to give more weight to data and data sources that confirm rather than disconfirm their prior assumptions and hypothesis. Review evidence obtained to make sure appropriate weight has been given to both confirming and disconfirming evidence" (Robinson & Lai, 2006:59).

No theory can altogether answer the unpredictable complexities of ethical dilemmas when researching in the human sciences. Although guidelines, codes and rules can help the researcher to have a point of reference, many times, they are of minimal help. Research can be seen as an unpredictable and spontaneous activity. This process can be ethical or unethical, and the ethical quality depends of the way in which the researcher builds relations.

Researchers have to have the ability and disposition to keep in view all that happens in the field. Over and above this, the researcher also needs to interrogate their own actions from an ethical viewpoint and ensure that they dedicate appropriate attention to these decisions. When embarking on your research, you need to become an ethical tool to yourself. Following the activities below, we will address the role of the researcher while undertaking fieldwork.

Stop and reflect

Divide into groups and pick one of the following five scenarios to discuss with your peers. Remain reflexive and aware of your opinions when discussing your opinions on these scenarios. Do not jump to the first thing you feel or think. Rather, carefully contemplate multiple views and opinions. Listen carefully to the viewpoints of your peers.

Scenario One: A researcher wants to study the classroom management and discipline styles of a group of teachers at a school. The researcher intends to employ hidden cameras in the classroom to reveal the truth about what goes on behind closed doors.
a Identify some of the ethical issues in this research design.
b Describe ways to improve the ethics component of this research design.
c What are alternative ways that this research could be designed?

Scenario Two: A researcher wants to study parental involvement of schoolgoing learners in a township community. The research would involve video and audio recordings of families and people in the community. The researcher pays a member of the community to help them with the research.
a What are the potential ethical hazards with this research design?
b What are the risks and benefits of this type of research?
c What type of consent would be necessary for ethical consideration in this study?

Scenario Three: A researcher wants to study the impact of large families versus small families on educational achievement and success. Personally, the researcher believes that overpopulation is a huge problem and that parents of many children are being irresponsible to the impact of overpopulation and poverty in the country and the world.
a Discuss the value judgements of the researcher and how these could impact on the research.
b How can the researcher avoid 'subjectivism' in the research?
c How would you design this research if you were the researcher?

Scenario Four: A researcher wants to interview teachers about high levels of absenteeism and disengagement at five local schools in a township community. The researcher intends to observe, run focus groups, and interview participants.
a What could go wrong with this research?
b How could you improve the ethical considerations for this study?
c Discuss the research design. What problems could you predict with the layout of this study?

Scenario Five: The researcher learns through personal communications that learners are being sexually harassed in toilet facilities at a school. The researcher wants to investigate what is going on.
a What ethical considerations should be made for this study?
b Design the ethical application for this study.
c If you were the ethical committee receiving this application, what warnings would you give this researcher?

Read the following scenario where two students are discussing fieldwork; it will help you recall the issues you have dealt with in this chapter.

(Two research students are discussing fieldwork)

Research student 1 (RS1): I have been reading a lot about values constraints in ethics sections of research books, but I don't understand what it is all about?

Research student 2 (RS2): I know, it is really difficult to understand how values impact on what we do when we are in the research context.

RS1: My supervisor keeps asking me about the external value of my research, the 'so what' nature of what I want to investigate; what is that?

RS2: Yes, I'm not exactly sure what I want to do in my research and why anybody else would want to read about it. I mean, I know our research is meant to add to the body of knowledge, but I am not sure exactly how.

RS1: But what about the values that have to do with the ethical nature of our research?

RS2: Yes, I remember my supervisor telling me about Milgram's study. This obedience research gave a lot of insight into the role of authority, or the researcher, and power relations in research settings. You remember – Milgram's research involved participants giving other participants perceived electric shocks at the command of the researcher. I can imagine that did not go down very well in the research community.

RS1: I'm sure that type of research would not be allowed today, or at least not without all kinds of strict consents and requirements.

RS2: Yes, these are considered to be **internal value constraints** – how the research is conducted, with the participants. The **external value constraints** have to do with the value of results, like your findings and what you do with them. But what we can learn from this is that it is important that we gather our evidence in ways that respect principles of confidentiality, privacy and truth-telling. This is the essence of internal value constraints, or ethics. It is relevant to evaluating the goodness of the research design and procedures.

RS1: Oh I see. So it ultimately comes down to being reflexive researchers in the field, and understanding how our opinions and judgements impact on how we research and what we are researching?

RS2: Yes. Now let's make sure we discuss this further with our research supervisors. I think we have only scratched the surface of ethics in research.

6.7 Demands on the researcher: What you don't read in research books

There is a vast number of texts that speak to the role of the researcher and the ethical 'recipes' that should be followed in order to do progressive, effective research in education. As Yin (2003) describes, the demands of a case study (or other social research methods and approaches) on your intellect, ego and emotions can be far greater than those of any other research strategies.

These difficulties are largely because data collection procedures are not automatic. The investigator needs to take advantage of unexpected opportunities rather than being trapped by them. At the same time, the investigator must exercise sufficient care against potentially biased procedures. The aim of this chapter is to inform you of the debates around ethics in research, and to equip you with the information needed to accurately and efficiently plan your research journey. However, there are also the 'unsaid' elements that are seldom the focus of methodology textbooks.

Ethical issues can be emotional, stressful and personally impactful. Research students have reported their heartbreak when working in impoverished environments around Africa. Witnessing acts that take place in schools that go against researchers' personal views, such as abuse, punishment, harassment, bullying, and corruption, can create a very emotionally draining fieldwork experience. Students have often spoken of wanting to 'betray' the research-er-participant boundaries. For example, by bringing food for children who are hungry; paying money to participants for their contributions because they know participants have no jobs or income; or reporting corrupt activities to officials and in so doing, betraying their confidentiality clauses. For further empirical evidence that shows how researchers have navigated their way through these challenging issues, see Sime (2008) and Braithwaite, Cockwill, O'Neill, & Rebane (2007). These authors comment on difficulties around ethics and participatory research, and how they overcame these, or managed them, while conducting research.

The intention of this section is for you to become aware of the nature of research in education, and how it can impact you as a researcher and as a person. Let us know take a look at reflections from the field, and see what we can learn from people who have been researchers in different contexts.

Tip

It is important that you do not deny or neglect your own wellbeing in the field. Make time to talk to your supervisor and colleagues during fieldwork. Keep a journal on your feelings during the process. Ensure that you take care of yourself as a person during the research process.

6.8 Conducting research in different contexts: Reflections from the field

Research in education has an ethical facet because it involves human participants, human behaviours and human attitudes, and the processes that contribute to these concepts. Within human interaction, there are always factors that may change your research design and plan. This section unpacks a few of the scenarios encountered in the field that require extra thought and action.

In Drake (2012), the researcher discusses some issues relevant to conducting research in the South African township context. The issue of safety and security when entering and leaving the township each day proved difficult at stages of the fieldwork. A few times there were episodes in township life that restricted access to the school. On one occasion, there were radical and intense riots going on. Community members were protesting against the lack of housing provision. Burning tyres in the main streets of the township, toyi-toying (shouting, dancing and singing), and prohibiting access into and out of the township, were all part of this protest. The South African police were monitoring the situation, ensuring the safety of the protesters and other people. They would not allow anyone to enter the township. The researcher could not gain access to the school for three weeks at one time.

Lee (1995) would describe this as situational danger – an unexpected crisis that needed to be dealt with in this research context. Lee also explains how data collection in challenging situations demands considerable ingenuity on the part of the researcher. The township researcher knew that in this climate and environment, it would be best to stay away.

The other factor that greatly influenced the researcher's ability to run interviews and focus groups was the strike action that took place during the fieldwork. Strike action ranged from go-slows, where teachers deliberately worked, taught, walked and behaved in a manner that was at a much slower in pace than usual, to leaving school early to protest at the local department of education offices. Striking is a normal occurrence in South African society, yet the researcher could not have planned for the severe impact these actions had on everyday functioning of school life in this context. Go-slows were taken seriously, with educators literally doing as little as they could throughout the day. The school day would also end early. This created fieldwork challenges that the researcher needed to overcome, as research plans could not go on as initially planned.

In Drake (2014), the researcher discusses additional ethical dilemmas that arose when embarking on research in township communities in South Africa. There were great difficulties cross-checking evidence as participants tried to cover up or hide certain practices that were observed during the observation fieldwork period. Robinson (1993) signals that the process of gaining agreement may not always bear any relationship to the accuracy of the participants' perceptions. This proved most applicable in the research context described here, as participants, at times, covered up certain incidents and behaviours in the school environment. Although they agreed with what they had said (while analysing the interview transcripts in the member-check process – see later), this process did not always accurately reflect the reality of school life. It ensured that participants were happy with what they had communicated about the issue, not the reality of the situation. **Member-checking** (Cohen, et al., 2000) means getting participants to check their transcripts, and then to check consensus among participants on events, incidents and behaviours.

Research participants may report on what they believe, or what they want to believe, and not on the real-life happenings in the school. Their espoused theory, which means what they believe or want to believe, is what they report on during the research process. "One source of fallibility is people's blindness to possible incongruence between their espoused theory, which is typically the source of their judgements about themselves, and their theory-in-use" (Robinson, 1993:118).

Another aspect the researcher needs to be extremely aware of was researcher 'bias' (Maxwell, 2005), and their own personal value judgements and opinions. Researchers have initial ideas about what township schools are like. There are numerous articles in newspapers and reports on the behaviour and events that occur in these environments. Researchers need to be aware of their existing preconceptions, and the selection of evidence that 'stands out' to them as researchers. In this case, this also created an awareness of the second threat Maxwell that cautions researchers to be aware of – the threat he expresses as 'reactivity'. This is generally understood as the influence of the researcher on the setting or individuals studied.

Hammersley and Atkinson (in Maxwell, 2005:106) describe how eliminating the actual influence of the researcher is impossible, and the goal of qualitative research is not to eliminate this influence, but to understand it and to use it productively. This aspect of ethical considerations should be continually reflected on, and addressed through specific interventions, for example, by setting up a 'cultural contact' as a neutral platform for participants of the research and the researchers themselves.

The intention of these reflections from the field is to show you, as novice researchers, that ethics is complicated and intricate, even for researchers who have been researching for many years. But with careful thought and consideration, and continual questioning about ethics through every stage of the research, you can embark on a research journey that will be continuously rewarding and enriching.

Conclusion

This chapter has introduced you to the discussions and debates around conducting ethical research in education. We have unpacked key terms, like objectivity, value freedom, and reflexivity that need to be considered when planning the ethical considerations in your research. You have also been exposed to problems that can arise in the field, through analysing and reflecting on actual research experience and the actual research process. This chapter serves as an introduction to the more theoretical debates around ethics. In the next chapter, you will gain a deeper and more detailed insight into practical ethics in the research process, and hopefully, become confident in the planning and execution of ethical matters in your research design and fieldwork. Ethics is one of the most important aspects of conducting research and this chapter has provided evidence as to why it demands your utmost care and attention.

Closing activities

Practical application activities

1 Now that we have unpacked many of the terms and ideas behind ethics in research, and you have been made aware of experiences from the field, you are required to look back at Table 6. 1 at the beginning of this chapter. With your research topic in your mind, start mind-mapping or making a journal of the important ethical considerations you will need to take in your research design. Make your considerations specific to your topic. Row by row in Table 1, think about what aspects you will need to be ethically sensitive to, or objective about, as you think through and plan your fieldwork and data collection. Once you have mind-mapped or written journal notes about your ethical considerations, make a time with your supervisor to discuss them. It is never too early to start thinking about the ethical nature of your research.

Self-reflection questions

2 What does 'ethics' mean to you?

3 What is your understanding of 'objectivism' and 'value judgements'?

Self-reflection activities

4 What key ethical considerations do you need to think about for your research?

5 What are some of the 'flags' or specific circumstances that you need to be especially aware of in terms of ethics in your research design?

Analysis and consolidation

6 Design a poster for a novice researcher who has no idea of what ethics in research is. Detail the most important things you have learned in this chapter. Share these in class, and discuss with your peers why you decided to focus on the information that you chose for your poster.

Bibliography

Babbie, E. & Mouton, J. 2011. *The practice of social research*. Cape Town: Oxford University Press.

Braithwaite, R., Cockwill, S., O'Neill, M. & Rebane, D. 2007. Insider participatory action research in disadvantaged post-industrial areas: The experiences of community members as they become community-based action researchers. *Action Research*, 5(1):61–74.

Cobb, D. 2014. Tales of a cross-cultural research journey: Navigating potholes, roadblocks and dead-ends. In J. Rath & C. Mutch (Eds). *Emerging critical scholarship in education: Navigating the doctoral journey*. Newcastle upon Tyne: Cambridge Scholars Publishing.

Cohen, L., Manion, L. & Morrison, K. 2000. *Research methods in education* (5th ed.). London: RoutledgeFalmer.

Crano, W. & Brever, M. 2002. *Principles and methods of social research* (2nd ed.). Mahwah, NJ: Lawrence Erlbaum Associates.

Creswell, J.W. 2014. Research design: Qualitative, quantitative and mixed methods approaches. Thousand Oaks, CA: SAGE.

Cribb, A. & Gewirtz, S. 2005. Navigating justice in practice: An exercise in grounding ethical theory. *Theory and Research in Education*, 3(3):327–342.

Drake, M. 2012. How the values in new South African policy manifest in a disadvantaged school setting. PhD thesis, University of Auckland, New Zealand.

Drake, M. 2014. Ethical complexities in fieldwork: A journey into values education in a South African school. In J. Rath & C. Mutch (Eds). *Emerging critical scholarship in education: Navigating the doctoral journey*. Newcastle upon Tyne: Cambridge Scholars Publishing.

Flick, U. 2006. *An introduction to qualitative research*. London: SAGE Publications.

Gewirtz, S. & Cribb, A. 2006. What to do about values in social research: The case for ethical reflexivity in the sociology of education. *British Journal of Sociology of Education*, 27(02):141–155.

Griffiths, M. 1998. *Educational research for social justice: Getting off the fence*. New York, NY: McGraw-Hill International.

Hammersley, M. 2011a. *Methodology: Who needs it?* London: SAGE Publications.

Hammersley, M. 2011b. Objectivity: A reconceptualisation. In M. Williams & W. Vogt (Eds). *The SAGE handbook of innovation in social research methods*. London: SAGE Publications.

Howe, K. & Eisenhart, M. 1990. Standards for qualitative (and quantitative) research: A prolegomenon. *Educational Researcher*, 19(4):2–9.

Kiana, S. 2014. Fieldwork in Iran: Traversing an environment of suspicion. In J. Rath & C. Mutch (Eds). *Emerging critical scholarship in education: Navigating the doctoral journey*. Newcastle upon Tyne: Cambridge Scholars Publishing.

Lee, R. 1995. *Dangerous Fieldwork*. London: Sage.

Mason, J. 2002. *Qualitative researching*. London: SAGE Publications.

Maxwell, J. 2005. *Qualitative research design: An interpretive approach* (2nd ed.). Thousand Oaks, CA: Sage.

McNamee, M. & Bridges, D. (Eds). 2002. *The ethics of educational research*. Oxford: Blackwell Publishing.

Mortari, L. & Harcourt, D. (2012). 'Living' ethical dilemmas for researchers when researching with children. *International Journal of Early Years Education*, 20(3):234–243.

Robinson, V. 1993. *Problem-based methodology: Research for the improvement of practice*. Oxford: Pergamon Press.

Robinson, V. & Lai, M. 2006. *Practitioner research for educators: A guide to improving classrooms and schools*. Thousand Oaks, CA: Corwin Press.

Sikes, P., Nixon, J. & Carr, W. (Eds). 2003. *The moral foundations of educational research: knowledge, inquiry and values*. New York, NY: McGraw-Hill International.

Sime, D. 2008. Ethical and methodological issues in engaging young people living in poverty with participatory research methods. *Children's geographies*, 6(1):63–78.

Simons, H. & Usher, R. (Eds). 2000. *Situated ethics in educational research*. New York, NY: RoutledgeFalmer.

Small, R. 2001. Codes are not enough: What philosophy can contribute to the ethics of educational research. *Journal of Philosophy of Education*, 15(3).

Strauss, A. 1987. *Qualitative analysis for social scientists*. Cambridge, MA: Cambridge University Press.

Tesar, M. 2014. Unmarked territories: Ethical challenges in archival research. In J. Rath & C. Mutch (Eds). *Emerging critical scholarship in education: Navigating the doctoral journey*. Newcastle upon Tyne: Cambridge Scholars Publishing.

Wassenaar, D. 2006. *Ethical issues in social science research*. In M. Blanche, K. Durrheim & D. Painter (Eds). *Research in practice: Applied methods for the social sciences*. Cape Town: University of Cape Town Press.

Yin, R. 2003. *Case study research: Design and methods*. London: Sage.

CHAPTER 7

Namhla Sotuku and Stunky Duku

Ethics in human sciences research

KEY CONCEPTS

Accidental deductive disclosure refers to the inadvertently included traits of individuals or groups that make them identifiable in research reports.

Capacity is the ability to acquire, retain, and evaluate information received and to make informed choices based on this evaluation.

Data cooking occurs when researchers withhold or report only those findings that fit the hypothesis.

Data trimming occurs when the researcher smooths over irregularities in the data to achieve a better 'fit' between actual and expected results.

Integrity is the quality of honesty, truth, truthfulness, and reliability.

Pseudonyms are made-up names used to refer to the participants in your research project, done to respond to the ethical principle of anonymity and confidentiality. Ensure that the names do not resemble any nicknames of the participants.

Research integrity is the process of proposing, doing and reporting research in accordance with accepted practices and principles. The accepted practices and principles are thus guided by honesty, truth, truthfulness and reliability.

LEARNING OUTCOMES

By the end of this chapter, you should be able to:

▶ Identify and study unethical case studies to sensitise yourself to situations in which ethical commitment becomes particularly salient.

▶ Learn how some researchers exploit human beings and thereby compromise research integrity.

▶ Acknowledge the importance of maintaining integrity in the execution of a research study.

▶ Discuss the major ethical values and principles in conducting research involving human participants.

▶ Reflect on how researchers anticipate and resolve various ethical issues that confront them, when conducting research involving human participants.

▶ Appreciate how, as student researchers, to avoid potential unethical decision-making when conducting research involving human participants.

Case study

Mrs Mana, a school principal, is reading the newspaper. She is drawn to a headline: "Education in crisis: Grade 3 learners fail annual national assessment". Below the headline are pictures of schoolchildren. In the background, the name of a school is clearly visible.

Mrs Mana: (*looking at the pictures*) Wow! Who did this? This is my school (*showing the newspaper pictures to another teacher*). Look!

Teacher Pam: This is Anje and Litho in Grade 3. Who took these pictures?

Mrs Mana: (*paging through the visitors' log book*) Oh! People are so devious. Do you remember the two ladies who visited us in May? The ones who introduced themselves as philanthropists, who help schools with fundraising. Apparently, they are researchers from a non-governmental organisation.

Teacher Pam: They asked us about our challenges and promised to buy the school some reading books.

Introduction

In the earlier chapters of this book you were introduced to the concept of research and to the process of conducting research. You would have realised that engaging in research gives one certain freedoms and privileges. These freedoms and privileges include the freedom to conduct investigations or search for knowledge, the right to disseminate findings and the opportunity to conduct research on human beings. However, it is important to note that such freedoms come with responsibilities. As a researcher, you have to act responsibly and with **integrity**.

The case study featuring Mrs Mana and Teacher Pam raises questions of how some researchers conduct themselves when collecting data. Do you think the two researchers acted with integrity? The case also raises questions of how best the two researchers should have behaved. This chapter seeks to engage you in examining the values and principles that should guide researchers as they conduct research involving human participants. What principles and values should researchers build into their work so that **research integrity** can be be maintained?

This chapter then discusses research involving human participants and the major ethical values in conducting human research.

7.1 Research involving human participants

In the introduction we pointed out that conducting research gives one certain freedoms and privileges. Conducting research involving human participants is one of those privileges. When such research is conducted, researchers need to maintain research integrity. Their practices when carrying out research should be guided by principles such as honesty, truthfulness, and reliability. However, history has revealed that researchers as early as the eighteenth century misused their freedoms and privileges. They exploited human beings and thereby compromised research integrity. This section presents examples of some infamously unethical case studies depicting how researchers compromised research integrity. (You will recognise them from Chapter 6, but they are worth examining again here.)

What is wrong with this research?

e.g.

Case study 1: The Tuskegee syphilis study

This now infamous study was conducted by the US Public Health Service in 1932. It aimed to determine the natural causes of syphilis by examining untreated cases of the disease. Four hundred American males from Tuskegee were recruited, but at no time in the course of the project were they asked to give consent to participate in the study. The particulars of what the study would entail were never discussed with the participants. For example, it was never explained to the participants that the survey was designed to detect syphilis, and that they were recruited because they had the disease.

(continued)

What is wrong with this research? *(continued)*

Case study 2: Stanley Milgram's 1963 research

In 1963 Stanley Milgram, a psychologist at a prestigious American university, conducted a study involving human participants. He wanted to understand the conditions under which individuals obey authority figures. He deceived people who volunteered to participate in his study into believing that they were involved in an experiment on the impact of punishment on memory. The participants read a series of word associations to individuals who were expected to repeat the words. If the participants to whom the words were read were unable to repeat words correctly, volunteers were asked to administer an 'electric shock' by means of a voltage meter with readings from 'slight' to 'severe' shock. They were required to increase the voltage for each wrong answer to see if delivering a shock would in fact enhance learning. However, the participants were deceived into thinking they were applying actual electrical shocks to another human being. Some participants protested on hearing cries of pain and witnessing other medical problems, and wanted to cease the experiment. The researcher in charge insisted that they continue, saying that he would take responsibility for the consequences. Surprisingly, some participants did continue.

Stop and reflect

1 After reading the cases, what is your reaction to what happened during the two experiments? Is this kind of research acceptable?
2 The examples of case studies presented here are not from Africa. Conduct a literature search of at least two examples of unethical case studies from Africa. The case studies should expose how the rights of individuals were violated during research studies.
3 Identify the nature of human rights violation in each case and suggest ways in which such violations could have been avoided.

We believe that after interrogating the case studies here, and also reflecting on what you learned from your research, you will by now have gained a better understanding and awareness of how some researchers' practices compromise research integrity. For example, in both the examples of unethical case studies presented here, the researchers were dishonest and thus violated the rights of the participants. The researchers mistreated the participants. They did not discuss the details of their studies or the real aims with the participants. Participants were therefore coerced into participation in the studies. Such practices led eventually to the process of developing a set of rules, values and principles to guide research involving human participants. This set of values and principles is very important for researchers. As a researcher, you always need to know that you have a responsibility to recognise and protect the rights and the wellbeing of the participants in your study. But how can researchers achieve this? What are the acceptable values and principles that guide research that involves human participants? The following section will examine the values and principles that should guide researchers as they engage in human research, so that research integrity can be maintained.

7.2 Major ethical values in conducting research involving human participants

Before we engage in a discussion on the ethical values that are key to conducting research involving human participants, let us examine the concept, 'ethics'.

Stop and reflect

Take few minutes and to reflect on the following questions:

▶ What comes into your mind when the term 'ethics' is mentioned?

▶ Where do people learn ethics?

▶ What exactly is unethical behaviour?

Provide examples to support your claims.

The term 'ethics' is understood to refer to values and principles by which a determination of what is the right and wrong thing to do, is made. Most people learn ethical norms and principles at home, school, in religious organisations, communities, and in other social settings. Because ethical norms seem to be everywhere, one might be tempted to regard them as common sense. However, we need to bear in mind that people have different perspectives and therefore they may interpret, apply and balance ethical norms in different ways in light of their values and life experiences.

Applying the concept of ethics to research involving human participants, means establishing the values and principles that should guide researchers as they conduct research on and about human beings, from inception through to completion and publication of results. Researchers are humans and they bring their own likes, dislikes, views and values to research projects; these sometimes compromise research integrity. Some researchers believe that they should remain detached from the participants. They stay detached because they claim to aspire to the goal of objectivity in the research process. The researchers in the Tuskegee syphilis study took this position and, in trying to achieve it, they deceived the participants.

This section examines the major ethical values and principles that researchers need to consider and adopt as guidelines in the process of conducting research involving human participants. The following major ethical values and principles are examined.

▶ Informed consent

▶ Beneficence (maximising benefits)

▶ Non-maleficence (minimising harm)

▶ Respect for anonymity and confidentiality

▶ Respect for privacy.

Before we examine each of these values and principles, let us take some time to examine how and where ethical values and principles feature when research involving human participants is conducted. In other words, where and how we can locate ethical issues within the research process. In earlier chapters, you were introduced to the process of conducting research. By now you will have learned that research is not an event, but a process. Once a researcher has identified an area of interest, reviewed related, relevant literature, he or she has to develop a research proposal. The research proposal outlines the researcher's plan of action so that the research study works well in the real world. The elements of a research proposal include key aspects like research methodology, data collection, samples, analysis of data, and interpretation of findings. In explaining the identified aspects when conducting research involving human participants, a researcher amongst other things, considers the following:

- ☑ **Where** the research will be conducted.
- ☑ **Whether** the research, or any like it, has been done before.
- ☑ **Who** will participate in the research.
- ☑ **The nature** of their participation.
- ☑ **How** the researcher will get the identified people to participate.
- ☑ **The effects** of the research on the participants.
- ☑ **Whether** the research design and methods pose any practical and ethical problems to those taking part, or to the site where the research will be conducted.

When it comes to ethical problems, these may include protecting the identity of the participants, their integrity, confidentiality of records, and data generated by the research. It is therefore very important that in the research process researchers identify ethical values and principles that they need to consider and adopt as guidelines. In the process of conducting research, researchers do not only identify ethical values, but they also review them for conformity to acceptable ethical principles and values. Addressing the identified aspects in a research proposal, before data are collected, helps the researcher to anticipate and resolve various ethical issues that might confront them when conducting research in the real world.

Now let us examine each of the values and principles listed earlier. Our discussion will focus on the key aspects of each ethical value and principle element, and how each value and principle is applied, practised and experienced when conducting research.

7.2.1   Informed consent

Earlier, we suggestd that there are issues that a researcher conducting research involving human participants has to consider. These issues include: Identifying who will participate in the research study, and how the researcher will get the identified people to participate. Before collecting data, the researcher needs to negotiate with identified participants and find out if they are willing to participate in the study. When a researcher negotiates with the identified participants, he or she is said to be seeking informed consent. Seeking participants' consent should not be treated as an event, but a process that needs to be negotiated and renegotiated throughout the research process.

Case study: How to seek participants' consent

Mandisa, a student reading for a Master of Education degree at a university in South Africa, conducted a study on Grade 3 teachers' practices in the teaching of reading in isiXhosa in two rural primary schools. She planned to interview Grade 3 teachers on how they teach reading in isiXhosa, and she also planned to observe them teaching reading in isiXhosa. These are the stages of the process she engaged in when negotiating participants' consent:

1 She sought permission and approval to collect research data, from the university at which she was registered for a Master's degree.

2 She sought approval from the provincial Department of Education. She needed to gain access to the schools in which the Grade 3 teachers who were to participate in study, worked.

3 She sought permission and approval from the school principal and the school governing body.

4 She sought permission from the Grade 3 teachers.

Stop and reflect

1 Why do you think it was necessary for Mandisa to go through this process?

2 What do you think the issues were when she negotiated Stages 3 and 4?

3 What do you think would have happened if she had negotiated consent with the teachers only?

4 Are there any other individuals or groups who need to be approached for consent? Why do you think they should be included?

Informed consent is a principle which ensures that participants in a research project have the right to be informed that they are being researched. They have to be afforded an opportunity to exercise their rights and choose whether or not to participate in a research project. Participants should exercise their free will and power of choice, without any undue pressure. Undue pressure may include: deceit, intervention of force, fraud, duress, or other forms of constraints or coercion. Let us now refer back to the first case study and to the examples of unethical research studies in section 7.1. How did the researchers deceive Mrs Mana and Teacher Pam into giving them information? How did the researchers in the examples of unethical research studies coerce or deceive the participants into taking part in the study?

As mentioned earlier, informed consent seeks to ensure that participants exercise their rights and choose whether or not to participate in a research project. However, not all participants might have the **capacity** and competence to give consent. Because of characteristics associated with age or disability, an individual may be rendered relatively powerless in exercising free will when choosing whether or not to participate in a research study. Sometimes, such participants may be less capable of understanding the potential harm. The competence of an individual in giving informed consent is partially determined by legal qualification and ability. In South Africa, for example, legal qualification is most often viewed in terms of age; individuals under the age 18 are considered to be legally unable to make certain decisions. Their rights are then legally protected by obtaining permission from parents or legal guardians (De Wit, 2013). In addition, people with cognitive or emotional disabilities are also identified as lacking the capacity to understand the nature and consequences of giving consent. Such people are referred to as vulnerable groups. It is imperative that vulnerable groups should not be taken advantage of in the name of science or research. Researchers investigating topics involving these individuals must take extreme care.

So what are the forms of obtaining consent from vulnerable groups, that is, individuals who might not have the competence to make certain decisions?. In particular, what are the forms of obtaining consent from individuals who are identified as having the capacity to make decisions? There are therefore two forms of obtaining informed consent:

▸ Direct consent
▸ Substitute consent.

The two forms of obtaining consent are negotiated through formal procedures. The formal procedures of negotiation include verbal and written consent. Verbal consent is verbally read to the participants for them to decide whether or not they want to participate in the study, while written consent involves reading, completing and signing a document.

7.2.1.1   Forms of obtaining informed consent

Direct consent is when an agreement to participate in a research project is obtained directly from the people identified to be involved in the research. For example, in Mandisa's case, she had to negotiate with the Grade 3 teachers she wanted to study. She had to get direct consent from them and thus obtain an agreement. Negotiating only with the school principal and obtaining permission from him or her on behalf of the teachers, is not direct consent.

Substitute consent or **third party consent** is given by someone other than the person to be involved in the in the study. Substitute consent may be obtained when it is determined that the person who is going to participate in the study does not have the capacity and competence to make the decision, or is dependent on others for his or her welfare (Nagy, 2006; De Wit, 2013). For example, when a researcher has identified children under the age of 18 as participants in a research study, the researcher would have to get permission from the children's parents or guardian. Children under the age of 18 are considered legally unable to make certain decisions. The researcher would have to obtain permission from parents and guardian for such children to participate in a research project. Parents and guardians will thus be involved in an agreement with the researcher. In addition, substitute consent may be obtained when people with cognitive or emotional disabilities are identified as possible participants. For both groups, the concern is that the individuals might not understand the nature and consequences of giving consent.

It is worth noting that although substitute consent may be sought, researchers need to adhere to the following requirements:

☑ The person who is going to be involved should be informed that he or she is being researched.

☑ The person to be involved should give an affirmative agreement to participate in the study.

☑ If the participant is underage:

▸ Firstly, the intended participants' individual assent needs to be sought. An assent is the individual child's (under the age of 18) affirmative agreement to participate in the research study. The assent form must be written at the appropriate reading level of the youngest participant, using simple terminology.

▸ Secondly, the individual's preferences and best interests should be considered.

Our discussion has highlighted the importance of seeking, obtaining participants' consent, and also ascertaining their capacity to give consent. But now we turn to what information the participants need to be given in order to decide whether they want to participate in the study.

7.2.1.2 Communicating information about research to identified participants

In addition to the issues discussed earlier another important element when seeking participants' consent, is communicating information about the research study. It is the responsibility of the researcher to ensure that the participants understand the information provided and can exercise their free power of choice, even if the individual is deemed legally incompetent.

The information that researchers need to disclose about their research studies includes:

The purpose of the study
- ☑ **Explanation about the selection** of the research participants.
- ☑ **Procedures/processes/methodology** to be followed.
- ☑ **A description any potential risks**, e.g. physical or mental harm, discomfort, any invasion of privacy and any threat to dignity.
- ☑ **How the study findings will be used**: any expected benefits either to the participants; or to contribution of knowledge to the field of study.
- ☑ **How the research findings** will be disseminated.
- ☑ **Methods that the researcher will use** to protect the anonymity and confidentiality.
- ☑ **Details of a person(s)** with whom the participants can discuss the study
- ☑ **A provision of the 'Non-coercive disclaimer'** which states that the participation is voluntary and no penalties are involved.
- ☑ **Finally, the freedom to withdraw** must be explained.

So how do researchers package all this information and make it available to identified participants?

The following are examples of documents that researchers design when seeking consent from people to participate in a research project. Remember, we mentioned that consent is negotiated through formal means, and these include verbal and written forms. Verbal consent is read aloud to the participants for them to decide whether or not they want to participate in the study. These two examples are for you to study so that you can link theory with practice.

Toolbox Documentation designed by researchers to obtain participants' consent

Example A

Title of the research project: Grade 5 learners' after-school reading practices.

Principal investigator and contact information: Mandisa Andazi . Student number: 2001999666, Truth University, 167 Sunnyside Road, East London. Contact number : 061 704 7259

Supervisor and contact information: Dr I Johannes. Truth University, Faculty of Education, 167 Sunnyside Road, East London. Contact number: 043 704 1589

(continued)

Example A *(continued)*

Purpose of the study: This study seeks to understand Grade 5 learners' after-school reading practices. The study will gather information on whether Grade 5 learners engage in reading, outside school hours; the texts they read; how they access these texts; and the reasons for their choices.

Procedures: Participants will be asked to complete a questionnaire and also to participate in individual interviews. The interviews will be held at a time convenient to them, and will be recorded only if they and their parents/guardian consent to that. Research findings will be used for academic purposes only.

Confidentiality: Your name, child's name and the name of the school will not be revealed at any stage of the research process.

Voluntary nature of participation: You and your child have the right to exercise your free will of choice. When you indicate that there are deviations from what was agreed on here, or have any other reasons, you and your child have right to withdraw from the project.

Participant's Agreement Statement (consent form)

I, **Peter Heck** (learner's parent/guardian) hereby give permission for my child **Zenande Tom** to participate in the research project conducted by Mandisa Andazi. The research project is on Grade 5 learners' after-school reading practices, and is part of course requirements for Ms Andazi's degree at Truth University.

I understand that my child is participating freely and without being forced in any way to do so. I give permission for the interview to be audio recorded. I also understand that my child has the right to withdraw from the interview at any time she or I feel the need to do so, and that will not prejudice her in any way.

I understand that this is a research project whose purpose is not necessarily to benefit my child or me personally or directly. I also understand that the researcher will have the freedom to publish the findings in academic journal(s).

I have received the telephone number of a person to contact should I need to speak about any issues which may arise in this exercise.

I understand that anonymity and confidentiality will be ensured throughout this study, and afterwards.

--------------------------------   -------------------------------
Signature of participant   Signature of parent/guardian

Date: ---------------------------

Signature of researcher ---------------------------------------

(continued)

Example B

167 Sunnyside Road
Truth University
East London
15 May 2015

Zamani Junior Primary
Chalumna

Dear Parent

Request for permission for your child to participate in a research project

My name is Mandisa Andazi. (student number: 2001999666), and I am a student at Truth University. I am currently registered for a Master's degree in Education. In order to meet the requirements for the degree, I have to conduct a research project.

I humbly request your permission to allow your child participate in my research project. The research seeks to understand Grade 5 learners' after-school reading practices. This study seeks to gather information on whether Grade 5 learners engage in reading after school hours, what the texts they read are, how they access them, and the reasons for their choices.

During the course of the research, the learners will complete a questionnaire, and also participate in individual interviews. The research activities will take place during school break time. I would like to record the interviews and therefore seek your permission to do so. Participation is voluntary, the study will not pose any harm to your child, and I will ensure that their anonymity and confidentiality is kept at all times during and after the research process.

Should you require further information, you can contact my supervisor, Dr I Johannes, senior lecturer in education research methodology, at this number: 043 704 1589, or email him at: johannes2@gmail.com.

Thank you.
Yours sincerely

------------------------------ [signature and date]
Mandisa Andazi

Please complete the section below and return it to the school. Please underline the appropriate response.

I, Jane Msomi (parent/guardian) give permission /do not give permission for my child, Litha Msomi, a learner in Grade 5 at Zamani Primary School, to participate in a research project on Grade 5 learners' after-school reading practices, conducted by Mandisa Andazi.

Signature (parent/ guardian)

Date

In some cases, even when researchers consider all the aspects involved in seeking participants' consent, obtaining consent can be a very challenging exercise. Here are two examples of researchers' experiences when seeking participants' consent:

Case studies: The challenges of seeking participants' consent

A Political climate challenges

Duku (2013) in her study reports on the participants' unwillingness to sign consent forms as the timing of the study coincided with political parties canvassing for votes and recruiting new members. It was one month before South Africa's first democratic general elections in 1994. Members of different political parties would go house to house in the rural areas canvassing people to vote for them. They would give people membership forms to complete to join the political parties. In one of the villages, Duku convened a meeting with the people she had identified as possible participants in her study. After presenting the nature of her study, and describing how the participants were to be involved, all the identified participants agreed that they would take part in the study. However, when she requested them to give their formal consent in writing they became suspicious and refused. The participants thought they were being coerced into joining a political party.

B Language preferences

Sifanelwe wanted to conduct her research in a village in Centane in the Eastern Cape. The most commonly-spoken language in the village is isiXhosa. When Sifanelwe tried to negotiate with possible participants on giving consent, they refused to give both verbal and written consent. The consent forms she brought with her were written in English only. This happened although the participants were all teachers, who understood English. In this instance, the unwillingness to sign the consent forms was specifically to do with the language of the consent form. It became clear that the use of a language which participants understand and are familiar with, is an enabling factor in obtaining consent, and is recommended.

7.2.1.3 Checking what we understand about informed consent

From our earlier discussion you will have learned that that informed consent comprises five important elements:

1 *Information:* Providing participants with all the information about the research project.
2 *Informing:* Informing participants that they are being researched
3 *Exercising free will:* Consent must be freely given. Participants have the right to choose whether or not they want to participate in a research project.
4 *Voluntariness:* Consent, although freely given, may be withdrawn at any time.
5 *Comprehension:* The researcher should ascertain the participants' capacity and competence to take informed decisions.

What about the other ethical issues confronting researchers, beyond informed consent? Our discussion now moves to the second ethical value and principle: beneficence.

7.2.2 Beneficence (maximising benefits)

As discussed in the earlier sections of this chapter, in the research process researchers have to identify ethical values and principles that they need to consider and adopt as guidelines. When deciding on research methodology and during data collection, researchers consider the following issues: the effects of the research on the participants; and whether the research design and methods pose any practical and ethical problems to those taking part, or to the site where it will be conducted. Some of the ethical problems include protecting the identity of the participants, protecting them from harm or exposure, honouring their integrity, and preserving the confidentiality of records and data generated by the research.

The implications of identifying ethical values and principles are that in conducting research which involves human participants, one should act in ways that benefit people, or at least in ways that minimise harm to others. The principle of beneficence relates to the ultimate or overall benefits of the research. It advocates that care must be taken to ensure that the intention of the research is to generate new knowledge. The new knowledge should produce benefits for participants themselves, for other individuals, or for society as a whole. This ethical principle involves acts of empathy, mercy, kindness, care, and charity, and is suggestive of altruism, love, humanity and promoting the good of others (Halai, 2006).

Some rules that underlie beneficence include the following:
▶ Protect and defend the rights of others.
▶ Prevent harm from occurring to others.
▶ Rescue people in danger.
▶ Help people with disabilities.

These rules are related to the principles of natural justice, which refers to equal share and fairness, and avoiding the exploitation or abuse of participants. The principle of justice for everyone compels researchers to protect the vulnerable and to promote the welfare and equality of all human beings.

Let us now examine the third ethical principle, non-maleficence, and identify how it differs from the principle of beneficence, discussed earlier.

7.2.3 Non-maleficence (minimising harm)

Some rules that underlie non-maleficence include the following:
▶ Do not kill.
▶ Do not cause pain.
▶ Do not cause offence.

This principle dictates preventing intentional harm and minimising potential harm. In practice, it means that research participants must not be subjected to any unnecessary risks or harm. Their participation in research should be identified as essential in achieving the goals of the research. This means that it must be proven beyond doubt that the goals of the research cannot be achieved without the participation of human participants. Moreover, the principle of minimising harm requires that the research involves a representative sample of the identified participants.

In addressing this principle, researchers should have a high level of sensitivity about what constitutes 'harm'. Harm in the context of research could be physical, psychological or emotional, social or economic in nature. For example, researchers should understand that if they enquire about intimate details of the participants' lives, they should be prepared to deal with opening old wounds or ongoing issues. Think of a research study that investigates the experiences of orphans as learners in a junior secondary schools. How could a researcher ensure that she does not cause any harm? Referring to the elements of research integrity, we identified that integrity includes truthfulness, honesty and reliability. In this instance, the researcher should not pressure the guardians or caregivers to grant permission to work with the children under pretence that the researcher or the project might help with their welfare. As a researcher, you should guard against promoting relationships of dependency with participants.

Let us also refer back to the opening case study. Mrs Mana and Teacher Pam were vulnerable as their school did not have sufficient teaching and learning resources. The researchers must have identified this vulnerability or susceptability and used it as a means to get information. Besides being dishonest about their purpose, the researchers used the vulnerability of Mrs Mana and Teacher Pam to their advantage. They were guilty of using 'softening up' techniques to get information from the participants who may have been unwilling to talk, had they known the real purpose of the visit.

Critical thinking challenge

In South Africa there is a high rate of violence targeting elderly people, especially women. Shana Mgedezi, a B Ed Honours student, wants to conduct a study on the effects of violence on elderly women. However, she feels such pity for them that she decides not to interview the elderly women. Instead, she interviews their caregivers, their children, and other family members. She argues that she wants to protect the elderly women and not to open old wounds.

Do you agree with Ms Mgedezi's practices? Support your response critically by drawing on information you have learned in this chapter and book.

In dealing with the principle of beneficence and non-maleficence, the American Educational Research Association (2005), and Fouka and Mantzorou (2011) suggest that researchers must consider all possible consequences of the research, and then balance the risks with appropriate benefits. They further suggest that if the risks outweigh the benefits, the study should be revised. Research ethics require that a favourable harms–benefit balance is maintained. It is for this reason that researchers, when they plan research projects, have to seriously consider the significance of their research. Much as the research project might involve advancing knowledge, thereby benefiting society, but researchers should also consider the potential harms to participants and find ways to minimise them.

The fourth ethical principle and value to be discussed is respect for anonymity and confidentiality.

7.2.4 Respect for anonymity and confidentiality

Anonymity refers to the researcher's undertaking to ensure that the participants' identities throughout the research are protected. Participants' identities may include their names, the names of the institution in which they work, their addresses, their relatives' names, their nicknames, etc. Their identities should be protected throughout the research process and after. This means that from the day the research idea is conceived, through writing a research proposal, data collection, data analysis, data interpretation, through to publication of results, participant anonymity is thought about and maintained. Anonymity assures research participants that they are protected by remaining unidentifiable. Anonymity can be achieved, for example, by assigning **pseudonyms** to participants. Researchers must check with the respondents if they are happy with the pseudonyms, as sometimes the pseudonyms assigned may coincidentally be the respondents' nicknames, or a brother/sister's name. This may be the reason why some researchers simply assign numbers or letters of the alphabet to the respondents, e.g. Respondent 1, 2; or Educator A, B.

Anonymity also includes the protection of the research site where the research is conducted. For example, if you are conducting research at a school, both the name of the school and the participants should remain unidentifiable.

Confidentiality of information refers to both the oral and written information shared by the individual with the researcher. Data collected during research and after should therefore be kept confidential. For example, if a researcher has selected a particular school as his research site, the data from that school must not be shared with other school communities. Confidentiality also promises the research participants that the findings will be presented in ways that ensure that individuals cannot be identified. It promises that the research records (interview transcripts, questionnaires, samples of work, photographs taken) will be kept confidential and that they will be secured in a locked place, and will not be shared with anyone without written permission from the participants.

On anonymity and confidentiality, Talarico (2013) cautions that even where the identities of participants and research sites have been made anonymous, there are potential risks of **accidental deductive disclosure**. He conceptualises deductive disclosure as the traits of individuals or groups that make them identifiable in research reports. This has been recognised as being more prevalent in qualitative research, where rich data about traits and characteristics of the individuals and research sites are presented. Remember how in the case study featuring Mrs Mana and Teacher Pam, the pictures taken by the researchers revealed the school's name.

Talarico (2013) advises that to prevent accidental deductive disclosure, researchers at times are forced to omit certain aspects of people's identities. This is done especially during data cleaning, a process in which the researcher reads data collected, tries to make sense of them, also trying to make sure that he or she has paid attention to ethical values and principles. In the real world, however, there are times when the ethical principles guiding research are challenged and questioned. Read the case study which gives an example of the principle of anonymity being questioned.

Case study: 'I want to be heard' – A researcher's experience of trying to ensure participants' anonymity

Joni is conducting research on the experiences of male teachers in the Foundation Phase (Grade R to 3). Amongst her respondents is Sive who presents himself as a gender activist. When Joni starts negotiating informed consent, she raises issues of confidentiality and anonymity. Amongst other things, she asks the respondents to complete consent forms. Sive does not want to sign the consent form.

Sive says: "Who told you that I wanted to be protected? I don't want to be unidentifiable and I also do not want my views to be anonymous. I will participate in your study on condition that my real name is mentioned. This will be evidence that this research is authentic, and other schools will then stop perpetuating gender inequalities."

Stop and reflect

If you were Joni, how would you respond to this scenario? Support your decisions.

Finally, we are going to examine respect and privacy as one of the ethical principles guiding research involving human participants.

7.2.5 Respect for privacy

As discussed previously, at the beginning of a research process, before a researcher can collect data, she or he negotiates informed consent with participants. Can you remember the five important elements of informed consent? Re-read these in section 7.2.1.3, if you need to.

A critical examination of what informed consent means, may reveal that when participants agree to participate in a research project, they are indirectly yielding up a certain amount of privacy. Much as that might be the case, one of the chief ethical principles guiding research is respect for privacy. The principle of respect for privacy has been identified as the point at which research goals and the right to privacy may come into conflict. Privacy has become a right that is highly treasured in contemporary Western society. But does total privacy exist in research when participants have agreed to participate in a research project?

In research, privacy is the freedom a participant has to determine the following aspects about his or her identity and private information:

▶ *Time*: When, during the research process, one's identity and private information should be shared or withheld from others.
▶ *Extent*: How much private information should be shared or withheld from others.
▶ *Circumstances*: Conditions under which the participants' identity and private information can be shared or withheld from others.

This means that even if people have agreed to participate in a research project, consent should also be negotiated on the amount of privacy to be maintained. If this is not done, it could result in an individual's rights being violated. Beauchamp & Childres (2001) believe that an invasion of privacy happens when private information, such as beliefs, attitudes, opinions and records, is shared without the participants' knowledge or consent. Participants' privacy may also be invaded when researchers study certain groups without their knowledge and without identifying themselves. Remember the case study at the beginning featuring Mrs Mana and Ms Pam, and the case study of unethical practices in the Tuskegee syphilis study in section 7.1? How was the privacy of the two groups violated?

Drawing from the discussion above, you should note that participants in a research project should determine when, how, and how much information about themselves should be shared or withheld from others. Some of the important factors in considering a potential invasion of privacy are now considered: sensitivity of the data; the setting in which the research takes place; and how public the information collected and finally published will be.

7.2.5.1 Sensitivity of the data

In the discussion on the principles of beneficence and non-maleficence, researchers are advised to exercise a high level of sensitivity about what constitutes 'harm'; for example, researchers should understand that if they enquire about intimate details of the participants' lives they should be prepared to deal with opening old wounds or perhaps unresolved pain.

Researchers must also exercise sensitivity about the information or data they collect during research. For example, data concerning sexual preferences represents information that many people would want to keep private. Such information is viewed as highly sensitive. Researchers should therefore protect participants' privacy. There is also information that is viewed as being situationally sensitive. Such information may include: age, weight, personal income, marital status, state of health, medical history, and other details that participants may regard as personal and private. As was discussed when seeking informed consent, negotiating such information is a process. Researchers should continuously negotiate with participants so as to protect their privacy. Participants should decide how public information about themselves should be imparted. Some information is surprisingly sensitive and researchers should be alert to the degree to which private information remains confidential. Whenever participants refuse to divulge personal information because they regard it an invasion of privacy, researchers ought to respect their views.

Let us now examine how the setting in which data is collected could impact on participants' privacy.

7.2.5.2 Setting in which the research takes place

Settings, like participants' homes, are construed as being private, so researchers should negotiate consent from participants, negotiate times (when to visit, length of an interview) if they are going to conduct research in these privates spaces. Researchers should therefore consider the setting in which the data are to be collected if undue invasion of privacy is to be avoided. For example, in your research report you can ensure a participant's confidentiality and anonymity, but you may be violating the participant's privacy when you visit him at his place of work and share with his supervisor the reason for your visit. Go back to the case study on how to seek participants' consent. What was your response to the question on the issues that Mandisa negotiated with the principal and the teachers? Do you think she needed to negotiate 'the setting' in which data were collected? If yes, why?

7.2.5.3 How public the information collected and published will be

When conducting research, researchers deal with data. They collect, analyse, interpret and present findings on them. Researchers should negotiate how much of the participants' private information should be made public or withheld from others. Moreover, researchers should negotiate with participants on how they should report on the information at their disposal. As indicated earlier, some of the data might be sensitive, depending on the nature of the research. Some information may even involve behaviour that could be considered embarrassing and potentially damaging to participants if revealed. In some cultures, revealing sacred information related to ceremonies like *ulwaluko* (initiation of boys in the Xhosa culture), is never appropriate.

Researchers are expected to publish. Some researchers when under pressure to publish, will alter the data they have collected. Data alteration involves **data trimming**, a process where researchers smooth irregularities to achieve a better fit between actual data collected and the expected results. Data alteration may also involve **data cooking**, a process where a researcher retains or reports only those findings that fit the hypothesis. Both these practices are ethically unacceptable, and cannot shelter behind the need for participant privacy.

Finally, on the principle of privacy, Drew (2007) points out that participants believe that their privacy is not threatened when only the researchers have access to their personal information and opinions; however, if these are then published in the media, it means that researchers have made personal information available to the general public. He cautions that such a practice is a breach of confidence and confidentiality, is unacceptable, and should never occur.

Doing what it takes: A South African example of the application of research ethics

In a recent study by Okeke, Adu, Rembe, Duku, Maphosa, Drake, Shumba and Sotuku (2014), strict adherence to research ethics was observed. The purpose of this study was to explore the effects of demographic variables on work-stimulated stressors and coping strategies among early childhood educators. The research team went through a rigorous process of ensuring respect to the research participants and their schools through the following processes:

▶ Applying for ethical clearance from the university to which the research team is attached as academics. This is a laborious activity involving completing a number of forms to ensure that all the stages of research abide by strict ethics.

▶ Seeking consent from the participating schools and research participants, in which the aims of the study and ethics involved in the study were outlined. During the interview process, the participants' consent to be electronically recorded was also sought.

Although this may not be an ideal approach to research ethics implementation, it represents a sound approach to deal with ethics in research that involves humans. As students who may be involved in collecting data in schools, this may guide your processes to achieve an ethics-sensitive study.

Conclusion

Engaging in research gives one freedoms and privileges. These freedoms and privileges include the freedom to conduct investigations and to search for knowledge, the right to disseminate findings, and the opportunity to conduct research on human beings. However, it is important to note that such freedoms come with responsibilities. Every researcher has the responsibility to protect and respect participants in a research study.

Researchers are humans and they bring their own preferences, views and values to research projects, and these sometimes compromise research integrity. This chapter presented key ethical values and principles that researchers should use as guidelines in conducting research involving human participants. These values and principles are important in conducting effective and meaningful research, and also in ensuring that as a researcher you do not engage in unethical conduct. Unethical conduct might compromise your research. The ethical values and principles guiding research include: informed consent, beneficence (maximising benefits), non-maleficence (minimising harm), respect for anonymity and confidentiality, and respect for privacy.

Much as these principles and values are universal, sometimes what they actually mean depends on the context and circumstances. Some participants may question them. However, such circumstances or occurences do not determine whether any of the values and principles apply. As a researcher, you are required to build ethical routines into your research project from inception to publication of findings. Your moral obligations do not begin and end with the signing of the letter of consent. Throughout your research, keep thinking and judging what your ethical obligations are. Although guidelines are suggested, each researcher must be responsible for the ethical issues within his or her own research project.

Closing activities

Analysis and consolidation

1 Identify the five major ethical values that researchers have to consider when conducting research involving human participants.

    a Make a summary of what each ethical issue identified in 1 above entails. Use the following table to structure your response.

Ethical value	Premise of the ethical value	Key aspects/elements of the ethical value

    b State whether the following statements are true or false. Support your claim.

       i When conducting research the researcher should inform participants about the nature of the research prior to participation.

       ii Ethical norms are common sense.

       iii Substitute consent is obtained directly from the person involved in the study.

       iv Circumstances during research determine whether and what ethical principles and values should be applied.

2 Doing human research includes collecting and analysing data about people. This has been identified as the point at which research goals and the right to privacy may conflict. Discuss four key issues that might affect privacy in research involving human participants.

Practical applications

3 Anje is conducting research on instructional strategies used by mathematics teachers. She has interviewed three teachers from a prominent school. Suggest and discuss ways in which she can undertake her research to ensure that the participants' identities throughout the research are protected.

4 Samuel Tendai is studying towards a Bachelor's degree in an African university. He is required to conduct a small-scale research study on parental involvement in their children's literacy development. Below is the consent form he designed for parents to complete.

Study Tendai's consent form and then respond to the following questions:

    a What are the strengths of Tendai's consent form? Support your claims.

    b What are the weaknesses of Tendai's consent form?

    c How would you improve this consent form?

I ------------------- mother/father/guardian (select appropriate option), of -------------------- (learner's name) understand that I have agreed to participate in a study conducted by Mr Samuel Tendai on parental involvement in their children's literacy development.

I also understand that my participation is voluntary.

Signature and date

---

5 Samantha, a student in B.Ed III, is planning to conduct a research project on the factors influencing student absenteeism. She intends to work with students registered for an undergraduate Bachelor's degree at two different universities. She plans to use one of her cellphone applications to conduct the study. Identify the potential ethical issues that she will confront and advise her on how to address them.

Bibliography

Babbie, E. & Mouton, J. 2002. *The practice of social research*. Cape Town, Oxford University Press (pp. 270–274).

Beauchamp, T.L. & Childres, J.F. 2001. *Principles of Biomedical Ethics* (5th ed.). Cape Town: Oxford University Press.

Burns, N. & Grove, S.K. 2005. *The practice of nursing research*: Conduct, critique and utilisation (5th ed.). St Louis, MO: Saunders.

Cochran-Smith, M. & Zeichner, K.M. (Eds). 2009. Studying Teacher Education: The Report of the AERA Panel on Research and Teacher Education. Published for the American Education Research Association by Lawrence Erlbaum Associates Inc (LEA). Taylor & Francis e-Library.

De Wit, G. 2013. Application for ethical clearance in conducting research. Accessed 15 February 2014 from: University of Fort Hare Govan Mbeki Research and Development Centre website: www.gmrdc@ufh.ac.za.

Drew, C.J. 2008. Chapter 3: Ethical issues in conducting research. In C.J. Drew, L.M. Hardman & J.L. Hosp. 2008. *Designing and Conducting Research in Education*. Google ebook. USA. SAGE Publications. Accessed 15 February 2014 from: http://www.sagepub.com/research ethics/ 03-Drew-45303.gxd9/7/2007.

Duku, N. 2013. 'Is my research ethical? Negotiating research ethical procedures in the real social world'. Paper presented 6–7 September 2013. SARAECE Regional Conference, University of Fort Hare, Eastern Cape Province, South Africa.

Fouka, G. & Mantzorou, M. 2011. What are the major ethical issues in conducting research? Is there conflict between research ethics and the nature of nursing? *Health Science Journal*, 5(1).

Halai, A. 2006. Ethics in Qualitative Research: Issues and challenges. Plenary address: Multi-disciplinary Qualitative Research in Developing Countries. Karachi, Pakistan: Aga Khan University. November, 2006.

Johnstone, M-J. 2009. Ethics and Advance Care Planning in a Culturally Diverse Society. *Journal of Transcultural Nursing*, 20:405–416. October 2009.

Nagy, N. 2006. Experimental methods for study of linguistic variation. In K. Brown (Ed). *Encyclopedia of Linguistics* (2nd ed.). Oxford: Elsevier. 4:390–394.

Okeke, C.I.O., Adu, E.O., Rembe, S., Duku, N., Maphosa, C., Drake, M.L., Shumba, J. & Sotuku, N 2014. The effects of demographic variables on work stimulated stressors and coping strategies among early childhood educators in East London Education District, unpublished manuscript, University of Fort Hare, East London Campus.

Orb, A., Eisenhauer, L. & Wynaden, D. 2001. Ethics in qualitative research. *Journal of Nursing Scholarship*, 33(1):93–96. Sigma Theta Tau International.

Reviere, J. 2011. Ethics in relation to research in nursing. British *Journal of Medical Psychology*, 1(3):341–348.

Rubin, D. 2000. Race and self esteem: A study of Latino and European-American students with learning disabilities. Unpublished Master's thesis, University of Utah, Salt Lake City.

Talarico J.F. 2013. Emotional intelligence and the relationship to resident performance: A multi-institutional study. *Journal of Clinical Anesthesia*, 25(3):181–187.

Part 2

Planning, designing and
conducting educational research

CHAPTER 8 Velisiwe Gasa, Patrick Mafora and Mncendisi Maphalala

The literature review

KEY CONCEPTS

Critical analysis means asking yourself whether you agree or disagree with a viewpoint and giving your reasons why. You need to stipulate what it is that makes you agree or disagree. When you analyse critically you test out your own views against those you are reading about. Then, as you read each study, you ask yourself if the evidence presented confirms your view; or does it perhaps provide a counter-argument that causes you to question your view? When you present a comprehensive and critical analysis, you need to use the existing literature to support your arguments, or the aims of your study. You should also be able to identify the limitations of the literature.

Evaluation of literature involves a comprehensive analysis of the similarities and differences between existing work and your own work.

Literature review is a critical review of existing knowledge on areas such as theories, critiques, methodologies, research findings, assessment and evaluations on a particular topic. It is not simply a summary to gather information from reports, journals and articles, but identifies similarities and differences between existing literatures and the work being undertaken. In short, it reviews what have already been done in the context of a topic, so the existing knowledge can be used to build up innovative ideas and concepts for further research.

Synthesis in the context of a literature review, refers to drawing material from different sources and integrating the material into one coherent argument.

LEARNING OUTCOMES

By the end of this chapter, you should be able to:

▶ Describe the purpose and importance of a literature review in a dissertation or thesis.

▶ Write a critical literature review.

▶ Use evaluation criteria to critique a literature review.

Case study: Finding the research topic for you

For Sibani, the spark of interest in her topic was largely inspired by the case of a student who was registered for a degree with one of the local higher education institutions while serving a prison sentence. The incarcerated student had completed an honours degree and then enrolled for a masters degree, passing the coursework with distinction. This outstanding performance made Sibani wonder what it was that motivated this student to achieve exceptionally despite the difficult conditions in prison. She became interested in the topic of the academic performance of all incarcerated students, but it remained an interest for quite some time. Then she met her former professor one day and shared what was becoming her new interest. Her professor advised her to read more literature about this interest, but Sibani kept procrastinating as usual. Then, after a media report that the Department of Correctional Services had trained close to 9,500 inmates as artisans over the past two years, she decided to search for literature to find out more about other incarcerated students who enrolled for degrees and achieved well.

(continued)

Case study *(continued)*

She read a range of books, journals, reports and papers, including textbooks on prisoner study and achievement. As she was considering studying for a masters degree herself, this gave her a context for carrying out further investigation into the topic of academic achievement of incarcerated students.

Now that you have read about Sibani's rewarding journey towards her study, you should be able to reflect on her case by answering the following questions:

▸ What was the advice that the professor gave to Sibani?

▸ If you were a professor, would you give this advice to your students? Support your answer.

▸ List sources that you need to consult when you are reviewing literature.

Introduction

A review of the literature is an essential component of any academic research project, be it a journal article, research study or dissertation. The literature review is regarded as a foundation on which a research project is built. This is why almost every research study begins with a review of the literature. The review is a careful examination of a body of literature that seeks to answer a research question for a particular study.

A literature search should help researchers to demonstrate the rationale for their research, and to describe how it fits within the wider research context in their area. The only way to achieve this in research is to undertake a literature review, that is, a review of material that has already been published, which may be relevant to the problem under investigation.

Through a literature review researchers have an opportunity to identify gaps in their field of knowledge that may warrant closer investigation. Researchers therefore need to demonstrate that their work will fill this gap by adding knowledge and understanding of the field of study.

This chapter provides researchers with a step-by-step logical approach to the process of undertaking a good literature review, which will help them justify their research and develop their thesis position.

8.1   Importance of literature review in a study

As already indicated, a **literature review** is a critical review of existing knowledge on areas such as theories, critiques, methodologies, research findings, assessment and evaluations on a particular topic. It is not simply a summary to gather information from reports, journals and articles, but identifies similarities and differences between existing literatures and the work being undertaken. In short, it reviews what have already been done in the context of a topic. Therefore, you can use the existing knowledge to build up innovative ideas and concepts for further research purpose.

A literature review serves several purposes in your academic research. You should be aware that academic research is always part of a dialogue among researchers. To be part of this dialogue, you, the researcher, needs to review literature in order to know what is going on in your field of interest and also to familiarise yourself with what exists within your topic or subject area. This may also create a protective shield for you against possible attack or critique by other researchers or experts in your area of interest. Your capabilities as a researcher will be shown in the quality of your review.

A good literature review shows that there is a theoretical base for the research project you are proposing to conduct. It should be clear how your research project fits in with what has already been done (providing a detailed context for your work). As you embark on your literature review, you may discover new knowledge, and areas that require further research as gaps may be revealed in the existing literature. You may end up undertaking a certain research project in response to a literature review.

Literature review is important for emerging researchers because they learn how relevant sources that will support their ideas and thoughts are selected. They learn how other's ideas and thinking are drawn into one's own argument in order to develop it, support it, defend it, or even protect it. It opens their eyes to the critical and important ethical matters involved in research generally, and in their area of study specifically. Literature review also helps them to explore those approaches and strategies that other researchers have used in order to construct a body of knowledge whose chapters, sections and paragraphs speak to one another, and to the reader. Furthermore, emerging researchers learn from others how to integrate their thoughts and ideas to avoid presenting arguments that are disjointed and incomplete to the extent that they become meaningless.

A literature review enables researchers to identify those ideas and thoughts which support or even oppose their own points of view, in order to engage both views critically in arguments. It gives them good reasons from pertinent sources to justify how and why their research study is worthwhile and important. Researchers learn from others how research aims and objectives are determined, constructed, and finally presented. Literature review helps to ground their research study and in doing so, gives it proper direction. Researchers also learn how to construct questionnaires, interview schedules, and how to draw conclusions so as to make valid findings which will lead ultimately to a sound and a balanced set of recommendations. As a process, a literature review enriches and empowers the researcher in many ways, some of which are beyond qualification or even quantification.

Putting the importance of literature review into context, let us relate it to the opening case study by highlighting some of the aspects that a literature review helped Sibani to uncover:

☑ **Developing a research question** Sibani knew that her topic of interest would be related to incarcerated students, but at this stage she needed more knowledge about the topic. Further searches and reading a range of literature helped her to know what is going on in this field of interest and also familiarise herself with what exists within her topic of interest. She decided to find out what motivates incarcerated students to achieve exceptionally despite the difficult conditions in prison.

☑ **Informing the study with theory** After developing an initial question, it was time for more reading. Sibani immersed herself in readings – both theoretical texts and existing research literature – on three concepts which related to her research topic: *incarcerated students*, *academic achievement* and *motivation*. Informed by all three sets of readings, she was able to proceed to her research project with more confidence.

☑ **Writing a literature review** Sibani made systematic notes on the key issues discussed in the published and unpublished sources she read. She developed the themes she had identified within the literature, and made critical comments on different issues. This process not only helped her to feel better-informed about the topic of her study, but she also felt more prepared for writing up her final report at the end of the project.

☑ **Designing the method** Reading and analysing the literature informed her about possible ways of collecting data. For example, she knew that she needed to cover all the students who were simultaneously serving their sentences in prison while registered for a particular degree in an institution of higher education. To make the research findings reliable and valid, she also knew that she had to involve non-incarcerated students registered for that particular degree in order to compare their performance.

Stop and reflect

The earlier information shows how crucial it was for Sibani to review the literature; this may well apply to your own study. Taking your own study and the information you have read in 8.1 into consideration, answer the following questions:

1 Mention four aspects that a literature review may help you to uncover.
2 Why is a literature review important in a study?
3 Why is a literature review important to new or novice researchers?
4 Can a literature review enrich and empower you beyond completion of your research project? How and why?

As you now have an understanding of how important it is for you to do a literature review, let us look at the elements of a literature review, as covered next.

8.2 Elements of a literature review

A literature review could be divided into three sections: an introduction, body, and conclusion.

8.2.1 The introduction

It is important to have a good introduction that clearly tells the reader what the literature will be about, by stating the approach you will take and putting forward the central ideas and purpose of the literature review. The introduction is meant to provide an appropriate context for reviewing the literature. An introduction essentially serves the purpose of informing the reader about the following:

▶ The parameters of the topic (what does it include and exclude?)
▶ How the review ties in with the identified research topic.

The introduction is meant to provide an appropriate context for reviewing the literature. It should therefore stimulate the interest of the reader to continue reading the whole section on literature review.

8.2.2 The body

This section summarises and evaluates the current state of knowledge in the field of study. It identifies major themes, the trends, or any findings that the researcher may agree or disagree with. In the body, the researcher has to discuss concisely what has already been written in relation to his or her problem and to identify current findings or insights about the topic, methodologies and theories. This information forms the basis for the formulation of questions that need further research and which remain unresolved.

8.2.3 The conclusion

The conclusion summarises major contributions of reviewed literature in the area being studied, and also highlights the gaps in research by showing inconsistencies in theory and findings. An indication of how the current study will deal with the identified flaws in research has to be stated. The researcher concludes by demonstrating how the previous studies inform the current study.

Let us now look at the guidelines for reviewing literature as it is provided in the section that follows.

8.3 Guidelines for reviewing literature

The literature review does not merely serve as a summary of what has been read. Its focus is more specific. The literature review is based on and directed by the research questions of the specific research project. In the literature review, previous research that is related to the central question of the current research is identified, evaluated, and synthesised. These processes culminate in a written submission that gives context to the research question of the study that is undertaken. This means that all literature that is reviewed is relevant *only* to the extent that it facilitates answering the research question of the current study, by providing and defining its framework.

Broadly speaking, the literature review should serve the following purposes:

- ☑ **Define and limit** your research problem.
- ☑ **Relate your study** to other studies on the topic.
- ☑ **Indicate the writer's insight** into existing work on the topic.
- ☑ **Point to existing gaps** in theory and research in the field.
- ☑ **Identify research** that has been conducted and does not warrant being repeated.

Collectively, these purposes of a literature review suggest that it helps develop a good working knowledge of the research topic and provides initial insight into the current study. In order to serve the intended purposes, the literature review should be conducted meticulously. It cannot be a haphazard or unsystematic process. The next section describes some key considerations for conducting a review.

8.3.1 Identify your question(s)

From the broad field of study that interests you, first identify the specific issue or issues that you wish to investigate. It is the issue (or issues) that you wish to research that determines and directs your reading. If your area of research interest is the motivation and resilience of female teachers, you would not read about the motivation of male soldiers. Rather, your reading would be focused on female teachers. The reading would be guided by the specific questions that you wish to answer about the teachers' motivation, not other aspects. The questions will determine which sources are critical to read; what are the related areas and the sources to consult; and what should be the scope of the reading. Once you have identified your questions you can proceed to search for literature, as explained next.

8.3.2 Search the literature

Literature includes everything that is written on a topic of interest. Because it has to be narrowed to the specific research question in order to be relevant, you should set criteria that define which literature to include and which to exclude. When conducting the actual search, use different keywords, paying attention to synonyms that could be used in different contexts. Sources can be identified in bibliographies and references in textbooks and journal articles, and from abstracting and citation database sources like ERIC, Google Scholar, ISI Proceedings, JSTOR, Scopus, ProQuest Dissertations and Theses Database, Web of Science, etc. Literature reviews may be available for some topics, or aspects of topics, but these may only be consulted in the development of your own literature review.

The literature that you have searched should be analysed and evaluated. This aspect will be dealt with next.

8.3.3 Critically analyse and evaluate

Critical analysis means asking yourself whether you agree or disagree with a viewpoint and giving a reason/s why. You need to stipulate what is it that makes you agree or disagree. When you analyse critically, you test out your own views against those you are reading about. Then, as you read each study, you ask yourself if the evidence presented confirms your view, or does it provide a counter-argument that causes you to question your view? When you present a comprehensive and critical analysis, you need to apply the existing literatures to support your arguments, or the aims of your study, and you should also be able to identify the limitations of literatures.

Evaluation of literature involves a comprehensive analysis of the similarities and differences between existing work and your own work.

Your reading, which should culminate in the writing of a literature review, should be critical and evaluative. While you may cite ideas, the material you read should not be repeated as is. Rather, you should evaluate it by indicating emerging trends and their significance with regard to, among other variables, their theoretical frameworks, arguments, methods, findings, and conclusions.

The questions you should ask when evaluating an individual source include determining whether the central argument it advances is logically formulated and convincingly defended; what constitutes the author's theoretical stance and the extent to which it is reconcilable with conclusions that are made; what evidence supports the author's contentions, and the extent to which the author discloses his or her assumptions and biases.

We would advise you to use sources that focus on key aspects of your research question and that are recent (although this should not preclude some theoretical 'classics' as well). Your review should reflect your critical engagement with the sources that you cite. For instance, it should point out strengths and weaknesses of the research methodology of cited studies, their theoretical frameworks, contradictions, controversies, and research gaps. You should also be in a position to differentiate between the authors' opinions and their research findings, and the extent to which their findings support their interpretations.

It is inevitable that you will agree with some authors and disagree with others when writing your review. You should present your own interpretations, not just state what others say. A key consideration should, therefore, be the author's standing and purpose of writing the views that you wish to cite. There is more merit in citing an author who is an authority on a topic than one who merely posts articles that are not peer-reviewed on the internet

Research findings carry more scientific merit than theoretical assertions for backing one's argument. Similarly, we would strongly advise you to refer to findings from studies conducted under similar or related contexts, than those that are not.

Literature analysis and evaluation should be done in conjunction with synthesis, as discussed next.

8.3.4 Synthesise

A **synthesis** in the context of literature review refers to drawing material from different sources and integrating that material into one coherent argument. A synthesised literature review should demonstrate your command of the field of study as demarcated by the research question. Major debates from key sources on the topic should not merely be presented one after the other. Rather, you should compare and contrast the emergent ideas, and outline what emerges from these diverse views and what are the gaps.

A synthesised review should provide a summary of key theoretical conceptions and research findings. It should be backed by evidence. The views of authors who draw similar conclusions should be presented together, and contrasted with views of those authors who draw different conclusions. It also serves as the theoretical context for the conclusions, implications and recommendations that will be subsequently made. All the aspects that have been discussed will help you, finally, to write the review.

8.3.5 Write the review

Through logical argument, the presentation of the review should show how the current research problem fits into what was previously researched. First identify a problem area and justify why it is an important topic to investigate. The review should communicate your specific point of view in relation to other views that are similar and those that differ. When outlining these commonalities and/or differences you should indicate whether the comparisons are in relation to theoretical arguments, classics or empirical research findings.

We strongly advise that you open the review with an overview which outlines what will and will not be covered. This overview should cohere with the subheadings that are subsequently used to sub-divide the review. The discussion in the review should follow a discernible pattern or structure. Some examples of discussion patterns are: themes, chronology, sector, development of ideas, or a combination of these elements.

To avoid disjointed and possibly incoherent arguments, use topic sentences to introduce a series of paragraphs that are related, and transitions between major sub-sections. Provide a conclusion which resolves the argument that was advanced in the review. In the case of theses, dissertations or journal articles that present original research, this conclusion should highlight the research question which the research addresses. The review should close with a summary which outlines what the literature implies.

When writing up your literature review, we recommend that you use each of your headings or themes to compare and contrast the differing views put forward in the relevant studies. You should never forget to explain how the literature that you reviewed relates to your investigation. Your literature review needs to tell an interesting 'story'. This story should lead up to how and why you are doing your investigation. The idea is not to present your story in a descriptive way, meaning it should not read like one thing after another. Rather, your story should be comparing, contrasting and evaluating the previous literature, as illustrated in Table 8.1.

TABLE 8.1: Examples of comparing, contrasting and evaluating previous literature

Descriptive	Analytical
• Summarises what other people have found without saying what these findings mean for your investigation. • Usually a chronological list of who discovered what, and when.	• Synthesises the work and succinctly passes judgement on the relative merits of research conducted in your field. • Reveals limitations or recognises the possibility of taking research further, allowing you to formulate and justify your aims for your investigation.
For example: "Green (1975) discovered that …" "In 1978, Black conducted experiments and found that …." "Later, Brown (1980) illustrated this in …"	For example: "There seems to be general agreement on x, (see White, 1987; Brown, 1980; Black, 1978; Green, 1975). However, Green (1975) sees x as a consequence of y, while Black (1978) puts x and y as …. While Green's work has some limitations in that it …, its main value lies in …"

(**Source:** Examples taken from University of Queensland: Writing the literature review)

8.3.5.1 Using the literature review to explain your findings

Previously, we mentioned that your literature review has two main purposes:

1 To place your investigation in the context of previous research and justify how you have approached your investigation.
2 To provide evidence to help explain the findings of your investigation.

In most cases, emerging researchers seem to forget the second purpose – that of using their literature review as evidence to explain their findings. When you are writing the discussion of your findings, you need to relate these back to the background literature. Referring back to your literature may help you to relate to these questions: Do your results confirm what was found before, or challenge it? Why might this be the case?

Table 8.2 gives an example on how you can refer back to your literature review in your discussion section.

TABLE 8.2: Example of how to refer back to a literature review

Finding	95% of the students you surveyed have problems managing their time at university.
What do you think about this?	I expected it to be less than that.
What makes you think that?	Research I read for my literature survey put the figure at 60–70%.
What conclusions can you draw from this?	There must be reasons why the figures are so different. The sample I surveyed included a large number of mature students, unlike the samples in the previous research. That was because the brief was to look at time management in a particular department, which had a high intake of post-work experience students.
Finished paragraph for Discussion section	The percentage of students surveyed who experienced problems with time management was much higher at 95% than the 60% reported in Jones (2006:33), or the 70% reported in Smith (2007a:17). This may be due to the large number of mature students recruited to this post-work experience course. Taylor (2004:16-21) describes the additional time commitment reported by students with young families, and the impact this may have on effective management of study time. The department recognises this, offering flexible seminar times. However, it may be that students would benefit from more advice in this area.

When you refer back to your literature, you should understand that there is a relationship between the literature review and the discussion section of your findings. An hourglass is used as an analogue to explain this relationship. We have shown you that your literature review usually starts broadly, and then narrows down to explain how previous research has influenced your specific investigation. But the discussion of your findings starts with the specific, by analysing your results, explaining what they mean for the outcome of your study, and then ends by widening out to assess how these results might contribute to your field of research as a whole. Figure 8.1 gives a brief diagram of how the relationship between the literature review and the discussion section of your findings should look like.

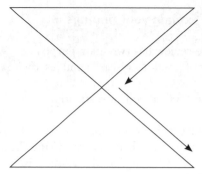

Literature review: Starts broad and narrows to show how past research relates to your project.

Discussion: Starts specific by explaining what your results show in relation to your study, then widens out again to say what this might mean for the field of research as a whole.

FIGURE 8.1: The relationship between the literature review and the discussion section of a study's findings (**Source:** Reproduced with permission of the University of Reading and the Association of Learning Development in Higher Education.).

When you are reviewing literature, it is very important to have the ability to detect whether you are on the right track or not. The information that follows may help you to discover this:

8.3.6 Detecting a good and a poor literature review

Table 8.3 will help to identify a good literature review and a poor literature review.

TABLE 8.3: Characteristics of a good literature review and a poor literature review

A good literature review...	A poor literature review is...
is a synthesis of available research	an annotated bibliography
is a critical evaluation	confined to description
has appropriate breadth and depth	narrow and shallow
has clarity and conciseness	confusing and longwinded
uses rigorous and consistent methods	constructed in an arbitrary way

Read the information box that may be useful to those students who are reviewing literature for the purpose of their postgraduate studies.

Tip

Revisit your literature review

In postgraduate studies (a PhD or long research project), you should understand that your literature review is more like a work-in-progress than a finished chapter. You should keep coming back to it as your study progresses. You may write your initial draft, put it aside, and then come back to it as the focus of your project shifts, or as you discover new research. You may end up re-structuring your literature review a number of times. Sometimes it becomes necessary to do a thorough redraft at the end before you submit. When writing up the discussion section of your findings, you may find that you need to redraft the focus of your literature review slightly to draw out those studies that are most important to your findings. This exercise allows you to remove studies that are less relevant, and to add others that turned out to be more significant than you initially thought.

As you continually review your literature, we recommend that you should simultaneously keep track of your references as outlined next.

8.3.7 Manage your references

Your review of literature should show that you are aware of, and have used and acknowledged key works in your area of research. You should keep track of both the authors, titles, and all the publication details of the material that you use. Your acknowledgements should be consistent and follow the same citation method, e.g. APA, Chicago, Harvard, Oxford, Vancouver. Failure to acknowledge the work of others, even when not done deliberately, is unacceptable. The failure to acknowledge the sources that you consulted is called plagiarism and, besides being unacceptable in academic practice and for publishing purposes, it makes it difficult for other researchers and readers to trace your original sources.

The standard requirement is that all sources that you paraphrase or quote directly should be acknowledged within the text. All works cited in text should also be listed in the reference list which is placed at the end of the text. Unlike the reference list which include only those sources that were cited, the bibliography includes *all* sources that were consulted, even if they are not cited. You can keep track of sources that you have used and format your citations as you write through licensed software tools that can be purchased, like EndNote, EndNote Web, CiteULike, RefWorks, and Papers. Some software, like Mendeley and Zotero, are freely available on the internet.

The choice of a reference management system will depend on your needs. Some common uses of reference systems include:

▶ Storage of details of cited materials whether added manually or imported from search engines
▶ Automatic generation of citations or reference lists following specific styles, e.g. APA 6th
▶ Searching and retrieving bibliographic records from library catalogues and journal indexing databases
▶ Attaching files, e.g. images, Word documents or PDFs
▶ Sharing folders or documents.

Before proceeding to the next section, which looks at the literature review routine, let us stop and reflect on what we have learned.

Stop and reflect

We hope that all this information has enriched your understanding of the literature review and you are in a better position to reflect on the following questions:
1 List the purposes that a literature review serves.
2 Discuss some key considerations for conducting a review.
3 Explain the criteria for analysing and evaluating literature.
4 Is there a pattern or a structure that you need to follow when you are writing your literature review? Support your answer.

8.4 Literature review routine

A literature review routine is centred around 'when, who, how, and where' you should search for literature. These aspects will be discussed next.

8.4.1 Who should do a literature review, and when?

Everyone who aspires to scholarship and wants to become an educationist, intellectual or academic should thirst for knowledge. Researchers are generally regarded as serious consumers of knowledge because before they can become better producers of knowledge they must first and foremost have been its consumers. Literature review, as an ordinary activity is meant to empower and enrich one's scope of thinking. But you need to be aware that this is a protracted and often tedious exercise. Reviewing, finding and retrieving the literature requires working for long periods of time. Most of the time will be spent in the library or using databases and online information sources. Despite the time that is spend on searching, you are also expected to read and re-read, and write and re-write. Yet, if you get yourself into the right frame of mind, discovering what other researchers have done can be fascinating and rewarding. You will inspire yourself by reading literature that challenges and also exercises your thinking, in that it strengthens your vision, analytical powers and style of argumentation.

A scholar must possess the desire to achieve excellence. You should be willing to immerse yourself in books and journals that address topical issues in your field of interest so as to keep abreast with current and topical issues that come and go. You need to constantly read so as to be aware of important matters that affect human life in all dimensions or aspects. You should be someone who is well-informed with respect to human life and society in its many diverse conditions and circumstances.

As a scholar or researcher, you need to develop the skills of how to do a literature review. This aspect is covered in the next section.

8.4.2 How do you review the literature?

Time planning and management of the search and review processes are crucial. You should avoid spending lengthy periods at a time searching, reading and reviewing. But if you are in the right frame of mind, capitalise on that mood and your own interest, and spend a sufficiently long and continuous period of time in the library or searching internet engines. Keep in mind that the purpose of the review process includes an analysis of each document to establish its validity and relevance to your study. Therefore, your analysis must be constructive, critical and objective. This validity and relevance will help you to identify ideas that are of specific interest in your chosen topic.

Your review should be a progressive development of ideas which demonstrate the authority for research in your area of interest. Consequently, most scholars will point out that there is no one correct or standard way in which to review literature or to write the review. However, notable features of a good review will include coherence, continuity, clarity, and fluency in the expression and development of ideas and argument. It is necessary to weave together your ideas in order to produce a piece of scholarly writing that will convey a clear and well-structured picture of the current situation, as mirrored through the lenses of past and current events. You should channel your readers to the key features you have identified in the literature that will underpin your research.

You should also know where to search for literature. This aspect is outlined next.

8.4.3 Where do you search for literature?

Today, knowledge is like a hare that is always on the run and tries to hide everywhere. Unlike in the past, when knowledge was primarily kept in the form of books mainly found in libraries; knowledge as mobile phenomenon can now be accessed from many sources on the internet. Different radio stations, television channels, newspapers, discussion groups and bulletin boards, and non-textual materials also carry current information on a daily basis. The non-textual formats such as video and audio formats, films and still, graphic and actual forms may also be useful to you as you search for information. However, as a scholar, you should try to build your own small library by investing in those sources that will empower you in the field of your own specialisation. Having your own library will save you time going in search of books at libraries that may be distant or not have the books you want to loan.

We also advise you to have a ready notebook or some kind of recordkeeping device in which you alphabetically record each source of information that you read for easy compiling later, either as a bibliography or references at the end of the research report. Your review should cover both published and unpublished sources, but unpublished sources should be used cautiously. These sources appear in many forms such as journals, booklets, reports and papers. Papers also appear in many forms such as conference proceedings, working, occasional, and position papers.

Furthermore, information is increasingly being released in electronic form on the Internet, in electronic journals and in intranets of particular organisations. Internet publications should also be cautiously used as they may not be refereed or editorially controlled. University-based research and development centres and their websites are also helpful sources of recent information. They publicise conferences and seminars which you may wish to attend so that you can listen to experts in the field that you are researching.

Let us think about what we have learned so far.

Critical thinking challenge

As a scholar or researcher, you need to read current sources since they are the source of latest, up-to-date information. With this statement, and the information you have read earlier, answer these questions:
1 Do you think it is necessary for you to do literature review: why or why not?
2 A scholar must possess the desire to achieve excellence. Do you agree? Support your answer.
3 What is included in the outstanding features of a good review?
4 Why should internet publications be used cautiously?
5 What is plagiarism and why is it unacceptable?

Conclusion

This chapter oriented you to what constitutes a literature review and described the three constituent elements of a literature review. The chapter argued that a literature review is not a stand-alone feature, but a significant pivot and basis for other components of the research process and the research report. This means that while the review of literature is grounded in the objectives of the study, it provides the rationale for the study and the context for considering the merits of the arguments advanced, the appropriateness of methods and techniques, and, finally, the soundness of findings.

The chapter described the key considerations you should make when conducting a search for literature and organising the reviewed literature into a logical and coherent unit that blends with the entire research report. In addition, the chapter outlined some evaluative criteria that you may use to assess and improve the quality of a literature review in a dissertation or thesis.

Overall, the chapter has led you through the process of searching for relevant literature and writing a critical literature review that is aligned to the study objectives and other aspects of the research project as presented in the dissertation or thesis.

Closing activities

Analysis and consolidation

Read the following extract drawn from the literature review of a student's research project. Use the criteria in the checklist, as well as the marking rubric that is given after the abstract to critique and assess the review:

Literature review: An example

This chapter aims to review the literature on relevant studies on personnel retention strategies in institutions.

Staff development is a variable that enhances teacher retention and improves workforce quality. Flatt and Jennifer (2006:5) describe ways to improve teacher retention; they state that educators should maintain a balance between optimism and realism. Training of mentors plays an integral part in teacher retention. Murray and Morrice (2003:40) indicate the fact that teachers enter their profession for intrinsic satisfaction of working with students, does not rule out the possibility that they will be motivated extrinsically as well. Increased flexibility for schools to remunerate their staff according to whether they possess scarce skills or are outstanding performers will encourage graduates to train in areas where there are shortages and enable schools to retain good and superior youth mentors as teachers (Webster & Wooden, 2006:185). Other retention strategies include: access to sick leave and paid leave, investment plans, better insurance cover, lower retirement age and better retirement plans that entice teachers to work on contract after retirement. Other incentives should include higher education as well as home ownership schemes. Work schedules need to be flexible enough to allow for part-time jobs (Murray & Morrice, 2003).

Therefore, research on teacher retention has been focused on those who opt to prolong their employment and how this continued employment can help enlighten those interested in retaining teachers in their institutions, as cited by Eugene (2005:4). There are substantive discussions about issues such as educational leadership, mentoring, and effective means of professional induction. Nonetheless, the challenge posed is how teachers and administrators can enhance unity in order to collaborate with one another so as to foster and maintain new generations of teachers (Walter, 2002). Several studies have been conducted on factors that bring about job retention among educators under various circumstances, and the results have shown similarities and differences, depending on what the researcher sets out to achieve. Steyn (1988:9–14) explains that the complexity of the concept of job retention assumes that certain aspects of the educator's background can influence their experience thereof, the implication being that job retention can be influenced by an individual's expectations. Steyn and Van Wyk (1999:37–38) talk of the difficulty of measuring educator satisfaction as brought about by individual's attitudes, which are abstract and difficult to express. In addition, attitudes can be formed by an individual's values, expectations and perceptions. Abu Saad and Isralowits (1991:773) also confirm the level of satisfaction experienced by an individual as a complex function of a) the degree to which different values connected with work and with its concomitant results are attained; b) the opportunities perceived for the attainment of these values; c) the relative advantages and disadvantages of the work situation compared with that of other people, and the personality and cultural determinants. Jacob (2008:25) identifies and explores the factors and conditions of moral leadership that affect the potential for teacher retention among Alternative Route Certification (ARC) teachers. Not only are ARC teachers drawn to the profession because of their own moral ideals, but findings reveal that they are also simultaneously responsive to principals' moral leadership. Specific traits such as attitudes, disposition, and actions that define moral leadership, are needed to foster teacher retention.

References

Flatt, Jennifer M. 2006. Stolpa. *Phi Kappa Phi Forum*, 86(3), Summer.

Webster, E., Marks, G. & Wooden, M. 2006. Reforming the Labour Market for Australian Teachers. *Australian Journal of Education*, 50(2):185–202.

Steyn, G.M. 1998. Teacher empowerment and the leadership role of principals. *South African Journal of Education*, 18(3):131–138.

Steyn, G.M. & Van Wyk, J.N. 1999. Job satisfaction of teachers. *South African Journal of Education*, 19(1):37–44.

Checklist for evaluating your literature review

Here is an example of the checklist to be used to critique the literature review abstract that is presented earlier.

Key considerations	Yes	No
1 Does the literature relate clearly to the student's research questions and objectives?		
2 Has the student included material that is interesting but does not contribute to the development of the argument?		
3 Has the student covered key theories?		
4 Has the student covered key literature or a representative sample?		
5 Are the sources used varied?		
6 Has the student shown the relationship inherent in the literature? (e.g. *juxtaposing views, similarities, differences*)		
7 Has the student highlighted those issues where his/her research will provide fresh insight?		
8 Is the literature up to date (as prescribed in your discipline)?		
9 Has the student engaged the literature? (e.g. *summary, synthesis, analysis & conclusions*)		
10 Has the student been objective in his/her discussion and assessment of other people's work?		
11 Has the student included references that are counter to his/her own opinion?		
12 Has the student outlined and clearly justified his/her own ideas?		
13 Is the student's argument coherent and cohesive – do the ideas link together?		
14 Is there a logical flow and coherence between different sections/paragraphs?		
15 Does the student's review lead to subsequent sections of the project report?		
16 Has the student acknowledged all sources consulted, fully and correctly?		
17 Has the student consistently used the same referencing technique (i.e. APA, Harvard, Chicago, etc.)		

Marking rubric

Here is an example of the marking rubric to be used to assess the Literature review abstract that is presented above.

Marking rubric	Excellent	Proficient	Average	Poor
Aim	Aim was clearly outlined and comprehensively justified	Aim was outlined and justified	Aim was outlined but not justified	Aim was not outlined or justified
Background	Provided a very comprehensive and detailed background; a wide and deep coverage of the topic	Showed a detailed background, but not comprehensive enough; sufficiently covered the work but a few areas not deep enough	A background with basic information; some key points missed; covered the topic at a general level	Lacked in significant details about the topic
Critical analysis	A comprehensive and critical analysis; applied the existing literature to support the arguments/the aim of study; identified the limitations of the literature	Some critical analysis; applied the existing literature to support some arguments/the aim of study; showed a few limitations in the literature	A limited critical analysis; presented the existing literature in a descriptive way; a limited analysis of the limitations of literature	No critical analysis; only described some existing literature; the limitations of literature were not mentioned
Evaluation	Showed a comprehensive analysis of the similarities and differences between existing work and the current work	Showed a basic analysis of the similarities and differences between existing work and the current work	Very limited analysis of the similarities and differences between existing work and the current work	Failed to analyse the similarities and differences between existing work and the current work
References	Referencing and citation style was correct and consistent between the text and the list of references	Referencing and citation style was mainly consistent between the text and the list of references	Some references were inconsistent between the text and the list of references	Many references were inconsistent between the text and the list of references

Bibliography

Boote, D.N. & Beile, P. 2005. Scholars before researchers: On the centrality of the dissertation literature review in research preparation. *Educational Researcher*, 34(6):3–15.

California Lutheran University. n.d. Developing your literature review, Available at [http://libguides.callutheran.edu/content.php?pid=587443&sid=4841827]. Accessed 20 August 2014.

Chan, C. 2009. *Assessment: Literature Review, Assessment Resources@HKU*, University of Hong Kong. Available at [http://ar.cetl.hku.hk]. Accessed 14 July 2014.

Galvan, J. 2006. *Writing literature reviews: A guide for students of the behavioural sciences* (3rd ed.). Glendale, CA: Pyrczak Publishing.

Hofstee, E. 2006. *Constructing a Good Dissertation: A Practical Guide to Finishing a Master's, MBA or PhD on Schedule* (pp.135–136). Sandton: EPE.

Koshy, V. 2005. *Action Research for Improving Practice: A Practical Guide*. London: Paul Chapman Publishing.

Levy, Y. & Ellis, T.J. 2006. A Systems Approach to Conduct an Effective Literature Review in Support of Information Systems Research. *Informing Science Journal*, 9:181–212.

Maphalala, M.C. 2014. The Consequences of School Violence for Female Learners. *Journal of Sociology and Social Anthropology*, 5(1):29–36.

Murray, N. & Beglar, D. 2009. *Writing dissertations and theses*. Harlow: Pearson Longman.

Rowley, J. & Slack, F. 2004. Conducting a literature review. *Management Research News*, 27(6):31–39.

Reardon, D.F. 2006. *Doing Your Undergraduate Project*. London: SAGE Publications Ltd.

Ridley, D.D. 2008. *The literature review: A step-by-step guide for students*. London: SAGE.

Saunders, M., Lewis, P. & Thornhill, A. 2000. *Research methods for business students* (2nd ed.). Essex: Prentice-Hall.

University of Queensland. n.d. Writing the literature review, Available at [http://www.uq.edu.au/student-services/phdwriting/phlink18.html]. Accessed 1 October 2014.

CHAPTER 9

Charl Wolhuter

Steps in the research process

KEY CONCEPTS

Descriptive research is a type of research that describes something, without seeking or offering any explanation or interpretation.

Edifice in the context of this chapter, edifice means the existing structure or body of available knowledge, including key concepts and the logical relations between these concepts.

Experimental research is where the researcher manipulates one variable, called the independent variable, in order to determine the effect of that variable on another variable, called the dependent variable.

Ex-post facto design this is where the researcher does not manipulate the variables; the variables, as they appear in their natural state, are used.

Interpretation to explain or to understand.

Lacunae is Latin for 'empty spaces', i.e. in this context, empty areas where no knowledge exists as yet.

Method comes from an ancient Greek word, meaning 'the way', and, in the context of this chapter, becomes 'the way to do research'.

Rationale is the reason for something to exist; in this context, the reason why a researcher should have a research problem to start a research project.

Synthesise means to bring together different, disparate elements, into one coherent whole.

Theory presents a set of concepts; also shows the relationships between these concepts. Often, these relationships are of a causal or explanatory nature, i.e. one concept is offered as the cause of or explanation for another.

Theory formation is where the body of scientific literature on a particular topic is surveyed and synthesised into a new unity, a new theory, for example, a study of published literature on substance abuse among adolescents.

LEARNING OUTCOMES

By the end of this chapter, you should be able to:

▶ Explain the steps in the research process, the essential features of each step, and why each step is necessary.

▶ Plan a research project; and, with the help of other chapters in this book, carry out such a project.

Case study: Why don't these learners perform?

You are an English teacher in a remote rural South African school where, sadly, like many other such schools in the country, all learners are from poverty-stricken homes. You notice that in your Grade 11 class, there are two distinct groups of learners: those who perform well (they consistently get above 65 per cent in English tests and examinations); and those who invariably fail. You want to investigate the reasons for this (see own practice as source of problems, later in this chapter), and also to use whatever explanations you might find, in order to improve the English competence of those learners who usually fail.

We will return to this case study at various places in the chapter, in order to illustrate and explain the various steps in the research process.

Introduction

This chapter will offer you a plan, or it may even serve as a manual, on how to conduct a research project, from the first step, namely, to search for a problem, until you find a possible solution to the problem, and then to write up your findings as a research report. In this sense, the chapter integrates most of what you will read in this book. The various sections of this chapter are all unpacked in more detail in other chapters of this volume. Therefore, in various places in this chapter, you will be referred to other chapters in the book, which will go into more detail on aspects of this chapter.

The chapter begins with an explanation on why you need to follow meticulously a series steps, when doing research. Then, in turn, each of these steps will be the focus of subsequent sections of the chapter. You will benefit most from this chapter by studying it in an interactive way, by actually planning your own research project, as you progress through this chapter. In subsequent features in this chapter, you will be guided on how to go about doing this.

9.1 Need for rigorous process in research

Research is the way in which scientific knowledge is created. Scientific knowledge can be defined as "methodically acquired, verified, systematised knowledge" (Stoker, 1969:1). This means the researcher has to give an account of the **method** he or she has used, when conducting his or her research. This method consists of a number of indispensable steps, namely:

- ☑ The statement of the problem
- ☑ The literature survey
- ☑ The hypothesis formulation
- ☑ An explanation of the research method
- ☑ The collection of the data
- ☑ The analysis of the data
- ☑ The interpretation of data
- ☑ The drawing of conclusions
- ☑ The writing up of the research report.

We will now discuss each of these steps in greater detail, starting with the statement of the research problem.

9.2 Statement of the problem (or the aim or topic/theme of the research): Your first step in conducting a research project

Under this heading, we now discuss, in turn, the necessity for a problem statement in forming the basis of a research project, the places or sources where you should look for a problem to research; and the requirements of a good research problem.

9.2.1 Rationale for a problem: Why you should have a problem, to start a research project

A research project begins with a research problem (or at least the researcher should formulate an aim or identify a topic/theme to research any **lacunae** in the existing corpus of scientific knowledge, which could yield research project(s). The absence of any problem would result in the collection of a mass of information, which would be quite useless (would serve no purpose), or would be the duplication of research which has been done already – and this would be a waste of time and resources. The absence of an inspiring problem would also result in an unmotivated researcher, who is unlikely to persevere in the difficult and testing road of research.

You will now ask the question often asked by the novice prospective researcher, namely: Where to find problems? To answer this challenging question, we shall now turn to:

9.2.2 Sources of research problems: Where should you look for a problem to research?

The following sources of research problems are suggested, mainly for students in the social sciences:

▶ In the existing corpus of literature the student will find lacunae (gaps in the existing knowledge base);
▶ From your own practice, if you are in a profession or occupation related to your field of study. For example, the teacher who wishes to conduct a research project in the field of education, could look into her own teaching practice and experience for a possible problem to research;
▶ From discussions with colleagues in your profession about problems they have experienced;
▶ From reports in the media.

A research problem cannot be formulated in any haphazard way. In order to form a solid basis of a research project, it should comply with a number of criteria. A good research problem can do a lot to facilitate the rest of the research project; it can even (and often) make the difference between success and failure.

9.2.3 Requirements of problem/topic selection: How do you know whether you have a good or suitable problem?

Choosing the wrong topic or problem for your research project can easily mean that your project will end in failure. Make sure that your problem complies with the following criteria:

▶ You must have the means (time, finance, knowledge, instruments) to research an answer to the problem;
▶ It must certainly be a problem that has not already been addressed by published research;
▶ You should formulate your problem in a manner, as clearly, briefly, and as simply as possible, preferably in the form of a question;

The following example is a practical exercise on how to identify a research problem.

> **Toolbox How to find your research problem**
>
> If you are a student in education, do the following exercise. (If you are a student in one of the other social sciences, you can also do the exercise; but of course, you should substitute your field of interest for that of education.)
>
> 1 Find copies of your daily newspaper for the past week (or go online and follow a news story for a week).
> 2 Cut out all the articles dealing with education.
> 3 Select one of the articles dealing with a topic, which is interesting, and develop from the content of that article a problem statement, keeping in mind all the guidelines given in this section.
> 4 Write down your problem statement, and keep it. You will be asked to return to it in later sections of this chapter.
> 5 As a side-exercise, consult some of the leading journals in your field. Do the published articles in recent editions deal with your chosen problem; or for that matter, with any of the critical issues you got from the local/national newspaper? The leading scientific journals are mostly based in the Western-European-North-American 'nerve centre' of the academic world; and they reflect the critical issues and interests of those parts of the world. This exercise will probably underscore the need for this book and its mission, namely, to build research capacity in Africa, and about Africa. In this regard, you may be interested to read the article by Wolhuter (2008), which shows how under-represented researchers from Africa are in one of the most prestigious journals. *Comparative Education Review.*

The next step in the research process is to conduct a thorough literature survey.

9.3 The literature survey: The next step in your research project

A thorough, sophisticated literature review is the foundation and inspiration for substantial, useful research (see Boote & Beile, 2005:3). The following section will first explain why a proper literature survey is an indispensable step in the research process, before turning to the way in which to conduct a literature survey.

9.3.1 Why a literature survey is necessary

It is through a literature survey that you will become acquainted with the latest state of knowledge on your problem/topic. The literature survey will tell you whether your problem is indeed a problem, whether the problem has possibly not been addressed by research already done at some time in the past. From a literature study, you will gain a fuller understanding of your own research problem. The literature survey frequently results in a refinement or improvement of the problem statement. The literature survey will also, in all likelihood, give you suggestions on the formulation of a hypothesis, and of the best methods available to research the problem – the next two steps in the research process.

Now that the reasons for a literature survey have been explained, the way to go about doing a good literature survey will be described.

9.3.2 Source basis for a literature survey: Where to find the literature for a literature survey

The library is your central source basis for a literature survey. For the most effective and efficient literature study, you would be well advised to consult your subject librarian at the outset. Identify a few keywords from your topic/problem statement; and key those words into the subject slot of your library catalogue.

Furthermore, do the same, i.e. also a keyword search, with respect to authoritative databases in your field of study, such as EBSCO-Host, Google Scholar, and in the fields of education, ERIC. However, such a keyword subject catalogue search of sources will not be sufficient. Supplement this search by combing through the editions of the past ten years of a number of the eminent journals in your field, and also of the most recent editions of books in the area of your topic. Ask your subject librarian for the Dewey shelf number of your field of research; and then go to that shelf in your library and consult all the books, especially those which have been published during the past ten years.

For many research projects, such a stock of published scholarly literature should not be the only literature to consult. Depending on your topic, you may well need to consult the following too:
- Dictionaries, in order to clarify key terms
- Subject encyclopedias; and
- Primary documents, such as legislative Acts, government reports, green and white papers, policy documents.

You have now amassed a stock of literature on your topic/problem. The next step (to which we go in the next section), is to work your way in a scientific manner through this body of literature.

9.3.3 How to go about surveying your field of literature

Once you have built up your stock of literature, as explained in the previous section, you should work carefully through each of the literature sources. Take thorough notes, as you work through the sources, whether on record cards, on loose sheets that you will file, in a notebook or electronically in a computer document. Reflect on what you read all the time; reflect with your problem statement in mind. Finally, you should **synthesise** your literature survey.

Towards your research report (whether it be a thesis, a dissertation, a book chapter, an article, or a monograph) you should now have a substantial section, in which to present the results of your literature study. You do not simply list your sources and present a summary of each; instead you need to build your own synthesis. Ideally, this synthesis should culminate in a theoretical framework for your research. Such a framework should reveal all the components/variables of your topic/theme/subject of research, and the relations between these components/variables. From this theoretical framework, *lacunae* in the existing **edifice** of knowledge should also be apparent – hence the need for your research.

Stop and reflect

Before you embark on a literature study for your research project, you are advised to study Chapter 8, *The literature review*, in this book. Now take your topic or problem statement and do a literature study, keeping carefully to the guidelines given earlier in this chapter.

9.4   Hypothesis formulation

9.4.1   What does the term 'hypothesis' mean?

A hypothesis is a provisional answer to the research problem, supported by research already done. In the following sections, we will explain why a hypothesis is an indispensable part of the research process, and how you should go about formulating a hypothesis.

9.4.2   Why the formulation of a hypothesis is a necessary step in your research process

There are simply too many facts in the world for the researcher to become acquainted with all of them, or to investigate everything in the world. Any scientific investigation/search/research must be for or against some view/proposition. Therefore, in order to demarcate their research, area, and to guide their collection of the data: that will try to answer the research question (the next step in the research process), the formulation of a hypothesis is essential to the researcher.

9.4.3   How to go about formulating your hypothesis/the requirements your hypothesis needs to meet

A hypothesis cannot be formulated in any random way; instead, it should meet a number of criteria. These are enumerated and discussed in the next section.
1. The hypothesis should, as stated in the definition above, be supported by research already done. This is one more reason for a thorough literature study. From the literature, and from a synthesis and a reflection on what you have read, especially from lacunae in the literature, you should get some idea of a suitable hypothesis for your research project. If you formulate a hypothesis that differs from or takes issue with what you have found in the literature, that is also acceptable, and even commendable; but then you must have a good reason why you disagree with the existing knowledge, i.e., you will have to substantiate your hypothesis thoroughly.
    For a practical example this first point, and the remaining points on the hypothesis, you will find one the end of this section.
2. The hypothesis should provide an answer to your research problem (once again, see definition of a hypothesis).
3   The hypothesis should be a researchable proposition; in other words, a proposition that can be investigated, and one for which you have the knowledge, time, and financial and infrastructural means to research.
4   The hypothesis should be formulated in as short, clear, and simple terms as possible.

In the example of hypothesis formation that follows, you will now find an illustration of these four requirements of a hypothesis, given as a practical example.

9.5 Research method: Choosing a method to investigate your research problem

After you have formulated you hypothesis, the next step in the research process is to test the hypothesis. You now have to choose an appropriate method to test the hypothesis.

9.5.1 Why your choice of a research method is important

As explained earlier the word 'method' comes from the ancient Greek word *methodologos*, which literally means 'the way', or 'the road'. As used here, as a part of the research process, it refers to the way in which you intend to conduct your research. The choice of and justification for a research method are a vital part of the research process. Bear in mind that at the outset of this chapter, research was defined as "methodically acquired, verified [...]. knowledge". Consequently, as a researcher, you will be required to state and to motivate (or justify) your choice of a research method. A large diversity of established, proven research methods exist. The next section will introduce you to this diversity, from which you will be able to choose an appropriate method to test your hypothesis, and to investigate your own research problem.

9.5.2 The variety of research methods

A myriad of research methods are available, from which you need to select the most suitable one. Keep in mind from this point that there are quantitative and qualitative research methods. You will first have to decide whether you should use a quantitative, or a qualitative method, or a combination of both. Good research may involve both.

▶ Quantitative methods may involve:
  › Sampling
  › Getting a representative sample
  › Measuring
  › Using statistical techniques to analyse your data.
▶ Qualitative methods may, in contrast:
  › Use a small number of data-rich subjects
  › Not be concerned with only the generalisability of the research findings.
  › Thoroughly investigate, interrogate and interpret a relatively small number of subjects, so as to throw up new perspectives on the theme, subject or problem under research.

You will very rarely use only one method in a research project. Usually, a researcher uses a number of methods. To distinguish between the variety of methods, and when they are to be used, Robson (2011) identified four levels of methods, namely:

- ☑ Research design
- ☑ Methods of data collection
- ☑ Methods of data analysis
- ☑ Methods of data interpretation.

A review of the spectrum of methods with respect to each level is now presented. Only a very brief overview can be given within the scope of this chapter. Before choosing the methods for your research project, you should consult other chapters in this book, where some of these methods are discussed in more detail, and also in other books on research methodology.

It is important that you make a thorough study of the basic, standard, authoritative research methodology books in your field. In fact, ideally you should have your own personal copy of each of these on your desk – readily available at any time – while you are busy with your research. In the field of education, for example, Leedy and Ormrod (2013); Gall, Gall & Borg (2007), and Neuman (2011) are widely regarded as authorities; and their books are used as standard reference works on research methodology.

9.5.3 Research design

Leedy and Ormrod (2013:74) define research design as "a general strategy for solving a research problem". De Wet, et al. (1982:12–13) distinguish between the following research designs:

- ▶ *Descriptive research*: This is research aimed at getting information on an existing situation, for example, research to measure how good the short-term memory of 17-year-old adolescents is.
- ▶ Theory formation: This is where the body of scientific literature on a particular topic is surveyed and synthesised into a new formulation, a new theory, for example, a study of published literature on substance abuse among adolescents.
- ▶ *Experimental research*: This is where the researcher manipulates one variable, called the independent variable, in order to determine the effect of that variable on another variable, called the dependent variable. In this context, to manipulate means the researcher deliberately changes the size/value/intensity of one variable, called the independent variable, in order to observe the effect on another variable. An example would be where the researcher wants to determine the effect of physical training (independent variable) on short-term memory (dependent variable). Different groups of people (research subjects) are then subjected to different regimes of physical training for a period of time. After a period of time, the researcher measures the short-term memory of the research subjects, and determines whether there is a relation between the amounts of physical training, which a subject has undergone, and the research subject's short-term memory.
- ▶ *Ex-post facto design*: This is where the researcher does not manipulate the variables; but the variables, as they appear in their natural state, are used. The following example from our ongoing school research project may use an ex-post facto design, as will be shown.

What if ...? Ex-post facto research design

In the research about the effect of cellphones on achievement in English language, the researcher has, in the natural course of events, two groups of learners available for the study: those with and those without cellphones. To determine the whether cellphone use has any possible effect on the achievement levels of the researcher-teacher's English learners, she simply compares the English results of those who possess cellphones with those who do not.

The classification of research design given here is only one of many, and is very broad. Before deciding on the best design for your research project, read Chapter 10 on Research design.

Once you have decided on a suitable research design, the next step is to choose a method or methods to collect the data.

9.5.4   The collection of data

The most common methods of collecting data include:

▶ *The questionnaire*: If you are doing research on how the South African voters view the various political parties and political leaders, the obvious way to probe them would be by means of a survey.

▶ *The interview*: In some instances, an interview is a better way of doing survey research than a questionnaire. Your research questions may be complex, and you want to make sure your research subjects understand each question put to them. In this case, an interview would be better than a questionnaire. The two main types of interview are: the individual interview (where the researcher interviews one research subject at a time); and the group interview (where the researcher interviews more than one research subject simultaneously).

▶ *The focus group discussion*: This is where between eight and 20 research subjects discuss a topic, with the researcher as the facilitator. The difference between a group interview and a focus group discussion is that with the group interview most communication is between the researcher and the research subject/s; whereas in a focus group discussion, most of the communication takes place between the research subjects themselves.

▶ *Observation*: If you want, for example, to research children's behaviour in a playground, the most obvious way would be to simply observe them.

▶ *Literature study*: In some research projects, the usual way to collect the data is by means of a study of the literature. If you want to do research on the 1994 elections in South Africa, the logical method of data collection would be to survey the publications of the local print media in 1994.

▶ *Documentary analysis*: In some research projects, the data are collected by means of a documentary analysis. If you, for example, want to do research on the historical evolution of a political party's views on education, then you would need to get hold of all the policy documents or statements of that party.

▶ *Tapping the existing databases*: Sometimes, the researcher is in the fortunate position where all the data needed are already available in existing databases. In education, for example, UNESCO hosts a vast database; and this is freely available on the website (http://www.uis.unesco.org).

These are the most common methods of data collection. Many other less commonly-used forms of data collection exist. An indication of these methods of data collection can be obtained from other research methodology books, as well as from published research articles, books, theses and dissertations. You are further advised to read Chapters 11, 12, 13, 14, 15, 16, 17, 18, 19 and 20, for more clarity on data-collection methods.

Data collection requires attention to research ethics. When your collection of data involves human beings, as research in the social sciences and humanities frequently does, you have to pay attention to research ethics. In an age of human rights, you should also – when conducting research – always respect the human rights of your research subjects.

Many institutions of higher education and all research institutions require ethical clearance before allowing research that involves human subjects. Many journals have an editorial policy only to accept articles involving human beings as research subjects on condition that a certificate of approval from the ethical clearance committee of the university of the author is submitted.

9.5.5 Analysis of data

To analyse the data means to look for patterns in the dataset. Once you have collected your data, you will now have to analyse the data mass, in order to make sense out of it. Data analysis, in the case of quantitative research, differs markedly from that of qualitative research.

9.5.5.1 Quantitative research

When you engage in quantitative research, you make use of statistical techniques. Several categories of statistical techniques exist:

▶ The first category is called descriptive statistics. Descriptive statistical techniques are used to summarise your data. The following are the most commonly used of these techniques: the mean, the median, the standard deviation, and the interquartile range. Let us return to the example of research on the short-term memory of adolescents. Suppose you took 1,000 adolescents and gave them a list of words to memorise for one minute. You would then test them to see how many words each one could recall after one minute. Now you have 1,000 values. In order to make sense of this mass of information, you calculate the average number of words that each adolescent could memorise. This value is the mean value. The concepts of median, standard deviation and interquartile range will be explained in later chapters in this book that deal with quantitative research.

▶ The second category of statistical techniques, inferential statistical techniques, is more complicated than descriptive statistical techniques. These techniques are used to determine whether two sets of data differ significantly. For example, (to return once again to the example of the research on the short-term memory of adolescents), you may wish to determine whether the short-term memory of male adolescents differs from that of female adolescents. You would then utilise inferential statistical techniques. Some of the most commonly used inferential statistical techniques are: Student's t-test; Analysis of variance (ANOVA); the Krushkal-Wallace test; the Mann-Whitney test; the Kolmogorov-Smirnov test; and the Chi-square test.

▶ A third category of statistical techniques is used to determine whether a relationship exists between two variables. These techniques include: correlation coefficients, such as Pearson's correlation coefficient, Spearman's rank-order correlation coefficient, and Kendall's coefficient of concordance. A correlation index is a measure of the relationship or co-variation between two variables. If you want to determine, for example, whether there is a relation or co-variance between adolescents' short-term memory and their achievement in history at school, Pearson's correlation coefficient would be an excellent technique to use. More advanced techniques of this type include: factor analysis, and cluster analysis, which fall beyond the scope of this chapter and book, but about which you can read in books on advanced statistical techniques.

This is a very superficial survey of the variety of statistical techniques available to the researcher. Two comments are appropriate here. Firstly, consult a statistician to assist you with choosing and applying the best statistical technique for your research project. Secondly, a full discussion of statistical methods, explaining the basic range of statistical techniques, their rationale, and their application potential, is not possible within the limitations of this chapter and book. However, given the importance of statistics as a research tool, we recommend strongly that you enrol for an introductory course in statistics. This is one of the best investments you could make, and it will yield dividends for the rest of your research career.

9.5.5.2 Qualitative research

As far as qualitative research is concerned, statistical methods are not the primary methodology. Instead, the emphasis is on interpretation, the next level of methodology. However, one highly-rated technique is ATLAS, a computer program, which is a valuable aid in qualitative data analysis. In this instance, you should also consult an ATLAS expert on the advisability of using ATLAS for analysing the data of your project – and if advisable, to assist you with the analysis.

While you could benefit greatly from an introductory course in statistics and in ATLAS analysis, both these topics are far too complex to be fully covered in this book. The data-analysis techniques outlined in this section are, however, unpacked in more detail in the four chapters in Part 3 of this book. Studying these chapters at this stage should increase your comprehension of the full range of data-analysis methods available to the researcher. It would also act as a scaffold, making it easier for you to work your way through a course in statistics and/or ATLAS analysis.

When you have completed the analysis your data, the analysed data should be interpreted, in order to make sense of your theme, problem and hypothesis.

9.5.6 Interpretation of the data

As a researcher, you cannot stop with an analysis of your data. After organising your data mass into manageable, understandable proportions, you should proceed to attach a particular meaning or understanding to your analysed data. Several methodological tools to enable you to interpret the data are at your disposal.

At the first level, a distinction can be made between three kinds or levels of **interpretation** of analysed data: description, interpretation, and critical analysis.

▶ The first level is description, the most elementary way of interpreting the data. This entails a mere systematic description of the data. An example is when you have studied the national Acts governing education in South Africa, and you then write a systematic account of these Acts and their contents.

▶ At a more advanced level, you could actively interpret and no longer merely report the data. For example, in research on the education system of France, you could interpret the French system in terms of the societal forces, such as the broad social system, history, economy, political system, etc. in France over a particular time period.

These are the factors which have shaped and given the French education system its particular character. Finally, the researcher could critically interrogate the analysed data, and also the existing state of knowledge, on a topic. For an example of the latter, read Wolhuter's (2011) critical survey on the state of research of doctoral education in South Africa. In Chapters 2, 3 and 4 these three forms of interpretation of data are unpacked in greater detail. Particular methods of data interpretation include: the historical method, ethnography, phenomenology, phenomenography, and the comparative method.

▶ The historical method arranges the data in a historical sequence, and reconstructs an integrative narrative. An example would be research on the South African education system. Current South African education is the outcome of a long process of historical evolution; and is the product of the forces at play at various times in history. In order to understand the present South African education system therefore, it would make sense, to reconstruct the historical development of the South African education system.

▶ Ethnography comes from the two Greek words, *ethnos* meaning a group of people with a common culture; and *graphos* meaning 'to describe'. Ethnography is about describing the unique culture of a small community, even the culture of a school, or of a specific class. For an example of a study using this method of data interpretation, see: Van der Westhuizen, et al., 2008.

▶ In an age of individualisation and human rights, the individual has become increasingly important; at the research level. This is true of many disciplines, not only in the humanities, but also in the social sciences. It is here where the methods of phenomenology and phenomenography appear to be most suitable. Phenomenology comprises the methods used by the researcher to reconstruct the individual's (research subject) experience of things, events and contexts, and especially the meanings he or she attaches to these situations. Here, the individual's personal frame of reference is reconstructed. For an example of this, read Milligan's (2003) research on how education influences the formation of identity among children in the Philippines.

▶ Phenomenography is a method, which was established by Ference Marton and his research associates at the University of Göteborg in Sweden in the 1980s, as a departure from phenomenology which attempts to reconstruct individuals' experience and their individual attachment of meaning. Unlike phenomenology's strict limitation to each individual's experience and attachment of meaning as unique, phenomenography goes on to try and classify individuals' experiences and their attachment of meaning by groups/categories of individuals. An example is Brew's (2001) study on how seniors experience research.

▶ The comparative method entails the comparison of different cases. In research into education, the method of international comparisons is frequently used (Crossley & Watson, 2011:103). The international comparative method means that education systems and institutions are compared, where they function in various national contexts. In this way, different countries can learn from one another's experiences in the field of education.

Before proceeding to the final step of the research process, namely, the writing up of your research, you should be aware of a major current concern in the established set of research methods. This concern is explained next.

A southern perspective

Within the scope of this book, a final, but very serious remark is apt, leaving you with a challenging assignment. The research methods surveyed in this chapter were all conceived in the mainstream of the international academic network: that is, Western Europe and North America. A case could be made that research methods are universal and not context-bound. Yet, how far the interests of the societies of the global South are served by these methods is also a moot point. Reflect on this question in the light of having read Chapter 1 on Afrocentricity as a research philosophy. This question, and the quest for a satisfactory answer, will probably occupy you for the rest of your research career. But it is worth pondering and pursuing.

    You should certainly come back to this question again, after you have worked your way through this book

9.6   Drawing conclusions

The research process culminates in the conclusions you draw. This section falls into four sections:

▸ In the first section, you should venture an answer to the research problem, on the basis of your results, which you have obtained from your data analysis and interpretation. It is important that this answer be substantiated by results from your data analysis and interpretation.

▸ Secondly, the new knowledge, which you have derived from your research, should be built into the existing edifice of scientific knowledge/theory. Remember, research was defined (at the start of the chapter) as methodically acquired, verified, systematised knowledge. Here, 'systematised' means that the new knowledge which your data analysis and interpretation have yielded, cannot be left in isolation, but should be integrated into the existing body of knowledge. Here, once again, the importance of a thorough literature study is underscored. The literature study will provide the theoretical structure into which you can build your own newly-established knowledge.

▸ Thirdly, ideally you should also use your research findings to make recommendations for the improvement of practice. We say 'ideally' as not all research lends itself readily to this. Theoretical ('blue sky') research is a case in point, in which case, you would state the limitations of your research. Here, you should be honest, and point out the shortcomings of your research in terms of, say, sample size or methods.

▸ This leads to the fourth and final part of the conclusion, namely, recommendations for further research.

9.7   Writing a research report

The high point of conducting a research project is the writing up of the research. It is necessary to do this is in order to disseminate your research findings, and to make them available to the wider academic community. This enables other researchers to read the results of your research as part of their literature survey, and, together with their own research, to integrate your research into the existing body of knowledge. Thus, you contribute to the progress of science. Failing to write up and disseminate the results of your research is not only a waste of research resources, but it denies the wider academic community the benefit of a new, interesting and worthwhile contribution to the corpus of knowledge.

A research report can take on many forms. These include a dissertation, a thesis, a monograph, an article in a scholarly journal, a book, or a chapter in a book, a conference paper, or an unpublished research report.

Toolbox Structuring a research report

The structure of the report is basically the same as the sequence of steps of the research process, as surveyed earlier in this chapter:

▶ *Title*: The title of your research report should be formulated with great care. The title should comply with the following criteria: Firstly, it should be able to draw attention and arouse interest in your potential readers; it should be serious but engaging and inspired. Secondly, the title should suggest the content. It should not be broader or narrower than the content. The title should give your reader a one-line synopsis of what the research report is all about. Finally, the title should not be too long. It should be as short as possible. Many scholarly journals have an editorial policy of limiting the number of words a title can contain, 15 words being the common maximum.

▶ *Research problem*: You should state your problem, motivate why it is a problem (a *lacunus* or gap in the body of published research, and/or an issue for which practice needs guidance), and why it is worth researching that problem.

▶ *Literature survey*

▶ *Hypothesis/hypotheses*

▶ *Research method*: You should explain your research method, and also motivate why your method is the best method to research your problem. As to how much detail you should give on the research method; the rule is that you must explain sufficient, so that the reader would be able to repeat your research. Remember, scientific knowledge was defined as "methodically acquired, *verified*, scientific knowledge". The verified implies that the research is replicable under the same conditions. Findings: In this section, you should report the outcome of your data analysis, as well as your interpretation of the analysed data.

▶ *Conclusion*: Here you should provide, on the basis of your findings, an answer to your research problem. You should also build your findings into the corpus of existing knowledge, and spell out the implications of your findings for the *improvement of practice*. Finally, you should declare the limitations of your research, and, in order to complete the research cycle, you should make recommendations for further research.

It is important to keep in mind that your research report should be written in clear and concise language. It is good practice to make use of a professional language editor to do a final language edit of your report. In fact, many journal editors require a certificate from an accredited language editor – certifying that your report had been properly language-edited – before they will publish your research. A research report is also not the place to use arrogant or bombastic language, or informal terms and slang. Furthermore, vilification, hate speech, and emotional language have no place in a research report.

Aspects of the writing of your research report are unpacked in more detail in other chapters of this book (chiefly in Part 4). Academic writing is more rigorous, and has more stringent requirements than you might think from the very brief discussion of the writing of a research report that has been done in this chapter. In Chapter 29, you can find a more detailed treatment of the requirements of academic writing. You are advised to read this chapter closely before you embark on the writing of a research report as it might well save you from the need to rewrite your report at a later stage.

In Chapters 26 and 27, you can read more about the specifics of respectively, reporting quantitative and qualitative research findings. One of the stringent requirements of academic writing is the need to be meticulous about citing and referencing literature and sources. These requirements merit a chapter of their own; and Chapter 28 takes you through referencing. Finally, the most prestigious research output is always in the form of publications (books, chapters in books, and above all, articles in peer-reviewed scholarly journals). That too is a field on its own with its own rules; however, you will be investing well in your research career by reading Chapter 30.

Conclusion

Now that you are more fully acquainted with the steps in the research process – identifying and formulating a research problem; how to conduct a literature survey; how to formulate a hypothesis; the choice and application of an appropriate research design; the methods of data collection, analysis and interpretation; and finally, the correct way of writing up your research – you are well equipped to embark on a research project of your own.

When you follow the steps set out in this chapter, backed up by what you have read in the others chapters, you have the necessary equipment to launch your research career, and to make your personal contribution to the world of science and of knowledge. We are sure you will find it rewarding – possibly one of the most rewarding things you attempt in life – and wish you every success.

Closing activities

Before you embark on a full research project of your own, it might be well worthwhile first doing the following activities as a 'dry run'. This will make it easier for you and save you a lot of time and wasted effort before you start in earnest on your own project.

1 From your own professional experience or outside observation, from the newspapers of the past week, and from three editions of different journals, identify two problems/themes, which you would be interested in researching.

2 With each of the problems/themes you have identified, go through all the steps in this stage of the research process: The formulation of a problem. Do a mini-literature research, involving one article or chapter in a book, on the problem/theme. Write a hypothesis and choose a research design, and the methods of data collection, analysis and interpretation. Write up these steps.

Bibliography

Boote, D.N. & Beile, P. 2005. Scholars before Researchers: On the Centrality of the Dissertation Literature Review in Research Preparation. *Educational Researcher*, 34(6):3–15.

Brew, A. 2001. Conceptions of research: a Phenomenographic study. *Studies in Higher Education*, 26:271–285.

Coombs, P.H. 1985. *The World Crisis in Education: The view from the eighties.* New York: Oxford University Press.

Crossley, M. & Watson, K. 2011. Comparative and international education. In J. Furlong & M. Law (Eds). 2011. *Disciplines in education: Their role in the future of educational research.* London: Routledge.

De Wet, J.J., Monteith, J.L.de K., Steyn, H.S. & Venter, P.A. 1982. *Navorsingsmetodes in die Opvoedkunde.* Durban: Butterworth.

Gall, M.D., Gall, J.P. & Borg, W.R. 2007. *Educational Research: An introduction.* Upper Saddle River, NJ: Pearson Education.

Leedy, P.D. & Ormrod, J.E. 2013. *Practical Research: Planning and Design.* Boston: Pearson.

Milligan, J.A. 2003. Teaching between the Cross and the Crescent Moon: Islamic Identity, Postcoloniality and Public Education in the Southern Philippines. *Comparative Education Review*, 47(4):468–492.

Neuman, W.L. 2011. *Social Research Methods: Qualitative and Quantitative Approaches*. Boston: Allyn & Bacon.

Robson, C. 2011. *Real World Research: a resource for users of social science research methods in applied settings*. Chichester, West Sussex: John Wiley.

Stoker, H.G. 1969. *Beginsels en metodes in die wetenskap*. Potchefstroom: Pro Rege.

UNESCO. 2014. Statistics. Available at http://www.uis.unesco.org. Accessed 29 July 2014.

Van der Westhuizen, P.C., Oosthuizen, I.J. & Wolhuter, C.C. 2008. The Relationship between an Effective Organizational Culture and Student Discipline in a Boarding School. *Education and Urban Society*, 40(2):205–225.

Wolhuter, C.C. 2008 Review of the Review: Constructing the identity of comparative education. *Research in Comparative and International Education*, 3(4):323–344.

Wolhuter, C.C. 2011. Research on doctoral education in South African education against the silhouette of its meteoric rise in international education research. *Perspectives in Education*, 29(3):126–138.

CHAPTER 10

Micheal van Wyk and Matshidiso Taole

Research design

KEY CONCEPTS

Design is the framework or plan of action used to conduct an investigation.

Research design is the blueprint which directs you in finding your way towards executing your plan for your research methodology.

Experimental design is a type of research design based on research by studying the causes, to establish the effects of the relationship between variables

Quasi-experimental design uses elements of both experimental and quasi-experimental whereby the treatment and control groups are compared in the study.

Transformative paradigm focuses on the experiences of individuals who suffer discrimination or oppression, and involves engaging in research that addresses power differentials.

LEARNING OUTCOMES

By the end of this chapter, you should be able to:

▶ Define and provide an example of a research design for your study.

▶ Explain the main functions of research design.

▶ Discuss the importance of having a research design before starting your study.

▶ Identify the components that need to be described in a research design.

▶ Discuss research design as a conceptually inclusive approach to research.

▶ Select whether to employ quantitative, qualitative or mixed methods approaches in the research study.

Case study: The *Vasa*: Spectacular but flawed in design

The King of Sweden, Gustav II, decided in the seventeenth century to build the most impressive warships so that Sweden could rule the waves. The King instructed shipbuilders to build a fleet of the best-equipped warships to conquer the world and expand his ideas for economic and political domination. The King commissioned his architects to design a warship, the *Vasa*, which would be one of largest ships ever built in the seventeenth century. The building work started in August 1628 and was completed eight months later. The ship was launched with great celebrations in Stockholm harbour. After the ceremony, the *Vasa*'s anchors were weighed and she sailed out of the harbour. A strong wind picked up and suddenly, the ship keeled over and sank in the harbour to the great dismay and disbelief of the King and his many guests. The King was disgusted and ordered an immediate investigation into this tragedy. Findings revealed that the ballast compartments had not been made large enough to balance the two big gundecks, as specified by the King, which made the warship unstable for sailing. It was also found that if the shipbuilders had added more ballast the ship would not have sunk. The *Vasa*, as the largest Swedish warship of its time, was well planned and built, meeting all criteria, but it lacked a general theory of design. The shipbuilders did not calculate stability as an essential component of a good design for the ship.

Introduction

This chapter defines research design and provides criteria for choosing an appropriate research design for your study. The main functions of research design for your study are discussed, with examples. It is important that you are empowered with this information so that you have a solid understanding of research design before starting your study. Several components that need to be included in a research design are highlighted. Lastly, criteria are provided for selecting whether to employ a quantitative, qualitative or mixed methods approach for your research study.

10.1 What is research design?

Obviously a good research design is well planned and its components work harmoniously together to fit the study. In this section, you will learn what exactly a research design is, and the specific functions it entails.

Punch (2011:62) defines research design as "[...] means all the issues involved in planning and executing a research project – from identifying the problem through to reporting and publishing the results". Wengraf (2002) is of the view that research design situates the researcher in the empirical world, and connects the research questions to the data and findings of the study. Further, Punch (2011:63) says it is a "[...] basic plan for a piece of research and includes four main ideas [...] the strategy, the conceptual framework, the question of what will be studied and the tools and the procedures for collecting and analysing empirical materials." It is your plan of action in which you decide how you will communicate your framework for the study.

It is evident from these definitions that a research design is a detailed plan of how you are going to conduct your research. Now that we have defined research design, the next section discusses the functions of a research design.

10.2 What are the functions of a research design?

Before you choose your research design, you need to know what the specific functions of your study's research design are. Any research design captures two very important aspects:
- The identification and development of specific processes and procedures of the research plan of action to conduct your research study; and
- The specific design that informs the procedures to ensure that the design is valid, accurate, and sets out objectives to be achieved.

Let us now discuss how to select a specific research design for the investigation.

10.2.1 Selecting a research design

It is important to decide at the outset the type of research design you want to use, that is, decide whether you want to use e quantitative, qualitative or mixed method design for your study. For the purpose of this chapter, we provide three types of research designs.

10.2.2.1 Study designs in quantitative research

In research design, there are different types of enquiry within qualitative, quantitative and mixed methods approaches that provide a specific direction for the purpose and procedures of the research.

For example, in quantitative research there are two types of designs that can be used:
- True experimental design
- Quasi-experimental design.

These designs will be explained in detail later, in section 10.3.

10.2.2.2 Qualitative research designs

In contrast to quantitative research design, qualitative research design demonstrates a different approach to research enquiry; this design relies on text and image data. (Silverman, 2011; Singleton & Straits, 2010). Creswell (2013) explains that a plethora of designs exist for this approach, as exemplified by the 28 that are identified by Tesch (1990), and the 22 identified by Wolcott (2009), as well as the five that Creswell (2013) identifies. The five designs identified by Creswell (2013) include:

- Narrative enquiry-based
- Phenomenology
- Ethnography
- Case study
- Grounded theory.

These five designs will also be explained in detail later, in section 10.3.

10.2.2.3 Mixed methods research design

In this section, we focus on the research design of the mixed methods approach. There is much literature about mixed methods design, indicating that it is an approach to enquiry involving collecting both quantitative and qualitative data.

Several authors describe the mixed methods approach as a combination of qualitative and quantitative designs which provides a more complete understanding of a research problem than either approach alone (Denzin & Lincoln, 2013; Creswell, 2013).

There are three basic mixed methods designs, namely;
- Convergent parallel
- Explanatory sequential
- Exploratory sequential mixed method designs.

These mixed methods designs will be explained in later sections of this chapter.

Before we focus on selecting types of quantitative designs, Figure 10.1 gives a brief constructive alignment of the major research design types.

FIGURE 10.1: Constructive alignment of major research designs

Of particular interest among the mixed methods designs is the convergent parallel mixed methods design because of its relevance to the research study that is being embarked upon in this research project. According to Creswell (2013:219), mixed methods design "is when the researcher collects both quantitative and qualitative data, analyses it separately and then compares the results to see if the findings confirm or disconfirm each other".

Before you continue with the next section of this chapter, complete the activity.

Stop and reflect

After studying the types of research designs, answer the following questions:
1 What is research design and why is it important to have an appropriate research design?
2 What are the functions of research design and why would you choose a particular research design?

In the following section, we will focus on the importance of selecting a type of quantitative research design.

10.3 Selecting a type of quantitative research design

There are several types of quantitative designs, which are chosen on the basis of three specific elements:
▸ The size/number of the population in the study under investigation
▸ The importance and reference of the research study
▸ The nature of the investigation of the phenomenon.

10.3.1 Studies based on the size or number of the population under investigation

In Table 10.1, a summary of types, objective/purpose and example of quantitative research studies based on size and number of the population is presented.

TABLE 10.1: Studies based on size and number of the population under investigation.

Type of study	Objective/Purpose of the type of study	Example of type of study
Cross-sectional studies	The aim of this type of study is targeted at exploring situations, problems, attitudes and issues using cross-sectional populations.	The extent of youth unemployment in South Africa
Pre- and post-test design studies	These studies, also called the before- and after studies, measure the effect of or change in a situation, aspect of a problem, or issue. This type of study is used to measure the impact or effectiveness of an intervention strategy.	The effects of teams, games and tournaments on achievement, retention and the attitudes of economics education students
Longitudinal studies	This type of study is researched over a period of time. In this design, the study is revisited several of times at regular intervals over a long period.	The extent of unemployment in South Africa 2000—2010: A longitudinal study

10.3.2 Study designs based on importance and reference period

In Table 10.2, a summary of the types of study based on importance and period of reference is provided.

TABLE 10.2: Study designs based on importance and reference period under investigation

Type of study	Objective/Purpose of the type of study	Example of type of study
Retrospective design	This design is to conduct, explore or study a phenomenon, event, problem, challenge or situation from available data for the period.	The relationship between levels of unemployment and street crime (which can be retrospective as well as prospective in design)
Prospective design	This design is common in studying a phenomenon, event, problem, challenge, or situation, but attempts to establish the outcome of the event or research study	The impact of parental involvement on the level of academic performance of their children.
Retrospective-prospective design	This type of design focuses on past trends of a study and compares with previous findings to conduct research in the future.	The impact of an advertising campaign for washing power on the sale of the product.

10.3.3 Studies based on nature of investigation

In this section, we discuss studies based on the nature of research which focus on exploring a phenomenon, event, problem or situations is tabulated. On the basis of the nature of the study, these are:
▸ Experimental designs
▸ Quasi-experimental designs

10.3.3.1 Experimental designs

Experimental design involves doing something and seeing what happen. That is, you manipulate variables. The variables are independent and dependent variables. In an experimental design, the independent variables are manipulated. Take a look at the following example to help you understand:

Manipulating variables in experimental design

In a study of the effects of cooperative teaching methods in performance improvement for Grade 5 learners, the independent variable will be the cooperative teaching method, and the dependent variable will be learner achievement. The dependent variable is the phenomenon you observe for change. In this example, the change we want to see is improved learner performance. The design will answer the important questions : Does the removal of the independent variable change the situation? or Does the adding of the independent variable change the situation? The researcher has two groups, the experiment group, and the control group. The experiment group will be the group that is exposed to cooperative teaching methods, whereas the control group will be the group that is not be exposed to cooperative teaching methods. In order to see the manipulation of an independent variable, in this case, cooperative teaching methods, we need to do a pretest before conducting the experiment. A pretest will tell us about learners' performance scores before the test, that is, before being taught using cooperative teaching methods. But we will also need a control group, that is, a group that is not exposed to cooperative teaching methods, in order to see if cooperative teaching methods make a difference in learners' performance.

Next, we explain randomly assigned groups and types of experimental research design.

10.3.3.2 Randomly assigned groups

Randomly assigning groups is done when the population to be studied is greater than the number of individuals you can study, that is, you have specified characteristics of subjects to include in the study. In the earlier example, all Grade 5 learners will be eligible to participate in the study. All subjects stand a chance of being selected for in the study. The researcher can put the names of all learners in a box and then draw them randomly. In this type of research design, the researcher has control over the experiment. The research design here focuses on the following kinds of questions: *who, what, when, where* and *how* the research is conducted.

Random assigning in experimental design e.g.

Suppose you decide to conduct an experiment to test the impact of a particular teaching method, the jigsaw cooperative learning method, on the academic performance of second-year economics students, to understand the effectiveness of the teaching method. In this study, the relationship between cause and effect is measured. The researcher has control over the *who* (economics students who participate in the experimental study) and the *what* (jigsaw teaching method) and its relationship to academic performance in economics students. In this type of design, economics students are randomly assigned to treatment and control groups to ensure that both groups are comparable.

Figure 10.2 shows the randomisation of an experimental design for the above example.

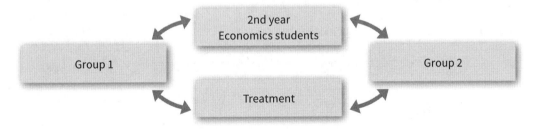

FIGURE 10.2: Randomly assigned groups

In random design, the second-year economics student population, and the experimental treatments are randomly assigned for the study. In this design, the unit of study, all second-year economics students, have an *equal* and *independent* chance of selection or being assigned to groups.

10.3.3.3 Types of experimental designs

In this section there are several different types of experimental designs that can be considered. A brief description of each is outlined.

▸ *One-shot case study*. This design is referred to as one-group post-test-only. It is used to determine whether an event, intervention or treatment has any effect on a group of participants. The dependent variable is measured once after the event, intervention or treatment, and conclusions are drawn.

- *Multi-group post-test-only design.* In this design more than one group is used, for example, you might have four to five experimental groups
- *Longitudinal case study design.* This design has features of both one-shot case study design and multi-group case study design, except that it provides for more measurements of the dependent variable.
- *One-group pretest–post-test design.* In this design there is measurement of a dependent variable within one group and there is no independent variable. The independent variable will be introduced and the dependent variable will be measured at a later stage.
- *Ex-post-facto design.*This design provides an alternative means by which a researcher can investigate the extent to which a specific independent variable might possibly affect the dependent variable of interest in the study.

10.3.3.4 Quasi-experimental design

Quasi-experiments are defined as experiments that do not have random assignment of research participants to two or more groups. This approach uses elements of both true experimental and quasi-experimental designs, whereby elements of variables are controlled by the researcher. As explained in section 10.3.3.2, random assignment can be used as a technique for controlling all known and unknown extraneous variables by equating the groups at the start of an experiment.

Quasi-experimental design

Several studies have indicated that early dropping out from school among youth has impacted on their later years regarding involvement in crime, unemployment, and general welfare. Research further puts these young people at a lower welfare and economic status compared with those who finish Grade 12 and further their tertiary studies. School dropouts among youth at high school level are most common in lower-income families. According to research studies, it is not possible to randomly assign these youth dropouts to the street kids group, or to say they get involved in crime, because this particular study focuses on the impact of early dropout compared with those who complete their post-school studies. In this case, the researcher can control the variables of the investigation in this type of design.

Stop and reflect

1 What is quasi-experimental design?
2 Contrast the differences between an experimental and a quasi-experimental design
3 What makes this a quasi-experimental rather than an experimental design?
4 Why is the greater incidence of school dropouts among lower income families a confounding factor to this study?

Now we will focus on the importance of selecting a type of qualitative research design.

10.4 Selecting types of qualitative research design

We look at some qualitative designs, such as the case study design, the narrative-based inquiry design, phenomenology, grounded theory, and ethnography.

10.4.1 Case study design

Case study designs have been repeatedly used in the fields of psychology, sociology and education. In addition to these fields, Merriam (2001) also suggests that the case study may be found in other fields that have ethnographic and historical orientations. Punch (2011:145) also emphasises that the case study is an empirical research method, which:

▶ Investigates a contemporary phenomenon within its real-life context.
▶ Is used when the boundaries between phenomena and context are not clearly evident.
▶ Relies on the use of multiple sources of evidence.

10.4.1.1 Defining a case study

Several authors provide definitions of the case study as a research design.

Punch (2011:4) defines a case study as "[…] a study of a bounded system, emphasising the unity and wholeness of that system, but confining the attention to those aspects that are relevant to the research at the time". Rule and Vaughn (2011:4) state that "the case study is an empirical inquiry that investigates a contemporary phenomenon within its real life context, especially when the boundaries between phenomenon and context are not clearly evident."

From these definitions, case studies are described as intensive descriptions and analyses of an individual, event, group, or community. In summary, case studies are types of qualitative research design.

In view of the definitions provided, Table 10.3 indicates specific features and examples of case study research design.

TABLE 10.3: Features and examples of case studies

Features of case studies	Example of cases
▶ Each case study has a specific boundary which is identified at an early stage of the study. ▶ The researcher is interested in each case study because of the unit of study to be clarified. ▶ Each case study investigates with the aim of preserving the wholeness and integrity of the case. To achieve the objective of the study, a problem must be established that is geared to specific features of the case.	▶ You are studying a single school, and this includes staff meetings, teachers, and classroom activities. ▶ You investigate a case of bullying at school in relation to age, gender and status. ▶ You investigate the case of gambling amongst women aged between 30-50 years, within specific income levels.

Think and link

A short introduction to case study research design is on YouTube at www.youtube.com/watch?v=bOqwfxhT2E0

10.4.1.2 Displaying case study designs

In this section, we will briefly describe the types of displaying case study designs. To illustrate this, Ritchie and Lewis(2003) identify several types of displaying case study designs:

▶ *Displaying range and diversity case study design.* After collecting and reporting the data, we need to describe classifications developed from within the data set of the case. In the reporting of data, there might be a range of attitudes, beliefs, judgements and action.

- *Displaying linkage case study design.* After collecting the data, patterns within the data set, detected linkages and associations between phenomena, often bring crucial insights during analysis. Through this, certain evidence needs to be conveyed to allow more sets of phenomena that may linked to the group, or be attached to a specific sub-group under investigation. In reporting the data, several important issues in displaying linkages in the data set are the evidence available to support the linkage, or the description of circumstances in which connections may change, and there may well be exceptions to the associations in the data.
- *Displaying typologies case study design.* Typologies define, describe and display the different segments in the project population, or different manifestations of the phenomena.

10.4.1.3 The rationale for using case study design

Rule and Vaughn (2011:7) explain that case studies provide a thick, rich description of the case under investigation. Literature indicates that case studies can be conducted and applied for a variety of research studies. The rationale for using this design is:
- To explore a general problem within a focused setting.
- To generate theoretical insights in developing new knowledge.
- To test existing theory in reference to the case.
- To shed light on other similar cases hence providing a level of generalisation that makes case studies more relevant to the study.

Before you go on to the next section on narrative design, read the following case study and complete the activity.

Case study: Investigating discrimination

Free State school staff guilty of hate speech
SAPA correspondent

The South African Human Rights Commission (SAHRC) has found a Bloemfontein school's staff guilty of hate speech towards black and coloured pupils. The school failed to create a learning environment free from harmful elements, such as racist utterances and demeaning remarks. This further violated both the right to education and children's rights. The commission made various recommendations for the school and the Free State education department. Free State education department spokesperson Howard Ndaba said no one had approached the department to complain of racism at the school, and when it tried to probe the matter, the department could not find anyone who was willing to give evidence. "We will now launch an internal investigation, but we can't proceed if no one is willing to give information." Ndaba said the department could not take action against the staff based on the SAHRC report because it did not contain allegations against particular staff members. The SAHRC found that the school staff's racist remarks constituted a clear incident of hate speech, and by extension, violated pupils' rights to equality and human dignity. Ndaba said the department welcomed the SAHRC report. "We will make sure we implement the recommendations of the report."

(**Source:** Adapted from *Mail & Guardian*, 25 July 2014: http://mg.co.za/article/2014-07-24-free-state-school-staff-guilty-of-hate-speech)

Stop and reflect

Read the case study on discrimination, and answer the following questions
1 What is the unit of analysis for this case study and how could this challenge be solved from an Afrocentric perspective?
2 Who are the participants in this case and what is the incident for investigation
3 What type of case study is this? Motivate your answer?

10.4.2 Narrative research design

In this section, we will focus on definitions, characteristics, types and data analysis components of narrative research, as a qualitative approach.

10.4.2.1 Defining narrative design

Narrative research is a branch of interpretive research where "words do the work" (Frank, 2000). The basic assumption of narrative research is that human beings and stories are intrinsically linked. This design involves:
▶ The description of the lives of individuals
▶ The collection of individuals' stories of their experiences
▶ The discussion of the meaning of those experiences

10.4.2.2 Characteristics of a narrative design

Narrative-based research is an attempt to increase understanding of central issues related to teaching and learning through the telling and retelling of participants' stories. There are six key characteristics of a narrative research design:
▶ Focuses on the experiences of individuals.
▶ Concerned with the chronology of an individual's experiences.
▶ Focuses on the construction of life stories based on data collected through active interviews. Active interviewing emphasises the collaborative construction of the story.
▶ Uses re-storying as a technique for constructing the narrative account.
▶ Incorporates context and place in the story.
▶ Reflects a collaborative approach that involves the researcher and the participant in the negotiation of the final text.

10.4.2.3 Types of narrative design

In this section, we briefly explain the types of narrative design:
▶ *Re-storying*. The process in which the researcher gathers stories; analyses them for key elements of the story such as the time, place, or plot; and rewrites the story to place it in a chronological sequence.
▶ *Oral history*. A method for collecting data from participants by asking them to share their experiences. There are two ways to develop oral histories, namely: interviews using structured or unstructured protocols; annals and chronicles. The participant constructs a timeline and divides it into segments of significant events or memories.
▶ *Storytelling*. Telling stories should become a normative part of the data collection process. The use of many stories can provide researchers with many opportunities to add to their understanding of the participants' experiences.

▶ *Autobiographical and biographical writing.* This involves engaging the participants in writing about their perceptions of their experiences. Autobiographical and biographical writing also has the potential to broaden the researcher's understanding of past events and experiences that have impacted the participants' experiences.

Now we focus on the data analysis of this research design.

10.4.2.4 Data analysis in narrative design

Narrative researchers take an empathetic stance towards the data. Narrative design also assumes that multiple truths co-exist. Therefore a text can be read many times and yield different interpretations each time it is read. Analysis of data in a narrative design includes:
▶ Data managing
▶ Reading
▶ Describing
▶ Classifying
▶ Interpreting
▶ Representing, visualising.

10.4.2.5 Different methods of analysis

There are several methods of data analysis that one can use in narrative research design. The data could be in the form of a text, transcript of recorded interviews, documents, stories and/or photos. The aim of the analysis is to understand the meaning that people create, or to understand what make sense to the participants, or even to understand why people do things and behave in the way they do.

▶ *Thematic analysis* .This is the analysis in qualitative research that focuses on identifying important information in the data and categorising it. The important information or themes should relate to the research question, and should describe the phenomenon under study. The researcher needs to read the data and identify possible themes. For example, in the study on how teachers experience curriculum change, possible themes from the research question: 'What are teachers' experiences of curriculum change?' would be positive experiences and negative experiences. It should be noted that the themes can be pre-determined or can be generated from the data.

▶ *Structural analysis.* Gall, et al. (2005) define structural analysis as involving a precise set of procedures for analysing qualitative data that do not need to be inferred from the data but are inherent features of the discourse, text, or events that the researchers are studying. Structural analysis is concerned with the way in which the narratives are organised, that is, the way in which words are used in the text. In particular, it involves the use of words, diagrams to analyse data, and making meaning or sense of the data. These can also be used to facilitate problem solving. Drawing makes explicit the emotions and brings out the creativity of the participants.

▶ *Interactional analysis/discourse analysis.* Communication forms the basis of human existence. People communicate to express their feelings, wishes, likes, or dislikes. Discourse analysis focuses on the use of words by participants to express themselves, air their opinions, or to interpret the world around them. Discourse analysis does not only deal with the literal meaning, but focuses on the deeper meaning. It takes into account the use of words by participants, participants' cultural and social orientations.

Let us now turn to the research design, phenomenology.

10.4.3 Phenomenology

In this section, we will briefly describe phenomenology as a research design.

10.4.3.1 Defining phenomenological study

Phenomenological study as a research design examines social experiences through the descriptions provided by the people involved. The social experiences are called the 'lived experiences' of participants in the study. The goal of phenomenological studies is to describe the experiences and their meaning for each subject.

Doing phenomenological research

In phenomenological studies, the researcher might want to conduct a study on the experiences of people living with AIDS. In this study, the researcher wants to get from the participants what it means to live with AIDS and how they feel about this. Importantly, the phenomenological study seeks to understand what it is to be human and how we construct knowledge. Data are presented from the perspective of the research participant(s).

Phenomenology emphasises the importance of personal perspective and interpretation, that is, meaning is constructed by the participants themselves. The researcher needs to 'bracket' his or her views and opinions about the phenomena under study. Information gathered in a phenomenological study can be used to inform, support or challenge policy and action. Using the same example, the researcher can use the information to inform the stakeholders on how best the disease can be managed, and what interventions are needed by the patients.

10.4.3.2 Types of phenomenology

There are two types of phenomenological studies to know about when deciding on a type of research design:
- Hermeneutical phenomenology
- Empirical, transcendental or psychological phenomenology.

These two types of phenomenological designs focus less on the interpretations of the researcher and more on a description of the experiences of participants. The researcher must first identify what she or he expects to discover and then deliberately put aside these ideas; this process is called bracketing (as you read earlier).

10.4.3.3 Data collection methods

Phenomenology involves gathering 'deep' information and perceptions through inductive, qualitative methods such as:
- Interviews
- Conversations
- Participant observation
- Action research
- Focus group discussions
- Analysis of personal texts.

Since this design deals with people, it is important that the researcher should establish a rapport and empathy to gain maximum information. Participants should not perceive the researcher as an outsider as this might hamper their openness to talking about their experiences.

10.4.3.4 Data analysis in phenomenology

Usually, phenomenological research yields large amounts of data, and so the researcher needs to:

- ☑ **Create and organise files** for data.
- ☑ **Read through texts**, make margin notes, form initial codes.
- ☑ **Describe personal experiences** through time and describe the essence of the phenomenon.
- ☑ **Develop significant statements**. Group these statements into meaning units or themes.
- ☑ **Include textural description** 'What happened?'
- ☑ **Use structural description**, 'How' the phenomenon was experienced (meaning).
- ☑ **Reflect** the 'essence'.
- ☑ **Present narration** of the 'essence' of the experience in tables, figures or discussions.

10.4.3.5 Challenges of phenomenology

There are several challenges in using phenomenology as a design, including:
▸ Understanding of the broader philosophical assumptions.
▸ Participants should be carefully selected.
▸ Bracketing of personal experiences may be difficult to apply.

10.4.4 Grounded theory

In this section, we briefly provide a definition and data analysis process when using grounded theory as a research design for your study.

10.4.4.1 Defining the concept

Grounded theory (GT) studies are a qualitative research approach. Grounded theory studies are those in which data are collected and analysed, and then a theory is developed that is situated in or generated from in the data. This means that grounded theory as a research design uses both an inductive and a deductive approach to theory development.

Corbin & Strauss, (2008:12) define GT as a "design to theorise and provide a conceptual ordering of an approach used in research design". GT is used to explain a phenomenon, its interrelatedness, and interpretations of the phenomena under investigation.

10.4.4.2 When to use grounded theory

Grounded theory design is based on the assumption that theory is generated from or grounded in the data from participants who have experienced a process. Grounded theory methods (GTM) can be used to explain a concept/process/phenomenon within a given context when no theory is currently available, and to understand the phenomenon. The objective of grounded theory as a design is intent on moving beyond description to discover/create theory, but also to extend the findings of the study.

10.4.4.3 GTM for data collection and analysis

When applying the GTM to data collection and analysis, the following issues are important:
▶ The collection of data, examining and building of theory, develops concurrently with the research process.
▶ During the GTM process, when interviews are transcribed and field notes are captured, the process of coding of data can start.
▶ Other data collection instruments can be used, such as observations.

To better understand the grounded theory method, look at the flow chart of the process for analysing collected data, in Figure 10.3.

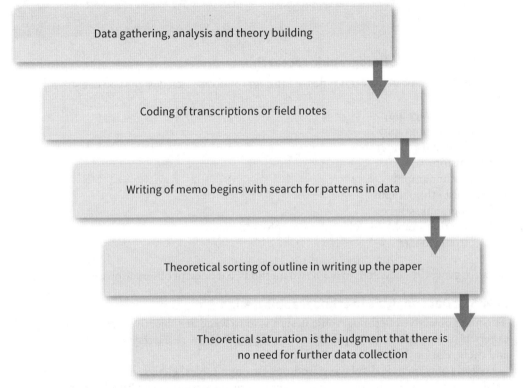

FIGURE 10.3: Integrated grounded theory method (IGTM)

10.4.5 Ethnography

In this section, ethnography as a research design will be explained. In addition, different types of ethnography will be discussed. We also discuss methods of analysis in ethnography and the challenges associated with ethnographic design.

10.4.5.1 Defining ethnography

Ethnographic studies involve the collection and analysis of data about cultural groups, communities or social settings. The researcher describes and interprets the shared learning, including patterns of values, behaviours, beliefs and language, of an entity or a unit. The researcher explores with the people their rituals and customs. An entire cultural group may be studied, or a sub-group in the culture, in this type of research.

Ethnographers interview people who are most knowledgeable about the culture, or the local people, in a particular setting. These people are referred to as key informants. For example, if a researcher needs to study the line of chieftainship of a particular clan, the researcher needs to consult the custodians, such as the elders to get the information. As Babbie and Mouton (2006) assert, the ethnographic researcher aims to learn new and different things from the people of the culture of interest to the researcher.

Think and link

Giampietro Gobo's book *Doing Ethnography* (2008: Chapter 5) is an excellent treatment of designing qualitative research. For the website connected to this chapter, look for Chapter 5 on www.sagepub.co.uk/gobo/resources.htm

10.4.5.2 Types of ethnographic research

The literature indicates several types of ethnographic research designs you can use for your research study:

- Realist ethnography
- Critical ethnography
- Confessional ethnography
- Life history
- Auto-ethnography
- Feminist ethnography
- Ethnographic studies
- Visual ethnography found in photographs and video
- Electronic media.

Data are generally collected through two methods: participant observations; and interviews.

10.4.5.3 Data analysis in ethnographic design

The main objective of ethnographic design is to to write an 'objective' account of the lived experiences of the participants. When analysing the data, the researcher will identify concepts and their relationships.

Analysis may include displaying findings through tables, charts, diagrams and figures. Analysis may also be semantic or include comparisons with other cultural groups.

After data analysis and collection, the researcher will then conduct a literature study to determine if any similar associations have already been uncovered by other researchers.

10.4.5.4 Challenges of ethnographic design

Every design has its own limitations or challenges. Let's look at the challenges of ethnographical designs:

- The time it takes to collect data is extensive. This design requires a prolonged engagement with the object of the study.
- A narrative form of writing might be challenging to authors more accustomed to traditional approaches.
- Profound sensitivity to the needs of individuals and groups under study is required. The researcher has to become fully immersed in the culture and lives of the people.
- Often there is a lack of sufficient funding to complete the project on time.

Before you continue with the next section on selecting mixed methods designs, read the ethnographic design case study and complete the activity.

Case study: *Boys in White*

In 1959, a group of researchers from the Chicago School of Medicine carried out a conceptually developed ethnographic study, eventually published as *Boys in White* (1961). The research group consisted of three researchers and four assistants. Team leader Everett Hughes, two co-researchers and four research assistants, spent three years on this research project. The team was granted ethical clearance to conduct the study in the School of Medicine because of increasing concern about students and their uncaring attitudes towards some patients. The research team were employed to collect data by attending classes to observe how students learn, and their attitude towards patients during their training. This study is rich in description, as depicted by Becker, et al. (1961:25-26) in the following extract:

In participant observation [...] the researcher participates in the daily lives of people he studies. We [...] did this by attending school with the students, following them from class to laboratory to hospital ward [...] We went with students to lectures and to the laboratories in which they studied the basic sciences, watched their activities, and engaged in casual conversation with them. We followed students to their fraternity houses and sat with them while they discussed their school experiences. We accompanied students on rounds with attending physicians, watched them examine patients on the wards and in the clinics, and sat in on discussion groups and oral exams. We had meals with the students and took night calls with them. We observed the participants in the daily activities of the school – which is to say that we were not hidden; our presence was known to everyone involved, to the students, their teachers, and their patients. Participating in the ordinary routine, we did so in the 'pseudo-role' of student. Not that we posed as students, for it was made clear to everyone that we were not students; but rather it was the students we participated with. When a lecture or class ended, we left with the students, not the teacher; we left the operating or delivery room when the student did, not when the patient or surgeon did, unless these happened to coincide. We went with the students wherever they went in the course of the day.

Findings revealed that 'positive' and 'negative' cases emerged to test preliminary observations, and review the data systematically. The research leaders, including Everett Hughes and his team, were conscious that critics might regard their findings as unpersuasive or anecdotal. The study was therefore intended as an 'experiment' in being more explicit about the modes of proof involved in analysis of this kind.

Critical thinking challenge

1 Identify the type of case study carried out in *Boys in White*, and describe it.
2 What is the unit of analysis in this type of case study?
3 In terms of this case study, what are the multiple sources of evidence?
4 Who does 'Boys in White' in the title refer to? Comment on this title.

10.5 Selecting mixed methods research design

As the name denotes, mixed methods research is a type of research in which a researcher combines elements of qualitative and quantitative approaches (e.g. uses qualitative and quantitative viewpoints, data collection, analysis, inference techniques) for the purpose of breadth and depth of understanding and corroboration (Johnson & Onwuegbuzie, 2007).

Teddlie and Tashakkori (2009) argue that mixed methods research includes at least one quantitative strand and one qualitative strand. They define a strand as a component of a study that encompasses the basic process of conducting quantitative or qualitative research: posing a question, collecting data, analysing data, and interpreting results, based on that study.

Mixing research methods can be a daunting task, so the researcher must have a specific reason for combining the two methods. After deciding to use a mixed methods approach, the researcher can employ the following stages to conduct the research:

▶ First, qualitative design is used to collect data through focus group interviews. After the interviews have been analysed, conclusions are made based on the results.

▶ Then the second stage is implemented to collect data by using structured questionnaires. The results of the first stage, in this case the focus group interviews, are then used to 'triangulate' findings of both the data collection instruments in line with the aim of the study.

Let us brifly examine the philosophical underpinnings of this research design for collecting data.

10.5.1 Philosophical underpinnings of mixed methods design

According to Teddlie and Tashakkori (2009), mixed methods design is underpinned by pragmatism and transformative perspectives. The latter focuses on the experiences of individuals who suffer from discrimination or oppression. Further, this perspective engages in research that addresses power differentials, in the research. De Vos, Strydom, Fouché & Delport (2005) (citing Creswell, Plano-Clark, et al., 2003:357) state that mixed methods design:

▶ Reports the results or findings of the study, that are both deductive and inductive in nature.

▶ Presents collected data that are both numerical and textual in nature.

▶ Is related to concurrent and sequential mixed designs in terms of using instruments such as surveys and interviews to triangulate the data collection process.

Before you continue with this chapter, log in to YouTube and watch this video.

Stop and reflect

On Web 8.1 -YouTube
Study the clip of John Creswell on the mixed methods approach. This is a useful tool to advance your understanding of this approach.
http://www.youtube.com/watch?v=10aNiTlpyX8

10.5.2 Reasons for using mixed methods

De Vos, et al. (2005) recommend that a researcher should carefully select a single mixed methods design that best matches the research problem and the research objectives of a study.

Some further reasons for choosing mixed methods as you design are suggested by several researchers in the following list.

▶ *When you want to explore a phenomenon from both perspectives by using different data collection methods.* The use of two or more data collection methods will assist in explaining the phenomena under study in more detail.

▶ *When you use two approaches, that is, qualitative and quantitative approaches to obtain complete information about the phenomena under study.* More confident decisions can be taken based on the results.

▶ *You can use quantitative data collection methods, such as questionnaires, then follow this with qualitative data collection methods, such as interviews, in order to validate the data you have gathered from using questionnaires.* Doing this will offer a more comprehensive set of evidence for studying a research problem, rather than using either quantitative or qualitative research alone.

▶ *When you need to make generalisations which combine both qualitative data collection methods and quantitative data collection methods,* the researcher is free to use all possible methods to address a research problem.

▶ *When you need to find an explanation for your findings.* Explanations encourage the use of multiple world views or paradigms. Therefore the researcher can decide which paradigm is most appropriate given their choice of a particular mixed methods design for a particular study.

▶ *When unexpected results emerge from the study,* follow-up research can be done using a different data collection method from the one used in the initial study.

10.5.3 Benefits of using mixed methods design

Here are the benefits of mixed method research designs:

▶ *Combines the qualitative and the quantitative methods.* The researcher can purposefully decide to use a combination of qualitative and quantitative data collection methods. For example, the researcher can use questionnaires (survey design) and focus group interviews for data collection for a single case study.

▶ *To broaden the mixed methods approach by using two or more data collection tools.* For example, the researcher employs semi-structured interviews, focus group interviews and observations as qualitative methods to explore the views of participants about challenges of implementing the new curricula but also uses open ended questions.

▶ *Uses one method of data collection and then uses the results to develop another method.* For example, the researcher can employ a questionnaire to identify teachers' views on promotion criteria for head of department, to collect data. This selective sampling of teachers (purposive sampling) is then followed up or extended to in-depth focus groups or face-to-face interviews.

▶ *Acts as a complementary approach.* In this case, the researcher uses quantitative and qualitative methods for collecting data. For example, a study is conducted on Grade 12 learners' views about career opportunities, a qualitative design is employed by using interviews with some learners; secondly, a questionnaire is used to explore the nature, scope and benefits of chartered accountancy as a career. These two methods are similar measures of different aspects of careers for Grade 12 learners.

▶ *The researcher employs mixed methods with the advantage of generating new findings* (knowledge/skills) or insights about the phenomenon under investigation.

10.5.4 Types of mixed methods research design

Creswell & Plano-Clark (2011) identify four types of mixed methods designs:

▶ Convergent parallel design
▶ Explanatory design
▶ Exploratory design
▶ Embedded design.

These types will be discussed in the sections that follow.

10.5.4.1 Convergent parallel mixed methods design

This method is sometimes referred to as the triangulation mixed methods research design. It is a one-phase design in which the researcher uses both qualitative and quantitative methods within the same timeframe. Convergent design is used when the researcher collects and analyses both quantitative and qualitative data during the same phase of the research process and then merges the two sets of results into an overall interpretation. The quantitative and the qualitative strands are conducted separately but concurrently, and merged at the point of interpretation. This means the researcher keeps the strands independent during analysis and then mixes the results during the overall interpretation.

10.5.4.2 Explanatory sequential mixed methods design

This is a two-phase mixed methods design which employs different stages in the study. For example, the researcher first uses focus group interviews. combined with observations, and follow it up with a short survey to explore teachers' perceptions of bullying on the school grounds. The researcher uses focus group interviews to collect data from the phenomenon. In this case the researcher collects data through interviews and survey to explore the extent of bullying at the school.

10.5.4.3 Exploratory mixed methods design

De Vos, et al. (2005) assert that the exploratory mixed methods design is used when a researcher first needs to explore a phenomenon using qualitative data, before attempting to measure or test it quantitatively. This means that the researcher builds a quantitative study on the results of a qualitative study. The researcher will link results from both strands since he or she wants to find out how quantitative results extend qualitative findings. The qualitative strand is considered exploratory, to be followed by further testing and verification during the quantitative data analysis phase. For example, the researcher can explore the challenge to teachers of implementing a new curriculum, using semi-structured interviews, and then using the resulting information to design a programme of intervention, and test it quantitatively using questionnaires.

Before you continue with the next section on embedded design, read the example for further clarity of this type of design.

Mixing methods in mathematics e.g.

After conducting a study on student performance in mathematics, the study employs an exploratory mixed methods design by first using observation of the teaching methods deployed in the mathematics classroom, and then following up with interviews with the teachers about teaching methods. A follow-up method with a questionnaire on different teaching methods and strategies for teaching mathematics is then used.

10.5.4.4 Embedded design

The purpose of embedded design is to provide a supportive and secondary role in a study, based primarily on the other types of data collected. Moreover, embedded design becomes a mixed methods approach when the researcher combines the collection and analysis of both quantitative and qualitative data within a traditional quantitative or qualitative research design.

Conclusion

Research design involves the extensive planning of your study. In designing your research, you have to consider the approach that is applicable to your topic and research questions. The approach can be qualitative, quantitative or the mixed methods approach. Each approach has a research design that is consistent with and appropriate to it. Your choice of research design should answer your research questions. Finding the right research design means different research designs can be used to study different research questions. It is important to note that each research design has its own strong points and its weak points, but your choice should always be informed by the purpose of your study.

Closing activities

Self-reflection questions

1 Revisit the opening case study, *The* Vasa: *Spectacular but flawed in design*, and answer the following question: What is the connection between research design and why the Vasa sank in the harbour?
2 If you have decided to use a research design for your particular study, identify the design and provide an example of the research design for your study.
3 What are the main functions of research design? Why is it important to have a research design before starting your study.
4 Identify the components/aspects that need to be described in a research design.
5 What are the differences between quantitative and qualitative research designs?

Analysis and consolidation

6 Identify two or more situations relating to your own area of interest where you think quantitative research designs might be more beneficial, and consider why this might be the case.

Practical applications

7 Is the research design you propose to adopt to conduct your study cross-sectional, longitudinal, experimental or comparative in nature? If possible, draw a diagram depicting your research design choice. Answer the following questions:
  a Why did you select this particular design for your study?
  b What, in your opinion, are the strengths, weaknesses, limitations and benefits of your selected design?
  c What constitutes your population or sampling?
  d How will you select the data, as well as do the data collection?
8 Write a proposal for conducting an ethnographic study of a particular group or occupational setting. This should review previous ethnographic studies of similar settings, and discuss any relevant methodological issues.
9 Use the case study, *Free State school staff guilty of hate speech*, to answer this question. You have been selected as part of the team to conduct a research study for your mini-dissertation. You should audio-record and transcribe a 20-minute interview with each, the principal, teachers, and learners, at a school. The interview should focus on any similar difficulties they have encountered at the school. Your team should then use the data to write an account of how learners change during such experiences, drawing upon the South African Human Rights Commission report, in your discussion.

Bibliography

Babbie, E. & Mouton, J. 2006. *The practice of social research* (3rd ed.). Cape Town: Oxford University Press.

Becker, H.S., Geer, B., Hughes, E.C. & Strauss, A. 1961. *Boys in White: Student culture in medical school*. Chicago: University of Chicago Press.

Bryman, A. 2006. *Social Research Methods* (4th ed.). Oxford: Oxford University Press.

Caracelli, V.J. & Greene, J.C. 1997. Data analysis strategies for mixed-method evaluation designs. *Educational Evaluation and Policy Analysis*, 15(2):195–207.

Corbin, J. & Strauss, A. 2008. *Basic qualitative research: Techniques and procedures for developing grounded theory*. Thousand Oaks, CA: Sage.

Creswell, J.W. & Cresswell, J.D. 2004. Mixed Methods Research: Developments, Debates and Dilemmas. In R.A. Swanson & E.F. Holton (Eds). *Foundations and Methods of Inquiry*. Berlin: Berrett-Koehler Publishers.

Creswell, J.W. & Plano Clark V.L.P. 2011. *Designing and Conducting Mixed Methods Research* (2nd ed.). London: Sage.

Creswell, J.W. 1999. Mixed-methods research: Introduction and application. In G. Cizek (Ed). *Handbook of educational policy*. San Diego, CA: Academic Press.

Creswell, J.W. 2007. Mixed methods approach. Online at: http://www.youtube.com/watch?v=10aNiTlpyX8.

Creswell, J.W., Plano-Clark, V.L., Gutmann, M. & Hanson, W. 2003. Advanced mixed methods research designs. In A. Tashakkori & C. Teddlie (Eds) *Handbook of mixed methods in social & behavioral research*. Thousand Oaks, CA: Sage (pp. 209–240).

De Vos, A.S., Strydom, H., Fouché, C.B. & Delport, C.S.L. 2005. *Research at Grassroots for the Social Sciences and Human Services Professionals* (3rd ed.). Cape Town: Van Schaik Publishers.

Denzin, N.K. & Lincoln, Y.S. 2013. *Strategies of Qualitative Inquiry* (4th ed.). London: Sage.

Frank, G. 2000. *Venus on Wheels: Two Decades of Dialogue and Disability, Biography and Being a Feminist in America*. Berkeley, CA: University of California Press.

Gall, J.P., Gall, M.D. & Borg, W.R. (Eds). 2005. *Applying educational research: A practical guide*. USA: Pearson Education.

Gobo, G. 2008. *Doing Ethnography:* Chapter 5. Online at: www.sagepub.co.uk/gobo/resources.htm.

Greene, J.C. 2007. *Mixed methods in social inquiry*. San Francisco: Jossey-Bass.

Greene, J.C., Caracelli, V.J. & Graham, W.F. 1989. Toward a conceptual framework for mixed-method evaluation designs. *Educational Evaluation and Policy Analysis*, 11(3):255–274.

Hancock, D.R & Algozzine, B. 2011. *Doing Case Study Research: A Practical Guide for Beginning Researchers*. Columbia University: Teachers College Press.

Henning, E. 2009. *Finding your way in qualitative research*. Pretoria: Van Schaik Publishers.

Johnson, R.B. & Onwuegbuzie, A.J. 2007. Mixed methods research: A research paradigm whose time has come. *Educational Researcher*, 33(7):14–26.

Kumar, R. 2013. *Research methodology: A step-by-step guide for beginners* (4th ed.). London: Sage.

Mackenzie, N. & Knipe, S. 2006. Research dilemmas: paradigms, methods and methodology. *Issues in Educational Research*, 16. http://www.iier.org.au/iier16/mackenzie.htm. Accessed on 15 March 2014.

Mail & Guardian. 2013. SAPA Reporter. *Roof of Tongaat Mall Collapse-A Tragedy.*19 November 2013.http://mg.co.za/article/2013-11-19-workers-trapped-under-roof-of-collapsed-tongaat-mall. Accessed 25 June 2014.

Mail & Guardian. 2014. SAPA correspondent. *Free State school staff guilty of hate speech*. http://mg.co.za/article/2014-07-24-free-state-school-staff-guilty-of-hate-speech. Accessed 25 July 2014.

Maxwell, J.A. 2013. *Qualitative Research Design: An interactive approach* (3rd ed.). London: SAGE.

McMillan J.H. & Schumacher, S. 2010. *Research in Education: Evidence-based Inquiry*. Cape Town: Pearson Education.

Merriam, S.B. 2001. *The new update on adult learning theory*. San Francisco: Jossey-Bass.

Punch, K. 2011. *Introduction to Social Research: Quantitative and qualitative approaches* (4th ed.). London: Sage.

Ritchie, J. & Lewis, J. (Eds). *Qualitative Research Practice: A guide for social science students and researchers*. London: Sage Publications.

Rule, P. & Vaughn, J. 2011. *Your guide to case study research*. Cape Town: Van Schaik Publishers.

Silverman, D. 2011. *Doing Qualitative Research*. (4th ed.). London: Sage.

Singleton, R.A. & Straits, B.C. 2010. *Approaches to Social Research* (5th ed.). New York and Oxford: Oxford University Press.

Teddlie, C. & Tashakkori, A. 2009. *Foundations of mixed methods research*. Thousand Oaks, CA: Sage.

Tesch, R. 1990. *Qualitative research: Analysis types and software tools*. Basingstoke, Hampshire: Falmer Press.

Thomas, G. 2013. *How to do your research project: A guide for students in education and applied social sciences* (2nd ed.). London: Sage.

Welman, J.C. and Kruger, S.J. 2004. *Research Methodology for the Business and Administrative Sciences* (2nd ed.). London: Oxford University Press.

Wengraf, T. 2002. Historicising the socio-theory and the constant comparative methods. In P. Chamberlayne, M. Rustin & T. Wengraf (Eds). *Biography and social policy in Europe: Experiences and life journeys*. Bristol: Polity Press.

Wolcott, H.F. 2009. *Writing up qualitative research*. Newbury Park, CA: Sage.

CHAPTER 11 Muzwa Mukwambo, Kenneth Ngcoza and Charles Chikunda

How researchers define and measure variables

KEY CONCEPTS

Concept is the abstract summary of a whole set of outlooks, behaviours, attitudes and characteristics, which we see as having something in common.

Constructs are theoretical constructions based on observations, yet they cannot be observed directly or indirectly.

Conceptualisation in research is a process of taking less-than-formed ideas and notions, and specifying them much more precisely so that we can get agreement on what we are talking about.

Operationalisation is the process of specifying how concepts will be measured.

Indicators are observations that we choose; they are considered a reflection of a variable we want to study.

Variable can mean an item of data collected in each sampling unit.

Measurement is understood to be structured steps/ways, methods or procedures used for generating data.

LEARNING OUTCOMES

By the end of this chapter, you should be able to:

▶ Understand research concepts/constructs.

▶ Define research concepts conceptually and operationally.

▶ Link concepts/constructs and variables.

▶ Explain the different types of variables and how they are measured.

▶ Understand why, in research planning, the researcher needs to know the different types of data, namely discrete (discontinuous) and continuous.

▶ Identify appropriate scales of measurement of variables, and use any given scale in the operationalisation of a measured variable.

▶ Describe the different types of errors and how they can be avoided in research work.

▶ Describe how a researcher addresses quality of research through ensuring that reliability, validity and triangulation are implemented.

Case study: Cell confusion

Lwazi and four participants work in a laboratory, where they conduct research on animal cells. The apparatus they use in the laboratory to supply electric power also uses dry electric cells. Tasked with conducting research to measure the life span of cells, Lwazi drafts a research proposal.

Lwazi gives the research proposal to the participants to read. He tells them, "Tomorrow, bring some cells; we want to measure their life span". Lwazi makes no effort to define what he means by a cell. Two of the participants do not bring anything the next day. They are uncertain whether Lwazi wants to measure the life span of an animal cell or the life span of an electric cell. The two protest, "But life span is universal to both". The other two participants take a guess and bring dry electric cells.

(continued)

Neglecting to define your terms and concepts when you embark on a research project is a recipe for failure. The reader is unable to contextualise, and has to take time trying to imagine and understand what is being researched, and why. To avoid such pitfalls it is imperative that the researcher uses a clear conceptualising process. It is the objective of this chapter to discuss what conceptualisation is.

Introduction

When designing a research study it is important to clarify how the fundamental concepts are defined and measured. This step assures the researcher and the beneficiaries of the research that the research is valid, trustworthy and dependable. So, research design needs to address the following questions: a) How are the concepts in the research defined? b) How are research concepts measured? c) Are the measurement methods precise enough to address validity?

This chapter will look at defining concepts in research work, conceptually and operationally. A discussion of the properties or levels of measurement, manifested in different measures, will be presented. Regardless of what method is used, measured variables can be underestimated or overestimated; in other words, variables are measured with some errors. This explains why we sometimes look for the mean for continuous variables, or alternatively, we allow for error. We include a section focusing on errors, as well as the qualities of measures, in particular, reliability and validity. The chapter closes with some questions for you to address.

11.1   What do we mean by concept?

A **concept** is a mental image that summarises a set of similar observations, feelings, ideas, perceptions, understanding, and so on. In other words, a concept is the abstract summary of a whole set of outlooks, behaviours, attitudes and characteristics which we see as having something in common. You may still be finding the idea of concept too abstract and difficult to really get a sense of. The simple task in the following activity will help you to understand what we mean by concept.

Stop and reflect

On a piece of paper, draw a house. Now compare the image you have drawn with a real house, any real house. Are they exactly the same? Almost certainly they are not. Indeed, in reality all houses are different, in terms of size, shape, design, materials used and colour. Nonetheless, they are all called houses. In other words, the word 'house' is only a label or term that is used to represent all houses existing in the real world. We call this term the 'concept' of house. Your drawing is based on the mental image that you use to summarise the set of ideas about real houses. Thus, the mental image is your conception of a house.

You may now have the following questions around concepts:

▸ Where do concepts come from?
▸ What is the purpose of concepts in life?

Providing answers to these questions adds some clarity to the whole idea of concept. In general, concepts are socially created. When people encounter or experience something that has features in common, they will form ideas about the associations. As we said earlier, concepts are mental images that summarise and represent the similarities between ideas. People then use terms, words or phrases, to refer to the ideas. These terms, etc. are known as concepts. In any society, concepts are created through mutual agreement on what meanings they represent. In contrast, scientific concepts are theoretical creations that are based on observations, but they cannot be observed directly or indirectly. We can only measure the things that the concepts summarise. An example is presented in Table 11.1 which gives two concepts, one from social sciences and the other from physical sciences (democracy and force). The table illustrates that both concepts cannot be observed directly or indirectly; rather, we can only measure the things that the concepts summarise.

TABLE 11.1: Illustration of concepts

Democracy	Force
The shift from apartheid to a democratic society popularised the concept of democracy in South Africa, as in many other formerly oppressed societies. But how can we measure the concept of democracy? We can only do this through measuring the indicators that are summarised in the concept of democracy, e.g. universal suffrage; freedom of association; racial and social inclusivity; a society built on freedom, equality and equity, among others.	Isaac Newton (1643—1727) developed the concept of force in what became known as his second law. His mathematical formula force = mass × acceleration (f = m.a) states that we can only observe the effects of force on an object by observing the change in the acceleration of a given object. Laboratory experiments confirm that we can only measure the things that the concept of force summarises, that is, mass and acceleration.

We now focus on the second question raised earlier, which is about the purpose of concepts in life in general. The answer to this question can be summarised as follows:

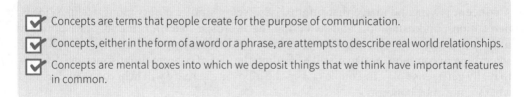

☑ Concepts are terms that people create for the purpose of communication.

☑ Concepts, either in the form of a word or a phrase, are attempts to describe real world relationships.

☑ Concepts are mental boxes into which we deposit things that we think have important features in common.

It is also important to remember that concepts are neither true nor false, just more or less useful. Another very important point to remember in research is what is known as the *fallacy of reification*: this is the mistake of regarding concepts as real and having an intrinsic objective existence. In the next section, we categorise concepts, with the first category appearing to have the quality of the fallacy of reification.

11.1.1 Further categorisation of concepts

The illustration in Table 11.1 may be slightly misleading, by giving the impression that all concepts are a bit fuzzy, or hard to pin down exactly. In fact, concepts can be assigned to three classes, namely:

☑ Direct observables

☑ **Indirect observables** (that is, not observed or experienced first-hand)

☑ Constructs.

Some examples of direct observable concepts are road, bird, weed, and so on. The examples of concepts in Table 11.1 (democracy, force) fall into the category of indirect observables. Other concepts in the category of indirect observables include worldview, science knowledge, philosophy, and many more. Finally, concepts like motivation, social justice, hunger, intelligence quotient (IQ), and others, are constructs. **Constructs** can be defined as theoretical formations based on perceptions and observations, although they cannot be observed directly or indirectly (Creswell, 2012). Democracy is a good example of a construct. In this chapter, we will refer to all direct observable concepts, indirect observable concepts and constructs, as concepts.

Stop and reflect

Make a table with four columns. Label the columns: Direct observable concepts, Indirect observable concepts, Constructs, and the last column must be labelled, Explanation. Now complete the table you have constructed by populating it with examples in the various categories. Don't forget to include an explanation for each entry.

11.2 Conceptualising and operationalising research concepts

In the previous section, we looked at the source and purpose of concepts in general. In this section, we focus on aligning concepts to research goals. It is always important to keep in mind that when doing research, we want to be quite clear about what it is we are actually measuring, studying, or observing. For this reason, there is a need to conceptualise and operationalise the concepts that we use in research.

11.2.1 What is conceptualisation?

Lee (2005) explains **conceptualisation** of research concepts as a process of taking very vague ideas and notions, and specifying them much more precisely so that we can get agreement about what we are talking about. Since people attach more than one meaning to a term, it is important to specify exactly what we mean (and *don't* mean) by the terms we use in our research. Read the case study of casual taxi talk in the following activity.

Stop and reflect

Case study: Multiple meanings in a taxi

One day, while travelling in a taxi I was drawn to a conversation between four young men. They were talking and laughing at the top of their voices, attracting the attention of the other passengers. I was not bothered because it is the thing I enjoy most about public transport. I quickly gathered that their casual talk was about ATMs. At first I thought they were discussing the fraud around automated teller machines at banks in the city. The conversation went on: "Uuh, so she is loaded, she gives you tons of cash?" said one. "You are supposed to spoil her, not the other way round," interjected another. "Haai muzala, you are such an embarrassment: you are making her your ATM, but you are the man …" the accusations went on. Eventually the storyteller shouted at top of his voice to emphasise the point: "No majita, you don't understand me, I mean assistant to madam – A-T-M!"

Think about the many meanings this anecdote suggests: What does the narrator think is being discussed? As the conversation develops, what do you (the reader) think is being discussed? What is actually being discussed?

The story echoes what we discussed in the first case study. This case becomes even more complicated when the concept being researched has multiple meanings. The reader, who wants to understand the research, is confronted with finding out from a spectrum of ideas, what the researcher intends to convey.

Research is conducted to solve a problem. This is the solution or outcome the reader wants. So, if conceptualisation is not properly done, the reader may later find that the research is intended for another area, not that of his or her interest. Also, the participants are affected when concepts are not fully conceptualised. This might affect the data generated from the research, as these participants will all have their own ideas which do not necessarily concur.

Stop and reflect

1 Remember the casual taxi talk story in the last activity? How many meanings are attached to the term, ATM?
2 Imagine you want to do research using the term ATM as your key concept: what do you think you need to do so that you have a common understanding of the concept with your research participants?

Toolbox Start conceptualising

In the process of conceptualisation you need to consider the following:
▶ Define your concepts in a way that reflects a common understanding (avoid personal, popular, or characteristic definitions, such as 'assistant to madam' for ATM).
▶ Remember that although concepts can neither be true nor false, they should be assessed by their usefulness in communicating with others and by their contribution to theoretical development (Lee, 2005). The point is that when you define the concept to be used in your research in a way that is too different, to obscure, or too unclear, you risk losing touch with the current theoretical debate because you cannot be sure you are talking about the same thing as is being discussed in the debate.

11.2.1.1 Dimensions of a concept

To clarify the notion of concepts, especially those complex ones (indirect observables and constructs), which we want to use in our research, we have to divide the concepts by aspect or dimension. A dimension is a specifiable aspect of a concept. Going back to the example of force, we need to divide the concept into two dimensions: that of mass and that of acceleration. The dimensions may continue; for example, in this case, acceleration will have to be divided further into measurable dimensions of velocity and time.

Another example from the socio-economic sphere is economic attitudes. The concept is not very clear or obvious. We need to focus on more specific aspects (dimensions) of economic attitudes, such as attitudes towards toll roads; or attitudes towards government policy on social grants; or attitudes towards government's policy on foreign direct investment in the country; or attitudes towards government regulation of corruption; and so on.

Always remember that which dimensions you should specify, depends on the research question that you pose at the beginning of your research. The final product of conceptualisation is to give a nominal or conceptual definition of the term as you use it in your research, so that other people know exactly what you are examining. Remember, too, that conceptual clarification is an ongoing process. It should begin before data are collected and analysed, although concepts may be further clarified during the process of analysis.

11.2.2   What is operationalisation?

Lee (2005) describes **operationalisation** as the process of developing measures or indicators of our concepts and showing how those indicators will be used to measure the concepts we are interested in. Put differently, operationalisation is the process of specifying how concepts will be measured. The question could be: What are these indicators or measures? An **indicator** is an observation that we choose to consider as a reflection of a variable we want to study. Going back to our example in Table 11.1, if we want to study or measure force, we have to specify the indicators that we are going to measure, in this case, mass and acceleration of the object on which force acts.

We can do the same with the concept of democracy. In other words, if you are operationalising the concept of democracy in your research, you need to ask yourself the following questions:
- What indicates the presence or absence of democracy in a particular society?
- How can you measure these indicators?

We can also draw from another example, that of economic development. To measure the economic development level of an economy, we usually use GNP per capita as an indicator. In this case, the variable or concept 'economic development' of different countries is indirectly measured by the numerical values of GNP per capita of those economies.

Having specified the concepts we want to analyse, we have to ask ourselves three questions about operationalisation (adapted from Lee, 2005):

1 How many indicators are necessary?
- The development of indicators for some concepts is straightforward, for example, for concepts such as age and level of education. For these simple concepts, one indicator is enough. However, developing indicators for some complex concepts, particularly those that are more abstract (as in direct observables and constructs) like inequality, human rights, corruption, racism, democracy, and many more, it becomes more problematic.

- As discussed previously, a complex concept can be divided into different dimensions. In order to fully capture the essence of the concept, we should create at least one indicator for each dimension. In general, the more complicated and abstract the concept, the more indicators you should develop. This is so that if, after data collection, you find that some indicators are not measuring what you have in mind, you will not be left with nothing to represent the concept.

2 How can the indicators be developed?

- First, you have to make sure that all the dimensions of the concept are covered. Then you have to specify the range of variation of your indicator. For instance, generally, there are only two attributes, male or female, for the concept, sex. However, in some research about sexuality, researchers may add more categories, say, the option transsexual, to capture the full meaning of sex in the context of transsexuality.
- Next, in similar fashion, you also determine the level of precision of the indicator. For example, when measuring educational level, you may simply divide the indicator into three categories: primary or below; secondary/high school level; and tertiary level. Alternatively, you may ask how many years of schooling your respondents have had. The first tends to be more precise than the last.

3 How can measuring instruments be constructed to measure the indicators?

- This question is related to your research design and methodology. For example, when you do a survey, the questions in your questionnaire will be your measuring instruments. However, if you, say, study the performance of schools in the Eastern Cape province, you will rely on statistical data collected by the regional authority, in this case, the Department of Basic Education.
- In general, there are three approaches for constructing measuring instruments:
  > *Verbal* or *self-report*. Such reports include replies to direct questions posed in a questionnaire or in an interview.
  > *Observation*. Researchers are the major data collecting instrument. For instance, we speculate that people will somehow be blocked by social convention in retrieving the meanings of foul language terminologies from their brain, so that the time for them to utter expletive will be longer than to utter normal words. In order to test this memory blocking hypothesis, we show different words, both normal and expletives, to the respondent, and then we observe the reaction time for them to recite the words, using stopwatch.
  > *Archival records*. These are the body of existing recorded information, for example, official statistics, patients' medical records, or school reports and university transcripts, etc.

11.2.3 Three ways to develop initial indicators

Basically, there are three ways that you can rely on to develop indicators for your research concepts.

1 Tried and tested indicators

In this case, as a researcher, you will use measures or indicators that have been used in other studies (Patton, 1996). These have already been tested. In this case, there is still a need to take note of the following:

✓ **Evaluate such measures to see whether they fit your research context.** You have to be considerate of the culture, language, accessibility of certain material, and terms or conditions of use, and many other considerations.

✓ **You may need to adapt them**, that is, adjusting and updating them to suit your research needs.

✓ **The advantage of using existing measures** is that you can compare with previous research and you also have the opportunity to build upon existing knowledge in the area.

2 Piloting indicators

▶ As a researcher you may opt to begin with a qualitative pilot study to 'test' the indicators that you have developed, or you have in mind. Usually this is done by using a less structured approach to data collection (Baker, 1994). For example, through observation or unstructured interviews of a sub-sample, you can gain an understanding of the motivations of actors and concerns that may be important to those in the target group. You can then design your indicators accordingly.

3 Consultation

▶ Consulting informants, from research participants to authority figures in the field you are studying, is another way that you may choose to use to develop indicators. For example, if you want to operationalise 'sexual harassment in the workplace', you may interview some victims or complainants, or ask some experts in labour unions responsible for fighting workplace sexual harassment, to see how the concept is understood, and the indicators used in measuring it. The advantage of this approach is that it may give insights into indicator construction as well as providing you with ideas that help in designing data collection instruments, such as the questionnaire, observation schedule, and so on.

11.3 Variables

Research entails describing and explaining the variation that occurs naturally in the natural environment, or the artificial environment. In an artificial environment, we create variation as a result of a manipulation. The variables are the names that are given to such variations that we intend to explain (Hannagan, 1997; Field, 2005).

In research work, variables can affect or change the results of a study (Heffener, 2014). All research studies have variables as these are needed to understand differences. The same variables are related to the concepts under study. Concepts and variables are discussed in the next section.

11.3.1 Concepts and variables

Conceptualisation as discussed in previous sections allows the researcher to develop a nominal definition (Mitchell, 2002). Once this is done, identification of variables and procedures to measure follows. Take for example the concept of incorporation of indigenous science with Western science teaching, which is defined as repeated use of cultural practices, community jargon or local examples, in science discourses to improve science understanding. This concept can be converted to a variable in many ways. One way could be by observing the frequency with which cultural practices, jargon and local examples appear in classroom discourse. Another way could be to ask learners how often they encounter cultural practices, social jargon, etc. in their science learning. A third way might be to ask teachers or learners to rate the use of the characteristics of indigenous science in Western science teaching, on a scale.

Variables are of different types. These are discussed next as we need to understand the term variable before we proceed to analyse the different types of variables.

It should be noted at this point that the term 'variable' has a dual sense. Variable can mean an item of data collected in each sampling unit, *and* it can mean a 'random variable'. A random variable is one used in the mathematical sense, but it is also one that takes different values according to a probability distribution. Here, we concentrate on discussing a variable in the mathematical sense, as follows next.

11.3.2 Classes of variables

Different classes of variables exist. These are: independent, dependent, control, and extraneous variables. Each of the mentioned type of variable has its own characteristics which makes it peculiar. It is important to identify the variables when conducting a research (Pietersen & Maree, 2012). The variables must be known by the researcher since they will have an effect on the research to be conducted. Let us discuss each of these variables, starting with independent variable.

11.3.2.1 Independent variable

An independent variable is a stimulus variable which can be physical, psychological, social, and so on, and cannot be changed by other variables (Matthews & Ross, 2010). Two types of independent variables exist: attribute and active variable. An active variable is manipulated to provide a stimulus to the dependent variable. This is achieved by changing the values of the active independent variable. For instance, temperature is an active independent variable manipulated to see how the heat energy absorbed, is changed. This also applies to increasing the pressure applied to one's shoulder to see the responsiveness to pain. Pressure applied and manipulated is the active independent variable. An attribute independent variable is not altered during a study. An example could be when the purpose is to study the effect of age on height. People of different ages are brought in to study their heights.

11.3.2.2 Dependent variable

A dependent variable, sometimes known as criterion measure, is a variable affected by an independent variable, and is the one the researcher is measuring. A dependent variable measures the response of the independent variable. In the examples given earlier, heat energy, pain and height are the dependent variable.

11.3.2.3 Control variable

A control variable is one which is kept constant during a study. It is controlled to balance its effect on the parameters. In a study of the relationship between pressure and volume, temperature is kept constant. Temperature, which is kept constant, is therefore the control variable.

11.3.2.4 Extraneous variable

An extraneous variable has an effect on the dependent and independent variable. However, it is not controlled. Sometimes, it is not controlled because no one knows how to control it, or how it affects the dependent or independent variable. Sometimes, research studies do not find evidence to support the hypothesis because of unnoticed extraneous variables that influence the results.

There are two types of extraneous variable, namely, participant variable and situational variable. A participant variable is related to the individual characteristics of each participating parameter. It may impact on how one responds. Factors determining a participant variable can include background differences, mood, anxiety, intelligence, awareness, and characteristics unique to an individual. Whereas a situational variable is related to factors in the environment; those factors which have an effect on how one responds. An example could be the amount of humidity in a room where a participant is answering questions. Humidity is taken as an extraneous variable.

Stop and reflect

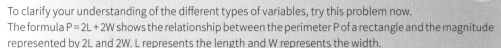

To clarify your understanding of the different types of variables, try this problem now.
The formula $P = 2L + 2W$ shows the relationship between the perimeter P of a rectangle and the magnitude represented by 2L and 2W. L represents the length and W represents the width.
1 Identify what types of variables P, L, and W are.
2 What could be said about the extraneous control variables?

Now that we have discussed variables and how they are related to concepts/constructs, our understanding of the types of variable will allow us to define a concept operationally, as we do next.

11.4 Defining a concept operationally

Understanding of a concept enables us to identify specific variables. The variables are measured using a set of identified procedures. The aim is to come up with some structured ways/steps or methods that really measure the concepts under study. The ways/steps or methods are what we can refer to as an algorithm. Such a process of connecting concepts to observation, direct or indirect, is referred as operationalisation.

It is fundamental to create strong operational definition for the independent variable and dependent variable. Operationally defining variables entails indicating what is measured, how the variables are measured, and the rules used to assign a value to what is observed, and finally, the interpretation of the value (Babbie, 2011).

A nominal definition of incorporation of indigenous science into Western science was given in an earlier section. Operationalisation of the same concept will have the same indicators given before, such as use of cultural practices, community jargon and local examples.

The scale of measurement given to the indicators is executed orally or is self-executed. The answer to each is either yes or no. Each indicator will have a score value ranging from 0 to 5. The value of the scores are added, with a score between 0 to 3 indicating none use of indigenous science in science discourses; a score of 4 suggests some incorporation of indigenous knowledge; and 5 is a clear indication that there is incorporation of indigenous knowledge.

As manifested, operationalisation provides the indicators which are the variables, including the measures, method(s) of data collection and generating, specific scoring of the responses, and interpretation of the scale scores.

Variables which are measured respond to unique research questions in the study. One of the benefits of making this kind of arrangement is to be sure of precision.

Precision when using scales of measurement is dependent on the information the research requires. It also depends on the graduation on the measurement tool used to measure. For example, a measurement of a diameter of 10m of a pond using a tape measure graduated in metres will be taken as 10±0,5m. If the tape measure is graduated in 10-centimetre intervals, the reading of 10m of the diameter of the pond will be 10 ± 0,05m.

For precision to be obtained when using scales of measurement it is important that the following are adhered to while formulating operational definitions:

☑ **Maintain consistency** with the conceptual definition.

☑ **Ensure that all variables responding to a concept are measured**, and methods used for measuring are described and clarified.

☑ **Ensure that the variables mentioned** are those which the other members in the community of practice are aware of.

If a researcher intends to bring in some other views, these must be explained: in other words, why the other variables are coming in. Critique from the other members in the community of practice might be helpful to prevent poorly-formulated operational definitions which yield inconsistency and poor data. Finally, as one of the last processes in operationalising a concept, one needs to show the variable's level of measurement in the research.

Stop and reflect

Do you think the use of operational definitions allows researchers to conduct studies where abstract concepts are being researched? Explain how an operational definition will allow such studies to be successfully conducted.

11.5 Measurement

Measurement is understood to be the structured steps, ways or methods and (algorithmic) procedures used for generating data (Cutcliffe & Harder, 2012). Symbols such as numbers, letters, and other symbols conforming to the structure of the properties of variables are assigned. Numbers are numerals with quantitative meaning and are amenable to statistical analysis, for example, age, height, or weight.

Algorithmic procedures for assigning labels to properties of variables are the most important component of measurement. Poorly-formulated rules can make data generation lose meaning. Also, compounded by the fact that some concepts cannot be measured directly but instead have to be counted, this creates a premise to clarify data types.

11.5.1 Data obtained from measurement or counting of variables

In quantitative research, two types of data generating processes are used, namely: measuring and counting. One might count the number of people in a family who are drug abusers. If you intend to find the height of a variable, you measure the value of the variable.

Alternatively, data can be generated by counting. Data generated by counting is referred as discrete (discontinuous) data; whereas data generated by measuring is referred as continuous data. Values of discontinuous variables assume integral whole numbers and, in most cases, are counts of items and also frequency. The values of continuous variables can take any value at any point along an uninterrupted scale. Some further examples are: length, mass, current, volume, and others. The distinction between continuous and discontinuous variables is important. Table 11.2 points out further characteristics of these two types of data.

TABLE 11.2: Subdivision of data types

	Data type	Definition	Examples
Discrete (discontinuous)	Nominal	Data have a name only and do not have order yet	Street, road, way, pass, fail
	Ordinal	Data can be put into categories and can be ordered, but without numerical scale	Very satisfactory, satisfactory, unsatisfactory
	Whole number data	Data can take the value of any whole number	Week 1, Week 2, Week 3 (any simple time series is suitable) Number of items (0; 1; 2; 3; 4; …)
Continuous	Measurement data	Data can take any numerical value	Length of an insect in cm (2; 2.3; 2.01; …)

Continuous data can be placed in certain levels. The levels are in the order of the strength of the scale being used. The next section discusses the levels based on Mann's (2011) suggestions on levels of measurement.

11.5.2 The levels of measurement scales

Mann (2011) suggests at least four levels of measurement scales. These levels were originally suggested by the psychologist Stanley Smith Stevens in 1955. The levels of measurement scale are used to describe the type, range and relationships among the values a variable can take. The four levels are: nominal, ordinal, interval, and ratio scale. Each of these scales has its own characteristics, which makes it suitable for measuring specific types of variables. However, each scale is hierarchical, mutually exclusive, and exhaustive. Each scale fuses the characteristics of the scale below it. Mutually exhaustive means that there must be sufficient categories that all the observations will fall into, in the research. Mutually exclusive means that the categories must be distinct enough that no observations will fall into more than one category. These four levels of measuring variables are now discussed.

11.5.2.1 Nominal scale of measurement

The nominal scale is one of the most elementary scales of measurement used to measure variables. The concept 'nominal' is derived from the Latin word *nomen*, meaning name. What it does is to identify groups into which different things may be classified. The groups are mutually exclusive. The probability of placing an individual item in more than one group is zero. Researchers often use this scale to study, for example, learners with difficulties in understanding mathematics and science; and those who understand these subjects. In this case, only two categories are present in which such learners can be placed. Other examples of variables which fall under nominal are gender (e.g. male, female), marital status (e.g. married spouse present, married spouse absent, widowed, separated, divorced, never married), nationality (e.g. South African, Namibian, Zimbabwean, Indian, French). Another illustration of nominal assignments would be the numbering of players in a football or netball team. Many more exist which can be used in the operationalisation of concepts.

The group name can be substituted by a number. Those with difficulties in understanding science and mathematics can be labelled as 1; and those without difficulties as 2. However, the numbers are a mere label, without a numerical value. Also, the sequence in which the numbers are used does not have a mathematical significance. This makes this scale of measurement suitable for qualitative research. In terms of level, the nominal scale of measurement is followed by the ordinal scale of measurement.

11.5.2.2 Ordinal scale of measurement

The ordinal scale of measurement of a variable has some similarity with the nominal scale of measurement. This scale categorises and also arranges the items under investigation into an order. Ordinal numbers are used to show rank order. Sequences range from the highest to the lowest number. An example could be the measure of conflict in an area, which can be ranked as low or high. Similarly, ordinal numbers are assigned to the sequence and do not indicate absolute values. Also, intervals between the categories are not equal

One particular example of an ordinal scale of measurement is the DAFOR scale, which is used to show abundance. Table 11.3 shows what the acronym DAFOR stands for:

TABLE 11.3: The DAFOR scale

Category	Score within the group
Dominant	5
Abundant	4
Frequent	3
Occasional	2
Rare	1

(**Source:** Adapted from Rich, Rebane, Fasham & Mcmeechan, 2005:203)

No simple relationship exists between the numerical values. The given order is always followed. This explains why some statistical operations like mean and standard deviation cannot be computed using the ordinal scale of measurement. The scale of measurement that follows the ordinal is the interval scale of measurement.

11.5.2.3 Interval scale of measurement

In addition to grouping and ordering, the interval scale of measurement recognises how far apart the units on the scale are. Unlike the nominal and the ordinal scales, which cannot successfully defend mathematical operations, the interval scale can. Some statistical operations such as the mean and standard deviation can be computed.

Mean is the mathematical average of all the terms. To find it, one needs to add up the values of all the terms and then divide by the total number of terms. Sometimes, we use the term arithmetic mean when we are discussing the mean, whereas standard deviation is a measure of how far away from the mean the measurements are.

Also, the interval scale of measurement accommodates the differences between, for example, 3rd and 4th, and 7th and 8th. Addition and subtraction can be carried out. However, the 8th is not twice the 4th. This is so because the interval scale does not have an absolute zero value. It shares this property with the nominal and ordinal scales since they also do not have an absolute zero value. Dates are good examples of an interval scale. Take, for example, the years 2001, 2005, and 2010, 2015. The interval between each point in the scale (one year) is equal. Ten years is required to reach the year 2015. Temperature is another example of an interval scale: 9° Fahrenheit is not three times 3° Fahrenheit. The Fahrenheit scale does not measure heat from zero, but it starts from -273°. Since this scale accommodates mathematical operations to a certain extent, it is suitable for mixed research work.

11.5.2.4 Ratio scale

The final scale is the ratio scale. It has all the properties of the other three scales. It differs from these other three in that it has an absolute zero. It uses ranking order and can be used for labelling. All the mathematical operations can be executed using the ratio scale. Measurement of weight, mass, length and others of this nature fall under ratio scale. A weight of 50 Newton is five times that of 10 Newton.

Each of the discussed scales of measurement has advantages and disadvantages. Sometimes, if we intend to offset the disadvantages we perform conversion from one scale to another. We now discuss one such conversion of scales.

11.5.3 Conversion of an interval to ordinal scale

It is not always possible to measure variables using the interval scale, and to analyse them using the same scale. Sometimes, this is because the recordings are too few. In such instances, an interval scale is downgraded to the ordinal scale. Downgrading should only be from strongest to weakest. Sometimes it is because the values of the variable read are too many, and some of the readings are of the same value. In such instances we proceed from the interval scale to the ordinal scale as will be described.

If the variable measured has values which are equal, their rankings will be tied together. These we then refer to as tied values or observations. Each of the tied values is assigned the value of the average of the ranking it would be given if there had been no ties. An illustration is given in Table 11.4, where the measurement of a variable length in millimetres (mm) is shown.

TABLE 11.4: Categorising continuous variables

Measured length (mm)	25	26	27; 27	28	29	30;30;30	31	32	33;33;33;33	34	35	36;36;36;36;36	37

The two extreme values 25 and 37 will be ranked as 1 and 23 respectively. Thereafter, 26 is ranked 2, and the two values of 27 occupy positions 3 and 4. The sum of 3 and 4 is 7, and the mean is 3.5, which is assigned as the ranking to each of them. This is done for each value to complete the table, as illustrated in Table 11.5.

TABLE 11.5: Ranking the tied variables

Measured length (mm)	25	26	27; 27	28	29	30;30;30	31	32	33;33;33;33	34	35	36;36;36;36;36	37
Rank	1	2	31/2 31/2	5	6	8; 8; 8	10	11	13.5;13.5;13,5;13.5	16	17	20;20;20;20	23

Although one method of converting an interval scale to an ordinal scale has been mentioned and analysed, there are several other ways. Anderberg (1973) suggests that there are 11 ways which can be used. He also suggests that each of the scales, nominal, ordinal, interval and ratio, can be converted to the other.

The order used to discuss the these measurement scales is from the weakest to the strongest, with the nominal being the weakest and the ratio scale the strongest, downgrading from the one above to the one below. In instances where a choice to select a measuring scale exists, it is recommended that the strongest must be selected.

Sometimes, conversion of scales of measurement is used to offset errors. Even though this is done we sometimes still get values with errors. We will now discuss how such errors arise, and the types which are known.

11.6 Measurement of error

When measuring a variable you can be as careful, and use as sophisticated a scale of measurement or apparatus as possible, but there is no guarantee that measurement obtained is exact (Blair, Menon & Bickart, 1991). Precautionary measures are put in place by researchers to minimise errors, but they still emerge (Tunks & Olness, 2002). Measured values are dependent on the skill of the observer, the apparatus used for measuring, and the environment in which the research is conducted. Regardless of the care put into operationalisation, errors still crop up. It is, however, best to know about these errors so that they can be prevented. Two types of errors are known, namely, systematic errors and random errors.

11.6.1 Systematic error

A systematic error is characterised by being predictable and reproducible. The error is consistent and in the same direction. The principal cause of systematic errors can be a persistent problem throughout the entire observation; or the use of erroneously calibrated apparatus; or a measuring technique that deflates or inflates the true value. An example is when an instrument reads 0,01 when not in use. A reading of more or less might be because it is not zeroed properly, or we say it has a zero error. Careful design of a measuring procedure eliminates systematic errors. The different forms of systematic error are:
▶ Social desirability (acquiescence bias)
▶ Leading questions
▶ Differences in subgroup responses in order of gender, ethnicity and age.

Social desirability error, also known as acquiescence bias error, occurs when the respondents answer to please the researcher. Only those answers which the respondents believe are desirable to the researcher, are given.

Systematic errors arising because of leading questions occur when the questions direct the respondents to answer in a particular way.

Finally, systematic errors arising because of differences in the subgroups are attributed to their different social identity, cultural beliefs, and even the socialisation patterns.

Careful construction of questions can reduce systematic errors. Even though a researcher may manage to remove systematic errors, another type of error remains. This type of error is known as random error.

11.6.2 Random error

Unlike systematic errors, random error, is not predictable. Random error is a statistical fluctuation in either direction, in the measured variable. Fluctuations can be attributed to the precision limitation of the measuring device (Fowler, 1991). Fluctuations might also be caused by how the respondent feels that particular day. The respondent might be in low spirits or high spirits, and this determines whether she or he responds to the question appropriately, or whether the measure will deliver the same value For example, the height of the same participant in a study may be measured as: 1,74m; 1,77m; 1,75m; and 1,73m. This could be because of limitations in measuring precision, from carelessness, inaccurate equipment, or poor method. Also, the environment in which the questions are executed might also allow for random errors to crop up. It is possible sometimes that we ignore the intensity of light, or time of day which might affect the way a respondent answers the questions. Another type of a random error is regression to the mean. This is observable when, in a particular instance, a respondent scores high, while in another instance with the same question or test, he or she scores low.

Acquiescence bias also occurs as random error. Also known as 'yea saying', acquiescence bias is essentially created when respondents tend to agree with whatever the interviewer presents to them. Perhaps the interviewer and the respondent become over-friendly during the interview, or the respondent feels that they have to give the 'right' answer, so as not to offend the interviewer.

Statistical or random errors can be avoided by taking large amounts of measurements. The researcher repeats the data-generating process using the same method and the mean of the data is found (see earlier in section 11.5.2.3 for an explanation of mean). Also, one can opt to use another technique to generate data and see if the results are in line with what was obtained before. An error estimate on a single-scale observation is taken as half of the scale. For example, the diameter of 23mm on a N\$1 coin, measured using a ruler graduated in mm, will be read as 23 ± 0,5mm. If numbers of measurement are available then the measured value is:

$$1/n \sum_0^n (x \pm ß/\sqrt{n^2})$$

Where n is the number of measurements done; x is each measurement done; $\sum_0^n ß$ is the error on a single measurement; and $ß/\sqrt{n^2}$ is referred to as the error on the mean. The consideration we give to errors in research is to ensure that quality in research is always addressed.

Stop and reflect

Suggest why some variables are measured to generate data, while others are counted in order to generate data. Give your own illustrative examples in each case.

11.7 Measurement of quality in research

The process used to measure concepts must provide stable results. One expects to get the same results if the same measurement process is repeated. In addition, if there are other measures carried out, the new results obtained must not show disparity with those results already known, or expected. In other words, the results must be consistent and they must be reliable. The operations must actually measure what they are supposed to measure. This means that the measures are valid in producing the correct measure of that outcome, and not another measure of a different outcome? Carefully constructed research questions and careful observations of the measure are the only way to guarantee reliability and validity. Psychometric instruments such as interviews, questionnaires and tests used to generate data usually guarantee validity and reliability since they are designed to have these characteristics, while reliability and validity assess quality in research (Flynn, Schroeder & Sakakibara, 1994).

11.7.1 Measurement of reliability

Reliability is the repeatability of the outcome of a measure, and is affected less by random errors. Repeatability occurs if the same results are produced when the data is generated again using the same method (Phelan & Wren, 2005). The process of measuring the variable yields a consistent value. However, for repeatability to be exercised, the conditions under which the measurement of the variable is operationalised need to be the same on all occasions in which reliability is being sought. Also, the use of the same type of scale of measurement is recommended for each of the occasions in which the measure is repeated to check its reliability. In some instances, the scale of measure might be changed, but the outcome of the measure must show the same results.

When re-measuring a variable using the same technique or another technique, time interval must be taken into consideration. This is so since some factors, such as mood, alertness, can change over the course of a given interval of hours. Another factor might be knowledge or skill which changes over the course of a week, or month.

Reliability becomes a challenge if a single observer is making measurements; the researcher might let subjectivity contaminate the observations (Moskal & Leydens, 2000). Instead, a critical colleague or peer can be invited to offset errors. It may also be a problem when multiple researchers are measuring the same variable. Their particular attitudes and beliefs may influence the results.

There are several methods used to evaluate reliability. They range from: test–retest; internal consistency; alternate forms; interrater and intrarater reliability. These methods are discussed next.

11.7.1.1 Test-retest reliability

If the measured variable in the concept under investigation does not fluctuate between an interval of time, then the degree to which the two measurements are related is known as the test–retest reliability of the measure. Gay, Mills and Airasian (2009) understand the notion of test–retest reliability as the consistency with which tests are answered, or when the measures remain relatively the same in each encounter. In other words, the measures in the encounters are stable, and stability is an indicator that the measures are similar. A high percentage of stability is an indicator of a high percentage of reliability. However, test–retest can also sensitise the respondent in such a way as might make the measurement unreliable (Joppe, 2000).

In a research study, data are generated, presented, analysed and conclusions are drawn. If the research is re-conducted say, two months or a year later, the test is still performing reliably if you have similar conclusions for both occasions.

As stated earlier, if the conditions under which the measures are conducted are changed, the chances of getting similar or congruent results diminish. Some of the factors which might render the results of the two conclusions different could be environmental: weather, lighting and temperature changes may have an effect on the two measures. Also, worldviews and attitudes are not static: it is probable that the second time you conduct the retest, an individual might have changed his or her worldview or attitude for any number of reasons.

11.7.1.2 Internal consistency

The use of multiple psychometric instruments to measure a concept is applied so as to address internal consistency. However, there must be a relationship between the psychometric instruments used. Internal consistency can be assessed by splitting the scale of measure, in which case the scale needs to have a long range. For example, a scale ranging from 0 to 30 can be split at 15. The two split parts are analysed, and if the results obtained from each part are similar, then there is internal consistency.

In internal consistency and test–retest reliability, the same type of questions in the instruments are used. This is not the case with alternate forms reliability.

11.7.1.3 Alternate forms reliability

This method is used to evaluate measurement reliability and is distinct from the other two discussed earlier in that the format of the psychometric measure is changed (Newby, 2010). Questions might be rewritten or reworded. This makes the questions different from one another, but they will still be consistent with one theme. The two sets of questions are then administered to the participants, and if the results are similar, this is consistent with alternate forms of reliability.

In the methods used to evaluate measurement reliability discussed so far, it is most likely that one observer is in control of administering the measures. In the case of interrater reliability the situation is different.

11.7.1.4 Interrater reliability

If more than one observer is present and they all compare their observations, interrater reliability is addressed if the results obtained from all the reporting observers are similar. Take a case of participatory action research, where the researcher reports her findings, and the subjects and a critical colleague are also in a position to comment on the observations made: if the reported observations are similar, then interrater reliability is addressed.

11.7.1.5 Intrarater reliability

Intrarater reliability happens when one observer assesses an individual on two or more occasions with the aim of finding out whether the results obtained are similar. This type of reliability is useful when assessing a subject, like mathematics, or physiology.

In order to have confidence in a measure, reliability must exist already, or occur before validity. We now discuss validity.

11.7.2 Validity

Validity, as a measure of quality, assesses whether what is measured is what is intended to be measured (Phelan & Wren, 2005). Does the operationalisation definition accurately reflect the concept the research is interested in? Does it measure what it purports to measure? A valid measure of a concept or construct is one that shows how:

- Closely related it is to other apparently valid measures.
- Closely related to the known or the supposed correlates of that concept.
- Not related to measures of unrelated concepts.

For example, a valid count of one's cattle in a kraal must correspond with the number of cows registered in the dipping tank register. In the case of measurement, an example is the measure of the pure melting point of ice at standard temperature and pressure, which must correspond with the standard known value of 0° C. The strands of validity are four, namely: content, criterion, face, and construct validity.

11.7.2.1 Face validity

Face validity exists if the concept under measurement relates more to the meaning of the concept under measure than to any other concept. A count of how many learners passed Grade 10 in a particular year, is a face validity of the pass rate for Grade 10 level. A measure of length in metres from one point of a circle to another point directly opposite it, is a face validity of the diameter of a circle.

11.7.2.2 Content validity

Content validity is addressed if the measure takes into account all the ranges manifested by the variable. To explore all the possible range, one seeks views from experts in the area, and also from reviewing the literature.

11.7.2.3 Criterion validity

In criterion validity, the idea of standard is brought in. A measure of a variable is compared with an unknown value. An example is when testing the boiling point of pure water. The moment the value obtained is in agreement with the standard known value, then there is criterion validity.

11.7.2.4 Construct validity

In construct validity, the measure obtained needs to resonate with other measures, as suggested in theory. It uses deductive routes to arrive at addressing construct validity.

11.7.3 Triangulation

Finally, to ensure that quality in research prevails, researchers talk of triangulation. Triangulation entails the use of two or more measures of the same variable to ensure quality (Coles & McGrath, 2010). Creswell and Miller (2000:126) define triangulation as "a validity procedure where researchers search for convergence among multiple and different sources of information to form themes or categories in a study". Four strands of validity exist, namely: methodological; data; theoretical; and research triangulation. Each type of triangulation entails the use of multiple ways to investigate the concept under discussion. For example, in methodological triangulation, two or more studies within a single study are used. This is also true for the three remaining types of triangulation.

Stop and reflect

How might failure to fully conceptualise a concept affect the quality of research? Write your answer as a set of guidelines for a new researcher.

Conclusion

In this chapter, we looked into the types of concepts, direct observable, indirect observable, and constructs. This allowed us to understand what concepts are, and enabled us to define them conceptually and operationally. Conceptual and operational definition of concepts is the key to planning in research studies. Conceptualisation shows the link between the concept and its components. Operationalisation of a concept provides specific rules to measure the variables which define the concept.

The idea of variables was developed to help you understand operationalisation of concepts. Variables, when acted upon by the proper measurement scale, will address reliability, validity and triangulation as parameters used as a gauge of quality in research studies. The treatment of different types of variables enables us to see how each type is related to the concept, and how it might be measured.

Measurement and counting were discussed as methods used for generating data. This led to a discussion of the different types of errors which arise in research work when measuring or counting. To address these errors, we discussed quality in research, in which we brought in the need for and importance of validity, reliability and triangulation.

Closing activities

Analysis and consolidation questions

1 Locate an article in an educational journal that gives an account of a research process.

  a Locate three concepts and describe how the researcher defines them.

  b Where does the researcher get the definition? Evaluate the definitions.

  c Describe the operational definition of the concepts. Evaluate the definitions in terms of reliability and validity.

  d Is the measure reliable? Why or why not?

  e Is the measure valid? Why or why not?

2 Describe the relationship between a conceptual definition and an operational definition of a concept/construct.

  a Is there any relationship between the two types of definition?

  b What are the components of the: i) conceptual definition; ii) operational definition?

3 Identify a research paper in an educational journal:

  a Which level of measurement does the researcher use: nominal, ordinal, interval or ratio?

  b Why does the researcher use this scale of measurement, according to Stevens' taxonomy?

  c What limitation, advantage, or disadvantage does Stevens' taxonomy have if the research is: i) qualitative; ii) quantitative?

  d How does the researcher address issues related to: i) systematic errors; ii) random errors?

  e How does the researcher address: i) reliability; ii) validity; ii) triangulation?

Bibliography

Anderberg, M.R. 1973. *Cluster analysis for applications.* New York: Academic Press.

Babbie, E. 2011. *The basics of social research.* Belmont, CA: Wadsworth Cengage Learning.

Baker, T.L. 1994. *Doing Social Research.* (2nd ed.). New York: McGraw-Hill.

Blair, J., Menon, G. & Bickart, B. 1991. Measurement effects in self vs. proxy responses to survey questions: An information-processing perspective. In P. Biemer, R. Groves, L. Lyberg, N. Mathiowetz & S. Sudman (Eds). *Measurement Errors in Surveys.* New York: John Wiley and Sons (pp. 145–166).

Coles, A. & McGrath, J. 2010. *Your educational research project handbook* (3rd ed.). Edinburgh: Pearson Education Limited.

Creswell, J.W. & Miller, D.L. 2000. Determining validity in qualitative enquiry. *Theory into Practice*, 39(3):124–131.

Creswell, J.W. 2012. *Educational research: Planning, conducting and evaluating quantitative and qualitative research* (4th ed.). Boston: Pearson Education.

Cutcliffe, J.R. & Harder, H.G. 2012. Methodological precision in qualitative research: Slavish adherence or "following the yellow brick road?". *The Qualitative Report*, 17(82):1–19.

Field, A. 2005. *Discovering statistics using SPSS.* London: Sage Publications.

Flynn, B.B., Schroeder, R.G. & Sakakibara, S. 1994. A framework for quality management research and associated measurement instrument. *Journal of Operational Management*, 11(4):339–366.

Fowler, F.J. 1991. Reducing interviewer-related error through interviewer training, supervision and other means. In P. Biemer, et al. (Eds). *Measurement Errors in Surveys.* New York: John Wiley and Sons (pp. 259–275).

Gay, L.R., Mills, G.E. & Airasian, P. 2009. *Educational research: Competences for analysis and application* (9th ed.). London: Pearson Education.

Grinnel, R.M. & Unrau, Y.A. 2010. *Social work research and evaluation: Foundation of evidence-based practice* (9th ed.). New York: Oxford University Press.

Hannagan, Y. 1997. *Mastering statistics* (3rd ed.). London: Macmillan Press Ltd.

Heffener, C.L. 2014. Defining variables. Retrieved 25 March 2015 from: http://Allpsych.com/research methods/definingvariables.

Joppe, M. 2000. The research process. Retrieved 23 October 2013 from: http://www.ryerson.ca/~mjoppe/rp.htm.

Lee, K. 2005. Conceptualization, operationalization and measurement. Retrieved 25 October 2014 from: www.cityu.edu.hk/dss/adpam/rm/handout/l4.doc.

Mann, P.S. 2011. *Introductory statistics: International student version* (7th ed.). Denver: John Wiley & Sons.

Matthews, B. & Ross, L. 2010. *Research methods: A practical guide for the social sciences.* (1st ed.). Edinburgh Gate: Pearson Education.

Mitchell, W.K. 2002. *Research methodology* (3rd ed.). Cape Town: Oxford University Press Southern Africa.

Moskal, B.M. & Leydens, J.A. 2000. Scoring rubric development: Validity and reliability. Retrieved 28 March 2015 from: http://pareonline.net/getvn.asp?v=7&n=10.

Newby, P. 2010. *Research methods for education* (1st ed.). Essex: Pearson Education.

Patton, M. 1996. *Utilization-focused evaluation* (3rd ed.). London: Sage Publication Ltd.

Phelan, C. & Wren, J. 2005. Exploring reliability in academic assessment. Retrieved 17 March 2015 from: https://www.uni.edu/chfasoa/reliabilityandvalidity.htm.

Pietersen, J. & Maree, K. 2012. Overview of statistical techniques. In K. Maree (Ed) *First steps in research.* Pietermaritzburg: Van Schaik Publishers (pp. 225–252).

Rich, T., Rebane, M., Fasham, M. & Mcmeechan, F. 2005. Methods for surveying habitats. In D. Hill, M. Fashman, G. Tucker, M. Shewry & P. Shaw (Eds). *Handbook of biodiversity methods survey, evaluation and monitoring.* Cambridge: Cambridge University Press (pp. 201–222).

Rumsey, D.J. 2011. Statistics for dummies. (2nd ed.). Retrieved 18 March 2015 from: http://www.dummies.com/store/product/Statistics-For-Dummies-2nd-Edition.productCd-0470911085.html15.

Silberstein, A. & Scott, S. 1991. Expenditure diary surveys and their associated errors. In P. Biemer, et al. (Eds). *Measurement Errors in Surveys.* New York: John Wiley and Sons (pp. 303–326).

Tunks, T. & Olness, F. 2002. Measurement and measurement error. Retrieved 25 October 2013 from http://www.physics.smu.edu/~olness/www/06fall1320/lab/01lab.pdf.

CHAPTER 12

Chinedu Okeke

Achieving qualitative validity, reliability and generalisability

KEY CONCEPTS

Epistemological issues relate to knowing what it is to know something.

Hierarchy of authority refers to the structure of influence and authority within an organisation, such as the school. Such a hierarchy of authority increases in power of control as it moves up, so that the principal holds the highest authority in the school.

Historicism a branch of philosophy that holds that all social and cultural phenomena are determined by history.

Humanism a philosophy that attaches much emphasis to human beings and to the study of the whole human in a rational approach which is concerned with the understanding of the uniqueness of humanity.

Neo-Kantianism a philosophy derived from the works of Immanuel Kant (1724—1804). Later philosophers whose ideas derive from Kant are referred to as neo-Kantians.

Ontological issues relate to knowledge of what kinds of knowledge exist in the world.

Phenomenon in the context of qualitative research, a phenomenon represents the behaviours or events you may be interested in investigating.

Philosophy of science a branch of philosophy that deals with the study of the foundations and methods of scientific knowledge. Its major concern is with the reliability and purpose of scientific knowledge.

Positivism a philosophy that emphasises that things can only be seen and observed. It believes in objective truth that waits 'out there' to be 'discovered'.

Pragmatism a philosophy of human action, which, in education, is concerned with the usefulness or utility of ideas. It is not only concerned with the search for truth like many other philosophies, but with what works.

LEARNING OUTCOMES

By the end of this chapter, you should be able to:

▶ Explain the meanings of both qualitative and quantitative research approaches.

▶ Describe briefly the origins of both research approaches.

▶ Describe the differences between qualitative and quantitative research.

▶ Identify the main criteria for checking the validity, reliability and generalisability of qualitative research findings.

▶ Understand how to demonstrate qualitative research validity and reliability.

▶ Understand how to interpret the credibility of qualitative research report.

Case study: Measuring credibility in qualitative research

Siyabonga is a Bachelor of Education (Hons) student entering the postgraduate research field for the first time in his educational career. Although Siyabonga has been introduced to the two approaches to research – the quantitative and qualitative approaches – he does not have a well-developed understanding of the various meanings and methodologies associated with them. He has just completed the research methods module and passed the summative examination, in fulfilment of course requirements. Siyabonga thinks he knows something about qualitative research. He wants to do qualitative research because he thinks it would enable him to avoid statistics and mathematics. This is the limit of his understanding of the qualitative research approach. Siyabonga does not know that the qualitative research approach means more than just the non-application of statistics. At the same time, Siyabonga does not know that qualitative research findings have different criteria which measure the credibility of those findings. He does not know that validity, reliability and generalisability mean different things in qualitative research. What is more, Siyabonga cannot even define qualitative research; nonetheless he is interested in conducting his study through the qualitative research approach.

What advice would you give to this particular student? Whatever your advice to him, the starting point for Siyabonga would be to read the rest of this chapter.

Introduction

In this chapter we want to look at one of the most interesting discussions in the conduct of research, regarding how both quantitative and qualitative researchers make claims that support the authenticity of their findings. This is about how qualitative researchers demonstrate that their research reports, and the processes leading to such reports, are valid, credible, and can be trusted. There have been debates among researchers for many years about whether the kind of research by qualitative researchers and the manner in which they conduct their research, can ever lead to findings that can be tested, trusted and generalised. By reading this chapter in conjunction with related chapters in this book, you will understand what qualitative researchers do when they set out to conduct research.

Experience has also shown that many postgraduate students who enter the research field are unsure of the differences between qualitative and quantitative research approaches. This is true particularly of those who want to pursue their studies through the qualitative approach, as we saw in the case of Siyabonga, but are often uncertain about what is involved. This chapter has been written with these students in mind, to help them find ways of demonstrating qualitative validity as well as reliability. To develop this chapter, we will:

- ☑ **Look** briefly at the meaning of qualitative approach.
- ☑ **Explore** the unique nature of qualitative data collection methods.
- ☑ **Identify** the characteristics of quantitative research approach.
- ☑ **Describe** the major differences between qualitative and quantitative research.
- ☑ **Discuss** the influence of the philosophy of science of the eighteenth and nineteenth centuries on the development of both research approaches.
- ☑ **Identify** the main criteria for checking qualitative validity and reliability.
- ☑ **Discuss** the main issues relating to the generalisability of qualitative research findings. Look briefly at the implications of our discussions to how you will conduct your own research.

Stop and reflect

As a follow-up to Siyabonga's case:
- ▶ What, in your view, could be the cause of Siyabonga's confusion about research approaches?
- ▶ How would you describe Siyabonga's confusion? Is it perhaps typical of students like him, or unusual?

12.1 Meaning of qualitative research approach

We want to start our discussion with an attempt to explain the meaning of qualitative research. It is important for us to begin with such an explanation because this section is at the heart of the rest of our discussions in this chapter. The word 'qualitative' implies a recognition of the research processes that result in the collection of fieldwork data, which cannot be reduced to quantification and measurement.

Qualitative research is concerned with the understanding of how a particular individual or group of individuals think, and the meanings they attach to their actions. In the quest to understand these meanings, qualitative researchers are encouraged to adopt ways that enable them to represent the voices or actual words of the participants in their research reports. You should note that this approach of using the participants' actual words in reporting research findings is what enables qualitative researchers to claim that their approach is 'thick' (meaning deep and substantial) and descriptive. Qualitative research approaches imply an emphasis or recognition of the processes and meanings that are not readily susceptible to measurement in terms of quantity, amount, intensity or frequency (Carney, Joiner & Tragou, 1997; Okeke, 2003; Wagner & Okeke, 2009; Okeke, 2010d).

Moreover, qualitative research approaches represent all kinds of research that are associated with the interpretive and/or naturalistic approaches. It is an umbrella term for all forms of humanistic research that emphasise the interpretation of meanings that are characteristic of the social world (Glesne & Peshkin, 1992). You will remember that Chapter 3 of this book deals with all aspects of interpretive research: read the discussions in this again if you have to, as doing so will complement our discussions in this section. It should also clear any doubts about what the qualitative research approach means. In 12.2 we want to explore the unique nature of the types of methods that qualitative researchers employ when collecting qualitative data during their fieldwork.

12.2 The unique nature of qualitative data collection methods

What you are about to learn is very important because it will enable you to understand further the uniqueness of qualitative data, and why the assessment of the findings emerging from such process requires criteria different from those meant for quantitative research findings. Qualitative researchers employ a number of data collection methods in the conduct of their research. These include participant observation; interviewing methods; focus group discussions (FGD); the use of diaries; the documentary approach; and edited topical life history approach. Let us briefly explain what qualitative researchers do when they employ any of these methods to collect fieldwork data:

12.2.1 Participant observation method of data collection

Participant observation is one of the methods that qualitative researchers employ when they go into the field to obtain information in the form of data. Participant observation requires the researcher's continuous involvement with the natural setting of the participants under study. It involves watching people, events or situations, and obtaining first-hand information relating to particular aspects of such events (Ujo, 2000). There are two types of observation, namely overt observation and covert observation, but before we proceed further, let us explain what these types of observation mean.

12.2.1.1 Overt observation

The word 'overt' entails a research process that is open to the knowledge and understanding of everyone in the environment where a particular research activity is taking place. Participant observation becomes overt where the identity of the researcher and the objectives and processes of her or his research activities are revealed to everyone who is involved in a particular environment where such research is taking place.

Consider a particular scenario in which you are conducting a case study on persistent lateness to school amongst Grade 11 learners in a particular school. You understand the school to comprise the learners, their teachers, the school's management team (SMT), the school's governing body (SGB), the learners' parents, the relevant department of education officials, and the wider community. So you are an overt researcher if the intentions of your research, as well as your actual research activities, are made known to all or most of the components of a particular school. Now let us look at the other type of observation.

12.2.1.2 Covert observation

There are many words related to the concept of 'covert', namely, hidden, secret, underground, and concealed, to name a few. You become covert when you decide to conceal or hide your identity during the research process in which you may be observing your participants. A covert researcher therefore is someone who does not want his or her identity or research intentions to be known, or openly seen by any or all of the components of, for example, the school in 12.2.1.1. The general idea is that when observers conceal their identities this enhances the quality of the outcome of the situation they may be observing. However, this type of observation goes with many ethical requirements, which you are required to observe as a researcher.

Firstly, by the time you begin your fieldwork you will be required to demonstrate how you will protect the rights of your participants. For instance, you will be asked to demonstrate how to obtain the consent of your participants. So you really cannot afford to hide your identity if you are to succeed in doing this. Again, where you intend to enter the personal lives of your participants in your study, it would be very problematic if you do so as a covert researcher. Most importantly, you could face legal action if it is found that you are a covert researcher where you have not obtained the relevant consent. You will remember that issues concerning research ethics and ethical considerations in research have been fully discussed in both Chapters 6 and 7. Refer to these chapters to complement our discussions in this section.

Secondly, we listed the different components of the school, in our discussions of overt observation in 12.2.1.1. Here, you should note that an essential aspect of the school components is that it operates in a **hierarchy of authority**, or chain of command, that must be observed by anyone entering the school. Such hierarchy of authority could hinder the activity of the covert participant observer. This is because, as a researcher seeking to enter the school space, you will not only be required to observe such chain of command, but such a requirement will make it very difficult for you to operate as a covert researcher in the contemporary school setting.

However, whether you are an overt or covert participant observer, what is very important about this method is that it enables you to gain first-hand knowledge about participants and their natural environment. This is also very important for the quality of the data being obtained. For a more detailed discussion on participant observation, refer to Chapter 16. Before we proceed to the other types of qualitative data collection methods, reflect on a few important questions.

Stop and reflect

From our discussions so far, consider some other advantages you can derive from using participant observation to improve the quality of your qualitative data:
1 Can you think what kind of data would be gathered from this method of data collection?
2 Can you think of any other data collection methods used by qualitative researchers? Write a short description of the method, its uses, and its advantages in qualitative research.

12.2.2 Interviewing method

Qualitative researchers also make use of the interviewing method, which is fully discussed in Chapter 17. To complement the discussions in that chapter, you should note that interviews can be sequential or structured, semi-structured and unstructured. Whatever form the interviewing takes, its major aim is to obtain information from the respondents through some kind of verbal interaction.

12.2.2.1 Unstructured, semi-structured, and structured interviews

In an unstructured interview, the researcher adopts an open-ended approach that allows the participants in the interview the freedom to respond in their own way. Such an approach to interviewing is usually and necessarily not systematic, and does not proceed with any form of listed or prepared questions.

On the other hand, the interview becomes semi-structured when the researcher decides to order his or her questions in such a way as to present the interview procedure to the respondents.

The structured interview is one in which the researcher carefully prepares the interview procedures. He or she will carefully review the questions and procedures before the interview meeting. Another name for structured interview is sequential, because the interview questions are presented in a sequence or order, in which the respondents are expected to respond. More so, the researcher using the structured approach consciously follows the sequence and may attempt to bring the respondent back to the sequence if she or he finds that the respondent is deviating from the sequence or structure of the interview process. The participant in a sequential or structured interview is also pre-informed on the nature of the interview, and may even be given the interview questions in advance. In recent years, both quantitative and qualitative researchers apply the structured interview method in the conduct of their study.

One very important thing you should know about interviewing as a qualitative data collection instrument relates to its strong ability to obtain information that may not be easily accessible through other means. Interviewing serves as a major research tool in investigating certain categories of participants. For example, you can use the interviewing approach when researching those who can neither read nor write, and with young children. Using the interview technique enables you to repeatedly enter the social space of the interviewee in ways that will encourage valid findings. We now proceed to the next section to look at another type of qualitative data collection method.

12.2.3 Focus group discussion method

Focus group discussion (FGD) is another data collection method which qualitative researchers use when they want to obtain fieldwork data. This method involves bringing together people or individuals who share similar characteristics, in a small group of between four and 12 people, for a discussion. FGD is a good approach when you want to stimulate people into revealing the underlying reasons for their behaviours and beliefs. According to Catterall and Maclaran (1997:12): "group interaction will be productive in widening the range of responses, activating forgotten details of experience and releasing inhibitions that may otherwise discourage participants from disclosing information".

Do the short activity next to help you reflect on our discussion of both interviews and focus group discussions.

Stop and reflect

Consider our discussions so far on interviews and the FGD method:
1 Can you think of any differences between interviews and FGD?
2 Describe by listing what your thoughts are on the differences.
3 How would you cater for these differences as you make decisions about your own fieldwork?
4 What would direct or influence your choice of data collection methods during your qualitative fieldwork?

A major difference between FGD and other group interviews is that in focus group discussions you as the researcher will simply take on the role of the moderator or facilitator. In this case, participants will engage in group discussions with one another while you play the role of their moderator as the discussions proceed. Again, whereas in other group interviews where the researcher takes on the role of the interviewer who directs the questions to the interviewee, in FGD you only perform a background role of facilitator or moderator. For more detailed discussions on FGD, read Chapter 19. Let us now look at the diary as an instrument of qualitative data collection.

12.2.4 Use of diaries as qualitative data collection instruments

A diary is a record in which people document events, which they feel are important to them. Another name for a diary is a journal. Such records of events will necessarily contain dates and the special reasons why such events are important to the individuals, that give a sense of why they have recorded the events. Although diaries are not very commonly used by researchers throughout sub-Saharan Africa, they are nonetheless an important qualitative data collection instrument.

The three types of diaries that are commonly used include the intimate diary, memoir, and the log:
- The *intimate* or *personal diary* represents a place where private thoughts and opinions may be recorded. Many now great and famous men and women kept this form of diary which gives us insight to their lives, ideas and times. Nelson Mandela is known to have kept such diaries during his lifetime.
- A second type of diary is the *memoir*, where selected events in one's life that are of special interest or memorable are recorded.
- The third type of diary is the *log*, which also performs a similar function to the memoir, though without involving the element of personal selection (Elliott, 1997; Okeke, 2010d).

In addition to the three types, diaries also take on different forms. The diary can be structured, where items are listed for the research participant to indicate how each item affects him or her, or it could contain a guide instructing the participant on what to do at every stage. The diary could be open with the participant user required to itemise important activities in his or her daily life. Whatever form the diary takes, its importance lies in its usefulness because a diary allows you as researcher to continue to obtain information from your research participants even when they are not in contact with you or in places you cannot reach owing to time differences.

Can you still remember our example of the study on persistent lateness to school amongst Grade 11 learners of a particular school? In the case of such research, you will certainly require the use of the diary if you are interested in obtaining credible and valid results. You can use the diary approach to capture those occurrences that may impact the learners' ability to get to school on time. Information about such occurrences or events in the lives of the learners cannot easily be captured through any other qualitative data collection methods. You can now see why the diary will continue to be a very important qualitative data collection technique for use by qualitative researchers. Continuing our discussions on the unique nature of qualitative data collection methods, we want to look at another important approach to data collection: This is the documentary approach, which forms the topic of our next discussion.

12.2.5 Documentary approach to qualitative data collection

Another qualitative data collection instrument is the documentary approach. This approach is also known as a secondary source of data collection. Refer to Chapter 20 to engage with this method of data collection in detail. For now, it is important for you to note that a secondary source of data collection is not a major qualitative data collection method. Instead, this approach simply plays a complementary role to other approaches and is also used by quantitative researchers. We will look at the quantitative research approach in 12.3. Before proceeding to the new section, let us look at one more qualitative data collection method.

12.2.6 Edited topical life history approach to qualitative data collection

Like the diary approach, the edited topical life history approach is not a very common qualitative data collection instrument among qualitative researchers in sub-Saharan Africa. However, it is a major research approach capable of adding value to the type of data we want to obtain as qualitative researchers. The edited topical life history approach is an attempt to obtain an account of the life of an individual, as recorded or given by the person or group of people who had lived or are still living within the context of such life. The most important data sources of this approach are autobiographies, memoirs, logs, letters, photographs, film, interviews, verbatim reports, observations, newspaper accounts, and court records.

Having explored the unique nature of qualitative data collection methods, we will take a brief look at the other type of research approach, the quantitative research approach in the following section.

Critical thinking challenge

Considering our discussions on the unique nature of qualitative research data collection methods:
1 Start to reflect on the nature of the data that you would obtain if you were to use any (or all) of the data collection approaches we discussed earlier. Make some notes on your reflections in relation to your own intended research.
2 Are you familiar with the questionnaire instrument and can you associate this instrument with any research approach? Can you think of any differences between data collected by qualitative methods, and data collected using the questionnaire instrument? (The questionnaire instrument is discussed in Chapter 18.)

12.3 What is quantitative research?

Although this chapter does not deal with quantitative research, the goal we have set for ourselves in this chapter will not be achieved if we fail to highlight some important features of quantitative research. By doing this, we lay the foundation for our discussion in 12.4 on the major differences between qualitative and quantitative research.

We have already explored the meaning of qualitative research. In this section you will learn how to identify research that is quantitative in orientation. To start with, you can easily identify a research approach by simply understanding the roles it is set to fulfil. Quantitative research is the branch of research which emphasises causal relationships between variables. Quantitative research is also known as variable analysis research (Hammersley, 1989; Okeke, 2009a).

This approach maintains that certain principles are fundamental to the conduct of research, and includes such ideas as:

▶ That the research enterprise must be accompanied by some elements of controlled experimentation;
▶ Giving clear demonstration of researcher objectivity and a total detachment from the subject;
▶ Showing evidence of the predictability and generalisation of research findings; that all scientific enterprise must be value-free (Obikeze, 1990; Okeke, 2003).

Being a field-testing enterprise, the quantitative research approach makes use of well-structured techniques including experimental, quasi-experimental, and survey methods. It relies strongly on the use of questionnaires, large population samples, variables, and hypothesis. You should now be able to associate the questionnaire instrument with a particular research approach – the quantitative research approach.

It is important too, for you to note that the operations of this research approach are guided by the assumptions that all human behaviour can be explained by what such researchers refer to as 'social facts', which derive from the natural law principle of deductive logic. This explains why quantitative researchers appear only to be interested in understanding distinguishing characteristics, elemental properties and empirical boundaries.

Using the questionnaire survey method, the researcher operating from this research approach will be more interested in measuring 'how much' or 'how often' because human social behaviour is only seen in terms of variables. Note that more information on quantitative research can be obtained from various chapters of this book, including Chapters 22, 23 and 24 and Chapter 26. These chapters will expand and complement your reading of the current chapter (Okeke, 2003; 2010d).

Now let us turn to the major differences between qualitative and quantitative research approaches, which will enable you to appreciate why findings emerging from both research approaches must be assessed differently, using different criteria.

12.4 Major differences between qualitative and quantitative research

Qualitative research can be differentiated from quantitative research methods in terms of the principles guiding their modes of enquiry. You should view these differences in relation to assumptions, purpose approaches, and the researcher's role in the actual fieldwork research process. These differences are represented in Table 12.1.

TABLE 12.1: Fundamental differences between qualitative and quantitative research

Quantitative approach	Qualitative approach
Assumptions	
Social facts have an objective reality	Reality is socially constructed
Primacy of methods. Variables can be identified and relationship measured	Primacy of subject matter. Phenomena are complex, interwoven and difficult to measure
Etic or outsider's point of view	Emic or insider's point of view
Purpose	
Generalisability	Contextualised
Predictions	Interpretation
Causal explanations	Understanding actors' perspectives
Approaches	
Begins with hypotheses and theories	Ends with hypotheses and grounded theory
Manipulation and control using formal instruments	Emergence and portrayal, researcher also assumes the role of an instrument
Experimentation, deductive and component analysis	Naturalistic, inductive and searches for patterns
Converts data to numerical indices and makes use of abstract language in write-up	Makes minor use of numerical indices and employs descriptive write-up
Researcher's role	
Detachment and impartiality	Personal involvement
Objective portrayal	Empathetic understanding

(**Source:** Adapted from Glesne and Peshkin, 1992:7)

From our discussions on the meaning of quantitative research in 12.3, and from the information in Table 12.1, you will discover that quantitative research relies on a well-established and systematic operating system. For example, with the hypothesis drawn and questionnaires constructed, the quantitative researcher is able to demonstrate the validity of the research instruments, as well as the perceived emerging findings even before data-gathering fieldwork is executed.

In other words, the assessment of quantitative research can effectively take place even in the absence of data. This means the quantitative researcher is able to show how data he or she has not even obtained can be assessed even before embarking on the actual fieldwork. At this point, it is important for you to understand that this approach to the assessment of unavailable fieldwork data is not possible with qualitative research design and execution. Why is this the situation with qualitative research data?

In the following section, 12.5, which deals with the assessment of qualitative research and the influence of the philosophy of science of the eighteenth and nineteenth centuries, we hope you will find the answer to the question posed in the last paragraph. But before reading on, do the following activity.

Stop and reflect

1 Think about the fundamental differences discussed in 12.4. You were asked earlier to reflect on the differences between the types of data collected from quantitative and qualitative research methods:

   a What were your reflections on the differences?

   b Are these differences becoming clearer to you now and do these differences make sense to you?

2 Engage in a group discussion with your peers to understand how you each feel about these differences:

   a Can you make sense from the fact that qualitative research findings should necessarily have different criteria for assessment from the criteria for assessing quantitative research findings?

   b What are your views overall about these?

12.5 Influence of philosophy of science of eighteenth and nineteenth centuries

In this section you will learn how the philosophy of science impacted the development of criteria for assessing qualitative research findings. In so doing, it is important for you to understand that research methodologies have a history. Such history is very long and it dates back to the philosophy of science in the eighteenth and nineteenth centuries. That history shows how the philosophy of science influenced the development of criteria for assessing the findings of research, whether it is qualitative or quantitative.

It is important for people who are starting out in research, as well as academics who teach research methods, to know something about the history of research methodology. It gives them a better understanding of the background and origins of current research methodologies. More so, it helps those entering the practice of research to be better equipped to make informed decisions about their choices of research methodologies.

What history are we talking about here? We are exploring the history of how the philosophy of science laid the foundations for two very important research traditions, namely, positivist-quantitative, and post-positivist or qualitative research traditions. Chapter 2 on positivism and Chapter 3 on interpretive research have helped you to fully understand our present discussions in 12.5. Find time to read them if you have not already done so.

Our discussions here take a fresh direction: to highlight how the philosophy of science in the eighteenth and nineteenth centuries has influenced how researchers view the findings they generate from both qualitative and quantitative fieldwork data. You should find this reading sufficiently interesting to begin to appreciate how the issues of validity, reliability and generalisability are achieved in qualitative research.

As a philosophical tradition, it is important to note that **positivism** was first made prominent in the works of the French philosopher Auguste Comte (1798–1857), who also developed the term 'sociology'. Central to positivism is the argument that observation cannot lead to the discovery of universal laws concerning a particular **phenomenon**, even though positivists argue that valid knowledge may result from such observation (Haack, 1995; Wagner & Okeke, 2009).

Observations of any phenomenon, according to positivism, must be backed by reasons, conjectures and theories regarding their forms, which include their shapes, structures, appearances and varieties. This is why positivists favour the hypothetical and deductive approaches to social enquiry. More so, this philosophical tradition emphasises the importance of the positive data of experience, pure logic and pure mathematics (Haralambos & Holborn, 1995).

Most importantly, you should note that it is from this thinking that 'validity' as a quantitative criterion for assessing credibility of research findings, developed. Thus "within the positivist terminology, validity resides amongst and is the result and culmination of other empirical conception: universal laws, evidence, objectivity, truth, actuality, deduction, reason, fact, and mathematical data" (Winter, 2000:7).

For many years, this type of reasoning strongly influenced the research tradition, resulting to a situation where all research enterprise appears to be measured from criteria established within these positivist traditions. You should realise by now that the importation of positivist research criteria in assessing the findings of post-positivist or humanist qualitative research is grossly inappropriate. The next section sets out to explain the specific functions that qualitative research performs, which results in obtaining different types of data that require different types of assessment criteria.

12.6 Functions of qualitative research

Qualitative research mainly explores the subjective aspects of an individual, or group of individuals being studied. Therefore, the principal function of qualitative research is to understand these subjective meanings that individuals make of the situations in their lives, which the researcher is interested in learning. An important aspect of qualitative research is that it is not interested in the quantitative measurement of the participants' behavioural characteristics. This central understanding influences the types of methods which qualitative researchers adopt when embarking on their studies.

Nonetheless, it is equally important to note that in every research enterprise, be it quantitative or qualitative, the researcher's main concern is to present a research report that is not only valid, but also reliable. However, validity and reliability, as represented in the positivist-quantitative tradition, are not appropriate for the evaluation of findings associated with qualitative research. According to Winter (2000:8), the situation is such that

> qualitative research sets itself up for failure when it attempts to follow the established procedures of quantitative research such as experimentation, efforts of replication, use of control groups, use of standardised formulas or the use of the pretest/post-test methods.

Historically, qualitative research arose out of the post-positivist refusal to accept the idea of a single, static or objective truth. Under the influence of the philosophy of science in the eighteenth and nineteenth centuries, post-positivism found expression in three main ideological movements, namely, **historicism**, **neo-Kantianism**, and the American **pragmatism** (Wagner & Okeke, 2009). The ideas of these three movements taken jointly are referred to as post-positivism or **humanism**. It is worth noting at this point that the ideas and beliefs of the historicists, neo-Kantians and pragmatists effectively laid the foundation for what is today known as the qualitative research approach.

Let us summarise our discussions on the influence of the philosophy of science in the eighteenth and nineteenth centuries, as well as on the functions of qualitative research. We want here to draw support from Winter (2000:10) who notes that "whether or not validity is essentially the same concept in qualitative and quantitative research, it would seem evident that the means by which this is to be achieved are different for each methodology".

Let us see how validity and reliability are demonstrated in qualitative research in the next section.

12.7   What is validity in qualitative research?

We hope that our discussion so far has increased your understanding about how qualitative researchers approach the evaluation of their findings. It should be clear to you why qualitative researchers want to do this very differently from quantitative researchers. You should now understand why qualitative researchers do not follow the ways of quantitative validity when demonstrating the credibility of their own research findings. Now let us learn how validity is demonstrated in qualitative research.

Many attempts have been made to replace the concept of validity as defined and used by quantitative researchers. According to Morse, Barrett, Mayan, Olson and Spiers (2002), in evaluating the quality and credibility of qualitative research processes and outcomes, the word trustworthiness becomes prominent. These authors claim that the concept of trustworthiness contains four aspects, namely:

> credibility, transferability, dependability and confirmability. Within these were specific methodological strategies for demonstrating qualitative rigor such as the audit trail, member checks when coding, categorising or confirming results with participants, peer debriefing, negative case analysis and structural corroboration (Morse, et al., 2002:14).

Many authors, such as Hupcey, 2002; Denzin & Lincoln, 2003; Smaling, 2003; Willis, 2007; Creswell, 2014, appear to support the earlier explanations about the demonstration of quality and rigour in qualitative research. You should note that this chapter reiterates the call of these authors on researchers and evaluators to look for and strive to maintain the methodological differences between the quantitative and qualitative approaches to research.

It is also important to note that during the fieldwork, quantitative researchers attempt to distance themselves as much as they possibly can from the research process, as a way of maintaining validity. However, qualitative researchers would argue that such 'distancing' will only make qualitative research findings questionable. Qualitative researchers maintain that you have to get very close to your participants in order to understand the very personal meanings that these participants attach to their actions.

12.7.1 Other steps towards achieving qualitative validity?

There are several other steps that a qualitative researcher will have to follow in order to achieve qualitative validity, including reflexive subjectivity, face validity, catalytic validity and triangulation (McCotter, 2001). Using the examples of Suzanne McCotter, let us see how the application of each of these four components would facilitate qualitative validity.

12.7.1.1 Reflexive subjectivity

This involves a high degree of openness on the part of a scrupulous researcher to clearly document the assumptions that have influenced the research process, from the inception of study until the report or findings of the study is published. Most importantly, reflexive subjectivity relates to clearly documenting how the researcher's assumptions are made manifest during the data collection process. It is a continuous process and resonates throughout every stage of the research until the report is completed.

12.7.1.2 Face validity

This is a process whereby the research findings are constructed through the participants in a study. Another name for face validity is response data, and this involves the recycling of the established categories, analytical themes and conclusions back to the participants in a study. According to Hodkinson (1998:562), this entails a situation where "research findings could have been constructed by the research participants yet been objectively discovered by the researcher".

12.7.1.3 Catalytic validity

Catalytic validity requires of the researcher to clearly show with documented evidence that the respondents or research participants have been actively involved in the research process, through the various methods that heor she has employed during the fieldwork leading to the data collection, analysis and research report.

12.7.1.4 Triangulation

Many authors (such as Wildy, 1999; McCotter, 2001; Creswell, 2014) maintain that triangulation requires the researcher to follow a multi-method approach to data collection. Simply put, triangulation involves mixing various methods and instruments which enable researchers to obtain a variety of information from the participants in a particular study.

The purpose of triangulation is to assist researchers to achieve or reach a point of comparison between methods in order to discover the similarities and differences in the responses of the participants. Something further to note about triangulation is that it arises from the need to achieve internal validity, and enables researchers to overcome any problems linked with the use of a single-method approach to data collection.

It follows that the use of multiple or mixed methods will help strengthen the outcomes of the research process in terms of findings. Such an approach will also assist researchers to avoid the presentation of assertions that may be misleading about the situation they have studied.

Having learned about how to achieve validity in qualitative research findings, our discussion now shifts to its related concept, reliability, in the next section.

12.8 What about reliability in qualitative research?

To start our discussion in this section, let us see what reliability means in quantitative research. Reliability in the quantitative context refers to the extent to which an instrument consistently measures and produces the kind of results it is intended to measure and produce. Many researchers have noted that the concept of reliability as it is used in quantitative research is misleading when applied to qualitative research. (We noted the major differences between qualitative and quantitative research studies in 12.4, arguing that these differences make the application of quantitative research reliability to the qualitative context both irrelevant and misleading.)

Lincoln and Guba (1985) note that the closest concept to reliability in qualitative research is dependability. This refers to the consistency of the entire research procedure that resonates through various stages of the research process. Of course, to check the dependability of qualitative research, the various stages leading to the research report have to come under scrutiny. These processes include the design of the study, methods of data collection and analysis, as well as method of interpreting or reporting the findings.

The requirement for achieving dependability means that you as researcher have to leave no stone unturned in explaining, detailing and documenting the processes, in a manner that enables the auditors and other readers of your report to believe in it. The next section takes a look at the issue of generalisability of qualitative research findings.

12.9 Achieving generalisability of qualitative research findings

This is another area where qualitative and quantitative research processes differ very markedly. For instance, quantitative research processes emphasise that quantity and its significance derives necessarily from the researcher's ability to represent the analysis and interpretation of data largely in numerical or statistical forms. By employing such quantitative data instruments as descriptive and inferential statistics (see Chapters 22 and 23); the quantitative researcher is able to reproduce a well-organised representation of the entire research process, mostly with the assistance of computer software such as the statistical package for the social sciences (SPSS). It is this process that enables the quantitative researcher to leave behind a well-documented process and, because of its replicability, such a process is usually counted as legitimate.

The process is not the same with qualitative research. The rationale for conducting a qualitative study is to explore the inner perspectives of individuals' everyday experiences concerning a particular phenomenon. It is important to note that the emphasis in qualitative research is not on the reproduction of a representative sample from a population. The qualitative researcher is necessarily interested in a deeper understanding of the behaviours of the individual or group of individuals being investigated. It is for this reason that the researcher tends to select those instruments that would enable him or her to conduct in-depth and critical analyses of the consciousness which the people in the study bring to the social context of the entire research situation. This consciousness is subjective and is always in a state of flux.

To reiterate, the aim of qualitative study is the understanding of the meanings that individuals involved in a particular action make of their situations. The qualitative researcher is simply interested in making sense of the situation, while he or she endeavours to represent the outcome in ways that reflect the purpose of the study. Since human behaviour is neither static nor fixed, but rather, fluid and ever-changing, you should note that assessing qualitative findings or reports through positivist-quantitative criteria would be misplaced and possibly amount to gross error.

Qualitative research processes are grounded in the observation of phenomena in a real world that is in a constant state of flux. It takes place in a situation that is specific in time and space, and as a result of that such processes, cannot be generalised to a different context. Therefore, generalisation of qualitative research findings in the context of quantitative research criteria would mean that the aim of qualitative research stands to be defeated. You may well want to ask what, then, qualitative generalisation is. Let us learn now what this concept means.

In qualitative research, generalisability is replaced by the concept of transferability. Smaling (2003:60) maintains that in assessing the transferability of qualitative research it is:

> the reader of the research reports not the researcher [who] determines whether analogies exist between the situation that has been researched and another situation which is of interest to the reader. The reader must have an adequate knowledge of the researched situation so that he can determine by himself whether there are sufficient relevant similarities that make it plausible that the research conclusions should hold in other situation.

What is very important to remember is that you, as the researcher, must try to carefully document all processes leading to the emerging research report. This process of documentation must consciously take off from the point of conceptualisation of a research idea, through to the fieldwork, until the research report is written. When you do this, readers of your research report will be left in no doubt of the processes leading to the research findings.

More so, in support of the above position, Smaling (2003) suggests that there are certain key elements of the qualitative research process that enable the researcher to prepare grounds for transferability. For instance, Smaling (2003:60) suggests that such a research report:

☑ **Must clearly state the status or position of the researcher,** as well as the role he or she played during the research process.

☑ **Should contain very clear information about the research participation.**

☑ **Should have detailed information about the research situation,** the conditions necessitating the study, and about the social contexts of the study.

☑ **Must have clear information about the methodology** followed.

☑ **Must clearly state the theoretical orientation** it followed and the rationale for the choice of the theoretical orientation.

☑ **The report itself must be descriptively thick.**

Before concluding this chapter, let us explore some of the implications of various aspects of our discussions in this chapter, so that you are able to conduct your research with confidence in your understanding research methodology.

12.10 Implications of the discussions in this chapter

It is important that students, new researchers, and even professionals enter the research field with a thorough grasp of the **epistemological** and **ontological issues** relating to the methodological choices they make. This chapter highlighted this essential information in its various sections, as it forms a very important part of your research career.

Before embarking on any study, whether qualitative or quantitative, it is imperative that you as a student or even research practitioner should endeavour to understand the epistemological and ontological standpoint of the method you choose to adopt. Such knowledge will enable you to choose the appropriate method.

Finally, in carrying out your own research activities, you have to understand that whether your findings are valid, reliable or generalisable resonates from the effect your research accounts, findings or reports make in the lives of those for whom the study was conducted.

Conclusion

We started our discussion with a brief look at the meaning of qualitative research and we also examined various tools used by qualitative researchers when they set out to obtain data.

The chapter then explored the main characteristics of the quantitative approach to research, and used a table format to represent the major differences between both qualitative and quantitative research approaches.

The influence of the philosophy of science of the eighteenth and nineteenth centuries on the development of both research approaches also informed part of our discussion. We saw how various ideas through positivism and post-positivism impacted the development of both the qualitative and quantitative research approaches. We also looked at the main criteria for checking qualitative validity and reliability.

Finally, the chapter looked at the implications of our discussions for how you will conduct your own research. You should now be in a sufficient position to make choices relating to your research methodology, as well as the criteria for checking the outcomes of your research endeavour.

Closing activities

Analysis and consolidation

A The following questions are set to enable you test yourself on the progress this chapter has enabled you to make.

1 Briefly define the concept of qualitative research.
2 Outline the main features of a qualitative study.
3 What are the main differences between qualitative and quantitative research? Use your own words to make the contrast.
4 Briefly describe the four steps a qualitative researcher will have to follow in order to achieve qualitative validity.

Practical application

B In this particular activity, you need to imagine inviting the student in our opening case, Siyabonga, for a discussion. In your discussion, ask him the following:

1 What has he learned from this chapter?
2 What aspects of the chapter has he has found most interesting?
3 Has he found any particular part most useful?
4 Now, since he is still interested in his qualitative study, invite Siyabonga to discuss with you how he would apply what he has learned in this chapter in demonstrating the credibility of his research findings. Record all Siyabonga's answers as you would if you were conducting an interview with him. Try and reflect the depth and detail of his responses.

Bibliography

Carney, J. H., Joiner, J. F., & Tragou, H. 1997. Categorizing, coding and manipulating qualitative data using the Word-Perfect Word Processor. *The Qualitative Report*, 3(1). Retrieved 15 April 2014 from: http://www.nova.edu/ssss/QR/QR3–1/carney.html.

Catterall, M. & Maclaran, P. 1997. Focus group data and qualitative analysis programs: Coding the moving picture as well as the snapshots. *Sociological Research Online*, 2(1). Retrieved 15 April 2014 from: http://www.socresonline.org.uk/socresonline/2/1/6.html.

Creswell, J.W. 2014. *Research design: Qualitative, quantitative and mixed methods approaches.* London: Sage.

Denzin, N.K. & Lincoln, Y.S. (Eds). 2003. *Strategies of qualitative inquiry.* London: Sage Publications.

Elliott, H. 1997. The use of diaries in sociological research on health experience. *Sociological Research Online*, 2(2). Retrieved 15 April 2014 from: http://www.socresonline.org.uk/socresonline/2/2/7.html.

Glesne, C. & Peshkin, A. 1992. *Becoming qualitative researcher: An introduction.* New York: Longman.

Golafshani, N. 2003. Understanding reliability and validity in qualitative research. *The Qualitative Report*, 8(4):597–607. Retrieved 26 July 2014 from: http://www.nova.edu/ssss/QR/QR8-4/golafshani.pdf.

Haack, S. 1995. Pragmatism. *The New Encyclopaedia Britannica*, Vol. 22. China: Grolier Incorporated, (pp. 514–515).

Hammersley, M. 1989. *The dilemma of qualitative method: Herbert Blumer and the Chicago tradition.* London: Routledge.

Haralambos, M., & Holborn, H. 1995. *Sociology: Themes and perspectives.* London: Collins Educational.

Hodkinson, P. 1998. The origins of a theory of career decision-making: A hermeneutical research. *British Educational Research Journal*, 24(5):557–572.

Hupcey, J. 2002. Maintaining validity: The development of the concept of trust. *International Journal of Qualitative Research*, 1(4):45–53. Retrieved 15 April 2014 from: http://www.ualberta.ca/~ijqm.

Lincoln, Y.S. & Guba, E.G. 1985. *Naturalistic inquiry.* Beverley Hills: Sage.

McCotter, S.S. 2001. The journey of a beginning researcher. *The Qualitative Report*, 3(1). Retrieved 15 April 2014 from: http://www.nova.edu/ssss/QR/QR6-2/mccotter.html.

Morse, J.M., Barrett, M., Mayan, M., Olson, K. & Spiers, J. 2002. Verification strategies for establishing reliability and validity in qualitative research. *International Journal of Qualitative Research*, 1(2): 13–22. Retrieved 15 April 2014 from: http://www.ualberta.ca/~ijqm.

Obikeze, D.S. 1990. *Methods of data analysis in the social and behavioural sciences.* Enugu: Auto-Century Publishers.

Okeke, C.I.O. 2003. *The gendered perception of schooling amongst secondary school students: A qualitative approach.* Unpublished doctoral thesis. Nsukka: University of Nigeria.

Okeke, C.I.O. 2009a. The experiences with qualitative validity in a classroom research: Issues Pertaining to value claims. *EDUCARE: International Journal for Educational Studies*, 2(1):1–16.

Okeke, C.I.O. 2010d. *Gender and schooling: A qualitative study of teens' perception of schooling in a Nigerian suburb.* Germany: VDM Publishing House.

Smaling, A. 2003. Inductive, analogical and communicative generalisation. *International Journal of Qualitative Methods*, 2(1):52–67. Retrieved 15 April 2014 from: http://www.ualberta.ca/~ijqm.

Ujo, A.A. 2000. *Understanding social research: A non-quantitative approach.* Kaduna: Anyaotu Enterprises Publishers.

Wagner, C. & Okeke, C.I.O. 2009. Quantitative or qualitative: Epistemological choices in research methodology curricula. In M. Garner, C. Wagner & B.B. Kawulich (Eds). *Teaching research methods in the Humanities and the Social Sciences.* London: Ashgate.

Ward, B. 1999. The edited topical life history: Its values and uses as a research tool. *Education Research and Perspectives*, 26(2):45–60.

Wildy, H. 1999. Statuses, lenses and crystals: Looking at qualitative research. *Education Research and Perspectives*, 26(2):61–72.

Willis, J. W. 2007. *Foundations of qualitative research: Interpretive and critical approaches.* London: Sage Publications.

Winter, G. 2000. A comparative discussion of the notion of validity in qualitative research. *The Qualitative Report*, 3(1). Retrieved 15 April 2014 from: http://www.nova.edu/ssss/QR/QR4-3/winter.html.

CHAPTER 13

Mutendwahothe Walter Lumadi

The logic of sampling

KEY CONCEPTS

Conscious bias is when the researcher is aware of reflecting a certain position or making certain choices, a bit like an intentional act of 'dishonesty'.

Non-probability sampling is a technique that gathers samples using a process which does not allow all the individuals within a population an equal chance of being selected.

Population is the total number of people who live all in the same geographical area; or, more generally, a large collection of individuals or objects with the same characteristics and the main focus of a scientific query.

Probability sampling is an approach in which every unit in the population has an equal chance of being selected for the sample. Probability can be accurately determined. The combination of these traits makes it possible to produce unbiased estimates of population totals, by weighting sampled units, according to their probability of selection.

Sample size is the total number of items taken from the population under study, which is ultimately used in statistical measurements. It is simple logic that a big sample should have a fair representation.

Sampling frame can be viewed as the source material from which a sample is drawn. It is a list of all those within a population that can be sampled, and may include individual participants.

Sampling is the process of selecting a few representatives (sample) from a bigger group (the sampling population), which then become the basis for predicting the outcome in the study.

Unconscious bias is the tendency to incline towards or favour a certain position owing to various factors, which you may not be aware of at the time.

LEARNING OUTCOMES

By the end of this chapter, you should be able to:

▶ Understand and apply the concept of sampling in research.

▶ Unpack the various types of sampling.

▶ Elaborate briefly on sampling techniques.

▶ Establish the relationship between probability and non-probability sampling.

▶ Clarify issues relating to conscious and unconscious sampling bias.

▶ Critically reflect on populations and sampling frames.

I am pleased to be announcing the results of all nine provinces today. The National Senior Certificate examinations in 2009 involved a total of 580 577 full-time candidates. Learners wrote a total of 197 papers in nearly 7,000 centres and the papers were marked by more than 30,000 markers. This meant that the marks of a total of around 12 million papers were captured during the entire process. I would like to commend KwaZulu-Natal as that province has shown an improvement in the pass rate of 3,5 per cent, up from 57,6 per cent in 2008 to 61,1 per cent in 2009. I am also pleased to report that the results in the Eastern Cape have stabilised at around 50 per cent. Both these provinces are essentially rural in character with high rates of poverty.

However, those in the Free State declined by 2,4 per cent, and the pass rates in the Western Cape and North West provinces have declined by 2,7 per cent and 0,5 per cent respectively. In addition, the pass rate in Limpopo declined by 5,4 per cent and that of the Northern Cape by a staggering 11 per cent. Gauteng's pass rate has also shown a decline of 4,6 per cent. Mpumalanga has registered the poorest performance with a pass rate of 47,9 per cent – a decline of 3,9 per cent. These disappointing results indicate that we need to take urgent steps to address the performance of the system which impacts on the performance of our learners.

(**Source:** Adapted from *Sunday Times*, 2010:11)

Introduction

This chapter argues for the logic of sampling in research. As a postgraduate student you need to decide on *what*, *who*, *how* and *why* of selecting your specific sampling for your research design and methodology. It is common that when writing your dissertation and thesis you, like many postgraduate students, will experience challenges with the purpose of sampling. If sampling is understood, half the battle is already won in writing up your research project for examination and funding purposes. In conducting research, students are often unable to directly observe each of the participants who happen to be in the population of the study. In order to address this challenge, they are compelled to collect data from the sampled participants and make use of the observation tool to make inferences about the population.

In fact, the type of correspondence theory between the sample and the size of the population is a crucial choice when a postgraduate student wants to know what proportion of the population displays a certain characteristic, such as a demographic feature.

Before you continue with the next section on the concept of sampling, read the opening case study of the Minister of Basic Education's announcement of the 2009 matric results again before answering the questions in the activity.

Stop and reflect

1 What is the population of provinces represented in the National Senior Certificate examinations?
  a Which sampling technique was used to identify KZN as the province that has shown an improvement in the pass rate?
  b What is the population of the 2009 Grade 12 examinations referred to by the Minister of Basic Education in the case study?
2 Which of the nine provinces is appears to be at the bottom of the provincial list in terms of performance? How do you know?

Continuing the introduction, the following section focuses on the concept of sampling.

13.1 The concept of sampling

It is of paramount importance that you should have a clear concept of sampling in research. Although various scholars define the concept of sampling differently, the definitions are intertwined and interrelated.

Tip

▸ Make sure that your sample is fair and representative.

▸ Avoid a population which is too big or too small.

▸ It is vital that you get access to the population of your sample; make sure you are able to.

13.1.1 Sample

When dealing with people, a sample may be defined as a set of respondents or participants selected from a larger population for the purpose of conducting a survey. The sample should be representative of the population so as to ensure that the findings can be generalised from the research sample to the population as a whole. We will use the opening case study to illustrate this. If we were to sample 10 per cent of the 7,000 centres where the matric examinations were written, a sample of 700 would be a fair representation. Although this sample may seem vast and wide, the representation is reasonably fair to all the provincial centres. See Table 13.1 for an example of this type of sampling.

13.1.2 Population

A population is a group of persons, objects, or items from which samples are taken for measurement; for instance, a population of cabinet ministers, mining engineers, medical doctors, or the dissertations and theses of postgraduate students. In our case study on Grade 12 results, the National Senior Certificate examinations in 2009 involved a total of 580,577 full-time candidates; thus 580,577 becomes our population. In order to draw conclusions about populations from samples, student researchers must use inferential statistics. Such statistics enable the researcher to determine the characteristics of a population by directly observing only a portion (or sample) of that population (you will find out more about inferential statistics in Chapter 23). Now look at the matric pass rate (Table 13.1, in descending order) for 2010 and 2011. Although some provinces registered a marked improvement, Eastern Cape, KwaZulu-Natal and Northern Cape show a slight decline. Eastern Cape has been languishing at the bottom of the provincial list for a number of years. Although some of the schools did well, most schools, especially in rural areas had poor results.

TABLE 13.1: South African NSC results by province, 2010–2011

Province	2011 %	2010 %	Difference
Eastern Cape	58,1	58,3	Declined by 0,2%
Limpopo	63,9	57,9	Improved by 6,0%
Mpumalanga	64,8	56,8	Improved by 8%
KwaZulu-Natal	68,1	70,7	Declined by 2,6%
Northern Cape	68,8	72,3	Declined by 3,5%
Free State	75,7	70,7	Improved by 5,0%
North West	77,8	75,7	Improved by 2,1%
Gauteng	81,3	78,6	Improved by 2,5%
Western Cape	82,9	76,8	Improved by 6,1%

(**Source:** *Sunday Times*, 11 January 2010:12)

Having familiarised yourself with the concept of sampling, try answering the questions in the activity.

Stop and reflect

1 Define the following concepts in your own words:
   a Population
   b Sampling.
2 Study the NSC results in Table 13.1 and answer these questions:
   a Eastern Cape (EC) is always languishing at the bottom of the provincial list. Which sampling technique was used which puts EC last in terms of performance in the table?
   b What is the difference in the percentage population between 2010 and 2011?
   c Which sampling technique would you use to sample the results of any province from the list in Table 13.1?

In the next section, you will focus on the required sample size.

13.1.3 Required sample size

Tip

▶ Identify the participants in you study.
▶ Know the formula to use and the size of the sample.

The required sample size may be calculated by making use of different formulas. This is entirely dependent on the collected data, which could be of qualitative or quantitative nature. A student researcher may use one of the formulas to construct a table that will give the optimal sample size, given a population size, confidence level, and a margin of error.

Study Table 13.2 which applies in determining the appropriate sample size for any study. Researchers believe that the scores given in the first column of the table give a sufficient confidence level at the value of 95 per cent; and a margin of error which is equivalent to 5 per cent. It goes further than this, however, because the value in the next column is the sample size that is required to generate a margin of error of ± 5 per cent for the entire population (Dooley, 2006:72). However, a 10 per cent interval, that is, a 10 per cent margin of error, may be considered unreasonably large.

TABLE 13.2: The required sample size

Population Size	Confidence = 95% Margin of Error				Confidence = 99% Margin of Error			
	5.0%	3.5%	2.5%	1.0%	5.0%	3.5%	2.5%	1.0%
10	10	10	10	10	10	10	10	10
20	19	20	20	20	19	20	20	20
30	28	29	29	30	29	29	30	30
50	44	47	48	50	47	48	49	50
75	63	69	72	74	67	71	73	75
100	80	89	94	99	87	93	96	99
150	108	126	137	148	122	135	142	149
200	132	160	177	196	154	174	186	198
250	152	190	215	244	182	211	229	246
300	169	217	251	291	207	246	270	295
400	196	265	318	384	250	309	348	391
500	217	306	377	475	285	365	421	485
600	234	340	432	565	315	416	490	579
700	248	370	481	653	341	462	554	672
800	260	396	526	739	363	503	615	763
1,000	278	440	606	906	399	575	727	943
1,200	291	474	674	1067	427	636	827	1119
1,500	306	515	759	1297	460	712	959	1376
2,000	322	563	869	1655	498	808	1141	1785
2,500	333	597	952	1984	524	879	1288	2173
3,500	346	641	1068	2565	558	977	1510	2890
5,000	357	678	1176	3288	586	1066	1734	3842
7,500	365	710	1275	4211	610	1147	1960	5165
10,000	370	727	1332	4899	622	1193	2098	6239
25,000	378	760	1448	6939	646	1285	2399	9972
50,000	381	772	1491	8056	655	1318	2520	12455
75,000	382	776	1506	8514	658	1330	2563	13583
100,000	383	778	1513	8762	659	1336	2585	14227
250,000	384	782	1527	9248	662	1347	2626	15555
500,000	384	783	1532	9423	663	1350	2640	16055
1,000,000	384	783	1534	9512	663	1352	2647	16317
2,500,000	384	784	1536	9567	663	1353	2651	16478
10,000,000	384	784	1536	9594	663	1354	2653	16560
100,000,000	384	784	1537	9603	663	1354	2654	16584
300,000,000	384	784	1537	9603	663	1354	2654	16586

Having studied the table on required sample size, you will understand how the concept of sampling applies in research. You will deduce that a sample is the sub-group of the population that the researcher is interested in. Sampling also has the added advantage of saving time and money, as working with an entire population is, for many reasons, generally impractical and uneconomical. An example of a sample is the free piece of sausage to taste that you are offered at the supermarket, which is designed to get you to buy a packet of sausages. A further example of a sample is a small sub-set of society that is surveyed in order to get an idea of the opinion of a society as a whole.

Now that you understand what a sample is, look at the following figure and respond to the questions on your left of the diagram, as they pertain to your own study.

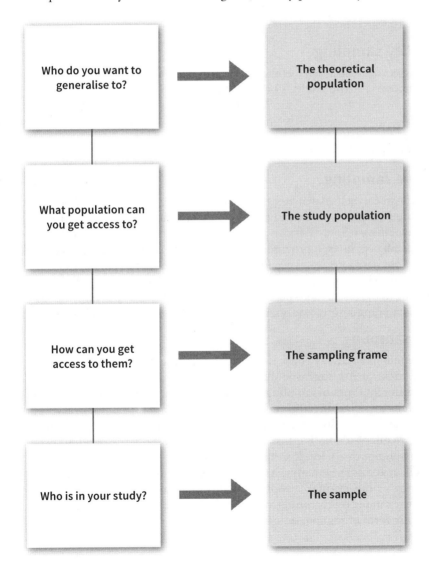

FIGURE 13.1: Sampling frame in research, after Tuckman, 1978:69

Before you continue with the next section on types of sampling, do the following activity.

13.2 Types of sampling

In this section, you will learn about the various types of sampling.

13.2.1 Probability sampling

This type of sampling occurs when each member of the **population** has the same probability or chance of being chosen for the study. The following are various types of probability sampling:

▶ Cluster sampling
▶ Random sampling
▶ Simple random sampling.

13.2.2 Purposive sampling

The concept of 'purposive' is self-explanatory. The researcher conducts research with an intention and purpose in mind, e.g. selecting the best three schools in mathematics and accounting achievement in each South African province. All the schools that have performed well in the identified subjects in each province will be sampled. It would be misleading if schools with a 0 per cent pass rate, or a very low pass rate, are to be sampled because the researcher's intention is to focus on the best schools. Sampling tends to be subjective and judgemental, according to the researcher's purpose. Since the sampling is determined largely by the researcher's own opinion or intention, the representation is rendered subjective.

13.2.3 No-rule sampling

This type takes a sample without any rules; the sample is representative if the population is homogeneous and consequently, one would have no selection bias.

There are several different types of sampling, that is, different ways of choosing a sample from a population. Guba and Lincoln (2007) take the view that sampling methods vary from simple to complex. When conducting research, it is virtually impossible to study the entire population that you are interested in. For instance, if you were to study the religious views of university students in South Africa, it would be absolutely impossible to survey every single university student across the country. As a result, researchers use samples as a way to gather data. Researchers will always make use of probability sampling, because this technique will reassure us that the sample is representative. We will also be able to estimate the errors that are involved in any form of random sampling.

13.3 How will you decide which type of sampling to use?

In most cases, statisticians and researchers prefer simple random sampling. It is the least complicated and easiest to understand. Further, when a researcher requires accurate data for any given sample, stratified random sampling will be more precise and relevant. When data on all participants are available, this separates them in terms of strata that appear to be applicable. However, if the sample is large enough and resources are adequate, it will be proper to utilise multi-stage sampling.

13.3.1 How are the results analysed?

When analysing the results, the main difference between the sampling types lies in the computation of the estimates of variance or standard deviation. The variance of the estimator will always be smaller if it came from a stratified random sample than from simple random sample, which is of the same size. As long as a small variance means accurate data, researchers will realise that it is consistent with stratified random sampling yielding good estimators, for a provided sample size.

Before you continue to the next section on sampling techniques, do the activity that follows.

Stop and reflect

With reference to the earlier discussion on the types of sampling, answer these questions:
1 What are the various types of probability sampling? Elaborate briefly on each of them.
2 How would you use purposive and no-rule sampling in your research study? Give suitable examples.
3 In your own words, suggest how you will define the following:
  ▶ Probability sampling
  ▶ Purposive sampling.
4 In your opinion, which type of sampling do you consider to be the best? Why?

In the following section, sampling techniques are interrogated from a research perspective.

13.4 Sampling techniques

Pitfall warning

Do not confuse the types of sampling with sampling techniques. Often, student researchers do not check whether the technique they choose is applicable to their study. How will you check?

Following on our discussions so far on the types of sampling, the following section focuses on the sampling techniques.

There are three main sampling techniques:

13.4.1 Random sampling technique

Random sampling is the least biased of all sampling techniques, which means there is no subjectivity: each member of the total population has an equal chance of being selected. For example, if you are seeking Gauteng Grade 12 learners' opinions about the overall pass rate, any learner would stand a chance of being randomly selected. Such a sample can be obtained using random number tables. In random sampling, the task is simply: = RAND (). When you type this into a cell, a random number in that cell will be produced. We will now briefly explain the terms 'random point', 'random line' and 'random area':

▸ *Random point sampling.* In this sampling technique, random number tables are used to obtain grid references for the points.
▸ *Random line sampling.* Here, too, pairs of grid references are obtained using random number tables, and marked on a map of the study area.
▸ *Random area sampling.* This is where random number tables generate coordinates which are used to mark the grid squares to be sampled.

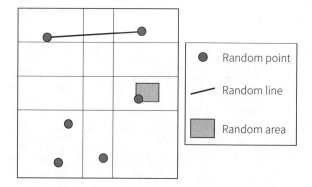

FIGURE 13.2: Random number grid

(**Source:** Durrheim, 2006:121)

Figure 13.2 illustrates a random number grid showing methods of generating random numbers, lines and areas. A brief discussion on systematic sampling follows.

13.4.2 Systematic sampling technique

Systematic sampling may be regarded as an approach of selecting a random sample from among a larger population. In systematic point sampling, a grid is used with the points positioned at the intersections of the grid lines (A), or in the middle of each grid square (B). This enables the researcher to carry out sampling at the closest feasible place. Sampling points for say, pebble data collection may be identified systematically along a transect line, e.g. every two metres or every tenth pebble. In the case of systematic line sampling, the northern part of the grid on a map can be used to identify transect lines (C & D).

Suppose the sum total of a population is 100, a random systematic sampling of 10 data points within that population would involve observing every 10th data point. A 'pattern' of grid squares to be sampled can be identified using a map of the study area, e.g. every third grid square down area (E) – the south-west corner – will then mark the corner of a quadrat. Patterns can be any aspect as long as they are regular (F).

13.4.3 Stratified sampling technique

This is used when the researcher wants to highlight specific sub-groups within the entire population. To ensure that there is a fair representation of the results, it is vital that sampling should be stratified well. Note that sampling is employed when the sampling frame comprises subsets of a *known* size. These subsets also consist of various proportions of the total. A brief discussion on this type of sampling follows.

13.4.3.1 Stratified systematic sampling

Leedy and Ormrod (2001:37) say that a population can be divided into known groups, and each group is sampled using a systematic approach. The number sampled in each group should be in proportion to its known size in the parent population. For example, the make-up of different social groups in the population of a town can be obtained, and then the number of questionnaires administered in different parts of the town can be stratified in line with this information. A systematic approach can still be used by surveying every fifth person.

A wide range of data and fieldwork situations can lend themselves to this approach. It is applicable wherever two study areas are compared, for instance, two large oceans of the world, such as the Indian and Atlantic; or a population with subsets of a known size, e.g. with distinctly varied ecology. A random point can be used to illustrate the number of measurements taken, which is representative of the whole size. If areas of both the Indian and Atlantic oceans were the study sites, there would probably be various types of subsets within these areas. When using random sampling, there is a likelihood that one or more of these may be missed completely. Stratified sampling will always take into account the proportional area of each ecosystem type in the oceans, and each could end up with a fair and systematic representation. If there were 40 samples taken in the oceans as a whole, and it became apparent that the waves accounted for 20 per cent of the total area, two samples will therefore need to be taken, which will eventually end up being identified as being random (A) or systematic (B).

Now that you have studied some sampling techniques, check your understanding, by answering the questions in the following activity.

Stop and reflect

1 Elaborate, explaining in detail, each of the following types of sampling techniques:
   a Random sampling
   b Systematic sampling
   c Stratified sampling.
2 Which sampling technique do you prefer for your study? Why do you prefer such a technique? Give relevant examples from your study.

Adding to the previous sections (13.3 & 13.4) on the types of sampling and sampling techniques, the following section now sheds light on probability and non-probability sampling.

13.5 Probability and non-probability sampling

13.5.1 Probability sampling

When each member of the population has a known probability, this is referred to as probability sampling. Examples of probability sampling, as you read earlier, are simple random sampling, stratified random sampling, and cluster sampling. Probability sampling has two common features:

▶ Each of the elements has a non-zero chance of being sampled.
▶ All the elements involve random selection at some point, for example, if the minister of basic education wants to select two learners who performed well in Grade 12 mathematics, all learners from all the provinces who achieved 100 per cent have an equal chance of being sampled.

Suppose we want to know how many fans in a school would wear a jersey featuring *Bafana Bafana* or *Amabokoboko* (Springboks) – the nicknames of South Africa's national football team and rugby team respectively – during an international game at the FNB or Loftus Versfeld stadiums. To answer this question in the context of the average number of South African fans in a school, would mean that everyone in the school would stand an equal chance of being sampled for the study. The same applies with sub-segments of the population. In a case where the researcher would like to obtain the opinions of primary and secondary school principals, a probability sample would mean that each school principal would have an equal chance of participating in the study. Essentially, probability sampling means that participants are selected at random and everyone has an equal and fair opportunity to participate in the study.

The last example shows that not every post-level one teacher, who is not a principal, stands an equal chance of selection: what makes this a probability sample is the fact that each person's probability is known. When every element in the population has the same probability of selection, this is known as an 'equal probability of selection' design. Such designs are also referred to as 'self-weighting' because all sampled units are given the same weight.

13.5.1.1 Simple random sample

According to Patton (1990:141), simple random sampling refers to the basic sampling technique assumed in statistical methods and computations. This simply means that for you to gather a simple random sample, you assign a number. A set of random numbers is then generated, and the units with such numbers are worthy of inclusion in the sample. A good example is the following: you are in possession of a population of 4,000 participants and you intend to choose a simple random sample of 400 participants. Firstly, each of the participants should be numbered from 1 to 4,000. Then you generate a list of 400 random numbers and the individuals assigned those numbers are the ones to be included in the sample.

13.5.1.2 Stratified sample

Stratified sampling may be viewed as a sampling skill in which the researcher divides the entire target population into various strata (sub-groups) and then randomly selects the final subjects proportionally from the different sub-groups. This type of sampling is used when the researcher wants to highlight specific sub-groups within a population (Cohen & Manion, 1994:120).

13.5.1.3 Cluster sampling

When it is impractical to compile an exhaustive list of the participants that make up the target population, cluster sampling may be both suitable and convenient. In most cases, the participants in the population are already grouped into sub-populations, and lists of those sub-populations already exist. For example, let us say the target population in a study is the home languages spoken by students at the University of Johannesburg. Although there is no list of all of these languages according to the categories the researcher is interested in, the researcher could create her own list of the dominant languages spoken in the Gauteng province, such as isiZulu, SeSotho, Sepedi, Tshivenda, Afrikaans and English and then obtain lists of students who speak those languages from the university database.

13.5.2 Non-probability sampling

According to De Vos (1998:111) this is a sampling technique that gathers samples using a process that does *not* allow all the individuals within a population an equal chance of being selected. The types of non-probability sampling include convenience sampling, consecutive sampling, quota sampling, judgemental sampling, and snowball sampling. Non-probability sampling is any sampling method where some elements of the population have no chance of selection (these are sometimes referred to as 'out-of-coverage' or 'under-covered'), or where the probability of selection cannot be accurately determined (Huysamen, 1996:88). In our ongoing case study, if we are focusing on schools that performed well in the so-called gateway subjects, such as mathematics and physical science, so all learners who were not registered for those subjects do not stand a chance of being sampled. Moreover, even if learners were registered for those subjects, the mere fact that they did not fare well in those subjects eliminates them completely. Here is another example: if there is a bursary to assist learners, who passed Tshivenda with excellent results, to study at certain institutions of higher learning, all learners who were not registered for this particular African language cannot apply because they do not meet the requirements, irrespective of their symbols in their own African language. Even if they got 100 per cent in their African language, they still would not qualify to apply because they are classified as out-of-coverage.

13.5.2.1 Purposive, or judgemental sample

This type of sample is selected based on the knowledge of a population and the purpose of the study. In Table 13.1, the Eastern Cape is at the bottom of the provincial list in terms of performance, followed by Limpopo. A novice researcher who wants to conduct research in the Eastern Cape would do it specifically on the basis of the poor results in the province. If, however, a researcher would like to investigate *why* learners' results are so consistently poor in the province, they would have to decide whether to use a teacher-centred design or a learner-centred design. After scrutinising these factors, the researcher would then suggest a way forward. However, a researcher whose study is focused on performance in mathematics and physical science, would go to the province with an already formed decision about the poor results in the area. For example, if a researcher is studying the high failure rate of Grade 12 learners in accounting, such a researcher would be compelled to interview the principals of high schools with a high failure rate in the National Senior Certificate examinations. Principals whose schools obtained a 0 to 10 per cent pass rate in the identified subject would obviously be sampled.

13.5.2.2 Snowball sample

A snowball sample is one in which the researcher collects data on the few members of the target population who can be located. Let us take this example: if a drama lecturer from one of the universities in the Eastern Cape is looking for five VhaVenda students to audition for *Muvhango* (the Tshivenda TV drama) in the Eastern Cape, any one person who is identified as such a student should be able to locate other members of the population whom they know. In fact, since these have to be students who are fluent in Tshivenda, a comparative rarity, because isiXhosa dominates in this province, they are likely to know other Tshivenda speakers. The students identified for auditions should be able to convince the panel that they are fluent in the language. The initial interviewee, who happens to be known to the researcher, refers the researcher to other interviewees. This process continues until all possible contacts have been tracked down.

13.5.2.3 Quota sample

This type of sample occurs when units are selected for a sample on the basis of pre-specified characteristics so that the total sample has the same distribution of characteristics assumed to exist in the population being studied (Moore, 1993:72). Suppose your research study is on gender equity in South Africa. When you conduct a national quota sample, you will be looking at MECs for education in all nine provinces in the country. Identify what proportion of the MEC population is female and what proportion is male, as well as what proportions of each gender fall into different political, religious, age, language and educational background categories. Here is an example of quota sampling:

Looking at a case of quota sampling

Non-probability sampling comes in various shapes and sizes, but the essence is that some kind of bias exists in the group of participants one is surveying. Let us think about it in the context of the leadership in a school setting. If the researcher asks female teachers why most of them are not school principals, the results are not representative of anything other than the opinion of female teachers who are not school principals. Male teachers are left out of the sample when only female teachers are interviewed, hence it is not representative. This effect, called snowballing (see above), creates a biased sample in which not everyone has an equal chance of being sampled.

Now that you have studied the example, you will see how the concepts of probability and non-probability sampling relate to conscious and unconscious sampling bias. Before you continue with the next section, establish how well you have understood the last discussion by doing the following activity.

Stop and reflect

1 Distinguish between probability and non-probability sampling.
2 How will you make use of these types of sampling in writing a chapter on research design and methodology? Give suitable examples.
3 In your opinion, what do you consider to be the importance of a sampling technique in conducting a research study?

Continuing from the earlier discussions on probability and non-probability sampling, the following section adds the dimension of what happens when conducting research with preconceived ideas, on the one hand; and without being aware of one's actions, on the other hand.

13.6 Issues in conscious and unconscious sampling bias

Tip

Recall Chapter 10 on research design and methodology: What does research design have to do with possible bias in your sampling methods?

In the following section, the concepts of conscious and unconscious bias are explained in relation to the sampling perspective. Errors occurring in the process of gathering the sample cause sampling bias, while errors in any process after that can cause selection bias.

13.6.1 Conscious sampling bias

Conscious bias is viewed as prejudice in favour of or against one thing, person, or group, compared with another, usually in a way considered to be unfair. Having bias involves pre-judging someone or something (Saunders, Lewis & Thornhill, 1998:96). When you are aware that you are biased, you are conscious of the fact that you are not giving the other person, situation or issue a fair chance.

When you are not aware of your bias, you will usually claim that you have not already made up your mind, and that you can be trusted to treat both sides fairly. Unconscious bias is possibly the more pernicious of the two, since it amounts to fooling yourself as to what your true feelings are. Most researchers are caught up in unconscious bias at some time. They do not always understand the way their brains work, particularly when it comes to cognitive assonance and dissonance (Sica, 2006). Look at the picture below (Figure 13.3) of the two coffee tables and see if you can determine the differences. Are these coffee tables of the same size and the same shape? Which of the tops is bigger?

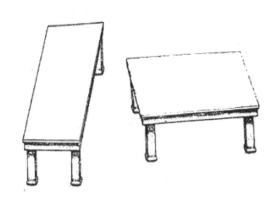

FIGURE 13.3: Size of tables

You would probably say: "Obviously they are not the same shape. The one on the left is clearly narrower and longer than the one on the right." Now take a piece of paper and either cut out or trace the table top on the left. Then lay your cut out or tracing over the top of the table top on the right. Which one is bigger? It is as you may have thought – they are identical in size, although not in shape. Sampling bias occurs when the sampling frame and the population are not consonant. This could happen if you were unable to obtain permission to access the list of the population you are interested in, which is a common occurrence among researchers. In conscious bias, if researchers are aware of their hidden bias, they can monitor and try to ameliorate hidden attitudes and covert agendas before they are expressed through behaviour. This compensation can include attention paying to language, body language, and to the stigmatisation felt by target groups (Borg & Gall, 1979:67).

13.6.2 Unconscious sampling bias

Unconscious bias is when you are not aware of your bias; you will claim that you have not already made up your mind, that you are impartial, and that you can be trusted to treat both sides fairly. Unconscious bias is the more dangerous of the two, since it amounts to deceiving yourself as to what your true feelings are. Most people are guilty of unconscious bias. They do not understand the way their brains work when it comes to cognitive assonance and dissonance, nor the extent of unexpressed prejudices.

Researchers have conscious and unconscious biases that can affect how they select units from the population for inclusion in their sample. For example, in approaching students from a particular religious background in a university, researchers may consciously choose to approach students that they feel are more like those who belong to a certain religion based on their manner of dress, their behaviour, their food preferences and lifestyle choices. This may even be viewed as an unconscious action. When a government minister of labour gives employment only to graduates from her place of birth, this becomes a conscious sampling bias. The question to ask here is: Why are all graduates from all the provinces not employed? Are they not employable? On the other hand, bias may be viewed as an unconscious act if it can be proved beyond reasonable doubt that such graduates were somehow disadvantaged by poverty, or in their examinations by a strike, or any other detrimental factors, and the minister had to somehow compensate for the disadvantage.

According to Dooley (2006:139), in unconscious sampling bias, the ability to distinguish friend from foe helped early humans survive, and the ability to quickly and automatically categorise people is a fundamental quality of the human mind. It is categories that dictate order to daily lives, and so people are also classified on many characteristics. This is also viewed as the foundation of stereotypes and prejudice. Recent scientific research has demonstrated that biases thought to be extinguished often remain as 'mental residue' in most people. [reference?]

In summary, sampling bias, or 'ascertainment bias' in medical concepts, is a bias in which a sample is collected in such a way that some members of the intended population are less likely to be included than others. "It results in a biased sample, a non-random sample of a population in which all individuals, were not equally likely to have been selected" (Ary, Jacobs & Razavieh, 2005:99). If this is not accounted for, results can be erroneously attributed to the phenomenon under study rather than to the method of sampling. Think about the following examples:

▶ *Pre-screening of trial participants*. A study to prove that diet and smoking do not affect a diabetes patient's health might mislead the younger generation. With diabetes there is always the danger of becoming blind, or having to have a limb amputated. Think about obesity in the USA, Europe and China: clearly, diet is a factor. Smoking is always risky and it always affects a person's health, regardless of whether they are at risk of diabetes or not, as it may result in cancer.

▶ *Exclusion bias results from exclusion of particular groups* (such as foreigners who are not allowed to vote in a foreign country) from the sample, for example, exclusion of subjects who have recently migrated into the study area (this may occur when people who have lost their identity documents or do not have such documents, are not available in a register).

Now that you have read about conscious and unconscious sampling bias, it is useful to test your understanding by responding to the following questions:

Critical thinking challenge

1 Distinguish between conscious and unconscious bias. Which do you think is more dangerous in a research study, and why?

2 When will a researcher be viewed as having conscious and unconscious bias in sampling? Give relevant examples from your own experience or study.

3 Give an example of a biased sample in any classroom situation of your choice.

In view of conscious and unconscious bias in sampling, the importance of populations and sampling frames will now be discussed.

13.7 Population and sampling frames

In this section you will begin to appreciate the importance of a sampling frame and population in a research study. The concept of population has already been defined earlier in this chapter. A sampling frame refers to the list from which participants are selected. A good sampling frame:

☑ **includes precise and concise data** which can be used to contact selected participants

☑ **includes all participants targeted** in the population

☑ **excludes all participants not targeted** in the population.

Moore (1993:87) argues that in many practical situations the frame is a matter of choice for the survey planner, and sometimes a critical one.

13.7.1 Sampling frame types and qualities

You should take note that the sampling frame is similar to the population you are studying, and may even be exactly the same. In choosing participants from the population to be included in your sample, probability sampling requires that you obtain a list of the population from which you want to select participants. In the case of the 580,577 learners who wrote the Grade 12 examinations, this would mean that we need to obtain a list of all learners who were registered for the National Senior Certificate examinations in their provinces in a particular year. To obtain this data, dedication from the researcher is needed, and expertise and commitment would be required from the provincial department of education.

The list would likely contain details about each learner (e.g. name, age, gender, subject registration and contact details). However, in more general cases, this is not possible. There is no way, for example, to identify all rats in the set of all rats. Where e-tolls are compulsory in Gauteng province, without activated cameras such as those used for speed prosecution, there is no way to identify which motorists using the highway routes will actually be liable to pay their way (in advance of the e-tolling stations). These imprecise populations are not amenable to sampling in any of the ways suggested later, nor can we apply statistical theory to them.

As a remedy, we seek a **sampling frame** which has the property that we can identify every single element and include any such in our sample. The most straightforward type of frame is a list of elements of the population (preferably the entire population) with appropriate contact information (Amin, 2005:95). In the most straightforward case, such as when dealing with a batch of material from a production run, or using a census, it is possible to identify and measure every single item in the population, and to include any one of them in our sample. However, in many other cases, this is not possible; either because it is cost-prohibitive (such as reaching every citizen of a country) or impossible (reaching all humans alive). Amin (2005) takes it a step further by maintaining that having established the frame, there are a number of ways for organising it to improve efficiency and effectiveness. It is at this stage that the researcher should decide whether the sample is in fact to be the whole population, in which case, it would be a census. A frame may also provide additional auxiliary information about its elements; when this information is related to variables or groups of interest, it may be used to improve survey design (Crook, 2001:34).

13.7.2 Challenges for sampling frames

Borg and Gall (1979:35) are of the view that the sampling frame must be representative of the population and this is a question outside the scope of statistical theory, demanding the judgement of experts in the particular subject matter being studied. Students at some universities encounter problems with their registration status. Sometimes they receive statements showing that they owe their full fees, which they are then supposed to settle before they write their examinations. Failure to do this will automatically mean that they do not get their results. The challenge with the above frames is that they omit registered students who are supposed to be writing their examinations. The irony is that the frames contain some unregistered students who will not write examinations; while some frames will contain multiple conflicting records for the same students. The conflicting information results in unnecessary confusion because students who are not in the frame have no prospect of being selected. Statistical theory informs people about the uncertainties in extrapolating from a sample to the frame. It should be expected that sample frames will always contain some errors which may result in bias. Once such sampling bias is identified, it should be minimised; one can only minimise since avoiding all bias is virtually impossible. In defining the frame, technical, economic and ethical issues also need to be taken into account (Patton, 1990:151).

Now that you have studied this discussion, it is important for you to test your insight by responding to the following questions:

Stop and reflect

1 What is a sampling frame? Describe it in your own words.

2 Give an example of a sampling frame in your study.

3 How will you use a sampling frame and population in your research study? Give a suitable example.

Conclusion

This chapter has focused on the importance of selecting sampling for your research design and methodology. In the discussion, the concepts of sampling, its types and techniques were briefly explained. Then probability and non-probability sampling, conscious and unconscious sampling bias were elaborated on. Population and sampling frames were contextualised from the logic of sampling. In conclusion, it could be said that sampling is viewed as the statistical technique of selecting the characteristics of a relatively small number of participants or items from a relatively large population of such participants or items. A valid inference about the characteristics of the entire population is drawn statistically.

Closing activities

Reflection questions

1 When do researchers need to use sample techniques?
2 Where and when would it be convenient for you to use sampling techniques in your study?
3 In Table 13.1, the provinces are arranged in descending order. Eastern Cape is often found languishing at the bottom of the provincial list in terms of performance. Which sampling technique was used to position provinces? Suggest some of the other reasons for the Eastern Cape's consistent poor performance in matric results.
4 Identify your own biases as a research student. How would you deal with unconscious bias?
5 Decide which of your biases you would address first. Explain why.

Bibliography

Amin, E.M. 2005. *Social science research: conception, methodology and analysis*. Kampala, Uganda: Makerere University Press.

Ary, D., Jacobs, L.C. & Razavieh, A. 2005. *Introduction to research in education*. New York: CBS Publishing.

Borg, W.R. & Gall, M.D. 1979. *Educational research*. New York: David Fulton.

Cohen, L. & Manion, L. 1994. *Research methods in education*. (4th ed.). London: Routledge.

Crook, C. 2001. The social character of knowing and learning: implications of cultural psychology for educational technology. *Journal of Information Technology for Teacher Education*, 10(1 & 2):19–36. Loughborough University, UK.

Crumpacker, L. & Van der Haegen, E. 1987. Pedagogy and prejudice: strategies for confronting homophobia in the classroom. *Women's Studies Quarterly*, 15(3–4):65–73.

De Vos, AS. 1998. *Research at grassroots: A primer for the caring professions*. Pretoria: Van Schaik.

Dooley, D. 2006. *Social research methods*. (2nd ed.). New York: Prentice-Hall.

Durrheim, K. 2006. Quantitative analysis. In M. Terre Blanche & K. Durrheim (Eds). *Research in practice: Applied methods for the social sciences*. Cape Town: University of Cape Town Press (pp. 96–122).

Guba, E. & Lincoln, Y. 2007. Competing paradigms in qualitative research, In N. Denzin & Y. Lincoln (Eds). *Handbook of qualitative research*. Thousand Oaks, CA: Sage (pp. 105–117).

Huysamen, GK. 1996. *Introductory statistics and research design for the behavioural sciences*. Cape Town: Academica.

Leedy, P.D. & Ormrod, J.E. 2001. *Practical research: planning and design* (7th ed.). Upper Saddle River, NJ: Merrill/Prentice-Hall.

Moore, N. 1993. *How to do research*. London: Teacher College Press.

Patton, M.Q. 1990. *Qualitative evaluation research methods* (2nd ed.). Newbury Park, CA: Sage.

Rose, P., Yoseph, G., Berrihun, G. & Nuresu, T. 1997. *Gender and primary schooling in Ethiopia*. IDS Research Report 31. Brighton: IDS.

Saunders, M., Lewis, P. & Thornhill, A. 1997. *Research methods for business students*. London: Pitman.

Schoenfeld, A.H. 1991. On mathematics as sense-making: An informal attack on the unfortunate divorce of formal and informal mathematics., In J. Voss, D.N. Perkins & J. Segal (Eds). *Informal reasoning and education*. Hillsdale, NJ: Lawrence Erlbaum.

Shapiro, A. 1999. Everybody belongs: changing negative attitudes toward classmates with disabilities. *Critical Education Practice*, 14.

Sica, G.T. 2006. Bias in research studies. *Radiology*, 238:780–789. Available online at http://radiology.rsna.org/content/238/3/780.full.

Sunday Times. 2010. Minister announces matric results. By M.W. Koekemoer. 11 January 2010.

Tuckman, B.W. 1978. *Conducting educational research* (4th ed.). New York: Harcourt Brace.

CHAPTER 14

Georgianna Duarte and Emma Miller

Survey research methods

KEY CONCEPTS

Interview survey is used to create a conversation between two or more people. Questions are asked by the interviewer to elicit responses or perceptions from the interviewee.

Primary data are a type of data that have not been gathered before, and are used when secondary data or information are not available. The data are observed or collected from first-hand experience. The advantage of primary data is that they should suit the researcher's purpose.

Surveys consist of a series of questions and other prompts to gather information from respondents.

Secondary data are a type of research that consists of data collected by someone other than the user. Common sources of secondary data include the national census or organisational databases.

Survey research is used in a variety of disciplines to assess thoughts, opinions and feelings, using a predetermined set of questions that are given to a sample of respondents.

Telephone survey is a method of opinion research where telephone calls are used to contact potential respondents.

LEARNING OUTCOMES

By the end of this chapter, you should be able to:

▶ Give a brief overview of survey research.

▶ Describe the diverse purposes of survey research.

▶ Identify the various types of survey research.

▶ Understand the strengths and weaknesses of surveys.

▶ Describe sampling procedures and methods.

▶ Outline and describe the guidelines for conducting survey research.

Case study: A classroom observation

This survey research took place at an early childhood development programme in Smitsville, a township in the Western Cape province of South Africa. The programme involved 240 children aged three to five years. The average class size was 40 children. The programme was located in a rural area, and its physical buildings were in poor condition. There were few resources, and a general shortage of early childhood materials and equipment. Many of the children were undernourished even though the region is an agricultural area, and the children mainly lived far from the centre. Some children appeared to be affected by fetal alcohol syndrome (FAS) due to the high use of alcohol in the region. During a classroom visit, the researcher observed a five-year-old boy who had difficulty following directions, listening to the teacher, and cooperating with other children. He spent hours wandering around, randomly selecting materials, and then tossing them on the ground. No one intervened and redirected or supported the child during the observation.

(continued)

Case study *(continued)*

How can we learn more about this learner to meet their educational and social needs?

In order to understand the learner, one might survey the teacher to learn about the strategies being utilised in the classroom. Through observation, parental surveys, and child interviews, the classroom teacher will gain a deeper understanding of the learning needs of the child.

Based on this observation, who might be surveyed to better understand the needs of this child?

The observation reflected a child having difficulty following directions, listening and cooperating. The teacher and parents would both be candidates for a survey focused on the unique characteristics of the child. For example, parents might complete a comprehensive survey about their child's development, learning style, preferences, and also characteristics of family life. Similarly, the teacher might complete a survey on child observations or teaching methods/strategies.

Based on this scenario, what types of surveys might we utilise to better understand the needs of the family and this child? We will explore this question in this chapter.

Introduction

Survey research is often used in assessing the thoughts, opinions, and feelings of a particular population or group. Many individuals participate in survey research when they use a new product, service, or are asked to review a restaurant or business. Survey research can be very specific, limited, or can even have global and widespread goals. Essentially, different academics and professionals in the liberal arts, education, psychology, science, and in business use survey research. Psychologists, educators and sociologists use survey research to analyse behaviour. Often, we become familiar with survey research when we are asked our opinions about a product, or a recent stay in a hotel. The trend is for survey research to be used to meet the more pragmatic needs of business and the media, for example, for evaluating political candidates, public health or transport services, and professional organisations.

A set of questions given to a predetermined sample of participants is what constitutes a survey. With a representative sample, one can describe the attitudes of the population from which the sample was drawn. Furthermore, one can compare the attitudes of different populations, as well as look for changes over a period of time. Having a good sample selection is significant because it allows one to generalise the findings from the sample to the population. This is the whole purpose of conducting survey research.

In quantitative and social sciences research, one of the most common types of tools is the survey. Firstly, survey research begins with the researcher selecting a sample of respondents from a population. Secondly, the researcher administers a standardised survey to the population. The person being surveyed, by online survey or a face-to-face interview, can complete or supply the data which are collected by the survey. Currently, the most commonly conducted surveys are through the internet (online) or a telephone interview. By using surveys, data can be collected from large or small populations.

Let us now examine how survey research is used in exploring the social behaviours of young children and the instructional strategies observed, in a rural setting.

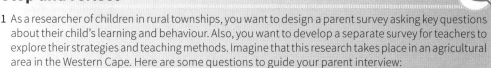

Stop and reflect

1 As a researcher of children in rural townships, you want to design a parent survey asking key questions about their child's learning and behaviour. Also, you want to develop a separate survey for teachers to explore their strategies and teaching methods. Imagine that this research takes place in an agricultural area in the Western Cape. Here are some questions to guide your parent interview:

   ▸ Does your child socialise with other children?

   ▸ Does your child select one activity at a time and maintain attention on that activity?

   ▸ Does your child follow instructions?

2 Now develop further questions for the parent interview survey, grouping and ordering them as makes most sense. Bear in mind that you are ultimately looking for data that will help teachers improve their teaching of these children (in the survey to be completed later).

14.1 The need for surveys

The purpose of a survey is to produce statistical estimates about some aspect of a population. This population can be small or large. The survey has two primary goals. The first is to minimise error in data collection. The second is to measure the error that is necessarily part of the measuring procedure.

Surveys are utilised to answer questions about experiences, opinions, and other characteristics of those participants in the study. The goal of a survey is to learn about the characteristics of the target population. There are numerous reasons for using a survey to better understand instructional strategies, methodology, and even demographics. For example, in South Africa there may be a need to examine the attrition rate of female graduate students versus male graduates in higher education. Similarly, a survey could be used to better understand what variables help learners in South African classrooms benefit from effective teaching strategies in early childhood education. Or, in contrast, a survey may be utilised to determine what courses are identified as most useful in a particular academic degree, and why they are perceived to be useful.

Surveys are often conducted because there is a need for specific information. Even when the information is available through other means, it is important to use surveys because survey research is efficient, easier, often a less expensive or a more accurate way to obtain the information. Using surveys allow the researcher to discover what a large number of people think about a particular issue. Surveys can be utilised for a wide range of topics and can be conducted relatively easily. When working on a local problem that might not have been addressed before, or there is little available research on the subject, a survey is useful.

If you are writing about children in a community and how they use their local park facilities, one of the best ways to learn about the community children is to go and talk to them. Another way of learning about their use of the park might be to observe their behaviour. These could be achieved through interviews, or through an online survey. After examining the usage of parks, you might explore if there are local reports, or publications that address the need for and use of community parks.

When one is working on a topic that is relatively new or original, and few publications exist on the topic being researched, surveys are the preferred method for collecting data. When a researcher collects data about a topic directly from the real work or activity, it is called **primary data**.

Methods for collecting primary data

Interviews can be a one-on-one, or small group format, of participants for a study. Interviews have the potential of providing a lot of information from a small group of people, and are useful when you want to obtain strong, knowledgeable opinions about a topic. Interviews are less structured than surveys.

Surveys. When the format of questioning is more structured, it is considered a survey and usually involves a large group of people. Surveys provide a limited amount of information from a large population of individuals, but are useful to learn what a larger population thinks about a topic.

Observations provide a researcher with insight about events, people, trends, and are useful when more information is needed without a biased interpretation. However, observations require documentation of clear and organised notes about the specific events in the researched world.

Analysis. When a researcher collects data and organises them in some meaningful fashion based on criteria, this is considered analysis. Analysis is used to identify a trend or pattern in the data. A type of analysis would be to record children's play using a complex climber, and then analyse specific types of play exhibited on the climber.

Returning to our community parks example, it might now be useful to examine if there is a connection between the cleaning or maintenance schedule of the park, the community usage, and the estimated attendance of events in the park. This second step is for the researcher to collect data and determine whether to utilise primary or **secondary data**. Primary data are data never gathered before, and they are used when secondary data are not available. The data are observed or collected from first-hand experience. The advantage of primary data is that they suit the researcher's purpose; the disadvantage is that to secure them is more costly and time-consuming than collecting secondary data.

Methods for collecting secondary data

Databases can hold substantial information previously collected and organised. Companies and other organisations have stored data that may be available to be utilised in conducting research. This data is considered valuable to a researcher since they will not require additional costs in either funding or time, which generating primary data would carry.

Websites provide a plethora of information to a researcher. However, it is important to remember that not all data found on the internet are valid, accurate or reliable. Great caution should be taken to ensure the validity of the data and of course any copyright implications.

Print material comes from newspapers, articles, journals, policy documents, and company reports.

Stop and reflect

Having developed an interview survey for parents, you now want to survey teachers on their perceptions of the behaviour of the children in their class:

1. What questions will you develop for the teacher survey? Do not repeat the parent interview questions, but think of questions that will help teachers improve their teaching strategies.
2. Are the data from your parent interview survey primary or secondary data? How can they be used in developing your teacher survey?

14.2 Purpose of the survey

The purpose of the survey is to produce statistics that are quantitative or numerical descriptions about some aspects of the target population. The primary way of collecting information is by asking people questions; their answers constitute the data to be analysed. Generally, the information is collected from only a fraction of the population. This is a sample, which is taken as representative of the larger population.

When you plan a survey, first consider who will be using the information you gather and for what purpose they want the specific information. For example, consider the case of a survey conducted in a school community about poor physical health performance. The information might be beneficial to administrators, parents, teachers and learners in making decisions, choices and plans. All these stakeholders have an interest in knowing how serious the health performance problem is. Is the problem due to the elimination of break periods? Is the problem due to the restricted amount of time allocated to physical education? Is the problem due to the decaying condition of play spaces, or their non-existence in the area? Stakeholders might also be interested in the various opinions in the school community about what the causes of this problem are. In addition, some new plans or policies might be put in place to reduce the problem as a result of some of the responses to open-ended questions. The researchers might have a better understanding of the problem if they are clear about the complexity of the problem, and gather factual data from different points of view.

Surveys can be used to obtain factual and attitudinal information, such as:

▸ *Factual information* on a survey administered only to learners might consist of their grade level, gender, and their behaviours. For example, a survey about academic performance in a student population might ask students about their academic average and how much time they spend on reading, writing, or in contact with their lecturers.

▸ *Attitudinal information* indicates how people feel and think about social conditions or about public policies designed to deal with specific conditions. A survey about academic performance might ask students for their opinions about how academic mentoring, accessibility of faculty, family responsibilities, financial concerns, or outside work, affect their studies.

The purpose of the survey is to identify and clearly define the target population and the group of people about whom you wish to know more. For example, you may only be interested in surveying school learners about academic performance. Focusing on a target learner population may provide valuable information about learners' perceptions of the problem, and their opinions about the causes of and solutions to poor performance. Perhaps your purpose is to compare attitudes and behaviours of high- and low-performing learners. In this case, your target population would include equal numbers of both types of learners. If your purpose is to gather information from all segments of the community – administrators, teachers, parents and learners – then you would obviously obtain more diverse viewpoints and fuller data.

14.3 Surveys as research instruments

Once you have identified a problem to research, the next step is to determine the instrument to collect the data. The most common instrument survey researchers use is the survey. You will remember that a **survey** is a means of examining the feelings, beliefs, experiences, perceptions, or attitudes of individuals or a group of people. The typical dictionary definition gives a clearer idea: 'A survey is a written or printed form used in gathering information on some subject or subjects consisting of a list of questions to be submitted to one or more persons.' As a data-collecting instrument, it can be structured or unstructured. The survey is used widely, and often takes the form of a very concise, pre-planned set of questions. Typically, it is designed to yield specific information to meet a particular need for research information. For example, we may want to find out why teachers use more convergent questions rather than divergent questions in an early childhood classroom. The research information is obtained from respondents who are normally from a related interest area.

14.3.1 Constructing the survey

Complex and attentive planning is required in constructing a survey in survey research. In constructing the survey, there are several steps in planning the questions that include:

- ☑ **First,** the researcher must review the information requirements necessitating a survey.
- ☑ **Second,** it is important to develop and prioritise a list of potential questions that will satisfy the information requirements.
- ☑ **Third,** one must assess each potential question carefully for cultural and linguistic appropriateness.
- ☑ **Fourth,** it is important to determine the types of questions to be asked.
- ☑ **Fifth,** the researcher must carefully decide on the specific wording of each question to be asked.
- ☑ **Sixth,** one must determine the structure of the survey to ensure order, meaning and relevance.
- ☑ **Seventh,** in constructing this instrument, one must carefully evaluate the actual overall survey and its purpose.

Constructing the survey is a critical process. If a survey is written poorly, or is incomplete, the results will not be worthwhile or representative of the sample. Surveys should produce valid and reliable demographically variable measures. Also, surveys should yield valid and reliable individual disparities such as self-report scales generate. These are some important considerations in creating a survey:

- ☑ **Cost savings:** The online survey is less expensive than paying for stationery, printing and postage in a regular mail survey.
- ☑ **Ease of editing/analysis:** Electronically, it is easier to edit, change and resubmit surveys, as well as to copy and organise data.
- ☑ **Faster transmission time:** Electronically, surveys can be delivered to recipients in seconds. Regular mail requires days for delivery and has more obstacles to receipt.
- ☑ **Easy use of pre-letters:** The researcher has efficient windows of time in sending invitations, response, and completed surveys in a short amount of time.
- ☑ **Better response rates:** Research shows that response rates on private networks are higher with electronic surveys than with paper surveys or interviews.
- ☑ **More candid responses:** Participants who complete an electronic survey report more honestly than those in paper surveys or interviews.
- ☑ **Wider audience electronically and faster response rate:** Owing to the speed and increasing use of the internet, participants can answer more rapidly and efficiently than on paper. Rather than just local coverage, the study has the potential for greater global coverage.

14.3.2 Using variables

Another important part of the survey involves the type of information you plan to collect to help answer your problem question(s). Variables are used in survey research to depict characteristics of the surveyed sample. Variables can include measurements such as ethnicity, socio-economic status, race, gender, and age.

14.4 Weaknesses in using electronic surveys

There are a number of significant weaknesses in using electronic surveys. The list below gives the most important weaknesses.

▶ *Limitations in demographics*: The population and sample may be limited to those who have access to or have a computer. There is also the concern of digital literacy and experience of internet applications.

▶ *Concerns of confidentiality*: It is difficult to guarantee or ensure anonymity and confidentiality in online surveys.

▶ *Layout and presentation issues*: When one constructs the format of a survey online, it may be challenging and the first of several versions. However, successive drafts will in time build experience and a useful skill.

▶ *Response rate*: Research has shown that email response rates are higher during the first few weeks, but as time passes, the return rate decreases.

14.5 The design of surveys

The design of a survey is critical. It is most important to carefully consider the population you are planning to survey in your research. Equally important is your identification of the individuals you plan to survey. Further significant decisions are where you will survey the sample, and how you plan to survey it. How long will the survey be? How much time will be needed to complete the survey? Can the individuals stop participating in the survey if they want to? What types of questions will be included in the survey?

Toolbox Preparing to conduct survey research

These questions and issues must be considered carefully as you prepare to conduct survey research:

▶ Who are you planning to survey? You must decide what group or groups you are focusing on as you formulate your research question.

▶ Why this group? Surveying this group or groups will be based on their accessibility and what the focus of the research is. It is critical to examine the purpose of your study in relation to the sample that you plan to survey.

▶ Why are you using a survey instrument? Surveys are designed to produce specific statistics about a target population.

▶ Does size matter? The size of the sample is very important: you need to revisit and re-examine it as you plan your study:

> Is your sample too broad in range?

> Is your sample too narrow in scope?

▶ Why does inclusion/exclusion matter? If the sample group excludes some people who are the target population, then the sample estimates will be skewed since you omitted those who matter. The same applies if you include people who are not the target population.

The next section deals with getting the best results from your survey in terms of the rate of response, and by asking the kinds of questions that will elicit full and interesting responses.

14.6 Guidelines for improving response rate

Having spent considerable time on the design of your research survey by carefully identifying your target group, you want to be sure of getting an adequate response. There are several significant ways to improve the response rate in administering a survey. These include:

- ☑ A letter of introduction
- ☑ A clear, concise explanation of the study
- ☑ A self-addressed stamped envelope, if you are using the mail system
- ☑ A monetary or other incentive (e.g. gift voucher, discount on product, service or fees)
- ☑ Making the process easy for the participant in terms of time, convenience and ease of use
- ☑ Sending a follow-up mailing to remind participants of the importance of their response
- ☑ Writing follow-up letters of encouragement or appreciation.

14.7 Guidelines for asking survey questions

It is most important to follow specific guidelines in selecting or developing appropriate questions for the survey. Before looking at the guidelines, you may also want to consider the following points and terms in creating the survey:

- ▶ Using question formats, particularly for populations that are multilingual or have varying levels of literacy, can be challenging.
- ▶ It is advisable to make sure that respondents are competent and willing to answer the questions of the survey.
- ▶ The questions must all be relevant, and shorter items are the most effective.
- ▶ It is important to avoid negative items, terms, the tone of questions, and especially to avoid biased items.

Toolbox Developing good survey questions

1 Avoid leading words in the questions of any survey.

There are many subtle word differences in meaning and this can produce significant variations in your results.

Example: 'could', 'should' and 'might' mean different things and produce differences in the responses to a particular question. In addition, strong words such as 'must', 'make', 'force', 'inhibit', 'change' and 'prohibit' represent control or restriction and can bias your results.

Example: The community should force you to attend political functions.

No one likes to be forced, and no one likes to be required to attend political meetings. This agreement scale question makes it sound doubly bad to attend political functions. Wording alternatives can be developed, such as simple statements like: The community should offer political informational meetings, or the community needs to offer community informational meetings.

(continued)

Toolbox *(continued)*

Example: How would you rate the talent of the popular actor?

This question tells you that the actor is popular. This type of wording can bias respondents. Try replacing the word 'popular' with 'well known', as in: How would you rate the well-known actor?

2 **Be sure to give mutually exclusive choices.**

All multiple choice response options should be mutually exclusive so that respondents can make clear choices. It is important to avoid creating ambiguity for respondents.

It is also important to review your survey and identify ways that respondents could get stuck with either giving too many or no correct answers.

3 **Ask direct and specific questions.**

Questions that are vague and do not communicate your intent can limit the usefulness of your results. Be sure that respondents know what you are asking.

Example: What suggestions do you have for improving the vegetarian menu in the cafeteria?

This question may be intended to obtain suggestions about improving the taste or quality of the particular food, but respondents may offer suggestions about variety, the different types of vegetarian diets to be accommodated, or even suggest using alternative ingredients.

4 **Be sure to include a 'prefer not to answer' option.**

Sometimes respondents may not want, or be able, to provide the information requested. Questions about marital status, family life, personal, political, or religious beliefs, and income, may be too intrusive and rejected by the respondent. For many individuals, privacy is an important issue. Assurances of confidentiality can be used to obtain private information. In many research studies, where respondents prefer not to answer, a pna option increases data quality and response rates for the rest of the survey, and generally many respondents appreciate this choice. Different cultural groups clearly answer differently, and may discontinue the survey entirely if the questions seem inappropriate or too invasive. Inform yourself about cultural sensitivities and build this understanding into carefully giving choices.

5 **Reflect and review to ensure that that you covered all possible choices.**

After carefully reviewing your survey, have you covered all your options and possibilities? If you are unsure whether you have or not, conduct a pretest.

6 **Use unbalanced scales carefully.**

Unbalanced scales may be appropriate for some situations and promote bias in others. For instance, a child care centre might use an Excellent–Very Good–Good–Fair scale, where 'Fair' is the lowest customer satisfaction point because they believe 'Fair' is unacceptable and requires the improvement of the centre. It is important to remember that if fair is the lowest point on a scale, a result of slightly better than Fair is most likely to be interpreted as not very good either. Also, scale points should have the same equal conceptual distance from one point to the next. For example, researchers have shown the points that are nearly equidistant to be the Strongly disagree–Disagree–Neutral–Agree–Strongly agree scale. Select and identify your bottom point as the worst possible situation or descriptor. Identify the top point as the best possible, and then evenly spread the labels for your scale points in-between. Try to tell what is wrong with the following example before reading the explanation.

Example: What is your opinion of the new diet yogurt? Pretty good; Great; Fantastic; Incredible; The best ever.

This question puts the middle of the scale at 'Fantastic', and the lowest possible rating as 'Pretty good'. This range of responses is not capable of collecting accurate opinions from respondents.

7 **Ask only one question at a time.**

There is often a temptation to ask multiple questions at once. This can cause problems for respondents and influence their responses.

The next section examines in detail the sample size of the population that you are planning to survey.

14.8 Sample size

How many people are you going to survey? Determine how many surveys you need to conduct. It is important to avoid having too few surveys because you won't have enough data to support any generalisations or findings you may make. At the same time, you do not want too many surveys because having too many surveys will be overwhelming when it comes to analysing your data. Similarly, if the sample size is too large, and the questions are not specific enough, you may end up with a large number of items unanswered, and this will be problematic in determining your results.

There are several challenges in securing the right sample for your research study. First, logistics need to be considered in determining the sample. Is the sample accessible, so respondents can answer the survey without hardship or inconvenience? For example, do they live close by; or do they live 200 kilometres away, and do not use the internet? A second challenge is the willingness to be part of the sample. Do the sample respondents even want to participate in the study? A third concern is the stability of the sample. For example, will the school or agency pull out of the sample midway because of transitional, financial, or political changes in its administration or leadership? Fourth, is the sample representative of the larger population? There is no basis for saying a sample is representative of the sampled population unless the sampling process gives each person selected a known probability of selection. While the sample size is an important process, how one is going to survey individuals is equally important. We deal with this next.

14.9 Process for surveying people

The survey method should be chosen carefully, based on the length of the survey and the types of questions. The researcher can choose to conduct his or her survey using different formats. For example, to do it in person by walking up to people and asking them questions; on paper using hand-out surveys and asking people to return them at a particular point; or even via the internet, either by directing respondents to a website link, or by sending an email. It is important to assess your questions for clarity and literacy level – both language and digital.

14.10 Determining the length of the survey

Determining the length of the survey depends largely on what the researcher is trying to discover. In addition, it also depends on how much information you want to gather. Longer surveys sometimes ask the same question in different ways to determine if people are being consistent in their responses. For the first survey, it is recommended to keep things simple. In surveys, shorter questions are generally considered more effective than longer questions.

14.11 Conducting surveys

After the survey is created, a comprehensive plan must be developed that outlines how, by whom, and to whom the survey will be administered. There are a number of ways to find a relevant sample group amongst your survey population. In addition, there are various considerations involved in administering the survey itself.

14.11.1 Administering a survey

For many researchers, it is challenging to ensure that the actual survey is answered in a timely manner. There are basic logistics in starting the survey. It is critical to identify a timeframe that is acceptable and convenient to participants in the survey. Equally important is to establish an appropriate and reasonable amount of time for the survey to be completed.

Deciding on the location of where to administer the survey is another important consideration. It is vital to make arrangements for the survey location well in advance. Second, it is valuable to pretest your survey to establish time, process, logistics, and other details that have not yet been considered. A pretest allows for reflection, adjustment, and corrections in the final data collection.

Administering the written survey can be conducted in several ways. The researcher can deliver the surveys to the schools, offices, or homes of the participants. In other studies, participants can pick up their survey at an established location or agency. Yet another method is mailing the survey directly to the home or workplace of the participant, and requesting that the survey be returned within a particular timeframe. Another efficient way of ensuring completeness is when the surveys are retrieved directly from the homes or workplaces of the participants.

14.11.2 Taking it personally

When deciding on the method of the data collection, it is important to consider how you would respond to the process. Many of us have terminated a survey, or stopped a call, or just not completed a survey. The important question to consider is, why? It is useful to consider the elements of how you would personally respond to a particular format.

14.12 Types of survey questions

What types of questions are you going to ask? Will it be an open-ended or closed question format about the focused topic? Using open-ended questions allows respondents the opportunity to answer in different ways. For example: How are you feeling today? In a closed question, the only possible response is either Good or Not good. Similarly, Did you feel that the new campus regulation about smoking was fair? can only elicit a Yes or No answer. Although a closed question is much easier to analyse, this type of question does not provide the rich data you may get with an open-ended question. Ultimately, what type of question you ask depends on what you want to discover.

14.13 Types of surveys

Diverse disciplines use a variety of surveys. There are many different types of surveys including self-administered surveys, **interview surveys**, **telephone surveys**, internet or online surveys, and focus group surveys. These surveys may vary in format, length and scope. Surveys may be about educational strategies, use of products, political or economic choices, or social issues. In addition, an important consideration in the selection and content of the survey is professional ethics (about which you read in Chapter 6 and 7 of this book) and which we will address in section 14.17. Table 14.1 describes how and what to consider in the selection of a survey.

TABLE 14.1: What to consider in the selection of a survey

Design	Who administers the survey	Setting	Survey structure	Cost
Mailed survey	Researcher	Individual	Mostly structured	Low
Group survey	Researcher	Group	Mostly structured	Very low
Phone survey	Professional	Individual	Structured	Moderate
In-person interview	Professional	Individual	Structured or unstructured	High
Web survey	Researcher	Individual	Mostly structured	Very low

14.13.1 The interview survey

An interview survey utilises both face-to-face or telephone formats to collect the necessary data. The researcher has a great deal of potential in influencing the quality of the collected data.

Tips for conducting a successful interview survey

▶ Clear and effective communication skills are needed in conducting the survey and collecting the data.

▶ The researcher should invest time and attention in building rapport, credibility and confidence with the participants in the study.

▶ The researcher must establish and build trust, and provide clarity of purpose. These attributes are all critical factors in the quality of the interview survey.

▶ The interview must be conducted in an authentic manner. In other words, the interviewer must be reflexive in their tone, pacing and non-verbal communication, in keeping with the participants' mood, demeanour and attitude.

14.13.2 The telephone survey

Using telephone surveys involves all of the preparation of face-to-face surveys, but can also create new problems because of their unfortunate reputation. A pitfall of the telephone survey method is that it is so much easier for an individual to hang up on a phone surveyor than to close the door in someone's face, or to walk out of the room. As a result, the number of calls needed to achieve a complete survey can be startling. One method to combat this pitfall is by using a computer: it allows for quick and random number dialling and for interviewers to type their answers using programs that automatically set up the data for analysis. Such programs include CATI (computer-assisted survey interview) that have made phone surveys a more cost- and time-effective method. CATI makes using the telephone survey a popular one among researchers. On the downside, however, respondents are becoming increasingly reluctant to answer phone surveys because they are often associated with telemarketing. As with face-to-face interviews, the telephone interviewer must be aware of their tone, repetition, expression, or lack of responsiveness during the survey.

14.14 Challenges of creating the survey

One of the main challenges in creating a survey is language. Considerations include using vocabulary or phrases that all respondents will understand, and carefully reviewing grammar, word choice, and expression (e.g. too formal, or too informal? too serious, or too casual?).

During the process of creating a survey, questions may be unclear or misleading to the participants. The researcher must carefully reflect on all the questions to ensure they are clear, not misleading, and free from bias.

Pitfalls in survey questions

Biased questions

A biased question encourages the participants to respond to the question in a certain way. The question might contain biased terminology, or be worded in a biased way. Some examples of biased questions include:

- ▶ Don't you agree that the increase in student parking is a problem for faculty?
  Revised question: Is student and faculty parking a problem?

- ▶ Many faculty members can't find a parking space; are you one of them?
  Revised question: Would you agree or disagree that parking is a problem?

Double-barrelled questions

These are frequently used in surveys. A double-barrelled question involves having more than one question embedded in it. Participants will often answer one but not both of the questions, or may disagree with a part of, or the entire question.

Example: Do you agree that parking is a problem and that the university administration should be working on an immediate solution this semester?

Revised question: Is campus parking a problem? (If the response to this question is Yes, then ask: Do you think the administration should be responsible for solving it?)

Confusing or wordy questions

The researcher must ensure that the questions are not confusing, too long, or vague. Confusing questions will lead to the participants being bewildered, and often result in unreliable answers.

Example: What do you think about parking? (This is confusing because the question isn't clear about what you're really asking regarding parking: Are you referring to student parking? Parking in handicapped spaces? The availability of parking in general?)

14.15   Strengths and weaknesses of the survey research method

As indicated at the outset, surveys are particularly good for producing precise descriptions of mass populations. Statistics SA provides accurate and reliable demographic information, and its census reports (based on a mass survey of the country) are a particularly useful source of detailed population information, statistics and trends. Surveys also allow for the collection of a great deal of data from a large number of people. However, they are often expensive and lengthy exercises, and the statistical information they produce is already dated by the time the results are published.

On the negative side, surveys share with experiments the disadvantage of artificiality. There is always a risk that people's answers to survey items may not reflect their true feelings or their subsequent actions. Surveys can also seem superficial, when compared with field research.

14.16 Selecting the sample size

You should consider changing the standard sampling and statistical analysis if the sample size is small (less than about 5,000), or if the sample size is a significant proportion of the population size, such as 20 per cent or more. Surveying a small sample size can include residents of a small town, village, or large city suburb. Other examples could include sampling learners in a class, employees in a company, or members of a professional organisation or group. Frequently, we experience survey calls in everyday life on education, the food and hospitality industries, medical or pharmaceutical professions. In each of these cases, the target population may vary from 30 or 40 to several thousand individuals.

The other side of the sample size coin involves surveying large populations, where the sample size is usually over 5,000. When the information needs depend heavily on the relationships between the survey questions so that patterns can be detected, a large amount of data must be collected from each respondent. Many surveys deal with large populations, such as all adults in South Africa, or all learners in Gauteng province. Target populations who respond to these surveys can often include hundreds of thousands or even millions of people. Textbooks tend to make the assumption that the sample size is small, compared with the population size in statistical and sampling analysis.

Critical thinking challenge

1 In the township of Ashton in the Western Cape, the community is mainly poor and resistant to change. Think about how you might survey the larger population about their ideas on alternative housing structures that are different from the breeze block units they are familiar with. Think about how you might address the problem of wind, debris, refuse and sewage in the proposed new plans and designs.

2 What type of survey would be most appropriate for this research? Develop your answer by supporting it with examples from your reading of this chapter.

14.17 Professional ethics in conducting surveys

Professional ethics is an important consideration in the selection and content of the survey. There is a widespread belief that studies are unethical if their sample size is not large enough to ensure adequate power or authority of the data collected. These authors have examined how sample size influences the balance that determines the ethical acceptability of a study: The balance between the burden that participants accept, and the clinical or scientific value that a study can be expected to produce. The average projected burden per participant remains constant as the sample size increases, but the projected study value does not increase as rapidly as the sample size if it is assumed to be proportional to power. This implies that the value per participant declines as the sample size increases, and that smaller studies therefore have more favourable ratios of projected value to participant burden. The ethical treatment of study participants therefore does not require consideration of whether the study power is less than the conventional goal of 80 per cent or 90 per cent. Lower power does not make a study unethical. This analysis addresses only ethical acceptability, not optimality; large studies may be desirable for other than ethical reasons.

Conclusion

Survey research is often used to assess thoughts, opinions, and feelings. A survey includes a predetermined set of questions. These questions are given to a sample, which can provide the researcher with a generalisation about the sample population. Surveys can be quantitative or qualitative in format and can be administered face-to-face, via telephone, or on the internet. There are two main sources for research: these are primary and secondary data. Different types of surveys contain both strengths and weaknesses that should be reviewed by the researcher in determining which instrument is be best for collecting the data. Primary data is data never collected before and typically more expensive to gather. Secondary data is data previously gathered (e.g. newspaper archives, policy documents, educational reports or public documents) that can be mined to obtain an answer to a particular question. This is less expensive since the data has already been collected. It is critical to ensure the protection of the participants' integrity and privacy, and that the research is conducted in an ethical manner.

Closing activities

For research students to have an opportunity to engage and reflect on survey research, the following steps are provided for meaningful practice. Each represents an opportunity for reflective practice and collaborative work.

Self-reflection questions

1 Reflect on the parent interview you developed earlier in this chapter, about the child's learning and social behaviour. How did you plan for parents to share this information? What did you think you would learn about the children that would help inform the teacher of more effective strategies?

2 Think of how you would have conducted your interview and the kinds of questions you asked: were there questions that needed to be reworded or changed? Which ones, and how would you rework them?

Practical applications

1 Identify a topic for a survey that is meaningful to your work or study. List the steps that you would take to determine if the survey design should be cross-sectional, successive independent samples, or longitudinal studies. (Refer to Chapter 10 on research design to remind yourself of these types.)

2 Construct an effective survey based on your topic.

3 On looking back at the different surveys you created earlier for the rural areas of Smitsville and Ashton, are these relevant in terms of your new topic? What have you learned from developing those surveys?

Analysis and consolidation

1 *Data analysis and design*

Design a matrix that compares the similarities and differences in analysing quantitative and qualitative data. Describe what analysis you would conduct for each of the different surveys used in the rural regions suggested earlier.

2 *Collecting survey data*

Describe the ways you would have collected the survey data for each of the townships in the Western Cape?

Bibliography

Allan, G. & Skinner, C. 1991. *Handbook for Research Learners in the Social Sciences*. London: The Falmer Press.

Alreck, P. & Settle, R. 2004. *The Survey Research Handbook* (3rd ed.). Los Angeles, CA: McGraw-Hill Publishing Company.

Babbie, E.R. 1995. *The practice of social research* (7th ed.). Belmont, CA: Wadsworth.

Creswell, J.W. 2013. *Research Design: Qualitative, Quantitative, and Mixed Methods Approaches* (4th ed.). Washington DC: Sage Publications.

Fox, J. & Tracy, P. 1986. *Randomized Response: A Method for Sensitive Surveys*. Beverly Hills, CA: Sage.

Fowler, F.J. Jr. 2013. *Survey Research Methods* (5th ed.). Washington DC: Sage Publications.

Frey, J.H. & Oishi, S.M. 1995. *How to Conduct Interviews by Telephone and in Person*. Washington DC: Sage Publications.

Garson, D. 2013. *Survey Research & Sampling 2013 Edition* (Statistical Associates "Blue Book" Series). New York City, NY: Routledge Publishing Company.

Nardi, P. 2013. *Doing Survey Research* (3rd ed.). Boulder, Colorado: Paradigm Publishers.

Rea, L. & Parker, R. 2005. *Designing and conducting survey research: A comprehensive guide*. Hoboken, NJ: John Wiley & Sons Publishing Company.

Weisberg, H., Krosnick, J.A. & Bowen, B. 1989. *An Introduction to Survey Research and Data Analysis*. New York City, NY: Scott Foresman Publications.

CHAPTER 15

Zhidong Zhang and Georgianna Duarte

Experimental methods and data collection

KEY CONCEPTS

Epistomology is concerned with what knowledge is, how we can acquire knowledge, and the relationship between knowers' beliefs and the world.

Experimental design is a set layout which follows the fundamental rationale of all experimental research methods. A given experimental design is a specific elaborated format of a given research method.

Interval scales provide the information not only about the rank-order feature, but also about that of equal distance between any two adjacent objects.

Inventories are sets of measurement instruments used to measure affective and non-cognitive dimensions such as personality, attitudes, beliefs, values, interests, and other emotional dimensions.

Logical positivism and **logical empiricism** together form neo-positivism, a perspective which holds that the purpose of both natural sciences and social sciences is to explore theoretical explanations so that they can be used to guide the scientific practice.

Measurement can be seen as a set of rules for assigning numbers to represent objects, traits, and attributes.

Nominal scale provides qualification information that gives the researcher categorical information; it only differentiates among objects or categories such as gender which has two categories, female or male.

Non-equivalent means not equal and is a term often used in research design to describe when the experimental conditions are not equal between two groups.

Numerical scale also called a ratio scale, it represents all the characteristics of the ordinal scale and interval scale. In addition, the numerical scale also includes the zero amount of the measure.

Ordinal scales also called rank order scale which provides rank-order information. This scale of measure is used to rank objects in terms of the quantity of a characteristic, or the object represented in a process.

Quantitative observation or **structured observation** is a quantitative data collection method with a set of quantitative rules or instruments. The data from the observation can be recorded in a numerical format as a measured value.

Survey is one of the inventory instruments which consists of a series of questions and other prompts for the purpose of gathering information from respondents.

Research hypothesis is a conjectural statement of variable relations in an experimental research study. The hypothesis is examined and proved by conducting a data analysis procedure.

Research setting is the environment in which research is carried out. Based on different foci and alternative perspectives, the research setting can be seen as the physical, social, and cultural site.

Test is a measurement instrument in education designed to measure the progress in knowledge aquisition and problem-solving skills development.

Case study: Using experimental design

A researcher from the University of Fort Hare in South Africa wants to study the effectiveness of different pedagogical strategies in teaching algebra. The researcher uses an experimental design which divides the class randomly into two groups, calling them 'group A' and 'group B'. The students cannot freely choose their own group. The two groups share equal characteristics at the beginning of the experiment since a random assignment procedure is used. In group A, the researcher uses a new pedagogical strategy to teach the algebra lesson. In group B, the researcher uses a standard pedagogical strategy to teach the algebra lesson. The researcher compares test scores at the end of the semester to evaluate the success of the new pedagogical strategy compared with the standard pedagogical strategy. At the end of the study, the results indicate that the students in the new pedagogical strategy group scored significantly higher on their final exam than the students in the standard teaching group.

Introduction

Research methods are divided into three main types: quantitative, qualitative, and mixed methods. The consensus in social sciences research circles accepts this breakdown of the research methods spectrum for the time being, regardless of its rationality. We plan to focus on experimental research methods, which are a fundamental and crucial part of research methods in educational and psychological sciences. It is not necessary, although still helpful, to start research methods by learning about them sequentially from quantitative methods, then to proceed to qualitative methods, and finally to mixed research methods.

The experimental research methods contain all characteristics of quantitative research methods, which are a set of systematic procedures by which researchers discover and explain the relations among the phenomena. Quantitative research is the numerical representation and manipulation of data collected for the purpose of describing and explaining the phenomena.

We start this chapter with a discussion of the characteristics, random rules and assumptions of quantitative research methods, and further examine the types of quantitative research methods, internal and external validity and their threat elements. **Measurement** and variables, as two crucial concepts, are introduced and a case study is progressively developed throughout the chapter to help research students understand the concepts: research design, and validity and threat elements.

15.1 Quantitative research methods

There are essentially two research designs/methods in quantitative research methods: experimental methods and quasi-experimental methods. The systematic procedures of the quantitative research possess several crucial characteristics:

▶ Accompanied by the development of scientific methodology, quantitative research has formed its own tradition.
▶ Methodology of quantitative research is rooted in a given set of epistemology paradigms.
▶ A research hypothesis is an indispensible component.
▶ The variable is a hub in connecting the raw data and the steps in the analysis.

Going over these characteristics can help us understand quantitative research, and help the researcher further the experimental research method and design. The *first* characteristic element informs us that there are several assumptions in quantitative research. For example, one assumption is that randomly selecting individuals can reach an impartial conclusion. Another assumption is that collecting and analysing information from each individual may indicates contingency, which means a future event or circumstance is possible but cannot be predicted with certainty. This contingency helps inform us of a conclusion with a necessity.

The *second* characteristic element is about epistemology paradigms. Epistemology directly influences and dominates research design, data collection, data analysis and explanations. You will remember that **epistemology** is concerned with what knowledge is, how we can acquire knowledge, and the relations between knowers' beliefs and the world. Much of the debate in this field has focused on the philosophical analysis of the nature of knowledge, and how it relates to connected notions such as truth, belief, and justification. For example, **logical positivism** or **logical empiricism** and interpretivism have very different explanations for the research study results. Thus, the quantitative researchers' explanations of a research study's results are unique and can be differentiated from the ones of other research methods (such as qualitative and mixed methods). Logical positivism/logical empiricism provides the quantitative methods an epistemological fundamental requires (Howell, 2013; Johnson & Christensen, 2012).

The *third* characteristic element is about the research hypothesis. A **research hypothesis** is a statement about an educated guess based on observation. The research hypothesis provides quantitative researchers with a scientific reasoning framework through which different research designs can be developed. A clear, logical hypothesis can transfer research conjecture into statistical hypothesis. For example, a careless research hypothesis, or one that is not carefully developed, may look great initially, but when researchers continue their work, and establish their statistical hypothesis, they may discover that the two hypotheses do not match. This is an important discovery for the researchers. Through an appropriate statistical procedure, based on reasonable research and statistical hypotheses, researchers can reach a robust statistical conclusion.

The *fourth* characteristic is about variables, which is the foundation of data collection and analysis. All data can only be analysed through variables. Sometimes the data can be directly recorded in a variable format, such as students' algebra achievements, which score between 0 and 100 continuously. More often, the raw data are indirectly recorded in the variable format by using coding techniques. For example, if we use a survey 5-status Likert scale, the information collected in each item can be transferred into a variable with five quantitative levels, such as 1, 2, 3, 4 and 5. So we can see that the variable is very critical in a quantitative research study.

15.2 Experimental research methods

Experimental methods have followed a format of logical positivism or logical empiricism. The philosopher August Comte represents this type of thinking in the logical positivism or logical empiricism school of thought. The assumptions in logical positivism and empiricism are that social facts have an objective reality. For example, in the opening case study of this chapter we want to obtain a conclusion about the differences between two pedagogical groups by comparing the students' achievements. One of the critical assumptions in logical positivism is that the variables can be identified and the relationships among them can be measured clearly. Essentially, research approaches usually begin with hypothesis and theory, and also researchers use formal instruments. They usually seek the norm and reduce the data to numerical indices. The research purposes of experimental research methods are usually to seek generalisability, causal explanations and predictions. For example, in the case study, if we find there is significantly different learner achievement in two different pedagogical groups, we can generalise that it is plausible that two different pedagogical strategies can be applied in any similar instructional environment (Howell, 2013).

Stop and reflect

Now that you have learned about quantitative and experimental research, see if you can answer the following questions:
1 What are four characteristics of quantitative research?
2 What is the relationship between quantitative research and experimental research?
3 How would you characterise the essence of logical positivism or logical empiricism?

15.3 Experimental methods and the 'random' rule

Experimental methods in research studies use controlled observations and measurements to test hypotheses. Their purpose is to determine cause-and-effect relationships. The random rule ensures that the design is able to eliminate threats from extraneous and confounding variables. Random rules include both random selection and random assignment of samples. Random selection of samples and random assignment of samples (which assigns individual members to experimental and control groups) are the fundamental requirements of the experimental research designs. These two essential features ensure that each individual member in the population has an equal chance of being chosen for the sample (Gay, Mills, & Airasian, 2012).

Random selection is a sampling procedure in which each member in the target population can be selected with an equal chance. For example, there are 1,000 Grade 5 learners in a school district. We can then define the school district as a population. We select 100 learners from the population by using a simply random selection procedure. This procedure ensures each Grade 5 learner in the school district has the same chance as others to be selected as a participant in a research project (Fink, 2003).

Random assignment is another procedure by which each individual or participant can be allocated into both an experimental group and control group. In other words, it ensures that each individual member in the study receives the equivalent opportunity to be allocated to either the treatment condition or the control condition. Just as there are random rules and controlled observations discussed here, it is important to recognise that there are specific assumptions about the objectivity of the process. These beliefs and assumptions are described in the next section. (Fink, 2009; Leedy, 2013).

15.4 Beliefs and assumptions about experimental methods

Experimental methods advocate that the nature of our reality of the world is objective and material (Leedy, 2013). This theory of knowledge is from scientific realism. Basically, the theory of knowledge searches for truth and is justified by the empirical confirmation of the hypotheses and universal scientific standards. The purpose of the experimental methods is to test hypotheses. The theory of knowledge is with a set of data. It is used to ferret out cause-and-effect relationships in educational and psychological sciences. In other words, through this procedure the researchers can explore the cause-and-effect relationship among a set of variables. Further, they can prove a theory with subtle different evidence or establish alternative models between the theory and the data.

The search for truth through, and the assumptions about, experimental methods must also include a focus on the assumptions of the variable relations.

15.4.1 The assumptions about variable relations

The phenomenon and events, and their relationships can be described and explained by a set of variables selected in the research design; other irrelevant variables called extraneous and confounding variables can be weeded out by using random selection and assignment techniques. The variable relations can be described in relationship maps. Such maps have been structured in analytical models such as regression models and path model. A regression model is a statistical structure or model that describe cause-and-effect relations between two groups of variables: predictors and the criterion variable. For example in the case study, we plan to examine the causal relation beteween the pedagogical strategy and students' achievement. We hypothesise that pedagogical strategy can predict students' achievement. Thus the pedagogical strategy is the predictor and students' achievement is the criterion variable.

The variable relationships can be described in path models. A path model is a path analysis which is a sequential multiple regression analysis. For example, we may initially be concerned about the relations between teachers' content knowledge of algebra and their use of a pedagogical strategy; and later we want to examine the relationship of pedagogical strategy and students' achievement. We intend to include all these relationships in one causal reation model. This composite model is called path model.

Based on regression and path models described here, we can classify the variable relations into three fundamental relationships:
- Correlational relationships
- Causal relationships
- Composite relationships.

The variable relations can be correlational. This means that correlational relationships indicate that two events change in a synchronised manner. For example, there has often been talk of a relationship between achievement in algebra and proficiency in a musical instrument. We cannot conclude that a student's high performance in a musical instrument might be because of their algebra achievement, and vice versa.

The variable relationship can be a causal relationship. This means that one variable causes a change in another variable. For example, in the opening case study, we believe that the pedagogical strategy can cause a change in students' achievements. The variables of pedagogical strategy and students' achievements have a causal relationship.

Finally, the variable relationships can be a composite relationship. A composite relationship consists of at least two simple causal relationships. In the previous path analysis, we took algebraic learning in which we included three variables: teachers' content knowledge of algebra, pedagogical strategy, and students' achievement. There are two direct causal relationships in this example: the causal relationship between teachers' content knowledge of algebra and pedagogical strategy; and the causal relationship between the pedagogical strategy and students' achievement. As we design a research study in which we want to include these two causal relationships in one analysis, we say the causal relationships are composite relationships (McMillan & Schumacher, 2010).

Now that you have read about the assumptions of the variable relations, it is important to understand the assumption of the generalisation of the sample to the population.

15.4.2 Assumption of generalisation of the sample to the population

Experimental methodologists assume that the information from a random sample of participants can be utilised precisely to estimate same information in the population. We use the previous example where we randomly select 100 Grade 5 learners in a given school district. We are interested in the mean of their algebra achievement; say 88 and then we reasonably expect that the population (1,000 learners in the school district) mean is also 88. There is an assumption that the researcher can generalise the results of their sample to the population, but it is critical to understand the assumption of random errors.

15.4.3 Assumptions about random errors

When experimental researchers conduct an experimental study to estimate population parameters with sample statistics, they believe there are errors between them. The errors are random because they are inherently unpredictable, and have null expected value.

What if ...?

Suppose we use the same school district as in the earlier example. We know the population mean from 1,000 pupils is 88.5, and the sample mean from 100 pupils is 88 in only one random sampling experimental design. The error is 88.5-88=0.5, which is due to random error. We further believe that if we can do N times of such kinds of random sampling experimental study, and N is sufficiently large, theoretically, the expectation of the sum of the errors is zero.

Philosophically, we are gradually approaching the truth of the phenomena when we increase the frequencies of random sampling time. If we use the earlier example again, we do more than one sampling: say we choose another 100 learners to measure their algebra mean. It is very possible that the second mean is different from the first one. The assumption of random error helps us understand that errors can be random, unpredictable, and have null expected value. In understanding the importance of random errors, we can now explore the various types of experimental research methods.

Stop and reflect

After learning about beliefs and assumptions in experimental research, you should be able to answer the following questions:
1 What are the assumptions of experimental research?
2 How do you use two random rules in experimental research?
3 What is the assumption of random errors?

15.5 Types of experimental research methods*

* Non-experimental research design has been excluded in this chapter. It can be understood as a different type of research design because it lacks manipulations and control of the independent variables.

There are two types of experimental research methods: true experimental and quasi-experimental research methods. In true experimental research methods, the participants are randomly assigned to groups for different levels of treatment. For example, in the opening case study, when the researchers divided the class randomly into two groups and called them 'group A' and 'group B', this research study took a true experimental design.

In quasi-experimental research methods, the participants are not randomly assigned to a treatment. Frequently, quasi-experiments are called natural experiments. This is because the membership in the treatment level is determined by the conditions which are beyond the control of the experimenter. For example, if a researcher plans to observe two different pedagogical strategies, small group teaching and project-based teaching, there are supposedly two natural Grade 5 classes, A and B. The researcher is allowed to choose either one to take for small group or for project-based teaching strategies. However, the researcher is not allowed to randomly reallocate these learners in the two classes. We can see that this does not satisfy the random assignment condition. Essentially, the power to generalise the results will be limited (Johnson & Christensen, 2012; Muijs, 2011; Teddlie & Tashakkori, 2009; Vogt, 2007).

Just as there are various types of research methods, there are unique experimental research settings. In the next section, you will learn about the context or environment in which research is conducted.

15.6 Experimental research settings

The **research setting** is a context or an environment in which a research study can be conducted. There are three different types of research settings in experimental research:
- laboratory settings
- field settings
- internet or 'virtual' settings.

For example, a laboratory experiment setting is the traditional one reflecting the traditional research epistemology; the study is conducted in a controlled environment. The laboratory provides a set of strict conditions where nearly all extraneous variables can be controlled. Often, researchers consider the experimental research setting as a strong experimental research environment because it is able to control for most of the extraneous variables. In other words, a laboratory environment can eliminate all 'noise' from the research environment. In contrast, a field experiment setting is a research environment in a real-life situation. An internet experiment setting is another research design in which the research setting is a virtual or online environment. (Shadish, Cook & Campbell, 2002; Reips, 2000).

Experimental research settings can vary from controlled to less controlled, and these are important decisions for the researcher. The researcher must consider the aspects of the design, and reflect on the rationale for that design, as will be seen in the next section.

15.7 Experimental design and rationale

Experimental design is a series of structures or frameworks based on experimental research rationales. Experimental research is only one kind of study that can test hypotheses to establish cause-effect relationships. The basic ideas are to establish compared conditions in experimental environments. The first strategy is to compare the change of the dependent variable before and after a treatment. The second strategy is to establish the control and experimental groups in terms of the random assignment principle. The purpose is to establish a baseline with the control group in order to compare the treatment variable in the experimental group (Johnson & Christensen, 2012).

There are several fundamental experimental research designs, including:

- ▶ Single-group post-test-only design
- ▶ One-group pretest–post-test design
- ▶ Post-test-only design with non-equivalent group
- ▶ Pretest–post-test control group design.

Besides the designs listed here, there are several other designs such as the Solomon four-group design, factorial design, repeated measures design, and time series design. These designs are all based on the designs we have already introduced, and will not be discussed here. We recommend that you refer to other research methods resources to find out more about these designs (Johnson & Christensen, 2012; McGillan & Schumacher, 2010).

15.7.1 Post-test-only design

The post-test-only designs consist of one-group post-test-only and post-test-only control group design. In one-group post-test, the researcher gives a single group of participants a treatment. The researcher then assesses the effect of the treatment. For example, the researcher asseses in terms of measuring the change of the dependent variable. Because there is no pretest and comparison with other treatments, the valid causal conclusions are very difficult to reach (McMillan, & Schumacher, 2010).

Figure 15.1 reflects a single-group post-test design where Group A receives only one intervention.

Single-Group Post-test-Only Design		
Group	Intervention	Post-test
A	X	O

FIGURE 15.1: Single-group post-test-only design

15.7.2 One-group pretest–post-test design

In this design, the participants in the group are given a pretest (O1), then the treatment (X), and then the post-test (O2). The pretest and post are the same; only they are given at two different times. In this design, the problem of comparison before and after treatment is solved. However, the treatment condition the contrast problem has not yet been solved. (McMillan & Schumacher, 2010).

Figure 15.2 shows Group A receiving one pretest, one intervention, and a post-test as part of the treatment.

Single-Group Pretest–Post-test Design			
Group	Pretest	Intervention	Post-test
A	O1	X	O2

FIGURE 15.2: Single-group pretest–post-test design

15.7.3   Post-test-only design with non-equivalent group

In this design, one group of participants received the treatment. While, the another group of participants received no treatment (or a different treatment). The term **non-equivalent** means group selection does not follow random assignment (McMillan, 2012).

Non-equivalent Groups Post-test-Only Control Group		
Group	Intervention	Post-test
A	X	O
B		O

FIGURE 15.3: Non-equivalent groups post-test-only control group

15.7.4   Pretest–Post-test control group design

In this pretest–post-test control group design, the researcher assigns the participants to an experimental and control group. Initially the participants are pretested on the dependent variable, O, and then the treatment X is administered. Then both experimental and control groups are post-tested on the dependent variable O again. The purpose of random assignment is to enable the researcher to reasonably rule out all possible threat factors of the internal validity.

The pretest–post-test control group design is an almost perfect experimental design. It is almost perfect because researchers believe they can control for all rival explanations. This design satisfies the condition of comparison before and after the treatment statuses of the dependent variables and the one of control and experimental group (McMillan, 2012; Leedy, 2013).

Figure 15.4 shows the randomised pretest-post-test control group design. Group A received the pretest, intervention, and the post-test, but Group B received both pretest and post-test, but no intervention.

Randomised Pretest–Post-test Control Group Design				
	Group	Pretest	Intervention	Post-test
Random assignment	A	O	X	O
	B	O		O

FIGURE 15.4: Randomised pretest-post-test control group design

There are several other preferred experimental designs in addition to the ones we have already discussed. Pretest–post-test control group design with more than one experimental group is to add more experimental group. This is a more efficient design that can report more than one experimental group results. In other words, this research design can increase the levels of the independent variable.

15.8 Internal and external validity

The ability to infer that a causal relationship exists between two variables is called internal validity. External validity is about the extent we can examine the results and how these can be generalised to and across population of persons, settings, times, outcomes and treatment variations (McMillan, 2012).

15.8.1 Internal validity

We frequently conduct research to determine cause-and-effect relationships in the context that we are studying. Internal validity occurs when a researcher controls all extraneous variables. The researcher also controls the only variable influencing the results of a study, which is the one being manipulated by the researcher. Basically, the variable the researcher intends to study is the focused variable affecting the results. But it does not affect some other unwanted variables.

There are some important guidelines to include:

▶ Can we conclude that changes in the independent variable actually influenced or impacted the observed changes in the dependent variable?
▶ Is there evidence that supports our conclusion?
▶ Is such a conclusion strong or weak?

With respect to internal validity, if a study demonstrates a high degree of internal validity, we can conclude there is evidence of causality. When a study has low internal validity, we can conclude there is little or no evidence of causality (Johnson & Christensen, 2012).

15.8.2 External validity

External validity is the degree to which the results of an empirical investigation can be generalised to and across individuals. External validity also refers to which the results can be generalised across settings and times. Generally, external validity is classified into two categories, which include population validity and ecological validity (Johnson & Christensen, 2012; McMillan, 2012).

15.8.3 Population validity

It is important to consider how representative the sample of the general population is. The more representative, the more confident we can be in generalising from the sample to the population. How widely does the finding apply? Generalising across populations happens when the research finding works across many different types of people, even those individuals not represented in the sample.

Ecological validity occurs when a result generalises across settings The types include: a) Interaction effect of testing; b) Interaction effects of selection biases and experimental treatment; c) Reactive affects of experimental arrangements; d) Multiple-treatment interference; and e) Experimenter effects (McMillan, 2012).

15.9 Extraneous and confounding variables and validity

Researchers would expect to obtain strong internal and external validities in the quantitative research studies. However, because of the complexity of research contexts and environments, there may be some variables which are out of the control of the researcher, which further threaten validity. Two kinds of variables are recognised which may threaten validity in quantitative research designs: extraneous variables and confounding variables (Johnson & Christensen, 2012; McMillan, 2012).

Any variable that you are not intentionally studying in the experimental research study is an extraneous variable, which produces an association between two variables that are not causally related.

When an extraneous variable impacts on the results of the research study systematically, it can distort causal relationships, and this variable is known as a confounding variable. A variable is recognised to be confounding because it leads to an alternative explanation, which then hides a true causal relationship. For example, a researcher has developed a new pedagogical strategy in algebra and is interested in examining the effectiveness of this strategy. Students are assigned to group A and group B; group A uses the new pedagogical strategy while group B uses a traditional pedagogical strategy. All students are given a pretest and it is supposed that group A students' achievement scores will demonstrate an obvious higher level than those of group B. One possible alternative explanation is that the higher scores may be from students' pre-knowledge of algebra. Thus the pre-knowledge is called an extraneous variable.

If we further examine group A students' pre-knowledge of algebra, we find that group A students have similar richer pre-knowledge of algebra than group B. In this situation, pre-knowledge of algebra systematically influences the causal relationship between the pedagogical strategy and students' achievement. Thus the pre-knowledge has been recognised as a confounding variable.

Clearly, researchers must be keenly aware of extraneous and confounding variables when they make conclusions about cause and effect.

15.9.1 Necessary conditions for causality

There are three conditions that are necessary to demonstrate that the variable A causes changes in the variable B. These conditions include:

▸ *Relationship condition*: Variable A and variable B are related.
▸ *Temporal antecedence condition*: There is a proper time order established.
▸ *Lack of alternative explanation condition*: Relationship between variable A and variable B must not be atributeable to any confounding extraneous variables.

For example, we may consider that a relationship exists between excessive consumption of soft drinks and the occurrence of a heart attack. So the researcher considers a correlation which exists between the consumption of soft drinks and the likelihood of having a heart attack. There are a few important questions to ask: Are we justified in concluding that soft drinks cause heart attacks? Does cigarette smoking and soft drink consumption contribute to heart attacks? Cigarette smoking is related to both of these variables. Individuals who drink few soft drinks are less likely to smoke cigarettes than are people who drink a lot of soft drinks. Similarly, the observed relationship between drinking soft drinks and heart attacks might be the result of the third variable of smoking. A researcher then needs to control for the effect of cigarette smoking in order to determine if this rival explanation accounts for the original relationship.

In brief, if any quantitative research design lacks of the necessary conditions for causality, random assignment procedures and careful considerations of the layouts for some elements may increasingly threat internal and external validities of the research study. The following section will discuss validity-threatening elements (Johnson & Christensen, 2012; McMillan, 2012).

15.10 Threats to internal and external validity

There are several significant threats to internal and external validity. The experimental design helps the investigator to control for threats to internal and external validity. The threats include:

1	History	6	Testing
2	Maturation	7	Instrumentation
3	Statistical regression	8	Design contamination
4	Selection	9	Compensatory rivalry
5	Experimental mortality	10	Resentful demoralisation.

The threats to internal validity compromise our confidence in stating that a relationship exists between the independent and dependent variables. Similarly, the threats to external validity compromise our confidence in showing whether the study's results are applicable to other groups (Gay, Mills, & Airasian, 2012; Johnson & Christensen, 2012; McMillan, 2012).

15.10.1 Threats to internal validity

There are several threats to internal validity, as discussed in the following sections.

15.10.1.1 The signicance of history

While the experiment was in progress, did some unanticipated event occur that affects the dependent variable? The threat of history is a threat for the one-group design but not for the two-group design. In other words, in the one group pretest-post-test design, the effect of the treatment is the difference in the pretest and post-test scores. The treatment or the history may be the resources of the difference.

Essentially, history is not a threat for the two-group (treatment/experimental and comparison/control) design because the comparison is between the treatment group and the comparison group. If the history threat occurs for both groups, the difference between the two groups is not related to the history event.

15.10.1.2 Maturation

The questions can be asked such as, were changes in the dependent variable due to normal developmental processes operating within the subject as a function of time? Maturation is a threat to one-group design. It is not a threat to the two-group design, if one assumes that participants in both groups change (mature) at the same rate. Consider these examples:

▶ *History* In a short experiment designed to investigate the effect of iPads in the classroom, participants missed some instruction because of a power failure at the school. The event of missing some instruction is related to the 'history', which can influence the research study results.

▶ *Maturation* The performance of Grade R children in a learning experiment begins decreasing after 45 minutes because of fatigue. This phenomenon means that the participants can acquire natural progress or recieve a common challenge in the study.

15.10.1.3 Statistical regression

Statistical regression is the result of a tendency for subjects selected on the bases of extreme scores to regress towards the mean on subsequent tests. For example, when measurement of the dependent variable is not perfectly reliable, there is a tendency for extreme scores to regress or move toward the mean. The amount of statistical regression is inversely related to the reliability of the test.

15.10.1.4 Selection

Selection refers to selecting participants for the various groups in the study. Are the groups equivalent at the beginning of this study?

▶ If subjects were selected by random sampling and random assignment, all have an equal chance of being in the treatment or comparison groups, and the groups are equivalent.
▶ Were subjects self-selected into experimental and comparison groups? This could affect the dependent variable.
▶ Selection is not a threat for the one-group design, but it is a threat for the two-group design.

15.10.1.5 Experimental mortality

Differential loss of participants across groups. Some important considerations might include: a) Did some participants drop out? b) Did this affect the results? c) Did about the same number of participants make it through the entire study in both experimental and comparison groups? and d) Is there a threat for any design with more than one group?

15.10.1.6 Testing

Did the pretest affect the scores on the post-test? A pretest may sensitise participants in unanticipated ways, and their performance on the post-test may be due to the pretest, not to the treatment, or, more likely, and interaction of the pretest and treatment. Testing is a threat to the one-group design and not a threat to the two-group design. Both groups are exposed to the pretest and so the difference between groups is not due to testing.

15.10.1.7 Instrumentation

Did any change occur during the study in the way the dependent variable was measured? This element poses a threat to the one-group design; not to the two-group design because we believe that there is an equal chance for two groups to be exposed to the same problem. Therefore two groups can balance the problem.

15.10.1.8 Design contamination

Did the comparison group know (or find out) about the experimental group? Did either group have a reason to want to make the research succeed? Did either group want the research to fail? Often, investigators must interview subjects after the experiment concludes in order to find out if design contamination occurred.

15.10.1.9 Compensatory rivalry

When subjects in some treatments receive goods or services perceived to be desirable and this becomes known to subjects in other groups, social competition may motivate the latter to attempt to reverse or reduce the anticipated effects of the desirable treatment levels. Saretsky (1972) calls this the 'John Henry effect' after the steel driver who, upon learning that his output was being compared with that of a steam drill, worked so hard that he outperformed the drill but died of overexertion.

15.10.1.10 Resentful demoralisation

If subjects learn that their group receives less desirable goods or services, they may experience feelings of resentment and demoralisation. Their response may be to perform at an abnormally low level, thereby increasing the magnitude of the difference between their performance and that of groups that receive the desirable goods or services.

15.10.2 Threats to external validity

There are six major threats to external validity (Gall, Gall & Borg, 2010; Springer, 2010), as discussed in the following sections.

15.10.2.1 Interaction effect of testing

Pre-testing interacts with the experimental treatment and causes some effect such that the results will not generalise to an untested population.

15.10.2.2 Interaction effects of selection biases and the experimental treatment

This is an effect of some selection factor of intact groups interacting with the experimental treatment that would not be the case if the groups were randomly selected.

15.10.2.3 Interaction effect of testing

In a physical performance experiment, the pretest cues the subjects to respond in a certain way to the experimental treatment that would not be the case if there were no pretest.

15.10.2.4 Interaction effects of experimental treatment

The results of an experiment in which the teaching method is the experimental treatment, used with a class of low achievers, does not generalise to heterogeneous-ability students.

15.10.2.5 Reactive effects of experimental arrangements

An effect that is due simply to the fact that subjects know that they are participating in an experiment and experiencing the novelty of it – the so-called Hawthorne effect.

15.10.2.6 Multiple-treatment interference

When the same subjects receive two or more treatments as in a repeated measures design, there may be a carry-over effect between treatments such the the results cannot be generalised to single treatments.

Stop and reflect

After reading about internal and external validity, can you describe it to a colleague? Think about the following in your description:

▶ What is internal and external validity?

▶ What are the threats to internal and external validity?

15.11 Measurement and data collection

The measurement of the data collection in quantitative research methods is a fundamental and crucial task. The measurement can be completed in just one step, however, sometimes it should be completed through more than one step. For example, students' algebra achievement is a kind of raw data which can be directly recorded in a data spreadsheet in a variable. Sometimes, the data cannot be directly recorded into the data spreadsheet in a variable format. The data should be coded by using a coding technique. In contrast, the measurement can be realised via quantitative concepts and variables. For example, a five-point scale can be coded into a five-level categorical variable. No matter what students' achievement is on the five-scale categorical data, they can all be described in a concept measurement. Researchers, in preparing their study, must understand following about the collection of data, the important concepts of measurement.

15.11.1 Concepts of measurement

Reynolds, Livingston and Willson (2009) define measurement as "a set of rules for assigning numbers to represent objects, traits, and attributes." For example, a mathematics test is a measuring tool. An examinee responds to the test items, and then the examiner makes a judgement following a set of rules. Many questions may arise in thinking about the concepts of measurement, as to what types of measures should be selected. The next section describes the various measurement scales as options in research design.

15.11.2   Types of measurement scales

There are four scales of measurement in quantitative research methods. A scale is a scheme for assigning scores to the characteristic being measured. The four scales are:

▶ Nominal scales
▶ Ordinal scales
▶ Interval scales
▶ Numerical scales.

Nominal scales provide qualitative information that informs the researcher categorical information. The nominal scale differentiates among the objects, such as gender, which has two categories: female and male. The nominal scale only differentiates among things, but cannot provide information of difference in the amount. For example, if hair colour has four categories: blonde, black, brown, red, we cannot evaluate any colour is greater or less than another one. However, we know they are different.

Ordinal scales also called rank order scales provide rank order information. This scale of measure is usually used to rank objects in terms of the quantity of a characteristic that the objects represent in a process. Perhaps when you assess a group of people's performances you know who is the best, and who is next best, and so forth, but you cannot measure the 'distance' between these people's performances.

Interval scales provide more information than nominal and ordinal scales. Interval scales provide the information not only about the rank order feature, but also about the feature of equal distance between any adjacent two objects. We can find many examples of interval scales in educational and psychological sciences. For example, in an algebra test, students A, B and C scored 85, 90 and 95 respectively. We understand that these scores are measured using an interval scale and they have equivalent distances between A and B, and B and C.

In addition, the interval scale does not have an absolute zero point. In other words, the zero point in interval scales does not mean it is true 'zero'. For example, the measure of temperature is a kind of interval scale; the temperature 0° F does not mean that there is not any temperature.

Numerical scales, also called **ratio scales**, are the highest level of measurement in quantitative methods; the numerical scale represents all the characteristics of the ordinal score and interval scale. In addition, the numerical scale also includes the zero amounts in the measure. Physical height and weight are such kinds of measure.

15.11.3   Measurement scales and variables

Measurement scales provide quantitative researchers with an excellent representation of process and result. Stated differently, the variables can be exactly described at four levels (Thorndike & Thorndike-Christ, 2010). There are four different variables from the measurement perspective:

▶ Nominal variables
▶ Ordinal variables
▶ Interval variables
▶ Numeric (ratio) variables.

The variable is a skilful representation in quantitative research. No matter what kinds of information we collect, we have to directly record and code it in a quantitative format called a variable (Allen & Yen, 2002).

There are many definitions of the variable. We prefer to use an operational definition based on our own understanding. In order to understand a variable, we have to follow two steps:

> ✅ **First,** the variable is just a concept, such as literacy achievement, a performance observation, or a simple construct like happiness.

> ✅ **Second,** we have to be able to define the problem space of the concepts, or we say we have a clear and logical range or category. For example, a Grade 5 mathematics test can be a variable; in fact, it is a continuous variable. In a conventional test, first, we know what the concept of the mathematics is; and second, we define the range from 0 to 100. A mathematics achievement can be a score in any number within the range from 0 to 100, including any decimal numbers within this range.

Another example is the assessment of a performance by observation with a Likert scale. We can develop the scale with five points to evaluate a performance: very poor, poor, average, very good, and excellent. We can further quantitatively scale them with 1, 2, 3, 4 and 5, correspondingly. However, we cannot define between any two adjacent points. For example, we cannot define any performance level between very good (4) and excellent (5). If we believe that any adjacent two points represent an equivalent distance, this variable is an interval variable. We can also see that we first define a performance – a concept; and secondly, we clearly define a category (Reynolds, Livingston & Willson (2009).

Critical thinking challenge

After reading about the various forms of measurement and the examples, develop a critical discussion by answering the following questions:

▶ What are measurement and measurement scales?

▶ What are variables

▶ How you can define a variable in your research study?

15.12 Data collection instruments

There are many instruments that are used to collect the data. Similarly, there are many instruments that reflect quantitative variable characteristics. These instruments include test, inventories, interviews and observations. They are ranked from more objective to less objective. There are also different instruments to collect data and then we code such kinds of data into variables (McMillan, 2012; Wright, 2008). There are many instruments in research, and the test is one way the researcher has participants respond to specific tasks.

15.12.1 Tests

A **test** is a designed cognitive or cognition-related task, which allows the examinee/testee to respond to the task. A set of implicit rules says that we assume the examiner and the examinee both understand the content knowledge and how to respond to the test item. Basically, there are two types of test:

▶ achievement tests

▶ aptitude tests.

Achievement tests measure and assess students' cognitive aspects, knowledge and skills, in a given content domain. There are two subtly different achievement tests: the standardised test, and instructor-constructed test. The standardised test is usually developed by a professional group of researchers and educators, and is administered, scored and interpreted in a standard manner. The instructor-constructed test can be conducted in a more flexible way. Standardised tests can be used to collect data for norm-referenced interpretations. The instructor-constructed test is generally used to measure and assess students' progress in both knowledge acquisition and problem-solving skills (Osterlind, 2010).

Aptitude tests, also called intelligence tests, are for predictive purposes. The predictive purpose means the test results can provide information about the examinees' scholastic aptitude in different cognitive dimensions, such as reasoning ability and mathematics ability, etc. Generally speaking, the test is designed to measure the cognitive skills, abilities and knowledge that students have accumulated for a long time. Aptitude tests have a broader spectrum in measuring cognitive and knowledge aspects. Put differently, aptitude tests can be used to measure knowledge and skills progress in a specific programme, especially in a school context. Achievement tests, on the other hand, attempt to measure cumulative experiences for individuals' academic prospects and other relevant aspects. Popular intelligence tests usually focus on the measurement of verbal ability, non-verbal ability, memory ability, reasoning, quantitative concepts, relational concepts, and many others (Reynolds, Livingston & Willson, 2009). Now we need to turn to other measurement methods used to measure affective and non-cognitive dimensions, which are called inventories or surveys.

15.12.2 Inventories and surveys

Inventories are a set of measurement instruments in quantitative research, which are used to measure affective and non-cognitive dimensions, such as personality, attitudes, beliefs, values, interests, and even other emotional and feeling disositional dimensions. These non-cognitive measures are usually more difficult to devise than those of knowledge and skills. The survey (about which you read in Chapter 14) is a popular instrument in the inventory category (Patten, 2011).

Pitfall warning

There are two pitfalls in this inventory research: the response set and social desirability. The response set is the tendency to answer most questions in the same direction. When the responder is not quite clear about the item the responder may follow his or her 'habit' to select a given option. Social desirability is that the responder selects the option which is based on a social norm and social desirability.

The **survey** is an important format in the inventory family. It is a self-report data collection instrument. Researchers collect information in other dimensions such options, beliefs, perceptions and other emotional aspects (Fink, 2003; 2009).

The structure of a survey usually consists of two parts: a scenario; and item sets. In the scenario part, the author describes the direction, purpose, background and illustration of how to select alternative options. An item set consists of a set of items. The amount of the items varies between 10 and even 100 or more items depending on the research purposes and different professional traditions. In education, 30 items can be a common example; in health professions and the child health sectors the surveys can consist of more than 100 items.

The most popular item format of the surveys takes a numerical rating scale, which includes a set of numbers with anchored endpoints.

Item stem and numerical rating scale with anchored endpoints (e.g.)

Question: How important is ethical education and training in graduate thesis preparation?

1	2	3	4	5
Least important	Less important	Neutral	Important	Very important

A strong survey usually represents a clear structure in format and expresses a meaningful theoretical construct (Johnson & Christensen, 2012).

15.12.3 Interview protocol

The interview protocol is a very effective data collection tool in quantitative research. According to Johnson and Christensen (2012:199), an "interview protocol is the data-collection instrument that includes the items, the response categories, the instructions, and so forth." It is a script prepared by the research designers. The interviewer reads and also interprets it if necessary, to the interviewees.

The interview protocol for a quantitative interview is to follow the standard procedures for all interviewees. It is believed that a standardised procedure can add to the enhancement of statistical validity. Researchers believe that the unified or standardised instrument or procedures allow all participants to receive similar or the same opportunity to respond to the same tasks.

The quantitative interview consists of closed questions. Interviewees only choose options from the interview questions in terms of the instructions, for example:

There are several pedagogical strategies that can be very helpful with learners, to facilitate problem-solving skill development in their algebraic learning. In your opinion, which one is the best one, from among the following:

a   Small group discussion
b   Problem-based learning

c   Role play
d   Simulated problem-solving environments?

Just as there is a protocol for the quantitative interview, there are other methods of data collection, including conducting observations.

15.12.4 Observations

Quantitative observation is also called structured observation. Researchers employ this method to systematically collect quantitative data. The chief purpose of quantitative observations is to examine the patterns of behaviours or actions. The observation environment may be a laboratory observation or a naturalistic observation. A laboratory observation means the researcher prepares a setting to observe the events and phenomena. A naturalistic observation is conducted in the real world. You should note that there may be different observation results even for the same observation focus, on different occasions or settings.

Sampling of the observations is a technical concern. When we plan to observe the events and phenomena, we have to have a focus. Stated differently, we have to 'sample' the events and phenomena. There are two different sampling methods:

▶ *Time-interval sampling*, which is to check for the events during a given time interval;
▶ *Event sampling*, which is to observe only after specific events have occurred (Johnson & Christensen, 2012).

Conclusion

This chapter has discussed experimental research and data collection. We started the discussion with experimental research characteristics and the epistemology of the experimental research methods to provide a theoretical consideration for researchers to explain their analytical results. We also used this discussion to further establish an association between research content domain theory and conclusions, based on applying the rationale of logical positivism/logical empiricism in the analysis.

Using the characteristics of experimental research, we discussed random rules including random selection and random assignment which guarantee each individual in the defined population an equivalent chance of being selected into the sample so as to reduce experimental errors.

We continued our topic discussion with the assumptions of experimental methods which provide a common base for researchers to build alternative experimental methods on. The variable is a crucial concept and any raw data should be recorded or coded into a variable, thus carrying out the analytical procedure. A generalisation rationale informs researchers that random sampling procedures guarantee analytical results, which can then be generalised and applied to a corresponding population.

Following the assumptions, we examined the types of experimental research methods and different designs. Throughout, internal and external validity were discussed. The threats to validity were briefly analysed. Finally, after covering to the concepts of measurement scale, popular data collection instruments, test, survey and observation were also discussed.

Closing activities

Practical application

Read the following short case and then write a full report by answering the questions that follow.

Bibliography

Allen, M.J. & Yen, W.M. 2002. *Introduction to Measurement Theory.* Long Grove, IL: Waveland Press Inc.

Fink, A. 2003. *How to sample in surveys.* Thousand Oaks, CA: SAGE Publications.

Fink, A. 2009. *How to conduct surveys: A step-by-step guide.* Thousand Oaks, CA: SAGE Publications.

Gall, M.D., Gall, J. & Borg, W.R. 2010. *Applying educational research.* San Francisco, CA: Pearson.

Gay, L.R., Mills, G.E. & Airasian P. 2012. *Educational research: Competencies for analysis and application.* San Francisco, CA: Pearson.

Howell, K.E. 2013. *An introduction to the philosophy of methodology.* Los Angeles, CA: SAGE Publications.

Johnson, B. & Christensen, L. 2012. *Educational research: Quantitative, qualitative, and mixed approaches.* Los Angeles, CA: SAGE Publications.

Leedy, P.D. & Ormrod, J.E. 2013. *Practical research: Planning and design.* San Francisco, CA: Pearson.

McMillan, J.H. 2012. *Educational research: Fundamentals for the consumer.* San Francisco, CA: Pearson.

McMillan, J.H. & Schumacher, S. 2010. *Research in eduation: Evidence-based inquiry.* San Francisco, CA: Pearson.

Muijs, D. 2011. *Doing quantitative research in education with SPSS.* Los Angeles, CA: SAGE Publications.

Osterlind, S.J. 2010. *Modern measurement: Theory, principles, and applications of mental appraisal.* San Francisco, CA: Pearson.

Patten, M.L. 2011. *Survey research: A practical guide.* Glendale, CA: Pyrczak Publishing.

Reips, U. 2000. The web experiment method: Advantages, disadvantages, and solutions. In M.H. Birnbaum (Ed). *Psychology experiments on the Internet.* New York, NY: Academic Press (pp. 89–117).

Reynolds, C.R., Livingston, R.B. & Willson, V. 2009. *Measurement and Assessment in education.* Upper Saddle River, NJ: Pearson.

Saretsky, G. 1975. *The John Henry effect: Potential confounder of experimental vs control group approach to the evaluation of educational innovations.* Paper presented at the American Educational Research Association's Annual Meeting, Washington DC, in April 1975.

Shadish, W.R., Cook. T.D. & Campbell, D.T. 2002. *Experimental and quasi-experimental designs for generalized causal inference.* Boston, MA: Houghton Mifflin Company.

Springer, K. 2010. Educational research: *A context approach.* Hoboken, NJ: John Wiley & Sons.

Teddlie, C. & Tashakkori, A. 2009. *Foundations of mixed methods research: Integrating quantitative and qualitative approaches in the social and behavioral sciences.* Los Angeles, CA: SAGE Publications.

Thorndike, R.M. & Thorndike-Christ, T. 2010. *Measurement and evaluation in psychology and Education.* San Francisco, CA: Pearson.

Vogt, W.P. 2007. *Quantitative research methods for professionals.* Boston, MA: Pearson.

Wright, R.J. 2008. *Educational assessment: Tests and measurements in the age of accountability.* Thousand Oaks, CA: SAGE Publications.

CHAPTER 16

George Chitiyo, Simon Taukeni and Morgan Chitiyo

The observation method

KEY CONCEPTS

Analogue observation refers to observations made in artificial settings such as clinical and laboratory environments. The environment has been manipulated by the researcher for the purpose of making the observations.

Complete observer As a complete observer, the researcher does not participate in the activities of the setting, and their role may or may not be known by those being observed.

Complete participant As a complete participant, the researcher immerses himself or herself in the culture of the participants, usually for extended periods of time. Their role as researchers is not known to the people being observed.

Data triangulation is an approach used in qualitative research as a means to minimise bias and increase trustworthiness of research findings, by using several methods and sources of data.

Emic perspective refers to an insider's perspective of the goings-on in a particular culture or community. It is the view held by those who, generally speaking, belong to that culture or community or those who have experienced the phenomenon.

Etic perspective In contrast to emic, this is an outsider's perspective of a phenomenon.

Naturalistic observation In contrast with analogue observation, this is a method which involves making observations of phenomena in the environment in which they naturally occur, using unobtrusive methods. There is no attempt made by the researcher to manipulate the environment.

Observer-as-participant As an observer-as-participant, the researcher does not participate in the activities of the setting, and their role is fully known by those being observed.

Participant-as-observer As a participant-as-observer, the researcher participates fully in the culture that they are observing, and the people being observed are aware of the person's role as researcher.

Phenomenology refers to the common meaning of a lived experience or perception held by those who experience it. A phenomenological perspective thus is the view held by the persons who have lived a particular experience and is thus a firsthand account given by the actors in a situation.

LEARNING OUTCOMES

By the end of this chapter, you should be able to:

▶ Define and describe the observation method.

▶ Identify different types of observation.

▶ Identify situations where observation is suitable.

▶ Identify the strengths and weaknesses of the observation method.

Case study: Gender interactions in a public setting

This was a very important opportunity for me and my fellow researcher Sipho, during our eight months of fieldwork, to observe first-hand gender interactions in a public setting. Previously, Sipho and I had just been holding interviews and focus groups with men and women separately.

There were about 10 men and 25 women at this meeting all of whom were volunteers in a health programme introduced by a non-governmental organisation the year before. All the women sat on the ground. Why? There were enough benches for everybody. Were the women afraid of the men? But they had told us in an all-female focus group that they did not feel threatened by the men.

In full view of everybody, one vocal woman, MaSibanda stood up and confidently walked towards the benches. The men's piercing eyes were fixed on her as if to tell her to go back and sit on the ground. She made herself comfortable on one of the empty benches. All the women were looking at the men as if to gauge their reaction. No words were exchanged, just loaded stares. No other woman dared follow MaSibanda.

During the meeting, it was mostly the men who spoke. The group leaders, a man and a woman, had to prod the women hard to share their views.

(This field notebook entry by Nozipho is a hypothetical example of a study addressing gender dynamics in a rural community in South Africa.)

Introduction

The field notes from Nozipho's field notebook highlight key issues about observation as a tool for data collection. Do people always do what they say they do? How much of the topic under study can be unearthed using observation? Do you think MaSibanda's action helped Nozipho and Sipho understand some aspect of gender interactions? Does the description of the setting help to place the findings in context? This chapter will help you understand some of the issues raised in this case study.

The extent to which a study's research questions are addressed depends on the quality of data gathered which, in turn, is also dependent upon the appropriateness of the method of data collection used. Observation is one of the most common strategies of data collection used in qualitative research, specifically in ethnographic studies. Other methods of data collection such as interviews and focus groups, are covered in Chapters 17 and 19 of this book. In this chapter, we will explore the observation method, highlighting the different types of observation, how to record field notes, the strengths and weaknesses of the method, and its applicability in different research settings. Among others, we will use the following examples to illustrate key points regarding the observation method: Freitag's (2005) study of women's participation in sports in Zimbabwe; Wamoyi, Wight, Plummer, Mshana and Ross's (2010) study of transactional sex in Tanzania; Pell, et al.'s (2013) study of antenatal care in Ghana, Kenya and Malawi; Wojcicki's (2000) study of commercial sex in South Africa; and; Singleton's (2012) study of perceptions of gender-based sexual violence in South Africa. In the next section, we will begin by defining observation.

16.1 What is the observation method?

Observation is one of several data collection methods used in qualitative enquiry across many research fields, including the social sciences, education, business, and health care. During observation, the researcher needs to use multiple senses to note what is happening, in order to get the best possible portrait of the phenomena being investigated and their context. The researcher uses observational techniques to understand the participants' actions, roles, and behaviours.

In such cases, the researcher is able to observe the actual phenomena of interest as they unfold or as the participants perform the behaviours or actions. Observation enables the researcher to take note of non-verbal communication and expression of feelings among the participants, as well as to see how they interact with one another. In the social and behavioural sciences, it is generally believed that attitudes and behaviours are not always congruent. Because people do not always do what they say they do, observation provides an important way of witnessing first-hand people's actions, behaviours, and interactions. Thus the researcher will be able to link the participants' words with their actions, particularly in situations where observation is used along-side other methods that capture the participants' views, such as interviewing or surveying.

One key feature of observation (particularly naturalistic observation) is that there is no intervention employed. The participants are not stimulated in any way, nor is there manipulation of conditions in their environment. Instead, the researcher goes to the natural setting where the participants are found, or where the phenomena naturally occur, and makes observations without manipulating any variables.

By natural environment, we refer to any setting that a researcher is interested in investigating. For example, in order to study the way of life of ghetto dwellers, you will have to visit the ghettos and make observations there. Similarly, in order to make observations of the interactions between teachers and students, you would need to go to a school setting. Several of the examples that are given in this chapter illustrate this important point where fieldwork observers conducted their fieldwork within the natural settings in which the participants resided or interacted. Conducting fieldwork observations in the natural setting ensures that the data collected are reliable and valid which, in turn, ensures the trustworthiness of the findings. Having defined the method, we now turn to the different types of observation.

16.2 Types of observation

We begin this section by explaining the difference between **naturalistic** and **analogue observations**. After that, we will focus on naturalistic enquiry and present the different types of observation that fall under it.

16.2.1 Naturalistic versus analogue observations

Naturalistic observations, on the one hand, involve the researcher making observations of phenomena in the environment in which they are naturally occur, usually using unobtrusive means. Analogue observations, on the other hand, are made in artificial settings such as clinical and laboratory settings; the environment has been manipulated by the researcher for the purpose of making the observations.

In certain contexts, analogue observations are also referred to as simulations. Simulations, also called role plays, are very common in clinical settings in the field of psychology. Norton and Hope (2001:60) describe role playing in clinical settings in the following terms:

> Role-played scenarios involve the simulation of an interaction between the client and another individual or a group in the clinical setting. Most commonly, clients are instructed to behave as they typically would and are asked to engage in one or more social inter-actions. For example, a client may be instructed to pretend that he or she had just been introduced to somebody at a party and to try to get to know the other person better. The subsequent conversation may last up to 10 minutes. Although in most cases the analogue situation is designed to approximate normal social conditions, the most basic question for the validity of analogue assessment is "Does the behavior exhibited by role plays correspond to behavior observed in more naturalistic situations?"

It is axiomatic that one of the major issues with simulations is their artificiality. This makes naturalistic observations appear superior to analogue observations. In a synthesis of research studies assessing social skills and anxiety, however, Norton and Hope established that there was moderate to high congruence in the findings from analogue and naturalistic observations. Nonetheless, one must always bear in mind that the field of study and the context of observation determine which method of observation can be used. This chapter mainly focuses on naturalistic observation. Before we turn to the different types of naturalistic observation, beginning with participant observation, try the activity that follows.

Stop and reflect

Now that you have been introduced to naturalistic observation, identify at least three examples of natural environments where observation can be used in your own field of study or research. What type(s) of behaviours, interactions, or phenomena can be observed in each of these environments?

16.2.2 Participant observation

There are two types of participant observation: **complete participant** and **participant-as-observer**. These are not completely distinct categories as the role of the participant observer at any one point during a research study can range on a continuum between these two points. As a complete participant, the researcher takes part fully in the activities occurring in the research setting, and their role of observer is not known to those being observed. When the researcher's role is participant-as-observer, they fully participate in the activities of the setting, and the people being observed are fully aware of the person's role as a researcher.

Participant observation is one of the most common types of data collection techniques within the observation method, and yet also the most involving. The researcher makes observations for extended periods of time, sometimes lasting up to several years.

Tip

As a researcher it is important that you have a non-judgmental attitude and interest in learning more about other people and their cultures if you are to be successfully assimilated into a different culture.

The main reason for immersion in the setting being studied is so that the researcher can gain an insider's perspective of the goings-on, called an **emic perspective**. The opposite of emic is **etic**, which is an outsider's perspective. Freitag (2005:18) exemplifies this concept of presenting an emic perspective as she seeks to describe the experiences and perceptions of Zimbabwean women towards sports, from their viewpoint. Her intention was to let the women relate their own stories, and she states that, "I made it a priority not to move into the research location wanting to prove my hypothesis. I intended to honestly convey the situation and thoughts of the people in the community through their perceptions, not mine".

As with Freitag, Singleton (2012:64), while acknowledging that there are many different interpretations and understandings of sexuality, states categorically that her aim in conducting a study of sexuality in KwaZulu-Natal in South Africa was "to give agency to the young women and men I came to know in Mpophomeni". One additional dimension that strengthened Singleton's efforts to represent the people's views adequately is that she learned the local language and conducted most of her interviews in isiZulu. Participant observation thus provides a vehicle through which the emic view can best be investigated and represented. The etic view can still be portrayed, but it will be subservient to the emic. After the following examples of participant observation, we will turn to the types of non-participant observation.

Going local: Participant observation exemplified

The researcher's role of *participant-as-observer* is typified by Freitag (2005) who conducted an ethnographic study in the town of Victoria Falls, Zimbabwe. The purpose of her study was to examine community opportunities for sports among women, as well as to examine women's attitudes towards sports. As a participant observer living in the community, she spent days mingling with the people of the community. During her first few weeks, she made as many new connections as she could, walking around the small town every morning familiarising herself with the people and the place. She would go to the local township to watch weekend soccer games, visit different market areas, and walk around the resort town taking pictures of things she found interesting such as little boys kicking balls made of plastic. She visited people's homes in the high-density areas. The relationships that she established gave her credibility with the locals, and it became easy for her to negotiate through her research activities and to collect the data for her study.

Other examples of this type of observer role include Wamoyi and colleagues (2010) and Singleton (2012). Wamoyi and colleagues' purpose was to understand young women's motivations for engaging in transactional sex in Mwanza, Tanzania. They used observation as the primary method of data collection across nine villages between 1999 and 2002. Although the fieldwork observers made it clear from the outset that they were observing the participants, because of the sensitive nature of the topic under investigation, they introduced themselves in the research communities as wanting to investigate factors related to young people's health in general, but did not disclose that they were specifically focusing on sexual health. The fieldwork observers in Wamoyi's study were complete participants in the research setting, living in the research communities for extended periods of time, befriending the locals and getting involved in all the activities and social events in which they took part.

Singleton's study of gender-based sexual violence took place in the township of Mpophomeni in KwaZulu-Natal in South Africa over a period of four years from 2001 to 2005. During this time, she participated extensively in community workshops, meetings, and other activities as the locals did. Such intensive involvement by both Wamoyi and colleagues, as well as Singleton, enabled them to gain very detailed emic perspectives of the issues they were investigating.

Naturalistic enquiry: Overt versus covert observations?

There are two types of naturalistic observations, namely overt and covert observations. Covert observations are done when members of the group being observed are unaware that they are being observed, whereas with overt observations, the people of the group are aware of the study and know that they are being observed. There are advantages and disadvantages to each of these methods of observation. For example, similar to the Hawthorne effect of participant reactivity to experimental arrangements, when observations are being performed overtly, participants may react differently if they are aware that they are being observed. The main advantages of covert observation are that the researcher will gain access to the research environment where people would otherwise not consent to being studied; and there is little or no 'participant reactivity'.

Although it gives the most accurate depiction of the phenomena being studied, covert observation is often criticised on ethical grounds. In addition to many institutional review boards (IRBs) frowning on covert techniques of observation, popular discipline-based organisations such as the American Psychological Association and American Sociological Association also generally disapprove of covert observation.

16.2.3 Non-participant observation

The role of the non-participant observer ranges between *observer-as-participant* and *complete observer*. In the role of observer-as-participant, the researcher does not participate in the activities of the community that is being studied and their role is clearly known by those being observed. A complete observer is at the opposite end of the spectrum from a complete participant. The researcher's interest is clearly spelt out: to observe the participants only with no intention of participating in their setting's activities, and the participants may or may not know that they are being observed.

It is not always the case that the researcher gets involved in the culture of the people being observed. As opposed to getting an emic perspective, a non-participant observer takes an etic approach. Non-participant observation is more focused as the researcher is able to simply concentrate on certain situations of interest to the researcher, rather than the totality of the context. For example, one can observe a lesson in progress during a class session using a video monitor. That way, the researcher observer does not disrupt the normal flow of the classroom environment. Another example is when an outsider, such as a university researcher, attends and observes school board meetings without participating in the discussions, a situation described by Fraenkel and colleagues (2012:446) as "sitting on the sidelines". Other examples given by Phillips (1996) include observation from a public place, such as a park bench or a window; and a midwifery example where one could observe the goings-on in labour wards using two-way mirrors or blinds. We will illustrate non-participant observation using a couple of examples from Wojcicki (2000), and Pell and colleagues (2013).

Looking without getting involved:
Non-participant observation exemplified

In a study of commercial sex work in Gauteng Province in South Africa, Wojcicki (2000) used non-participant observation (specifically, *observer-as-participant*) as well as interviews and survey methodology to collect data from her participants who included commercial sex workers and other categories of respondents. She reported that during times that she was not conducting interviews, sometimes she sat in a bar or hotel lobby, just as an observer, watching the interactions between the sex workers and their clients. Her observations in taverns and in other such places gave her a phenomenological perspective of these settings. Through observation she learned that foreign women, particularly from Eastern Europe or Taiwan comprised about a third of the population of women in brothels in the northern suburbs of Johannesburg. Likewise, she noted that women from Madagascar were also part of the brothel population in these suburbs, unlike in other similar places elsewhere. A specific account narrated by Wojcicki (2000:354) follows, which reinforces the point about the value of observation in any setting, be it participant or non-participant:

(continued)

Looking without getting involved:
Non-participant observation exemplified *(continued)*

In one of the middle range Hillbrow hotels, which tends to have more foreign sex-workers (primarily from Zambia, Swaziland and Mozambique), and Coloured South Africans, two women (after being interviewed) were eager to get clients, but were wearing jeans or pants. The clients that they were chatting with told the women that they wanted to see their legs and advised that they go and put on mini-skirts. Observing these interactions and speaking to the women as they went up to their hotel rooms, I noted how quickly the women came downstairs in different attire. In one instance, a woman changed to a see-through mini-skirt with thong underwear. Both women [...] acted speedily to satisfy client desires [...] Women will not be ashamed to call out to men in the bar, 'Hey, are you ready to be naughty?' Another woman articulated the competition and the difficulties quite clearly.

An example of a study which may fall somewhere between observer-as-participant and complete observer was reported by Pell and colleagues (2013). These researchers explored factors that influence attendance and utilisation of antenatal care services among women at several sites in Ghana, Kenya, and Malawi. Pell and colleagues were only interested in the aspect of antenatal care attendance and utilisation in the communities and at health care facilities. Local fieldworkers made their observations at the healthcare facilities that offered antenatal care services, as well as in the communities where the women lived. Although they often spent time in the research settings, in this study, the fieldworkers' role was only that of observer and there was no mention of their involvement in the culture of the communities that they observed.

The vignette by Wojcicki illustrates how as an observer you would also need to pay attention to what is said by participants in the research setting as this provides a rich context within which the findings can be interpreted. The examples that we have just looked at lead us into the next section of our discussion - recording field notes.

Critical thinking challenge

Using the examples you came up with in the previous section, identify the most suitable type of method of observing the phenomena from among participant (complete participant and participant-as-observer) and non-participant (complete observer and observer-as-participant) observation methods. Justify your choice. There is no wrong answer; the context of the study is the major determining factor.

16.3 Recording observation data using field notes

Data from observations are recorded in the form of field notes. It is imperative that as a qualitative researcher you keep a field notebook in which to record daily notes. This is where you write everything that you encounter in the field setting, descriptions of places visited, people interacted with, events attended, feelings harboured, and emotions experienced - literally everything. Because observations themselves are not structured per se, field notes do not have to be recorded in any standardised way; you simply record everything you see, smell, taste, feel, or hear at the very moment when you make these observations. Although there are no guides to be followed, such as those used when conducting key informant interviews or focus group discussions, Patton (2002) and Lofland and colleagues (2006) recommend that field notes must include the following key elements:

- ☑ *A description of what has been observed*: whenever possible, you should record your observations immediately afterwards so that you do not forget the details of what you saw, felt, or heard. With the plethora of technology these days, recording field notes can be made simple by dictating what you want to capture using a smartphone, tablet, an iPad application, or a computer program, for later transcription.

- ☑ *Descriptive information* about the setting, the people present, and activities that occurred; people's behaviour, interactions, actions, or feelings are likely to be influenced by the physical and social environment in which they are being observed. (We will illustrate this point later in the chapter using a hypothetical example to show how a study's setting can possibly influence participants' views, thereby necessitating a thorough description of the fieldwork setting.)

- ☑ *Verbatim quotations of what people said*; sometimes it is necessary to capture exactly what the participants said in their own words. Such quotes will help validate or explain why people do what they do, thereby minimising bias due to subjective interpretations of people's actions by the researcher.

- ☑ *The observer's feelings and their reactions* to what has been observed during the moment that they experience such feelings; to some degree, this will help to keep the researcher's subjectivities in check.

- ☑ *The observer's own interpretations of the situation* and hence their perception of the meaning of what they have observed; including your own preliminary views of the observation data will inform later interpretations during data analysis.

As the observer, you should spend a considerable amount of time every day during fieldwork writing notes. Lofland and colleagues (2006:111) stress that "all the energy and enthusiasm generated by actually being out and about mucking around in some setting must be matched by cloistered rigour in writing down what has taken place". The purpose of observation is defeated if as a researcher, you do not make timely and detailed field notes, especially considering that field notes provide a rich context within which the findings of the study must be interpreted.

Don't procrastinate with recording field notes

The longer you put off recording field notes, the more you will lose the finer details of the phenomena you are investigating. It is best to record your observations immediately after you make them, that is, write them out.

At the end of each day you need to spend a considerable amount of time expanding your daily notes, making sure to add as much detail as possible while the memory of what transpired is still fresh in your mind. In Wamoyi and colleagues' (2010) study, the fieldworkers spent one to two hours each day dedicated to the writing of field notes. In addition, they also prepared a summary report after every field visit. Such a practice is commendable as it gives credence to the data. Similarly, Freitag (2005) reports about keeping a daily personal journal, as well as daily personal reflections of her experiences during her fieldwork in Victoria Falls.

Now that we have addressed the topic of recording field notes and provided guidelines for doing so, we can state with certainty that the quality of field notes is thoroughly enhanced if you would take time to provide a description of the setting in which observations are taking place. This subject of description of setting is the topic of the next section.

16.4 Description of the fieldwork setting

The researcher needs to make a complete and full description of the fieldwork setting in order to provide a context within which the findings of his or her study must be understood. As Patton (2002) noted, such a description should use descriptive rather than interpretive adjectives that show the researcher's own interpretation of the setting. A description of the setting includes the physical environment such as the school, classroom, community centre, hospital, house, or any other physical facility or place, where the study is taking place, or at least where the researcher is making their observations. The reason why it is necessary to provide a description of the physical setting is that the physical environment will most likely have an effect on the participants, and how they respond to or perceive a programme that might be going on at that location.

What is place? Describing the physical setting

To illustrate the point about the importance of describing the setting, we will use a hypothetical example of a researcher who is interested in studying the morale and job satisfaction of teachers in two suburban schools. Interviews conducted with teachers at the two schools revealed clear differences in the levels of morale and job satisfaction at the two sites. From interview findings, staff at school A seemed to be happy and quite satisfied with their working conditions (apart from their low salaries) while those at school B seemed to be very unhappy with everything. The difference in the settings is illustrated in Table 16.1. At school B, apart from meagre salaries, teachers' morale is also bound to be influenced by unfavourable working conditions, particularly the dilapidated physical facilities. Failure on the part of the researcher to take note of the physical environment may lead to erroneous conclusions.

TABLE 16.1: Description of school settings

School A	School B
New, state-of-the-art buildings Toilets are always clean and have running water	Dilapidated buildings Toilets are often blocked and do not always have running water Roofs of almost all the buildings have caved in Floors are all cracked Windows are broken The classrooms do not provide shelter from the rain during the rainy season, nor protection from gusty winds during the dry season
All classrooms are equipped with computers	Only the principal's office has a computer
Teachers have a 'conference room' where they each have a station to work from.	There are no teacher offices, nor a 'conference room' of any kind for teachers to work outside their classrooms.

In addition to the physical environment, the human and social environment also needs to be considered. This, too, has a bearing on how people's perceptions are shaped. According to Patton (2002:283):

> In describing the social environment, the observer looks for the ways in which people organize themselves into groups and subgroups. Patterns and frequency of interactions, the direction of communication patterns, and changes in these patterns tell us things about the social environment. How people group together can be illuminative and important. All-male versus all-female groupings, male-female interactions, and interactions among people with different background characteristics, racial identities, and/or ages alert the observer to patterns in the social ecology of the program.

Who is here? Describing the human and social environment **e.g.**

Expanding the hypothetical scenario of teacher morale and job satisfaction at the two suburban schools introduced earlier, there is also a marked difference in the management styles employed at the schools. Mr Sibanda, the principal of school A, believes in shared governance. He always consults with the teachers before making decisions. Staff meetings are enjoyable to attend, and teachers feel free to voice their concerns without fear of intimidation or victimisation. A schedule of staff meetings for the whole school term is posted in the conference room so that all staff members can plan ahead of time to attend. The situation at school B is not quite the same. The principal, Mrs Zulu, runs the school with an iron fist. She hands down orders and never consults with her staff. No teacher dares speak back to her. Staff meetings are erratically announced, usually a day or two before. During meetings, Mrs Zulu does not share the agenda with her staff, the mood during these meetings is tense, and communication is extremely one-sided.

You will notice that we deliberately exaggerated the example which we described here, but it is for a purpose: to make the point about the need for the researcher to make observations of both the physical and social settings and record them as accurately as possible in the form of field notes. Regardless of their level of enthusiasm or motivation, teachers working in school B under Mrs Zulu's leadership are likely to express lower levels of morale than their counterparts in school A. Simply arriving at conclusions using interview data while neglecting to provide a context within which the teachers work will be misleading.

Now that we have addressed the issues of recording field notes and description of the field-work setting, we turn to a discussion of the application and suitability of naturalistic observation.

Stop and reflect

Write, in a few sentences, the most memorable feelings, emotions and experiences you had in the past hour. Now, also do the same for feelings, emotions and experiences you had three days ago at about lunchtime. Did you find that for the second part, you had to stop and think in order to remember what you did three days ago? This simple exercise illustrates the importance of recording field notes in a timely manner if one is to capture the intricate details of the 'goings-on', particularly the feelings and emotions you had at the time.

16.5 Application and suitability of the observation method

Naturalistic enquiry generally requires the use of unobtrusive methods where the flow of events is least disrupted. To quote Adler and Adler (1998:81):

> Qualitative observation is fundamentally naturalistic in essence; it occurs in the natural context of occurrence, among the actors who would naturally be participating in the interaction, and follows the natural stream of everyday life. As such, it enjoys the advantage of drawing the observer into the phenomenological complexity of the world, where connections, correlations, and causes can be witnessed as and how they unfold.

Using unobtrusive methods ensures that the researcher obtains an unadulterated account of the true nature of the phenomena under observation. One can thus be fairly confident about the reliability and validity of one's data, and, consequently, one's findings. The concept of phenomenology mentioned by Adler and Adler refers to the common meaning of a lived experience or perception, held by those who experience it. Depending on the extent of their involvement in the field setting, the observer could as well be part of those who share the experience, and thus they can be well placed to describe it with a considerable degree of accuracy.

To illustrate this point, Wojcicki (2000), in studying sex work in Gauteng, South Africa, was able to gain important insights through observing the interactions of sex workers with their clients in bars and hotel lobbies. She was also able to get a **phenomenological perspective** of the atmosphere in taverns, which none of her other data collection methods had revealed. There might not have been a better place for Wojcicki to study the interactions of sex workers with their clients than the bars and hotel lobbies. Certain phenomena can only be studied through observation. Crowd behaviour is a standard example of this. In the field of business research, Zikmund, Babin, Karr, and Griffin (2012) showed how toy manufacturers are able to utilise observation to understand children's preferences for toys. Because young children are not able to express their reactions to products, market researchers observe them while they play with a toy, doll, or game. Thus, the researchers can generally gauge the level of interest in different products by observing potential target customers interact with the products.

Apart from your research topic being able to determine whether to use observation, Lofland and colleagues (2006) discuss how a study's setting can also determine what method of data collection to use. Naturalistic observation might be suited to situations where the participants are located in a specific 'place'. Examples of situations that call for observation because participants are located in a specific place include the following situations: when one wants to study the lives of children who live on the streets; how children form friendships in child-care settings; the interactions of teachers and students in the school environment; how commercial sex workers solicit potential clients in night clubs in red-light districts; how married couples behave in public places such as restaurants; and behaviours of gamblers in casinos. Although you will be able to use other methods of data collection for topics like these, observation is especially attractive as either a stand-alone method or as one that is used for **data triangulation**.

The ease or difficulty of gaining access to a research site usually makes the observation method more appealing than other techniques, such as interviewing or experimentation. Ethical considerations aside (not that they are not important), if the process of negotiating access to a research site is complicated because the protocols for interviewing or experimentation are not easily understood, the observation method becomes a viable option, particularly if the phenomena to be observed are of a public nature. We reiterate, though, that researchers will need to comply with the requirements of their ethical review boards before they engage in any research endeavours that involve human or non-human subjects.

An ethical dilemma

Jabulani is an academic in a developing country. He is intending to conduct research on the process of election rigging. One of the best ways to gather data is perhaps to physically observe the voting process at polling stations. It is impossible for him to have access to data at polling stations as a researcher.

However, in the event, Jabulani gets accredited as an election supervisor who would have the prerogative of seeing the ballot tallies at several polling stations. He would also be witness to voter intimidation which he envisages will happen at the polling stations. For most of the time during the voting process, including ballot counting and tallying, he has a spy webcam attached to his shirt. He notices several anomalies in the data that were collated at the local stations and the figures reported to the electoral commission, not to mention the level of voter intimidation carried out by partisan law enforcement agents. This is perfect data for his study.

Here are some ethical considerations from this scenario. Is it okay that Jabulani does not disclose his real intention of researching election rigging before being accredited? Should he use the discreetly collected data for his study?

Now that we have addressed situations when observation can be used as well as ethical issues that must be considered, the next section addresses strengths of the observation method.

16.6 Strengths of the observation method

Compared with self-reported data, such as from surveys or interviews, data collected through observation are free from respondent bias. Sometimes when people are responding to surveys or interview questions, they tend to give socially desirable responses. In addition, survey or interview data are often riddled with memory bias and inaccuracies. We present you with an example here about how observation data were used to verify the accuracy of verbal reports given by interview respondents and focus group participants.

How can observation help to verify the accuracy of verbal reports?

A researcher was involved in the evaluation of a child supplementary feeding programme which was implemented by a non-governmental organisation in a number of drought-stricken rural communities of South Africa during the drought of 2004. The parents of the children who were receiving the free food were very appreciative of the intervention and did not want the programme to end. For that reason, from all the interviews and focus groups that were conducted with the mothers of the 1–5-year-olds, the participants' responses seemed exaggerated (in a positive way, though). Some mothers even stated that the children's bones were showing signs of increased strength due to the porridge that they were receiving. This information could not be verified. The programme staff who were working in these communities told the researcher that the mothers were exaggerating the facts so that they would continue to receive support. Programme staff indicated that they were not noticing any physical change in the children's appearance over the several months that the programme had been in place, and that they had been observing the children. Nevertheless, they echoed the same sentiments as the mothers, that the children were better off with the supplementary porridge than without it as this might be the only real meal the children were getting in a day.

As can be seen from this example, observation helps verify the information obtained through other data collection techniques, in this case, interviews and focus groups. Over-reliance on one method of data collection can sometimes lead to biased or erroneous conclusions.

It is generally desirable in research to use multiple methods of data collection so that findings from one approach can be corroborated using another approach. Observation complements other ways of collecting data such as experimentation, interviews, focus groups, and surveys, hence providing an important strategy for data triangulation. According to Adler and Adler (1998), observation is not only a basic form of research, but it is also the one that is most likely to be used for data triangulation.

Validating findings: Observation is useful for triangulation

Here, we describe Singleton's (2012) example introduced briefly earlier and show how she used observation to triangulate her findings. Singleton's ethnographic study was conducted in the township of Mpophomeni in KwaZulu-Natal in South Africa. Her purpose was to examine the disparity between the law and local beliefs and practices regarding gender-based sexual violence. The study took place from 2001 to 2005. The participants included a score of young men and women between the ages of 18 and 35. Occurring in phases, her methods of data collection included a survey, in-depth interviews, and extensive participant observation in community workshops and meetings.

Singleton wrote about how, through observation, she witnessed tension that existed during workshops between the advocates of modern or Western definitions of rape, and those who strongly supported local views and traditional practices. Singleton (2012:71) noted how, during one workshop, participants "clearly expressed anxiety about the notion of gender equality". Corroborating findings from other data collection methods, her observations helped her gain a deeper understanding of the extent of the participants' strong views on the subject.

Like Singleton, findings from Pell and colleagues' (2013) study of antenatal care attendance among young women in Ghana, Kenya and Malawi showed that observations validated findings from interviews, and vice versa. For example, in Malawi, both interviews and observations showed the researchers that inadequate infrastructure was a hindrance for all recommended procedures of antenatal care to be carried out at all the health care facilities. In Kenya, observations confirmed the data from interviews about the variation of charges for antenatal care services across different health facilities that the participating mothers had reported.

Through observation, Freitag (2005) was able to verify the stories that were told by the locals using photographs of sports facilities and incidences when she saw women actually participating in sports. Cliggett and Wyssmann (2009), in a study of strategies employed by Zambian teachers to earn alternative incomes, used observations to complement the data they obtained from mainly formal interviews with educators in a town and rural village. This helped validate findings from the participants' narratives.

16.7 Weaknesses of the observation method

Observation can be used to describe how certain behaviours occur or how activities are carried out. Through mere observation, however, one cannot tell why the actions happen in the way they do, or why certain people behave the way they do. Answers to the why questions would require the use of other methods of data collection, such as interviewing.

Another limitation of naturalistic observation is that one usually has to wait for certain behaviours or actions to occur in order to observe them, and the waiting period is indeterminate. For instance, if researchers want to observe how commercial sex workers solicit potential clients in a nightclub, they may have to wait for a long time before they see such actions occur, assuming that there are potential clients to be asked. Unlike in interviews, where one can prompt respondents to answer specific questions, when observing, one usually cannot prompt certain actions, except when using simulations or role plays.

Observer bias can be a limitation on observations. According to Zikmund, Babin, Karr and Griffin (2012) observer bias is a distortion of measurement resulting from the cognitive behaviour or actions of a witnessing observer. An observer can have their own prejudices, subjectivity, or strong views about a certain subject, and having to describe its occurrence may evoke those tendencies such that they report what they see using their preconceived ideas. Such observer biases can undermine the trustworthiness of the data that are collected. Freitag (2005:18), in her ethnographic study of women's involvement in sports in Victoria Falls, noted:

> I felt that it would be difficult to truly see life through an African perspective and that a large number of personal biases could arise from my recent introduction to Critical Studies. I was hoping that I could view a third-world society in a non-judgmental manner and attempt to see it through the perspective of the local worldview [...] I currently find it difficult to look at any interaction between people or in the structure of social and political institutions without wondering whether there is intent to discriminate or a resulting inequality.

What counts as evidence is sometimes hazy in observation because what is observed depends on when, where, and for how long the observation is done, how many observers there are, and how they perceive what they observe. It also depends on what is taken to be evidence of, or a proxy for, an underlying latent construct. Observers need to decide what the *observation evidence* is. For example, is the degree of wear and tear on a book in the school library an indication of its popularity, or carelessness by its readers, or of destructive behaviour by students? Failure to decide what constitutes observation evidence will likely result in one making inaccurate conclusions about the issue under study.

The quality of observation data also depends to a very large extent on the level of competence of the fieldworkers. The concept of 'garbage-in:garbage-out' applies. Poorly-trained observers will generate poor field notes and hence produce unreliable data. An example is given in Katzer, Cook and Crouch (1978) in which a group of scientists at a meeting all witnessed the same event and yet, when asked to write what they witnessed, only one description out of 40 was close to what actually happened. Patton (2002) highlights the needs for scientific enquiry that uses observation to ensure that the observers are thoroughly and adequately trained for fieldwork. Such training includes learning to pay attention to detail, learning how to write descriptively and practising it, as well as being meticulous in documenting field notes.

Conclusion

In this chapter, we have used several examples drawn mainly from African contexts to illustrate different aspects of the observation method, including types of observation. The first distinction one needs to note is between analogue and naturalistic observations. Analogue observations are simulated or role-played scenarios. However, the chapter focused largely on naturalistic observations where the researcher performs their observations in the natural setting in which the phenomena of interest will be occurring naturally. The researcher thus gets a phenomenological perspective of the subject under investigation.

Two types of naturalistic enquiry were defined and exemplified: participant and non-participant observation. Establishing rapport with local people is an important ingredient for the success of participant observation. With non-participant observation, the researchers only concern themselves with observing specific behaviours or actions rather than the totality of the context.

One of the key lessons from this chapter is about field notes: failure to record them makes the whole observation exercise futile. We provided general characteristics that field notes need to have, noting that there is no specific guide to be followed in writing field notes, except to record them as close to the event or observation as possible.

In discussing findings collected through observations, it is important for you to take note of, and provide a description of the setting of the study as this most often has an influence on the participants' behaviours, feelings, or actions.

Lastly, we urge researchers also to consider the merits and demerits of observation within the particular context that they want to use such a method.

Closing activities

Self-reflection questions

1 Explain the difference between participant and non-participant observation.
2 Give examples of situations in your own field of study or work that could be investigated using both participant and non-participant observation.

Practical application questions

3 Identify one topic or issue that would require the use of naturalistic observation, select the most appropriate type of observation, and describe how you would go about conducting the fieldwork observations.
4 Using the example you identified in 3, discuss what other methods of data triangulation would be appropriate for your study.

Analysis and consolidation

5 With a partner, choose an observable phenomenon to observe for up to one hour (for example, students' interaction in the college cafeteria; the process of checking out books in the library; or pedestrian behaviour at a busy intersection). Conduct your observations separately and write your own field notes. Afterwards, come together to discuss and compare findings.
6 Discuss ways through which the validity of your findings could be enhanced.

Bibliography

Adler, P. A., & Adler, P. A. 1998. Observational techniques. In Denzin, N. K. & Lincoln, Y. S. (Eds). *Collecting and interpreting qualitative materials* (pp. 79–109). Thousand Oaks, CA: Sage Publications Inc.

Check, J. & Schutt, R. K. 2012. *Research methods in education.* Thousand Oaks: Sage.

Cliggett, L. & Wyssmann, B. 2009. Crimes against the future: Zambian teachers' alternative income generation and the undermining of education. *Africa Today,* 55(3):25–43.

Cohen, L., Manion, L. & Morrison, K. 2011. *Research methods in Education* (7th ed.). New York: Routledge.

Fraenkel, J.R., Wallen, N.E. & Hyun, H.H. 2012. *How to design and evaluate research in education* (8th ed.). New York, NY: McGraw-Hill.

Freitag, A.J. 2005. Women and sport in Africa: An ethnographic study in Victoria Falls, Zimbabwe. Master's thesis. Paper 2760

Johnson, B. & Christensen, L. 2012. *Educational research: quantitative, qualitative and mixed approaches* (4th ed.). London: SAGE Publications, Inc.

Katzer, J., Cook, K.H. & Wayne, W.W. 1978. *Evaluating Information: A guide for users of social science research.* Reading, MA: Addison-Wesley.

Kawulich, B.B. 2005. Participant observation as a data collection method. In *Forum: Qualitative Social Research*, 6(2).

Lofland, J., Snow, D., Anderson, L. & Lofland, L.H. 2006. *Analyzing social settings: a guide to qualitative observation and analysis* (4ᵗʰ ed.). Belmont, CA, USA: Thomson Wadsworth.

Mathison, S. 1988. Why triangulate? *Educational Researcher*, 13–17.

Norton, P.J. & Hope, D.A. 2001. Analogue observational methods in the assessment of social functioning in adults. *Psychological Assessment*, 13(1):59.

Patton, Q.M. 2002. *Qualitative research & evaluation methods* (3ʳᵈ ed.). Thousand Oaks, CA: Sage Publications Inc.

Pell, C., Meñaca, A., Were, F., Afrah, N.A., Chatio, S., Manda-Taylor, L. & Pool, R. 2013. Factors affecting antenatal care attendance: results from qualitative studies in Ghana, Kenya and Malawi. *PloS one*, 8(1), e53747. Retrieved 15 February 2014.

Phillips, R. 1996. Observation as a method of data collection in qualitative research. *British Journal of Midwifery*, 4:22–9.

Simpson, M. & Tuson, J. 2003. *Using observations in small-scale research: A beginner's guide*. Glasgow: University of Glasgow, the SCRE Centre.

Singleton, J.L. 2012. The South African Sexual Offences Act and Local Meanings of Coercion and Consent in KwaZulu-Natal: Universal Human Rights? *African Studies Review*, 55(2):59–75.

Walshe, C., Ewing, G. & Griffiths, J. 2012. Using observation as a data collection method to help understand patient and professional roles and actions in palliative care settings. *Palliative medicine*, 26(8):1048–1054.

Wamoyi, J., Wight, D., Plummer, M., Mshana, G.H. & Ross, D. 2010. Research on transactional sex amongst young people in rural northern Tanzania: An ethnography of young women's motivations and negotiation. *Reproductive Health*, 7, doi:10.1186/1742-4755-7-2. Retrieved 15 February 2014 from http://www.reproductive-health-journal.com/content/pdf/1742-4755-2.pdf.

Wojcicki, J.M. 2000. Sex-work, stigma and violence in the "new" South Africa: An ethnographic study of sex for money exchange in Gauteng Province. (Order No. 9979058, University of California, Los Angeles). ProQuest Dissertations and Theses, 555-555 p. Retrieved 15 February 2014 from http://search.proquest.com/docview/304583244?accountid=28833 (304583244).

Zikmund, W., Babin, B., Carr, J. & Griffin, M. 2013. *Business research methods*. Mason, OH, USA: Cengage Learning.

CHAPTER 17

Francis Dakwa

The interview method

KEY CONCEPTS

Interview is a formal meeting in which one or more people consult, question or evaluate another person.

Afrocentrism is a cultural ideology and worldview, originating in the United States and dedicated to the history and consciousness of black people of African origin.

Cultural sensitivity refers to cultural awareness and an understanding that there are differences in cultures.

Conceptual framework is the set of assumptions, expectations, beliefs, and theories that support and inform research.

Ethical issues are concerns with standards of conduct, and moral fundamentals and moral philosophy.

Beneficence is a concept stating that researchers should have the welfare of the research participants as the goal of research.

Non-maleficence is a commitment to avoid ham to interviewees.

Research ethics is the application of the fundamentals of ethical principles of planning, conducting and reporting research.

Vulnerable children are young people at risk of being physically or emotionally harmed.

LEARNING OUTCOMES

By the end of this chapter, you should be able to:

▶ Define the interview research method as it relates to African perspectives.

▶ Briefly describe the different types of interviews.

▶ Analyse the viability of the interview research methods within other methods.

▶ Assess the relevance and applicability of the interview method within Afrocentric dimensions.

▶ Define conceptual frameworks and ethical issues related to research interviews.

▶ Discuss the significance of interview research methods on children.

▶ Analyse the implications of conducting research interviews on children with disabilities and vulnerable children.

Case study: The plight of Dinginkosi

Dinginkosi is a 14-year-old orphaned boy living in Chief Makwena's village in the Tsholotsho district in Zimbabwe. He has long since dropped out of school because both his parents died of HIV and AIDS two years ago when Dinginkosi was completing his primary education. His relatives, Thembinkosi (his late mother's brother) and his sister Nothando, who act as his guardians, are unable to support him because they are in financial straits themselves.

Introduction

Dinginkosi's case is a clear example of issues prevalent within an African situation. The interviewer's dilemma lies in trying to enter and understand Dinginkosi's world, as he or she conducts interviews with the different personalities surrounding the boy's life. This chapter will unveil contextual issues related to interviewing people within Afrocentric dimensions. Problems related to types of interviews, their strengths and weaknesses will be discussed. The chapter will also examine strategies to be employed in interviewing children, as well as those with disabilities. You will, as a research student, analyse the effective application of ethical issues to be considered when conducting research interviews with your participants. You will also be exposed to the need for cultural sensitivity as you try to involve participants fully in your interviews. Observation of cultural norms and values will immensely enrich your interviewing skills. Ethical issues surrounding research interviews will also be presented from an African perspective. First, we try to define what the research interview approach entails.

17.1 What is the interview approach?

An interview is a face-to-face conversational engagement between two people where questions are asked by the interviewer in order to elicit responses that can be analysed within qualitative research situations. The major objective of qualitative interviewing is to enable the researcher to measure what the interviewees say so that they can capture the information and interpret it in the research analysis. The interview, as a research technique, consists of questions by the interviewer and oral responses by the research participants. Note the emphasis on oral engagements between the interviewer and interviewees. Let us further clarify the need to record responses so that you, as a researcher, can analyse these on your own and come up with results, a discussion of findings, conclusions, and recommendations for your research.

An interview is not a haphazard affair; it is planned. You do not want to interview your learners on, for instance, thieves who broke into their hostel; and, a day later, you interview the same learners about why they pursue their romantic interests during school hours; and next day, you ask them to come up with reasons why they don't respect their teachers enough to wash their dusty cars over the weekends. It sounds like a mix-up of research interests and intentions, and so it is. Your interviews should be planned to follow an ordered and rational research pattern:

- ☑ **Determine your topic** (issues for interview):
- ☑ **Define your problem**.
- ☑ **Specify your objectives** for the study. Please note that you have the option to use the objective model or the purpose of the study model, but not both because you will, here be discussing one and the same issue.
- ☑ **In your methodology, select appropriate subjects** (respondents) to be interviewed.

Having read generally about the interview as a research method, think about the questions raised in the next activity.

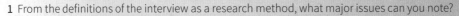
17.2 Types of interviews

In this section, you will be introduced to different types of interviews. Although interviews are usually applicable to qualitative research, quantitative research, to some extent, also benefits from the interview method of research.

17.2.1 Qualitative research interview

The qualitative research interview seeks to describe and reveal the meanings of central themes and issues in the lives of the people being interviewed. The main purpose of a qualitative research interview is to understand the meaning of what the interviewees say (Rubin & Rubin, 1995). A qualitative interview is a research tool, and a good interviewer must prepare questions in advance, and later analyse responses and report results. Qualitative interviewing is an adventure in learning about teaching in different countries and communities, their cultural views and references, their problems and solutions, and how their practices are similar and different from your own. The way you interview depends on what you want to know. It is a process in which you find out what others feel and think about their worlds, in other words, their specific situations.

Qualitative interviewing is part of ethnography, a systematic study of particular ethnic groups, for instance, Shona, Zulu, or Venda culture. Every culture is unique and the interviewer would need to understand and be sensitive to issues related to particular cultures.

17.2.2 Informal conversational interview

In the informal conversational interview, an oral approach is maintained. There are no predetermined questions. Consequently, the interview remains as open and adaptive as possible to the interviewees.

17.2.3 General interview guide approach

The general interview guide approach is intended to ensure that the same general areas of information are collected from each interviewee. This approach provides more focus than the conversational approach. However, the method still allows some measure of freedom and adaptability in obtaining information from the respondent interviewees.

17.2.4 Standardised open-ended interview

In this type of interview, the same open-ended questions are asked of all interviewees. This approach facilitates faster interviews, which can be more easily analysed and compared. Such interviews should be appropriate within a qualitative research situation, where the researcher would analyse interviewees' different opinions. We look at closed fixed-response interviews next.

17.2.5 Closed fixed-response interview

In a closed fixed-response interview, all interviewees are asked the same questions and required to select answers from among the same set of alternatives. Such an interview would be suitable for researchers not experienced in interviewing. In the next section, we look at cultural interviews.

17.2.6 Cultural interview

The cultural interview focuses on the norms, values, understandings, as well as the taken-for-granted rules of behaviour of a group, community or society. In a cultural interview, one would have to take cognisance of the norms and values of, for example, Shona, Ndebele or Shangani culture. This will lead to successful and effective cultural interviewing.

17.2.7 Personal (structured) interviews

This is a face-to-face, two-way communication between the interviewer and the respondents. The personal interview is carried out in a planned manner and is also referred to as a structured interview. This type of interview requires a lot of preparation, rapport-building and sensitive probing. Respondents are encouraged to answer questions freely, completely and pertinently. Responses are recorded. In a structured interview, the interviewer asks each respondent a series of pre-established questions with a limited set of response categories. The structured interview resembles more closely a human encounter than the questionnaire format of receiving questions from an unknown person.

17.2.8 Unstructured interviews

An unstructured interview does not have any set format, although the interviewer may have some key questions formulated in advance. The unstructured interview may seem free and random, like a conversation, but researchers know that with preparation and awareness it can often produce very rich and informative responses.

17.2.9 Focus group interviews

These are unstructured interviews which involve a moderator leading a discussion between a small group of respondents on a specific topic. Membership of an ideal focus group ranges from six and 12 members. The purpose of such a focus group interview is to triangulate data from other sources (Mangham, 2003). The triangulation would emanate from the group discussions.

17.2.10 In-depth interviews

The in-depth interview, also known as depth interview or unstructured interview, is a type of interview which researchers use to elicit information in order to achieve a holistic understanding of the interviewees' point of view or situation. In-depth interviewing can also be used to explore interesting areas for further investigation. An in-depth interview is, again, like a conversation with an individual, conducted by a trained person, that usually collects specific information about the interviewee. Such interviews can also be applied when an agency or researcher does not know much about a population and wants to obtain primary ideas from the participants. Information obtained through in-depth interviews can be used to develop quantitative surveys once interviewers have a better understanding of what is going on with their participants. Sometimes, an in-depth interview would give you all the information you need without conducting another survey.

   In-depth interviews can be used together with focus groups or in place of focus group interviews. They may probe deeper into a person's feelings, attitudes and beliefs about issues surrounding the interviewees. Information obtained through in-depth interviewing can only be qualitative in nature.

17.2.11 Telephone interviews

The main objective of telephone interviewing is to enable data to be collected from geographically scattered samples more cheaply, efficiently and quickly than through field interviewing, and to avoid the traditional limitations of postal surveys. The problems with phoning have to do with obtaining adequately representative samples of the general population, as well as adequate response rates. There have also been doubts expressed concerning the quality of the data, compared with face-to-face interviews (Durrant, et al., 2010).

The telephone interview is the most accepted approach for quantitative data collection. It is a principal survey method and the most widely used survey modality in industrialised nations Besides cost and time savings, some further advantages of telephone interviews include the ability to reach geographically dispersed respondents as well as interview safety.

Pitfall warning

Problems can arise in telephone interviews because of limited telephone coverage in some areas, own response rates, language issues and the absence of visual non-verbal cues. Can you think why or how each of these may present a problem?

Tip

From an African viewpoint, one would need to raise a few concerns and observations:

▶ Given accessibility to the mobile phone system, most individuals on the African continent have access to telecommunication services.

▶ However, conducting telephone interviews would always be a costly exercise for the interviewer, whether by fixed line or mobile services.

▶ Another observation would stem from the cultural perspective, where you could not interview anyone you choose within a family, customary or socio-ethnic situation.

▶ Can you add any tips about similar concerns, from your particular cultural or socio-ethnic situation?

17.2.12 Internet interviews

An internet interview or online interview is a new form of online research. It is used with very geographically dispersed populations. Online interviewing can be used with individuals or groups that are often difficult to meet in person, such as the less physically mobile – those with disabilities, or in prison, or hospitals. This method may also be suitable for isolated groups like drug dealers, terminally-ill patients, or those living in dangerous places like war zones. It can also be used to reach target groups where the audience is unknown or chooses to be anonymous.

Having examined the possibilities of telephone and internet interviews, you may now want to try the next activity.

17.3 Strengths and weaknesses of the interview method

In this section, we review the strengths and weaknesses of the interview research method in broad outline. Many more strengths and weaknesses emerge in different situations, but we are concerned here with those that persist generally, beyond the situational.

17.3.1 Strengths

▶ Interviews are appropriate when dealing with illiterate people.
▶ They are also useful for children with disabilities and intellectual impairments.
▶ In an interview, the interviewer can probe if the respondent's answer is too brief, or there is no initial response.
▶ The interviewer gives interviewees flexibility in dealing with unstructured questions, which often produces more interesting and meaningful results.

Let us now examine some weaknesses of the interview method.

17.3.2 Weaknesses

▶ Interviews are expensive and time-consuming as the researcher would have to personally contact each respondent.
▶ Interviewees might be influenced by the presence of the interviewer which may pose as an intimidation factor.
▶ Some interviews might not be open or frank enough for fear of victimisation of the interviewees.
▶ Dishonest practices may crop up where the interviewees may hide useful information.

After studying the strengths and weaknesses of interviews, you need to stop and reflect on the questions, and suggest your own views.

In the next section you will study reasons why interviewees do not respond to interview questions.

17.4 Reasons for non-response in interviews

Considerable effort, time and expense go into developing interview instruments and organising the interview process. It is an obvious concern, then, when the researcher gets an inadequate or no response from interviewees. The reasons are complex and not always explainable, but it essential to start understanding why. The following factors can influence non-response to interview questions:

▶ Researchers' behaviour and attitudes can have an influence on responses.
▶ Researchers' experience of the interview process may be a limiting factor.
▶ The issue of interviewer and interviewee remuneration may play a role.
▶ Interviewee behaviour, attitudes and motivation may play a part in non-response.

Continuing our discussion of non-response we now look at how the interviewer's personality and organisational skills can affect interviewee responses.

17.4.1 How the interviewer affects responses from participants

▶ The interviewer can draw out responses by the manner of his or her presentation of questions.
▶ The interviewer's extrovert personality (charisma) could provoke certain responses.
▶ The interviewer could obtain responses by his or her efficient organisation of the interview process.
▶ The interviewer can earn the cooperation of the interviewees by creating rapport and respect.

Let us now examine more closely how the interviewer affects interviewees' responses to survey questions.

17.4.2 How the interviewer affects interviewees' responses to survey questions

▶ The interviewer's observable characteristics may evoke feelings of trust, respect, seriousness of purpose, or the opposite.
▶ Interviewer's actions in the survey interview process, like waiting for answers, speaking more slowly or clearly, checking on the attention, understanding or comfort of the interviewee.
▶ The interviewer's thorough preparation for the interview, such as being on time and having the required materials to hand, their background knowledge of the current situation, and their solution-finding approach when things do not go exactly according to plan (as they seldom do).
▶ Thorough preparation of respondents by the interviewer so that they are aware of the purpose of the interview, how long it will take, what will be the outcome of the process.

You may need to analyse the questions in the activity that follows, to help clarify your understanding of responses in interviews.

Stop and reflect

1 Consider any two reasons why interviewers would fail to get responses to their questions. Explain why you think this happens.
2 How can you as an interviewer influence responses? Explain such influence is important to know about, and perhaps what you could do to avoid it.

17.5 Debate on reliability and validity of interviews

A problematic area of interviews is described by John Dean and William Whyte (1958) in their article, *Interview and authentic self*. They cite the problem where the interviewer may not be able to determine whether the interviewee is telling the truth in his or her responses to interview questions. The authors highlight the susceptibility of the interview technique to a variety of distortions, hence the interview should be viewed with the possibility of ulterior motives and subjectivity in mind.

On the same theme, Hammersley (2003), in his article, *Recent radical criticism of interview studies: Any implications for the sociology of education?*, warns against overdependence among qualitative researchers on interview data. He particularly singles out social and educational researchers like those in the mass media and their audiences whom he judges have become obsessed with the idea of interviews as a means of discovering and researching some secret or sensational realities.

There are no ready answers to the debate about achieving validity and reliability in qualitative research, especially when using the interview method. We can only urge awareness, as suggested here of distortions and limitations. We also recommend that you re-read the relevant parts of Chapter 12 again, to clarify the issues.

17.6 The African perspective

In this section, we attempt to analyse the different views of scholars who have done research on the impact of Afrocentrism in research

Mkabela (2005), in her paper entitled, *Using the Afrocentric method in researching indigenous African culture*, highlights the need to take cognisance of the cultural aspirations, understandings and practices of African indigenous people, and to relate these to research. It is incumbent upon the researcher or interviewer to observe and understand culturally-sensitive issues as the researcher interviews respondents to questionnaires, or in conducting surveys and group focus and individual interviews.

Knowledge about indigenous people is vital before a researcher prepares to interview respondents on any research issues. If you are interviewing women or children from any African ethnic group, for instance, Yorubas, Shanganis, Bembas or Vendas, would you be able to walk in and interview them? What are the cultural issues at stake? Supposing you want to carry out research in Chief Chiweshe's area and you intend to interview the headmen in villages there: how should go about this activity? Such questions cannot be ignored because they impinge crucially on effective research within the African sphere.

It is vital for the researchers to empathise and identify with the people being studied in order to understand how they see things. We would go further and say 'Get into their shoes and walk with them.' If you, for instance, intend to interview Tswana young men on their views on sexuality and marriage, do you simply pick a sample and start the interview? The answer of course is definitely not. As a good researcher, you would take time to know the people, listen to their views on a subject, and involve them in the interview process. In the next section we examine the need to involve participants in research interviews.

17.7   Interviewees as participants and not as spectators

For research to be successful, there is need to involve indigenous communities as fully participating members of the research enterprise. If you are researching, for instance, Kikuyu herdmen on the impact of cattle in traditional economic structures, you would need to involve the actual herdmen in the interviews.

Involve these herdmen even in the design of your interview. Much research has failed to yield intended results because the interviewer imposes his or her views on cultural groups.

Africans, as observed by Mkabela and Luthuli (1997), are known for their clear orientation to collective values and a collective sense of responsibility. A researcher intending to interview people in villages within the Shona culture would not simply walk in and carry out his or her mission. Researchers should first do their homework and find out the structures and responsible contact people who will advise them on the procedures to be followed.

One other aspect of Afrocentrism to be discussed is uBuntu/hunhu/unhu. You could cautiously translate this as humaneness – the dignity and personal features a human being displays in order to earn respect from those around him. However, this translation does to fully convey the simplicity – and paradoxical complexity – of this concept, which is why we say 'cautiously'. A researcher would have to understand the dress code particular to that culture or ethnic group and, if possible, put on that attire as you approach the group in question. As a researcher, you could attempt to eat the local food, follow the expected greetings rituals, and display the expected manners within that culture. In uBuntu/unhu/hunhu, you display the expected behaviour that would lead others around you to regard and respect you as a human being. As soon as you earn that respect from respondents within a particular African culture you can conduct your interview with confidence because you have earned the needed respect and created the rapport to accomplish effective outcomes in your research.

Consider the research issues raised in the next activity. You should choose an African situation familiar to you.

Critical thinking challenge

Select a particular African socio-ethnic group (one that you are familiar with would be ideal, but if not, remember to do your homework thoroughly on whichever you end up choosing) for your interview:

1 Define the research problem.

2 Create a topic for your research.

3 Define the methodology of your research and sample your subjects

Note: The African perspectives discussed in this section should be embedded throughout your research proposal.

17.8 Towards a culturally sensitive-research approach

Linda Tillman (2009) approaches research from an African-American perspective. We will sift through a few central issues highlighted by Tillman and attempt to apply them to interview research. Note that although she is speaking to the African-American experience, we will apply Tillman's views to the African continent and context.

The application of a culturally-sensitive research approach can be a catalyst for educational change (Lee & Slaughter-Defoe, 1995). Educational research should characterise African identities, cultural solidarity, as well as education for self-reliance.

Tillman observes that culturally-sensitive research approaches both recognise ethnicity, and position culture. Tillman also observes that the cultural, historical and contemporary experiences of black people serve in an emancipatory role. A researcher interviewing members of the black community would reflect and take part in their journey towards emancipation, independence and, indeed, empowerment. Tillman also raises the issue of culturally congruent research methods, as well as the need to utilise culturally-specific research techniques. Culturally-sensitive research approaches apply qualitative methods such as interviews (individual, group, life history, etc.). The history part of the interview would necessarily incorporate the oral history traditions of the African people.

Critical thinking challenge

Critically examine some examples from your particular African situation, while you reflect on Tillman's African-American perspective. What in particular resonates in your situation? What seems unfamiliar or insignificant?

17.9 Conceptual framework

The conceptual framework of research encompasses concepts, assumptions, expectations, beliefs and theories that support and inform your research. A conceptual framework would explain to you either graphically or in narrative form the main things to be studied, the key factors, concepts or variables as well as the presumed relationship between these variables and research issues. (Miles & Huberman, 1994). You would need, in the next section, to study the diagram and link it to a research situation you are involved in.

FIGURE 17.1: How the conceptual framework links components of research design

Stop and reflect

Imagine you have been invited to conduct interviews at Chitengu Secondary School in the Zaka district in Masvingo, Zimbabwe, where teachers think the head of the school and top administrators have been the cause of the poor A-level examination results experienced over the past four years. Using the information supplied in Figure 17.1, explain how you would conduct your interviews, as part of your investigation.

In the next section we discuss the relationship between the conceptual framework and interviews as a viable research method.

17.10 Relationship between conceptual framework and interview research method

In considering the relationship between conceptual frameworks and interview research method, you would need to take into account what you think is taking place with the issues, settings and people you plan to study. Apart from examining the theories, beliefs and prior research findings, you also need to look closely into literature, preliminary studies, as well as the personal background of your participants. What we are emphasising here is that you, as a responsible researcher, need to understand the people and issues you are studying.

In the next section, we consider ethical issues related to research interviews.

17.11 Ethical issues

Throughout this chapter, and indeed this book, we place ethics and ethical considerations at the heart of research.

17.11.1 Informed consent

You would need to inform research subjects about the purpose of your interviews, as well as the main features of your interview design. You need to consider carefully, and make prior arrangements to find out who should provide the consent. Within many African cultures, you will meet instances of classified or confidential information which cannot be divulged at any cost, hence the need for informed consent. Subjects to be interviewed will need to agree to the release of any identifiable information needed in your research.

17.11.2 Confidentiality

The principle of confidentiality demands that you act in accordance with the trust placed in you as a researcher. Confidentiality is an obligation arising from your clients' trust in you. Their trust would restrict any disclosure of information about clients other than the purpose for which this information was originally disclosed by your interviewees. When recording information from your interviewees, it is advised you use pseudonyms to protect the identity of your clients.

17.11.3 Autonomy

Autonomy refers to the interviewees' right of privacy. As an interviewer, you do not force subjects to talk if they do not feel like talking. Allow them to withdraw from the interview if they want to, because they are not obliged to take part. Suppose you come across a group of children playing games in a field and you ask to interview them. As children rightly do when confronted by a stranger making strange requests, they all run away. Although you may be dumbfounded, it is their right to flee from the situation. It is their autonomy. If you make an appointment to meet kraal head Zikomu at his village, for instance, and he does not pitch up, you do not ask him why and you do not persist with trying to get an interview. It is his right not to attend the interview. That is his autonomy. Autonomy expresses respect for the client's right to be self-determining. The respondent should be given the freedom to voluntarily participate in an interview, or not.

17.11.4 Beneficence

Beneficence entails that you act in the best interests of the interviewee. It is a concept in research ethics which states that research should have the welfare of the research participants as a goal of research.. Your conduct should be above board and the interview process should be conducted with efficiency and the knowledge that informs practice. The principle of beneficence demands that you respect the interests of interviewees whose capacity for autonomy may be diminished owing to immaturity, lack of understanding, extreme distress, serious disturbance, or any other significant personal constraints. As a researcher, you need to safeguard the interests of your clients by avoiding or minimising harm to interviewees (Bosede, 2010).

17.11.5 Non-maleficence

Non-maleficence is your commitment to avoid harm to the interviewee. This would involve avoiding sexual, financial, emotional, or any other form of client exploitation. This would also entail avoiding incompetent practices. You should absolutely refrain from offering your services to your subjects or carrying on with the interview process when you are unfit to do so owing to illness, personal circumstances, or worse, intoxication.

Stop and reflect

You want to investigate the effects of the oral tradition on the education of secondary schoolgirls in your particular cultural situation. What ethical principles would you incorporate in your interview? Make a list and explain each item in the context of the research you want to carry out.

In the next section, we analyse the effectiveness of the interview research method as compared to other research methods.

17.12 Interview approach versus other research methods – a comparative analysis

In this section, we compare the interview method of research with other methods, for instance, questionnaires and observations. Interviews, as you know, can apply in both qualitative and quantitative research. When interviews are unstructured, in other words, open-ended with regard to questions asked by the researcher, a qualitative research paradigm is employed. On the other hand, if the questions are structured, the data and results often lead to a quantitative analysis, hence a quantitative paradigm to the research is applied.

With unstructured interviews, focus group interviews, observations and content analysis, the researcher uncovers biases, values and experiences in the form of words, pictures and objects. The research is therefore inductive and is also qualitative in nature. On the other hand, when the researcher uses questionnaires, inventories and computer-based applications, he or she is utilising numbers and statistics. This research is deductive rather than inductive because it is based on reasoning and logic. In a qualitative research the design emerges as the study unfolds, whereas in a quantitative approach the researcher carefully designs all aspects of the study prior to collection of data. An unstructured interview or observation would flourish in a natural setting. However, a structured interview or questionnaire would be highly controlled.

Interviews are particularly useful for getting the story behind participants' experiences. The interviewer can pursue in-depth information around the topic. However, interviews may also be useful as a follow-up to certain responses to questionnaires, for instance, to further investigate a puzzling, unclear or incomplete response.

In most research, both the qualitative and quantitative approaches are employed. A research instrument can use both structured and unstructured questions, where the interviewer solicits views/opinions of interviewees. At the same time, the researcher needs to quantify the data through closed questions. The researcher can triangulate the results by comparing responses from an unstructured interview, questionnaire and observations, in an attempt to validate his or her findings. Triangulation will also test the reliability of his or her results, and this will enrich the research.

The next section has been included to equip you with the skills for interviewing young children.

17.13　Research ethics on interviewing young children

While research ethics are used in the universal sense, in this section, we want to highlight ethical considerations particular to interviewing children in research activities. We will also attempt, throughout our discussion, to zero in on African perspectives related to interviewing children and young people.

The ESOMAR World Research Codes and Guidelines (2009) stipulate specific guidelines for interviewing children and young people. The researcher should take special care and precautions when interviewing children. The welfare of the child is the overriding factor where they must neither be disturbed nor harmed by the experience of being interviewed. On the other hand, the researcher, guardian or parent of the child should be confident that the safety rights and interests of the child are fully safeguarded. Within an African context, the relevant authorities, who may include school heads, education officers and teachers in charge (TICs), must be confident that all research carried out with children and young people is conducted to the highest ethical standards, and that there can be no question of any possible abuse of children involved in the interview.

The interview process should observe common sense and good research practice when involving different age groups of children. If you, for instance, want to interview children under the age of 12 years in a village, you would need to obtain permission to do so from the parents or guardians. No child of this young age should be approached for an interview unless he or she is accompanied by an adult. Because of the vulnerability of children, the identity and credentials of the interviewer must be ascertained. In many African societies, strangers are thoroughly scrutinised by heads of the village or clan structures before they are allowed into the village or cultural group. Research interviews should take into account the degree of maturity of the child. Questions asked should be graded according to the level of maturity, in other words, the different age groups of children should be taken into consideration in designing the questions to be asked in the interview.

As we have said, in research ethics involving children, there should be a balance between the researcher's aims and protection of any participants. The United Nations Convention on the Rights of the Child (1989: Article 12) stipulates that state parties should ensure that the child who is capable of forming his or her own views has the right to express those views freely in all matters affecting the child. In this case, the views of the child within an interview situation should be given due weight in accordance with the age and maturity of the child. In many African countries, there are Acts and policies in place to protect children engaged in research interviews such that the authorities now require to examine the instruments to be employed on children before permission is granted to carry out the research. This is particularly vital because some questions could be harmful to the child, especially where the child's feelings are concerned and where hisor her relationships with other children, family and authorities, as well as the institutions concerned, would be detrimentally affected. Researchers would need to understand the policies prevailing in any situations involving children. They should also understand the political climate prevailing within a particular country, region or indeed, at village or community level. It is incumbent on the researcher to conduct a prior search, do thorough homework, to ascertain that the intended research instrument respects the country's code of ethics. This would protect the children, community and institution, as well as the researcher.

17.13.1 Helsinki Declaration (1964)

Current ethical principles for conducting research with children arise from the Nuremberg Trials which took place after World War II, as well as the Nuremberg Code which emerged from these trials (UCL Research Ethics Committee, 2004, online). This Code sets out statements of certain moral, ethical and legal principles relating to research involving human subjects, vis-à-vis children. The Declaration of Helsinki emerged from the Nuremberg Trials and Code and was amended in 1989 to the Helsinki Declaration, and again in 1996. It includes an examination of the issue of children as research subjects with regard to informed consent.

According to the Helsinki Declaration, adequate information must be provided to the research participants and participation in the research must be freely volunteered. The participant can withdraw at any time from the research. The Declaration further states that when the subject in research is a minor, in other words, a child, permission from the responsible relative replaces that of the participant in accordance with national legislation. Informed consent should be obtained in writing. In addition, the guidelines indicate that whenever the minor is able to give consent, the minor's consent must be obtained in addition to the consent of the minor's legal guardian. The Helsinki Declaration is therefore emphatic on the need for consent from *both* the child, *and* the parent or guardian of the child.

Parental consent or guardian's consent is required where it is believed that the child is not competent to consent. Although the child's consent is advisable, the power to consent in legal terms belongs to the parent or legal guardian. People consenting on behalf of the child only do so legally provided participation in the interview is of benefit to the child.

In the next section, we will examine the relevance of meaningful consent and issues of confidentiality related to interviews on children.

17.13.2 Towards meaningful consent and issues of confidentiality

Children under the age of 18 years in many African countries are referred to as children under the legal age of majority, and would need to be protected in a research situation, especially if they are undertaking studies in an institution. However, in some cultural contexts, the age of majority has been drastically lowered to 15 or 16 years to allow for socio-ethnic accommodations. In such cases, the child is regarded as responsible enough to consent to being interviewed, and the parental or guardian consent issue falls away. In current trends, children are increasingly seen as having rights and responsibilities of their own, and, as such, could agree to be interviewed on any research issues without recourse to parental or guardian consent Confidentiality can be overridden if the child is identified as in danger. Here, the researcher would have to use his or her discretion and be absolutely clear what constitutes 'danger' in terms of research situations involving children. Practical examples would arise where the researcher is aware that the child being interviewed is under the influence of alcohol or drugs. The interviewee may need treatment or psychological attention and so confidentiality of information in this case would have to be compromised for the benefit of the child.

Having read about the implications of research interviews on children, think about the questions raised in the next activity.

Stop and reflect

1 Discuss any three considerations in interviewing children within your particular African situation

2 Examine protocols you would observe before interviewing children within African perspectives.

3 Discuss the advantages of the application of the Helsinki Declaration proposals to Africa today.

In the next section we focus on ethical issues as they relate to persons with disabilities.

17.14 Ethical guidance for research among people with disabilities

The National Disability Authority (2009) emphasises that any research ethics involving human subjects should be framed and conducted in a manner that respects the human rights of individuals. The United Nations Convention in the rights of persons with disabilities highlights the following issues which the researcher should bear in mind in interviewing persons with disabilities: respect for inherent dignity; individual autonomy; freedom to make own choices; independence of persons; equality; full and effective participation in inclusion in society; respect for difference; as well as accessibility.

There is now a shift from doing research on persons with disabilities to doing research with them (Research Governance Framework of Health, 2005a). Participatory approaches would only enhance the efficacy of the research. However, participatory approaches should seek and work on validity and reliability of findings. Morgan (2007) laments that there is universally little participation in research by children with disabilities.

There is a particular need for good practice in research involving people with disabilities. The United Nations Convention on the rights of persons with disabilities (2006) emphasises the need to adhere to ethical approaches applicable to persons with disabilities throughout the research process. Basically, the ethical principles applied to the other communities of people without disabilities that we have already discussed also apply to people with disabilities When interviewing people with disabilities, it is essential to recognise the diversity of the population, which might include people with visual impairments (blind or partially sighted), those who are deaf, as well as people with intellectual disabilities.

There is also a need for accessibility considerations, in other words, conducting interviews at venues that are accessible and safe as well as providing appropriate disability awareness training for interviewers. It is unethical to place extremely burdensome demands on research subjects with disabilities. The needs of people with disabilities should be considered in the sampling strategies and there is also need to adapt the method, length and intensity of the research interview to participants. For example, it is essential to provide material in easy-to-read formats for participants with intellectual disabilities, and the interviewer would need to use sign language (or employ an interpreter who can sign) when interviewing children who are deaf.

Having analysed ethical issues relating the interview for people with disabilities, you can think about them in context by engaging in the challenge that follows.

Critical thinking challenge

Critically examine the issues you need to consider in involving the following categories of disability in research interviews:

▶ Children who are blind

▶ Children who are deaf

▶ Children with intellectual disabilities.

In the next section, we discuss interview consideration as they relate to vulnerable children.

17.15 Considerations for orphans and other vulnerable children (OVCs)

Extreme care should be taken when interviewing children who have suffered abuse, and children affected by HIV and AIDS. Such experiences should be incorporated in research interviews because the suffering and trauma, the abuse and the ravages of HIV and AIDS have caused untold havoc and disruption to the lives and wellbeing of these children. In whatever sphere they are found, OVCs have a story to tell, a disturbing one, which the world must know so that action can be taken to put things right, especially in Africa. The work of Horizons (2005), as a Population Council funded by USAID in Africa, deserves mention because considerable research has already been conducted, where such children have been involved.

Horizons recognised that there were methodological and ethical gaps in conducting research on OVCs in sub-Saharan Africa and, indeed, in other parts of Africa. Horizons has, through its work in Zimbabwe and Rwanda, drawn up research measures and ethical guidelines that help in understanding and measuring the psychosocial dimensions of vulnerability. To this end, test responses have been developed to improve psychosocial outcomes and protect children, while collecting data for these purposes. In Zimbabwe, researchers tested and refined measures of psychosocial wellbeing which informed later research in Rwanda that in turn, tested new measures of social support, grief, maltreatment and marginalisation (www.ncbi.ntm.gov).

In conducting interviews involving children's and parental feelings and past experiences, it is vital to consider whether the participants have the emotional resilience to cope with being asked to talk about their painful experiences. Children who have been abused are a particularly vulnerable group and, as such, researchers must exercise extra measures to protect these children, as well as themselves as researchers.

Finally, in the conclusion, we draw together the major concerns of interviews, as well as areas for further research.

Conclusion

In the opening case study, you would have thought about Dinginkosi's plight in relation to research interview issues surrounding him. As we developed this chapter, you deepened your understanding of the significance of observing ethical issues when we interview children, people with disabilities, and other vulnerable children. The chapter drew on Afrocentric approaches to interviewing people in African cultures. Other issues highlighted indicated that different cultures within African perspectives are not specific about the age of majority of children for whom parental consent should be obtained before interviewing the children. You learned that all children are the most vulnerable group of interviewees, especially in the context of internet or online interviews. This could be a valuable area needing further research. If current indicators are correct that the exposure of children to pornography and violence, as well as those who target children on the internet, the work of researchers is made more difficult and dangerous. We therefore need to investigate how effectively modern technology like the internet could be positively harnessed within the interview research method process.

As we close our chapter, you should engage with the following questions and activities to apply and consolidate what you have learned.

Closing activities

Analysis and consolidation

1 Name any five types of interviews and explain their purpose.

2 What are the weaknesses or drawbacks of interviews? Develop your answer as a set of pitfall warnings.

3 Discuss the ethical issues to consider when interviewing children who are blind. Conclude your discussion with a short set of guidelines for such interviews.

4 Imagine you have to organise an interview with the parents of two schoolchildren who recently died of HIV and AIDS. These were the parents' only children. What considerations will you take into account, and why?

Practical application

5 You are investigating a particular rural African situation where villagers have requested their chief for boreholes to be drilled in their fields because drought has affected their crop yields for the past three years. Plan, develop and organise appropriate interviews and suggest the possible outcomes. Write your answer as a report that includes fully developed interview plans, etc. supported with reasons.

Bibliography

Alderson, P. & Morrow, V. 2004. *Ethics, social research and consulting with children and young people.* Lilford: Barnados.

Atkinson, J.M. 2007. Protecting or empowering the vulnerable: Mental illness, communication and the research process. *Research Ethics Review*, 3(4):134–8.

Bliss, C., Higson-Smith, C. & Sithole, L. 2013. *Fundamentals of social research methods: An African perspective.* (5ᵗʰ ed.). Cape Town: Juta.

Bosede, A.F. 2010. Ethical principles of guidance and counseling. *International Journal of Tropical Medicine*, 5(2):50–63.

Boyce, C. & Neale, P. 2006. *Conducting in depth interviews: A guide for designing and conducting in-depth interviews for evaluation input.* Pathfinder International.

Casale, M., Lane, T., Sello, L., Kuo, C. & Cluver, L. 2013. Conducting health survey research in a deep rural South African community: Challenges and adaptive strategies. *Health Research Policy and Systems*, 11.

Chimedza, R.M. & Mutasa, J. 2003. *Some developmental, cultural and linguistic aspects of deafness.* Harare: Zimbabwe Open University.

Chimedza, R.M. & Petersen, N. 2003. *Educational considerations for students with hearing impairments.* Harare: Zimbabwe Open University.

Christensen, P. & James, A. 2000. *Research with children. Perspectives and practices.* London: Falmer Press.

Cohen, L. & Manion, L. 2004. *Research methods in Education.* London: Croom Helm.

Commission on Stateus of People with Disabilities. 1991. A strategy for equality: Report of the Commission on the Status of People with Disabilities. Stationery Office. Dublin.

Dakwa, F.E. 2009. Views of children with visual impairment on the challenges of inclusion. *Zimbabwe Journal of Educational Research*, 1(3):76–88.

Dakwa, F.E. 2011. A reflection of teachers' perceptions on the inclusion of children with visual impairment. *Zimbabwe International Journal of Open and Distance Learning*, 1(1) 56–60.

Dakwa, F.E. 2014. Inclusion of children with visual impairments in regular schools – A Zimbabwean perspective. *International Journal of Academic Research in Progressive Education and Development*, 3(1):89–97.

Dawad, S. & Veenstra, N. 2007. Comparative health systems research in a context of HIV/AIDS: Lessons from a multi-country study in South Africa, Tanzania and Zambia. Challenges of conducting research interviews on children with disabilities in Africa.

Dean, J. & Whyte, W. 1958. Interview and authentic self. *Human Organisation*, 17(2).

Denzin, N.K. & Lincoln, Y.S. 2000. *Handbook of qualitative research.* Thousand Oaks. CA: Sage.

Dillard, C. 2000. The substance of things hoped for, the evidence of things not seen: Examining an endarkened feminist epistemology in educational research and leadership. *Qualitative Studies in Education*, 13:661–681.

Durrant, G.B., Groves, R.M., Staetsky, L. & Steele, F. 2010. Effects of interviewer attitudes and behaviours on refusal in household surveys. *Public Opinion Quarterly*, 74(1):1–36.

ESOMAR: *World Research Codes and Guidelines.* 2009. Online. Accessed 17 March 2014.

ESOMAR: *World Research Library.* 2014. Online at: http//www.esomar.org/knowledge-and-standards/codes and guidelines. Accessed 19 March 2014.

Fraenkel, J.R. & Wallen, M.E. 1996. *How to design and evaluate research in education.* London: McGraw Hill.

Gillian, A. 2002. Participation and power. *Africa Insight*, 32(1):25–29.

Goka, T. 2006. The naive researcher doing social research in Africa. *International Journal of Social Research Methodology*, 9(1):61–73.

Gorin, S., Hooper, C.A., Dyson, C. & Cabral, C. 2008. Ethical challenges in conducting research with hard-to-reach families. *Child Abuse Review*, 17(4):275–287.

Gorman-Smith, D. 2003. Prevention of anti social behaviour in females. In D.P. Farrington & J. Cold (Eds). *Primary prevention of antisocial behaviour.* Cambridge: Cambridge University Press (pp. 212–317).

Hallahan, D.P. & Kauffman, J.M. 2006. *Exceptional learners: An introduction to special education.* Boston: Pearson.

Hammersley, M. 2003. Recent radical criticisms of interview studies: Any implications for the sociology of education? *British Journal of the Sociology of Education*, 24(1):119–126.

Heward, W.L. & Orlansky, M.D. 2009. *Exceptional children*. London: Merrill.

Horizons. 2005. Population Council (USAID).

Horizons/USAID. 2007. Psychosocial benefits of a mentoring program for youth-headed households in Rwanda.

Inform. 2013. *Conducting safe and ethical research with children* NSPCC facts sheet. http://nspcc.org.UK/inform/research.briefings/ethical-research.fac.

Kaar, M. 2009. *A critical investigation of the merits and drawbacks of in-depth interviews. A guide for designing and conducting in-depth interviews for evaluation input*. Pathfinder International.

Kershaw, T. 1992. Afrocentrism and the Afrocentric method. *The Western Journal of Black Studies*, 16(3):160–168.

King, N.M. & Churchill, I.R. 2000. Ethical principles guiding research on child and adolescent subjects. *Journal of Interpersonal Violence*, 15(7):710–724.

Kirk, S.A., Gallagher, J.J., Annastasiow, M.J. & Coleman, M.R. 2006. *Educating exceptional children* (14th ed.). Boston: Houghton Mifflin.

Kvale, S. 1996 *Interview: An introduction to qualitative research interviewing*. Thousand Oaks, CA: Sage.

Lee, C.D. & Slaughter-Defoe, D.T. 1995. Historical and sociocultural influences on African American education. In J.A. Banks & C.A.M. Banks (Eds). *Handbook of Research on Multicultural Education*. New York: Macmillan (pp. 348–371).

Mangham, I.L. 2003. Character and virtue in an era of turbulent capitalism. In H. Tsoukas & C. Knudsen (Eds). *The Oxford Handbook of Organization Theory: Meta-theoretical perspectives*. Oxford: Oxford University Press.

Mapara, J. & Mudzanire, B. (Eds) 2013 *Ubuntu/Unhu philosophy: A brief Shona perspective*. Harare: Bhabhu Books.

Masson, J. 2000. Researching children's perspectives: Legal Issues. In A. Lewis & G. Lindsay. *Researching: Children's perspectives*. Birmingham: Oxford University Press.

Mathee, M., Harpham, T., Maicken, N., Barnes, B.; Lagerson, S., Feit, M., Swart, A. & Naidoo, S. 2000. Overcoming challenges in urban health research in developing countries: A research note. *International Journal of Social Research Methodology*, 13(2):171–178.

McNamara, C. 1999. *General guidelines for conducting interviews http://www.napnp.org/library/evaluation/interview. htm*. Accessed 19 March 2014.

Miles, M.B. & Huberman, A.M. 1994. Qualitative data analysis: A sourcebook of new methods (2nd ed.). Beverley Hills, CA: Sage Publications.

Mkabela, N. & Luthuli, P.C. 1997. *Towards an African philosophy of education*. Pretoria: Kagiso Tertiary.

Mkabela, Q. 2005. Using the Afrocentric methods in researching indigenous African culture. *The Qualitative Report*, 10(1)3:178–189.

Morgan, R. 2007. *Disability and Research Ethics Governance in Ireland. A Draft Report for the NDA*. Dublin: NDA.

Musengi, M. & Dakwa, F.E. 2010 & 2011. Language dilemmas of the deaf child: An educator's View point. *NAWA Journal of Language and Communication*, 4(2) Dec 2010 & 5(1) June 2011.

Olson, K. & Peytchev, A. 2007. Effect of interviews experience on interviewer pace and interviewer attitudes. *Public Opinion Quarterly*, 71(2):273–286.

Orb, A., Eienhauer, L. & Wynaden, D. (2000) Ethics in qualitative research. *Journal of Nursing Scholarship*, 33, 1, 93–96.

Resnik, D.B. 2011. *What is ethics in research of why is it important? Natural Institute of Environmental Health Sciences: Your Environment, Your Health*. US Department of Health and Health Services.

Rubin, H. & Rubin, I. 1995. *Qualitative interviewing: The art of hearing data*. Thousand Oaks. CA: Sage.

Schenk, K.D., Michaelis, A., Sapiano, T.N., Brown, L. & Weiss, E. 2010. Improving the lives of vulnerable children: Implications of Horizon's research among orphans and other children affected by AIDS. *Public Health Reports: March–April*,125(2):325–336.

Sitko, N.J. 2013. *Qualitative methods: Data analysis and validation*. Indaba Agricultural Policy Research Institute.

Smith, D.D. 2001. *Introduction to special education. Teaching in an age of opportunity*. Boston: Allyn & Bacon.

Swain, R. 2000. Awareness and decision making in professional ethics. The new code of the psychological society of Ireland. *European Psychologist*, 5(1):19–27.

Tillman, L.C. 2009. *The SAGE Handbook of African American Education*. New York, NY: Sage

United Nations. 2006. *Convention on the rights of persons with disabilities*. http://ww.un.org/disabilities. Accessed 21 March 2014.

Walklate, S. 2000. Researching victims. In R.D. King & E. Wincup (Eds). *Doing Research on Crime and Justice*. Oxford: Oxford University Press (pp. 183–201).

Walmsley, J. 2004. Inclusive learning disability research: The non-disabled researcher's role. *British Journal of Learning Disabilities*, 2(2):65–71.

Walmsley, J. 2004. Normalisation, emancipatory research and inclusive research in learning disability. *Disability and Society*, 16:187–285.

Wiles, R., Crow, G., Heath, S. & Charles, V. 2007. The management of confidentiality and anonymity in social research. *International Journal of Social Research Methodology*, 1–2.

CHAPTER 18

Emily Ganga and Mncendisi Maphalala

The questionnaire approach

KEY CONCEPTS

Close-ended or closed refers to questions that are restricted, structured, not flexible.

Double-barrelled questions have multiple parts.

Open-ended refers to questions that are unrestricted, flexible or unstructured

Question is a request for information or for a reply; it usually ends with a question mark.

Questionnaire is a document containing questions designed to elicit information appropriate for analysis.

LEARNING OUTCOMES

By the end of this chapter, you should be able to:

▶ Describe the concept of questionnaire instrument.

▶ Distinguish between types of questions in questionnaires.

▶ Explain the rationale for the use of the questionnaire in a study.

▶ Suggest strengths and weaknesses of a questionnaire.

▶ Describe questionnaire construction, analysis and interpretation.

▶ Construct questionnaire types covering the introduction, instructions, question wording, rating scales, and closing statement.

▶ Demonstrate understanding of questionnaire layout and format.

▶ Discuss pilot testing of the questionnaire.

▶ Examine ethical considerations in using a questionnaire.

▶ Analyse methods of data analysis used for questionnaires.

Case study: Choosing a research instrument

Nelisa is a young student following a Bachelor's degree programme at a university in South Africa. Among her many subjects is a 'Research methods and statistics' course which she passes so well that she is permitted to proceed with the research project. Her departmental guidelines to research suggest five chapters for the study. She has completed the first and second chapters of her research study. She realises when she gets to her third chapter that she needs to plan and collect data for analysis. She and her tutor sit to discuss the methodology. The two deliberate on an ideal instrument that would collect data from the 50 participants whom Nelisa has identified as her study sample. She and her tutor list data collection tools, such as interview schedules, questionnaires, observation guides, checklists, and document analysis. Being a beginner in research, it would be more appealing for her to work with an instrument that is easier to prepare and administer. Since Nelisa has decided to collect both qualitative and quantitative data, she and her tutor agree that the questionnaire would be the most flexible tool. It would help to elicit participants' opinions and attitudes on her topic.

Introduction

The case study about Nelisa endeavours to describe a typical learning situation in which students may find themselves as they enter and go through the research process. From reading the earlier chapters of this book, you may have noted that engaging in a research project is usually a requirement for students to fulfil, as part of most degree programmes. Nelisa and her tutor probably talked about a number of highlights of the questionnaire. Why does one decide to use a questionnaire? What are the different types of questions and questionnaires? How is a questionnaire constructed and administered? What are the pros and cons of using questionnaires? How is questionnaire data analysed?

This chapter will provide detail that will help you to answer these and other questions relating to the questionnaire approach in research. It is also our wish that as you read this chapter, you can comfortably engage in the activities we provide. The bibliography at the end of this chapter provides a further reading list to widen your concept and scope about the questionnaire as a research tool that you will find most useful in your studies. We start by discussing the concept of the questionnaire.

18.1 Concept of the questionnaire instrument

From Nelisa's case, you might have learned that one of the commonest data collection tools used in research is the **questionnaire**. The questionnaire is a form of enquiry that contains systematically arranged series of questions that are given to research participants to elicit data for a study. The data may, for instance, contain the opinions and attitudes of the participants on a chosen research topic. It is most appropriate where survey information is required. It can be administered by the researcher, or by others in the absence of the researcher. Although the questionnaire is frequently used where quantitative data is required, it can also be structured as an open-ended tool to collect qualitative data. To determine the appropriateness of using a particular type of a questionnaire, the researcher has to consider the problem under investigation, the objectives of the study, or the hypothetical statement of the enquiry. The questionnaire should consider the *what*, *who*, *where*, *when* and *how* of the research situation at hand.

According to Babbie (2010), a questionnaire is a document containing questions designed to elicit information appropriate for analysis. It is a form prepared and distributed to obtain responses to certain questions. Questionnaires allow the same participants an opportunity to hear or read the same questions. It is one of the most appropriate and dependable tools because it is so easy to use to extract data from many people. The questionnaire is an ideal tool because it permits group administration, without allowing participants to confer on responses. It usually appears in a standardised format, especially in the instructions that participants should follow. Time for answering is not usually fixed, as one would have in the case of an interview. Today, a questionnaire has become a versatile research tool which can take various formats depending on its purpose.

A questionnaire is designed to motivate the research participants to give responses towards completing the study. It does not make participants look for answers in texts or by doing internet searches for correct answers. In fact, it provides instructions and clarification in clear, simple language for the respondent. Most questionnaires would begin by asking for simple details such as the demographics of the participants in section one, moving from simple to more complex questions. Sidhu (2003:133–134) advises that "[...] opening questions create a favourable attitude before any progress is made towards the questions which are a bit delicate or intimate." The categories in which questions are placed in a questionnaire should enable the participant to proceed in answering without difficulty, as one moves incrementally from simple to more complex ones. The researcher is also allowed creativity in the construction of a questionnaire, e.g. use of pictorials, graphics and tables.

The researcher can either construct the questionnaire, or obtain a ready-made one from published texts, the internet, or some research organisations. A good example of a ready-made questionnaire is the student version of the *Utrecht Work Engagement Scale (UWES) and Psychological Capital Questionnaire (PCQ)* that was obtained from the internet and was used in a collaborative cross-cultural study on the 'Psychological capital and work engagement' treatise, by Ganga and Motswalakgoro (2013).

Questionnaire types may vary in purpose, size and appearance, but they should be able to collect information which can be used subsequently as data for analysis. The questions listed by the researcher should be able to gather information by asking the participant directly about the issue at hand. Though it may take time to design the various types of questionnaires for the participants, it is vital to consider costs of production, distribution, collection, and analysing the results. A tentative budget should be in place for this purpose. Now, before we discuss the types of questionnaires, we would like you to understand the kinds of questions most often used in a questionnaire.

Stop and reflect

After the brainstorming exercise with her tutor, Nelisa was asked to read more about the questionnaire, in preparation for constructing one. Do some further reading yourself to understand the concept of a questionnaire as a research tool, and then respond to these questions:

1 What is a questionnaire?
2 What is its purpose in research?
3 List some of the features you may find in a questionnaire.

18.2 Questions in a questionnaire

The word, '**question**', is the stem or foundation of all questionnaires. Good questions are specific and will attract good answers for a research study or enquiry. Neuman (2000) says that question writing is an art that requires skill, practice, patience and creativity. Good questioning begins with introductory remarks and instructions for clarifying issues in order to maintain valid and reliable results. Good questioning motivates the respondents to provide the information or data. It is most appropriate for participants who can read and write. It remains one of the most common methods of gathering data, mainly because it is not time-consuming and gives reliable results.

Cohen, Manion and Morrison (2011) suggest that the larger the size of the sample, the more structured, closed and numerical the questionnaire may be; yet the smaller the sample, the more open and wordy the questionnaire may become. In other words, the questionnaire for a larger sample is more quantitative in nature, while one for a smaller sample is normally qualitative. The questionnaire could be postal, internet, or a face-to-face 'clipboard' in type (Denscombe, 2007),depending on available resources.

For participants to fully comprehend the questions forming a questionnaire, it is vital that the questions are free from the following possible limitations:

▶ ambiguity
▶ unnecessary jargon
▶ bias
▶ emotionally-charged terms
▶ double-barrelled questions (See Figure 18.1 for further ideas on questioning).

Basically, questions in a questionnaire fall within two main categories. These are:

▶ **Close-ended**, also known as closed or structured types
▶ **Open-ended** or unstructured, where participants engage in free responses.

Each type of questioning has advantages and disadvantages. In the next two sections we discuss the characteristics, strengths and weaknesses of the two basic types of questions.

18.2.1 Close-ended questions

Common among close-ended questions are those requiring yes or no responses; true or false responses; and ones with rating scales. In each of these cases, you may notice that responses are fixed and allow limited choice. Compared to open-ended questions, they take a longer time to construct, but a shorter time to complete. Expected responses are somewhat rigid, and participants may not shift towards freely writing their preferred alternatives. Respondents are usually instructed to tick, place a cross, shade, circle, underline, or bold their preferred answers.

These types of questions function better in evaluative studies. In such studies, participants find themselves choosing the most appropriate answers as they see fit. Administration of these types of questions enables researchers to analyse results in a much simpler fashion than in open-ended cases. Responses are easier to compare, code and analyse. Even less literate persons may find it easier to respond, especially if the language remains simple and straightforward.

However, the major drawback is that participants are forced to respond only to given alternatives. In such a situation, participants may find it boring and sometimes very unsatisfactory to be forced into feelings or responses they do not feel or approve of. Also, too many responses may confuse some participants. Responses that are too simplistic may be given to very complex matters. The opposite is evident in free-response or open-ended questions, a discussion of which follows.

18.2.2 Open-ended questions

In open-ended questions, participants are afforded an opportunity to share detail. Here, participants provide answers in their own words. There are no pre-fixed alternatives, as in close-ended cases. There is more space provided for responses than in close-ended questions.

Unlike close-ended questions, open-ended questions provide for an extension of views because they allow for unlimited detail from participants. The respondents are able to clarify their creative responses as they move from simple to more complex questions. The participants' deep thinking can be revealing because responses are then qualified. Any anticipated responses are uncovered here as participants try to clarify their views.

In some instances, participants may end up providing more detail than is required or relevant. Questions can sometimes intimidate participants and, in such cases, the participants may end up getting lost. They then provide irrelevant responses or no answers at all. An incomplete questionnaire can distort the coding procedure.

Summarised in Figure 18.1 are the strengths and weaknesses of open- and close-ended questions used in the construction of a questionnaire.

Advantages of Open Questions	Disadvantages of Open Questions
Unlimited responses, respondents can qualify and clarify their responses, unanticipated findings are discovered, responses range from simple to complex, creativity, self-expression, rich detail and revelation of respondent's logic and thinking process.	Different detail in responses obtained, sometimes irrelevent responses, difficult comparisons and analysis, coding difficulties, some respondents may lose direction, time, thought and effort is necessary, some questions may be intimidating for respondents and answers may take a lot of space on the questionnaire.

CLOSED VERSUS OPEN QUESTIONS

Advantages of Closed Questions	Disadvantages of Closed Questions
Quicker and easier for respondents to answer, respondents' answers are easier to compare, answers are easier to code and analyse, fewer irrelevant answers to questions, easier to answer for less literate persons, and replication is easier.	Less-informed participants may answer too easily, listed responses may miss other choices that respondents may prefer, too many responses may confuse participants, questions may be misinterpreted, respondents may give simplistic answers to complex issues, and participants may be forced to make choices they may not prefer.

FIGURE 18.1: Open- and close-ended questions juxtaposed

As the researcher selects questions, it is vital that he or she is cautious about the pros and cons of questioning procedures, so that maximum effort goes into making each instrument understood by each respondent. Some of the drawbacks of questionnaires can be countered by using the questionnaire in conjunction with other research tools in the same study. This is known as instrument triangulation, which you have read about in several other chapters in this book.

18.2.3 Other types of groupings for questions

Other groupings of questions in a questionnaire include contingency ones that are answered only if the respondent has answered a previous one. For example, a child might answer well on how drugs taste if he or she has tested them before. Where identical response categories are provided, the questions form a matrix with response rate along the top, thus providing efficient use of space and time. The other common types of questions are: dichotomous types that carry two options; nominal-polytomous types that carry two unordered options; ordinal-polytomous that carry more than two ordered options; and bounded continuous ones where the respondent is presented with a continuous scale.

18.3.4 Types of questionnaires

The various types of questions one may choose from will differentiate between types of questionnaires. In deciding to construct a questionnaire, there are essentially two types:
▶ Online questionnaires
▶ Paper-based questionnaires.

In online questionnaires, completion can be conducted through email or by following a link that will take the participant to the questionnaire. All communications about the completion of the questionnaire are sent electronically to the participants.

In a paper-based questionnaire, questions are written or printed on a sheet of paper and the participant responds to the questions by writing the answers in the spaces provided on the questionnaire. Paper-based questionnaires can be administered in a number of ways including: individually; by mail; in group settings; and by dropping off the completed questionnaire at an agreed location.

The advantage many researchers and participants experience in using a questionnaire is that of the interviewer's absence. This allows the participant to be more objective and honest in giving responses. Completion is done at the interviewee's own pace. However, the researcher carries the task of making timeous follow-up on questionnaire return rate. For faster action by the participants, there is often a need to provide participants with a questionnaire cover letter that specifies the purpose and the importance of the research. This procedure applies to both the self-completion questionnaires that we mentioned before.

Stop and reflect

1 Distinguish between open-ended and close-ended questions.
2 What factors guide a researcher in question selection?

18.3 Rationale for using a questionnaire in a research study

The number of the advantages of a questionnaire seem to outweigh the disadvantages as is reflected in the discussion that follows. Let us now examine the strengths and weaknesses of using a questionnaire in research studies.

18.3.1 Strengths of questionnaires

There is general agreement on the following strengths of a questionnaire:

- ☑ The questionnaire can be quite affordable if properly planned.
- ☑ If properly constructed, the researcher may assign other people to administer it.
- ☑ Questionnaires allow participants adequate time to make their responses.
- ☑ There is greater uniformity in measurement because the same tool is utilised across all selected participants.
- ☑ Data gathered are easier to analyse than those from interviews and focus group discussions.
- ☑ Any questions that may be embarrassing for some participants can be answered in complete privacy.
- ☑ Participants are able to consult, where there may be a need to do so.
- ☑ Questionnaires can be answered at participants' own pace and time because they are not seen as tests for assessment.
- ☑ Little or no training is required for coding, analysis and interpretation of data.
- ☑ Researchers may end up with data that are not like those from other sources. Such information could be sensitive yet quite useful as means of interpreting or solving a pending issue.
- ☑ Questionnaires can be answered by many research participants simultaneously, thus saving time.

18.3.2 Weaknesses of questionnaires

Although the questionnaire has numerous advantages, it also has significant disadvantages, as discussed now. Researchers are therefore encouraged to find ways of countering the drawbacks by using the technique in conjunction with other data collection tools. We list some of the weaknesses here:

▸ Questionnaires do not provide the flexibility sometimes noted in interviews. So it is sometimes advisable to use this tool in conjunction with interviews as a means of authenticating data.

▸ Most people are generally better able to express their views verbally than in writing. However, many researchers try to curb this limitation by making the tool available to participants in alternative languages, from which a participant can choose.

▸ Questionnaires can be answered only when they are sufficiently easy and straightforward. It is advisable for researchers to simplify the language in order to achieve a 100 per cent return rate.

▸ Biased questions may distort findings, therefore, researchers should be aware of possible bias in the questions.

▸ The answers given by participants to mail questionnaires are seen as final. Data triangulation may help to overcome this limitation.

▸ If a questionnaire is not administered face-to-face but by post, email attachment or online, there is a possibility of not getting many questionnaires back. In order to increase the response rate the researcher may need to call participants directly if they have not responded to the questionnaire and ask them politely if they have any questions or if they need help with completing the questionnaire. You may also consider completing the questionnaire as an interview by phone.

Now we lead you to some practical understandings of how the questionnaire is constructed. In 18.4 we explore the construction of a questionnaire as a data-gathering instrument for efficiency in your research process.

Stop and reflect

How can one deal with a lack of question flexibility when collecting data through a questionnaire?

18.4 Overview of questionnaire construction, analysis and interpretation

The most important points to be taken into account in designing a questionnaire are that it takes time and effort, and that the questionnaire will be re-drafted a number of times before being finalised. Any good researcher must make available adequate time for the construction of the questionnaire. According to Martin (2006), in constructing a good questionnaire, it is important to consider a number of issues, covering:

▸ The wording and ordering of questions
▸ Selection and wording of response categories
▸ Formatting
▸ The mode of administration of the questionnaire.

By completing a questionnaire, data are collected indirectly, thus replacing face-to-face interaction with respondents. Unlike interviews, questionnaires provide time for respondents to think about their answers. Most advantageous of all is the issue of confidentiality and anonymity in using a questionnaire to elicit data from the participants. They are usually an inexpensive way of gathering data. However, it may be quite difficult to monitor and control conferring by participants who experience the same situation. Only a short space of time is used to elicit a large amounts of information.

Denscombe (2007) advises researchers to make adequate consultations and trials, or by submitting to other area specialists before trial use or pilot-testing in order to allow collection of precise, valid and reliable data. Each question must be justified in its contribution to the purpose of study. A careful exploration of the intended hypothesis within the topic is essential, as well as scrutinising texts or literature in order to frame questions that probe crucial issues about the topic being studied.

Creswell (2009) and Frankel & Wallen (2010) assert that the data collected by questionnaires can be presented in table form covering the frequencies, totals, percentages, as well as averages such as the mean. Any descriptive or narrative data can be converted into brief notes before being cumulated under various categories. The process then necessitates calculation of the correlation coefficient in order to establish the relationships among the data. Any conclusions that are made about data from a questionnaire should take into consideration the percentage of the responses. On this note, Sidhu (2003) advises that the lower the percentage of responses, the lower the reliability of the data collected. Therefore, researchers utilising responses from questionnaires should be sure to find ways of enhancing the credibility of data collected.

18.4.1 Steps in constructing a questionnaire

Any good questionnaire is well organised and clear. The response options do not confuse participants but help them to respond without difficulty. There is no bias in the flow of the responses because all the response options are provided. In most cases the flow in a good questionnaire encourages the participants to complete the instrument without leaving any gaps mostly because work usually flows from simple to complex.

Peterson (2000:14) presents seven distinct tasks that are needed to achieve a quality questionnaire. A good questionnaire constructor would aim to accomplish the following tasks if he or she is to develop a quality questionnaire. The flow chart in Figure 18.2 presents each of the tasks explained here:

▶ Review the information requirements necessitating a questionnaire. In other words, various constructs that form the tool should be listed. In most cases, research questions guide review of information requirements.
▶ Develop and prioritise a list of potential questions that will satisfy the information requirements. This procedure will ensure that no important detail is left out.
▶ Assess each potential question carefully. It is vital to go through the question carefully in order to verify its content.
▶ Determine the types of questions to be asked. Are you going to use qualitative or quantitative research methodologies?
▶ Decide on the specific wording of each question to be asked. Will it be open- or close-ended?
▶ Determine the structure of the questionnaire, e.g. many start with basic demographics, while others prefer to place such details at the end of the questionnaire.
▶ Evaluate the questionnaire. Is it good enough to elicit details from the calibre of your clients? Eventually the questionnaire has to pass evaluation processes that also entail scrutiny by other specialists in the area of study.

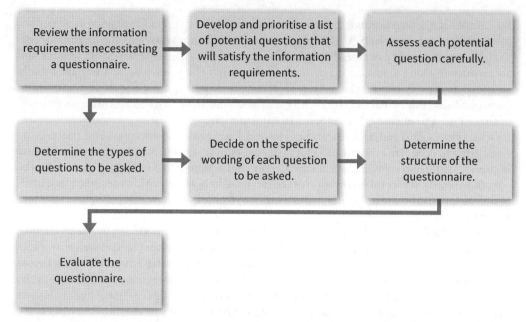

FIGURE 18.2: Tasks to obtain a good questionnaire

(**Source:** Stages adapted from Peterson, 2000:14)

In contrast to Peterson's stages in constructing a questionnaire in Figure 18.2, Swisher (1980), holds the following criteria to be important in constructing a good-quality questionnaire:

▸ Format and layout – it can be a structured or unstructured format.
▸ Question writing – can have vertical or horizontal alignment.
▸ Question sequencing – usually from simple to complex.
▸ Organisation
▸ A cover letter – that introduces the enquiry.

After construction, questionnaires may be administered personally by the researcher, encouraging some rapport and a higher response rate. Other researchers may prefer to administer the questionnaire electronically or by mail. This can be less expensive and much faster if participants have access to internet, and there are no problems of postal delays. Where some participants are unable to access electronic devices, this can result in a low response rate. In such instances, the researcher needs to follow up using available means. The following challenge helps you think about issues on how to assemble a good questionnaire, before we look at specific questionnaire features in 18.5.

Stop and reflect

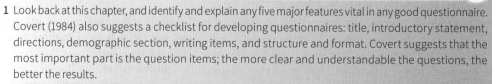

1 Look back at this chapter, and identify and explain any five major features vital in any good questionnaire. Covert (1984) also suggests a checklist for developing questionnaires: title, introductory statement, directions, demographic section, writing items, and structure and format. Covert suggests that the most important part is the question items; the more clear and understandable the questions, the better the results.

2 What would you consider in constructing a good questionnaire?

18.5 Questionnaire structure

The questionnaire has some distinct parts and a particular organisation.

18.5.1 Introduction in a questionnaire

A good questionnaire should contain introductory statements, clear instructions, and a closing statement. The general purpose of the questionnaire is given in the introduction. It is followed by a request for cooperation, information about anonymity, and confidentiality procedures. A cover letter can be added to the questionnaire or a short introduction should also be printed on the questionnaire so that the questionnaire becomes a self-explanatory.

18.5.2 Questionnaire instructions

It is vital that the researcher lists general instructions on how to go through the survey, either in the introduction, or within each section. The participants will want to know how the instrument is to be completed. Depending on the topic being investigated, an appeal for cooperation, a few words to introduce the researcher and his or her affiliation or institution need to be included. It may also be necessary to inform participants about deadlines in order to facilitate achievement of a high of questionnaire response rates.

An example of an introductory statement included on a questionnaire is the following:

Getting started: An introductory statement (e.g.)

My name is............. (provide your name), and I am a student at Blue University. Thank you for taking time to complete this questionnaire. You have been selected to complete the questionnaire as one of the current Course 1 university lecturers. This study is commissioned by the Department of Academic Development at Blue University to determine your experience with academic literacy levels of Course 1 teacher education students at Blue University. Feedback gathered from this survey will help develop intervention programmes for students' academic literacy development. Participation is voluntary and you are free to withdraw at any point. You are also free to choose not to answer questions that you are not comfortable with. This survey is confidential. You will not be individually identified in any information or reports produced from these data. Feedback from the survey will be available to lecturers on completion of the report. If you have any queries about the survey, please send them to me at the following email address ....

The instructions at the beginning of a self-administered questionnaire are necessary as they guide the participants on how to complete it. This is required to facilitate a proper response. For close-ended questions including multiple-choice, yes or no, and rating scales, respondents should be given instructions about answer formats. For instance, the participants need to be told where to place the star (*) or a cross (x) when referring to their correct answer in a closed-question response. For open-ended questions, respondents should be given some guidance as to the length and detail of answers to be provided.

18.5.3 A closing statement

A closing statement on a questionnaire comes right at the end and it is aimed at thanking participants for completing the questions. A closing statement also serves another purpose: of informing the participant about what to do with the questionnaire once they have completed it. This is important in the case of self-administered questionnaires in which the researcher is not present. The next section explains how to word questions and response options in a questionnaire.

18.6 Wording in questions

The wording of questions and response options in a questionnaire is very important. Asking a question without using the proper wording would yield results that would be of little value to the research being conducted. Kent (1993) provides three conditions to maximise the possibility of obtaining valid responses:

☑ The participants must understand the questions, and understand them in the same way as all other participants.

☑ Participants must be able to provide the answers.

☑ Participants must be willing to provide the information.

Where researchers overlook making questions clear and unambiguous, participants often do not know exactly what the researcher is looking for. Researchers should also avoid asking questions that have multiple parts. This is called a **double-barrelled** question. Use the simplest words possible because respondents may vary in the way they understand the language used. However, it is important to remember that simple words are sometimes vague and ambiguous. Researchers should know that vague questions produce vague answers.

Good questioning frequently begins by posing simpler questions before the more sensitive ones. The simpler ones will eventually lead to answering the more important ones. Difficult questions force participants to struggle to complete the questionnaire. In these cases, the difficult questions are usually left untackled. The aim remains targeting a 100 per cent return rate in the responses given by each participant on the questionnaire. The idea is to aim at having every research question receive adequate feedback. Figure 18.3 attempts to summarise suggestions for asking worthwhile questions in a questionnaire.

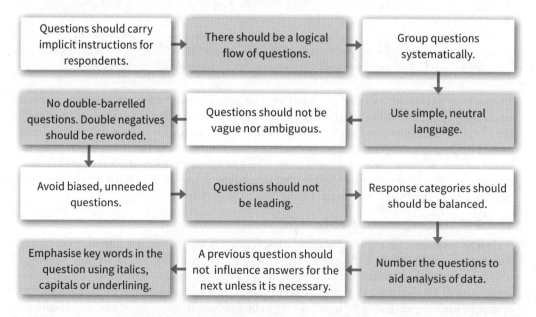

FIGURE 18.3: Characteristics of good questioning

18.6.1 Rating scales

In assessing attitudes, a rating scale is used to yield "a single score that indicates both the direction and intensity of a person's attitude" (Henderson, Morris & Fitz-Gibbon, 1978:84). The scoring method for most rating scales is based on the idea of measuring the intensity, substance, or potency of a variable, where each item must differentiate those respondents with a favourable attitude from those with an unfavourable attitude. The questions items should permit a broad spectrum of feelings, from strongly accepted through neutral to strongly unaccepted.

According to Weisberg, Krosnick and Bowen (1996), if a rating scale is to be used in a questionnaire, three decisions must be made:

☑ **Firstly,** the decision is how many points to include in the scale. It is usually a good idea to construct scales with fewer than seven points, because psychological research indicates that people have difficulty reliably making more than seven distinctions.

☑ **Secondly,** the decision is whether to provide a middle alternative in a scale. It is generally good to include a middle alternative because it represents the best description of some respondents' feelings.

☑ **Thirdly,** the decision is how many points to assign to the labelled words. Verbal labels help to clarify the meanings of scale points for respondents. It is best not to mix labelling words with numbers.

There are three major rating scales that are commonly used in questionnaire development: Thurstone, Likert, and semantic differential. We will discuss each rating scale type as it is used in a questionnaire format.

18.6.1.1 Thurstone scale

Created by Louis Thurstone, a psychologist who pioneered psychometrics in the US, the Thurstone scale is intended to develop a format for generating groups of indicators of a variable that have an empirical structure among them. The Thurstone technique begins with a set of belief statements about an issue, e.g. you want to rank the reasons for studying at a certain university. You would then put together a list of items (about 10 items) and ask participants to assign scores between 1 to 11 to each item. By assigning scores, they are ranking the items in order of which is the weakest indicator, through to which is the strongest indicator, as illustrated in the following example:

Using a ranking scale

I am studying for this qualification at this particular institution because of: [Rate the reasons provided below in terms of how much you agree with them, from 1 (agree least) to 11 (agree most).]

The overall reputation of the institution		The location of the institution	
The institution's reputation in my chosen subject area		It is the only institution offering this programme	
Family members have studied at this institution before		Funding was available to me to study at this particular institution	
It was recommended to me by my teachers		My financial sponsor advised or encouraged me to enrol here	
The cost of the programme compared with other institutions		Graduates from this institution have good career and employment prospects	

Once the respondents have scored the items, the researcher examines the scores assigned to each item by all the respondents, to determine which items the respondents agreed upon the most. The researcher is then able to ascertain the participant's most preferred choice.

18.6.1.2. Likert rating scale

Likert rating scales are the most commonly-used scales in social sciences research. Invented by the psychologist, Rensis Likert, it is an effective tool popularly used in questionnaires because of its easy construction, high reliability and successful adaptation to measure many types of characteristics. On the Likert rating scale, a participant indicates agreement or disagreement with a variety of statements on an intensity scale. The five-point "strongly agree" to "strongly disagree" format is used. Responses are added across the items to generate a score. The Likert scale typically has the following format in a questionnaire:

In relation to your chosen research area, and your supervisor(s):	Strongly agree	Agree	Disagree	Strongly disagree
1 I chose to study at this institution because of its academic and research reputation.	☐	☐	☐	☐
2 The costs of the programmes in this institution are cheaper compared with other institutions.	☐	☐	☐	☐

The Likert scale provides direct and reliable assessment of attitudes when scales are well constructed and they lend themselves well to item analysis procedures.

18.6.1.3. Semantic differential scale

A semantic differential scale provides an indirect measure of how a person feels about a concept, object, or another person. It asks a participant to rate how they feel about a particular idea, concept, or subject, based on a seven-point rating scale. The scale measures subjective feelings about something by using a set of scales anchored at their extreme points by words of opposite meaning (Edwards, Thomas, Rosenfeld & Booth-Kewley, 1997). Participants mark the place on the scale continuum between the adjectives that best express their perceptions, attitudes, feelings, and so on. The results of semantic differential scales can be used to assess respondents' overall perceptions of various concepts or issues. For instance, the example of the semantic differential scale below attempts to find out participant's weighting on the usefulness of their university's academic development programme.

Would you say the university's academic development programme is useful?	7	Very useful
	6	
	5	
	4	
	3	
	2	
	1	Not useful

Before continuing to our next section on questionnaire layout and format, it is vital to note that, unlike other rating scales, the semantic differential scale does not have a neutral or middle selection. A participant must choose one or the other adjective.

18.7 Questionnaire layout or format

The layout or format used in a questionnaire is very important because the face validity determines manner in which it will be accepted by its users. Babbie (2001) points out that the appearance and arrangement of the questionnaire should be clear, neat, and easy to follow. Very often respondents seem to decide whether or not they will participate based on the appearance and the length of questionnaires. A shorter questionnaire stands a better chance of being completed than a longer one. Our observations as researchers have shown that long questionnaires will only be completed if the respondent is involved with or interested in the topics under discussion.

The questionnaire layout is crucial for self-completed and mailed questionnaires because the researcher will not be available to make verbal clarifications to the respondent. Remember, it is the questionnaire's appearance that persuades the respondent to agree to answer. Neuman (2000) suggests that good mailed questionnaires should include:

▶ A polite and professional cover letter on letterhead stationery
▶ Identification of the analyst or evaluator by name, institution, capacity
▶ Telephone or facsimile (fax) numbers for clarification questions
▶ A statement of appreciation for participation.

Read the example of a cover note here.

COVER NOTE FOR THE TEACHER'S QUESTIONNAIRE

Great Zimbabwe University
Faculty of Education
PO Box 1235
Masvingo, Zimbabwe
14 February 2015

Dear Participant

I am…………… (name of student researcher), a student at the above university. I am currently carrying out a study on the 'Effects of counselling on the academic performance of victims of drought in Ngaone homelands'. Would you kindly assist in my research by completing my questionnaire as truthfully as possible. Your cooperation in this matter will enable me to………………………………………………………… (complete the statement).

Participation is voluntary and you may choose to withdraw at any stage of the research process without any penalty. The information you provide will be treated with strict confidentiality and will be used for academic research purposes only. There are no monetary benefits for participation. If you are agreeable to participating in this enquiry, please read and sign the attached consent form before you begin completing the questionnaire.

Thank you.
Yours faithfully

Mr/Mrs/Ms.--- Cell no: +263 ----------------------------

email:-----------------------------

Basically, the format and layout in a questionnaire must be physically and logically consistent. If well sequenced, respondents will find it easy to follow instructions. It is the researcher's duty to make the questionnaire interesting by improving the layout, its design and the sequencing of questions.

Respondents are required to check one response from a series of responses provided. This may be a square or circle next to each response for the respondent to check or fill in, or the respondent might be instructed to circle their response. The selected option or method used should be made clear and displayed prominently next to the question. This enables the respondent to locate the response easily. An incorrectly entered response may cause data to be incorrectly recorded.

In sequencing the questions in a questionnaire, logical questioning should proceed from simple to more complex ones. A good questionnaire could begin with screening questions. These questions establish whether one should complete the questionnaire or not. These should be simple, non-challenging questions to help to capture the interest of the respondents.

Transition questions are meant to establish a smooth flow of ideas. Some questions are called skips. Such questions may be phrased as follows: 'If Yes, then answer questions 6–8'; and 'If No, proceed to answer question 5'. Towards the end of the questionnaire, more difficult questions can be introduced. When the questionnaire has been constructed it is pilot-tested to test its suitability for use.

18.8 The questionnaire pilot test

The researcher should test the questionnaire on a small sample of his or her participants first before the instrument is fully utilised. The pilot study is meant to identify any faults in the questioning. It is easier for others to notice question ambiguity than to allow oneself to validate one's own instrument. Piloting helps the researcher to check on and correct each question prior to administering the final questionnaire. Having done your pilot survey, you can then make amendments that will help to maximise your response rate and minimise errors. This is the most important step in preparing a questionnaire. The pilot test helps to see how clear the researcher's instructions, questions, and the participant's answers are.

A small group of participants must be chosen for this purpose and they should be representative of the group to be surveyed. After explaining the purpose of the pilot test, the participants should be allowed to read and answer the questions without interruption. When they are finished, the researcher can ask them to critique the cover letter, instructions, and each of the questions and answers. The researcher will then finalise the questionnaire taking into consideration the input of pilot participants, thus reducing faults in the instrument.

18.9 Ethical considerations in using a questionnaire

As you work with a questionnaire or other data collection tools, you need to be aware of ethical considerations that safeguard you as the researcher and any other people you involve in your study. Among the ethical considerations are issues of autonomy, justice, beneficence and non-maleficence of human research participants. Throughout this book, there have been many discussions concerning ethical considerations, e.g. Chapters 6 and 7. Most universities and colleges have their own research ethics guidelines, e.g. Unisa's Policy on Research Ethics (2007). These are guidelines for professional conduct or behaviour. We encourage that you read widely on this aspect before you attempt to administer a questionnaire.

Alongside ethical guidelines are vital documents that you will need to familiarise yourself with. These may include consent and assent forms for the participants, without which your questionnaire may not be accepted for use. Below is an example of an incomplete consent form to be used in a study involving both children and adults. Try to complete its blanks in groups or as individuals in order to make it a functional document. We have provided the basic format and components for you. You can use the topic you are researching, or another topic, to construct a meaningful consent form.

INFORMED CONSENT FORM FOR: ------------------------------------- (Adults)

Important: Take your time to study this form carefully before you make a decision to fill it in or not to. I also suggest that you discuss the issue with the child before telling me of your decision. Feel free to ask questions and for clarification from me if something is not be clear as I explain the procedure.

Name of researcher: -------------------------------------

Designation/Position: -----------------------------------

Email: ----------------------------- Mobile cell number: ----------------------------------

Student number and institution: ---

Research topic: --

----

1 Purpose of study

I ask your permission to allow your child -------------------------------------(name of child) to participate in my study by responding to a questionnaire on issues related to the above topic. The study aims to find out how ------------------------------- This is in line with documenting and recommending how best to --

2 Benefits, freedom, discomfort and the right to help

There are neither direct nor financial benefits, but you are assured of safety, autonomy, respect and confidentiality throughout the research process. At the end of my study, I promise to present my findings using only pseudonyms (not your real names) in order to protect your own and your child's identity. Feel free to ask questions and for clarification. If my questioning might inadvertently cause any emotional discomfort, please be assured that my intention is not to cause any harm. I promise to remain supportive and patient with your child at all times.

3 Sampling

I have decided to select ------------------------------- participants for this enquiry knowing that they ------------------------------- Participation remains voluntary, but your positive decision, together with the minor's, is welcome at your convenient time.

---

4 Period of study

The questionnaire administration will run over a period of two weeks, in which I intend to ---------------------------------- The first visit is meant for distributing the questionnaires at each centre, followed by another visit after _____ days to collect completed sheets. Every effort will be made to avoid disturbing school lessons.

5 Sharing the findings

At the end of my study, the children's voices will be heard and the rest of the selected participants will be informed about the findings. I intend to run a workshop in the district. A written report will be sent to the ministries of Education, Sport, Arts and Culture offices for sharing with participants and other interested stakeholders.

6 The right to withdraw participation

Your child has the right to ask questions, not answer any of the questions, or to withdraw without any penalty. Your signature will indicate your understanding of this agreement and granting permission for the minor to participate. A copy of the signed consent form will be returned to you for your future reference. Another copy of the signed form will be retained by the child. You may return the form unsigned if you do not wish to continue.

7 Commitment

I, ---------------------------- being the ----------------------------- (designation) responsible for the general welfare and security of ----------------------------- (name of child) hereby give my consent that the bearer ---------------------------- (your name) goes through her or his research work with my child for as long as the child remains physically, psychologically, emotionally, and socially safe. I have read the foregoing information, have asked for necessary clarifications, and I am satisfied that the child can choose to participate.

Thank you.

Details of Guardian(s)/Person(s) giving consent

Name of Guardian/Person giving consent: -----------------------------------

Relationship to child/Designation: ---------------------------------------

Cellphone/Telephone number --

Witness ------------------------ Signed ------------------------- Date ---------------------

Only non-harmful procedures should be followed in any study, and the least stressful operations implemented especially where vulnerable populations are involved. The researchers' obligation should be to respect the participants' freedom to choose at all times by getting child assent to participation. The term, 'assent' means that the child shows some form of agreement to participate without necessarily comprehending the full significance of the research that is necessary to give informed consent. The assent form also carries the name and signature of the adult (parent/guardian) offering his or her consent. In any research involving human beings, it is vital to safeguard the welfare, dignity and rights of all participants. This remains the primary obligation for the researcher.

18.10 Analysis of questionnaire data

Analysis of questionnaire data involves coding questions and responses and deciding how to aggregate the data for use by the researcher. This can be done successfully by using simple frequency counts for closed-ended questions or using a categorisation of the written answers to open-ended questions. Based upon Kent's (1993) suggestions for qualitative data reduction, open-ended questions can be analysed with the following data processing operations:

▶ Paraphrasing and summarising what respondents have answered
▶ Classifying responses into suitable categories
▶ Converting questionnaire data into quasi-quantitative data
▶ Undertaking content analysis.

For open-ended questionnaires, Tesch's qualitative model of data analysis that groups findings into themes and sub-categories (Tesch, 1990, in Ganga, 2013) can be used to analyse qualitative data. The model is a systematic process of examining, selecting, categorising, comparing, synthesising and interpreting data. It addresses the initial sub-problems or research questions. Data from an open-ended questionnaire are mostly verbal.

Data that are obtained from the questionnaire are presented in the form of tables, graphs or histograms using statistical analysis. Both descriptive and inferential statistics can be employed in the analysis of questionnaire data. Statistics are useful for describing the results of measuring single variables, or for constructing and evaluating multi-item scales. The statistics include frequency distributions, graphs, and measures of central tendency and variation, and other reliability tests.

Other statistics are used to describe the association among variables and to control other variables. For instance, cross-tabulation is one simple technique for measuring association and controlling other variables. All these statistics are termed descriptive statistics, because they describe the distribution of and relationship among variables. Please refer to Chapter 22 for further information.

Statisticians can also use inferential statistics to estimate the degree of confidence that can be placed in generalisations from a sample to the population from which the sample was selected. Again, we refer you to Chapter 23 for more detail on inferential statistics.

Conclusion

The content of this chapter is not exhaustive; the authors have instead tried to unearth some aspects of the questionnaire that may be useful in research work. Questionnaires may be used successfully if properly triangulated with other data collection methods discussed in this text. To round off this chapter, we suggest that you take another look at your learning objectives and see if you have accomplished them.

Tackle the activities that follow with the help of this chapter, other chapters in the book, and any other relevant sources. We hope that this chapter has helped to widen your scope and understanding of the questionnaire instrument in research. As a student working under the supervision of a tutor, you will find the questionnaire one of the most exciting and useful methods as you plan to collect research data. Many researchers in and outside South Africa prefer the use of a questionnaire because it entails minimal problems when it is properly constructed and utilised. Skilful questionnaire design carries some important advantages for students too.

The chapter has comprehensively looked at the different types of questions, questionnaires, questionnaire construction, its administration, strengths, weaknesses and analysis of questionnaire data. Try all the questions and activities in the following section to consolidate your understanding of this important research tool.

Closing activities

1 Imagine you are carrying out a research study on: The effects of drug abuse on the academic performance of teenagers in Limpopo Province; or your own choice of a topic. Attempt the following questions based on good questioning formats.

   a Construct any two simple and neutral questions that you can use with teenage participants.

   b How would you guard against double-barrelled questions?

   c State any two questions that you consider leading. How would you modify them?

   d Discuss examples of unbiased, balanced questions for use in a questionnaire.

   e Why would it be advisable to consider each of the following in designing a questionnaire:

   ▶ Costs of production?

   ▶ Questionnaire administration?

   ▶ Method of analysis?

2 In groups, discuss some of the pros and cons of the questionnaires you have constructed. How would you endeavour to counter each of the questionnaire's limitations?

   a Explain the uses of closed, open, and contingency questions.

   b Formulate five closed and open-ended questions related to a particular research question, aim or a research topic.

3 Below are some badly formulated questions. Identify and list the main errors, and then redraft each question to address these errors and explain the changes that you have made.

   Question 1 You say that you are not in favour of school on Saturday morning.
   Question 2 Do you approve of your school's unreasonable cellphone policy?
   Question 3 What is your current age?
   ▶ 10 or less
   ▶ 10 to 20
   ▶ 20 to 30
   ▶ 30 or greater.

   Question 4 When was the last time you attended quality assurance and staff development workshops?

4 Select an individual/group research topic where a questionnaire could be one of the best data collection tools. Craft two or three research questions or state a hypothesis. Try and construct a 10-item questionnaire appropriate for use in the research. Explain how you would administer it.

   a Practise pilot testing the 10-item questionnaire on fellow students.

   b Justify the inclusion of each type of question in the questionnaire.

   c How would you prefer to analyse the collected research data, and why?

Bibliography

Babbie, E.R. 2011. *The Basics of Social Research* (5th ed.). Belmont, CA: Wadsworth.

Babbie, E.R. 2012. *The Practice of Social Research* (13th ed.). Belmont: Wadsworth/Cengage Learning.

Barnes, S. 2001. *Questionnaire Design and Construction*, Institute for Learning and Research Technology, University of Bristol http://www.survey.bris.ac.uk/support/wp-content/uploads/2011/02/question_design.pdf.

Chavan, S.K. 2010. Steps in Questionnaire Construction, Annasaheb Vartak College, Mumbai, India http://www.managementparadise.com/forums/marketing-research/202422-steps-questionnaire-construction.html.

Cohen, L., Manion, L. & Morrison, K. 2011. *How to do a Research Project: A Guide for Undergraduate Students* (7th ed.). London: Routledge.

Covert, R. W. 1984. A checklist for developing questionnaires. *Evaluation News*, 5(3):74–78.

Creswell, J.W. 2002, 2009. *Research Design; Qualitative and Quantitative Approaches:* London: Sage.

Denscombe, M. 2007. *The Good Research Guide for Small Scale Social Research Projects* (3rd ed.). Berkshire: McGraw Hill

Desai, V. & Potter, R.B. 2010. *Doing Developmental Research* (3rd ed.). New Delhi: Vistaar Publications (SAGE).

Dillman, D. 2000. *Constructing the questionnaire: Mail and internet surveys.* New York: John Wiley & Sons.

Edwards, J. E., Thomas, M. D., Rosenfeld, P., & Booth-Kewley, S. 1997. *How to conduct organizational surveys: A step-by-step guide.* Thousand Oaks, CA: Sage.

Fraenkel, J.R. & Wallen, N.E. 2010. *How to design and evaluate research in education.* New York, MacGraw-Hill.

Ganga, B.S. & Motswalakgoro, T.J. 2013. *Psychological Capital and Work Engagement: A Cross-cultural Study* (unpublished BA Hons treatise in Industrial and Organisational Psychology) Port Elizabeth: Nelson Mandela Metropolitan University.

Ganga, E. 2013. *The Effects of Double Orphanhood on the Learning and Cognition of Children in Child-Headed Households* (DEd thesis) University of South Africa, available @ *umkn-dsp01.unisa.ac.za/bitstream/handle/10500/.../thesis_ganga_e.pdf?*

Gilbert, N. 2011. *Researching Social Life* (3rd ed.) London: Sage.

Henderson, M., Morris, L., Fitz-Gibbon, C. 1987. *How to measure attitudes.* London: Sage.

Kent, R.A. 1993. *Marketing research in action.* London: Routledge.

Maphalala, M.C. 2006. Educator's Experiences in Implementing the Revised National Curriculum Statement in the GET Band. PhD thesis. University of Zululand: KwaZulu-Natal.

Martin, E. 2006. Survey Questionnaire Construction, Research Report Series (13), US Census Bureau, Washington DC. http://www.census.gov/srd/papers/pdf/rsm2006-13.pdf.

McMillan, J. & Schumacher, S. 2001. *Research in Education: A Conceptual Introduction.* New York: Harper Collins College.

Nachmias, C. & Nachmias, D. 2008. *Research Methods in Social Sciences.* New York: Worth.

Neuman, W.L. 2000. *Social research methods: Qualitative and quantitative approaches* (4th ed.). Boston: Allyn & Bacon.

Peterson, R.A. 2000. *Constructing Effective Questionnaires.* Thousand Oaks, CA: SAGE Publications.

Sheatsley, P.B. 1983. Questionnaire construction and item writing. In P.H. Rossi, J.D. Wright & A.B. Anderson (Eds). *Handbook of survey research.* San Diego: Academic (pp. 195–230).

Sidhu, K.S. 2003. *Methodology of Research in Education.* New Delhi: Sterling Publishers Ltd.

Swisher, R. 1980. Criteria for the design of mail questionnaires. *Journal of Education for Librarianship*, 21(2):159–165.

Unisa. 2007. *Policy on Research Ethics.* Pretoria: Unisa.

Weisberg, H.F., Krosnick, J.A. & Bowen, B.D. 1996. *An introduction to survey research, polling, and data analysis.* Thousand Oaks, CA: Sage.

Yin, R.K. (Ed). 2003. *Case Study Research, Design and Methods.* New Delhi: SAGE.

CHAPTER 19

Mishack Gumbo and Mncendisi Maphalala

The focus group discussion method

KEY CONCEPTS

Focus group is a data gathering method in which a group of participants is involved in a discussion where the researcher moderates the discussion.

Moderator of a focus group is, in most cases, the researcher himself or herself, who facilitates the focus group discussion for purposes of data gathering.

Qualitative research is predominantly exploratory research. It can be used to create an understanding about the problem under investigation as the research gathers data from participants in a social setting through their opinions, reasons and motivations. Qualitative research can also facilitate the development of ideas or hypotheses for potential quantitative research.

Method is a certain kind of procedure to accomplish or approach a study. Methods can either be established or systematic ones used. Specific to research, research method refers to the process of gathering data for purposes of answering the research question(s).

Sample size refers to the representative number of a target population, which is intended to participate in the study, for purposes of data gathering.

LEARNING OUTCOMES

By the end of this chapter, you should be able to:

▸ Define the focus group in your own words.

▸ Differentiate between types of focus groups.

▸ Know when and why you can use the focus group.

▸ Understand the strengths and weaknesses of focus group discussion.

▸ Understand and motivate an ideal sample size for the focus group.

▸ Plan and implement the focus group discussion method.

▸ Understand the knowledge and skills that you should have in order to implement the focus group.

▸ Understand the possible impact of culture on the focus group.

▸ Understand the strategies of focus group data analysis.

▸ Deliberate on the ethics around the focus group method.

Case study: Investigating college students' views

The researchers in this study investigated students' views on vocational education and training in three schools and three TVET colleges in South Africa. The researchers sampled six focus groups of 10 students each, totalling 60 students. These students were supposed to be spread across three provinces, with a gender balance among the participants. The focus groups covered the spread of institutional types, i.e. three schools and three colleges, one of each per province, across rural and urban, high, medium and poor performing institutions. The study was on four vocational areas of hospitality, construction, hairdressing and IT/business and enterprise skills.

Owing to limited timeframes, colleges were selected on the basis of institutional types using departmental college campus lists. Schools were selected on the basis of their proximity to the selected colleges as potential feeder schools to these colleges, as well as according to their academic performance.

The researchers contacted colleges during April 2010, sending a letter that stipulated the desired profile of focus groups in terms of age, programme of study, and gender, along with consent forms for under-age learners. Owing to time and distance constraints, a more rigorous sampling frame was not obtainable from the institutions against which students could be selected randomly. Therefore, the researchers asked the contact persons at college campuses and schools to select the students.

There were some problems with the composition and size of focus groups. Contact people tended to select students on the basis of the students' availability, which was in turn, limited by the programmes on offer at the schools and colleges at the time of the investigation. Thus, the researchers did not achieve their initial plan in terms of the sample size. Table 19.1 provides the breakdown of the sample by institutional type, province and gender.

TABLE 19.1 Composition of focus group

Province	School			College		
	Male	Female	Total	Male	Female	Total
Eastern Cape (poorly performing, rural)	6	4	10	6	3	9
KwaZulu-Natal (mixed, medium performing)	2	8	10	5	3	8
Western Cape (high performing, urban)	2	10	12	2	7	9
Total	10	22	**32**	13	13	**26**
Total interviewed: 58						

(**Source:** Adapted from Needham and Papier, 2011:18)

Keep in mind this opening case study because you will refer to it again later in this chapter.

Introduction

Chapter 18 developed your understanding of the questionnaire approach. Chapter 19 is about the focus group discussion method. The focus group method has assumed a very important role over the past few years as an effective way of collecting qualitative data. This chapter introduces this method to you and provides you with important information that will help in your choice and execution of the focus group discussion method.

This chapter discusses when can you use focus group, the strengths and limitations of the focus group method, types of focus groups that you can choose from, ideal size for focus groups, planning and implementing the focus group method, skills, knowledge and roles that you will require and use for focus group, data analysis and interpretation in focus group, the impact of culture on focus groups, and ethics in focus group use.

19.1 Focus group discussion defined

Focus groups were first used as a market research technique in the 1920s. Sociologists used focus groups in marketing and election campaigns to bring together small groups of unrelated individuals to discuss a new product, or a political candidate. By conducting focus group discussions researchers sought to understand the motivation of the participants in choosing a particular product over the other or preferring a particular political candidate over the other. Focus groups were at that stage called focused interview. Since then, researchers working in different fields use focus groups intensively.

Focus group is a form of qualitative research method in which you can ask a group of people about their perceptions, opinions, beliefs and attitudes towards a product, a service, concept, advertisement, idea, packaging, and so on. You should not confuse focus group with focus interview. Focus group relies on the interaction within the group, based on topics that the researcher supplies. The main difference between these types of interviews is that in a group interview the focus is on researcher–participant interaction, whereas in focus group participants interact with each other, with the researcher monitoring and directing the discussion.

Try out the questions in activity now.

Stop and reflect

Reflect on the definition of focus group discussion. What have you learned so far? When and in which areas were focus groups first used? How can you define focus group? How can you differentiate between focus group and group interview?

19.2 When and why to use focus group discussion

Researchers use focus groups in qualitative research for a variety of purposes, such as the following:

▶ **Market research**: Focus groups are an economical way of gathering a relatively large amount of qualitative data from multiple human subjects. In what ways do you think the use of focus group by the researchers in the opening case study was economical? Companies often employ market researchers to conduct focus group interviews with consumer target groups. The purpose is to gather these groups' feelings, thoughts and attitudes about a particular product in order to increase the marketability of their products. Three purposes for which researchers can use focus groups in this field include clinical, exploratory and phenomenological:

  › *Clinical purposes*: focus groups uncover consumers' underlying feelings, attitudes, beliefs, opinions, and the subconscious causes of certain behaviour.
  › *Exploratory purposes*: focus groups help generate, develop and screen ideas and concepts.
  › *Phenomenological purposes*: focus groups help discover consumers' shared everyday life experiences, such as their thoughts, feelings and behaviour.

▶ **Evaluation research**: You can use focus groups to evaluate a particular programme, e.g. an educational programme to help measure its success, strengths and weaknesses.

▶ **Development of content for a new programme**: You can use a focus group to interview a target group for which you want to offer a new programme.

▶ **Evaluation of issues and programmes within the criminal justice system**: You can use a focus group to gain insight into community policing programme.

▶ **Collection of data from people traditionally referred to as difficult**: You can use a focus group to gather data from people who may feel unsafe, disenfranchised or are otherwise reluctant to participate in research, e.g. AIDS patients, welfare recipients, drug users and prisoners.

▶ **Medical sociology**: You can use a focus group to access stigmatised populations about topics like fertility, grief, depression and cancer.

▶ **Access to experiences and attitudes of marginalised groups**: Marginalised groups can include radical or ethnic groups, sexual minorities, women, children, the mentally and physically challenged groups. Focus groups serve as safer places for these people to share their experiences and perspectives. Consider the following scenario about researching internet dating (adapted from Hesse-Biber & Leavy, 2011:164)

Stop and reflect

A researcher is interested in internet dating among a population of individuals who are around 30 years old. The researcher wants answers to the following questions for which he or she is considering a focus group:

▶ Why do people turn to internet dating?

▶ In what ways are internet first dates qualitatively different from non-internet first dates?

How would this researcher select a focus group?

Think about what you have learned in section 19.2 and answer the questions in the Critical thinking challenge that follows.

Critical thinking challenge

Think about a research problem that you can investigate using the focus group discussion method. Which purpose does the problem you have identified suit? State your own purpose if the problem you have identified does not fall in any of those given in section 19.2. State the problem and the questions you will ask.

Let us now focus on the strengths and weaknesses of focus groups.

19.3 Strengths and weaknesses of focus group discussion

As with all research methods, there are certain strengths and weaknesses that you should bear in mind.

19.3.1 Strengths of focus groups

Focus groups have the following strengths:

▶ Focus groups are an economical, fast, and efficient method for obtaining data. You can conveniently use focus groups to gather data from multiple participants, thereby increasing the overall number of participants in a qualitative study.

▶ Interaction between participants is the crucial feature of focus groups in the sense that:
  ⟩ Participants' interaction highlights their view of the world, the language that they use about an issue, and their values and beliefs about a situation;
  ⟩ Participants' interaction enables them to ask one another questions;
  ⟩ Participants' interaction enables them to re-evaluate and reconsider their own understandings of specific experiences;
  ⟩ Interactions that occur among the participants can yield important data, can create the possibility for more spontaneous responses, and can provide a setting where participants can discuss personal problems and offer possible solutions.

▶ Focus groups elicit information in a way that allows you to find out why an issue is salient and what is salient about it. As a result, as a researcher, you can understand the gap between what people say and what they do.

▶ In a focus group, if participants reveal multiple understandings and meanings, you are able to offer multiple explanations for their behaviour and attitudes.

▶ Focus groups give participants the opportunity to take part in decision-making processes. You can give them a chance to work collaboratively with you, and this can empower them.

▶ If a group works well, trust develops and the group may explore solutions to a particular problem as a unit, rather than as individuals. Thus, belonging to a group can increase participants' sense of cohesiveness and help them to feel safe in sharing information.

▶ Participants can become a forum for change, both during the focus group meeting, and afterwards.

▶ Respondents can answer and build on one another's responses and therefore improve the richness of data being gathered.

▶ Focus groups provide information from people who can reveal insights about actual conditions and situations;

▶ Focus groups provide flexibility, high face validity and relatively low cost and quick results (compare with Chapter 12 on measuring qualitative validity, reliability and generalisability);

▶ A researcher can gain greater insight into why certain opinions are held by focus group members.

▶ Focus groups provide information directly from individuals who are interested in the issue or who hold expert knowledge on a topic about which researchers know little.

▶ Focus groups provide a representation of diverse opinions and ideas.

▶ Focus groups provide a relatively low cost and efficient way to generate a great deal of information;

▶ In focus groups, the environment is socially oriented which is necessary for qualatative research.

19.3.2 Weaknesses of focus groups

Although focus group research has many advantages, it also has certain weaknesses, which include the following:

▶ As a moderator, you have less control over the data produced than in either quantitative studies or one-to-one interviewing. You need to allow participants to talk to one another, ask questions and express doubts and opinions, while you have very little control over the interaction other than generally keeping participants focused on the topic.

- By its nature, focus group research is open-ended and cannot be entirely predetermined.
- Context and culture influence individual participants in such a way that they express collective views rather than individual views. You may not always find it easy to distinguish an individual's view from the group's views.
- You may find it difficult to convene focus groups because of not being able to find a representative sample.
- Owing to the dynamism of focus group, members may discourage certain individuals from participating, particularly the unconfident, reserved ones, or even those who experience communication problems, or who have special needs.
- Some participants may not feel free to express sensitive or personal information in a group context. These individuals prefer personal interviews.
- The survey results may not fully represent the opinion of the larger target population, which makes it difficult to generalise results to larger populations.
- Focus groups are susceptible to facilitator bias, which can undermine the validity and reliability of findings.
- A few vocal individuals can side-track or dominate the discussions.
- Participants may abandon their original views in search of consensus within the group.

The strengths can serve as a motivation for your choice of focus groups in your study, but you should also think about how you will address the weaknesses of focus groups.

Now try the questions in the next challenge.

Critical thinking challenge

What have you learned this far in section 19.3? Mention and briefly explain the strong points about focus group. Do the same with weaknesses of the focus group. Revisit the opening case study and identify and motivate the strengths and weaknesses that the researchers might have encountered. For the research problem that you stated in section 19.2, what role do you think the strengths of focus group discussion will play? Identify weaknesses that can specifically impact on your focus group discussion. How do you plan to address these weaknesses?

The next section focuses on the types of focus groups.

19.4 Types of focus group discussion

Different focus groups serve different purposes, such as in the following instances:

19.4.1 Moderator-dependent focus groups

All types of focus groups in this section depend on a moderator. But the role is very clear in a moderator-dependent focus group. In this type of focus group the moderator organises the group and the interaction among the participants, and asks the group questions and facilitates the discussion.

19.4.2 Two-way focus groups

A two-way focus group involves two focus groups which allow one focus group to watch and listen to another focus group, and then discuss the observations made. By hearing what another group thinks, this listening focus group opens up more discussions and may lead the second group to different conclusions than those it has reached without hearing another group's opinions.

19.4.3 Dual moderator focus groups

In a dual moderator focus group, the moderator makes sure that the session progresses smoothly, while a co-moderator takes care of covering all topics and ensures that relevant developments in the discussion are explored further. Discussions with only one moderator can sometimes draw the focus away from the main point; two moderators can ensure a more productive session.

19.4.4 Duelling moderator focus groups

Duelling moderator focus groups use two moderators who play devil's advocate with each other. The two moderators take opposite positions in a discussion. Because one purpose of focus groups is to shed light on new ways of thinking, a contrary viewpoint added to the mix often facilitates new ideas.

19.4.5 Client participant focus groups

Client participant focus groups involve the client who directs the focus group while he or she is also part of the focus group, either in secret or openly. This focus group gives clients more control over the discussion. If there are specific areas that the client wants covered, for example, he can lead the discussion where he wants it to go. Client participant focus groups provide the opportunity for one or more client representatives to participate in the discussion, either covertly or overtly.

19.4.6 Respondent moderator focus groups

In a respondent moderator focus group, one of the participants takes on the temporary role of the moderator. This type of focus group is ideal because the person asking the questions often influences participants' answers. Therefore, different people take on the moderator's role to increase the chances of varied, more honest responses.

19.4.7 Mini focus groups

Mini focus groups involve a number of between four or five participants compared to a regular size focus group that may have six to 12 participants. Depending on the client and subject matter, you may prefer the more intimate approach in this type of focus group because the number of participants is small and therefore more manageable.

19.4.8 Online focus groups

Technological advances have now made it possible to link participants electronically. Participants share images, data and their responses on their computer, tablet or smartphone screens. Conducting this type of focus group saves you travelling time and costs. Chat-based focus groups, and webcam and audio-based focus groups are examples of online focus groups. To conduct the online focus groups effectively, you should ensure that participants have access to the internet, a webcam and earphones, and resources such as computer and internet search capacity.

19.4.9 Teleconference focus groups

You can conduct teleconference focus groups on a telephone network. A conference call hook-up makes it possible for you to conduct a focus group discussion with people in several different places, at the same time. This focus group has the potential to increase participation of those selected. The advantage of a teleconference focus group is that it suits busy people who you may find it difficult to get together in one place at one time. However, this type of focus group will make you lose out on non-verbal cues of participants.

19.4.10 Piggyback focus groups

Piggyback focus groups are useful when participants have gathered for a purpose other than for a focus group, for example during their free time, meals or after work. The aim is not to interrupt the primary purpose of the participants' gathering. However, you can target the participants' meeting arrangement to do focus group work. This strategy works well with professional associations or interest groups. For example, if you want to conduct focus groups with the school principals in a particular region, find out when the principals get together for regional meetings and arrange to conduct focus groups while the principals are already assembled.

You should consider aspects of your study like research questions to decide on the type of a focus group. Resources are the other important aspect that can help you decide on the type of a focus group. For example, if you want to use an online focus group, you should ensure that each of the recruited participants has access to a computer and internet facilities, and that he or she will be available on the date of the online discussion.

Critical thinking challenge

In section 19.4 you learned about the types of focus groups. Without referring back to section 19.4, write down and explain these types of focus groups. What aspects will determine your choice of the type of focus group to use? What type of focus group did the researchers in the opening case study use? What type of focus group did you choose for the research questions that you generated in the Critical thinking challenge in section 19.2? Motivate your answer.

To these types of focus group you should also add thinking about the sample size that you will recruit.

19.5 An ideal sample size for a focus group

You should consider reading this section concurrently with Chapter 13 on sampling. The research question and research design guide your assembly of a focus group, including the sample size and number of groups. For example, in a single qualitative case study, you may want to consider multiple focus groups because you really want to gather as much of the data surrounding the case under investigation as you can. However, research literature presents different opinions about the sample size. The nature of an individual researcher's study determines the sample size. A sample size of between six and 12 participants can provide sufficient diversity for the information required, and is an acceptable and manageable size. A focus group with more than 10 participants may be difficult to control for an inexperienced moderator, and it limits each person's opportunity to share insights and observations. In contrast, participants in a smaller group may feel too uncomfortable to talk. Yet another opinion states that in most studies the number of participants in focus groups range between eight and 16, but you could still consider smaller and higher numbers depending on the purpose, circumstances, resources, and research timeframes. In the end, the nature and scope of your study should determine your needs in terms of sample size, or even the number and composition of focus groups. But, most importantly, your decision should be the outcome of a discussion between you and your research supervisor.

A common thinking about the focus group is that homogeneity should guide the sampling of the group, i.e. to a greater extent, the group members should exhibit common characteristics, such as, they work at the same institution, they come from the same region, they are of the same employment rank, they belong to the same age category, and so on. The group can also be heterogeneous in order to enhance the element of diversity in the data collected, so as to enable good triangulation in the analysis and thus enhancement of the validity of the study. In most cases, the focus group is a naturally occurring entity, such as a group that works in the same institution. Another important rationale is staying with a reasonable sample for practical reasons, i.e. to allow effective manageability of the group.

In deciding about the sample size you should consider possible withdrawal of participants from your study. Therefore, you should consider pushing your sample to at least 10 or 12. If some participants decide to withdraw from the discussion, you will most probably still be left with a reasonable number, say eight or seven. Too small a sample can give you the problem of being left with one or no participants. In the school environment, for example, you may be confronted by withdrawal of teachers who you have chosen for your sample due to their redeployment, extended leave based on personal circumstances, changing of subjects or grades within the same school, and so on. Facing issues like this will frustrate you if you have not already thought out their impact on your sample. Also, if you did not plan your questions well, this may discourage the group from participating. You should, however, note that in a single case study you may also sample only one participant from whom you will extract the data that you intend getting. This single participant can be your most important data source. The effort that you make in creating a rapport with this participant will ensure being able to spend extended hours with him or her.

Multiple focus groups can also determine the sample size, which allows you to assess the extent to which saturation has been reached, whether data saturation, i.e. when information occurs so repeatedly that you can anticipate it, and the collection of more data appears to have no additional interpretive worth; or theoretical saturation, i.e. when you can assume that your emergent theory is adequately developed to fit any future data you collect. Multiple focus groups play a very important role in determining saturation, in covering more data on the investigated phenomenon, and in increasing the validity of the study.

Critical thinking challenge

After reading section 19.5, you should now have an idea about an ideal size of sample for the focus group and what factors might influence your sample size. Have you thought about the size of the focus group for your identified research problem and questions in the Critical thinking challenge in 19.2? What was the sample size of each of the six focus groups used in the opening case study? What were the constraints that the researchers faced? How could the researchers have planned for the constraints that they faced? How big is your sample and why? Is there a need to review the sample size after you read section 19.5? Explain your review to your colleague or supervisor. If you were to consider multiple focus groups, estimate the size of each group and indicate how many groups there will be.

Now that you have learned about the issues surrounding the sample of a focus group, let us look at planning and implementing the focus group.

19.6 Planning and implementing the focus group

It is very important to do careful planning before implementing the focus group. Let us now look at what steps to take in planning the focus group.

19.6.1 Pre-focus group discussion

In planning the focus group, a pre-focus group discussion is very important. The issues that should be addressed at this pre-focus group discussion are explored now.

19.6.1.1 Reading and thinking about the research questions

It is always advisable to first read up on the focus group and its use before any attempt to use it. By the time you use focus groups you should have developed your methodology chapter, which includes the methodology literature sources that you have accessed to substantiate your decisions and choices about the focus group. You should also have designed your data gathering instruments.

Prepare the questions that you intend asking during the focus group. These questions should be about crucial information that you intend getting from the participants as far as the focus of your study is concerned. The main research question and research design ultimately guide how you will construct the focus group. The questions should preferably be semi-structured questions, which will provide you with a list and prepare you to ask each of the questions on the list. Most important is to be prepared to ask follow-up or prompting questions. Experienced researchers can actually use themes instead of asking the actual questions to help stimulate the discussion. Since you are not that experienced as yet, you should stick to the list of your planned questions.

19.6.1.2 Preparing resources

Your planning for the focus group should include putting in place the resources you will need. You should have thought well in advance about the cost of conducting the focus group and made funds available for it. If you decide to be the moderator or facilitator, the main human resource you need is a note taker. Another obvious resource that you need is a recording device to use with the consent of the participants. You may wonder why you need a note taker when you will be using a recorder. This is because you do not want to rely wholly on recording technology. You need a note taker to capture certain logistics that cannot be captured in a recording, e.g. the seating arrangement and assigning voices to the participants for analysis purposes. So, as you plan for your focus group, think about all the resources that you will need and assemble them appropriately.

19.6.1.3 Practising introduction and questions

Reflect on and practise your introduction and the questions you are going to ask the participants. You should impress upon the focus group to remain interested in staying with you in the discussion. As part of your introduction, you should plan to restate the purpose of your study even if you might have stated it during the recruitment of participants. Practice also helps you deal with issues of anxiety and confidence prior to the discussion session.

19.6.1.4 Planning to arrive early

You should arrive at the venue at least an hour before the session starts depending on whether you have made all the necessary arrangements. If arrangements have not yet been made you should then consider an earlier arrival time. It is crucial to realise that if you fail your participants on the time aspect you may end up with no one in the venue. If your participants are working they do not have the time to wait for your late arrival. Even if they are not working, it is always better to keep to the agreed arrangements.

19.6.1.5 Assembling the required equipment

Equipment that has not been assembled in advance due to security reasons can be assembled when you arrive at the venue of the focus group session. As part of assembling the equipment and/or resources, you should pretest them in order to ensure their proper functioning.

19.6.1.6 Making the environment conducive for focus group discussion

You should take extra care to create a safe environment in which participants can express genuine disagreement. Make an effort for sessions to be relaxed, e.g. the seating arrangements in a conducive room should be in a circle so that participants can comfortably face and see one another to enhance interaction. The participants should be able to talk to one another, not to the researcher. A conference-style room is ideal for the focus group. A neutral place is essential to avoid positive or negative associations with the site or building. For example, instead of interviewing teachers in their schools, you should rather choose a neutral place such as a community centre or building where they usually hold their meetings away from the school. A relaxed environment can promote openness and the willingness of the participants to talk.

19.6.2 During the focus group discussion

After careful planning of your focus group, the next steps are implementing the various stages of the focus group discussion.

19.6.2.1 Welcoming the group

Now that you have practised how you are going to approach the introduction and welcoming, you should warmly welcome the group. Agree with the focus group members at this stage whether they consent to the use of a recording device.

19.6.2.2 Setting ground rules and norms

Be careful when you introduce ground rules not to be too instructive, which may close down the focus group from the beginning. The ground rules should include an announcement about how you have planned the discussion to go. You can negotiate with the focus group members the use of cellphones, breaks, and so on, and how you will handle the agreed-upon way forward. You can actually ask for the switching off and putting out of view of cellphones by turning off yours and that of the note taker first, to prevent any disturbance once the discussion has started.

19.6.2.3 Addressing ethical issues and confidentiality

Explain the purpose of the focus group discussion to the participants. Explain the objectives of your research and state the risks and benefits to the participants and the community. Avoid creating false expectations in getting participants' cooperation. Assure the participants of their confidentiality, i.e. that you will not use the participants' actual names. You should ask the participants not to disclose, outside of the discussion, the name of a fellow participant nor talk about what he or she has said. It is vital that you obtain the participants' informed consent. Since this is a group, or even a few groups, you have the options of a written informed consent or to record the process of informed consent. Written informed concern is ideal for purposes of having a document if it is required by any stakeholder that you are accountable to.

19.6.2.4 Presenting questions one by one (including prompting)

You may want to start with a general comment to get the discussion going, and wait for responses from the participants. Your general comment may not necessarily be about yielding the required information, e.g. "Curriculum implementation can be a complex issue". Then, invite a wide range of commentary by asking participants for their experiences, thoughts and definitions as you take advantage to prompt in the process. Some examples of prompting may include: "Please tell me more about that"; "Could you explain what you mean by …"; and "Can you tell me something else about …". Use the silence or neutrality technique to allow participants to think about the questions you ask and to clarify any information that they can provide. One way of using the silence technique is to refrain from nodding your head, raising eyebrows, agreeing, disagreeing, praising or refuting any comment that the participants make. Limit your participation once the discussion starts, ask the question and let the participants react to it without you having to provide direction. Do not play the counsellor's or educator's role by providing commentary on every contribution. You can remain neutral by asking open-ended questions and avoiding leading questions.

Adopt the active listening strategy because it will help you in maintaining the interest of the participants. Active listening involves maintaining your lively posture, focusing your eyes on the participant making a comment at that point, noting what participants are saying so that you do not forget your prompting points and aspects, and so on. Restrain yourself from dominating the focus group discussion. As you move from one question to another, and at the end of the discussion, synthesise what the participants have said.

Note that the opinion of every member of the group is important. Make it your responsibility to encourage all the focus group members to participate actively in the discussion, including the reluctant members. You should also be prepared to ensure that one individual does not dominate the focus group discussion session.

At the end of the discussion, thank the group for participating in the discussion.

Then there needs to be a debriefing session at the end. The purposes of debriefing include the following:

- ☑ To record any additional information that the participants in the debriefing may provide. An audiotape cannot capture nonverbal communication such as gestures, facial expressions, eye contact, tension, which help to illuminate the findings.
- ☑ You can take advantage of debriefing to clarify issues that could confuse the focus group.
- ☑ To address questions that did not work well and clarify the reasons why they did.
- ☑ To capture any information that confirms or disconfirms data collected in sessions conducted already.
- ☑ To provide a space to discuss new topics that the focus group suggests.
- ☑ To identify gaps in the gathered information so that you can fill these gaps in the subsequent focus groups.
- ☑ To note the information such as cultural norms, fact checking or specifics about your study, that you should consider researching outside the focus group setting.
- ☑ You can also take advantage of debriefing to discuss areas of concern like group dynamics and questions that surfaced during the focus group.
- ☑ As a moderator, you and your note taker, have an opportunity to give each other constructive feedback.

Critical thinking challenge

In order to develop the kind of plan you envisage, you need knowledge and skills for conducting focus groups.

19.7 Required knowledge, skills and role of moderators in focus groups

It is important for the focus group to have a moderating team. Some reasons for a skilled moderator include:

▶ One or two people may dominate the discussion, so you should control that skilfully.
▶ When the entire group is silent, you should exercise your expertise on how to proceed with the discussion.
▶ When one or more people start to ask you questions, you should know how to respond. There may be a need to collect data from a number of focus groups and systematically deal with this bulk of data during the analysis.

Moderators or facilitators need to be competent because they have to face numerous tasks and manage different behavioural patterns. Moderators need to possess good interpersonal skills and personal qualities, be good listeners, stay non-judgmental and, above all, be adaptable.

The moderating team comprises the moderator or facilitator, and the assistant moderator or note taker. The tasks of moderators or facilitators are to:

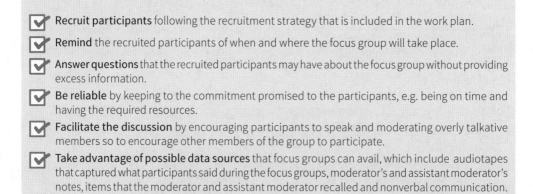

☑ **Recruit participants** following the recruitment strategy that is included in the work plan.

☑ **Remind** the recruited participants of when and where the focus group will take place.

☑ **Answer questions** that the recruited participants may have about the focus group without providing excess information.

☑ **Be reliable** by keeping to the commitment promised to the participants, e.g. being on time and having the required resources.

☑ **Facilitate the discussion** by encouraging participants to speak and moderating overly talkative members so to encourage other members of the group to participate.

☑ **Take advantage of possible data sources** that focus groups can avail, which include audiotapes that captured what participants said during the focus groups, moderator's and assistant moderator's notes, items that the moderator and assistant moderator recalled and nonverbal communication.

You will now realise that you need to be knowledgeable and skilled in techniques for building rapport in focus groups. Note the suggested techniques that you can use to promote rapport.

▶ Maintain a relaxed and positive atmosphere for the participants.

▶ Be friendly to the participants.

▶ Smile with and at the participants.

▶ Keep eye contact with participants.

▶ Try your best to speak in a pleasant tone of voice.

▶ Relax your body language so that you are accessible to the participants.

▶ Include appropriate humour where you can.

▶ Restrain yourself from rushing the participants to respond to your questions.

▶ Promote mutual respect among group members.

▶ Determine ground rules before you start the focus group.

▶ Exercise self control, be humble and appreciative.

▶ Guard against unnecessarily repeating or rewording all that participants say.

▶ Be aware of 'talking down' to your participants.

▶ Avoid scolding your participants either for what they say in their responses or for their personal characteristics or behaviour.

▶ In the same way, avoid permitting participants to berate or bully other participants in the group.

▶ Restrain yourself from compelling the participants to respond to a question at all, or even to respond in the way you expect them to.

Furthermore, you need considerable knowledge and skills in how to handle participants' different personalities and emotional states, which take a lifetime to learn, but here are some ideas that will help.

Seriously ...

▶ In a careful and polite way, control the overly talkative participant. You can manage such a participant by thanking him or her for their contribution and encourage others to come in with their contributions.

▶ Agree with the participants on the ground rules, e.g. discourage them from interrupting any speaker who is making a contribution, or from being aggressive.

▶ Be on the alert for the shy participants and offer them an opportunity to speak. You could pause the discussion and ask if someone else has something to say.

▶ In the event that one participant becomes angry because of what another participant says, calm the offended participant's anger by assuring him or her of the sensitivity of the issue at hand, and then divert the discussion from the offender and offended persons to the issue itself.

▶ If a participant starts to cry, try to diagnose the reasons for his or her distress. If the participant becomes upset because of an issue that is related to group dynamics, revisit the ground rules to remind the participants about what the group agreed to.

▶ Look out for signs of fatigue among the participants. If the participants start to look tired, become impatient or unfocused, it is better to take a break, or have them stand up and take some short exercise.

There are also two moderation styles that you can adopt:

▶ Passive, non-directive moderation is a style in which the moderator-observer limits his or her role by asking just enough questions. The moderator-observer also prompts in a limited way. Rather, the moderator-observer only reinforces the discussion so that it can go on.

▶ Directive or active moderation is a style in which the moderator-observer is heavily involved, especially in terms of providing direction to the discussion and bringing it on track if the participants start to take the discussion off the track.

The assistant moderator takes care of the recording of the focus group's discussions. The recording happens through the use of audio or video equipment, but the assistant moderator should also take notes. The assistant moderator should ensure the proper arrangement of the environment where the group discussion will take place. The arrangement of the environment means planning for possible late coming of participants, seating, refreshments, data verification, and help with data analysis and interpretation.

Managing more than one focus group can be complicated. Sometimes appointing a co-moderator is useful to perform the following tasks:

☑ **Take responsibility** to prepare the room for the discussion, by arranging food, seating and tables.

☑ **Prepare the audio recorder and microphones**, as well as ensuring that this equipment is in good working order.

☑ **Manage the recording of the discussions** and label and change the tapes or discs.

☑ **Welcome** and greet the participants.

☑ **Serve the participants** with refreshments and allocate them name tags.

☑ **Hand a list** to the moderator with the names of all the participants.

☑ **Manage the challenges** that arise during group discussions.

☑ **If the co-moderator has planned incentives** for participants, he or she should distribute these incentives at the end of the group discussion.

Critical thinking challenge

Reflect on what you have learned in section 19.7. Relate the knowledge and skills that the researchers have shown and to what extent, in executing the focus group in the opening case study. Do you agree that the researchers needed an assistant moderator, and if so or not, why? Think about the knowledge and skills required in order to effectively conduct the type of focus group you chose for your research questions in the Critical thinking challenge in section 19.3. Relate how you will apply your knowledge and skills in your focus group discussion.

The next section deliberates on data analysis.

19.8 Data analysis and interpretation in focus group research

For greater understanding of this section, you should consult Chapters 22 and 25 on quantitative data analysis and qualitative data analysis, respectively. As you collect focus group data, you should analyse them. Analysis means bringing order to your data by developing patterns, categories and descriptive units. Data analysis focuses on aspects that include words, tone, context, non-verbals, and so on. In data analysis you convert the recorded data on tapes to transcripts. Your analysis should draw a comparison of discussions of similar themes. It is unusual to assign percentages in the results of data from focus groups.

The analysis of focus group data involves three steps explained as follows:

1 *Indexing* is about reading the transcript to familiarise yourself with the data and to allocate codes to each piece of data, e.g. on the margins. These codes categorise pieces of the text about a common viewpoint related either to a key question or central purpose of the study.
2 *Management* focuses on collecting and bringing together extracts with the same assigned code. To execute the management of data you could manually cut up individual responses and cluster similar extracts, opt for a word processor to cut and paste extracts, or use the software designed for qualitative data analysis, e.g. Atlas.ti.
3 *Interpretation* is about the development of a summary statement about the categories of text. The statements often turn into themes to be reported during the write up of the findings.

The analysis enables you to write up the findings of the study eventually.

Critical thinking challenge

Section 19.8 has exposed you to how to analyse data from focus group sessions. Explain in detail how you will use the information in section 19.8 to analyse data that you will gather through the type of focus group that you chose in the Critical thinking challenge in section 19.4.

There are certain cultural dynamics of focus group, which you need to be aware of as these dynamics may impact either positively or negatively on your study.

19.9 The impact of culture on focus groups

Beware of cultural dynamics that have an impact on group members. Cultural meanings can be anything from dress to gestures and language. A brief pre-discussion session with the group might help clear up any cultural expectations and clashes that may surface during the focus group discussions. Clearing up these meanings will help you to know and observe certain cultural boundaries. This cultural knowledge will also help you to bring the perspective of meaning into the analysis of data that relate to culture. What are the meanings that participants communicate by how they have dressed on the day? What meaning can certain remarks carry from a cultural perspective? What meaning can emanate from the participants' body language and gestures? Also, note that as much as participants' culture may influence the focus group, yours as a researcher can also influence how participants will react to the discussions. Dress sends a certain impression to the participants. It is just as important to mind your opening remarks and expression, as well as your body language towards the participants.

But cultural differences can also yield valuable information in bringing other perspectives from the focus group to the findings. You should therefore, as part of prompting, tease out the meanings that seem to surface from certain gestures and talk. Trace the meaning of concepts that participants seem to express. It is common that in a discussion participants like to code-switch to their home language. You should listen carefully to capture meanings from the participants' home language and let them explain the concepts as they know them in their language.

Now think about the questions in the Critical thinking challenge below.

Critical thinking challenge

How can culture affect the focus group discussion? How do you plan to manage the influence of culture specifically in the focus group that you chose as your data collection method?

Cultural issues also imply ethics in focus groups.

19.10 Ethics in focus group research

Ethical considerations for focus groups are the same as they are for most other methods of social research. However, you should exercise great caution in your handling of ethics in focus groups because there is greater chance that confidential information may leak out because of the interactive nature of the focus group. You should declare information about the purpose and role that participants will play in a focus group. You should be honest and inform participants about your expectations of them. You should develop a plan for handling sensitive information, such as participants' confidentiality. You should also advise participants to keep the information revealed during the focus group discussion confidential.

Critical thinking challenge

In this last section 19.10, you learned about ethics in focus groups. How did the researchers in the opening case study approach ethics in their research project? Apply this knowledge in your focus group and explain how you will handle ethics in your own research.

Conclusion

Focus group discussion is one of the most valuable methods of data gathering in research. However, you need to carefully plan and implement the focus group method if you are considering using it in your study. This chapter has drawn your attention to the important aspects of the focus group to build your knowledge. Making an effort to read more on the use of the focus groups will greatly help you understand how to implement the focus group method effectively. This chapter has provided essential information about understanding, planning for, and implementing the focus group method, so you can consider it with confidence in your own research.

Focus group, as a method of data gathering, deals with the primary sources of data, in this case, the members of the discussion group. In Chapter 20 you will learn about gathering data from secondary sources of data.

Closing activities

Self-reflection questions

1 What is your definition of focus group?

2 What are the different types of focus group?

   a Think of a research problem that will require you to use focus group as your method of data collection.

   b Based on the knowledge you acquired in this chapter, state the type of focus group that you will consider for your research problem.

Analysis and consolidation

3 When and why can you use focus group? Give a reason or reasons why you would consider the type of focus group you chose for your research problem.

4 What are the strengths and weaknesses of focus group? Think about and state practical strengths and weaknesses of the focus group you chose for your research problem.

5 What is the ideal sample size for focus group? How big will the size of your focus group be?

Practical applications

6 How can you plan and implement the focus group method?

   a Practically outline your plan for the chosen focus group. Do this by following the logical steps you have learned about in 19.6 of this chapter.

   b Find a group of your colleagues and try out your focus group plan with them.

7 Discuss the knowledge, skills and roles required for the implementation of focus group.

   a Ask for feedback from your colleagues about how you fared in your trial.

   b Also, do your own self-assessment and think of the areas where you need to improve.

   c What is the possible impact of culture on focus groups?

   d How can you analyse the focus group data?

   e What ethical issues surround focus groups and how can you manage them?

Bibliography

Association for Institutional Research. 2012. Conducting focus group with college students: Strategies to ensure success. *AIR Professional File*, 127:1–16.

Basch, C. 1987. Focus group interview: An under-utilised research technique for improving theory and practice in health education. *Health Education Quarterly*, 14(41):1–8.

Billson, J.M. 2006. Conducting focus group research across cultures: Consistency and comparability. Available at: www.welldev.org.uk/research/workingpaperpdf/27-WORp1-27.pdf. Accessed 8 January 2014.

Eliot, S. 2005. Guidelines for conducting a focus group. Available at: http://assessment.aas.duke.edu/documents/How_to_Conduct_a_Focus_Group.pdf. Accessed 8 January 2014.

Fife, E.M. 2007. Using focus groups for student evaluation of teaching. *MountainRise, the International Journal of the Scholarship of Teaching and Learning*, Spring.

Gibbs, A. 1997. *Focus groups, social research update*. Guildford: University of Surrey.

Goss J.D. & Leinbach, T.R. 1996. Focus groups as alternative research practice. *Area*, 28(2):115–23.

Hesse-Biber, S.N. & Leavy, P. 2011. *The Practice of Qualitative Research* (2nd ed.). London: Sage.

Holbrook, B. & Jackson, P. 1996. Shopping around: Focus group research in North London. *Area*, 28(2):136–42.

Homan, R. 1991. *Ethics in Social Research*. Harlow: Longman.

Kitzinger, J. 1995 Qualitative research: Introducing focus groups, *British Medical Journal*, 311:299–302.

Kitzinger, J. 2008. The methodology of focus groups: The importance of interaction between research participants. *Sociology of Health & Illness*, 16(1):103–123.

Kress, V.E. & Shoffner, M.F. 2007. Focus groups: A practical and applied research approach for counselors. *Journal of Counseling & Development*, 85:189–195.

Kreuger, R.A. 1988. *Focus groups: A practical guide for applied research*. London: Sage.

Krueger, R A. & Casey, M.A. 2000. *Focus Groups: A Practical Guide for Applied Research* (3rd ed.). Thousand Oaks, CA: Sage Publications.

Krueger, R.A. 1994. *Focus groups: A practical guide for applied research* (2nd ed.). Thousand Oaks, CA: Sage.

Lankshear, A.J. 1993. The use of focus groups in a study of attitudes to student nurse assessment. *Journal of Advanced Nursing*, 18:1986–89.

Litosseliti, L. 2003. *Using focus groups in research*. London: MPG Books Ltd.

Mack, N., Woodsong, C., Macqueen, K.M., Guest, G. & Namey, E. 2009. *Qualitative Research Methods: A data collector's field guide*. North Carolina: Family Health International.

Merton, R.K., Gollin, A.E. & Kendall, P.L. 1956. *The focused interview: A manual of problems and procedures*. New York: The Free Press.

Morgan, D.L. & Kreuger, R.A. 1993. When to use focus groups and why. In Morgan, D.L. (Ed). *Successful focus groups*. London: Sage

Morgan, D.L. 1997. *Focus groups as qualitative research*. Thousand Oaks, CA: Sage.

Needham, S. & Papier, J. 2011. Practical matters: What young people think about vocational education in South Africa. Available at: www.skillsdevelopment.org/PDF/What-young-people-think-about-vocational-education-in-South-Africa-report.pdf. Accessed 8 August 2014.

Onwuegbuzie, A.J., Dickinson, W.B., Leech, N.L. & Zoran, A.G. 2009. A qualitative framework for collecting and analyzing data in focus group research. *International Journal of Qualitative Methods*, 8(3):1–19.

Padgett, D.K. 2008. *Qualitative methods in social work research* (2nd ed.). California: Sage.

Powell, R.A., Single, H.M. & Lloyd, K.R. 1996. Focus groups in mental health research: Enhancing the validity of user and provider questionnaires. *International Journal of Social Psychology*, 42(3):193–206.

Race K.E., Hotch, D.F. & Parker, T. 1994. Rehabilitation program evaluation: Use of focus groups to empower clients. *Evaluation Review*, 18(6):730–40.

Rennekamp, R.A. & Nall, N.A. 2008. Using focus groups in program development and evaluation. Lexington: University of Kentucky Cooperative Extension. Available at: www.ca.uky.edu/AgPSD/Focus.pdf. Accessed 8 January 2014.

Sagoe, D. 2012. Precincts and prospects in the use of focus groups in social and behavioural science research. *The Qualitative Report*, 17:1-16. Available at: www.nova.edu/ssss/QR/QR17/sagoe.pdf. Accessed 4 January 2014.

Smith J.A., Scammon, D.L. & Beck, S.L. 1995. Using patient focus groups for new patient services. *Joint Commission Journal on Quality Improvement*, 21(1):22–31.

Stewart, D.W. & Shamdasani, P.N. 1990. *Focus groups: Theory and practice*. Thousand Oaks, CA: Sage.

Yin, R.K. 2011. *Qualitative research from start to finish*. New York/London: The Guilford Press.

CHAPTER 20

Velisiwe Gasa and Patrick Mafora

Using secondary sources of data

KEY CONCEPTS

Data are the information you collect as a researcher. May be generated as audio- or video-recorded interviews, questionnaires, field diaries and documentary evidence, so it is very important for the researcher to design an effective, personal system to organise the data.

Data analysis is, in general terms, the process of making interpretations of the data that have been collected and possibly constructing theories based on the researcher's interpretations.

Ethics is concerned with ethical principles and adherence to professional codes. These principles need to be at the centre of data gathering, data analysis and writing up of projects.

Secondary sources of data are collected by someone other than the user. Simply put, data are considered to be secondary in a research study when they were previously collected by the researcher or other researchers for different purposes. The data are readily available and are being reused, that is, the data are explored, analysed and interpreted in the context of the new research question(s); not the research question(s) they were initially collected to answer.

LEARNING OUTCOMES

By the end of this chapter, you should be able to:

▶ Distinguish between primary and secondary data.

▶ Discuss the advantages and disadvantages of using secondary data.

▶ Evaluate the suitability of secondary data for answering research question(s).

Case study: Sibani chooses secondary sources

After Sibani has engaged with a lot of literature research (as you may remember from Chapter 8) and has read widely on planning, designing and conducting educational research (Chapters 9, 10, 15) she knows that it is practically impossible and makes no sense for her to collect and analyse primary data. She becomes aware that generating longitudinal data from scratch is usually impossible; and, even if it is possible, could easily cost her a lot of money that she does not have. She knows too that with longitudinal data, a set of well-run surveys could take up to six years to obtain coverage, plus the analysis time. This would prove unviable for her Master's dissertation as the university has its own completion timeframe. She therefore opts for data which are readily available and have been collected by other researchers for other studies. Such data are called secondary data. She takes advantage of the fact that secondary sources can give a geographical and international spread. She is also aware that these sources are library-based or internet-based, and are usually much faster to access.

Sibani embarks on her journey of exploring secondary data with Dillon, Madden and Firtle's (1994:66) advice at heart: "The first prerequisite for locating appropriate secondary data is intellectual curiosity. You should never begin a half-hearted search with the assumption that what is being sought is so unique that no one else has ever bothered to collect it and publish it. On the contrary, assume there are corollary, secondary data that should help provide definition and scope for the primary research effort."

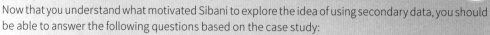
Introduction

This chapter focuses on the merits of using secondary sources of data. It gives practical examples on why some researchers opt to use them. It clearly states that the purpose of undertaking a research study is to answer one or more research question(s). The question(s) are usually answered through data collected specifically for the study. This is called primary data. It is noted in the case study that sometimes it is not always practically possible or sensible to collect and analyse primary data. In such cases, the researcher may use data which are readily available, having been collected by other researchers for other studies. Such data are called secondary data and are used to answer the research question(s) for which they were not specifically collected. Secondary data can be obtained from a myriad of sources that might include published printed material, electronic material, or even unprocessed or raw data. The data can be used in research studies following either a quantitative or a qualitative design, or in mixed methods studies. Researchers who choose to use secondary data should exercise extra caution as they use the data for purposes and contexts for which the data were not specifically collected.

20.1 Definition and purpose of secondary sources of data

What defines data secondary is the different purpose that they are being used for. The same data which were primary in the initial study become secondary when used for a different purpose.

To put it simply, we may say a secondary source is something written about a primary source. You can think of secondary sources as second-hand information. If I tell you something, I am the primary source. If you tell someone else what I told you, you are the secondary source. Secondary data are, therefore, not necessarily inferior. Their quality and usefulness depends on the extent to which they help to answer the new research question(s).

The researcher's key guides regarding the location of secondary data are the research question(s) to be answered, and a thorough knowledge of related literature. Secondary data can be traced by following up on original research reports of surveys, observations and field experiments in the reference lists of published printed and electronic materials (books, journals, e-journals). The data can also be located through tertiary literature like indexes and data archived catalogues. Unpublished personal or corporate records like diaries, letters, minutes of meetings, and reports also serve as sources of secondary data.

Putting the purpose of secondary sources of data into context, let us relate it to the opening case study and see how Sibani planned to use her secondary sources of data in her own study. The next case study will reveal her plan:

Once you understand the purpose of secondary data, we advise you on how to make an informed decision on using the secondary data. This aspect will be covered now.

20.2 Decision path for using secondary data

The flow chart in Figure 20.1 on page 358 presents a decision path that should be followed when using secondary data. This flow chart, which was suggested by Joselyn (1977:15), is divided into two stages. The first stage portrays the relevance of the data to the research objectives (applicability to the project objectives). The final stage relates to questions about the accuracy of secondary data (accuracy of the data). The flow chart provides questions where answers are sought. If answers are in the affirmative (Yes), one may proceed with the use of secondary data. If answers are negative (No), one must stop using the secondary data.

Now that you have made an informed decision to use secondary data, you need to get pointers in order to evaluate your decision. This will be covered by the following section.

20.3 Considerations before using secondary data

You are unlikely to be familiar with data that you did not collect. You should, therefore, first familiarise yourself with the data before they can be used. You should know how the data were collected; what were the response categories for each question; and, details of the population and sample.

Secondary data should also be evaluated for appropriateness before they can be used in the new study. Some of the issues to consider are:

▶ *Availability*: The data should be readily available, timely, organised, useful and in a simple form. If not primary data should be collected. It should also be easily manipulated to satisfy the changing and ad hoc requirements of management for information.

▶ *Accuracy*: The data source should be dependable and the methodology that was used should also be appropriate for the research question.

▶ *Relevance*: The data should be current and help answer the new research question.

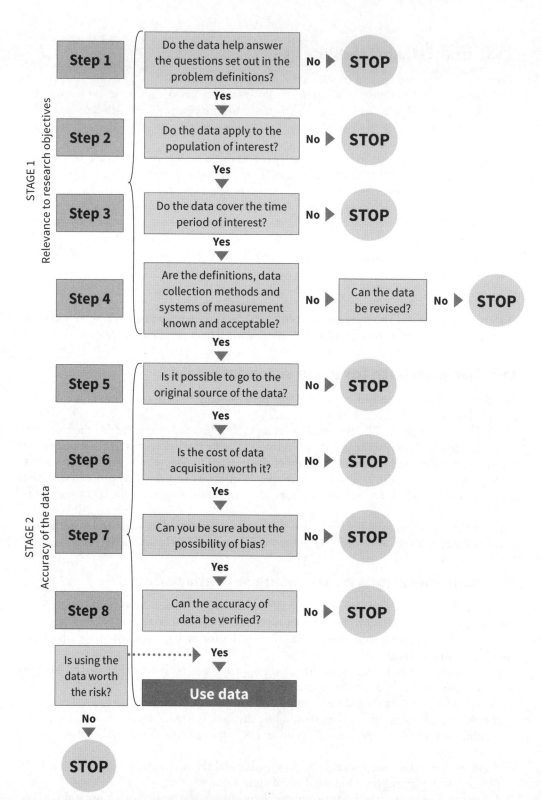

FIGURE 20.1: Flow chart on decision-making to use secondary data

- *Sufficiency*: The data should be extensive enough to address all dimensions of the problem.
- *Authenticity*: The genuineness of the document or source should be evaluated with regard to its soundness and authorship.
- *Credibility*: Caution should be exercised as to whether the original author has given a true account of the situation, or has distorted it in some way to make the situation look better. If any distortion was applied, the integrity and accuracy of your study may be affected.
- *Representativeness*: Careful consideration should be given to how typical or atypical the documents being sourced are, in order that you can recognise limits to the conclusions. Bear in mind that the physical survival and availability of documents may limit the representation of documents.
- *Meaning*: You need to be concerned with how well you will be able to understand the document, especially if it is old, in another language, or contains elements you are unfamiliar with.

Further, Stein (2002) highlights another six criteria for consideration:
- Authorship
- Authority of the author
- Authority of the material
- Authority of the site or organisation
- Currency (i.e. is it up-to-date?)
- Pressure groups or objectivity.

After you have taken an informed decision to use secondary data, it is also important to know how the data that you intend to use are classified. This aspect is outlined now.

20.4 Classification of secondary data

Secondary sources of information are divided into two categories: internal and external sources of data.

20.4.1 Internal sources of data

Internal sources of data are usually obtainable from the organisation that you are employed in, or registered at. Most organisations collect information about their day-to-day operations or activities, for example, schools collect data on the number of registered learners, their biographical details, and their academic performance. These sources are ready to be used, although they often require further processing.

20.4.2 External sources of data

External sources of data are obtainable from published materials, computerised databases and from companies that collect and sell common pools of data. These sources are mainly obtained from the local and national government agencies, trade and professional associations, commercial services and national and international institutions such as universities, research institutes, financial institutions and some non-governmental organisations.

The next section covers the main sources of data which emanate from the two categories discussed in section 20.4.

20.5 Main sources of secondary data

The most authentic type of secondary data is the published printed source such as books or reference books and journals or periodicals. Their credibility depends on the writers, publishing company, and time and date of publication.

Today books are available on almost any topic you want to research. Magazines and newspapers also form part of secondary data although their credibility is sometimes questioned.

Secondary data can also be obtained from *published electronic sources* on the internet. These sources can be in the form of e-journals, e-books, and generally websites or weblogs.

Secondary data can also be obtained from *unpublished personal records*. These sources can be in the form of diaries, letters, or government records. Diaries are personal records of ordinary and famous citizens. Those of ordinary citizens are rarely available whereas those of famous (or infamous) people are usually accessible in one way or another.

Another authentic type of secondary data can be *government records*, such as census data or population statistics, health records, educational institutions' records, constitutional and legislative archives or public sector records. Other records may be from *non-governmental organisations'* survey and research data, or from *private companies*.

Ahmed Kathrada's Robben Island diaries e.g.

Ahmed Kathrada's Robben Island diaries are the most famous example of personal records that you may be able to obtain. Ahmed Kathrada's personal 'bits and pieces' are available online. One of the most interesting 'pieces' is the diary in which Kathrada, a struggle veteran and one of Nelson Mandela's oldest personal friends, discusses their prison sentence to Robben Island. Another good example of the letters of famous people that can be accessed widely are the letters that Nelson Mandela wrote to his wife Winnie while in prison.

A few of the sources mentioned in section 20.5 will be briefly explained now.

20.5.1 Books and reference materials

Books or reference materials sometimes provide secondary source material. For example, the book, *The Mind of South Africa: The Rise and Fall of Apartheid*, by Allister Sparks, published in 1990, could be used as a secondary source to learn about accounts of South Africa's agonising history and its transition from apartheid to democracy. Some reference materials are in the form of handbooks, manuals, encyclopedias, and dictionaries. Bear in mind that trying to categorise into types of sources can get tricky, because a secondary source may also be a primary source. Some books can be seen as both a secondary and a primary source, depending on how you are using them and the nature of your research. If you are commenting on the narratives or accounts of events, the book would be a secondary source; but if you are writing a book review, the same book becomes a primary source, because you are commenting on, evaluating, and discussing the author's ideas.

20.5.2 Scholarly and professional journals

Scholarly journals generally contain reports of original research or experimentation written by experts in specific fields. They usually contain articles which have undergone a peer review process whereby other experts in the same field, review the content of the article for accuracy, originality, and relevance.

20.5.3 Literature review articles

Literature review articles assemble and review original research dealing with a specific topic. These reviews are usually written by experts in the field and may be the first written overview of a topic area. These articles discuss and list all the relevant publications from which the information is derived.

20.5.4 Trade journals

Trade journals contain articles that discuss practical information concerning various fields or industries. These journals provide people in these fields with information relating to that field, trade or industry.

20.5.5 Technical reports

Technical reports are accounts of work done on research projects regardless of whether they are completed or ongoing research projects. These reports are written to provide research results to colleagues, research institutions, governments, and other interested researchers.

20.5.6 Official statistics

Official statistics are demographic statistics collected by governments and their various agencies, bureaus, and departments. Government statistics may include:
- Population censuses
- Social, education or economic surveys, household expenditure surveys
- Import/export and trade statistics
- Economic and production statistics
- Jobs and employment statistics
- Agricultural statistics.

For example, Statistics South Africa collects huge amounts of information that usually covers long periods of time. These statistics can be useful to researchers because they are easily obtainable and provide a comprehensive source of information. Gill (1993:3), however, posits a caution on using official statistics as they are "characterised by unreliability, data gaps, over-aggregation, inaccuracies, mutual inconsistencies, and lack of timely reporting". He emphasises that you should critically analyse any statistics from whatever source for accuracy and validity. He also suggests some of the reasons why the problems mentioned exist:
- A large number of interviewers or data collectors are required to collect a sizeable scale of official surveys. In order to reach those numbers sometimes under-skilled interviewers are contracted.
- The survey area is often large, and research team is sometimes limited in its adequate supervision of interviewers, and the entire research process.
- Human and technical resource limitations sometimes prevent timely and accurate reporting of results.

20.5.7 Trade and industrial associations

Trade associations in most cases produce a trade directory and, perhaps, a yearbook but it is advisable to check with them what kind of data they publish. Commercial services which operate under different commercial organisations charge for their information. Firstly, they need to fund the collection of the data, which is often wide-ranging in its content; and secondly, it is with the purpose of making money from selling these data to interested parties that they are engaged in it at all.

20.5.8 National and international institutions

National and international institutions produce economic reviews, university research reports, journals and articles. For example, national and international agencies such as the World Bank; Statistics South Africa; the Human Sciences Research Council (HSRC); the South African Social Attitude Survey (SASAS); the Research Data Management Centre; and the South African census produce an abundance of secondary data which can prove extremely useful to many researchers. Although some of these institutions do not require payment in the form of money, there are access conditions and copyright implications that you need to abide by. A good example of access conditions and copyright is taken from HSRC and is provided here.

Why access conditions and copyright?

The HSRC has clear access conditions and copyright so, in accessing the data, you have to give assurance that:

▸ The data and documentation will not be duplicated, redistributed or sold without prior approval from the HSRC.

▸ The data will be used for statistical and scientific research purposes only, and the confidentiality of individuals or organisations in the data will be preserved at all times, and that no attempt will be made to obtain or derive information relating specifically to identifiable individuals or organisations.

▸ The HSRC must be informed of any books, articles, conference papers, theses, dissertations, reports or other publications resulting from work based in whole or in part on the data and documentation.

▸ The HSRC must be acknowledged in all published and unpublished works based on the data, according to the citation as stated in the study information file or the web page metadata field, citation.

▸ For archiving and bibliographic purposes an electronic copy of all reports and publications based on the requested data must be sent to the HSRC.

▸ The collector of the data, the HSRC, and the relevant funding agencies bear no responsibility for use of the data or for interpretations or inferences based upon such uses.

▸ By retrieval of the data you signify your agreement to comply with the above-stated terms and conditions and give your assurance that the use of statistical data obtained from the HSRC will conform to widely-accepted standards of practice and legal restrictions that are intended to protect the confidentiality of respondents.

▸ Failure to comply with the above is considered infringement of the intellectual property rights of the HSRC.

The access conditions and copyright as required by any institution should be upheld all the time when secondary sources of data are being used. You need to check first if these access conditions apply in any secondary sources of data that you intend to use in order to avoid any infringement of intellectual property rights. Before proceeding to the next section, which looks at the usefulness of secondary data, let us stop and reflect on what we have learned.

Stop and reflect

1 Look at the HSRC access conditions and copyright in the last section. Can you explain why you think it is necessary to follow them?
2 How is published secondary data classified?
3 List the various internal sources of secondary data and explain their benefits to the researcher.
4 Describe the importance of the government census data as a major source of secondary data.
5 What are the different sources of secondary data, including internal sources and external sources?

20.6 The usefulness of secondary data

No matter the form, secondary data play an important part when it is not possible to get primary data. They also play a crucial part when respondents are not willing to reveal certain essential information. Sometimes primary data may not exist at all, and in such a situation, one has to confine the research to secondary data. For example, if your research is on sexuality, you need to be aware that some populations in Africa still find it taboo to discuss this matter. You may find that participants are not willing to give the information you want for your research. So, in this case, you could collect data from published printed sources, published electronic sources or government records.

Consulting secondary sources should make you realise that the exact information you want to uncover is already available through secondary sources. This may help you to eliminate the need and expense of carrying out your own primary research. The researchers who collected the original data may stipulate how difficult it was conducting their primary research. This is because the details of how the information was collected are included in the readily available secondary data. These details usually include the procedures used in data collection and the difficulties encountered in conducting the primary research. This may help you to make an informed decision about whether the research is worth pursuing despite the difficulties.

20.6.1 Published printed sources

As mentioned in section 20.5, the most authentic type of secondary data is published printed sources, such as books and journals or periodicals. The use of books may start before you have selected the topic. Their use stretches beyond topic selection because they provide insight into how much work has already been done on the same topic. These sources can continuously help you to prepare your literature review.

Journals and periodicals are becoming more important as far as data collection is concerned. The reason is that they often provide more up-to-date information than books and sometimes maintain important theoretical discourses that are emerging. They can give you more specific information on your particular research topic rather than more general topics.

Magazines and newspapers are also effective in sparking ideas, but their reliability can be questioned. A good story sells even if the truth is a bit twisted or sensationalised, and that is sometimes how magazines and newspapers operate. Newspapers are most useful in cases where the information can only be obtained from them, for example, in the field of political studies when one deals with rare cases. However, you should be aware that new sources are preferred to old sources. You should not confine yourself to accounts of the past (in whatever form), reading them as the final word, since new technology and new research often brings new facts and views to light.

20.6.2 Published electronic sources

Published electronic sources on the internet are also becoming more useful in the world of research. These sources consist of e-journals, e-books, general websites or weblogs. The internet is becoming more accessible, fast and available to the masses. Advancements in published electronic sources can be seen in much of information that is now been carried and transmitted. Most of the information that is not available in printed form is available on the internet.

Although the credibility of the internet was very questionable in the past, nowadays it is more reliable and trustworthy. This is because in the past accredited journals and books were seldom published on the internet. Nowadays almost every journal and book is available online. These sources can mainly be accessed free, but for some you may have to pay, register or subscribe in order to gain access. The latest journals are difficult to retrieve without subscription but if your university has an e-library you can access any journal. This gives you an opportunity to view, print and place an order for sources that are not available.

Can you trust it?

Note that we say 'more reliable and trustworthy' not 'completely reliable and trustworthy' when describing internet sources. You need to use your latent knowledge of websites and always cross check, and cross check again.

Generally, websites are also easily accessible but they sometimes do not contain reliable information. It is advisable that you check their content for the reliability before quoting from them (see pitfall warning above).

Diaries written by different people, called weblogs, are also becoming increasingly popular to use. The information in weblogs is as reliable as personal written diaries, but much more immediate.

News sources are known to reach wide audiences. Some can be generally classified under literature, along with industry surveys, compilations from computerised databases and information systems.

20.6.3 Unpublished personal records

Unpublished personal records in the form of diaries, letters or government records have proved to be useful. Diaries can be very useful when you are conducting a descriptive research. Letters like diaries are also a rich source that can be accessible or rarely accessible but their reliability should be checked before using them. Government records, such as census data or population statistics, health records, educational institutions' records, or public sector records; as well as other records from non-governmental organisations' survey data; or private companies, can be important for marketing, management, humanities and social science research. Despite the usefulness of secondary data, you should be aware that these data have advantages and disadvantages, as discussed in the next section.

20.7 The advantages and disadvantages of secondary data

The use of secondary data in research brings strengths and weaknesses to a research project.

20.7.1 Advantages

The most basic strength is that the sources of data are easily accessible, and access to data is possible when it is not easy to get primary data.

▸ With the availability of online access, secondary sources are more openly accessed. This offers convenience and generally standardised usage methods for all sources of secondary data.

▸ The use of secondary data allows researchers access to valuable information for little or no cost at all.

▸ Using secondary data is much less expensive than if you had to carry out the research yourself, even when the data have to be purchased.

▸ Secondary data provides initial insight into the research problem and points to additional primary data that should be collected in a study.

▸ A considerable amount of time is saved when secondary data are used, as the data do not have to be collected in raw form, or be prepared for analysis. Very often, these phases have already been completed.

▸ Duplication of effort is avoided because researchers use available good data rather than collecting primary data.

▸ When it comes to the analysis of secondary data, this is faster when compared with formal primary data gathering and analysis exercises.

▸ It lends itself to trend analysis as it offers a relatively easy way to monitor change over time, since it only depends on the level of data disaggregation.

▸ Its analysis carries a form of human skills development as data collectors with limited research training or technical expertise can be trained to conduct a secondary data review.

▸ The breadth of data available makes it easy for individual researchers to obtain large amounts of data that they would have a difficult time collecting. Many of these data sets are also longitudinal, meaning that the same data have been collected from the same population over several different time periods.

▸ Their analysis allows researchers to look at trends and changes of phenomena over time. In most cases, the data collection process is often guided by expertise and professionalism that may not be available to individual researchers or small research projects.

▸ The data collection for many accredited agencies is often performed by personnel who specialise in certain tasks and have many years of experience in that particular area, and with that particular survey. This is in contrast to smaller research projects as sometimes data is collected by students who do not have that same level of required expertise.

20.7.2 Disadvantages

The main weakness associated with the use of secondary data in a research project is that the researcher cannot vouch for the quality of the data with certainty.

▸ The researcher is unable to make informed judgements as he or she does not know about factors related to the initial research process, such as what accounts for the response rate, whether the data is accurate, or is it as recent as it may be reported.

▸ The researcher who uses secondary data has no control over what is contained in the data set. This can limit the analysis or alter the original questions the researcher seeks to answer. If the proper interpretation and analysis of data are missed they do not help the researcher understand *why* something happened.

> The researchers may never know if the data, instruments or data collection methods have been altered over time, been censored, weighted, or deleted.
> The data may not cover the scope of the current study sufficiently in terms of period, research questions, and sample.
> The geographical region desired, for the years desired, or the specific population that the researcher is interested in studying may also limit the use of the available data.
> The researchers may find that the boundaries of geographical areas have been redefined; units of measurement and school grades may also have changed.

▶ The data may be available in a form that does not match the researcher's envisaged analysis, such as using different age categories.
> The variables may have been defined or categorised differently from what the researcher would have chosen. For example, the race may be defined as 'black' or 'white' instead of containing every major race category as it is now understood in southern Africa.
> The important variables, such as individual or group values, beliefs, or reasons that may be underlying current trends, may not be revealed.

▶ The data may also be blighted by the original researcher's prejudice or the secondary researcher's out-of-context interpretation of them.
> The availability of the desired information may be hampered by the data collectors as they decide what to collect and what to omit. Sometimes data collectors may have vested interests; even if they compile the data, they may have reasons for wishing to present a more optimistic or pessimistic set of results for their organisation.
> Inexperienced researchers can easily become overwhelmed by the volume of data available and fail to exercise selectivity with a caution. Sometimes it may happen that sources conflict with one another.

▶ Another setback may be that the researcher does not know exactly how the data collection process was done, and how well it was done. Mostly, researchers need to read between the lines because they are not privy to some of the information. It may not be easy to validate if there was poor documentation of the secondary data set or electronic format incompatibilities. It may also be true that secondary data are only as good as the research that produced them.
> The researchers may not know how seriously the data may have been affected by problems such as low response rate or respondent misunderstanding of specific survey questions.
> The researchers may not know what the conditions were that led to the data production. It might be that they were originally gathered to persuade, justify, or otherwise convey a particular point of view, or were intended for consumption by particular groups, which differ from the current project.
> The researchers must guess at what the author(s) meant by the terms, cultural and sub-cultural references, jargon, or idiomatic expressions they used. New researchers may be aware that definitions used in the data may have changed over time, and may end up drawing erroneous conclusions.

▶ It is expensive to pay for year's subscription to commercial data providers, the supply of data from data archives, and requesting special tabulations from government survey sources.

▶ If the data are required by thesis writers, to obtain coverage of a set of well-run surveys, especially longitudinal data, could take a number of years. For example, if the researcher wants to use statistics, he or she may get out-of-date data because censuses mostly take place at 10-year intervals.

- Most of the secondary data are not clean (in the sense of straightforward and ready to use) and need to be cleaned up, to be checked against other sources, and organisations need to be contacted to clarify some issues, like copyright and confidentiality. All these are time-consuming exercises. Sometimes it is not easy to obtain current data, and inevitably, secondary data are dated.
- Researchers who use secondary data are deprived of the opportunity to do interviews, frame a questionnaire, and handle SPSS, or other statistical packages. These researchers lose out on the training advantage of the research process, meaning their research craft training diminishes. As they do not conduct fieldwork, they are unable to estimate inaccuracies in measurement through standard deviation and standard error because these are sometimes not published in secondary sources.

A great deal of information has been given to you in this chapter. Let us now give you an opportunity to reflect on the information provided to you.

Stop and reflect

The information in this chapter has been to enrich your understanding of secondary sources of data, and you should be in a good position to answer the following questions:

1 Why are secondary data important?
2 Discuss the role of new information technologies in collecting secondary data.
3 What are the advantages and disadvantages of secondary data?
4 Why does the reliability of published statistics vary over time?

20.8 Ethical issues in the use of secondary data

You need to be aware that secondary data are generally owned by a person or institution other than the researcher doing the secondary analysis. The data can be freely available, but sometimes they are not freely available for further analysis. Mostly data that are classified as freely available can be obtained from the internet, from books or another public forums. This data is seen as public domain and permission for further use and analysis is implied. Even if explicit permission for use of this particular data is not required, you are still expected to acknowledge the person who owns or originated the original data. If the data are not freely available, explicit and written permission for the use of the data must be obtained from those who own, or originated the data.

   You should bear in mind that the size of the forum when you analyse whether the secondary data may have changed. You may want to use or publish in a wider forum than originally indicated to participants. In such instances, the participants must be approached in order to gain permission for such use. When you analyse secondary data, you may want to get further information or to interview, observe or test the participants who were involved during the collection of the primary data (which have now become secondary data). In such cases, you may not directly contact the participants. If you do this you will be impinging on the participants' right to anonymity and confidentiality as stated in the original research. What you need to do is to provide full information letters about the research to the researcher who collected the primary data. You have to ask him or her to approach the participants with your letter. If the participants indicate their willingness to be approached by you, then you may personally proceed to negotiate fully informed consent from the participants.

It is your responsibility to ensure that further analysis of the data is conducted appropriately. You must be clear about how different variables and indicators are defined and weightings are allocated. If it is a qualitative data, you must include a clarification of concepts as employed. Use the appropriate analysis tools that are specified by the owners of the data as far as they are provided and prescribed. For instance, the IDB analyser is provided by the International Association for the Evaluation of Educational Achievement (IEA) to analyse the Progress in International Reading Literacy Study (PIRLS) or Trends in Mathematics and Science Study (TIMSS) data.

Researchers who use secondary data sometimes assume that it may not raise the same kinds of ethical considerations as primary data would. However, this view is rarely accepted by ethics committees. They require researchers to check the nature of data. It is debatable whether secondary data present almost no ethical dilemmas since the data are already in the public domain in some way and have been anonymised. You need to be aware that even if the data have been anonymised, there is still a risk that participants could become identifiable. The greater the sensitivity of the information you are mining, the more you need to protect and assure the participants. Even if the existing data do not require full ethics application, a letter explaining the research and seeking permission for the use of the data should be acquired.

Critical thinking challenge

You need to discuss the following questions in a group and give practical examples.

1 What ethical issues are involved in the use of secondary data?
2 Is it true that secondary data present no ethical dilemmas? Support your answer.

Conclusion

In this chapter, the merits of using secondary sources of data were brought forth and explored. The pros and cons of using secondary sources of data were discussed at length in order to help you to make informed decisions. You were made aware that secondary data may be sufficient to solve the problem, or at least they may help you to better understand the problem under study. But a key consideration when deciding to use such data should be the extent to which the data meet the purpose of the new research, or help to answer the research question. Not even every piece of data available would meet this requirement. It is therefore important that before making use of secondary data, you should evaluate both the data themselves and their source. Particular attention should be paid to definitions used, measurement error, source bias, reliability, and the time span and dates of the secondary data. Overall, you should be able to find that the advantages of using secondary data outweigh the disadvantages.

Closing activities

Self-reflection questions

1 How can you distinguish secondary data from primary data?
2 Explain the criteria for evaluating the quality of secondary data, with examples.
3 Discuss the task of locating published secondary data that are appropriate for a researcher.
4 What considerations should you bear in mind before using secondary data?

Practical applications

5 You need to work as a group to classify the source scenarios provided below. You have to indicate if they fall under secondary data or not. Ask each other questions for further clarity.

I am writing an essay on Nelson Mandela for my History class. I have used articles from Wikipedia and another online encyclopedia. What am I using?	When I was at a Reed Dance ceremony a few years ago, I found an old spear; I did research and found out it has been made by the Zulu warriors. What is my old spear?
My sister found an old wedding dress in one of our old tin trunks. My father said it belonged to my grandmother. What is the wedding dress?	At school we use textbooks to learn about the history and geography of the African continent. When we use textbooks, what are we using?
I was watching eNCA and one of the reporters said he had heard good reviews about a new sports movie. When he talks about the movie, what is he doing?	I found a letter to one of my friends in the locker room after school the other day. I know it's private, but I want to read it! What is the letter?
When I do homework about the South African government and I read commentaries by the Constitutional Court on heritage monuments cases, what am I reading?	My friend Sibani said I should read a book that she really likes. She told me about it, and it sounds really good! When Sibani talks about the book, what is she?
I like to read *Bona* magazine. I really like the articles written by people about African actors. When I read these stories, what am I reading?	My mom has CDs of my grandparents telling stories about when they were kids. We love to listen to these at family gatherings. What are we listening to?

6 Think of any topic and research questions that you intend to collect secondary data on, then use the checklist below to evaluate if your research goals will be achieved through secondary data sources.

Evaluated item	Yes	No
Does the data have comprehensive information to help answer the research question(s)?		
Does the data cover the population that you wish to study?		
Can unwanted data be separated from data you wish to use?		
Do measures and units used in the data match those of your study?		
Are the data current?		
Does the data cover all variables that you seek to measure?		
Is the methodology clearly described?		
Is the data source credible?		
Is the data source reliable?		
Has the data been recorded accurately?		
Does the benefit of using the data outweigh the associated costs?		

Bibliography

Arthur, J., Waring, M., Coe, R. & Hedges, L.V. 2012. *Research Methods and Methodologies in Education*. Thousand Oaks, CA: Sage Publications.

Blaikie, N. 2010. Designing Social Research. Cambridge: Polity Press.

Chapman, S. & McNeill, P. 2005. *Research Methods*. Abington, Oxon: Routledge.

Crawford, I.M. 1997. *Marketing Research and Information Systems*. Rome: FAO Corporate Document Repository.

Daas, P. & Arends-Toth, J. 2012. *Secondary data collection*. Netherlands: Statistics Netherlands.

Dillon, W.R., Madden, T. & Firtle, N.H. 1994. *Marketing Research in a Research Environment* (3rd ed.). Burr Ridge, IL: Irwin.

Gill, G.J. 1993. *OK, the data's lousy, but it's all we got (being a critique of conventional methods)*. London: International Institute for Environment and Development.

Gorard, S. & Taylor, C. 2004. *Combining Methods in Educational and Social Research*. New York: McGraw-Hill Education.

Joselyn, R.W. 1977. *Designing the marketing research*. New York: Petrocellis/Charter.

Saunders, M., Lewis, P. & Thornhill, A. 2000. *Research Methods for Business Students* (2nd ed.). Essex: Prentice-Hall.

Smith, E. 2008. *Using Secondary Data in Educational and Social Research*. London: McGraw-Hill Education.

Stein, S. 2002. *Sociology on the web: A student guide*. Harlow, England: Prentice-Hall.

Vartanian, T.P. 2011. *Secondary Data Analysis*. New York: Oxford University Press.

Walliman, N. 2006. *Social Research Methods*. London: Sage Publications Inc.

CHAPTER 21

Mishack Gumbo

The pilot study

KEY CONCEPTS

Pilot study involves running a trial of the main study in order to ensure the main study's feasibility and validity.

Main study is the actual study after conducting its pilot or test study.

Feasibility in research, means the likelihood that the study can be conducted considering factors such as the appropriateness of the research methods chosen.

Pretest means to test or pilot the study before conducting it in order to ensure the study's feasibility and validity.

Research instruments are a designed or adopted/adapted standardised tool used for gathering research data.

Findings is the information discovered after or in the process of conducting research.

LEARNING OUTCOMES

By the end of this chapter, you should be able to:

▶ Express your understanding and describe the value of a pilot study.

▶ Explain the reasons for piloting your study.

▶ Discuss the advantages and disadvantages of a pilot study.

▶ Understand what to report in a pilot study's findings.

Case study: Pilot study at the Faculty of Education at Thutong University

This pilot study launched an investigation into the views of postgraduate students on the cultural factors that play a role in the supervision of their studies. The cultural backgrounds of both the students and the supervisors contribute to the relationships that are formed during postgraduate supervision work.

The study was conducted with students registered in the master's and doctoral programmes in the Faculty of Education at Thutong University. The researchers used a mixed-methods approach that informed the interviews, survey and observation that took place. The data collection instruments were applied for the first time. As a result, this study was regarded as a pilot study. A random sampling was used for the survey and purposive sampling for the interviews.

One hundred master's students and 50 doctoral students, from a target population of 450 students, participated in the survey. Six master's students and six doctoral students were selected from the survey group for the interview and to be observed with their supervisors in during the supervision process.

The study yielded the following preliminary findings: misunderstanding that students sometimes experience between their supervisors and themselves; a culture of openness and support by a few supervisors; distance between the supervisor and student brought upon by cultural prejudice.

Introduction

Chapter 20 looked at secondary sources of data. This chapter now looks at the pilot study as a means of pre-testing the main study through data gathering methods and processes. The opening case study incorporates a pilot study, which this chapter will keep referring to in order to enhance your understanding. Pilot studies receive little attention in research training and literature. Many conducted pilot studies, such as that in opening case study, merely report the findings of the study instead of feedback on the processes and data gathering instruments, which can help to validate and make the main study feasible. The current chapter fits well in the many chapters in this book, to address the methodological issues. Therefore, the purpose of the current chapter is to help you understand a pilot study, to know the reasons why you should pilot your study, and how you should treat the findings of a pilot study.

21.1 Understanding the pilot study

21.1.1 What is a pilot study?

A pilot study is about running a trial of the main study. You trial-run your main study in order to ensure its feasibility and validity. In other words, a pilot study is about pilot testing the main study. There are other terms that researchers use to refer to a pilot study, such as experimental, exploratory, test, preliminary, trial, try out. Researchers mostly pilot the method sections of their studies because it is the 'how' of the study that the researchers want to validate. A pilot study is therefore a small investigation with an aim to test the feasibility and validity of procedures and to gather information prior to the main study.

You can use a pilot study in qualitative, quantitative or mixed methods studies. For example, you can use a qualitative pilot study to develop interview schedule, which includes the questions to ask. You can actually administer s questionnaire on a very small sample such as ten. There may be a need to change or modify certain aspects of the questionnaire based on the feedback you will receive from participants in the pilot study before you conduct the main study. Thus, you can design a pilot study to test whether the study is worth pursuing and what changes you need to make to the questionnaire.

The pilot study pretests a research instrument. In a big study in which there is a need to design a few research instruments you need pilot studies, which become the mini versions of the main study. Thus, a pilot study addresses important methodological concerns that you may encounter in the main study.

21.1.2 A pilot study is a feasibility study

To build on your understanding of a pilot study, let us briefly focus on a pilot study as a feasibility study. To test the feasibility of procedures means to test if the methods of the main study are feasible to implement when taking into account certain factors in the research field, e.g. participants' understanding of the questionnaire, resources needed, time it will take to complete the questionnaire and how that may influence the attitude of the participants. Based on these factors, the intended design for the main study may or may not work. So, a pilot study helps you to address these factors beforehand to ensure the feasibility of the main study. It helps to ascertain that you may conduct the study after you have tested it out. A pilot study thus happens prior to the main study. Example A explains how you can pilot your questionnaire for purposes of feasibility.

A

> The pilot of a questionnaire survey can begin with interviews to establish the issues that you need to address in an interview questionnaire. Then you can pilot the wording and order of the questions. Finally, you can test the research process, such as the different ways of conducting interviews, as well as precautionary procedures you have planned to overcome problems such as poor recording and response rates.

(**Source:** Adapted from Van Teijlingen & Hundley, 2013:824).

Based on the procedures explained in A, you can make the necessary changes to the main study prior to conducting it, guided by the feedback that you got from the participants in the pilot study.

Did you notice in A that you need to first trial-run your main study in order to ensure its feasibility and to resolve the issues that may affect the planned goal of your main study beforehand?

B and C now demonstrate feasibility in simple practical ways.

B

> A home-based baker takes out the first pan of cookies from the oven and asks her family or friends to taste them. She wants to know if they are good, even though she is confident that she prepared the mixture properly. This is so that something can be done to improve the quality of the cookie dough before baking the rest, if this first batch is not quite right.

C

> When changing a printer cartridge, you should always run a test page, or you might find that the whole document that you print after changing the cartridge still does not look good enough. This may cost you resources such as your old cartridge going to waste as it did not need changing, wasted paper, time, and so on.

21.1.3 A pilot study is not the main study, or a small sample study

You should not confuse a pilot study with a small sample study, such as is described under 21.3.1. A pilot study may not be small in all research projects, especially if it is a survey pilot study. Do you think that the study reported in the opening case study is a pilot study or the main study? The researchers treated this pilot study both as a pilot and main study. They treated it as the main study because they reported the findings of the study, not the gaps that the participants might have identified. They treated the pilot study as a pilot because they piloted their research instruments. The researchers intended to conduct the second cycle of the study. The expectations will therefore be that they should explain how they modified their instruments based of the participants' feedback in the pilot study. Feedback about the gaps in the pilot study is what this chapter emphasises.

21.1.4 The value of a pilot study in research

An Ashanti proverb states that *you should never test the depth of a river with both your feet.* In reference to a pilot study, getting into the river with both your feet resembles conducting the main study without pre-testing it. You would want to take a long stick to test the depth of the river before you attempt to cross it. If you take the long stick as a pilot study, it means that you will first pilot the main study before you conduct it. In the river, you check the depth so that you will not sink. You pilot the main study so that it will not fail. Therefore, you should avoid taking a risk, and pilot test the main study first. It is far better to be sure whether your study is worth spending time, resources, energy, etc., on, before discovering later that all this was a waste.

As a student, you should seriously consider piloting your main study because that is part of your candidature training. You will gain knowledge and skills on how to effectively implement your research plan in the field. You should realise that even experienced researchers value of piloting their studies first. You will not want to be disappointed by realising only when you are at the point of gathering data, that the research participants find it difficult to understand the items you have asked them to respond to. You could prevent this disappointment by piloting your research instruments first. There are also administrative, resource related, managerial and scientific issues, which create a need to conduct a pilot study prior to the main study.

The value of pilot studies lies in their pragmatism, as they offer adaptation to the research field. Pilot studies can minimise data collection problems. Just getting into the field can provide you with fascinating information and observations. However, that can result in you not knowing where to start if you did not pilot the study first. Specifically on grounded theory application, researchers' choices do not focus on the decisions that go before initial data collection, which can result in two major problems:

▶ The process of identifying relevant groups in data collection can be very long. Depending on your own theoretical sensitivity, the process may result in an erroneous and biased theoretical proposition.
▶ Failure to pilot the study first is an indication of insensitivity or unawareness about contextual dynamics. Contextual sensitivity should guide the choice of groups in order to guide the theoretical purpose.

As a researcher, you should not undermine the importance of an insider's perspective that relates to awareness of context. Insider's perspective guides the proposition of locally informed and significant contributions to theory. A pilot study is a mechanism that can help to build a well-grounded knowledge development and to construct a tangible theory. A pilot study can also help to acquire early contextual sensitivity through the collection of essential information. Contextual sensitivity helps in the effective research design and development of greater awareness of dynamic events, agents and circumstances that can positively modify the flow of the research process and affect decision making.

21.1.5 Misconceptions about the pilot study

There is a tendency to devalue a pilot study in research due to the existing misconceptions. Addressing these misconceptions will help you to appreciate the value of a pilot study. Existing misconceptions include the following:

▶ A pilot study is a small study that you as a student do, which you can complete quickly. In contrast, a pilot study demands effort just like the main study. As a researcher, you should make a commitment to pilot your study so that you can learn the potential and areas that you should improve in the main study. You will be able to make the necessary revisions and adjustments in the main study.

▶ A pilot study is a small study that does not require any funding. You should fully budget for a pilot study as part of the main study. You need the necessary resources for a pilot study. However, there is challenge that, pilot studies are partly about testing the feasibility of the main study. Funders may not support pilot studies because they think that the outcome of the pilot studies may suggest that the main study is not feasible. For most studies you will conduct a pilot study on a small scale. So, you should consider keeping the costs as low as possible so that you do not discourage funders.

▶ A pilot study is a small study that has limited funding. Do not be mistaken; big national projects may demand bigger funding amounts for their pilot studies.

▶ A pilot study is a small single centre study that does not require resources like the main study. However, there can be a need for multiple pilot studies for the main study depending on the complexities and nature of such studies, e.g. mixed-methods, multi-methods, longitudinal, etc. studies. Mixed methods refer to mixing methods under a quantitative-qualitative study, e.g. a survey, observation, taking photographs, unstructured individual interviews, and so on. On the other hand, multi-methods are about using more than one method for data gathering under a quantitative study or a qualitative study, e.g. structured individual interviews, focus group interviews, document analysis and observation in a single qualitative study. Longitudinal studies happen over an extended period of time. The complexities of studies you conduct can thus determine the amount of resources you need. In fact, some pilot studies may need a significant investment of resources, making it difficult to discontinue the research after an unsuccessful pilot study. Therefore, you might be tempted to make considerable changes in the main study rather than deciding that the proposed study is not possible without resources, time, population, and so on. Funders might be reluctant to fund a further study if the pilot has been substantial as they might view the research as no longer original, especially if you publish the results from the pilot study. Therefore, you should approach pilot studies with great care in relation to politics that impact on resource provision.

▶ A pilot study is a small study that is similar in size as someone else's published study with just a small sample. However, you should not mistake a pilot study for the main study, which you undertake on a small scale. The purpose of a pilot study is dissimilar to that of the main study. The main study reports the findings of the study. In a pilot study you report what you have learned and what improvements you can make in the main study.

It is thus clear that a pilot study is pre-testing the main study in order to can make the necessary adjustments before conducting the main study. Figure 21.1 shows that a pilot study precedes the main study. As shown in Figure 21.1, you should plan and conduct the pilot study, account for what you have learnt during the pilot study, make the necessary modifications in the main study, and implement the main study.

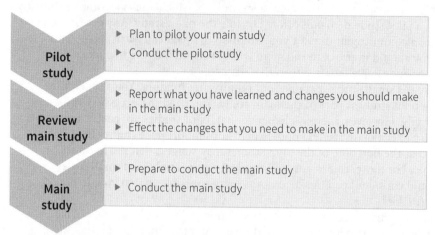

FIGURE 21.1: The process of piloting the main study

Now answer the questions in the challenge that follows.

Critical thinking challenge

You have learned some important points in this section about what a pilot study is and what it is not. Share these important points with a colleague. Make sure that you include your own understanding of a pilot study, different terms used to define a pilot study, and explain the value of a pilot study in a research project. In addition, explain the misconceptions that exist about pilot studies.

21.2 Reasons for a pilot study

Let us try to get behind and into why a pilot study is necessary: what can it tell us to warrant the effort in time and resources?

21.2.1 What are the reasons for a pilot study?

Let us consider Murphy's law of a pilot study: "Anything that can go wrong will go wrong" (Van Teijlingen & Hundley, 2002:33). Also consider the Chinese expression that states, "to ensure that the things that do go wrong, go wrong during the pilot study so that we can fix them before we start the full study". Both these laws and expressions indicate the importance of piloting the main study. This importance leads to the reasons why you should pilot your study. These reasons relate to the general aspects that a pilot study addresses for the main study, and the aspects that relate specifically to methodological issues. The pilot study enables the researcher to:

☑ Assess the feasibility of a full-scale study or survey.

☑ Design a research protocol.

☑ Assess whether the research protocol is realistic and workable.

☑ Assess the likely success of proposed recruitment approaches.

☑ Determine what resources, such as finance or staff, are needed for a planned study;

☑ Develop a research question and research plan.

☑ Receive training in as many elements of the research process as possible.

☑ Convince funding bodies that the research team is competent and knowledgeable.

☑ Convince funding bodies that the main study is feasible and worth funding.

☑ Convince other stakeholders that the main study is worth supporting.

☑ Develop and test adequacy of research instruments.

☑ Establish whether the sampling frame and technique are effective.

☑ Identify logistical problems which might occur using proposed methods.

☑ Estimate variability in outcomes to help determine sample size.

☑ Collect preliminary data.

☑ Assess the suggested data analysis strategies in order to reveal possible problems.

☑ Ascertain the theoretical relevance and feasibility of a sampling frame.

☑ Employ data from pilot findings to rework the stages of the main data collection to strengthen your audit trail so that you tighten the rigour of the study.

These reasons suggest that pilot studies are a crucial element of a good study design. However, piloting a study does not obviously mean that the main study will be free of challenges. The situation in the field might have changed by the time you conduct the main study. For example, you might find that some teachers that you sampled who agreed to participate in your study have been redeployed. But still, a pilot study enhances chances of success with regard to other aspects of the study. Redeployed teachers becomes an aspect that you could not foresee, otherwise you could have planned for this possible change if it surfaced during the pilot study.

21.2.2 The role of a pilot study in improving internal validity

Accounting for trustworthiness of a study is one of the pillars of sound scientific research. A pilot study has a role to play in improving the internal validity, particularly of a questionnaire. It does this by:

▶ Pre-testing the questionnaire on the participants sampled for a pilot study before you can administer it in the main study;

▶ Seeking the opinions of the participants on the readability, soundness, flow, etc of a questionnaire so that you can address issues of ambiguities and unclear questions;

- Monitoring the time the participants take to complete the questionnaire so that you can adjudge if the time is reasonable or whether you should cut out unnecessary or ambiguous questions to make up for a shorter time;
- Checking if the questions yield sufficient range of responses from the participants;
- Finding out if you can interpret the participants' responses in accordance with the needed information;
- Ascertaining if the participants have answered all the questions;
- Re-phrasing the questions that participants did not answer as expected; and
- Re-piloting the study if the extent of revision of the questionnaire is large.

You could design your questionnaire items in such a way that they look orderly, but it may pose certain problems to the respondents. Also consult Chapter 18 on the questionnaire approach. Therefore, pilot studies can help correct issues of ambiguity, difficult questions, double barrel questions, and so forth, so that you do not accommodate loopholes in the finalised questionnaire.

21.2.3 The role of a pilot study in the Delphi data collection method: an example

According to Skulmoski, Hartman and Krahn (2007), the Delphi method gives an illustration of where the pilot study features. The Delphi method is a repetitive process to collect and distil the judgements of experts, using a series of questionnaires interspersed with feedback. You develop a series of questionnaires and administer them logically as you conduct the study in a few rounds with the same participants. You develop the subsequent questionnaire based on the results of the previous questionnaire. The process stops when you think that the data gathered answer the research question. Four features characterise the Delphi method:

- Anonymity allows participants free expression of their opinions. You can evaluate participants' decisions on their merit rather than on who has proposed the idea.
- Iteration, which is the main distinguishing characteristic, allows the participants to refine their views in the light of progressing from round to round of the project.
- You can control feedback, i.e. you can provide feedback to the participants in the process, inform them of other participants' perspectives, and thus provide them the opportunity to clarify or change their views.
- The statistical aggregation of the group response allows for a quantitative analysis and interpretation of data.

The role of a pilot study is to test and adjust the Delphi questionnaire. The pilot study does this to improve comprehension and to solve any procedural problems. There might be a need to pretest subsequent questionnaires as well. The Delphi pilot suits inexperienced researchers who run the risk of being too ambitious about the scope of their studies. Such researchers may also think too limitedly about the time it will take a participant to fully respond to the Delphi survey. Therefore, the Delphi method helps the inexperienced researcher not to rush their studies.

To conclude this section, go through the questions in the challenge and answer them.

21.3 Advantages and disadvantages of pilot studies

21.3.1 Advantages

One of the advantages of conducting a pilot study is that it can give a warning about three things that could go wrong, which are that a pilot study can:
- give an indication about where the main research project could fail.
- give a warning about where you may not be following the research protocols.
- signal the inappropriateness or complication of the proposed methods or instruments.

The following are the advantages of a pilot study:
- You conduct a pilot study before the main study in an attempt to avoid wasting time and money on inadequately designed project.
- A pilot study prepares you in gaining valuable insight about the main study. Should anything be missing in the pilot study, you can still add it in the main study to improve the chances of a clear outcome.
- A pilot study provides proof that the main study has the potential to succeed.
- A pilot study can help identify the design issues before conducting the main study.
- In quantitative studies a pilot study permits a preliminary testing of the hypothesis that leads to testing more precise hypothesis in the main study.
- A pilot study often provides you with ideas, approaches and clues you may not have foreseen before conducting the pilot study.
- A pilot study permits a thorough check of the planned statistical and analytical procedures, giving you a chance to evaluate their usefulness for the data. You may then be able to make needed alterations in the data collection methods.
- A pilot study can greatly reduce the number of unanticipated problems because you have an opportunity to redesign parts of your study to overcome difficulties that a pilot study reveals.
- In a pilot study you may try out a number of alternative measures and then select those that produce the clearest results for the main study.

21.3.2 Disadvantages

In addition to the advantages of a pilot study be aware of the following limitations:
- You will most probably conduct a pilot study on a much smaller scale than your intended research study. Consequently, the findings of the main study may vary from the findings of a pilot study. That is why you should consider not to report the findings of a pilot study. Rather, report the feedback about the instruments and processes from the participants and how they helped you to improve the main study.

- A pilot study may not be appropriate for case studies. You should therefore take great care when you pilot a case study due to its uniqueness.
- You mostly can only conduct a pilot study with members of the relevant population, but not on those who will form part of the sample for the main study.
- A pilot study is normally small in comparison with the main study and can therefore provide only limited information on the sources and magnitude of the variation of response measures.

A pilot study reveals gaps

Note that in accordance with the first limitation, a pilot study is not mainly about reporting the findings: the main aim of a pilot study is to report the gaps that the pilot study reveals about the planned main study.

If your study follows a case study design, be cautious, particularly in multiple case studies or in single case studies that employ multi-method. A case study does not suggest simplicity; it needs rigorous investigation with an aim to study the phenomenon in-depth. Therefore you may not overlook the need to pilot your study.

The third limitation is about objectivity. It is not advisable to include the same participants of a pilot study in the main study. These participants have already seen the research instrument. Their responses in the pilot study will most probably influence the responses in the main study. These participants have the benefit of seeing the instrument for the second time. How could you advise the researchers in opening case study about their sample?

Section 21.3.3 has already been partly addressed in the last limitation.

21.3.3 Managing instances where it is not possible to pilot your study

There are instances where it may be impossible to pilot your study. The impossibility is due to factors that are beyond your control and that can impact on the main study. An obvious factor is when the target population is so small that you can only consider it for the main study. There is, however, an alternative to validate your instruments. In piloting an interview questionnaire, for example, you can use the interviewing-the-investigator technique (also called interviewing-the-interviewer technique).

Interviewing-the-investigator technique works more or less like a role-playing technique. Your supervisor, or another expert, becomes the interviewer, while you as an investigator become the interviewee. There may be a need for a third person who acts as an observer. The participants should approach this exercise as they would the pilot project in the real situation. You as an investigator should have prepared your interview schedule and other documents that relate to it, e.g. consent letter(s), as well as any resources that you need, such as a recording device, a researcher's journal, and so on. It would be even better to either arrange the interview space to represent the real space at the site of the main study, or to conduct the trial interview there.

The interviewer, who happens to be the supervisor or an expert, should start by asking the interviewee for his/her consent to participate in the study and to record the interview. The interviewee should then sign the consent letter. The interviewer can proceed to ask the interviewee the questions in the interview schedule, as well as any prompting questions. The various role players can now reflect on how the interview went. They can reflect on clarity or issues of ambiguity, whether the responses yielded the information that was expected, time spent on the interview, checking if the data you recorded came out clearly on the recording device, checking if there was any need for additional resources, checking the phrasing of the consent letters, bias management, and many other things. You and the 'expert' can then listen to the recorded interview and discuss it. You can re-conduct the interview until you are satisfied that you have thrashed out anything bothering you about the interview. The participants should even consider swopping roles, and also allowing the observer to play the interview or interviewee roles. Going through these processes is, of course, time-consuming, but equally an exercise worth spending time on for the sake of building quality into the main study. The participation of the supervisor should be limited if you cannot avoid it at all, since supervisors can also bring bias into the study. You should rather involve another expert.

Another technique that you can consider is the study monitoring seminar technique, which is bigger in scope than a pilot study, or the interviewing-the-investigator technique. The scope is bigger because you can apply it throughout the study even to check on aspects outside of methodology, e.g. literature study. However, you and your supervisor can narrow it down only to the methodology, if you want to. The supervisor, in agreement with you, organises the study monitoring seminar by scheduling support seminars for you in the faculty, where he/she can invite a few expert colleagues in the field and fellow students to participate in such seminars. The seminars can be very enriching to you. The supervisor of this chapter's author organised a seminar when the author was doing his doctoral degree. The author benefited substantially as he had the opportunity to interact with the academic audience. The audience helped by suggesting relevant ideas and literature that the author incorporated in his study later on.

Now, try the questions in the challenge.

Critical thinking challenge

Think back on what you have learned in this section.
1 Write about the advantages and disadvantages of a pilot study. Discuss what techniques you can use when you cannot pilot your study.
2 Find two colleagues with whom you can role play the interviewing-the-investigator technique. Make notes about what you learned as you role play the technique. What is the value of a study monitoring seminar technique for your study?

21.4 How should you treat the findings of a pilot study?

21.4.1 A brief overview of the challenges of a pilot study

Should you report the pilot findings in your main study? What is your opinion on this matter? This section addresses this question. Keep in mind the purpose of a pilot study, which is to test the feasibility of the main study. It is important to keep in mind that despite all the efforts, a pilot study may not render the main study problem free. You may not see into other hidden challenges during a pilot study. The situation in the field might have changed to some extent by the time you conduct the main study, as stated in section 21.3.1. Challenges may not be obvious until you conduct the main study.

The next sections respond to the challenges of reporting the findings of a pilot study.

21.4.2 What not to include from the pilot study in the main study

The findings of a pilot study are not the focus of the pilot study itself. Therefore, it is not advisable to report the pilot findings as part of the main study's findings. Including the findings in the main study may contaminate the main study. You may not even make an effort to analyse the findings of a pilot study. The focus of a pilot study relates to the study's purpose, which is about getting feedback from the participants about how they experienced the questionnaire in the process of filling it, or how they experienced the interview questions in the process of being interviewed. The feedback that the participants give helps to improve the questionnaire for the main study. Since a pilot study is a trial run, you should report as part of the main study only lessons that you have learnt and corrections you have made in the main study. Again look at the opening case study. What have the authors reported in that case study? Why do you think so?

Also, you may not include the pilot participants in the main study. As indicated in section 21.3.2, the pilot participants have already been exposed to the data collection instrument; the main study may be biased if you include them in the main study. (See Chapter 6 about issues of objectivity.) Sometimes, however, it may be challenging to exclude the pilot participants because to do so will result in too small a sample in the main study. This problem arises especially where you have decided on cluster samples, for example, from schools, prisons or hospitals. However, you cannot just include a pilot sample in the main study. You should exercise caution where you cannot avoid including the pilot sample in the main study. Alternatively, you can conduct a sensitivity analysis to assess the extent to which the process of piloting the study influences the size of the intervention effect.

21.4.3 Findings of a qualitative pilot study

The purpose of a pilot study guides what you should report about the findings. You could use some or all of your pilot data as part of the main study. This is because qualitative data collection and analysis is often progressive and a second or subsequent interview in a series is often more effective than the previous one. As an interviewer, you might have gained insights from the previous interviews that other researchers used, to improve interview schedules and specific questions. Hence, there may be insignificant difference between a pilot study and the main study. In practical terms, you can conduct 18 focus group interviews. You will listen to the recordings or read through the transcripts of the first three or four to improve the interview questions. You may also want to improve on how you introduce the issues in the group interview, or even add new topics. Therefore, although there is no specific pilot study, analysis of the earlier focus groups can help to improve the later ones. Thus, to start with data analysis as soon as data collection starts elicits your reflections as a researcher so that you can make the necessary improvements in the following stages of data gathering.

A pilot study should, however, be intentional. You should plan it in advance. It is not convincing enough to assume that integrating data collection for the improvement of the subsequent collections is simply a pilot study if you had no intention to consciously conduct any pilot investigation. That also has implications on the approach of reporting your pilot findings. Thus, the idea of a pilot study as experimental, exploratory, test, preliminary, trial, or even try-out, still holds and you should not confuse it with the other means of dealing with data.

21.4.4 The influence of context on pilot findings

Contextual factors play a role in pilot findings. Three examples on reporting the pilot findings will illustrate the influence of context in this section. These examples shed light for the inexperienced doctoral candidate who is entering the field of inductive qualitative enquiry.

The examples also reveal how pilot studies can contribute towards making decisions about the design of grounded theory studies. Each example shows the researcher's efforts in deciding on a research design that is relevant to his or her research question and context. The examples cover the following aspects:

▶ Objectives of the study
▶ Reasons for conducting a pilot study
▶ Strategies for collecting data and analysing them
▶ How the pilot study contributed towards contextual sensitivity
▶ How the pilot study assisted in designing the subsequent stages of the study.

What if …? Librarians in Syria

This pilot study was about the role of academic librarians in the strategic planning of information systems in higher education. It is based on public universities in Syria.

Objectives of the study
The objective of the study was to inquire into the role of academic librarians in information systems strategic planning in Syria's public universities.

Reasons for conducting the pilot study
▶ The first reason was about the exploration of identities that were emerging from the organisational environment in the Syrian public higher education.
▶ The second reason was to identify key informants, because the number of public higher education organisations in Syria is small.

Strategies for collecting data and analysing them
The researchers in this pilot study employed a snowball selection strategy. They used this selection strategy to identify key informants from four public Syrian universities. The researchers first implemented the snowball selection strategy by conducting a holistic meta-enquiry in the higher education ministry. The researchers used open interviews to gather data from the higher education ministry, while they used semi structured interviews to gather data from the higher education organisations. For data analysis, the researchers used open coding and embrionary axial coding.

How the pilot study contributed towards contextual sensitivity
The pilot study produced the processes of planning and management, which currently were silent and not documented. The results of the pilot study indicated unplanned academic librarians' contribution in delivering information services in the entire university environment. The pilot study further helped to identify a number of formal and informal collaborations and co-operations between different stakeholders.

How the pilot study assisted in designing the subsequent stages of the study
The pilot study assisted in the following ways:
▶ The researchers were able to identify initial set of informants to interview.
▶ The researchers managed to identify the initial categories that they used in designing the interview scripts for the following stage.
▶ The pilot ensured the feasibility of the study.
▶ The higher education leaders and professional stakeholders were interested in the study.
▶ The first open coding helped to focus the objectives of the study on questioning the processes that sustain the unstructured and non-formalised contribution of academic librarians.

What if ...? Chinese medicine

The researchers enquired into the identification of barriers to knowledge sharing in inter-professional collaboration between traditional and Western medicine health care practitioners. The study was conducted in China.

Objectives of the study

The study investigated the barriers to sharing knowledge between Western medicine and traditional medicine practitioners in China.

Reasons for conducting the pilot study

▶ The first reason for the study was to create an understanding of the current situation in the health care institutions in China. The focus areas in the study were collaboration, interaction and sharing of knowledge between the traditional medicine and Western medicine practitioners.

▶ The second reason for the study was to create an understanding of the nature of the relationships between the two practising groups and the processes in the organisation which supported these relationships.

Strategies for collecting data and analysing them

The researchers used a purposive sampling technique to select seven health care professionals and workers for interviews. The researchers used the techniques of open coding, axial coding and constant comparison to analyse data. This pilot study improved the researcher's skills with respect to conducting semi structured interviews. The researcher applied the acquired skills to approach potential participants, select a suitable interview environment, engage in deep conversation with the participants, and probed and followed up the emerging topics. The pilot study created awareness in the researcher about the challenges in the research process. These challenges included processes of negotiating access to potential informants, the impact of participants' heavy workloads on access, cultural disposition to disclose information in interviews, and the held views about the status between the researcher and surgeons. The pilot study helped the researcher to minimise these problems, which ensured the success of data collection during the main study. The pilot study also helped the researchers to develop an insight about hospital procedures and communication channels. Furthermore, the pilot study cast light about the implications for narrowing the focus of the study, sampling, designing initial interview scripts and designing the next stages of the study.

How the pilot study contributed towards contextual sensitivity

The pilot study revealed problems about knowledge sharing between traditional Chinese medicine and western medicine practitioners in the Chinese hospital environment. The government decided to accommodate these two groups of medical practitioners in the same physical institutions. Next, the government expected the groups to collaborate. However, the findings of the pilot study showed that these groups did not seem to interact naturally or harmoniously.

How the pilot study assisted in designing the subsequent stages of the study

The pilot study validated the research question. The pilot study also confirmed the gap in the study. The pilot study assured the researchers of the relevance of the selected case study in conducting the study. Therefore, the researchers managed to secure access to interview participants. The researchers could generate the first set of categories to guide the following steps of the data collection.

What if ...? Incorporating indigenous technology

This study was about the implications of indigenous technologies for a technology education curriculum.

Objectives of the study

The objective of the study was to develop a model for a Technology Education curriculum that could facilitate the transformation of the existing Technology Education curriculum in schools to incorporate the richness of indigenous technologies.

Reasons for conducting the pilot study
- ▶ The first reason was to explore the nature and understanding of indigenous technologies from a Technology Education perspective.
- ▶ The second reason was to explore a way to accommodate the richness of indigenous technologies in the Technology Education curriculum.

Strategies for collecting data and analysing them

This was an action research study. Five Technology teachers who teach Grades 7 to 9 participated in action research cycles in terms of a series of plenary meetings, interviews, document analysis and observation. Grade 7 learners also participated in practical class activities with these teachers. The researcher co-observed with the teachers. The researcher used open coding, axial coding and selective coding strategies to analyse data and identified thematic categories that would enable the design of a model ultimately. This pilot study helped the researcher, who was a doctoral candidate at that time, to sharpen his negotiation skills into the site of investigation, lead discussions during plenary meetings, use probing techniques during interviews, observe and co-plan class activities with the teachers.

How the pilot study contributed towards contextual sensitivity

The pilot study revealed some degree of neglect of indigenous technologies in the Technology Education curriculum. Though the Technology Education curriculum policy specifically mentioned indigenous technologies, teachers seemed not to take up the opportunity to integrate indigenous technologies in their practice. It came out clearly that teacher workshops did not train them on the integration of indigenous technologies in their practice. Thus, the pilot study created awareness about the legitimacy of integrating indigenous technologies as policy grants. There was a need to show them how to integrate indigenous technologies.

How the pilot study assisted in designing the subsequent stages of the study

The pilot study confirmed the research question that the researcher planned for the study. The researcher made some changes to improve on data collection methods. He tightened the observation instrument by including a list of specific items to observe. He also brought the interviews to a much earlier stage rather than keep them only at the end of the action research cycles. He deemed it necessary to include the school principals of the two schools for the main study in the interviews. He changed the individual structured interviews into free-attitude interviews to allow more relaxation on the part of the interviewees to share information. He reduced the plenary meetings about lesson planning that integrated indigenous technologies to three by combining some of them, and changed document analysis meeting into an analysis sheet to give to teachers to analyse the textbooks that they used. He added the post-cycle reflection meeting to co-evaluate the cycle activities with the teachers.

You will see from these three examples that feedback from the pilot study can help you to revisit data gathering methods and processes in order that you can correct the gaps revealed by the pilot study. Therefore, you will be able to take care of poor planning at this stage before you encounter it in the main study. A doctoral candidate, Fonger (2011), attests to the fact that a pilot study helped him to learn about and implement observation in mathematics education. Experienced researchers, Forgasz and Keur (1997), corroborate this helpfulness; they conducted a pilot study in mathematics education and appreciated the fact that the pilot study helped them to review their research design.

Reflect on this section and answer the questions in the challenge.

Critical thinking challenge

This last section has addressed the challenges of reporting the findings of a pilot study in the main study. What should your focus be in reporting the findings? Based on the tips you have learned about designing a questionnaire in Chapter 18: about the questionnaire approach, think about a research problem that you intend investigating, the research methods that you will use, and the sample. Follow the pattern of the three examples in section 21.4.4, to demonstrate the contribution of your pilot study towards the main study.

Conclusion

This chapter has tried to achieve the following:
▶ It provided a background for a pilot study (which includes the motivation for this chapter on pilot study).
▶ It defined and explained the value of a pilot study.
▶ It captured the advantages and critically deliberated on the limitations of a pilot study.
▶ It addressed the challenges for reporting the pilot findings.

The chapter defined a pilot study as a preliminary investigation that you should embark on with the idea of solidifying the feasibility of the main study, and to improve data gathering methods based of the findings of a pilot study. A pilot study helps in skilling and enhancing the knowledge of inexperienced researchers. Advanced researchers can benefit from conducting a pilot study as well. Besides from researchers benefiting from a pilot study, this chapter emphasised the importance of piloting the main study.

For postgraduate candidates registered for their Master's or doctoral studies, it is important that supervisors make sure that these Master's and doctoral candidates pilot their studies and give an account as part of their report writing, of how piloting their studies improved their data collection methods.

Analysing fieldwork data, which the next part of this book will address, can be done much more effectively if a study has been properly piloted.

Closing activities

Self-reflection questions

1 Define a pilot study.

2 What is the value of a pilot study in the research project?

3 What are the existing misconceptions about a pilot study and how can you counteract these misconceptions?

4 Explain the reasons for piloting your study.

5 Discuss the advantages and disadvantages of a pilot study.

6 What exactly are you supposed to report from the pilot study in your main study?

7 Revisit the opening case study. Based on the understanding that you have gained in this chapter, how would you have approached the study in that particular case?

Practical applications

8 As part of your research study, develop a plan to conduct a pilot study.

Think about the general and methodology specific aspects surrounding your study that the pilot study will address and improve on.

Use the following template to account for the improvement of your main study:

▶ Title of the study.

▶ Objectives of the study.

▶ Reasons for conducting the pilot study.

▶ Strategies for collecting data and analysing them.

▶ How the pilot study contributed towards contextual sensitivity.

▶ How the pilot study assisted in designing the subsequent stages of the study.

9 Finally, think about a way you are going to report the improvements you factored in this template as part of writing up your dissertation, thesis or article.

Bibliography

Chenail, R.J. 2011. Interviewing the Investigator: Strategies for addressing instrumentation and researcher bias concerns in qualitative research. *The Qualitative Report*, 16(1):255–262. Available online at: www.nova.edu/ssss/QR/QR16-1/interviewing.pdf.

Cortner, T., Intrator, S., Kelemen, M. & Sato, M. 2000. What graduate students say about their preparation for doing qualitative dissertations: A pilot study. Paper presented at American Educational Research Association. New Orleans, USA.

De Vaus, D.A. 1993. *Survey in Social Research* (3rd ed.). London: UCL Press.

Flyvbjerg, B. 2006. Five misunderstandings about case-study research. *Qualitative Inquiry*, 12(2): 219–245.

Fonger, N.L. 2011. Lessons learned as a novice researcher: A pilot study in mathematics education. *The Hilltop Review*, 4(2):55–62. Available online at: http://scholarworks.wmich.edu/hilltopreview/vol4/iss2/10. Accessed on 22 December 2013.

Forgasz, H.J. & Keur, B. 1997. The role of the pilot study in mathematics education research. *The Mathematics Educator*, 2(2):187–196.

Foster, R.L. 2013. What a pilot study is and what it is not. *Journal for Specialists in Pediatric Nursing*, 18:1–2.

Gumbo, M.T. 2003. Indigenous technologies: Implications for a technology education curriculum. Unpublished PhD thesis. Pretoria: Vista University.

Gumbo, M.T. 2014. An action research pilot study on the integration of indigenous technology in Technology Education. *Mediterranean Journal of Social Sciences*, 5(10):386–392.

Kraemer, H.C., Mintz, J., Noda, A., Tinklenberg, J. & Yesavage, J.A. 2006. Caution regarding the use of pilot studies to guide power calculations for study proposals. *Arch Gen Psychiatry*, 63:484–489.

Lancaster, G.A., Dodd, S. & Williamson, P.R. 2004. Design and analysis of pilot studies: Recommendations for good practice. *Journal of Evaluation in Clinical Practice*, 10(2): 307–312.

Nunes, B.M., Martins, T., Zhou, J., Alajamy, L.M. & Al-Mamari, S. 2010. Contextual sensitivity in grounded theory: The role of pilot studies. *The Electronic Journal of Business Research Methods*, 8(2):73-84. Available online at: www.ejbrm.com. Accessed 22 December 2013.

Polit, D.F., Beck, C.T., Hungler, B.P. 2001. *Essentials of nursing research: Methods, appraisal, and utilisation* (5ᵗʰ ed.). Philadelphia: Lippincott.

Reiss, C.R. n.d. The importance of pilot studies in the development of large-scale seawater desalination plants. Available online at: www.twdb.state.tx.us/publications/reports/numbered_reports/doc/R363/C5.pdf. Accessed 19 January 2014.

Sampson, H. 2004. Navigating the waves: The usefulness of a pilot in qualitative research. *Qualitative Research*, 4:383–402.

Skulmoski, G.J., Hartman, F.T. & Krahn, J. 2007. The Delphi method for graduate research. *Journal of Information Technology Education*, 6:1–21.

Thabane, L., Ma, J., Chu, R., Cheng, J., Ismaila, A., Rios, L.P., Robson, R., Thabane, M., Giangregorio, L. & Goldsmith, C.H. 2010. A tutorial on pilot studies: The what, why and how. *BMC Medical Research Methodology*, 10:1.

Van Teijlingen, E.R. & Hundley, V. 2001. The importance of pilot studies. *Social Research Update*, 35. Available online at: http://sru.soc.survey.ac.uk?SRU35.html.

Van Teijlingen, E.R. & Hundley, V. 2002. The importance of pilot studies. *Nursing Standard*, 16(40):33–36.

Van Teijlingen, E.R. & Hundley, V. 2013. Pilot study. In M.S. Lewis-Beck, A. Bryman & T. F. Liao (Eds). *The SAGE Encyclopedia of Social Science Research Methods*. Thousand Oaks: SAGE (pp. 824–825).

Whitheley, A. & Whitheley, J. 2005. The familiarization study in qualitative research: From theory to practice: Graduate School of Business Working Paper 51. Perth, Australia.

Part 3

Analysing fieldwork data

CHAPTER 22

Bruno Yawe and John Mubazi

Quantitative data analysis: Descriptive statistics

KEY CONCEPTS

A histogram is a graphical representation of the distribution of data.

A measure of central tendency or location is the centre of gravity of data distribution.

A measure of disparity or dispersion measures the spread of data distribution from the centre of gravity.

Measurement is a procedure in which a researcher assigns numerals (numbers or other symbols) to empirical properties (variables) according to specified rules.

Assignment means mapping where numerals or numbers are mapped onto objects or events.

Rule specifies the procedure a researcher uses to assign numerals or numbers to objects or events.

Arithmetic mean is the amount which, when multiplied by the number of items, gives the total for the group.

Interpolation is a simple mathematical technique which estimates an unknown value by utilising immediately surrounding known values.

Frequency polygon or curve (line chart) presents a frequency distribution pictorially and is an alternative to a histogram.

Ogive or cumulative chart/frequency/line graph shows who or what falls above or below a particular point.

Nominal is a level of measurement where the data or variables are merely named.

Ordinal is a level of measurement which orders the sequence or indicates the rank ordering of items.

Interval is a level of measurement which assigns spaces of equal intervals to numbers.

Ratio is a level or scale of measurement which represents values measured in equal units from absolute zero.

LEARNING OUTCOMES

By the end of this chapter, you should be able to:

▶ Explain the meaning and functions of the measures of central tendency and dispersion.

▶ Name the different categories of these measures.

▶ Outline the different kinds of measures of location and disparity.

▶ Differentiate between these measures.

▶ Discuss the implications of these various measures of central tendency and dispersion.

▶ Try out some reflective activities.

As part of a class assignment in an educational statistics class in the College of Education and External Studies at Makerere University in Uganda, an instructor compiled the data below. A uniform class interval was used starting from point 30—34 to construct an exclusive grouped frequency distribution for the data:

Classes	f_i (a)	Class mid-points x_i(b)	f_ix_i	cf
30 – 34	4	32	128	4
35 – 39	7	37	259	11
40 – 44	15	42	630	26
45 – 49	11	47	517	37
45 – 49	8	52	416	45
55 – 59	5	57	285	50
	$\sum = 50$		$\sum = 2{,}235$	

Measures of central tendency or location, the arithmetic mean, the median, and the mode, were computed to convey to the head of department an idea of the class performance. The instructor was also required to comment on the findings:

Arithmetic mean $= \bar{x} = \dfrac{2{,}235}{50} = 44.7$.

Median $=$ Mdn $= 39.5 + 4.7 = 44.2$

Mode $=$ Mo $= 39.5 + \dfrac{10}{3} = 42.8$, a crude one would be 42.

In addition, the instructor was required to compute one measure of disparity or dispersion, the standard deviation, and to plot the histogram and frequency polygon for pictorial analysis.

Introduction

Over the years, our experience has shown that students require tools in the area of quantitative data analysis and descriptive statistics in particular, to competently report their research findings. The purpose or objective of this chapter is to look at quantitative data analysis with particular reference to descriptive statistics. This is important since it will enable you to understand the essential quantitative data analysis tools in the area of descriptive statistics. Without these tools, the outcome of research may be of little value to you and others. In order to achieve our objective, this chapter presents the measures of location and disparity, outlines their various types, and explains them with examples. The chapter also examines their relative use, as well as discussing their relative advantages and disadvantages. In addition, an exploration of organisation and graphing quantitative data has been carried out. Descriptive statistics reinforce the planning, designing and conducting of educational research and are also useful in reporting and the dissemination of research findings. This is demonstrated in the case study, and this chapter will explore what happened when the head of department requested the instructor to make available the required information for pictorial analysis.

22.1 Measurements

Once you have collected your quantitative data, you need to use descriptive statistics to convey the important aspects of their distribution. The two broad features of the distribution are measures of **central tendency** and measures of **dispersion**. A measure of central tendency or location is the centre of gravity of a data distribution, while a measure of disparity or dispersion measures the spread of a data distribution from the centre of gravity. The most commonly used measures of central tendency are the mean, median, and mode. Conversely, measures of dispersion which include the variance and the standard deviation indicate the extent to which the collected data differ from the sample mean.

Quantitative data are data that can be measured numerically. **Measurement** is a procedure in which a researcher assigns numerals (numbers or other symbols) to empirical properties (variables) according to specified rules. Things that can be measured precisely such as the number of attendees at an event, the temperature in a given location, or a person's height can be considered quantitative data.

A numeral is a symbol of the form I, II, III, … or 1, 2, 3, … and has no quantitative meaning unless you give it such a meaning. A numeral can be used to identify phenomena, objects, or persons. Numerals that are given quantitative meaning become numbers that are amenable to quantitative analyses. **Assignment** means mapping and numerals or numbers are mapped onto objects or events. A **rule** specifies the procedure a researcher uses to assign numerals or numbers to objects or events. The numerical structure of the measurements must be similar, in its relations and operations, to the structure of the indicators.

There are four levels or scales of measuring, namely, nominal, ordinal, interval, and ratio:

▶ The **nominal** level is where the data or variables are merely named, and is considered the lowest or weakest type of data.
▶ The **ordinal** level orders the sequence or indicates the rank ordering of items, and is characterised by categories that are ranked in terms of values.
▶ The **interval** level assigns spaces of equal intervals to numbers. At this level of measurement, mathematical calculations are possible: the numbers can be added and subtracted but not multiplied or divided.
▶ **Ratio** level or scale represents values measured in equal units from absolute zero, a defined, natural, or non-arbitrary zero point. The numbers or scores can be multiplied and divided, which is not possible to do with lower levels.

All levels of measurement are successively built on one another such that a higher level of measurement has all the properties of the lower ones.

Now that we have discussed issues surrounding measurements, we will look at how these measurements are used in practice. We start by looking at how they are used in computing the measures of **central tendency** or **location**.

22.2 Measures of central tendency or location

Representative measures or measures of location or central tendency are those that are used to represent a set of data or data distribution. They are commonly called averages and are the most well-known measures of numeric data. They are single values intended as representatives which can neatly characterise a whole group. There are different types of averages to suit different situations and requirements but the most commonly used is the arithmetic mean.

22.2.1 The mean

22.2.1.1 The arithmetic mean

The **arithmetic mean** or the mean is the most common measure and is the amount which, when multiplied by the number of items, gives the total for the group. For non-grouped data is the sum of the variables divided by its total number. Observations: $x_i = (x_1, x_2, ..., x_n) = (15, 7, 11, 4, 8)$, N = 5 therefore the arithmetic mean is 45/5 = 9.

The following formula yields the arithmetic mean: $\bar{x} = \dfrac{\sum_1^n x_i}{n}$ where:

▸ $\bar{x}$ is the arithmetic mean;

▸ $\sum_1^n x_i$ is the sum of all observations; and

▸ n is the number of observations.

This example is about computing the arithmetic mean from the raw data: Suppose that the following data have been collected by asking 50 students the number of kilometres they travel to their university each day (to the nearest kilometre). Find the mean distance travelled.

18	22	28	25	12	25	18	26	27	14
28	25	29	4	28	25	25	16	23	24
13	23	30	22	19	22	29	26	7	18
24	29	19	24	24	23	3	20	15	32
23	29	25	10	21	35	31	24	21	8

Solution
You will notice that the previous formula for computing the mean can be employed to calculate the mean for the data provided. In so doing, the sum of the distances travelled is 1,091 kilometres. Because we have 50 observations, we compute the mean by dividing the sum by the number of observations (1,091/50) which yields 21.82 kilometres. This means that the average distance travelled to the university by each student is 21.82 kilometres.

Besides the arithmetic mean or the mean, there are other means, for example:
▸ Weighted mean
▸ Harmonic mean
▸ Geometric mean.

These are explained in the sections that follow.

22.2.1.2 Weighted mean

A weighted mean is meant to solve a problem arising from combining the means of a number of groups to form a grand mean. In this case the means of a number of groups are thought of as x-values and their constituent numbers or weights as (frequency) f-values.

Examples include the calculation of grade point average (GPA). The formula is:

$$x - \frac{\Sigma xw}{\Sigma w}$$

Where w_i is the weight of the ith observation and $n = \Sigma w_i$.

> This example shows how a weighted mean or average can be used to compute the final score of a student given different weights of each examination element:
>
> Rating system: Exercise(s) 0.15 or 15%
> Test(s) 0.10 or 10%
> Exam 0.75 or 75%
>
> $$\frac{70 \times 0.15 + 62 \times 0.10 + 58 \times 0.75}{100} = 10.5 + 6.2 + 42.5 = 60.2\%$$
>
> If they were of equal weights then it would be a matter of adding scores off the total, the simple or arithmetic mean.

22.2.1.3 Harmonic mean

A harmonic mean is a specialised average or measure of location generally used to average rates or ratios with the advantage of taking little account of extreme values. It is the reciprocal of the arithmetic mean of the sum of the reciprocals, expressed as:

$$H = \frac{1}{\frac{1}{N}\Sigma \frac{1}{X}}$$

If weighted,

$$H = \frac{\Sigma W}{\frac{1}{N}\Sigma \frac{1}{WX}}$$

> This example shows how the harmonic mean can be used to compute the average speed of cycling up and down hill:
>
> Given uphill and downhill cycling of 10 and 30 miles per hour respectively, find the average speed.
>
> $$\frac{1}{10} + \frac{1}{30} = \frac{4}{30}$$ Since it is a reciprocal, it follows $2 \times \frac{30}{4} = 15$ MPH.

According to Francis (2008:124), symbolically the harmonic mean (hm) of x_1, x_2, x_n is given by:

$$hm = \frac{n}{\Sigma \frac{1}{X}}$$

> This simple example shows how the harmonic mean (hm) formula can be used:
>
> If $x_i = 2, 4, 6$ then hm = $\dfrac{3}{\frac{1}{2} + \frac{1}{4} + \frac{1}{6}} = \dfrac{3}{0.5 + 0.25 + 0.17}$
>
> $$= 3.27$$

Depending on the basis of measurement, rates can be averaged using either the harmonic mean or the arithmetic mean (Francis, 2008:124-5). Since a rate is always expressed in terms of the ratio of two units, the criteria for choosing which is appropriate is:

▶ If the rates are being averaged over *constant numerator units, the harmonic mean* is used.
▶ If the rates are being averaged over *constant denominator units, the arithmetic mean* is used.

22.2.1.4 Geometric mean

The geometric mean is a specialised measure of location, generally used to average proportional increases or changes such as percentages or index numbers. It is defined as the n-th root of the product of *n* values. Because of the way it is defined, it takes little account of extremes and occasionally is used as an alternative to the arithmetic mean.

The geometric mean rate of return gives the mean percentage return of an investment over time. Francis (2008:123) gives the Financial Times (FT) Index as the most well-known example of its practical use, calculated as the geometric mean of a set of selected share values. Other applications include compound interest over several years, total sales growth, and population growth.

There are several ways of calculating the geometric mean that include a calculator with the help of logarithms or with a computer command line.

22.2.2 The median

A median is the middle point (not necessarily a value) of a series or set of data arranged in order of magnitude, ascending (increasing) or descending (decreasing). It halves the distribution into two equal parts. When n is odd, the median value is (n+1)/2. When n is even, there is no unique middle or central value. The convention in such a case is to use the mean of the middle two items to give a (practical) median.

There are two methods commonly employed for estimating the median, namely:

▶ Using an interpolation formula
▶ Graphical interpolation.

Interpolation in this context is a simple mathematical technique which estimates an unknown value by utilising immediately surrounding known values.

For computation, given a grouped frequency distribution, identify the class or group that contains the median item using the cumulative frequencies and the fact that the median is exactly half way along the distribution. The formulas below will provide a theoretical value for the median within the class:

$$Mdn = L + \frac{n1}{n2}W$$

where L is the lower class boundary of the median class

n_1 is the number of frequency that must be covered in the median class to reach the median item, that is, (N/2) – f_{cb} (cumulative frequency below)
n_2 is the sum of all the frequency in the median class
w is the class width, assuming all classes are equal and continuity.

$$Mdn = L + i\,\frac{(\frac{N}{2} - Cfb)}{fw}$$

where L = Like above, is the exact lower boundary of that group in which the median happens to fall.

i = Like w above, is the class interval or width.

N/2 is the median definition for even numbers. When calculating or estimating the median value in a grouped frequency distribution, the $(\Sigma f+1)/2$ th $= N/2$ th theoretical item.

N = Total number of items in the distribution.

C_{fb}= Cumulative frequency below that group in which the median happens to fall.

f_w = Actual frequency within that group in which the median falls.

This example shows how the formulas above can be used. The table presents the frequency as well as the cumulative frequency. Using the formula for computing the median, determine the median distance travelled by students to the university.

Kilometres travelled to university	Frequency	Cumulative frequency	As a %
0–5	2	2	4
5–10	3	5	10
10–15	4	9	18
15–20	7	16	32
20–25	20	36	72
25–30	11	47	94
30–35	3	50	100

Solution

The median = 20.5 + (9/20)5 = 20.5 + (0.45 x 5) = 22.75   first formula

or

= 20.5 + 5[(25 – 16)/20] = 20.5 + 2.25 = 22.75   second formula

In one of the graphical methods, a percentage cumulative frequency curve or ogive is drawn and the value of the variable that corresponds to the 50 per cent point (i.e. halfway along the distribution) is read off and gives the median estimate (see section 22.12). Alternatively, greater than (>) and less than (<) cumulative frequency curves intersect at a median value where the frequency is divided into two equal parts.

According to Francis (2008:113), using a cumulative **frequency polygon** rather than an **ogive** yield the result identical to that obtained using a formula. An **ogive** approach accurately drawn yield better results.

The median has at least three advantages as a measure of central tendency. namely:

1 It is an appropriate alternative to the mean when extreme values are present at one or both ends of a set of distribution.

2 It can be used when certain end values of a set of distribution are difficult to get, expensive to have, or impossible to obtain.

3 Unlike the mean that cannot be calculated if the data values are non-numerical, the median can be used with non-numeric data provided the measurements can be naturally ordered.

The median has also one advantage over the mean in that it can assume a value equal to one of the original items. However, it is difficult to handle theoretically in more advanced statistical work and its use is therefore restricted to basic level analysis.

Now that we have looked at the second measure of central tendency or location, the median, we turn to the third, the mode.

22.2.3 The mode

Sometimes a set of data is obtained where it is appropriate to measure a representative or average value in terms of popularity or most liked or common. In this instance the mode is more representative of the data than the mean or median because it is the value which occurs most frequently. With grouped data, like the mean and the median, it cannot be determined exactly but crudely estimated as the middle of the class with most frequency. It may have one value (uni), two values (bi), or more than two values (multi).

There are two computational methods, the interpolation formula; and the graphical using a histogram (see section 22.7). In the case of the interpolation method, a formula can be utilised:

$$Mo = L + \frac{D1}{D1 + D2} W$$

where L is the lower class boundary of the modal class (like for the median).
D_1 is the difference between modal class frequency and frequency of preceding class.
D_2 is the difference between the frequency of the modal class and frequency of the following class.
w is the class width or size, like for the median.

This example shows how the formula above can be used to compute the mode. The table presents the frequency as well as the cumulative frequency. Using the formula, determine the modal distance travelled by students to the university.

Kilometres travelled to university	Frequency	Cumulative frequency	As a %
0–5	2	2	4
5–10	3	5	10
10–15	4	9	18
15–20	7	16	32
20–25	20	36	72
25–30	11	47	94
30–35	3	50	100

Solution
The mode: $D_1 = 20 - 7 = 13$; $D_2 = 20 - 11 = 9$; $L = 20.5$; and $W = 5$
Substituting we get $20.5 + [13/(13+9)]5 = 20.5 + (13/22)5 = 20.5 + 2.95 = 23.45$

The mode has two advantages, namely:
1 When or where 'most popular' matters, the mode is an alternative to the mean or median; and
2 The mode can be used even in the presence of open classes or isolated extreme values.

In terms of disadvantages:
1 The mode may not exist or be unique.
2 In cases of further analysis, unlike the mean and the median, the mode has no 'natural' measure of dispersion to twin with.
3 Like the median, the mode is not used in advanced statistical work.

Looking at the third measure of central tendency or location, the mode, finishes the three types of these measures namely the mean, the median, and the mode. Before looking at the measures of disparity or dispersion in the next section, 22.3, we conclude section 22.2 by looking at the relationship between the three measures of location in the following section 22.2.4.

22.2.4 The relationship between the mean, median, and the mode

The mean is the most common and easier measure of central tendency. With a normal (symmetric) distribution, the mean, median and mode all coincide at the point of symmetry. The distribution is symmetric if the observations are balanced or approximately evenly distributed about its middle and the centre of the data divides a graph of the distribution into two 'mirror images'.

   If the distribution is not symmetric, it is asymmetric. There are two asymmetric situations: Positive (+) or right-skewed that has the tail on the right which normally means that we start from the left with the mode then the median and finally the mean. When negative (-) or left-skewed, the tail is on the left meaning that we start with the mean then the median and finally the mode. The effect or leverage of the extreme values exerted on the mean is manifested in its being pulled closer to them or towards the tail of the distribution.

   Diagrammatically, the mode falls under the main peak or hump of the curve, the median divide the area under the curve into two equal parts, and the mean marks the center of gravity of the area under the curve.

This diagram shows that when the distribution is symmetric, the mean, the median, and the mode coincide. It also shows the positions of the left and the right tails of a distribution.

Left tail   Right tail

Mean
Median
Mode

A mean is an expected value for whatever is measured. Its importance lies in the fact that decisions can be based on this measure and a lot of time can be saved.

Now that we have completed looking at the measures of location or central tendency, we turn to looking at the measures of disparity or dispersion in the next section, 22.3.

Stop and reflect

What is 'typical' in the measures of location, central location or tendency?

22.3 Measures of dispersion or disparity

Dispersion or **disparity** is the statistical name for the spread or variability of data. Measures of variability are concerned with the degree of variation or departure from the central value or score because in a given set of data the actual values/members can vary a great deal.

These measures describe how spread out or scattered a set or distribution of numeric data is. There are different bases on which the spread of the data can be measured:
1 *Overall spread of items.* This measure is called the range.
2 *Central percentage of spread of items.* These measures have links with the median:
   a) the 10 to 90 percentile range.
   b) the quartile deviation.
3 *Spread about the mean.* This is concerned with measuring the distance between the items and their common mean. There are two measures of this type:
   a) the mean deviation.
   b) the standard deviation.

After this brief introduction, we now turn to the types of the measures of dispersion or disparity starting with the range in 22.3.1.

22.3.1 Overall spread of items: Range

The range is the simplest measure of dispersion available in statistical analysis defined as the numerical difference between the 'smallest and largest values of the items in a set or distribution'. If it is small, the distribution is said to be *homogeneous* (compact) and if large, it is said to be *heterogeneous* (Wangusa, 2007:61).

a) Non-grouped
The range is the difference between the largest and the smallest value in the distribution.

This is an example of finding a range from ungrouped data:

Item	1	2	3	4	5	TOTAL	Ranges:
A	5	4	5	6	5	25 Mean for A = 5	A = 6 – 4 = 2. B = 7 – 2 = 5.
B	5	7	6	5	2	25 Mean for B = 5	

b) For grouped data with frequency distribution
In this case it is the upper value of the highest class minus the lower value of the lowest class.

This example shows how to get a range from grouped data using the distance travelled by students to the university.

Kilometres travelled to university
0 – 5
5 – 10
10 – 15
15 – 20
20 – 25
25 – 30
30 – 35

Using class limits the range is L 0 – 5; H 30 – 35: range is 35 – 0 = 35.
Using class boundaries the range is 35.5 – 0.5 = 35.

After looking at the range, we now turn to some other measures of disparity or dispersion under section 22.3.2.

22.3.2 Quantile, quartile deviation or semi-interquartile range, quartile coefficient of dispersion and quartile measure of skewness

22.3.2.1 Quantile
A quantile or fractile collectively split a set or distribution of items up into equal portions. It is the value of an item which lies at a particular place along an ordered set or distribution, the most well-known being the median.

The most important example of a quantile is called a quartile, and these are described together with their use in calculating measures of dispersion and skewness. The three quartiles split a distribution up into four equal parts and can be identified as the numerical value of the $(n+1)/4^{th}$, the median, and the $3(n+1)/4^{th}$ items. The quartiles of a distribution can be estimated using either
1 A generalised linear interpolation, or
2 A cumulative frequency curve.

The generalised interpolation formula to estimate the value of some defined quantile, Q, is given as follows: $Q = L_Q + [(P_Q – F_{Q–1})/f_Q)]C_Q$
Where L_Q = Lower boundary of the quantile class
P_Q = Position of quantile in the distribution
$F_{Q–1}$ = Cum. freq. of the class prior to the quantile class
F_Q = Actual frequency of the quantile class
C_Q = quantile class width

Other types of quantiles are deciles and percentiles that split a distribution into ten and one hundred equal parts respectively.

22.3.2.2 Quartile deviation or semi-interquartile range

This is a measure of dispersion that is paired naturally with the median and is defined as the range covered by the first and the third quartiles divided by two: qd = $(Q_3 - Q_1)/2$ = *semi-interquartile range*, the average distance between the median and the quartiles. Therefore, approximately 50 per cent of all items are found within one quartile deviation either side of the median.

Wangusa (2007:63) argues that the lower quartile and the upper quartile vary less from sample to sample than the outer quartiles. In addition, Wangusa maintains that the quartile deviation is far more stable than the inter-quartile range.

22.3.2.3 Quartile coefficient of dispersion

Quartile coefficient of dispersion (qcd) = [(quartile deviation)/median] × 100 per cent. It measures the quartile deviation as a percentage of the median in the same way the coefficient of variation measures the standard deviation as a percentage of the mean. Thus it is a relative measure of variation.

22.3.2.4 Quartile measure of skewness

This enables a measure of skewness to be calculated in terms of the quartiles. For a symmetric distribution, the median (Q_2) lies exactly halfway between the other two quartiles. If a distribution is positively skewed, the median is pulled closer to Q_1 and if negatively skewed, it is pulled closer to Q_3.

This coefficient is the quartile measure of skewness (qsk) = $\dfrac{Q_1 + Q_3 - 2Q_2}{Q_3 - Q_1}$

Where qsk < 0 implies that there is left or negative skew.
qsk = 0 implies that there is no skew.
Qsk > 0 implies that there is right or positive skew.

22.3.3 Mean deviation

Mean deviation is one of two under the *spread about the mean* basis on which the data spread can be measured, as seen earlier. It is a measure of dispersion that gives the average absolute difference between each item and the mean. It is the sum of absolute values from the mean divided by the number of observations:

$$MD = \Sigma \frac{|x_i - Mean|}{N} \qquad \text{non-grouped}$$

$$= \Sigma \frac{|x_i - Mean|}{\Sigma f_i} f_i \qquad \text{grouped}$$

This is an example of computing a mean deviation from raw or ungrouped data using the formula above:

Item	1	2	3	4	5	Total	Mean deviation:
A	5	4	5	6	5	25 Mean for A = 5	A = 0, 1, 0, 1, 0 = 2 = 2/5
B	5	7	6	5	2	25 Mean for B = 5	B = 0, 2, 1, 0, 3 = 6 = 6/5

We now turn to the second measure under the *spread about the mean* basis on which the data spread can be measured as seen earlier, the standard deviation.

22.3.4 Standard deviation and variance (mean square deviation)

The standard deviation is usually reported together with the mean because it measures the extent of deviation or departure from it, "the average spread around the mean" (Newbold, et al., 2010:77). In words, the standard deviation can be defined as 'the root of the mean of the squares of deviations from the common mean' of a set of values. According to Francis (2008:136), it is an adaptation of the mean deviation and it is an ideal partner for the mean. It is a natural partner to the arithmetic mean in the following respects:

▸ *By definition*: It is defined in terms of the mean.
▸ *Further statistical work*: The normal distribution commonly used in statistical analysis can only be specified in terms of both the mean and standard deviation.

Two special measures based on it are relative measure of dispersion called the coefficient of variation and the Pearson's measure of skewness.

22.3.4.1 Standard deviation

Standard deviation is the square root of the variance. The symbols are S or SD for sample and σ for universe or population. According to Newbold, et al. (2010:76-77), the denominator of the formula to compute *s* is *n-1* as rationalised by mathematical statisticians.

$$SD = \sqrt{\sum_{i=1}^{n} \frac{(x_i - Mean)^2}{N}}$$

The larger the value, the higher is the variability and vice-versa. If the value is close to the mean, this would imply a high degree of scatter. The standard deviation should be approximately 'one-sixth' of the range for roughly symmetric distributions. For moderately skewed distributions, it will be slightly larger. All items should be within three (3) standard deviations of the mean, 95 per cent within two (2), and 50 per cent within 0.67.

22.3.4.2 Variance (σ^2 or SD^2/s^2)

Variance (σ^2 or SD^2/s^2) or simply the standard deviation squared is also known as *mean square deviation* (Wangusa, (2007:64).

22.3.4.3 Uses of both standard deviation and variance

▸ To compare one or more sets of observations in order to decide whether they differ significantly from each other.
▸ To compare the performance of an individual member/case with that of the whole group.
▸ To transform raw data into standard scores.

Table 22.1 compares the advantages and disadvantages of the measures of dispersion or disparity thus far looked at:

TABLE 22.1: Advantages and disadvantages of some measures of dispersion

Measures	Advantages	Disadvantages
Range	▶ It is a simple concept and easy to calculate.	▶ Only uses two extreme observations therefore there is loss of information; or it only takes two values into account thus affected by extreme values. ▶ It has no natural partner in a measure of location and is not used in further advanced statistical work.
Mean deviation	▶ All values are considered. ▶ It is not difficult to understand. ▶ It is useful for comparing the variability between distributions of like nature.	▶ It is rarely used because it moves from one to another observation and is thus time consuming. ▶ In practice it can be complicated and awkward to calculate if the mean is anything other than a whole number. ▶ Because of the modulus sign, it is virtually impossible to handle theoretically and thus is not used in more advanced analysis; nor is it good for further mathematical manipulations.
Standard deviation	▶ Unlike the range, it can be regarded as truly representative of the data by taking into account all data values in its calculation. ▶ It was derived as a practical and theoretical alternative to the mean deviation because this is awkward to handle both practically and theoretically. ▶ It overcomes the inconveniences of the variance given in square units by taking its square root.	
Variance	▶ It is quite useful as a measure of dispersion and is used for numerous purposes in more advanced statistical analysis.	▶ It is measured in square units which is a practical drawback.

We now turn to the first of the two special measures based on the standard deviation, in section 22.3.5.

22.3.5 Relative dispersion, the coefficient of variation (or variation coefficient)

The standard deviation is an absolute measure of dispersion where we express variation in the same units as the original data. If we have two or more distributions with different units, we can unfortunately not compare them.

The standard deviation cannot be the sole basis for comparing distributions. If we have a standard deviation of 10 and a mean of 5, the values vary by an amount twice as large as the mean itself. If, on the other hand, we have a standard deviation of 10 and a mean of 5,000, the variation relative to the mean is insignificant. Therefore, we cannot know the dispersion of a set of data until we know the standard deviation and the mean, and how the standard deviation compares with the mean.

What we need is a relative measure that will give us a feel for the magnitude of the deviation, relative to the magnitude of the mean. The *coefficient of variation (CV)* is one such measure of dispersion. It relates the standard deviation and the Mean by expressing the standard deviation as a percentage of the mean provided the mean is positive (Newbold et al., 2010:79). The unit of measure then is 'per cent' rather than the same units as the original data.

$$\text{Population coefficient of variation} = CV = \frac{\sigma (100)}{\text{Population mean}}$$

or population relative variation.

$$\text{Sample coefficient of variation} = CV = \frac{SD \times 100}{\text{Sample mean}}$$

or sample relative variation.

Absolute variation is simply $\sigma \times 100$ or standard deviation $\times$ 100, while

$$\text{Relative variation} = \frac{\text{Absolute variation}}{\text{Average}}$$

Since the standard deviation is being divided by the Mean, the actual units of measurement cancel each other out, leaving the measure unit-free and thus very useful for relative comparison.

Finally in section 22.3, the measures of disparity or dispersion look at the second of the two special measures based on the standard deviation, Pearson's measure of skewness, in section 22.3.6, next.

22.3.6 Pearson's measure of skewness

Measure of skewness show how evenly a set of items is distributed. It is a description of the extent of the non-symmetry (or 'lopsided') of a distribution, given in terms of measures of location and dispersion. For most practical purposes, it is usual to require a measure of skewness to be unit-free (a coefficient) and the following expression, the *Pearson's measure of skewness (Psk)* is of this type:

$$Psk = \frac{\text{Mean} - \text{mode}}{\text{Standard deviation}}$$

$$= \frac{3(\text{Mean} - \text{median})}{\text{Standard deviation}}$$

Psk = < 0 shows that there is left or negative skew.
Psk = 0 signifies no skew, a symmetric distribution.
Psk = > 0 means that there is right or positive skew.

The greater the value of Psk, irrespective of the sign, the more is the distribution skewed. For moderately skewed distributions, Mean – mode = 3(Mean – median). This is particularly useful if, for a given set of data, it is either only the mean and the median that are known, or the mode is particularly unrepresentative.

Stop and reflect

Distinguish between the quartile and Pearson's measure of skewness.

22.4 Computing descriptive statistics using Microsoft Excel

Now that we have examined the formulae of computing the various descriptive statistics, let us demonstrate how to use Microsoft Excel to compute the descriptive statistics. Microsoft Excel uses the formulae presented earlier on, to compute descriptive statistics. Descriptive statistics can be computed by typing data for each variable in a specific column and following these steps:

▸ Go to **Tools**
▸ Select **Data analysis**
▸ Select **Descriptive statistics**
▸ Select **Input range** to highlight the variables whose descriptive statistics you want to compute. If there are labels in the first row, select this.
▸ For the **Output range**, select **New worksheet apply**
▸ Select **Summary statistics**
▸ Finally, click the **OK** button.

Using the earlier example of the distances travelled to your university in kilometres and having typed the various distances in one column, following the listed steps will give you a new worksheet which appears as the following screen. Use the earlier example on the distances and type the various distances in one column. Now follow the listed steps and you will get a new worksheet, as shown in Figure 22.1, whose results are presented in Table 22.2.

Column1	
Mean	21.82
Standard Error	1.011
Median	23.5
Mode	25
Standard Deviation	7.148
Sample Variance	51.09
Kurtosis	0.548
Skewness	-0.89
Range	32
Minimum	3
Maximum	35
Sum	1091
Count	50

FIGURE 22.1: Descriptive statistics using Microsoft Excel

TABLE 22.2: Descriptive statistics for the distances travelled to your university using Microsoft Excel

Column 1	
Mean	21.8200
Standard error	1.0108
Median	23.5000
Mode	25.0000
Standard deviation	7.1477
Sample variance	51.0894
Kurtosis	0.5480
Skewness	−0.8921
Range	32.0000
Minimum	3.0000
Maximum	35.0000
Sum	1091.0000
Count	50.0000

Suppose that we have several variables in several columns. With several variables in several columns, Microsoft Excel reports descriptive statistics for each variable by column.

22.5 Organisation and graphing quantitative data

The communication of scientific research requires decisions about how to present quantitative data. Many options are available for presenting data, especially with the increasing capabilities of word-processing, spreadsheets, and graphics software for creating tables and graphs. Quantitative data can be presented using frequency tables and cumulative frequency tables. Building on the frequency table and the cumulative frequency tables, we can graphically present quantitative data by means of a histogram; frequency polygon; and cumulative frequency curve or ogive. In what follows, we show how to construct frequency tables, cumulative frequency tables, and later demonstrate the steps to go through to construct a frequency polygon and a cumulative frequency curve.

22.6 Constructing frequency tables

Frequency tables summarise a set of numerical data by grouping the data into a frequency distribution or frequency table. There are various steps towards the presentation of quantitative data using a frequency table.

How to construct a frequency distribution table and compute the median using the interpolation formulas

Using data from an earlier example in section 22.2.1.1, construct a frequency distribution table.

Solution

In what follows, we set out the various steps toward presenting quantitative data using a frequency table.

Step 1 From the raw data we find the largest and the smallest values. This will allow us to see the range (or spread) of the data. In this case 35 = largest and 3 = smallest. Therefore, the range of the data is 32.

Step 2 Choose the number of groups or intervals the table should have. There are no hard and fast rules to this but it is conventional to have between 6 and 10 intervals. In this case let us take seven intervals.

Step 3 Decide how large each interval should be. It is best when choosing the class interval to make the size of each group a 'round' integer. For example, 5, 10, 20, 100 or 1,000. To give some indication of the size we can take the range obtained from step 1 and divide by the number of classes required. For this example, 32/7 = 4.57. This would be a difficult number to work with therefore it would be best to round upwards, making each interval equal to 5.

Step 4 Ensure that the boundaries are clear and unambiguous. Because the data we are using looks to be discrete (i.e. whole numbers with gaps that can be counted precisely) we could use the intervals: a) 0 to 4 kilometres; b) 5 to 9 kilometres; and so on.

Alternatively we could define the intervals as if they refer to continuous data where there are no gaps, as follows: a) 0 but under 5 kilometres; b) 5 but under 10 kilometres; and so on.

In fact, all data that has been measured (e.g. distances, times) is continuous by its very nature. It may look discrete, but that is the result of rounding figures to the nearest whole number.

Step 5 Use the tally method to construct the table as shown below.

Kilometres travelled to university	Number of students
0 but under 5	2
5 but under 10	3
10 but under 15	4
15 but under 20	7
20 but under 25	20
25 but under 30	11
30 but under 35	3

If you compile this frequency table using Microsoft Excel, the groups are differently defined, by default, as: a) Greater than 0, but no more than 5; b) Greater than 5, but no more than 10; c) Greater than 10, but no more than 15; and so on.

Hence the number of employees in the groups will differ slightly. For example, a data value of 15 exactly would go into the third group with Excel's default definition but it goes into the fourth group (15 but under 20) when we tally manually. The table compiled in Excel looks like this:

Kilometres travelled to university	Number of students
>0 up to 5	2
>5 up to 10	3
>10 up to 15	5
>15 up to 20	8
>20 up to 25	20
>25 up to 30	10
>30 up to 35	2

22.7 Histograms

Often, researchers want to know the distribution of their data. To this end, they construct a histogram. *A histogram is a graphical representation of the distribution of data.* The histogram depicts data shown in frequency tables. It resembles the vertical (or column) bar chart. However, there are some very important differences, which are as follows:

▶ The bars on a histogram are *adjacent*, whereas in a bar chart they are separated. This is because the scale on a histogram's horizontal axis is usually continuous, while on a bar chart it is usually discrete.

▶ When analysing the histogram, it is the **area** of the bar which is important, not just the height as with bar charts. Constructing a histogram with equal class intervals is relatively simple. We follow the same routine as with bar charts but shrink the gaps to zero, as we will shortly see.

However, when there are open-ended or unequal class intervals, you must be more cautious when constructing a histogram of such data. To construct a histogram using Excel, you may need some assistance from your tutor.

Toolbox Using Microsoft Excel to create a histogram

If you want to draw a histogram for the 'distance travelled to university' data, you need to re-arrange as follows the output for the histogram in Step 5 described earlier. This is done manually on the spreadsheet, with a view to labelling on the subsequent output of Chartwizard.

Kilometres travelled to university	Number of students
>0 up to 5	2
>5 up to 10	3
>10 up to 15	5
>15 up to 20	8
>20 up to 25	20
>25 up to 30	10
>30 up to 35	2

For raw data, as we have already seen, Excel uses the **Data analysis** option of **Tools** to place such data in a frequency table. For data in the form of a frequency table, we use **Chartwizard** to prepare a bar-chart of the data and then edit this to close the gaps between the bars.

Select the **Column** chart option from **ChartWizard**. The resulting histogram had three main areas for improvement:

1 The relevant labelling of axes during the **Chart options** window;

2 The group values needing to be entered in full, as shown on the previous page (this was done before calling up **Chartwizard**); and

3 The bars needed to be made adjacent. This last operation was effected by right-clicking on any of the bars and then **Format data series/Options** allows the bars' gap width to be shrunk to zero so that the bars are adjacent to one another.

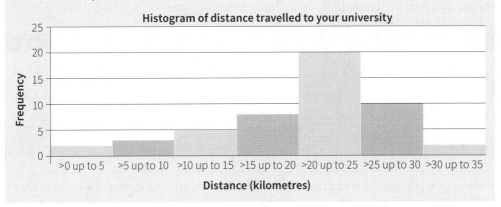

22.8 Cumulative frequency tables

In some cases it may be useful to present the data in such a manner that we can see the frequency of a variable that lies above or below a certain value. For example, the table below is constructed from the original 'kilometres travelled to university' data by using the total cumulative frequency *below or equal to the upper class boundary (UCB)* of each group as shown in Table 22.3.

TABLE 22.3 Frequency and cumulative frequency of kilometres travelled to university

| Kilometres travelled to university | | Number of students | |
Lower class boundary	Upper class boundary	Frequency	Cumulative frequency
0	5	2	2
5	10	3	5
10	15	4	9
15	20	7	16
20	25	20	36
25	30	11	47
30	35	3	50

The cumulative frequency of 36 refers to 36 values (of students' mileage) that were less than or equal to 25 kilometres, etc.

22.9 Cumulative frequency curves (or ogives)

The cumulative frequency curve, also known as the ogive, is useful when undertaking a complete analysis of a dataset in terms of its median and quartile values (see earlier in this chapter and later in this book). The first step when constructing an ogive is to create a cumulative frequency table, which may be either a cumulative frequency 'less than' or cumulative frequency 'more than'. For the purpose of this exercise we confine our interest to a cumulative frequency 'less than' curve. We will see later that the **cumulative frequency as a percentage of total frequency** is often used and this is what has been plotted. Table 22.4 presents the cumulative frequency as a percentage of total frequency for the distance travelled to university.

TABLE 22.4 Frequency, cumulative frequency, and cumulative frequency as percentage of total frequency of kilometres travelled to university

Kilometres travelled to university	Number of students	Cumulative frequency	As a %
0 but under 5	2	2	4
5 but under 10	3	5	10
10 but under 15	4	9	18
15 but under 20	7	16	32
20 but under 25	20	36	72
25 but under 30	11	47	94
30 but under 35	3	50	100

▶ Note: the cumulative frequency refers to the total number of distances which are less than the upper limit of the class interval.
▶ The % cumulative frequency is then scaled on the 'Y' axis while the upper group boundaries are scaled on the 'X' axis. Note that this scale should be relative to group interval sizes.
▶ The cumulative frequency of zero should be assigned to the lowest limit of the data. In this case that is the lower boundary of the first group, a distance of 0.

Toolbox How to construct a cumulative frequency curve (ogive)

In order to construct a cumulative frequency curve or ogive we revert to the cumulative frequency table and plot the **cumulative frequency** on the **vertical axis** while the **lower class boundary** is plotted on the horizontal axis. Using the cumulative frequency table of the distance travelled to university data, we can plot the cumulative frequency curve or ogive, as shown below.

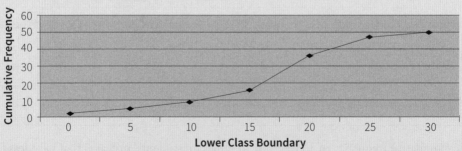

Cumulative frequency curve (ogive) of kilometres travelled to university

Researchers use the cumulative frequency when analysing data. The value of the cumulative frequency indicates the number of elements in the dataset that lie below the value in question.

Conclusion

In this chapter we have discussed the meaning of measurement, the meaning and the practice of the measures of central tendency or location, and disparity or dispersion, as well as the pictorial data presentation. You are now well grounded in these meanings, as well as the various concepts that are linked with them. Always keep in mind the various functions that these measures and pictorial means of data presentation perform in the field of research. We also noted various advantages and disadvantages associated with these measures and means of data presentation. You should now be able to contrast and explain the differences between these two categories of measures of central tendency or location, and dispersion or disparity. Further, we outlined their many functions so as to make sense of the task of research. In doing this we exploited both quantitative as well as the pictorial data presentation or reporting. The pictorial aspect is useful for those who may still lack confidence in dealing with quantitative data. A number of activities and reflections have been carefully designed in this chapter to help you understand and engage with the ideas it contains.

Closing activities

Analysis and consolidation

1 What is the method which researchers use to infer meaning from data and to determine what conclusions are justified?
2 What is a frequency distribution?
3 Name some methods for graphically representing a frequency distribution. When should each be used?
4 What is a summary statistic?
5 Name three measures of central tendency and three measures of dispersion. Briefly explain their functions and relative advantages and disadvantages.

Practical applications

6 Suppose the observation of incomes of inhabitants of a country is as follows:

Individual	A	B	C	D	E	F	G	H	I	J
Income (US$ per head)	95	120	80	150	50	130	70	90	110	105

Calculate the range, mean absolute deviation, and sample variance and standard deviation.
7 State whether the following statements are true or false:
   a The mode is a measure of variability.
   b A distribution is said to be symmetric if the mean is equal to the mode and the median.
   c A distribution is negatively skewed if the right tail is longer.
8 Suppose that 20 students' scores in an examination are as follows:
   97, 92, 88, 75, 83, 67, 89, 55, 72, 78, 81, 91, 57, 63, 67, 74, 87, 84, 98, 46.
   Construct a frequency table starting with class interval 40-49.
   Use the frequency table above to:
   a Form a cumulative frequency column.
   b Find a mean mark, median, mode and the inter-quartile range, and give comments on your findings.
   c Plot the histogram and frequency polygon on the same graph.
   d Compute the quartile deviation and comment on your results.

9 Carry out a field and/or library search to yield raw data on which to use graphical and numerical procedures involving processing, summarising, analysing and interpreting, so as to make sense of the data, that is, changing data into knowledge that leads to better decision-making.

Micro-classroom-based research

10 Gather data on the height of your classmates. Enter the data into Microsoft Excel and generate the descriptive statistics associated with the data collected. Interpret your results.

Bibliography

Centers for Disease Control and Prevention. 2009. Evaluation Briefs No. 20.: http://www.cdc.gov/HealthyYouth/evaluation/pdf/brief20.pdf. Accessed 2 August 2013.

Gillan, G.J., C.D. Wickens, J.G. Hollands & C.M. Carswell. 1998 Guidelines for Presenting Quantitative Data in HFES Publications. *Human Factors*, 40(1):28–41.

Frankfort-Nachmias, C. & Nachmias, D. 2003 *Research Methods in the Social Sciences* (5th ed.) London: Arnold.

Francis, A. 2008 *Business Mathematics and Statistics* (6th ed.). London: South-Western Cengage Learning.

Newbold, P., Calson, W.L. & Thorne, B. 2010 *Statistics for Business and Economics* (7th Global ed.). New York, London: Pearson.

Wangusa, T. 2007. *Essentials of Research Methodology in Human and Social Sciences*. Kampala: Bow and Arrow Publishers Ltd.

Wilcox, W.R. 2012. Definitions of descriptive statistics of a single variable generated by the Descriptive Statistics tool in Excel's Data Analysis Accessed 27 March 2014 from: *people.clarkson.edu/~wwilcox/ES100/descdefn.do.*

CHAPTER 23

Quantitative data analysis: Inferential statistics

KEY CONCEPTS

Bivariate hypothesis is a hypothesis involving two variables, with one dependent variable (DV) and one independent variable (IV).

Hypothesis is a claim about a given population parameter, such as the claim to the effect that all the students in a given class, have a mean IQ that differs from the international mean IQ.

Inferential statistics The provider of tools for inferential data analysis is interested in studying a given sample, and drawing inference, that is, making deductions or generalisations on the population from which the sample was chosen.

Null hypothesis usually denoted H_0, is one that nullifies the research hypothesis.

Research hypothesis usually denoted H_1, is one that postulates the existence of a difference (e.g. between males and females) on the means of a variable; or the relationship between variables in which a researcher has an interest.

Univariate hypothesis is a hypothesis involving only one variable, such as the IQ of a student.

LEARNING OUTCOMES

By the end of this chapter, you should be able to:

▶ Define inferential statistics in a way that distinguishes it from the descriptive statistics that you covered in Chapter 22 of this book.

▶ Compare and contrast the following pairs of concepts that are useful in inferential statistics: Population versus sample; parameter versus statistic.

▶ Discuss the estimation of population parameters and tests of hypotheses on population parameters as the major branches of inferential statistics.

▶ Distinguish between point estimation and confidence interval estimation, and how each is used, plus the pertinent terminology, such as confidence level.

▶ Carry out the procedure for the testing of hypotheses on population parameters, and the pertinent terminology, such as research hypothesis, null hypothesis, significance level.

▶ Extend the concept of testing of hypotheses on population parameters, to the case of bivariate hypotheses, that is, hypotheses that involve relating two variables.

▶ Appreciate the available statistical techniques for the testing of bivariate hypotheses, and to know when and how each is used.

CHAPTER 23 Quantitative data analysis: Inferential statistics   413

Case study: Getting to grips with inferential statistics

Consider the following conversation between a university student and her professor. The student has finished collecting her positivist research data using a questionnaire, but is stuck on the way forward:

Professor: Welcome to my office. What can I do for you? You look very happy.

Student: I feel happy that I have collected my data, and, given the coaching I got on descriptive statistics, what more do I need?

Professor: Are you sure you are finished?

Student: Yes, prof, of course, why not?

Professor: Do you think the frequency tables, and the pertinent percentages, plus the measures of central tendency and dispersion are adequate for you to test bivariate (i.e. two-variable) hypotheses?

Student: What are bivariate hypotheses?

Professor: Check your first objective: Are you not relating the sex of a student to academic performance? Does that not hypothesise a relationship between two variables, namely 'academic performance' (a numerical dependent variable, DV) and 'sex' (an independent variable, IV)? Is that not a two-variable or 'bivariate' hypothesis? Does that not require Student's two-sample t-test?

Student: Prof! Stop there before I abandon the course!

Introduction

Having covered several chapters in this book relating to positivism or quantitative research, starting with Chapter 2, this chapter is intended to help researchers such as the student in the opening case, who are now grappling with the use of inferential statistics. We want to help them graduate from descriptive statistics (covered in Chapter 22) to deductive inferential statistics, which is useful in testing hypotheses. Remember that right from the first chapter, we have stressed that positivist research is interested in testing theories. And because theories are usually broad, they have to be broken into hypotheses for the purpose of testing them. So the importance of this chapter for a positivist researcher cannot be over-emphasised. This chapter is intended to reduce the 'statistical anxiety', so common among most researchers, which occurs when individuals encounter statistics in any form, at any level.

By the end of the chapter we hope to reduce any statistical anxiety you are feeling. To help you, this chapter starts with a contrast between the descriptive statistics which you covered in Chapter 22, and the inferential statistics in this chapter, emphasising that the latter builds on the former. The next two sections, 23.2 and 23.3 respectively, introduce the two major branches of inferential statistics, and hence inferential data analysis: the estimation of population parameters and the testing of hypotheses on population parameters. In section 23.4, we extend the idea of testing of hypotheses on population parameters to the bivariate case, that is, we introduce the idea of testing hypotheses that involve two variables. This will be consolidated in sections 23.5 on comparative data analysis, and 23.6 on correlative data analysis. Be sure to try all the closing activities to round off this consolidation. Let us now turn to what the term inferential statistics means.

23.1 What is inferential statistics?

While the descriptive statistics that you covered in Chapter 22, provide the tools for descriptive data analysis, and is interested in collecting, processing and analysing data for purposes of describing a specific sample, inferential statistics provides the tools for inferential data analysis. Inferential data analysis is interested in going beyond the sample selected, and drawing inferences, that is, making deductions or generalisations, on the population from which the sample being described was chosen.

Four basic concepts that are useful in inferential statistics, and hence inferential data analysis, are the study population and its parameters; the sample chosen from the population and its statistics. A population is the mass of all units of analysis (e.g. students in a university course; learners in a school), in which the researcher has an interest. The numerical characteristics of a given population are officially referred to as the parameters of the population. Thus for a given population, its parameters include the population size (N), the population mean (μ), the population variance (σ^2) and the population standard deviation (σ). However, due to constraints (e.g. skill, time and cost), the researcher usually selects a random sample, that is part of a given population, for purposes of studying the population.

The numerical characteristics of a given sample are officially referred to as the statistics of the sample. Thus for a given sample, its statistics include the sample size (n), the sample mean ($\bar{x}$), the sample variance (s^2), and the sample standard deviation (s). So **inferential statistics**, which provides tools for inferential data analysis, can officially be defined as an attempt by a researcher to draw inferences or make deductions about population parameters using sample statistics. The next two sections of the chapter, 23.2 and 23.3, respectively, introduce two major branches of inferential statistics, and hence inferential data analysis: the estimation of population parameters; and the testing of hypotheses on population parameters. Do the activity next to check your understanding so far.

Stop and reflect

1 In the introductory section, we defined descriptive statistics and inferential statistics, which are obviously branches of a discipline called statistics. Do an internet search for the definition of statistics.
2 Apart from distinguishing the branches of statistics as descriptive or inferential, how else can statistics be categorised, and why?

23.2 Estimation of population parameters

The world we live in is full of uncertainties, and researchers are not exempt. Indeed, if we knew everything we wanted to know, there would be no need for research. Inferential statistics offers positivist researchers the tools for the estimation of unknown parameters of a given research population. These tools are introduced with the following example:

Introducing the concept of estimation

An education psychologist wants to 'estimate' the mean intelligence quotient (IQ) of all the students in a large class. The psychologist takes a random sample of size, 100 students from the class, which sample yielded a sample mean IQ of 80.0 with a sample standard deviation of 5.0. Using those sample results, that is sample statistics, what inference can the researcher draw about the unknown mean IQ (μ) of all the students in the class?

(continued)

Solution

Note that this research question requires the researcher to estimate the unknown population parameter (μ), the mean IQ of all the students in the class. We have been told that the researcher took a random sample of size, n = 100 students, and got a sample mean IQ, x̄ = 80.0, with a sample standard deviation, s = 5.0. The researcher can hence estimate the unknown population parameter (μ) in at least two ways, namely point estimation and confidence interval estimation.

23.2.1 Point estimation

One way of estimating an unknown population parameter, is to provide a single figure, known as a point estimate of the parameter. For example, in the example 'Introducing the concept of estimation', the point estimate of the population mean IQ of all the students in the class, would be the sample mean IQ the 100 sampled students scored, that is, x̄ = 80.0. However, while the actual value of the unknown parameter, could be quite close to the point estimate, there is a possibility that the actual value of the parameter is very far from this point estimate. Thus to be more confident of an estimate, a researcher could consider confidence interval estimation.

23.2.2 Confidence interval estimation

The educational psychological researcher can be more confident of the estimate if he/ she states that the actual value of the unknown population parameter (μ), lies within a given interval, with some high probability or confidence level, say 90, 95 or 99 per cent. Statisticians have shown that to get the confidence interval estimate of the mean (μ) of a given population, all a researcher needs to do is to take a random sample of a reasonable size (n), and to compute the corresponding sample statistics, namely the sample mean (x̄) and the sample standard deviation (s), and hence the standard error (SE) of the mean, which is given by:

$$SE = \frac{s}{\sqrt{n}} \quad\text{..} (23.1)$$

Hence, for example, the 90 per cent confidence interval estimate of μ is given by:

x̄ ± 1.65 SE .... (23.2A)

Relatedly, the 95 per cent confidence interval estimate for μ, is given by:

x̄ ± 1.96 SE .... (23.2B)

And the 99 per cent confidence interval estimate for μ, is given by:

x̄ ± 2.58 SE .... (23.2C)

Note that the 95 per cent confidence level is the most popular in social science research although some of our examples may not stick to it. You will see this more clearly in the following example.

Introducing confidence interval estimation

In the example, 'Introducing the concept of estimation', the educational researcher took a random sample of size, n = 100 students, and got a sample mean IQ, $\bar{x}$ = 80.0, with a sample standard deviation, s = 5.0. Help the researcher to establish a 90 per cent confidence interval estimate for the mean IQ of all the students in the class.

Solution
From expression (23.2A), the 90 per cent confidence interval estimate of the population mean, μ, is given by:

$\bar{x} \pm 1.65$ SE ....(23.2A) Now, from Expression (23.1), the standard error (SE) of the mean, is given by:

$$SE = \frac{s}{\sqrt{n}} = \frac{5.0}{\sqrt{100}} = \frac{5.0}{10} = 0.5 \quad ....(23.3)$$

Substituting this and $\bar{x}$ = 80.0 in Expression (23.2A), the 90 per cent confidence interval estimate of the population mean, μ will be:

$$80.0 \pm 1.65 \times 0.5$$
$$80.0 \pm 0.825$$

that is

$$80.0 - 0.825 \text{ to } 80.0 + 0.825$$
$$\text{or } 79.175 \text{ to } 80.825 \quad ....(23.4)$$

After the *Stop and reflect* activity, in the next section 23.3, we will turn to another branch of inferential statistics, namely the testing of claims or hypotheses on population parameters.

Stop and reflect

In the last section, we introduced the concept of estimation of population parameters as a branch of inferential statistics. This concept is in turn useful in educational measurement evaluation (EME). Do an internet search to find out:
a) What the term EME means.
b) How the estimation of population parameters is useful in EME.

23.3 Testing of hypotheses on population parameters

We now turn to another branch of inferential statistics, namely the testing of hypotheses on population parameters. Let us look at an example to introduce how a hypothesis on a population parameter is tested:

Introducing testing a hypothesis on a parameter

Suppose the educational researcher cited in the example, 'Introducing the concept of estimation' and the example, 'Introducing confidence interval estimation', having been prompted by teacher complaints, hypothesises that the population of all the students in the class, has a mean IQ that differs from the international mean IQ of 100.0. We can help the researcher to test whether this hypothesis is acceptable. How do we go about it?

Solution
If we let μ to stand for the mean IQ for the population of all the students in the class, we shall be testing the **research hypothesis**:

H_1 : The mean IQ of the population differs from 100.0 .... (23.5A)
(i.e. $\mu \neq 100.0$)

against the **null hypothesis**:

H_0 : The mean IQ of the population does not differ from 100.0 .... (23.5B)
(i.e. $\mu = 100.0$)

Note that a hypothesis is made about a given population, and hence about a population parameter. For example, in expression (23.4), the hypothesis is made about μ, the mean IQ of the population of all the students in the class. Note also that the null hypothesis, H_0 (e.g. expression 23.4B), true to its name, nullifies the **research hypothesis**, H_1 (e.g. expression 23.4A). However, it is worth noting that H_1 and H_0 are complementary, meaning that if one of them is accepted, the other is rejected. Strictly speaking though, statistical techniques such as those in the remaining part of this chapter, and summarised in Table 23.1, test the null (and not the research) hypotheses. This is why null hypotheses are at times referred to as statistical hypotheses.

One way to test the null hypothesis, H_0 (in expression 23.4B) is to calculate a chosen high confidence interval estimate, usually 95 per cent or 0.95 in the social sciences, and seeing whether the hypothesised value of the parameter in question (e.g. 100.0 in expression 23.4), lies within this confidence interval estimate. If it does, the null hypothesis is accepted at the chosen acceptance or confidence level. Whatever the acceptance or confidence level chosen, say 95 per cent or 0.95, the remaining percentage, in this case 5 per cent or 0.05, is referred to as the rejection, significance or critical level used, and this is usually denoted as α. Hence we usually come across the expression $\alpha = 5\%$ or $\alpha = 0.05$ in positivist or quantitative statistical reports.

For example in expression (23.4), we established the 90 per cent confidence interval estimate for the mean IQ of the population of all the students in the class, as ranging from 79.175 to 80.825. Clearly then, the hypothesised value of the mean IQ, 100.0 in expression (23.4) does not lie within this 90 per cent confidence interval estimate. Actually, the hypothesised value of the mean IQ, 100.0 is higher than the computed 90 per cent confidence interval estimate. Thus, we reject the null hypothesis, H_0 in expression 23.5B, and accept the research or alternative hypothesis, H_1 in Expression 23.4A. In other words, we infer that at the 90 per cent or 0.90 confidence level (or 10 per cent or 0.10 significance level), the mean IQ for the population of all the students in the class significantly differed from (or was much lower than) the international mean IQ of 100.0. Having looked at testing a univariate hypothesis, that is a hypothesis involving one variable, now stop and reflect, before going on to the next section 23.4.

23.4 Types of variables as determinants of the statistical tools for testing bivariate hypotheses on population parameters

In section 23.3, we introduced the concept of testing a hypothesis. However, for simplicity, the **hypothesis** we tested was **univariate**, that is, it involved only one variable, namely the IQ of a student. In the remaining sections of this chapter, starting with this one, we will go further and test **bivariate hypotheses**. These are hypotheses that are typically found in social research, involving two variables, with one dependent variable (DV) and one independent variable (IV). It is worth noting at the outset, that the types of DV and IV in a given hypothesis (e.g. whether categorical or numerical) determine which statistical tool to use to test the hypothesis, as suggested in Table 23.1.

TABLE 23.1: Types of IV and DV as determinants of statistical tools for testing bivariate hypotheses

Nature of IV	Nature of DV	Statistical tool
Binary categorical	Numerical	Student's two-sample t-test (section 23.5.1)
Categorical with at least two categories	Numerical	Sir Ronald Fisher's analysis of variance (section 23.5.2)
Numerical	Numerical	Karl Pearson's linear correlation coefficient (section 23.6.1)
Ordinal or ranked	Ordinal or ranked	Charles Spearman's rank correlation coefficient (section 23.6.2)
Categorical	Categorical	Karl Pearson's Chi-square (section 23.6.3).

The first row in Table 23.1, suggests that if a researcher is interested in comparing the mean values of a numerical dependent variable (DV), such as when a score in a test varies on the two categories of a binary categorical independent variable (IV), that is a categorical variable such as sex with only two categories, then the statistical tool of interest is Student's two-sample t-test. Other rows can be interpreted similarly. Sections 23.5 and 23.6 respectively will expand on Table 23.1.

23.5 Comparative data analysis

The first two rows in Table 23.1 jointly exemplify cases where a researcher is interested in comparing the mean values of a numerical DV on the categories of a categorical IV. So the two suggested tools, namely Student's t-test and Fisher's ANOVA, are statistical tools for comparative data analysis. The details on the two techniques will be dealt with in this section 23.5.

23.5.1 Comparing values of a numerical DV on the values of a binary categorical IV: Student's two-sample t-test

With Student's two-sample t-test, as suggested by the first row in Table 23.1, a researcher is interested in comparing the mean values of a numerical dependent variable (DV) on the two categories of a binary categorical independent variable (IV). We need an example on this.

Using the t-test e.g.

This example is from Babirye-Kakeeto's (1993) MEd dissertation, one of whose objectives was to test whether the performance in history (a numerical DV) of a student, differed according to the sex of the student (a binary categorical IV, with the categories, boys and girls). In other words, if μ_b and μ_g represented the mean performances for all the boys and all the girls respectively, then Babirye-Kakeeto's study in this respect, involved the testing of the research hypothesis:

H_1 : The mean performances for the two populations differed significantly ....(23.6A)

   (i.e. $\mu_b \neq \mu_g$),

against the null hypothesis:

H_0 : The mean performances for the two populations did not differ significantly .... (23.6B)

   (i.e. $\mu_b = \mu_g$)

To test the null hypothesis, H_0 (Expression 23.6B), Babirye-Kakeeto (1993) sampled 305 students (152 boys and 153 girls) from three school in Kampala District in Uganda, basing on their performances in History in the Uganda National Examinations Board exams. The resulting sample data or statistics are presented in Table 23.2.

TABLE 23.2: Sample statistics from Babirye-Kakeeto's (1993) study

Sample size	Sample mean	Sample std deviation
$n_b = 152$	$\bar{x}_b = 34.4$	$S_b = 13.0$
$n_g = 153$	$\bar{x}_g = 33.9$	$S_g = 14.0$

In Table 23.2, n stood for the sample size; the subscripts b and g stood for boys and girls respectively, while x̄ stood for the sample mean and s for the sample standard deviation. The sample means in Table 23.2 suggested that the boys performed better than the girls. But was the difference statistically significant? To answer such a question, Babirye-Kakeeto (1993) or a similar study, can compute Student's two-sample t statistic:

$$t = \frac{\bar{x}_b - \bar{x}_g}{\sqrt{\dfrac{S_b^2}{n_b} + \dfrac{S_g^2}{n_g}}} \quad \text{.................................. (23.7)}$$

(continued)

Thus, substituting from Table 23.2 into expression (23.7), Student's two-sample t statistic in Babirye-Kakeeto's (1993) study translated to:

$$t = \frac{34.4 - 33.9}{\sqrt{\dfrac{13.0^2}{152} + \dfrac{14.0^2}{153}}}$$

$$= \frac{0.5}{\sqrt{\dfrac{169.0}{152} + \dfrac{196.0}{153}}}$$

$$= \frac{0.5}{\sqrt{1.11 + 1.28}}$$

$$= \frac{0.5}{\sqrt{2.39}}$$

$$= \frac{0.5}{1.55}$$

$$t = 0.32 \dotfill (23.8)$$

Note that if the value of t is negative, then its sign should be ignored. That is its absolute value should be taken. Note that Babirye-Kakeeto's (1993) computed or observed t statistic (expression 23.8) was not computed for its sake. Rather, it was to help her to test her null hypothesis (expression 23.6B) on the equality between the two mean performances for the given two populations of students. In testing the null hypothesis (expression 23.6B), she was actually posing the question: was her computed or observed t statistic (expression 23.8) statistically significant, that is, exceeded some critical, significance or rejection value, for her to reject the null hypothesis (expression 23.6B)? Critical Student's two-sample t values, denoted t_c, have been tabulated in Table 23.3

TABLE 23.3: Critical t statistic values

α levels for two-tailed test						
df	.20	.10	.05	.02	.01	.001
1	3.078	6.314	12.706	31.821	63.657	636.619
2	1.886	2.920	4.303	6.965	9.925	31.598
3	1.638	2.353	3.182	4.541	5.841	12.924
4	1.533	2.132	2.776	3.747	4.604	8.610
5	1.476	2.015	2.571	3.365	4.032	6.869
6	1.440	1.943	2.447	3.143	3.707	5.959
7	1.415	1.895	2.365	2.998	3.499	5.408
8	1.397	1.860	2.306	2.896	3.355	5.041
9	1.383	1.833	2.262	2.821	3.250	4.781
10	1.372	1.812	2.228	2.764	3.169	4.587
11	1.363	1.796	2.201	2.718	3.106	4.437
12	1.356	1.782	2.179	2.681	3.055	4.318
13	1.350	1.771	2.160	2.650	3.012	4.221
14	1.345	1.761	2.145	2.624	2.977	4.140

| α levels for two-tailed test | | | | | | |
df	.20	.10	.05	.02	.01	.001
15	1.341	1.753	2.131	2.602	2.947	4.073
16	1.337	1.746	2.120	2.583	2.921	4.015
17	1.333	1.740	2.110	2.567	2.898	3.965
18	1.330	1.734	2.101	2.552	2.870	3.922
19	1.328	1.729	2.093	2.539	2.861	3.883
20	1.325	1.725	2.086	2.528	2.845	3.850
21	1.323	1.721	2.080	2.518	2.831	3.819
22	1.321	1.717	2.074	2.508	2.819	3.792
23	1.319	1.714	2.069	2.500	2.807	3.767
24	1.318	1.711	2.064	2.492	2.797	3.745
25	1.316	1.708	2.060	2.485	2.787	3.725
26	1.315	1.706	2.056	2.479	2.779	3.707
27	1.314	1.703	2.052	2.473	2.771	3.690
28	1.313	1.701	2.048	2.467	2.763	3.674
29	1.311	1.699	2.045	2.462	2.756	3.659
30	1.310	1.697	2.042	2.457	2.750	3.646
40	1.303	1.684	2.021	2.423	2.704	3.551
60	1.296	1.671	2.000	2.390	2.660	3.460
120	1.289	1.658	1.980	2.358	2.617	3.373
?	1.282	1.645	1.960	2.326	2.576	3.291

* To be significant, the t obtained from the data must be equal to or larger than the value in Table 23.3

(**Source:** Amin, M.E.. 2004, Foundations of statistical inference for the social sciences. Kampala, Uganda: Makerere University Press, p. 326, Appendix 5)

To read off any critical Student's two-sample t value (from Table 23.3), a researcher such as Babirye-Kakeeto (1993) takes more or less the steps as given in the Toolbox.

Toolbox Reading the critical t values table

Step 1 Choose an appropriate critical, significance or rejection level, α

Babirye-Kakeeto chose α = 5 per cent or 0.05, which is the most popular in the social sciences, including education, in which she researched. She checked for this in the top row of Table 23.3, noting the column in which it falls.

Step 2 Get the so-called number of degrees of freedom (df), associated with the test

For Student's two-sample t statistic (expression 23.7) the number of degrees of freedom (df) is given by the sum of the sizes of the two samples used, less two. Thus algebraically:

$$df = n_b + n_g - 2 \quad\text{... (23.9)}$$

(continued)

PART 3 ANALYSING FIELDWORK DATA

Toolbox Reading the critical t values table *(continued)*

Thus according to Table 23.2, because Babirye-Kakeeto (1993) used samples of sizes, $n_b = 152$ and $n_g = 153$, the number of degrees of freedom (df) associated with his Student's two-sample t statistic, was df $= 152 + 153 - 2 = 303$. Identify this df $= 303$ (taking? since 303 exceeded 120) in the left-most column of Table 23.3, noting the row in which it falls.

Step 3   Read off the required critical t value
Where the column identified in step 1 and the row in step 2 meet, was Babirye-Kakeeto's (1993) required critical t value:

$t_c = 1.960$ .... (23.10)

Step 4   Make inference
Note that Babirye-Kakeeto's (1993) computed or observed Student's two-sample t value (0.32 in expression 23.8) did not exceed her critical t value (1.960 in expression 23.10). Thus, at the $\alpha = 5$ per cent or 0.05 level of significance, Babirye-Kakeeto accepted her null hypothesis, H0 (expression 23.6B) and rejected her 'research' or alternative hypothesis, H1 (expression 23.6A).

In other words, she inferred that at the 5 per cent or 0.05 level of significance, the mean performances in history for the two populations of students, namely that of the boys and that of the girls, did not differ significantly. The difference, then, in the sample means in Table 23.2, suggesting that the boys ($\bar{x}_b = 34.4$) scored higher than the girls ($\bar{x}_g = 33.9$), could be attributed to chance. Hence she recommended that "there should be no discrimination based on the criterion of sex, while selecting history students for secondary school" (Babirye-Kakeeto, 1993:48).

Let us now look at a technique that generalises the t-test technique, by allowing the categorical IV to have two or more categories.

23.5.2 Comparing values of a numerical DV on the values of a categorical IV with at least two categories: Fisher's analysis of variance

With Fisher's analysis of variance (ANOVA) test, as suggested by the second row in Table 23.1, a researcher is interested in comparing the mean values of a numerical dependent variable (DV) on the categorics of a categorical independent variable (IV), with at least two categories. An example will be helpful here.

Using ANOVA

Babirye-Kakeeto (1993), might have been interested in testing whether the performance of a student in history (a numerical DV) differed according to the school (a categorical IV, with three categories, namely School 1, School 2; and School 3) a student was in. In other words, if μ_1, μ_2, and μ_3 represented the mean performances in History for all the students in School 1, for all the students in School 2 and for all the students in School 3 respectively, then Babirye-Kakeeto's study in this regard would involve testing the research hypothesis:

(continued)

H_1 : The mean performances for at least two of the three populations ....(23.11A)
    that is, the three schools, differed significantly (i.e. $\mu_1 \neq \mu_2$
    and/ or $\mu_1 \neq \mu_3$ and/ or $\mu_2 \neq \mu_3$),

against the null hypothesis:

H_0 : The mean performances for all the three populations, that is the ....(23.11B)
    three schools did not differ significantly (i.e. $\mu_1 = \mu_2 = \mu_3$)

To test the null hypothesis, H_0 (Expression 23.11B), Babirye-Kakeeto would then use the analysis of variance (ANOVA) test which is a generalisation of Student's two-sample t-test. Being a generalisation, you can read about it in such sources as research and/or statistics textbooks, dissertations, conference papers, book chapters, and journal articles. However, you will soon note that ANOVA has very tedious calculations, making it more manageable if you use a computer package such as the statistical package for social scientists (SPSS). Chapter 24 will further clarify this for you.

Stop and reflect

In section 23.5, we have introduced Student's two-sample t-test and Sir Ronald Fisher's analysis of variance (ANOVA) tests.

1 However, Student was a pseudonym for William Sealy Gosset. Do an internet search (e.g. http:// en.wikipedia.org/ wiki/ William_Gosset) to find out why Gosset had to use the pseudonym, together with other details about him such as when, where and how long he lived, plus his contribution to inferential statistics.

2 Repeat 1, but for Sir Ronald Fisher and his ANOVA (e.g. use: http://en.wikipedia.org/wiki/ Ronald_Fisher).

23.6 Correlative data analysis

The last three rows in Table 23.1, exemplify cases where a researcher is correlating the values of a DV with the values of an IV of a similar type as per the dichotomy of variables. So the three suggested tools, namely Pearson's linear correlation coefficient (PLCC) test, Spearman's rank correlation coefficient (SRCC) test and Pearson's Chi-square test, are statistical tools for correlative data analysis. The details on the three tools will be dealt with in this section 23.6 of this chapter. Let us start with Pearson's linear correlation.

23.6.1 Correlating two numerical variables: Karl Pearson's linear correlation coefficient test

With Karl Pearson's linear correlation coefficient (PLCC) test, as suggested by the third row in Table 23.1, a researcher is interested in how a dependent variable (DV) and an independent variable (IV) that are both numerical, correlate, that is vary with one another. We shall use an example to clarify this.

Using Pearson's linear correlation coefficient test

This example is from Kakooza's (1997) doctoral thesis, one of whose objectives was to test whether the achievement by a learner in adult literacy (a numerical DV) was positively related to the number of lessons attended by the learner (a numerical IV). In other words, Kakooza's study involved testing the research hypothesis:

H_1 : The two numerical variables were positively linearly correlated, ...(23.12A)

against the null hypothesis:

H_0 : The two numerical variables were not linearly correlated ....(23.12B)

To test the null hypothesis, H_0 (expression 23.12B), Kakooza (1997) targeted 258 illiterate learners in two districts in Uganda and had them instructed after recording their ages. After nine months of instruction, the learners whose number had reduced to 75, were given an adult literacy test. Letting x and y be the independent and dependent variables (IV and DV), that is the number of lessons attended by a learner and the achievement of the learner in the test respectively, the resulting sample data, that is, sample statistics were as in Table 23.4:

TABLE 23.4: Algebraic form of the sample statistics from Kakooza's (1997) study

Learner	Attendance x	Achievement y
1	x_1	y_1
2	x_2	y_2
.	.	.
.	.	.
.	.	.
75	x_{75}	y_{75}

From data such as those in Table 23.4, Kakooza could compute Karl Pearson's linear correlation coefficient (PLCC), a statistic given by:

$$r = \frac{n\Sigma xy - \Sigma x \Sigma y}{\sqrt{n\Sigma x^2 - (\Sigma x)^2}\sqrt{n\Sigma y^2 - (\Sigma y)^2}} \quad\text{.................(23.13)}$$

Where as you saw in Chapter 22, Σ is the Greek letter capital sigma, the equivalent of capital S, which is a symbol for the order to sum. Thus if you have a sample of say 75 observations $(x_1, x_2 \ldots x_{75})$ made on some variable x, then Σx is an order to sum all of them. That is $\Sigma x = x_1 + x_2 + \ldots + x_{75}$. Similarly. if you have a sample of say 75 observations $(y_1, y_2 \ldots y_{75})$ made on some variable y, then Σy is an order to sum all of them. That is $\Sigma y = y_1 + y_2 + \ldots + y_{75}$.

Also Σxy is an order to sum all the products of the corresponding observations $(x_1 y_1, x_2 y_2 \ldots x_{75} y_{75})$. In other words, $\Sigma xy = x_1 y_1 + x_2 y_2 + \ldots + x_{75} y_{75}$. Using the same logic, Σx^2 is an order to sum all the squares of the observations on x (i.e. $x_1{}^2, x_2{}^2 \ldots x_{75}{}^2$). In other words, $\Sigma x^2 = x_1{}^2 + x_2{}^2 + \ldots + x_{75}{}^2$. Similarly, $\Sigma y^2 = y_1{}^2 + y_2{}^2 + \ldots + y_{75}{}^2$. Thus from Table 23.4, the summations necessary for use in expression (23.13), will be computed as in Table 23.5:

TABLE 23.5: Summations for Kakooza (1997) to use in expression (23.13)

Learner	Attendance	Achievement	Product	Square of attendance	Square of achievement
	x	y	xy	x^2	y^2
1	x_1	y_1	$x_1 y_1$	$x_1^{\,2}$	$y_1^{\,2}$
2	x_2	y_2	$x_2 y_2$	$x_2^{\,2}$	$y_2^{\,2}$
.	.	.	.	.	.
.	.	.	.	.	.
.	.	.	.	.	.
75	x_{75}	y_{75}	$x_{75} y_{75}$	$x_{75}^{\,2}$	$y_{75}^{\,2}$
Sums	$\Sigma x = 1{,}172$	$\Sigma y = 2{,}835$	$\Sigma xy = 45{,}445$	$\Sigma x^2 = 20{,}108$	$\Sigma y^2 = 115{,}748$

Thus, substituting from Table 23.5 into expression (23.13), Pearson's linear correlation coefficient (PLCC) in Kakooza's study translated to:

$$r = \frac{75 \times 45{,}445 - 1{,}172 \times 2{,}835}{\sqrt{75 \times 20{,}108 - 1{,}172^2}\ \sqrt{75 \times 115{,}748 - 2{,}835^2}}$$

$$= \frac{3{,}408{,}375 - 3{,}322{,}620}{\sqrt{1{,}508{,}100 - 1{,}373{,}58}\ \sqrt{8{,}681{,}100 - 8{,}037{,}225}}$$

$$= \frac{85{,}755}{\sqrt{134{,}516}\ \sqrt{643{,}875}}$$

$$= \frac{85{,}755}{366{,}76 \times 802{,}42}$$

$$= \frac{85{,}755}{294{,}294{,}91}$$

$$r = 0{,}29 \quad\ldots\ldots\ldots\ldots\ldots\ldots\ldots\ldots\ldots\ldots\ldots\ldots\ldots\ldots\ldots\ldots\ldots\ldots\ldots\ldots\ldots\ldots\ldots\ (23.14)$$

Note that the arithmetic sign of Karl Pearson's linear correlation coefficient (PLCC, r) suggests the direction of linear correlation. That is, a negative value implies a negative linear correlation, that is, as one of the variables increases, the second one decreases. A zero value implies zero or no linear correlation, that is, there does not seem to be any linear relationship between the two variables. Lastly, a positive value (e.g. that in expression 23.14) implies a positive linear correlation, that is, both variables tend to increase or decrease together. Secondly, PLCC (r) can only take values between -1 and 1 inclusive (i.e. $-1 \leq r \leq 1$), which is a good arithmetic check on the accuracy of whatever PLCC (r) that you compute.

Note also that Kakooza's (1997) computed or observed r statistic (expression 23.14) was not computed for its own sake. Rather, it was to help her to test the null hypothesis, H_0 (expression 23.12B) on the absence of linear correlation, that is, for the linear independence, between the two numerical variables. In testing the null hypothesis, H_0 (expression 23.12B), she was actually posing the question: was her computed or observed r statistic (expression 23.14) statistically significant, that is, exceeded some critical, significance or rejection value, for her to reject the null hypothesis, H_0 (expression 23.12B)? Critical Pearson's linear correlation coefficient (PLCC) r values, denoted r_c, have been tabulated, and given to us in Table 23.6:

TABLE 23.6: Critical PLCC r values

(df= n – 2)	α Level for two-tailed test				
	.10	.05	.02	.01	.001
1	.98769	.99692	.999507	.999877	.9999988
2	.90000	.95000	.98000	.990000	.99900
3	.8054	.8783	.93433	.95873	.99116
4	.7293	.8114	.8822	.91720	.97406
5	.6694	.7545	.8329	.8745	.95074
6	.6215	.7067	.7887	.8343	.92493
7	.5822	.6664	.7498	.7977	.8982
8	.5494	.6319	.7155	.7646	.8721
9	.5214	.6021	.6851	.7348	.8371
10	.4973	.5760	.6581	.7079	.8233
11	4762	.5529	.6339	.6835	.8010
12	.4575	.5324	.6120	.6614	.7800
13	.4409	.5139	.5923	.6411	.7603
14	.4259	.4973	.5742	.6226	.7420
15	.4124	.4821	.5577	.6055	.7246
16	.4000	.4683	.5425	.5897	.7084
17	.3887	.4555	.5285	.5751	.6932
18	.3783	.4438	.5155	.5614	.6787
19	.3687	.4329	.5034	.5487	.6652
20	.3598	.4227	.4921	.5368	.6524
25	.3233	.3809	.4451	.4869	.5974
30	.2960	.3494	.4093	.4487	.5541
35	.2746	.3246	.3810	.4182	.5189
40	.2573	.3044	.3578	.3932	.4896
45	.2428	.2875	.3384	.3721	.4648
50	.2306	.2732	.3218	.3541	.4433
60	.2108	.2500	.2948	.3248	.4078
70	.1954	.2319	.2737	.3017	.3799
80	.1829	.2172	.2565	.2830	.3568
90	.1726	.2050	.2422	.2673	.3375
100	.1638	.1946	.2301	.2540	.3211

*To be significant, the r obtained from the data must be equal to or larger than the value in Table 23.6

(**Source:** Amin, M.E. 2004, Foundations of statistical inference for the social sciences. Kampala, Uganda: Makerere University Press, p. 327, Appendix 6)

To read off any critical PLCC r value from Table 23.6, a researcher such as Kakooza (1997) takes more or fewer steps, in the following Toolbox.

Toolbox Reading the critical t values table

Step 1   Choose an appropriate critical, significance or rejection level, α
Kakooza (1997) chose α = 5% or 0.05, the most popular in the social sciences including Education in which she researched. She checked for this in the top row of Table 23.6, noting the column in which it falls.

Step 2 Get the so-called number of degrees of freedom (df) associated with the test
For Pearson's linear correlation coefficient (PLCC) r statistic (Expression 23.13), the number of degrees of freedom (df) is given by the number of paired scores, that is, the sample size used, less two. Thus, algebraically:

$$df = n - 2 \dotfill (23.15)$$

Thus according to Table 23.5, because Kakooza (1997) used a sample of size, n = 75 learners or paired scores, the number of degrees of freedom (df) associated with her PLCC r statistic was df = 75 – 2 = 73. Identify this df = 73 (taking 70 which is nearest to 73) in the left-most column of Table 23.6, noting the row in which it falls.

Step 3   Read off the required critical PLCC r value
Where the column identified in step 1 and the row in step 2 meet, was Kakooza's (1997) required critical PLCC:

$$rc = 0.2319 \dotfill (23.16)$$

Step 4   Make the inference

Note that the (absolute) value of Kakooza's (1997) computed or observed PLCC r value (0.29 in expression 23.14) exceeded her critical r value (0.2319 in expression 23.16). Thus, at the α = 5 per cent or 0.05 level of significance, Kakooza rejected her null hypothesis, H_0 (expression 23.12B) and accepted the research or alternative hypothesis, H_1 (expression 23.12A). In other words, she inferred that the two numerical variables (attendance in terms of the number of lessons attended and the achievement in adult literacy respectively) were significantly positively linearly correlated.

This means those learners who attended more lessons, also tended to achieve higher in the adult literacy test. Having observed that the adult learners had many constraints (e.g. planting crops, guarding their crops from pests, carrying water), which made it difficult for them to attend classes, Kakooza (1997:54) recommended that, "local councils [...] take literacy as one for developing their areas and should therefore alert the appropriate officials in the Game Department to fight vermin and pests and lessen the burden of guarding crops by adult literacy learners".

We now outline a technique that is closely related to that of Pearson's linear correlation, that is, Spearman's rank correlation.

23.6.2 Correlating two ordinal or ranked variables: Spearman's rank correlation coefficient test

With Spearman's rank correlation coefficient (SRCC) test, as suggested by the fourth row in Table 23.1, a researcher is interested in how a dependent variable (DV) and an independent variable (IV) that are both ordinal or ranked, correlate, that is vary with one another. Let us look at an example.

Using Spearman's rank correlation coefficient test

Kakooza (1997) might have been interested in testing whether the learners' positions or ranks on their achievement in adult literacy (an ordinal or ranked DV) were positively related to their positions or ranks on attendance, that is the number of lessons they attended (an ordinal or ranked IV). In other words, her study could have involved testing the research hypothesis:

H_1: The two ordinal or ranked variables were significantly correlated, ...(23.17A)
  against the null hypothesis:

H_0: The two ordinal or ranked variables were not significantly correlated ....(23.17B)

To test the null hypothesis, H_0 (expression 23.17B), Kakooza could then have used Charles Spearman's rank correlation (SRCC) test, which is an approximation of Karl Pearson's linear correlation coefficient (PLCC) test. Being an approximation of PLCC, the calculations for both SRCC and PLCC are similar, especially when using a computer package such as the statistical package for social scientists (SPSS) is used, as you will see in Chapter 24.

Now, having given details on Pearson's linear correlation, and outlined Spearman's rank correlation, let us also outline a technique that is intended to correlate two categorical variables.

23.6.3 Correlating two categorical variables: Pearson's Chi-square test

With Pearson's Chi-square (χ^2) test, as suggested by the bottom row in Table 23.1, a researcher is interested in how a dependent variable (DV) and an independent variable (IV) that are both categorical, correlate, that is, vary between one another. An example is called for now.

Using the Chi-square test

Balyesiima's (1992) MEd dissertation had as an objective to test whether the performance in economics (a DV categorised as high, moderate and low) differed according to the attitude of a student toward economics (an IV categorised as good, fair and poor). In other words, Balyesiima's study involved testing the research hypothesis:

H_1: The two categorical variables were significantly correlated, ...(23.18A)
  against the null hypothesis:

H_0: The two categorical variables were not significantly correlated ....(23.18B)
  (i.e. they were independent)

(continued)

Using the Chi-square test *(continued)*

To test the null hypothesis, H$_0$ (expression 23.18B), Balyesiima randomly selected 296 senior six students from seven schools in three districts of Uganda. He administered a questionnaire tapping the students' attitudes towards economics, and eventually gave them a test in economics, noting their respective achievements, resulting into the data in Table 23.7:

TABLE 23.7: Attitude vs Performance in Economics in Balyesiima's (1992) study

Attitude	Performance			Total
	High	Moderate	Low	
Good	33	31	33	97
Fair	63	54	60	177
Poor	10	7	5	22
Total	106	92	98	296

For such a data set as in Table 23.7, the positions of the nine observed frequencies (i.e. 33, 31 . . ., 7 and 5) are referred to as the cells in the cross-tabulation. In order to correlate the two categorical variables (in this case, attitude and performance), a researcher such as Balyesiima (1992) uses the Chi-square technique. However, due to space limitations, the details on the technique could not be given in the chapter, and hence you can follow it up in textbooks on research methods and statistics.

Stop and reflect

In section 23.6, we introduced three techniques, with the first and the third, attributed to one person, Karl Pearson. The second technique is attributed to Charles Spearman.
1 Do an internet search (e.g. http:// en.wikipedia.org/ wiki/ Karl_Pearson) to find out other details about Karl Pearson, such as when, where and how long he lived, together with his contribution to inferential statistics, to the extent of being named the 'father of modern statistics'.
2 Repeat 1 but for Charles Spearman and his rank correlation coefficient (e.g. try: http:// en.wikipedia. org/ wiki/ Charles_Spearman).

Conclusion

This chapter has been one of several chapters in this book related to positivism or quantitative research, starting with Chapter 2. The chapter is intended to help researchers like yourself, who are now grappling with the use of inferential statistics. We started with a contrast between descriptive statistics that you covered in Chapter 22 and inferential statistics, stressing that the latter builds on the former to make generalisations on a population from which the sample was chosen.

Four basic concepts that are useful in inferential statistics, namely a population and its parameters; a sample, and its statistics were introduced. With that background, the chapter had seven more sections. Sections 23.2 and 23.3 respectively introduced two major branches of inferential statistics, and hence inferential data analysis: the estimation of population parameters and the testing of hypotheses on population parameters. In section 23.4, we extended the idea of testing of hypotheses on population parameters to the bivariate case, that is, we introduced the idea of testing hypotheses that involve two variables. This was consolidated in sections 23.5 on comparative data analysis; and 23.6 on correlative data analysis. These two sections (23.5 and 23.6) allowed you to see some of the main statistical calculations at work. Try all the end-of-chapter questions to be sure you have a solid foundation in inferential statistics. We hope that this chapter has gone some way to reduce the statistics anxiety in you.

Closing activities

Reflective questions

Question 1
In this chapter, we have introduced inferential statistics, while in Chapter 22 you read about descriptive statistics. How do the two branches of statistics a) differ; and b) relate?

Practical applications

Question 2
Revisit the example 'Introducing confidence interval estimation' and the Toolbox on 'Confidence interval estimation', and establish the a) 95 per cent; and b) 99 per cent confidence interval estimates respectively, for μ, the mean IQ of all the students in the class. (You will remember, however, that the 95 per cent confidence level is the most popular in social sciences research.)

Question 3
Revisit the example, 'Introducing testing a hypothesis on a parameter', and test the null hypothesis at the a) 95 per cent; and b) 99 per cent confidence levels, respectively.

Question 4
Revisit the example, 'Using the t-test', and test Babirye-Kakeeto's (1993) null hypothesis at the a) 90 per cent; and b) 99 per cent confidence levels, respectively.

Question 5
Revisit the example, 'Using Pearson's linear correlation coefficient (PLCC)', and test Kakooza's (1997) null hypothesis at the a) 90 per cent; and b) 99 per cent confidence levels, respectively.

Analysis and consolidation

Question 6
A researcher who fears or dreads statistics is not up to the job; conversely a researcher who has no fear of statistics may also not be up to the job. Discuss.

Bibliography

Amin, M.E. 2004. *Foundations of statistical inference for the social sciences.* Kampala, Uganda: Makerere University Press.

Babirye-Kakeeto, M. 1993. *Relationship between English language and History performance at Ordinary Level in Kampala secondary schools.* Unpublished Master of Education dissertation, Makerere University, Kampala, Uganda.

Balyesiima, D.F. 1992. *Evaluation of students' attitude to, and performance in tests involving essay, objective and data response questions for A-level Economics in selected schools in Kampala, Mpigi and Mukono Districts.* Unpublished Master of Education dissertation, Makerere University, Kampala, Uganda.

Coombs, C.H. 1964. *The theory of data analysis.* New York, US: Wiley.

http:// en.wikipedia.org/ wiki/ Charles_Spearman

http://en.wikipedia.org/ wiki/ Karl_Pearson

http:// en.wikipedia.org/ wiki/ Ronald_Fisher

http:// en.wikipedia.org/ wiki/ William_Gosset

Kakooza, T. 1997. *Correlates of achievement in adult literacy using pedagogical and andragogical methods of teaching.* Unpublished PhD in Education thesis, Makerere University, Kampala, Uganda.

Stevens, S.S. 1951. Mathematics, measurement, and psychophysics. In S.S. Stevens (Ed). *Handbook of experimental psychology.* New York, US: Wiley.

Recommendation

In this chapter, especially in the *Stop and reflect* activities, we have directed you to the internet as a possible source of material for further reading. Now that you have finished this chapter, please read the relevant chapters in the book for the reasons given in brackets:

Chapter 2 (In Chapter 23 you dealt with how data that are collected during positivist research are analysed deductively. So if you re-read Chapter 2, which gave the philosophical basis of the positivist research paradigm, you will find both chapters clearer.)

Chapter 11 (The data for the inferential analysis that you have dealt with in Chapter 23, have to be properly defined and quantitatively measured. Thus it is important for you to revisit Chapter 11 to have this issue consolidated.)

Chapter 13 (The data for inferential analysis that you have dealt with in Chapter 23, have to result from reasonably large samples that are randomly selected. Chapter 13 emphasises this sampling issue. Read it again.)

Chapter 15 (Experimental methods of data collection are of special relevance in positivist research in general, and the inferential analysis that you have read about in Chapter 23, in particular. So you need to re-read Chapter 15.)

Chapter 18 (The questionnaire as a tool for data collection is of special significance for positivist researchers, especially when planning to use inferential data analysis, the topic of Chapter 23. Look at Chapter 18 again.)

Chapter 22 (Descriptive data analysis which employs tools collectively known as descriptive statistics, the subject of Chapter 22, precedes inferential data analysis which employs tools collectively known as inferential statistics, the essence of Chapter 23. This makes it imperative for you to again read Chapter 22.)

Chapter 24 (SPSS facilitates descriptive and inferential data analyses, which you learned about in Chapters 22 and 23 respectively. Reading the following Chapter 24 will make all three chapters clearer to you.)

Chapter 26 (If the proceedings and findings of positivist research are not going to be reported, then the research is futile. By reading Chapter 26, you will be in a better position to write positivist research reports.)

CHAPTER 24

Chrysogonus Nwaigwe

Application of the statistical package for the social sciences (SPSS)

KEY CONCEPTS

Computer output refers to results of computer analysis.

Computer software is programs developed for various applications using a computer.
A program is a set of coded instructions in the language a computer understands, to enable it execute some actions.

Data view is the environment in which data are entered for analysis.

Default software is a program that is originally installed on a computer during manufacturing.

Dialog (also Dialogue) box is a rectangular box on a computer screen containing options for instructions to be given to the computer to perform an operation.

Label column is a column in a spreadsheet in which the full names of the variables can be entered.

Log on is to enter into an environment on a computer, for example, the SPSS environment.

Name column is a column in a spreadsheet in which names of the variables may be entered as abbreviations, or in full if the characters can be accommodated in the column.

Numeric (adjective) is used to describe a quantitative variable, examples, volume, weight, length, etc. that must be entered as numbers.

P-value is a probability value for interpretation of some statistical results, especially in statistical inference.

String (adjective) is used to describe a qualitative variable, examples, gender, educational level, marital status, etc. that must be entered as alphabets or a combination of alphabets and numbers.

Type (noun) is used to describe the nature of a variable, numeric, string, etc.

Variable view is the environment in which variables are named and defined in terms of types and sizes.

LEARNING OUTCOMES

By the end of this chapter, you should be able to:

▶ Explain the meaning of SPSS.

▶ Describe the origin of SPSS and the need for SPSS.

▶ Enter data in SPSS.

▶ Use SPSS to calculate frequencies, percentages, mean, standard, and other descriptive measures.

▶ Draw charts.

▶ Use SPSS to perform a reliability test, regression and correlation analysis, t-test, and one-way ANOVA.

▶ Interpret results of SPSS output.

Introduction

Statistics is understood as a popular tool for research. Most research procedures are anchored on quantitative data analyses. Modern quantitative data analyses are done with ease through the use of **computer software**. This ensures accuracy, reduction of labour and time. It also ensures easy interpretation of results. For example, if you have done statistical analysis using the statistical analysis package for the social sciences (SPSS), you do not need to look up for the table (critical) value of the statistic in a statistical table; all you need to do is to make use of the **P-value** often seen as sig. 2 tailed in the **computer output**. The use of the P-value will be dealt with in a later section in this chapter. In the next section, we discuss the use of SPSS for statistical analysis.

24.1 Using SPSS to analyse statistical data

The Statistical Package for Social Sciences (SPSS) is one of the earliest computer software packages for analysing statistical data. Its origin dates back to 1968, when it was developed by Norman Nie, Hadlai Hull and Dale Bent (http//www.spss.com.hk/corpinfo/history.htm), three graduate students from different professional backgrounds. The initial work on SPSS was done at Stanford University in California, out of the need to quickly analyse volumes of social sciences data gathered through various research methods.

SPSS has since gained enormous popularity in the fields of applied statistics, natural and social sciences, and engineering. It has also proved useful in educational research. Although there are other statistical packages, such as Mini-Tab and SAS, none has been as widely used as the SPSS.

There are several versions of SPSS. The later versions range from Version 11.0 to Version 21.0. Our teaching of the applications of the SPSS in this book will be mostly based on Version 17.0 of the SPSS. The choice of this version has no special significance, other than that it is a version in current use. However, once you are able to use one version of the SPSS, you can use any other version with ease.

There are very few differences in the use of SPSS among various versions of the software. Before reading this chapter, it is assumed that the reader has studied the preliminary chapters of this book on descriptive and inferential statistics and is now acquainted with various statistical techniques and when to use them. Our task in this chapter is to teach the reader how the various statistical techniques treated in Chapter 22 and Chapter 23 can be carried out with SPSS. Other statistical techniques found in SPSS that are outside the scope of this book can, however, be carried out with less stress if the reader has successfully begun to use any version of SPSS for statistical analyses.

Although there are a number of books on the use of SPSS, we try to address the unique needs of the African student in computer use, a subject only recently introduced to the school curriculum, in this book. Our chapter further focuses on SPSS in an educational research context rather than discussing SPSS on its own. In the next section, we describe the components of the SPSS.

24.2 Components of the SPSS

It is important to note that the SPSS program does not usually come as **default software** in most computer systems. So you need to ensure that your system has SPSS installed on it. If the SPSS program is installed on a computer, it is usually found among the desktop shortcut icons; otherwise, click on the Start button and then click on "All Programs" to check if SPSS is already installed on your system. Let us suppose that you have successfully ensured that SPSS is installed on your system, to **log on** to the SPSS environment to view the components [SPSS17.0, type in data, OK, Variable View, define your variables, Data View, enter your data], double click on the SPSS icon on the desktop, or on the "All Programs" menu. This takes you to a dialogue box in the SPSS environment which asks you what you would like to do (You have five options to choose from). The dialogue box and the options are shown in Figure 24.1.

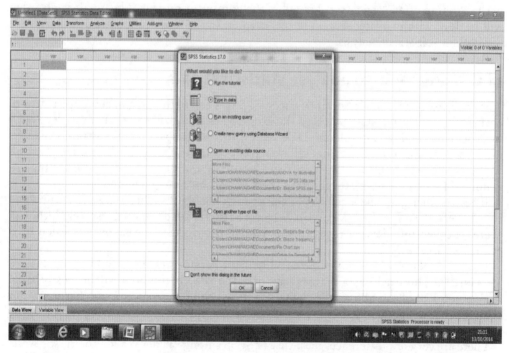

FIGURE 24.1: A typical view of SPSS when you click on the SPSS icon on a desktop

Take your cursor to the small circle beside the option "Type in data" and click on it. The **dialog box** disappears leaving only the spreadsheet on the SPSS environment (see Figure 24.2).

FIGURE 24.2: A typical view of SPSS data view spreadsheet

At the bottom of the spreadsheet, you will see two options **"Data View"** and **"Variable View"**. Usually, before entering data into the SPSS spreadsheet, the variables on which the data were collected have to be defined. Clicking on the "Variable View Icon" enables you to enter into a new environment where you have to define the variables (see Figure 24.3).

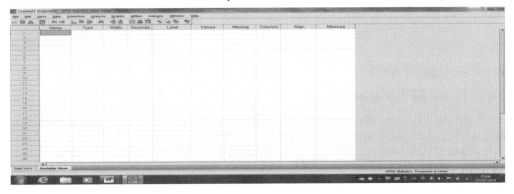

FIGURE 24.3: A typical view of SPSS variable view spreadsheet

We will discuss how to properly define variables later in section 24.3.1. When you have finished defining your variables, click on the "Data View" to begin entering your data; this takes you back to the SPSS spreadsheet with each defined variable appearing on top of a separate column of the spreadsheet. You can now enter the data on each variable in the appropriate column.

Suppose the variables "Height" and "Weight" of some persons were defined in the "Variable View", when you go back to the "Data View", the spreadsheet appears as in Figure 24.4.

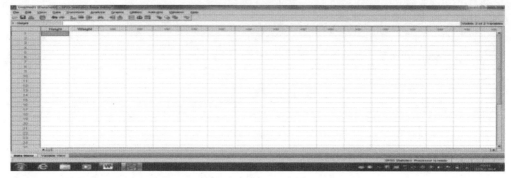

FIGURE 24.4: A typical view of SPSS data view after defining variables

Some menus such as File, Edit, View, Data, Transform, Analyze, Graphs, Utilities, Add-ons, Window and Help can be found at the most top left-hand corner of the SPSS spreadsheet. We will explain those needed for the understanding of this chapter as the need arises.

Stop and reflect

▸ Think of installing a version of SPSS in your personal computer.

▸ Could you attempt logging on to SPSS.

In the next section, we describe how the SPSS works.

24.3 How SPSS works

In this section, we are going to teach you how to use the SPSS to carry out some fundamental and specific statistical analyses. In Section 24.2 we mentioned the "Variable View" and definition of variables as a preliminary and fundamental step that must be taken before entering the data for analysis in "SPSS Spreadsheet". The definition of variables is important for distinction among the outputs of various variables and easy interpretation of the outputs. If the variables are not defined before entering the data in the spreadsheet, the default variables, VAR00001, VAR00002, VAR00003, etc., are displayed as the variable names for the first, second and third variables respectively, and it continues in that order. In section 24.3.1, we are going to systematically guide the reader on how to define variables in SPSS.

24.3.1 Definition of variables in SPSS

In this section, we provide a guide on how we can properly define variables in SPSS. As we mentioned in Section 24.3, to define your variables in SPSS [Variable View, Name, Type (numeric/string), OK, Width Column, Decimal Column (for numeric variables only), Values Column, enter the value for each variable, enter the label for the variable, Add, OK (when all variables are added)], click on the "Variable View Icon" at the bottom of the "SPSS Spreadsheet". Enter each variable name in a separate rectangular box under "Name". It is preferable to enter the abbreviations for the variables in the "Name Column" and enter the full names for the variables in the "Label Column"; for example, "edustatus" can be entered for educational status in the "**Name Column**" while it can be entered fully in the "**Label Column**".

1 Can you think of variables you often come across in your discipline? List them now, with details.
2 Now think of short names for each that unambiguously capture their essence.

Variable names are not case sensitive (i.e. upper and lower case letters may be used). However, spaces, dots and punctuation marks are illegal characters in defining variable names; for example, "edu.status" or "edu status" is an unacceptable variable name in SPSS. Some versions of SPSS allow only limited number of characters to be entered as a variable name but Version 17.0 allows a good number of characters to be entered as a variable name. In practice, it is better to use few characters to define a variable so that it will enter in one rectangular box in the "Name Column". The full name of the variable, as we mentioned in this sub-section may be given in the "Label Column".

After entering the variable name, use your right arrow key to take your cursor to the next column "**Type**". Click on the small square box in the column with dotted lines. This enables you to define the type of variable that you have entered. Choose **numeric** or **string** and click on "OK". Note that you can also define a string variable as numeric if you intend to enter the data in numeric form, example, if you wish to enter gender as a numeric variable you can use 1 to represent male and 2 to represent female. This may also be indicated in the "Label Column".

To specify the maximum number of characters to enter for each variable, click on the "Width Column" and specify the number of characters. After that, take your cursor to the "Decimals Column" and define the number of decimal places.

Now, if you wish to enter the name of your variable which you have entered as abbreviation in full, take your cursor to the "Values Column" and enter the values and the corresponding labels. For example, you may enter "1" as the value and male as the label and click on the "Add" menu in the dialogue box, similarly, enter "2" as the value and female as the corresponding label and click on "Add". Click on "OK" when you are sure, you have entered all the values and their labels for a particular variable (see Figure 24.5).

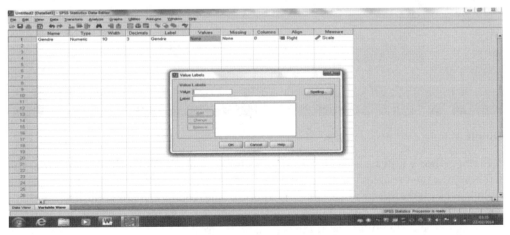

FIGURE 24.5: A typical view of SPSS variable view when variables are to be given labels

After defining your variables, click on the "Data View" as we have mentioned in section 24.3. Each defined variable name appears on the spreadsheet as a separate column. Enter the data for each variable, column wise under each variable. In the next section, we are going to explain how SPSS can be used to carry out some descriptive and inferential statistical analysis.

24.4 How does the SPSS work?

In this section, we shall describe how to use the SPSS to calculate percentages, means and standard deviations and other descriptive measures. We shall also describe how to use the SPSS to perform the t-test, Chi-square test, analysis of variance (ANOVA), correlation, regression and reliability analysis, such as Cronbach's alpha and split-half. The steps that must be followed to achieve each described statistical analysis will be given. We provide a guide on how to interpret results from SPSS. At the end of this section, careful understanding of the steps would enable the reader to run the described statistical analysis without further help. In section 24.4.1, we describe how to use SPSS to calculate frequencies and percentages.

24.4.1 Using SPSS for calculations of frequencies and percentages

In this section, we will explain how to calculate frequencies and percentages using SPSS. [enter your data, Analyze, Descriptive Statistics, Frequencies, highlight the variables, click on the arrow pointing to the right, OK]. For example, enter data on gender to calculate the frequencies and percentages of male and female students at attendance in a meeting. Look at the top of the Spreadsheet and click on "Analyze", click on "Descriptive Statistics", click on "Frequencies", as shown in Figure 24.6.

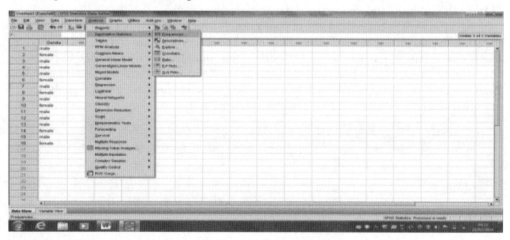

FIGURE 24.6: A typical view of SPSS for frequency and percentage analysis

A dialogue box with two adjacent rectangular boxes appears. The rectangular box at the left contains the variables you have entered data on them while the rectangular box at the right hand with the heading "Variables" is empty. In the rectangular box at the left, highlight the variables you wish to calculate the frequencies and percentages on and click on the arrow pointing to the rectangular box at the right (see Figure 24.7).

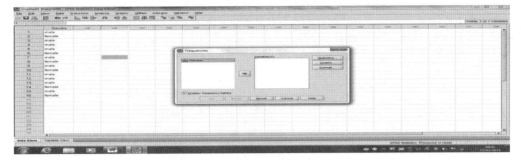

FIGURE 24.7: SPSS view in course of doing percentage and frequency view

This will automatically transfer the highlighted variable(s) to the rectangular boxes at the right. Click on "OK" at the bottom of the dialogue box and the results showing the frequencies and percentages are automatically displayed for each of the variables entered in the right rectangular box for analysis.

In order to obtain the mean, mode, median, measures of deviation, click on the "Statistics" beside the right rectangular box and check on the box for any descriptive measure you wish to include in the analysis and click "OK" and the results are displayed. In the section 24.4.2, we describe how to use SPSS to plot charts.

24.4.2 Plotting charts with SPSS

To draw a chart with the SPSS, go to the Variable View and define your variables appropriately. Enter your data in the Data View [Graph, Gallery, choose chart, drag the chart, drag variable label for X axis to the axis, drag variable label for Y axis to the axis, Titles/Footnotes, enter your title(s), Apply, OK]. Click on Graphs at the top of the spreadsheet for Data View. Go to the "Gallery" to choose the kind of chart you require, to describe your data; for example, click on Bar to display several types of bar charts. Click on the type of bar chart you require and drag it to the rectangular box where you see "Drag a Gallery Chart" to use it as your reference point.

Label the X and Y axes and drag the labels to the space for the X or Y axis, as the case may be. Click on Titles/Footnotes to give a title to your chart, then click on "Title 1" to type in the first title of your chart in the space "Content" with a rectangular box. If there are more titles, subtitles or footnotes, click on "Title 2", subtitle or footnotes, as the case may be, to enter more titles, subtitle or footnotes. Click on "Apply" at the bottom of the rectangular box adjacent to the graph. Click on OK and the chart is automatically displayed. If, for example, you try plotting a simple bar chart with the following data:

TABLE 24.1: Number of students in different levels in a university department

Level	Number
Year I	68
Year II	34
Year III	168
Year IV	158
Year V	92

you will produce the chart in Figure 24.8. It is important to note that if we want the chart to appear as rectangular bars (like the one in Figure 24.8) the level of students has to be defined as a string variable; otherwise, the bars will appear as lines.

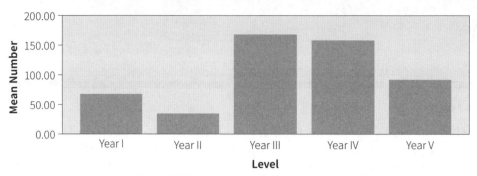

FIGURE 24.8: A simple bar chart of the number of students in a university department

It is also important to note that, alternatively, you can give a title to your chart by clicking on the "G Graph" on top of your chart and typing in the title of your chart.

Suppose, we wish to represent the above data with a pie chart, we will go to the "Gallery" and choose Pie/Polar, a sample pie chart is then displayed, drag the sample pie chart to the space "Drag a Gallery chart here to use it as your starting point". Drag the Number of students to the "Angle Variable" and student level to "Slice by". Enter the title of your pie chart as we explained earlier and click on OK to display your chart. Using the data in Table 24.1 to plot a pie chart will produce the pie chart in Figure 24.9.

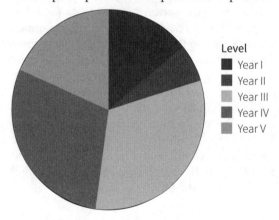

FIGURE 24.9: Pie chart of the number of students at each level in a university department

In order to plot an ogive with SPSS, define your class boundaries as a string variable in the Variable View. Define your cumulative frequency as a numeric variable, go to the Data View and enter your data. Click on "Graph" and go to Chart Builder. Click on "Gallery" and choose "Line". Drag the type of line graph you want to the space above as in the bar chart and pie chart operations. Drag the variable showing the class boundaries to the X-axis and the cumulative frequency to the Y-axis. Give a title to your graph as usual and click on "OK" and the ogive is displayed.

For example, plotting an ogive with Table 24. 2 below will produce the following ogive:

TABLE 24.2: Allowance in (Naira) of a group of students in a secondary school

Allowance group	Frequency	Cumulative frequency
139.6–181.5	9	9
161.5–180.5	20	29
180.5–200.5	33	62
200.5–220.5	25	87
220.5–240.5	11	98
240.5–260.5	4	102

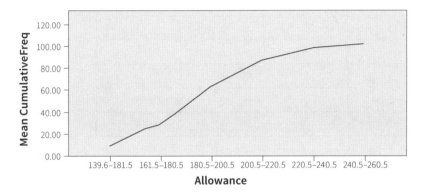

FIGURE 24.10: Ogive of allowance (in Naira) of a group of students in a secondary school

Stop and reflect

1 Can you think of any problem in your discipline that you can solve in with a chart?
2 Try drawing the chart with SPSS.

In section 24.4.3, we describe how to use the SPSS to perform a reliability test.

24.4.3 Using SPSS to perform a reliability test

In order to use the SPSS to perform a reliability test, define your variables in the "Variable View" as numeric variables. Enter your data appropriately in the "Data View". Click [Analyze, scale, Reliability Analysis, highlight the items for analysis, arrow sign opposite the items, Model, select your test, OK] on Analyze, choose scale, follow the arrow in front of the scale and choose "Reliability Analysis". Highlight the items you wish to perform the reliability test on. Click on the arrow opposite the items. This automatically selects the highlighted items for the test. Go to "Model", choose Alpha if you wish to obtain the Cronbach's Alpha. You can also choose any other test such as Split-half, Gultman, Parrel or Strict Parrel from the Model selection. Click on "OK" and the result is displayed. For example, if you use Table 24.3:

TABLE 24.3: Internal consistency of students' rating of teacher using five different criteria

Item 1	Item 2	Item 3	Item 4	Item 5
4	2	2	5	2
5	1	1	4	3
4	4	3	3	2
3	1	4	5	5
3	5	4	4	5
3	5	4	4	5
3	5	5	3	4
5	5	5	5	3
5	4	5	5	3
5	2	2	4	3
3	2	2	3	5
4	3	3	4	4

To perform a reliability test using Cronbach's Alpha it will produce the following result, in Table 24.4:

TABLE 24.4: Reliability statistics

Cronbach's Alpha	N of Items
.298	5

In the next section 24.4.4, we explain how SPSS can be used to carry out a correlation analysis.

24.4.4 Analysis of correlation with SPSS

In order to use SPSS to do correlation cnalysis, define your variables in the Variable View as numeric. Enter your data appropriately in the Data View. Click [Analyze, Correlate, make your choice of correlation, highlight your variables, arrow sign, opposite the variables, choose test, OK] on Analyze, choose correlate, follow the arrow on correlate and choose the type of correlation you wish to do, bivariate, partial or distances.

For example, click on Bivariate and you will see that a dialogue box with two rectangular boxes appears. Highlight the variables for bivariate correlation and click on the arrow pointing to the rectangular box for variables. The variables will automatically leave the rectangular box for bivariate correlations and enter the rectangular box for variables.

At the bottom of the two rectangular boxes, choose the type of bivariate correlation you wish to do: Pearson, Kendall or Spearman. For example, when you click on Pearson to choose it, "A good mark" must appear in the small box for Pearson so that you can be sure that you have chosen it. Click on "OK" and the result of the analysis is displayed; for example, using Table 24.5 below to do a bivariate Pearson correlation analysis will produce the output in Table 24.6.

TABLE 24.5: Weight and height of a group of teenagers

Weight (kg)	Height (cm)
60	2.00
70	2.50
56	3.00
62	2.78
64	2.60

TABLE 24.6: Output of correlations between weight and height

		Weight	Height
Weight	Pearson correlation	1	−.252
	Sig. (2-tailed)		.683
	N	5	5
Height	Pearson correlation	−.252	1
	Sig. (2-tailed)	.683	
	N	5	5

In section 24.4.5, we are going to describe how to use SPSS to perform a regression analysis.

24.4.5   Using SPSS for regression analysis

To use SPSS for regression analysis, define your variables as was explained for correlation (section 24.4.4). Enter the appropriate data for all the variables defined. Click [Analyze, Regression, choose type of regression, specify dependent and independent variables, method, choose method, statistics, specify estimates, Continue, OK] on Analyse, choose Regression, move your cursor to the arrow on Regression and choose the type of regression you want to run and a dialogue box appears showing the variables and prompting you to specify which variable is dependent and which is independent.

Highlight the dependent variable and click on the arrow pointing to "Dependent". Also highlight the independent variables and click on the arrow pointing to "Independent(s)". Immediately below "Independent(s)", you see "Method". The default method is "Enter". Leave it on the default if you wish to run ordinary regression; otherwise click on the arrow on "Enter" and choose an alternative type of regression you wish to run, then stepwise, Remove, Backward, or Forward.

After that, go to "Statistics" on the box and specify all the estimates you wish to obtain, be it R Square Change, Durbin-Watson, etc. Click on "Continue" and click on "OK" to have the output displayed.

Consider using SPSS to run a regression analysis of the data as in Table 24.7.

TABLE 24.7: Monthly income and expenditure of a group of lecturers (in Naira)

Income	Expenditure
170000	94000
260000	155000
120000	83000
150000	90000
450000	358000
222000	180000
300000	268000
170000	70000
120000	65000
140000	56000

In this case, we take income as our independent variable and expenditure as our dependent variable and define each of them as a numeric variable in the "Variable View". The data for each variable are then entered in the "Data View". We then follow the steps in this section to run the regression analysis. The following output, as shown in Table 24.8, Table 24.9 and Table 24.10, is produced.

TABLE 24.8: Summary of the statistics

Model Summary[b]										
					Change Statistics					
Model	R	R Square	Adjusted R Square	Std. Error of the Estimate	R Square Change	F Change	df1	df2	Sig. F Change	Durbin-Watson
1	.966[a]	.933	.925	27629.89522	.933	111.389	1	8	.000	2.386

a. Predictions: (Constant), Income
b. Dependant Variable: Expenditure

TABLE 24.9: ANOVA table on expenditure and income

Model		Sum of Squares	Df	Mean Square	F	Sig.
1	Regression	8.504E10	1	8.504E10	111.389	.000[a]
	Residual	6.107E9	8	7.634E8		
	Total	9.114E10	9			

TABLE 24.10: Coefficents of the model

Model		Unstandardised coefficients		Standardised coefficients	t	Sig.
		Std. Error	Beta			
1	(Constant)	−55681.920	20659.431		−2.695	.027
	Income	.940	.089	.966	10.554	.000

Our example on regression analysis involves only one independent variable, but sometimes a regression analysis involves one dependent variable and two or more independent variables. This is called multiple regression analysis. The procedure is the same with our earlier explanation, but one needs to highlight each of the independent variables and click on the arrow pointing to the "Independent(s)" each time to enter the variable as an independent variable. In the next section, we are going to describe how to use SPSS for the analysis of Chi-square contingency table.

24.4.6 Using SPSS for analysis of Chi-square contingency table

In order to use SPSS to analyse a Chi-square contingency table, one needs to define three variables in the "Variable View", namely, the variable represented in the row of the table, the variable represented in the column of the table, and the observed frequencies. When this is done, go to the "Data View" to enter your data. When you enter each observed frequency, enter its positions in the table (the row number and the column number) under the variables representing the row and column respectively.

For example, to represent the contingency table in Table 24.11 in SPSS, proceed in the following way:

TABLE 24.11: Ratings of a group of people on the performance of three political parties in a state in Nigeria

Political party	Rating		
	Bad	Fair	Good
PDP	76	80	44
APC	150	35	15
APGA	19	11	170

Observe that the political parties are represented in the rows. The ratings are represented in the columns. Therefore, go to the "Variable View". Define the following variables, observed frequency as "Observedfreq", political party as "Politicalparty" and rating can be written in full. Go to the "Data View". Enter your data as in Table 24.12.

TABLE 24.12: Illustration on how to enter data in Chi-square contingency table in SPSS data view

Observedfreq	Politicalparty	Rating
76	1	1
80	1	2
44	1	3
150	2	1
35	2	2
15	2	3
19	3	1
11	3	2
170	3	3

That is, the observed frequency 76 is in the first row and first column, 80 is in the first row and second column and the other observed frequencies follow in that order. After you have entered the data, click [data, weight cases, highlight the observed frequency variable, arrow sign opposite the observed frequency, OK, Analyse, Descriptives, Crosstabs, highlight the row variable, highlight the column variable, Statistics, Chi-square, Continue, OK] on "Data" on top of the "Data View Spreadsheet", select "weight cases" by taking your cursor to it and clicking on it. The first dialogue box appears. Click on the small circle for "weight cases by".

Then highlight the variable "Observedfreq" and click on the arrow by the right pointing to the "Frequency Variable". This enables "Observedfreq" to enter into the space "Frequency Variable". Click "OK" and a screen appears with the inscription "Weight by Observedfreq". Go to the Menu Bar on top of the screen and click on "Analyze", choose "Descriptives", follow the arrow on "Descriptives" and click on "Crosstabs".

A second dialogue box appears, highlight "Politicalparty" in the dialogue box and click on the arrow by the right pointing to the "Row(s)" in the dialogue box. This enables the variable "Politicalparty" to enter the space for "Row(s)" in the dialogue box. Similarly, highlight the variable "Rating" and click on the arrow by the right pointing to "Columns". This enables the variable rating to be entered into the space for "Column(s)".

Look at the top right of the dialogue box and click on "Statistics", a third dialogue box appears on the second dialogue box, click on the small rectangular box for Chi-square and click on "Continue". Click "OK" to have the output displayed. The following output was obtained for the data.

TABLE 24.13: Chi-square tests

	Value	df	Asymp. Sig. (2-sided)
Pearson Chi-square	341.998[a]	4	.000
Likelihood ratio	351.855	4	.000
Linear-by-linear association	105.897	1	.000
N of valid cases	600		

Note: 0 cells (.0%) would have expected a count less than 5. The minimum expected count is 42.00.

In section 24.4.7, we describe how to use the SPSS for analysis involving the t-test.

24.4.7 T-test analysis of data using SPSS

Recall that in a t-test, data are collected on one variable from one or two samples. Therefore, in order to do a t-test analysis using SPSS, define the variable on which data were collected as usual in the "Variable View" as a numeric variable. If it involves two samples, define a string variable in the "Variable View" which could be called "Group".

When that is done, go to the "Data View" and enter all the data for the two groups under one variable, that is, the variable that the data were collected on. Under the string defined variable, "Group" enter the name of the first group for all the data from the first group, and enter the name of the second group for all the data from the second group. After that, look up at the top of the "Data View Spreadsheet" and click on Analyze, choose "Compare Means". Follow the arrow on "Compare Means", choose "Independent Sample t-test", a dialogue box appears, highlight the test variable. Click on the arrow by the right pointing to "Test Variable(s)", then highlight group. Click on the arrow by the right pointing to "Group Variable".

Once that is done, the SPSS prompts you to define your groups, "Group (?)". Click on "Define Groups". Now enter the name of the first group for "Group 1". Similarly, for Group 2, enter the name of the second group. Click on "Continue" and then click on "OK" to have the output displayed.

Suppose you want to do a Paired Samples t-test: when you follow the arrow on "Compare Means", choose Paired Samples t-test instead of Independent Samples t-test. A dialogue box appears, highlight the two defined variables and click on the arrow by the right. This enables the two variables to be entered simultaneously for analysis. Click on "OK" to have the output displayed.

Consider, for example, the data in Table 24.14 consisting of scores in a statistics course for two independent groups, "Boys" and "Girls", in a class:

TABLE 24.14: Scores of students in a statistics course

Boys	Girls
45	45
67	67
89	65
24	66
65	56

Table 24.15 presents the way the data should appear in the "SPSS Data Spreadsheet".

TABLE 24.15: An illustration of how data should be entered in SPSS for independent sample t-test

Scores	Group
45	Boy
67	Boy
89	Boy
24	Boy
65	Boy
45	Girl
67	Girl
65	Girl
66	Girl
56	Girl

The two groups involved in this analysis are boys and girls. If we follow the description of the Independent t-test procedure in this section, we have the output produced as in Table 24.16 and Table 24.17.

TABLE 24.16: Group statistics

	Group	N	Mean	Std. Deviation	Std. Error Mean
Scores	Boy	5	58.0000	24.57641	10.99091
	Girl	5	59.8000	9.36483	4.18808

TABLE 24.17: Independent samples calculated t values and the significance

		Independent Samples Test								
		Levene's Test for Equality of Variances		t-test for Equality of Means						
									95% Confidence interval of the Difference	
		F	Sig.	t	df	Sig. (2-tailed)	Mean Difference	Std. Error Difference	Lower	Upper
Scores	Equal variances assumed	3.571	.095	−.153	8	.882	−1.80000	11.76180	−28.92277	25.32277
	Equal variances not assumed		1	−.153	5.138	.884	−1.80000	11.76180	−31.79272	28.19272

Consider another set of data where the opinions of people of two different groups are rated on some items about a particular aspect of life or a programme. This kind of research is popular in social sciences and education. For example, suppose a survey is carried out about the performance of a particular governor in a state in two different areas, urban and rural; and the responses of people to the listed items is rated on a five-point Likert scale: Strongly agree (5); Agree (4); Undecided (3); Disagree (2); and Strongly disagree (1).

Items

1 The state governor has improved rural electrification.
2 The state governor has improved the quality of roads in the state.
3 The state governor has made potable water accessible to people in both urban and rural communities.
4 The state governor has reduced the level of unemployment in the state.
5 The facilities and quality of education in the state have improved.
6 The state governor has made good health care accessible to communities in the state.

Suppose seven people each from the urban and rural communities were involved in the survey, and each person responded to each of the six items. Notice here that two different groups are involved, urban and rural, and you want to test if there is a significant difference in the mean responses of the two groups on each of the items. In this case, each of the six items will be defined in the "Variable View" as a numeric variable and another variable defined as string variable to represent place – urban or rural. After that, go to the "Data View" of SPSS and enter the responses of the seven people each from the rural and urban on the six items, as in Table 24.18.

TABLE 24.18: An illustration of how data with multiple test variables should be entered in SPSS for independent sample t-test

Item 1	Item 2	Item 3	Item 4	Item 5	Item 6	Place
5	5	4	4	5	4	Urban
5	5	4	4	5	4	Urban
4	5	4	4	5	4	Urban
5	5	4	4	5	4	Urban
2	5	4	4	5	4	Urban
2	5	2	4	5	4	Urban
1	5	2	3	5	4	Urban
5	1	4	5	5	4	Rural
4	1	4	5	4	5	Rural
5	2	4	5	4	5	Rural
5	2	4	5	4	5	Rural
5	2	5	5	4	5	Rural
5	2	5	5	4	2	Rural
2	2	5	5	4	2	Rural

The data in the first seven rows of the table represent the responses on each of the six items of the seven persons selected from the urban set for the survey. The first row represents the responses of the first person from urban, second row the responses of the second person from urban, in that order. Similarly, the last seven rows in the table represent the responses on each of the six items of the seven persons selected from the rural set.

Follow the following procedure in 24.4.7, "Analyse", "Compare Means", "Independent Samples Test", then highlight all the items (1 to 6) and enter them as your "Test Variable(s)" by clicking on the arrow pointing to "Test Variable(s)". Highlight "Place" and enter it as your group variable by clicking on the arrow pointing to "Group Variable", then click on "Define Groups" to enter urban and rural as your Group 1 and Group 2 respectively, click on "Continue" and "OK" to have the output displayed, as in Table 24.19.

TABLE 24.19: Independent samples calculated t values and the significance for t-test involving multiple items

		Levene's Test for Equality of Variances		t-test for Equality of Means						
									95% Confidence interval of the Difference	
		F	Sig.	t	df	Sig. (2-tailed)	Mean Difference	Std. Error Difference	Lower	Upper
Item 1	Equal variances assumed	4.214	.063	−1.285	12	.223	−1.00000	.77810	−2.69543	.69534
	Equal variances not assumed			−1.285	10.393	.227	−1.00000	.77810	−2.72488	.72488
Item 2	Equal variances assumed	26.667	.000	17.816	12	.000	3.28571	.18443	2.88388	3.68755
	Equal variances not assumed			17.816	6.000	.000	3.28571	.18443	2.83444	3.73699
Item 3	Equal variances assumed	4.129	.065	−2.378	12	.035	−1.00000	.42056	−1.191632	−.08368
	Equal variances not assumed			−2.378	9.303	.041	−1.00000	.42056	−1.94667	−.05333
Item 4	Equal variances assumed	5.760	.034	−8.000	12	.000	−1.14286	.14286	−1.45412	−.83160
	Equal variances not assumed			−8.000	6.000	.000	−1.14286	.14286	−1.49242	−.79330
Item 5	Equal variances assumed	5.760	.034	6.000	12	.000	.85714	.14286	.54588	1.16840
	Equal variances not assumed			6.000	6.000	.001	.85714	.14286	.50758	1.20670
Item 6	Equal variances assumed	19.200	.001	.000	12	1.000	.00000	.53452	−1.16462	1.16462
	Equal variances not assumed			.000	6.000	1.000	.00000	.53452	−1.30793	1.30793

Sometimes a t-test involves only one sample (group); in this case, also follow the arrow on "Compare Means", choose One-Sample t-test, and a dialogue box appears. Highlight the variable. Click on the arrow pointing to the right (Note that in this case, only one variable needs to be defined). Beneath the rectangular box for "Test Variable(s)", you will see a small rectangular box for "Test Value", click inside the box, then type in your test value. Remember that the "Test Value" for "One-Sample" t-test is either a hypothesised value or the population value, otherwise called population parameter. Click on "OK" after entering the "Test Value" to have the output displayed.

We have illustrated the use of SPSS for t-test with an Independent Samples t-test. Illustrations of the two other types of t-test described here are left for the reader to do as activities. In section 24.4.8, we will describe how SPSS can be used to carry out data analysis involving analysis of variance.

24.4.8 Using SPSS for the analysis of variance (ANOVA)

You will recall that the ANOVA technique is used to test if the means of three or more groups are equal. There are different kinds of ANOVA techniques, but we will limit ourselves to the use of SPSS for One-Way-Analysis of Variance. The use of SPSS for other techniques of ANOVA other than One-Way-ANOVA is not within the scope of this chapter.

In order to use SPSS to do ANOVA, go to the "Variable View" and define the dependent variables and the group (factor). It is important to note that in this case, both the dependent variable and the factor have to be defined as numeric in the "Variable View". After defining the factor as numeric, move your cursor horizontally to the "Label Column" and enter the name of the group again. Further, move your cursor to "Values Column", click on the square box with dotted lines in front of "None", a dialogue box appears, requesting you to enter an arbitrary value for each label.

For example, if your group is made up of three methods of teaching: seminar, question-and-answer, and lecture, you could enter "1" as the value, and seminar as the label. Click on "Add" in the dialogue box. Enter "2" as value, and question-and-answer as the label, and click on "Add". Enter "3" as the value, and lecture as the label", click on "Add", and click on "OK".

It is important to note that going to the "Label" and "Values" columns in the "Variable View" when doing ANOVA is only necessary if you wish to do a "Post-Hoc Analysis", otherwise, you would just name the variable and specify the type and proceed to the "Data View" to enter your data. The data from different groups are entered in one column (under one dependent variable name), as in t-test discussed in 24.4.7, but are distinguished by entering the arbitrary number for that group under the variable defining the factor.

After you have entered the data, click [define variables properly, enter your data, Analyze, Compare Means, choose test, select the dependent variable, select the factor variable, Post-Hoc, choose post hoc test, Continue, OK] on "Analyse" and go to "Compare Means"; follow the arrow to the right of "Compare Means" and choose "One-Way-ANOVA". Highlight the dependent variable and click on the arrow pointing to the "Dependent List"; highlight the variable defining the group (factor). Click on the arrow pointing to "Factor". If you wish to do a post-hoc analysis, click on "Post Hoc" in the dialogue box, then choose the type of post-hoc analysis you wish to run by checking on the square box beside it. Click on "Continue" and then click on "OK" to have the output displayed.

Suppose you want to use SPSS to run the analysis of data collected on the three methods, seminar, question-and-answer, and lecture, in teaching calculus (see Loftus & Loftus, 1988:325), as shown in Table 24.20.

TABLE 24.20: Final exam score for students in each of three teaching method situations

Seminar	Question-and-answer	Lecture
94	83	80
90	86	85
95	89	81
89	87	81

Thus, in the SPSS "Data View", the data should appear as in Table 24: 21.

TABLE 24.21: Illustration of how to enter data for ANOVA in SPSS Data View

Score	Method
94	1
90	1
95	1
89	1
83	2
86	2
89	2
87	2
80	3
85	3
81	3
81	3

After entering the data, proceed to "Analyze, Compare Means" One-Way-ANOVA. Enter score as the dependent variable and method as the factor and continue as described in earlier in this section.

The output of the data in Table 24.21 with the Least Square Difference (LSD) chosen as the test for Post-Hoc Analysis is given below:

TABLE 24.22: ANOVA table on scores of students in three teaching methods

	Sum of Squares	Df	Mean Square	F	Sig.
Between Groups	211.167	2	105.583	15.971	.001
Within Groups	59.500	9	6.611		
Total	270.667	11			

TABLE 24.23: LSD multiple comparison of scores of students in three teaching methods

(I) Method	(J) Method	Mean Difference (I-J)	Std. Error	Sig	95% Confidence Interval	
					Lower Bound	Upper Bound
1.00	2.00	5.75000*	1.81812	.012	1.6371	9.8629
	3.00	10.25000*	1.81812	.000	6.1371	14.3629
2.00	1.00	−5.75000*	1.81812	.012	−9.8629	−1.6371
	3.00	4.50000*	1.81812	.035	.3871	8.6129
3.00	1.00	−10.25000*	1.81812	.000	−14.3629	−6.1371
	2.00	−4.50000*	1.81812	.035	−8.6129	−.3871

* The mean difference is significant at the 0.05 level.

Suppose you are carrying out research in which you need to use ANOVA to analyse the difference in the means of three or more groups (methods) with multiple items as in the case of the t-test in Table 24.18, enter the data as in Table 24.18, but define the group or method as numeric.

Suppose there are three items (questions) to measure the efficiency of three methods in doing a job. If three persons were involved in each method and a five-point Likert scale was used, the data should be entered as in Table 24.24 below.

TABLE 24.24: Illustration of how to enter data in SPSS Data View for ANOVA involving multiple items

Item 1	Item 2	Item 3	Method
5	4	5	1
4	4	5	1
5	3	4	2
1	3	5	2
2	3	5	3
3	1	2	3

Table 24.24 shows that data in the last two rows were from Method III, data in the next two rows were from Method II and the first two rows after the row containing the column headings were from Method I. The analysis follows the same procedure as explained for the procedure for ANOVA in this section. In section 24.4.9, we explain how to interpret results of data analysis with SPSS.

Stop and reflect

1 Can you think of any problems in your discipline that you could solve with any of the statistical tools mentioned in this chapter?
2 Can you apply the SPSS to solve the problems?

24.4.9 Interpretation of results from SPSS

The basic difference in interpretation of results from SPSS and that of a manually-computed operation is in the probability value, otherwise called P-Value. All other results from the SPSS output have the same interpretations and are the same with those computed manually.

The SPSS uses the P-Value Approach for analyses of data. This approach obtains a P-Value for the statistics computed. The P-Value is often seen in SPSS output as "Sig." or "sig. (2-tailed)" as mentioned in the introductory section of this chapter. Therefore, rather than the conventional method of comparing the calculated value with the tabulated value, you compare the P-value of the computed statistic with the level of significance, often 0.05. If the P-Value is less than 0.05, it shows there is significant difference between the computed value and the parameter of the given population. So you do not accept the null hypothesis which says there is no significant difference between the computed value and the parameter.

For example, the P-Value in Table 24.22 shows that there is significant difference in the means of the methods since the P-Value (0.001) is less than 0.05. The P-Value for the Pearson Chi-square in Table 24.13 shows that the ratings are independent of the political party that the respondents belong to, since P-Value (0.000) is less than 0.05. The P-Value in Table 24.10 shows that there is significant relationship between the dependent variable and the independent variable since the P-Value (0.000) is less than 0.05. Though, most of the P-Values here are 0.000, but it does not mean that the P-Value takes that value every time. In the next section, we are going to discuss the category of people that should use SPSS.

Stop and reflect

Try to observe differences between interpretation of statistical results with P-Value approach and the conventional method of using table values.

24.5 Who should use SPSS?

The SPSS covers a number of statistical tools for analysis of research data. Most of these tools are necessary for research in Statistics as a discipline, Economics (especially in the area of econometric research), Biological Sciences, Chemistry, Teaching methods, Management, Public Health, Biometrics, Pharmaceutical Sciences, Social Sciences, Environmental Sciences, and some aspects of Engineering.

The user of SPSS is expected to be familiar with the statistical tools and procedure relevant to his or her discipline. The user is also expected to be computer literate and conversant with basic computer operations. The SPSS does not give the user the knowledge of statistical tools, but assumes that the user has already acquired the knowledge of when to use each statistical tool, and the rudiments of the tool. Therefore, the SPSS should not be used in isolation but in line with the user's knowledge of statistics and statistical tools. In the next section, we discuss the necessary skills for the use of the SPSS.

24.6 Necessary skills for using SPSS

As we mentioned earlier in section 24.3, to use SPSS we need to acquire computer skills and be conversant with the basic computer operations. We need to be knowledgeable in statistics. These are important because they guide us on how to properly define the variables and enter the data for analysis. They also help us to understand the output and properly interpret the results. In the next section, we discuss the criticisms of the SPSS.

24.7 Criticisms of the SPSS

SPSS has been criticised as it does not cover statistical tools in some areas, such as operational research techniques, or some aspects of time series analysis.

There is not enough flexibility among various versions of the SPSS. For example, if an analysis is done with one version of the SPSS and the output is copied to another computer system that does not have exactly that version of the SPSS as that in which the analysis was done, opening the output and printing it from that system becomes a problem.

Copying output from SPSS to Microsoft Word also poses a problem in the sense that there is no version yet that makes provision for highlighting the entire output at the same time, and copying it and pasting it in Microsoft Word. Thus one needs to copy the results in the output one-by-one and go to Word to paste it each time.

Conclusion

In this chapter, we have tried to present the meaning of SPSS, its origin and usefulness to the researcher. We have explained extensively how to log on to SPSS and define different types of variables (numeric/string/etc.).

Above all, we explained and gave illustrations of how to enter data in SPSS and carry out some statistical analyses on descriptive and inferential statistics. We have also shown and explained how to interpret results from SPSS output. Do the closing activities to consolidate your learning in this chapter.

Closing activities

Practical applications
Use the SPSS to answer all questions.
1 Given the following measurements of weight of six patients in kg, 60, 78, 45, 65, 51, 64.
   a   Obtain the mean weight of the patients.
   b   Using a One-Sample t-test, test if the mean weight is significantly different from 60 kg.
2 A department in a university schedules a meeting for students in the department; the following was the attendance of the students by year: Year 1, 68; Year II, 65; Year III, 45; Year IV, 50. Obtain the percentage of student attendance by year.
3 Given that the temperature of 10 patients in degrees Centigrade was taken before and after treatment for malaria, as shown in Table 24.25, use a Paired-Sample t-test to test if there is significant difference between the temperature of the patients before and after treatment.

TABLE 24.25: Temperature (°C) of patients before and after treatment for malaria

Temp. before	30	35	37	37	38	39	39	39.6	36	37.8
Temperature after	32	35	37	38	38.5	37.9	37	35.4	36	37

4 Use the data in Table 24.25 to draw a histogram.
5 With the aid of SPSS, use Chi-square to test if crime is significantly independent of gender, in Table 24.26.

TABLE 24.26: Number of cases of different crimes committed in town X by gender

Crime	Murder	Rape	Robbery	Kidnapping	Drugs	Fraud	Total
Male	345	825	805	505	1225	1070	4775
Female	230	275	345	172	659	654	2335

6 With the aid of SPSS, run a multiple regression analysis of the data in Table 24.27.

TABLE 24.27: Hypothetical data on input variables and output of four farms

Output (Naira)	Farm size (hectares)	Labour (Naira)	Capital (Naira)
46000	2	14000	15000
58000	3	14000	20000
98000	5	20000	35000
108000	5	47000	25000

Bibliography

Loftus, G.R. & Loftus, E.F. 1988. *Essence of Statistics* (2nd ed.). New York: Alfred A. Knopf

CHAPTER 25

Nosisi Feza

Qualitative data analysis

KEY CONCEPTS

Empirical evidence is information collected through observations, interviews, documents; also called scientific information.

Low inference describes an observation or analysis where the observer takes in everything that goes on in a situation (often in a classroom, or teaching/learning situation) or the data, without making any judgement or evaluation of the events, transactions, etc. Contrasts with **high inference**, which is used to describe an observation in which the observer makes a judgement or evaluation about what went on.

Novice researcher is a new, developing researcher who is still learning the science and skills of conducting research.

Raw data is collected information for research purposes that has not yet been analysed or formatted.

Synthesis is a combination of different ideas towards developing a new idea or theory.

Systematic search is using ordered questions to guide the search for ideas and information.

Triangulation means two or more methods are used to respond to a question.

Trustworthiness is the quality of being able to rely on a thing's validity and integrity; having confidence in ideas produced.

Validity in qualitative research, is said to exist when the claims made by the researcher match the participants' views of the results.

LEARNING OUTCOMES

By the end of this chapter, you should be able to:

▶ Review different methods of analysis used in qualitative research and the rationale behind each method presented.

▶ Understand the need to use more than one method for strengthening the validity of your results.

▶ Demonstrate, through activities, your own conceptualisation of the methods learned.

▶ Understand and 'own' methods of analysis in order to be able to use them successfully.

▶ Analyse data using the case studies provided and following given criteria to do so.

▶ Conduct your own research project employing an analysis method/s of your choice to produce a report or research article.

▶ Explore and familiarise yourself with the qualitative analysis software available to you.

Case study: How I'm doing in maths

One of the major challenges faced in South African education is learners' poor performance in mathematics and science. A number of researchers have investigated the factors that influence this poor performance and advanced a number of factors, such as poor socio-economic status of learners and their communities, scarcity of qualified mathematics teachers, and poorly resourced schools. Little is known about the views of learners concerning their performance. Researcher Mono (pseudonym) conducted a single case study investigating a learner's views about his own mathematics performance. Here is an extract from the interview data documented, between the learner and researcher Mono.

Mono: How was your performance in mathematics in your June exams?

Learner: I scored 52% for mathematics.

Mono: Were you happy about your score?

Learner: Very happy.

Mono: Can you tell me what made you so happy?

Learner: I usually score below 40% and now I have improved to 52%, way over the pass mark.

Mono: What is your pass mark?

Learner: The pass mark is 30%, but our teacher only accepts 40%.

Mono: Do you think you can do better than that?

Learner: I don't know, it is so hard to do mathematics for me. When I have homework, I don't have anyone to help me at home. My mother comes home late after work and she is always too tired to help me. This time I was helped by my friend Sifiso because he was worried about me always being punished at school for not doing homework. He explains better than my teacher and I can ask him any time I don't understand.

Mono: Do you ever ask your teacher for help? Does your teacher know that you do not have help at home?

Learner: No, I don't ask my teacher for help. It is too embarrassing in the classroom. And we are not allowed to disturb teachers when they are in the staffroom. My teacher never asks me, why I am not doing my homework. He just punishes me by making me stay after school for an hour.

Mono: Do you do your homework when you have to stay after school?

Learner: No, I don't do my work. I don't know how to do it. Until my friend Sifiso stayed with me one day. Now we work together at my home after school, and then we go and play.

The dialogue in this case study gives the raw data collected by researcher Mono. In order to bring meaning and understanding of the views expressed by the learner, this data must be analysed by Mono. This chapter introduces different methods of analysing data and the rationale behind choosing a particular method.

Introduction

Careful and deep understanding of a complex situation is the key to qualitative enquiry. Unravelling the hidden motives of experienced actions can only happen when time and focus is given to the particular studied behaviour. Such practice can only occur in a qualitative enquiry. This chapter aims to guide and challenge **novice researchers** through an introduction to the different methods of analysis in qualitative research and how such methods are used to disentangle information needed to advise or assist in solving problems using **empirical evidence**. Also, the technology assistance given by different software in the market will be introduced, focusing on the ability of a particular software in analysing qualitative data.

Qualitative researchers are a diverse group of people spread globally who endeavour to implement critical interpretive approaches that will enable them to make intellectual interpretations of complex problems and sometimes alarming situations that make up day-to-day experiences. For example, in the opening case study, researcher Mono seeks to understand from the learner's point of view the reasons for poor performance in mathematics in South Africa. Mono selected a single case study to achieve his objective, from many research strategies. Each strategy requires certain data sources and techniques. Returning to Mono's case study, he used interviews to collect data and might also have used audio-tape or field notes to record the data.

This kind of data is complex because it uses words not numbers; in other cases, gestures, expressions, photos and videos are also observed and interpreted. This complexity does not support a single way of analysing qualitative data. Instead, it demands creativity, discipline, and a systematic approach. Srivastava and Hopwood (2009) note the flexibility of qualitative analysis in allowing researchers to turn **raw data** into results. There is no single recipe for the change that transforms raw data. However, if qualitative analysis is conducted efficiently, it changes data to results.

This chapter gives you a map to guide and direct your own research ends. The complexity of qualitative analysis takes the notion of a formulated rule for analysis to a level where it is purely a creation that is informed by the aim of responding to the questions the researcher investigates. For example, the life history mode might be a biography using the same data sources as ethnographic research, such as interviews, documents, archives and participant observation. The analysis of such data might require sorting, coding, interpreting, etc. This chapter then argues that data analysis is the systematic search for meaning. Qualitative enquiry has developed a number of such systematic approaches that assist researchers in revealing meaning from the data.

This chapter discusses the approaches of qualitative research in analysing data, how to maintain validity in the qualitative analysis; what the different analysis models are;, the different types of data analysis software packages; finally it concludes by highlighting important parts of the chapter and provides activities for you to do.

25.1 Approaches of qualitative research

Qualitative research uses diverse approaches. Qualitative scholars discriminate between these diverse approaches from a kind of punitive socialisation, and tend to favour one approach more than others (Glesne, 2015). For example, scholars call their approaches case study, ethnography, life history, narrative analysis, oral history, discourse analysis, action research, grounded theory, heuristic enquiry, biography, and so forth.

Each approach brings its own theoretical tradition, such as case studies where there are fewer participants and the researcher spends more time with them. Ethnography requires the researcher to be part of the community being studied, with the aim of understanding the culture of the participants over a longer period of time. Grounded theory, in contrast, works with a minimum of 30 participants and often more, with the aim of forming theory from their responses. Each approach highlights certain applications, such as observation, interview and participation for ethnography, with case studies possibly choosing one or two only, and participation being optional. Each approach favours certain procedures to analyse data, such as thematic, constant comparison, word count, etc.

This chapter then focuses on the procedures used to analyse data, specifically the analysis models used by qualitative scholars. The strength of an analysis model relies on its **validity**. The analysis should make sure that the results of the analysis can be trusted by readers. Validity is discussed next to ensure that every researcher maintains it as a central principle during analysis.

25.2 Validity

Glesne (2015) and Carcary (2008) argue that research design of the study and data collection need to attend to the validity or **trustworthiness** of the results thoroughly, otherwise the whole work will be in vain. Creswell (1998) then suggests eight authentication measures that a researcher should follow. Those procedures are:

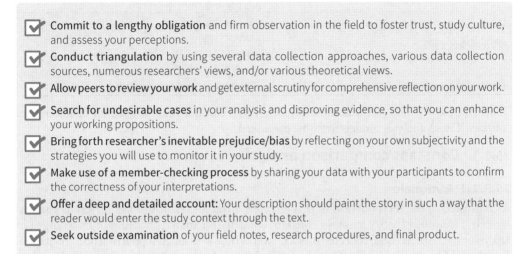

- ☑ **Commit to a lengthy obligation** and firm observation in the field to foster trust, study culture, and assess your perceptions.
- ☑ **Conduct triangulation** by using several data collection approaches, various data collection sources, numerous researchers' views, and/or various theoretical views.
- ☑ **Allow peers to review your work** and get external scrutiny for comprehensive reflection on your work.
- ☑ **Search for undesirable cases** in your analysis and disproving evidence, so that you can enhance your working propositions.
- ☑ **Bring forth researcher's inevitable prejudice/bias** by reflecting on your own subjectivity and the strategies you will use to monitor it in your study.
- ☑ **Make use of a member-checking process** by sharing your data with your participants to confirm the correctness of your interpretations.
- ☑ **Offer a deep and detailed account:** Your description should paint the story in such a way that the reader would enter the study context through the text.
- ☑ **Seek outside examination** of your field notes, research procedures, and final product.

With all these procedures in mind, the power of the findings in quantitative analysis lies in the expertise that is applied while analysing the data (Miles, Huberman & Saldana, 2014). Each model has its own strengths, hence Glesne (2015); Onwuegbuzie and Teddlie (2003); Greene, Caracelli & Graham (1989), contend that using various data analysis tools in qualitative research strengthens validity and representation.

Stop and reflect

- ▶ Going back to the interview by researcher Mono in the opening case study, choose one procedure you will use to make sure that the data are trustworthy.
- ▶ Write a brief explanation on what makes you choose this procedure.

25.3 Qualitative research analysis models

Approaches in qualitative research tend to use similar methods to collect the data, such as interviews, participant observations, focus groups, etc., indicating an overlap in both analysis and data collection. However, qualitative researchers might use different approaches or methods to analyse data (Glesne, 2015). Therefore, any discussion on the analysis models is inclusive of many diverse approaches used by qualitative scholars.

Certain approaches are used as tools to discuss the diverse analysis models. Onwuegbuzie, et al. (2012), in their synthesis of qualitative analysis, discuss the relationship between sources of data and qualitative analysis, which give a clear representation of the overlaps in data analysis techniques. Table 25.1 presents these relationships using data sources and analysis models discussed in this chapter.

TABLE 25.1: Relationship between type of analysis model and data source

Data source	Qualitative analysis model
Interviews Focus groups	Componential analysis Domain analysis Taxonomic analysis Thematic analysis Constant comparison analysis
Observations	Keyword-in-context Domain analysis Taxonomic analysis Thematic analysis
Photographs, videos	Constant comparison analysis

Table 25.1 clearly indicates that most data analysis techniques can be used for different data sources. These analysis models are now discussed.

25.3.1 Constant comparison analysis

25.3.1.1 Rationale

As indicated in the introduction of this chapter, different traditions use different analysis models. Grounded theory employs constant comparison analysis because of its strength in analysing data that has been collected over a period of time with much supporting documentation. Leech and Onwuegbuzie (2007) assert that this method can be adjusted to analyse data collected in one single round or single cases, too.

25.3.1.2 Purpose

The constant comparison analysis method or technique can be employed with the purpose of ascertaining themes obtainable through the data (Leech & Onwuegbuzie, 2007).

25.3.1.3 Principle

According to Tesch (1990), constant comparison analysis's main tool is comparison. The researcher's role is to read through the entire collected data, then group them into manageable parts for comprehension. These parts of data are then put into similar categories using a **low-inference** analysis to describe them. The main aim is to bring together similarities and contrasts between these low inferences. When all the data has inferences, the inferences are grouped together according to their similarities and contrasts and codes emerge. In summary, the researcher creates groups/categories, forming borders of such categories, allocating similar sentences or words to categories, summarising each group of sentences by giving it a category, discovering sentences or phrases that contradict the grouped data, with the aim of discovering patterns (Tesch, 1990; Boeijie, 2002). Then, when patterns are discovered, such patterns bring out themes or a theme that must be supported by the groups. This method promotes member-checking where a researcher returns to where the data were collected and checks if the codes, themes and claims made describe the participants' statements (Merriam, 1998; Leech & Onwuegbuzie, 2007). This practice strengthens the validity of the findings of the study.

Let us look at the example of a case study that investigated the culture of a school in the Eastern Cape of South Africa through observation at the school and in the classrooms (Feza, 2012:43):

The big stone building, typical of a rural town in the Eastern Cape, stands in the middle of the small town. Boys and girls wearing grey and white sit under a tall tree. This building houses a mixed school, starting from Grade R through to Grade 9. All teachers in the school speak Afrikaans during break time in the staffroom; however, the medium of instruction at the school is English. This is one of the few stone buildings to be found in this small town. Inside this building are two sections, for learners and for teachers/administration, respectively. The school management side consists of the principal's office, with well-polished trophies dating as far as the early 1900s; a secretary's office; a staffroom that is well decorated with shelves, tablecloths and flowers, neatly arranged (both the staffroom and the principal's office have wooden floors, and the secretary's office has tiled floors and a security gate). The second section of classrooms is behind the secretary's office with a tiled path that becomes pavement at the back. The front of the classrooms is full of litter and clutter, and the classrooms are dusty. Each classroom has more than 45 children and is very noisy. The learner population is 99 per cent black, while the teacher population is 90 per cent white. The posters hanging in the classrooms walls are flying loose and torn.

The staffroom

A classroom

Stop and reflect

▶ Read the whole vignette again to gain a good sense of it.

▶ Group together fragments that describe similar things (look at the following examples):

The big stone building, typical of a rural town in the Eastern Cape, stands in the middle of the small town. (*An old school building*)

All teachers in the school speak Afrikaans during break time in the staffroom; however, the medium of instruction at the school is English. (*Afrikaans first-language teachers*)

This is one of the few stone buildings to be found in this small town. Inside this building are two sections, for learners and teachers/administration, respectively. (*An old building in traditional school arrangement*)

The school management side consists of the principal's office, with well-polished trophies dating as far as the early 1900s; a secretary's office; a staffroom that is well decorated with shelves, tablecloths and flowers, neatly arranged (both the staffroom and the principal's office have wooden floors, and the secretary's office has tiled floors and a security gate). (*Old established successful school*)

The second section of classrooms is behind the secretary's office with a tiled path that becomes pavement at the back. The front of the classrooms is full of litter and clutter, and the classrooms are dusty. (*Neglected classrooms*)

(continued)

The front of the classrooms is full of litter and clutter, and the classrooms are dusty. Each classroom has more than 45 children and is very noisy. The learner population is 99 per cent black while the teacher population is 90 per cent white. The posters hanging in the classrooms walls are flying loose and torn. (*Dense classrooms dominated by many black learners, with white teachers*).

1 Give each fragment a descriptive code (for example, check the descriptive codes in brackets above).
2 Respond to these questions before firmly establishing the categories/codes.
3 What is the core message of each sentence? What is the relationship between sentences? Are there any contradictions?
4 Give your own categories/descriptive codes. Do you have common categories? What do similarities/ differences do your common categories have?
5 Compare the categories. What do these categories say about one another? Are there any similarities or disparities?
6 Summarise the categories. What are the emerging themes?
7 Support each theme with empirical evidence from the vignette.

25.3.2 Thematic analysis

25.3.2.1 Rationale

Thematic analysis is a quest to ascertain themes that surface as being significant in the narrative of the occurrence (Feraday & Muir-Cochrane, 2006). Rice and Ezzy (1999) also suggest that this quest requires vigilant and repeated reading of the data.

25.3.2.2 Purpose

The aim of thematic analysis is to uncover themes that are prominent in the data. Also, the objective of finding the thematic links is to assist the shaping and interpretation of the emerging themes (Attridge-Stirling, 2001:387). According to Attridge-Stirling, thematic analysis tries to uncover significant themes from the data. Therefore, data should be allowed to speak, demanding that a researcher to engage with them rigorously.

25.3.2.3 Principle

In Glesne's (2015) terms, thematic analysis uses coding as a first step in analysis that will be followed by separating of data using those codes to form data clusters for further analysis. The role of the researcher is therefore to code data first.

Feza (2012) typed out all her data and numbered each row. Then she annotated the data in each row. Annotations are low-inference phrases that summarise the content of each row (Ely, Anzul, Friedman, Garner & Steinmetz, 1991) for conducting descriptive analysis. For example, when annotating the sentence "There is lot of noise from learners in some classrooms that are without teachers", she wrote "(noisy unattended learners)". The low inference in brackets describes the observation in the sentence, with no judgement made at all.

Feza then grouped these annotations into a table to look for patterns; in this step, she was conducting interpretative analysis. She then colour-coded the annotations according to similarities and also highlighted the odd ones. The emerging patterns became the codes that she analysed further, using analytical memos, as suggested by Ely, et al. (1991).

Feza then used analytical memos to engage and create a dialogue with the data. As indicated by Glesne (2015), in this method, themes emerge from the data following further analysis of the codes and descriptions. "Themes are assertions that have a high degree of generality" (Spradley, 1980:141). This statement suggests that the researcher needs to carry the responsibility of each theme as it makes a valid claim that needs to be supported by the data.

Going back to Feza's approach, her final analysis stage was the analytical stage. In this stage she employed colour coding, searching for patterns and discrepancies using Miles, et al.'s (2014) suggestions. She was looking for relationships and odd cases that did not confirm the emerging patterns. In her description, she shared that she struggled to see any relationships until she took three days, completely away from the data.

After being away from the data for three days, she decided to use visual basics from Microsoft Word (by clicking 'Insert' and then exploring the smart art graphics gallery) as a tool to assist her. She also read her literature review again and used it in her analysis. She brought together all the photos, data codes and classroom artefacts, and the raw data, to employ an interactive process of looking back and confirming codes (Miles, et al., 2014).

A story began to emerge, but before she concluded on her observations, she invited peers and a senior researcher to critically look at her data in her research log and give her feedback. She reflected on her journey by writing analytical memos of reflections and returned to the data with peer feedback. Themes emerged from the visual basics.

Mixed messages

This example is from Feza's analytical memo about her case study of the culture of the school in the Eastern Cape:

> The school displays two messages: one is a message about having resources in the administration block, and a well-organised environment. However, in the classrooms a different message emerges: noisy, filthy classrooms and learners with no textbooks. The observations indicate that the school has two different faces.

25.3.3 Domain analysis

25.3.3.1 Rationale

Spradley (1980) uses the ethnographic approach in describing domain analysis. One of the data collection techniques in ethnographic approaches is participant observations. Participant observations are documented in the researcher's own words in field notes. These words have cultural domains that are embedded in the words written in the field notes, which will not just materialise on their own.

25.3.3.2 Purpose

The main objective of domain analysis is to explore, through the narrative, for cover expressions, encompassed terms and semantic associations (Spradley, 1980). The semantic relationships in the data highlight the meanings of the social conditions of the participants, and also how the social situation and cultural meanings connect. The task of the researcher is to confirm the cultural areas that interpret and reveal the challenges of the participants as shown in their accounts, without reproducing the researcher's assumptions (Atkinson & Abu El Haj, 1996:439).

25.3.3.3 Principle

Atkinson and Abu El Haj (1996) propose four steps that a researcher needs to take in conducting domain analysis.

Toolbox Using the four-step approach in domain analysis

1 Identifying the domains

The researcher should first highlight the concrete instances, and categories will come from the practical issues raised by the participants more than from the language they are communicated in. The researcher must acquaint herself or himself with the text by reading through it numerous times. Data could be indexed or annotated line by line, using descriptive phrases as categories.

2 Creating a classification of sub-categories

After the researcher has documented the primary categories, other topics that materialise from the data will be described as tributary sub-sets. The researcher should not rely on the primary categories only, but arrange the concrete data into identified main categories. This approach will assist in putting together the actual phrases and allow sub-categories to come out of the participants' own words. In this way, the participants' most important categories will emerge.

3 Specifying the components

This step permits the researcher to grasp what the study has been looking for. The participants, through sub-categories that have been identified, respond to the question of the study. This is the step where challenges and successes are identified in the topic being researched. The researcher is able to identify key issues that have emerged from the data. The question of the study is responded to, and more has come out that may speak to policy makers and planners.

4 Relating the domains

Now the researcher's role is to ascertain associations between primary domains, using the research question of the study as the guide. Also, the researcher needs to find associations between sub-categories focusing on the research question of the study. At this stage, the researcher is constructing the overall picture. This part of analysis is tedious as the researcher needs to explore the actual quotations of the participants that link one sub-category to the alternative, in relation to stimulus and significance.

Stop and reflect

Use the interview of researcher Mono in the opening case study to respond to the following:
1 Use your own words in writing the purpose of Mono's interview.
2 Now that you have a purpose formulated try and design the questions of the study.
3 Use the data from the interview to respond to the following questions:
   a) What are the social situations and cultural domains that are the interviewee's responses?
   b) What are the relationships between the social situations and the cultural domains you mentioned above?
4 What are your own biases regarding this interview that may influence your analysis.
5 How are you going to deal with them? Remember Spradley (1980) asserts that the domains should reflect the participants' concerns not the researcher's pre-defined categories.

25.3.4 Componential analysis

25.3.4.1 Rationale

Leech and Onwuegbuzie (2007) propose that the componential analysis be conducted after the main domains have been established. Componential analysis involves a search for the attributes of terms in each domain. Researchers move from looking at similarities based on the semantic relationship governing a domain to differences among symbols within a domain that are based on relationships other than semantic relationships. Each subset within a domain or taxonomy consists of a contrast set, that is, terms that are both alike and different.

25.3.4.2 Purpose

According to Leech and Onwuegbuzie (2007), the aim of using componential analysis is to ascertain the variance between sub-sections of areas. Componential analysis is described as a logical exploration for characteristics of qualities related by cultural signs. Therefore, domain analysis and componential analysis can be employed together for analysis.

25.3.4.3 Principle

Spradley (1980) asserts that componential analysis unpacks chunks of meaning that participants link with their own cultural meanings. Read the example of an episode from an interview with a Grade 4 learner from a rural school in the Eastern Cape.

What if …?   e.g.

Interviewer: What do you think you need to get a better education?
Learner: I would like my school to have a garden. My grandfather used to plant food in our home farming land that is huge. Now the land is not used and no one knows how to farm the land. The school garden will teach me skills on how to plant vegetables and how to take care of them. I will then take the knowledge to my grandfather's land and plant there. My grandfather is no more and we have no food since he passed on. I would also like my school to farm chickens and teach us how to do this so that our school can have funds for learning resources. When I know how to take care of chickens I can also teach my mom and we can start a chicken run at home.

The cultural domains that emerge from this episode are as follows:
▶ Education
▶ Curriculum
▶ Rural learner.

Spradley (1979) suggests eight steps that are involved in the componential analysis as follows:

☑ **Choose a dissimilarity statement** to analyse.
☑ **Record differences** previously revealed.
☑ **Make a paradigm** schedule.
☑ **Ascertain dimensions** of contrasts which have dual values.

Applying these steps in a componential analysis of the Eastern Cape rural learner's situation gives us:

- The *cultural domain* is: education
- The *contrast set* is: school, farming land, but no food.
- Record *differences previously revealed*:
  - the school does not teach the rural learner to survive in the rural community
  - the school does not assist the learner in using the available farming land
  - the school may be able to help the learner succeed, however, that is not certain as the learner goes to school with no food
  - the farming land may assist the rural learner to learn, but there is no education available about farming
  - the farming land is of no help to the learner as the learner cannot farm
  - the farming land is not helping the learner to succeed because it is not used
  - having no food does not help the learner to learn
  - the farming land might provide food but there are no skills on how to use it
  - teaching the learner how to farm might assist the learner, but the school does not provide such in the current curriculum.

A componential analysis table can be used to respond to the question 'Is education able to assist the rural child?' The table then has contrast set, words used by the learner that are dissimilar, which are: school, farming land, no food. Then dimensions of contrasts are also created in Table 25.2.

TABLE 25.2: Componential analysis table

Contrast set	Dimensions of contrasts		
	Does it help the rural learner to learn?	Does the school curriculum help the learner to develop skills needed?	Does home environment help the learner to succeed?
School	No	No	No
Farming land	Maybe	Maybe	Maybe
No food	No	No	No

Table 25.2 indicates that school is not helping the rural learner to learn. Therefore the school in all dimensions shows that it is irrelevant. The farming land also indicates that it has potential for helping the rural learner. The lack of food is also detrimental to the learner's learning success.

This table gives some indication of the results, but in order to make this an inference, more interviews should be conducted to support and validate these findings.

25.3.5 Keywords-in-context

25.3.5.1 Rationale

According to Fielding and Lee (1998), keywords-in-context exposes how the participants use words in a setting, by matching words "that appear before and after keywords" (Leech & Onwuegbuzie, 2007:566). This kind of analysis therefore focuses on how the participants use words in explaining the phenomena in situations. Fielding and Lee (1998) say this is the exploration of the philosophy behind the use of words.

25.3.5.2 Purpose

Keywords-in-context analysis is useful when data is not rich, or there are arguments that are of interest to the researcher. Keywords-in-context analysis assists in detecting some fundamental relationships the participant is inferring through his or verbal explanation. However, this analysis method is limited because an investigator might lose the meaning of the words within the context they are used in, especially if the words around the keyword are inadequate.

25.3.5.3 Principle

Leech & Onwuegbuzie (2007) suggest the following steps in performing this type of analysis:
▶ *Reading all the data and finding the main words that are used most often*, or in an unusual manner, is the main objective of the researcher. For example, the interview of the rural learner will be used to identify keywords by underlining them:

Learner: I would like my school to have a garden. My grandfather used to plant food in our home farming land that is huge. Now the land is not used and no one knows how to farm the land. The school garden will teach me skills on how to plant vegetables and how to take care of them. I will then take the knowledge to my grandfather's land and plant. My grandfather is no more and we have no food since he passed on. I would also like my school to farm chickens and teach us how to do that so that our school can have funds for learning resources. When I know how to take care of chickens I can also teach my mom and we can start a chicken run at home.

The keywords from our example are: *school*, *garden*, *to plant*, and *farm*. Table 25.3 presents these words.

TABLE 25.3: Keywords, words before keywords, and words after keywords

Keyword	Words before	Words after
school	Would like, like my, that our	To have, to farm, can have
garden	Have a, school	Will teach
to plant	Used to, how to,	Food, vegetables
farm	Home, school to	Land, chickens

Table 25.3 also indicates that the learner would like the school to teach farming, and have a school garden that will teach learners how to plant to eradicate poverty at home. This analysis brings out relationships that the participant would like to see in her schooling. The relationship between home needs and school curriculum is emerging from this analysis.

Leech & Onwuegbuzie's other strategies for choosing keywords are as follows:

▶ *Theories or literature on empirical studies can be used to choose keywords.*
  While this is another strategy for choosing keywords, the researcher can also identify theories that influence the participant, for example, rurality influences this participant.

▶ *Keywords should be chosen because of frequent use or repetition.*
  Looking at the selected keywords in the example, all of them are used more than once.

▶ *Keywords could also be used throughout the study.*
  In this case, the researcher should look at the whole interview to see which words are used throughout.

The models of analysis discussed in this chapter can be performed manually or by using software packages which will be the subject of our next discussion.

25.4 Qualitative data analysis software packages

Qualitative research is growing and is so used widely in different applications that the field has its own software packages which researchers can use to analyse qualitative data. The list of qualitative analysis software in the market includes: ATLAS.ti, MAXQDA, and NVIVO. In this chapter, only ATLAS.ti is discussed.

25.4.1 Rationale

The ATLAS.ti software package is used to analyse a range of qualitative data, such as field notes, observations, interviews, textual sources, and other forms of qualitative data. The software allows a researcher to conduct constant comparison analysis, thematic analysis, domain analysis, componential analysis, and keyword-in-context analysis, as defined in this chapter. The software itself is able to engage with the researcher as he or she uses it. For example, ATLAS.ti has a welcome wizard that gives the researcher a comprehensive experience of the functions of the software. This chapter can only give an overview of how ATLAS.ti works, but the knowledge workbench of ATLAS.ti teaches you about all the features of the program and how to use them. ATLAS.ti gives support to its customers in a diverse ways. The support centre (http://support.atlasti.com) permits you to surf their knowledge base and gives you help options that allow you to track solutions to your problems. The online support or forum is available at: http://forum.atlasti.com/index.php.

25.4.2 Purpose

Manual qualitative analysis is time-consuming as it involves many stages that lead to final analysis. For example, thematic analysis requires that the raw data that are typed up should also be numbered and each line should be annotated with low inferences. Doing all this manually takes a great deal of time, whereas using software makes it more efficient. A huge benefit is that the researcher does not lose control of engaging with the data, as ATLAS.ti allows the researcher to conduct the following analysis activities:

▶ Creating codes
▶ Assigning codes to segments

- Create quotations
- Open coding.

25.4.3 Principle

ATLAS.ti uses its own language that does not specifically mean the same things as English. For example, in the list of activities a researcher can conduct in ATLAS.ti, there is the creation of quotations. Quotations in language and also generally are not created by the researcher but extracted from participants' direct words. However, in this case, creation of quotations means selection of important data that might later be coded, like audio, words, or pictures. Each term used in ATLAS.ti will be explained with the create quotation function.

ATLAS.ti has a welcome wizard that gives you the following options:
- You can open an existing hermeneutic unit. A hermeneutic unit is your research project that you might have already uploaded on ATLAS.ti and which you are working on.
- Or you can create a new hermeneutic unit.
- Or you can just continue with the program. In this case, you may want to learn about the program first before you start anything.

When you just continue with the program ATLAS.ti will display its knowledge workbench. The main features of the knowledge workbench are as follows:
- The Hermeneutic Unit where all the project documents are, such as memos, codes, all the files and documents uploaded for the research project. They will be found under this unit.
- The Hermeneutic Unit Editor. This tool is the main editing tool of ATLAS.ti. This tool provides access to all other editing tools needed. It consists of:
  - The Main Menu. This menu gives you access to the different parts of your project, such as your verbatim document, your codes, memos, etc.
  - The Primary Document Pane. This window allows you to view your documents, work on them if you want to mark important data, or even code the data.

25.4.3.1 Creating a Hermeneutic Unit (HU)

The researcher selects the 'Create a hermeneutic unit' option, and names it when asked to do so. Then choose file option and save to the selected file folder. It is recommended that you have your own USB drive to save your file in, unless you are working on ATLAS.ti on your own computer, but back-up is always recommended. Now that you have opened an HU, prepare to send your data to the file.

Please note that ATLAS.ti works with electronic data files that are text-based, therefore the interviews need to be transcribed before being transferred to ATLAS.ti. Also, it supports graphics and has limited support for audio data. Once your data are ready, you need to assign it.

25.4.3.2 Assigning documents

Choose 'Documents/Assign' from the main menu, select one or more files to upload from the dialogue window, and click open. You can upload more than one document at a time by using the control key.

25.4.4 Working with the documents

25.4.4.1 Create quotations

Creating quotations is marking segments of the documents that are important, and assigning codes to them. These segments may be textual, graphic or audio, and any of them can be marked. This method is used in constant comparison analysis. To do this in ATLAS.ti:

▸ Select the segment from the document.
▸ Move the cursor into the selected segment, and right-click to open the context menu.
▸ Choose 'Create free quotation'.
▸ Your quotation will show in the drop-down list.

25.4.4.2 Coding documents

Please note that the margin area of the document should be on, so that you can be able to see the action. To code a selected part or section of the document you have four different types of coding you can use:

1 *Open coding.* When you link a new node with existing segments or quotation. A node is a term used in code. You do this by selecting the segment, choose code from the main menu, enter a name for your code and click OK.
2 *Code by list.* When you want to assign existing codes to quotations or text.
3 *In-Vivo coding.* When the text is good enough to be a code by itself.
4 *Quick coding.* When you want to use a currently selected code to code a segment or text.

Stop and reflect

Visit your institution's library and find out which qualitative analysis software your institution affiliates to and discover more on how to access the software. Most software has a limited trial time you can sign up, perhaps a week. Sign up and go through the tutorials of the software, while you document the following:
1 What tools does the software provide that were used in the different analysis this chapter has introduced?
2 What new terms does the software use?
3 With each analysis method please list the tools from your software.
4 Design a study and write the questions of the study
5 Write your design of the study with more focus to the analysis of the results.
6 Choose software you would prefer and list the reasons of your preference.

Conclusion

This chapter guides the novice researcher in conceptualising qualitative analysis. It brings forth the importance of qualitative analysis in responding to complex questions about behaviour. It highlights the strength in triangulating data sources, analysis methods, data with literature and analysis amongst colleagues.

It discusses the five methods of analysis selected for this chapter: componential analysis, domain analysis, taxonomic analysis, thematic analysis, and constant comparison analysis.

The discussion of the methods highlights each method's strengths and shortcomings. The chapter emphasises the importance of triangulating the analysis methods to strengthen the credibility of the findings.

Qualitative analysis methods described in this chapter continue to develop as researchers employ them in their research projects. The software package this chapter introduces were developed from the analysis methods already discussed, hence their tools match those used in all different methods of analysis in qualitative research. As a novice researcher, it is in your best interest to read more about these methods to benefit your research journey.

Closing activities

Practical applications

1 Without assistance, use the following vignette to conduct a constant comparison analysis from a case study that investigates the culture of the school in the province of KwaZulu-Natal in South Africa.

> This independent school is located in a suburban area of Kwa-Zulu-Natal. The school building is set amongst suburban homes and government offices. The schoolyard has limited space in front and is used for walking only. Parking is allocated in the school grounds behind the school building. Entering the school, you are welcomed by administrative offices and a foyer. The walls in the foyer display pictures of school learners with trophies and sports awards. Most teachers in the school are over 40 years of age; even the administrator is in her late fifties. The school principal is about to retire, having only one year left to go. The school teaching staff comprise 14 white South Africans and two Indian South Africans. The school is very clean, even the classrooms and the grounds. Learners are all dressed in uniforms of the same colour. In the school passages there are displays of learner's art work and some pictures of learners in sport clothes with their teachers. The school enrolment is mixed, with 40 per cent white South African learners, 32 per cent black learners, mixed with immigrant learners, and 28 per cent South African Indian students.

Use the vignette to respond to the following questions and activities:
a Annotate each sentence of the vignette (use low inference phrases)
b Look for similar annotations and group them
c Find what is common about the grouped annotations and also what is different
d Write down an analytical memo of observations
e List the codes that emerged from the patterns (similarities) and odd occurrences.
f Go back to your inferences and look for odd occurrences or disparities.
g Write your emerging themes with supporting evidence from your data.

2 The following narrative is from researcher Mono's interview:
a Identify the domains found in this narrative following step one of the domain analysis method:

> *Learner:* No, I don't ask my teacher for help. It is too embarrassing in the classroom. And we are not allowed to disturb teachers when they are in the staffroom. My teacher never asks me, why I am not doing my homework. He just punishes me by making me stay after school for an hour.

b The following domains were identified by another researcher about the above narrative:
> *Domains:* teacher-driven learning, learner passivity
> Support or contest the listed domains comparing them with your own, using data from the narrative.

3 In this case study, the researcher conducted interviews with the school's mathematics teacher to understand the teacher's practice.

> *Researcher:* How long have you been in this school?
>
> *Teacher:* I have just arrived in this school in May of this year. I am teaching African learners for the first time. I am a qualified high school teacher and throughout my work experience, I taught high school mathematics. Therefore, it is also my first time teaching primary and junior secondary mathematics classes. Unfortunately, these learners here are so behind because they did not have a teacher for the first two terms of the year. Also, their reading skills are poor, making it difficult for them to work independently. During my entire teaching career, which is now two decades, I have never seen nor experienced a situation like this. The OBE curriculum the [education] department expects us to teach is not working. The man, Spady himself, who brought OBE to this country, said it in the newspapers: "OBE is not working in South African schools", but still we are expected to do it. There is a system of condoning kids even if they are behind. Education is being politicised by bringing democracy in the classroom.

Read this episode twice before responding to the following questions:
a   How is the education culture defined by the teacher?
b   What are the domains that come from this episode? List them.
c   Select a contrast set from the paragraph for analysis and list it
d   Draw a componential analysis table.
e   Find dimensions of difference which have dual values (yes or no answers).
f   Conduct a componential analysis
g   Write down your observations.
h   What is the completed paradigm of this paragraph?
i   What would you highlight as the strengths of this method of analysis?
j   What are the weaknesses you find in this method of analysis?

4   Use the episode that follows to conduct a keywords-in-context analysis, following the steps suggested by Leech and Onwuegbuzie (2007).

This episode is from a case study of African learners' learning experiences in a mixed school. The episode is an interview with a teacher who teaches these learners mathematics.

> *Teacher:* Lots of the time they look at the problem and think it's too much information. Then I verbalise it for them and focus on the keywords, and then they can work on it. Sometimes I have to sit with them and I ask them to look if the numbers are going up or down before they decide if they need to add or multiply, or they need to subtract or divide.
>
> Their English is different to standard English and therefore, before they solve problems, they need to read them first, translate them to their own language, then begin to think about how they are going to solve the problem and what skills they need to use. We treat them as others instead of acknowledging their difference.
>
> Unfortunately, I have to prepare them for the state tests. Therefore, I do not have time to assist them with their English needs, but only to drill them the mathematics knowledge. When they return to the mainstream class they regress and become poor performers again. Their English is not recognised as its own language, so the school does not see it as the home language.

5 Research project

Now that you have experienced how to use different methods of analysis qualitatively, do your own study. Design and conduct in-depth interviews with a person you admire, or someone you regard as a role model, about understanding the effects of home, community/neighbourhood, and parenting in his/her life, towards achieving what you identify as successful in his/her life. The number of interviews will be determined by the purpose of your study and your continuous engagement with the data. Then do the following:

▶ Give a rich background on how you selected your participant.

▶ Transcribe your data.

▶ Choose the method of analysis that will respond well to your research questions.

▶ Discuss your choice of analysis method and show its credibility.

▶ Analyse the data manually.

▶ Analyse the data using an available software at your university.

▶ Triangulate the analysis from these two techniques and write a report on the outcomes highlighting similarities and differences.

▶ Write a report with high focus on the analysis and strategy used to report the findings of your study.

▶ Develop a research article from this study and prepare a presentation.

Please note that your instrument should focus on the questions that respond to your objectives.

Bibliography

Atkinson, S. & Abu El Haj, M. 1996. How to do (or not to do): Domain analysis for qualitative public health data. *Health Policy and Planning*, 11(4):438–442, Oxford University Press.

Attridge-Stirling, J. 2001. Thematic networks: an analytic tool for qualitative research. *Qualitative Research*, 1(3):385–405.

Boeije, H. 2002. A Purposeful Approach to the Constant Comparative Method in the Analysis of Qualitative Interviews. *Quantity & Quality*, 36:391–409.

Carcary, M. 2008. The Research Audit Trial – Enhancing Trustworthiness in Qualitative Inquiry. *The Electronic Journal of Business Research Methods*, 7(1):11–14.

Creswell, J. 1998. *Qualitative enquiry and research design: Choosing among five traditions*. Thousand Oaks, CA: Sage Publications.

Denzin, N.K. & Giardina, M.D. 2001. Qualitative Enquiry and Global Crises. In N.K. Denzin & M.D. Giardina (Eds). *Qualitative Enquiry and Global Crises*. California: Walnut Creek.

Ely, M., Anzul, M., Friedman, T., Garner, D. & Steinmetz, A.M. 1991. *Doing qualitative research: Circles within circles*. London: Falmer Press.

Fereday, J. & Muir-Cochrane, E. 2006. Demonstrating rigor using thematic analysis: A hybrid approach of inductive and deductive coding and theme development. *International Journal of Qualitative Methods*, 5(1). (online) available at: http://www.ualberta.ca/~iiqm/backissues/5_1/pdf/fereday.pdf. Accessed 6 January 2014.

Feza, N. 2012. My culture, my learning capital, my tool for thought. In N. Tutelea (Ed). Germany: LAP LAMBERT Academic Publishing.

Fielding, N.G. & Lee, R.M. 1998. *Computer analysis and qualitative research*. Thousand Oaks, CA: Sage.

Glaser, B.G. & Strauss, A.L. 1967. *The discovery of grounded theory: Strategies for qualitative research*. Chicago: Aldine.

Glesne, C. 2015. Becoming *Qualitative Researchers: An Introduction* (5th ed.). Pearson: Boston.

Greene, J.C., Caracelli, V.J. & Graham, W.F. 1989. Toward a conceptual framework for mixed-method evaluation designs. *Educational Evaluation and Policy Analysis*, 11:255–274.

Jacob, E. 1987. Qualitative Research Traditions: A Review. *Review of Educational Research*, 57(1):1–50.

Kincheloe, J. 2001. Describing the bricolage: Conceptualizing a new rigor in qualitative research. *Qualitative Enquiry*, 7(6):679–692.

Leech, N.L. & Onwuegbuzie, A.J. 2007. An Array of Qualitative Data Analysis Tools: A Call for Data Analysis Triangulation. *School Psychology Quarterly*, 22(4):557–584.

Leech, N.L. & Onwuegbuzie, A.J. 2008. Qualitative data analysis: A compendium of techniques for school psychology research and beyond. *School Psychology Quarterly*, 23:587–604. doi:10.1037/1045-3830.23.4.587.

Merriam, S.B. 1998. *Qualitative research and case study applications in education* (2nd ed.). San Francisco: Jossey-Bass.

Miles, M.B., Huberman, A.M. & Saldana, J. 2014. *Qualitative data analysis: An expanded sourcebook* (3rd ed.). University of Arizona: Sage.

Onwuegbuzie, A.J. & Teddlie, C. 2003. A framework for analysing data in mixed methods research. In A. Tashakkori & C. Teddlie. *A framework for analysing data in mixed methods and behavioural research*. Thousand Oaks, CA: Sage.

Onwuegbuzie, A.J., Leech, N.L. & Collins, K.M.T. 2012. Qualitative Analysis Techniques for the Review of the Literature. *The Qualitative Report*, 17 (56):1–28.

Perez, M.S. & Canella, G.S. 2011. Using Critical Analysis for Critical Qualitative Research Purposes. In N.K Denzin & M.D. Giardina (Eds). *Qualitative Enquiry and Global Crises*, California: Walnut Creek.

Rice, P. & Ezzy, D. 1999. *Qualitative research methods: A health focus*. Melbourne, Australia: Oxford University Press.

Spradley, J.P. 1979. *The ethnographic interview*. Fort Worth, TX: Holt, Rinehart & Winston.

Spradley, J.P. 1980. *Participant Observations*. New York: Holt, Rinehart & Winston.

Srivastava, P. & Hopwood, N. 2009. A Practical Iterative Framework for Qualitative Data Analysis. *International Journal of Qualitative Methods*, 8(1):6–84.

Tesch, R. 1990. *Qualitative Research. Analysis Types and Software*. London: Falmer Press.

Using ATLAS.ti for Qualitative Data Analysis http://www.stanford.edu/group/ssds/cgi-bin/drupal/files/Guides

Using MAXQDA for Qualitative Data Analysis. http://www.maxqda.com.

Using NVIVO for Qualitative Data Analysis. http://www.qsrinternational.com/products_nvivo.asp.

Part 4

Reporting and disseminating research findings

CHAPTER 26

Oladele Arowolo and Bongani Bantwini

Presentation of quantitative research reports

KEY CONCEPTS

Data analysis involves relating a set of data on a particular variable to another data set defining another variable or variables, to establish a pattern and determine relationships.

Data consolidation involves deriving measures or indicators from raw data.

Data from primary and secondary sources primary data sources may consist of data generated from field surveys using questionnaires, conducted by the researcher; secondary data sources are published data, often available in government records such as census reports on education, population, employment, agriculture, etc.

Data triangulation involves using different sources of information in order to increase the validity of a study.

Dependent and independent variables refer to the variables of interest to study, e.g. education might be a dependent variable in income distribution; independent variables are explanatory variables, used to explain the patterns of variations within the independent variable.

Problem conceptualisation is the inventing or contriving of an idea or explanation, and formulating it mentally; conceptualisation is the process of development and clarification of ideas or concepts.

Quantitative research is based on 'scientific' facts or evidence which can be verified, thus assuring the absence of self-interest or bias in the conclusions derived.

Research methodology refers to the process adopted in conducting research, consisting of identification of data sources, data collection, procedures, data consolidation and data analysis, based on a framework.

LEARNING OUTCOMES

By the end of this chapter, you should be able to:

▶ Define the basic characteristics of a quantitative research study.

▶ Identify the steps to be taken in conducting a quantitative research study.

▶ Understand the major differences between quantitative and qualitative research.

▶ Explain why a quantitative approach is preferred in certain kinds of research.

▶ Understand the basic skills required in conducting quantitative research.

▶ Develop elements of a quantitative research report to present to different categories of audience.

Case study: The interrelationship between education and development

A study of two contrasting communities in Mpumalanga province has confirmed what seems to be well-established in the literature on the relationship between education and poverty in South Africa. Community A is predominantly urban, while community B is largely rural. The two communities can also be differentiated on the scale of education: community A has a much higher proportion of adults with secondary and higher levels of education completed, compared with community B where most of the adult population has low levels of education. This explains in part the very strong correlation between the level of education and the observed standard of living in the two communities. Visible unemployment is much higher in community B than in A, more so among the youth where the unemployment rate stands at 61 per cent in community B, compared with 20 per cent in community A. Indeed, the two communities exhibit vastly different levels of performance on all the other available indicators of development, including health status, access to safe drinking water, electricity for lighting and heating, standard housing, and supply of amenities. It is clear that in order to raise the standard of living and reduce poverty levels in community B, concerted efforts must be made to increase investment in education in the community.

Introduction

This chapter focuses on the presentation of a quantitative research report. The chapter brings together different aspects of the research process in a way that even non-quantitative researchers can benefit. Quantitative research is important because we now live in an age in which almost every aspect of life is quantified: who you are; level of education attained; the amount of calories consumed per day; weight gained or lost; hours of sleep; income earned, etc. This suggests that we can hardly avoid some measure of quantification in a research that involves understanding relationships among people, places or things.

This chapter looks at the processes in quantitative research, from the formulation of a research topic, identification of study population, data collection, to data analysis and interpretation, and conclusion of the study. In summary, the chapter considers the following:

▶ Characteristics of quantitative research that serve as a basis for presentation.
▶ Clear statement of the research problem, and the attempt being made through the study to resolve aspects of the problem.
▶ Methodology, including data sources and approaches to data collection, data analysis plan, and consolidation of data.
▶ Presentation of results and discussion.
▶ Conclusions – with a focus on the significance of the findings in terms of a contribution to knowledge and possible policy implications.

One of the learning objectives of this chapter is to enhance your ability as a researcher to understand how to present the various aspects of a completed research study that has used the quantitative approach. After working through this chapter, you will have a clear understanding of the different steps to follow in preparing, as well as presenting, a quantitative research report.

Critical to the process is the 'Introduction' section to the report. As you introduce your report, you should paint a clear picture of what the research is all about and why the topic chosen is of such significance. The introductory section should also address the structure of the report with a justification for the sequence of the sections.

Another vital learning objective is **problem conceptualisation**. This has to do with how you have come to define the issues for the research and how you explain them. How relevant is your research topic to the current development challenges being faced by your country or community? The answer to this question will provide a sound justification for conducting the research. Why the choice of the quantitative approach? If the subject of study has evoked controversy in the literature but without consensus, the choice of a quantitative method is critical to resolving issues around that subject. Quantitative approaches allow you to choose among a variety of statistical and analytical methods that could be used to demonstrate the objectivity of your findings (see Chapter 12).

In defining the research objectives and choice of analytical techniques, you learn more by undertaking an extensive review of relevant literature on the subject of your research. From the review of literature you will be able to identify a theoretical position or a set of hypotheses relevant to your study. Literature review exposes you to the range of similar work already carried out by others in the field of study, and this prevents you from simply duplicating what has been done. If you must duplicate a previous study in another population or context, a literature review also serves as a basis for justification of your own efforts.

An equally important learning objective is the ability to describe the process involved in data collection from primary and/or secondary sources, and their advantages and limitations. Once you are clear of your data sources and their limitations, there is justification for your study method or the approach adopted for your research. The same applies to the framework or structure adopted for analysing the data collected. The question here is how will you present your analysed data in a logical way? Among the numerous variables generated from your data, how will you establish relationships? Obviously, you are not going to establish relationships among all of them, so you need to choose the minimum number of independent variables for your analysis.

The quantitative approach also involves an understanding of the procedure for **data consolidation** – turning your raw data to the objectives you want to measure, or indicators. Once your data sets are consolidated, your research process can move on to the choice of statistical techniques applicable to your study. You are most likely to use a computer for data analysis and you need to understand the variety of computer software packages relevant to your research work. This goes hand in hand with your choice of statistical techniques for presenting your data.

Another outcome of this chapter is the presentation of research findings, including comments on data reliability; estimates of population from the sampled elements; and interpretation of results of statistical analysis. Your work is not only done by generating a set of indicators from your data; you should justify your findings by determining the quality of the data, and the confidence attached to your sample statistics, through statistical tests.

Discussion of your research findings is important in your presentation. You should be able to present how your findings point in a particular direction, similar to or different from other findings in the literature. How is your research significant in its findings? How useful are the findings for any future studies or perhaps for state policy? In short, what is the significance of the results of your research in terms of contribution to knowledge and/or policy?

With the above objectives in mind, you should be able to structure your research report in a logical manner. In addition, these objectives are important in guiding your research process from the beginning to the end.

26.1 Characteristics of quantitative research

In addressing the characteristics of a quantitative report, it is perhaps necessary to ask the question: What does a quantitative research study try to do?

What distinguishes quantitative research from other approaches is methodology. Quantitative methods, by definition, place emphasis on objective measurements and the numerical analysis of data collected. You can do this through various approaches such as polls, questionnaires, or surveys. In essence, quantitative research focuses on gathering numerical data and generalising it across groups of people.

A quantitative research report may be descriptive and/or analytical.

26.1.1 Descriptive research

A descriptive research report establishes relationship among variables. For example, if A and B represent two communities in Mpumalanga province, a study of income of households in relation to highest level of education attained by household heads, in the two communities can generate data, say, on average household income in which the average is higher in A than in B. The same study may produce data on levels of education attained by household heads, in which household heads in community A are better educated than in community B. A more rigorous description of income and educational differentials may use any of the conventional statistical techniques to determine the strength or degree of difference between average household income in A compared to B; or significance of difference between the means of income of A and B. The same can be done for differences in highest level of education attained by household heads in the two communities.

Still on descriptive statistics, you can use tabulated data to establish a relationship or association, or lack of it, between say, level of educational attainment and income earned annually by household heads. In essence, one of the major tasks of descriptive statistics is that of presenting data, of organising and condensing them, with numerical summaries (such as average, proportion, total, etc.), or by illustrating with tables or graphs.

26.1.2 Analytical research

Analytical research reports, on the other hand, establish causality between one variable and other variables, say education in relation to income, occupation, place of residence whether rural or urban, number of hours worked, etc.

Otherwise known as *inferential* statistics, analytical statistics is concerned with developing and utilising techniques for properly analysing, or drawing inferences from numerical information, as you will have read in Chapter 23 on inferential statistics. For example, in establishing relationships between variables, you may collect data on people with different levels of educational attainment, and their reported characteristics in the other variables such as income, access to medical facilities, quality of housing, etc., at a given period of time. The data set can be analysed using appropriate statistical techniques to determine the degree of relationship or correlation, between education, as a *dependent variable*, and any of the other *explanatory variables*, the variables associated with variations in education such as income, age, gender, industry or occupation, etc. You may also wish to establish the proportion of variations in education jointly explained by the dependent variables, or multiple correlations; or use education to predict type of work done or income in a regression model.

Therefore, a **quantitative research** report is based on 'scientific' facts or evidence which can be verified, thus assuring the absence of self-interest or bias in the conclusions derived.

In addition, given that the data you collect cover a representative sample of the population, findings from quantitative research can be generalised to the larger population from which the sample was selected for the study. This characteristic is important and should be borne in mind when the researcher is determining a sampling procedure to be employed and the sample size n in relation to the population *N*.

Consequently, it is required that a valid research design forms the basis of data collection in survey investigations. Having conceptualised the research problem, a valid design must be based on an accurate definition of the study population *p* in relation to the sample *s* obtained from it. Given the significance of a research design in establishing the validity of evidence from a survey, it may be important for you to refer to Chapter 10 again.

Perhaps most critical to quantitative research is the integrity of the data used in the analysis and presentation of evidence. Data quality is about the reliability and accuracy of the information being analysed, that is, the indicators, and the adequacy of statistical techniques used in the presentation of data.

Stop and reflect

At this point, you should be able to make a distinction between descriptive and analytical research. How do you understand the differences? You should also think about the different statistical techniques available to measuring relationships between variables.

When numbers are assigned to characteristics being observed it becomes *measurement*, for example:
1 No schooling
2 Primary education only
3 Secondary education
4 Tertiary education, but not university
5 University education.

This kind of measurement often generates four types of data:
▸ Nominal – numbers indicating differences in kind
▸ Ordinal – differences in kind, plus rank observations in order of importance
▸ Interval – differences in kind, plus rank size observations, and intervals/differences comparable
▸ Ratio – defines one value compared to another value.

Each of these requires the application of appropriate statistical concepts and techniques.

The integrity or quality of your data being presented in a research report depends on three things: the reliability of the sources of data; the adequacy of the measures you derive; and the statistical techniques you apply.

Stop and reflect

You should now be able to distinguish between qualitative and quantitative variables in research. Do you understand the difference between nominal and ordinal data? Having understood these differences, you should be in a position to describe data measurement appropriate to nominal and ordinal data.

Some of the advantages and disadvantages of using quantitative methods as opposed to qualitative approaches are summarised in Table 26.1.

TABLE 26.1: The advantages and disadvantages of using quantitative research methods

Advantages	Disadvantages
Allows research to be conducted on a large scale, involving a greater number of subjects and a lot of information, and enhancing the generalisation of the results.	Quantitative research is more costly than using qualitative research.
Provides precise, quantitative, numerical data thereby allowing for greater objectivity and accuracy of results.	While the quantitative method is more efficient and able to test hypotheses, it may miss contextual detail.
Applying well-established standards means that the research can be replicated, and then analysed and compared with similar studies.	The development of standard questions by researchers can lead to 'structural bias' and false representation, where the data actually reflect the view of the researcher instead of the participating subject.
It is easy to summarise vast sources of information, make comparisons across categories and over time, and allows quantitative predictions to be made.	Results provide less detail on behaviour, attitudes, and motivation.
Personal bias can be avoided by researchers, as the research results are relatively independent of the researcher (e.g. statistical significance).	Results are limited as they provide numerical descriptions rather than detailed narratives, and generally provide less elaborate accounts of human perception.
Testing and validating already constructed theories about how and why phenomena occur, as well as testing hypotheses that are constructed before the data are collected.	The researcher might miss out on phenomena occurring because of the focus on theory or hypothesis testing rather than on theory or hypothesis generation.
Can generalise research findings when the data are based on random samples of sufficient size, and/or when the research has been replicated on many different populations and sub-populations.	Knowledge produced might be too abstract and general for direct application to specific local situations, contexts, and individuals.

Stop and reflect

Based on the information in Table 26.1 on the advantages and disadvantages of quantitative research, what do you think your own strengths and weaknesses in adopting this approach are? In which specific areas do you still feel uncomfortable using the quantitative approach? As you read this chapter further, you should be able to fill in such gaps.

26.2 Basic steps in preparing quantitative research

Following some basic steps will enable you to clearly articulate the introduction to your research and address methodology issues, including: the analytical framework; the data collection approaches and consolidation of the data analysed; and a synthesis of information generated. Using a step-by-step process will show you how to discuss the results of your research, and draw conclusions from your research results.

What if you get stuck?

New insights into the research problem can be addressed by generating fresh evidence from the same or a different population, or through the application of a refined methodology, or both.

26.2.1 Getting started

In making the preparation of a quantitative research report, you should first be mindful of the specific requirements for presentation, whether it is for publication or as a power point presentation. Requirements are often stated in terms of length, structure, referencing style and related editorial policies and guidelines. The same considerations apply to research reports that are meant for submission as theses or dissertations for a university degree programme.

Your adherence to requirements for report presentation is very critical to its acceptance. It is also possible that the clients of your research extend beyond the academic audience to government institutions, agencies or organisations that provide funds for such research activities. In most cases, the authorising government department or funding agency will provide you with what is called the 'terms of reference' (ToR) for the research work. The ToR will often contain information that will guide you in the design of the study, data collection and analysis, and the processes to be followed in preparing and presenting your study report.

The next section takes you through the contents of an introductory section, as a first step to your presentation.

26.2.2 Step 1: Introduction

In preparing your quantitative research report, the introductory section should contain a logical and succinct account of the statement of research problem, past efforts to address this problem, and the need for new insights into the problem for possible resolution. You could address new insights into the research problem through the generation of fresh evidence from the same or a different population, or through the application of a refined methodology, or both.

Your introductory section should be clearly presented, and information about the whole report succinctly summarised in a way that will engage the interest of your reader. You should try and answer the following questions in your introduction: 'Why is the subject of this research considered so important to you as a researcher?' or, 'What is the significance of the issues for this research in the literature on the subject?' The introductory section offers you space to explain the purpose and objectives of your research and the potential contribution it offers to knowledge and to the policy environment.

It is therefore important that this section addresses the statement of the problem for research. For example, it is possible that there are conflicting findings reported in the literature and in the body of evidence generated by official statistics on the relationship between gender and access to development opportunities in South Africa. You might want to establish the basis for conflicting findings reported in the literature by using a more rigorous definition of discrimination, or through application of a new methodology, or a combination of analytical techniques. Alternatively, the purpose of your research might be to contribute to the growing body of evidence which supports the view that irrespective of class, education and place of residence, gender discrimination is overwhelmingly against the access of females to economic opportunities. At this point, you should think through your research problem and be able to engage in the search for relevant literature on the subject.

In the introductory section, it is also important for you to provide information on alternative positions on the subject, and where the official or government policy is located in the discourse. If government policy is in line with the international conventions and treaties or conference agreements on the subject, say, gender discrimination and education, it will be necessary to outline and discuss the different shades of opinions on the subject in the country of study, and why there are such differences. If, in spite of government gender policy promulgated 20 years back and increasing investment in education, there is evidence of widespread and persistent gender discrimination, the problem statement should attempt to describe the reasons most cited in the literature. This could provide a basis for your research investigation, and the proposed methodology as a means of resolving the conflicting results from the literature.

Your introductory section may be combined with a literature review, or treated separately, depending on the requirements of the publishing company, journal, or the audience for which your research report is intended. The review of the literature should be specific to the subject of the research and focused on the issues to be addressed (Chapter 8, on literature review, is essential reading).

Stop and reflect

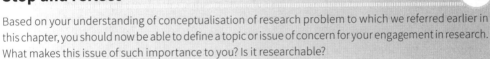

Based on your understanding of conceptualisation of research problem to which we referred earlier in this chapter, you should now be able to define a topic or issue of concern for your engagement in research. What makes this issue of such importance to you? Is it researchable?

The next section, or second step, focuses your attention on methodology issues in quantitative research.

26.2.3 Step 2: Methodology

The methodology of quantitative research is perhaps its most distinguishing characteristic. In presenting your quantitative research report, therefore, you should place emphasis on the methodology or the approaches to the study. There are three related elements to **research methodology**, namely:

▶ The analytical framework
▶ The data collection approaches
▶ Consolidation of the data analysed and synthesis of information generated.

Each of the three elements of methodology listed above should be clearly addressed and presented in your quantitative research report.

26.2.3.1 Analytical framework

The analytical framework for presentation of research results is often based on a conceptual model, a theory or hypothesis to be tested (see Chapter 9). For example, the opening case study of this chapter looks at the relationship between the highest level of education attained by household heads in two Mpumalanga communities, and selected social, economic and demographic indicators of development such as income, health status, access to electricity, housing type, etc. The case study explores these relationships as a way of predicting the future trends in the income of household heads in the study population. The analytical question to be addressed in the report is: How much education advancement will be required to achieve a given level of say, income, health status, etc., in the communities?

Stop and reflect

26.2.3.2 Data collection

By design, quantitative research is often based on data from primary or secondary sources, or a combination of both. This is critical in the presentation of your research design, given that your research design has significant implications for the interpretation of results.

It is essential that a valid research design forms the basis of your data collection in survey investigations. Having conceptualised the research problem, a valid design must be based on an accurate definition of the study population p in relation to the sample s obtained from it. Given the significance of research design in establishing the validity of evidence from a survey, we will treat this subject in some detail, even if this leads to some overlap with related topics in this book. In essence, the presentation of a quantitative research report should include a clear description of its research design as follows in this section.

In terms of data sources, two major sources are distinguished in the literature; namely, data from secondary and primary sources.

a) *Data from secondary sources*
  > Data obtained from secondary sources include the following:
  • Census data on population, agriculture, education, employment, etc.
  • Data from official government records, such as education, immigration, trade statistics, agricultural production, mining records, etc.
  • Organisational sources like annual reports on government performance, reports on project evaluation findings, from e.g. World Bank, United Nations agencies, etc.
  • Data from review of literature on the subject of research.

In the case study cited earlier, the research relied on data from secondary sources, namely, official data on education; population census reports; special survey reports on demography and health; and official government reports on social and economic development in South Africa. In presenting a quantitative report, you need to pay attention to the approaches you have used and describe them in clear terms.

You could use multiple methods to ascertain the validity of data collected from secondary sources, as well as those generated from surveys. The process of compiling evaluation material based on multi-methods, referred to as **triangulation**, has proved useful in determining whether there is convergence or not. Triangulation means comparing the available evidence or indicators from different sources to ensure that findings are not attributable to a method anomaly. However, where divergent results emerge, alternative, and likely more complex, explanations are generated from discussion groups and interview results. Thus, triangulation allows you to more confidently interpret data from official sources and those derived from programme reports, against those generated from field investigations.

b) *Data from primary sources*
> Data from primary sources often involve structured or semi-structured research instruments targeting potential respondents that are the units of analysis for the study. You should look at Chapters 17 and 18 again, which address this subject in detail.

It is particularly important for you to pay careful attention to the presentation of method of data collection in quantitative research report, since the integrity of the data used in the analysis is critical to the quality of the research itself. Once the method of data collection is determined, the next step is for you to choose the most appropriate approach to the administration of the questionnaire. Chapter 18 provides a more detailed discussion of the subject. There are three major conventional approaches to questionnaire administration in social studies:
▶ Self-administration
▶ Mail method
▶ Interviews.

Whichever approach you adopt in your research should be described in the presentation. Chapter 14 addresses survey research, and you should familiarise yourself with the basic definitions and procedure for primary data collection.

Since most quantitative research works use sampling as a way of addressing the population, your quantitative research design should ensure that the sampling frame, procedure for sample selection, determination of sample size in relation to the study population, and related statistical considerations are well defined and justified. Your presentation should describe clearly the procedure used in selecting the sample.

A sample frame is the first consideration in element sampling. Sample frame refers to a list comprising a set of physical units from which the actual sample is selected. When the actual physical listing of all sampling units is difficult, an equivalent procedure is the *frame*. A frame includes physical lists and also procedures that can account for all the sampling units without the physical effort of actually listing them. In area sampling, for example, the frame consists of maps, but the frame can be constructed without mapping the entire population.

The frame consists of previously available descriptions of the material in the form of maps, lists, directories, etc., from which sample units may be constructed and a set of units selected. Frame specification should define the geographical scope of the survey and the categories of materials covered, as well as the date and source of the frame. A frame should be adequate; the initial frame may require emendation or construction, particularly in the later stages of multi-stage sampling, before they may be considered adequate. For example Statistics South Africa (2013) has developed what is referred to as a new Business Sampling Frame (BSF), based on the value-added tax (VAT) database, derived from the South Africa Revenue Service (SARS).

In element sampling, a frame is considered perfect if every element appears on the list separately once, and only once. In a complete and perfect frame, every element must appear in only one listing. For example, a perfect frame for primary school teachers in a given municipality should consist of all currently (the period in reference) registered at:
▶ Primary schools, whether private or public school; as
▶ Teachers, regardless of gender, race, or any distinguishing background characteristics; in a designated municipal area.

In order to ensure reliability of your findings and place confidence in your sample estimates, you should have an optimal sample size. Chapter 13 develops and explains to the logic of sampling. The researcher is often confronted with the question: What per cent sample do I need? The concern is about the adequacy of precision that a given per cent sample could yield.

It is important to note that:
n is an important factor in $S^{2/n}$, or variance

Variance $= (1 - f)\, s^{2/n}$

$$s = \frac{\sqrt{1 - fs}}{\sqrt{n}}$$

The variance of the sample depends not only on the sample size n, but also on the sample design.

Let us assume that the acceptable precision as V^2, the variance of the mean. The cost of the sample can be stated in terms of n, the sample size.

For a desired variance $V2$, or standard error V, how large should the sample be?
Assume v = 0.01
Then,

$$N = n' = \frac{(p)\,(q)}{(V2)}$$

If $p = 0.5$, $q = 0.5$

$$n' = \frac{(0.5)\,(0.5)}{(0.01)^2}$$

$$n' = \frac{0.25}{0.0001} = 2{,}500 \text{ either for a population of 1 million or 100 million.}$$

This 'methodology' section places emphasis on the subject of sampling in relation to the study population. Now you should be able to answer the question: 'How large a sample size do I need for my study?' In addition to Chapters 13 on the logic of sampling, Chapter 14 on survey research methods, and Chapters 15 to 18 which address data collection methods, should be read as the basis for defining aspects of quantitative research.

If your research design is adequate, and results are based on sample size that is sufficiently large and representative of the population, quantitative research findings can be generalised to the population. This is an important characteristic of quantitative research; it means that you do not have to study the whole population, which is often very costly, before making general statements about its features or characteristics. Related to this characteristic is the predictive utility of quantitative methods; based on appropriate statistical techniques, the analysis of data collected can be used to establish relationships among variables and or predict the course of their development in future.

A well-designed quantitative research study can easily be replicated or repeated. This is so because the data sources are defined, the measures used are known, and the entire research process is documented. Therefore, you can conduct the same study within the same population at other times, or elsewhere, and be guaranteed verifiable results.

Toolbox Getting permission to go ahead

You should now be able to identify and describe the different data sources for your research, and how you are going to gain access to these sources. If you need data from primary sources using questionnaires or other forms of structured or semi-structured schedules, you should think in advance whether you need to get official permission to conduct interviews among the intended population of study. In some cases, you may have to go through official ethics clearance. (See Chapters 6 and 7 for more on research ethics procedures.)

26.2.3.3 Coding, data processing and analysis

How you handle collected data from fieldwork should be clearly presented in the report. In terms of procedure, once the fieldwork is completed, you need to carefully edit all the returned questionnaires whether they are completed or not and prepare to enter the data into the computer for processing and analysis. You should also examine each questionnaire returned to determine the extent of completeness, missing cases and inconsistences in the questions answered. For illustration, a child born to woman in the study cannot be older than his or her biological mother. This is why editing of the returned questionnaire schedules is of critical importance to data quality.

At this point, you should determine what computer programme should be used for data processing, for instance, the statistical package for the social sciences (SPSS) or any other suitable software package. The step-by-step procedure for using the SPSS is addressed in detail in Chapter 24.

26.2.3.4 Consolidation of data analysed

Apart from making generalisations, one of the goals of quantitative research is to establish a relationship between a dependent variable, that is, the object of your study; and a set of independent variables, referred to as explanatory variables.

Using the opening case study for this chapter as illustration, you may be interested in why incomes earned by household heads vary by their different education background characteristics. In this example, if education is measured in terms of highest level attained by household heads in the selected communities, data collected from household heads on their incomes in rand per annum, health status, and housing type, could be used to explain the patterns of variations in their education. Thus, education is the dependent variable, while income, health status and housing type are used as the explanatory or independent variables. You may then derive measures of association among the different variables in the study population using relevant statistical techniques.

The above requires that you prepare a tabulation plan to guide your selection of variables, the relationships you want to establish, and how many tables you plan to generate through cross tabulations. Remember that from only seven variables, it is possible to generate seven (factorial) combinations or tables, i.e. $7 \times 6 \times 5 \times 4 \times 3 \times 2 = 5,040$ tables in all.

Consolidation of data involves analysis and synthesis of data, using conventional statistical techniques, application of computer-based models in use in the study area, or related techniques. Having collected data on education levels of heads of household, the next thing to do is to consolidate the data by deriving estimates of proportions of households in each education category: No school; Primary completed; Secondary completed; Tertiary but not university; University education. In the case study of two Mpumalanga communities, development indicators include measures of poverty, education completed, unemployment rate, access to safe drinking water, electricity, and other amenities.

26.2.4 Step 3: Preparation of results

Every research study anticipates results based on the patterns generated by the data and the outputs from computer and/or statistical applications.

The results represent the findings from your research, and there are several ways of preparing the results of data analysed in a quantitative study. However, your presentation of results should follow a logical sequence. For example, the opening case study in this chapter involves a dependent variable, education, and multiple independent variables – income, health status, unemployment rate, etc. – in which you would like to show the general distribution of sample by each variable, and measure relationships among variables.

You may at the same time wish to estimate means and the proportions and their variance distributions, test for significance, as well as demonstrate relationships in testing hypotheses between the two hypothetical Mpumalanga communities. In this type of situation, the following sequence of presentation and interpretation of results is suggested:

- Frequency distribution
- Patterns and strength of association
- Measures of central tendency
- Measures of dispersion
- Significance tests
- Correlation – simple, multiple
- Analysis of variance
- Regression – simple, linear, multiple
- Advanced modules: for example, factor analysis.

This sequence suggests a move from simple descriptive data to complex analysis of relationships among variables in the study. This does not mean that all quantitative reports must use all the methods of statistical analysis mentioned above. It is possible that your presentation is descriptive enough without any form of analysis. Even if analysis is done, your preparation might require the use of one of the analytical techniques or a combination of them.

At each stage in your preparation, you should feel free to use tables such as one-way frequency, two-way cross tabulation, three-way cross tabulation, etc., complemented by graphic illustrations. Some of the analytical tools automatically generate graphs for illustration and display of results, as in regression estimates in which both the equation defining the regression line and the graph are generated by the computer.

Whenever a table is presented, it is important to address the important figures in the table as a pointer to the direction of results generated by the analysis of data. Merely producing a table without reference to it is not useful; at the same time, it may be too much to refer to all the figures in a table given that the table itself is provided to give a summary view of the data set or information being presented.

It is useful in presenting your quantitative research report to illustrate it with graphs, maps and diagrams. Table 26.2 shows the distribution of adult population by highest level of education attained in the two communities adopted as case study in this chapter.

TABLE 26.2: Highest level of education completed by adults (%) in two communities

Highest level of education completed	Community	
	A (%)	B (%)
No schooling	35	8
Primary	48	15
Secondary	10	44
Tertiary but no university	4	20
University 1st degree	2	10
University higher degree	1	3
TOTAL	100	100

Figure 26.1 illustrates the data in Table 26.2 on educational distribution of the adult population in the two communities.

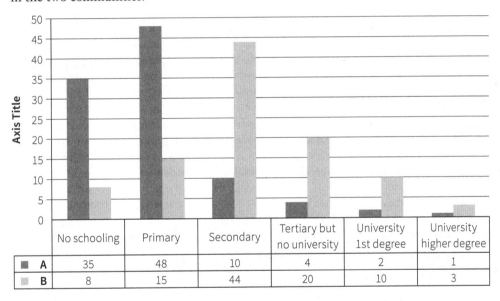

		No schooling	Primary	Secondary	Tertiary but no university	University 1st degree	University higher degree
■	A	35	48	10	4	2	1
▨	B	8	15	44	20	10	3

FIGURE 26.1: Highest level of education completed by adults (%) in two communities

Whenever the choice of a graph is made, such as tables, the presentation should address the features of the graph, including interpretation of the data transformation. In a time series or trend analysis, graphic illustrations seem to show the observed trends better than tables; but the choice is yours to make, depending on the type of audience and the message being conveyed.

In addressing numbers or data in the report, you should use absolute or total figures sparingly; rather, ratios, proportions or percentages, means, and summary measures are preferred.

If the presentation aspires to a higher level of rigour, descriptive statistics presented as measures of central tendency, for example, should be qualified by measures of dispersion, such as variance or standard deviation.

The same argument goes for estimation of proportion or percentage in the research report. If, say, the study found that 20.6 per cent of females, as opposed to 11.2 per cent of males have no formal schooling, it may be necessary to discuss this further through analysis of the significance of the proportions; and also to determine if the observed difference between the proportion of uneducated among females compared to males is statistically significant. There are procedures available for making such computations in all basic introductory texts on social statistics.

As the level of statistical rigour progresses, the presentation of results often demands greater attention to detail. Interpretation of the results of analysis, say, using correlation or regression, may be required so as to drive home the meaning of the statistics and implications for your research findings.

Stop and reflect

You should be able to reflect on the step-by-step rigour in statistics as you move from simple descriptive to analytical statistics. You are encouraged to read the related chapters (22 and 23) in this book carefully to see how the presentation of results is done, from interpretation of frequency distribution to more advanced statistical measures.

26.2.5 Step 4: Discussion

In presenting your quantitative research report, the discussion section should aim at consolidating the research experience in such a manner that the conclusion reached is understandable. It should be a succinct summary of the research experience and a justification of findings. Your discussion section should consider the following points:

- ☑ **the research design and implications** for the interpretation of results
- ☑ **data collection experience** and ways in which data quality might be affected
- ☑ **the tabulation plan** and treatment of missing data
- ☑ **editing and data cleaning** processes
- ☑ **robustness of selected statistical techniques** and/or computer software package used, together with the assumptions made
- ☑ **the level of confidence** in the results generated by analysis.

The discussion on data collection should not be a repetition of your research design and the processes involved in questionnaire design and administration. However, mention should be made of the importance of the research design, particularly the adequacy of the sampling frame and the choice of sampling fraction in the determination of sample size, as well as the usefulness of the simple random method in the selection of elements into the sample. This section should also reflect on your field experience in data collection as it might affect the quality of data collected, including editing of schedules, checks introduced while coding and entering the data for computer processing. For example, if the period of data collection is fairly long, say, three weeks or more, certain environmental or cultural factors might affect aspects of the characteristics of the study population beyond what the data or literature could reveal.

Equally important in the discussion section is consideration of the definitions and measures you used in the research, especially if there are alternative measures or definitions of the variables in the report. For example, in the case study of the two Mpumalanga communities, poverty is addressed generally; but there are several indicators of poverty, such as quality of housing, unemployment, health status, and access to electricity. Therefore, you should discuss issues related to the measurement of variables used, and clearly show how the particular measure adopted in your research is better than the alternative(s). It is also possible that for a single variable, say, education, there are several measures in use; in such a situation, you should discuss the justification for use or non-use of alternative measures of education in your research.

Your discussion section should also focus briefly on justification for the choice of statistical techniques or the program package employed in the analysis of data collected. Such justification can at times be inferred from the results obtained and their usefulness in addressing the research problem. Above all, your presentation in this section should mention the overall reliability of data and the degree of confidence imposed on interpretation of results.

Conclusion

In this chapter, you have followed the process of conducting and presenting your quantitative research report. A well-articulated introduction is important to your presentation because it contains the justification for your study and tries to convince your audience about its importance.

Problem conceptualisation in research has also been addressed. This has to do with how you have come to define the issues for the research and have explained them.

In defining the research objectives and choice of analytical techniques, you learn more about your topic or problem by undertaking an extensive review of relevant literature on the subject of your research. You are able to identify a theoretical position or a set of hypotheses relevant to your study.

Your ability to describe the process involved in data collection has also been addressed, from primary and/or secondary sources, and their advantages and limitations. Focus has also been given to the logical presentation of your analysed data and how to establish relationships among variables.

The quantitative approach also involves an understanding of the procedure for data consolidation – turning your raw data to the objectives you want to measure, or indicators. Once your data sets are consolidated, your research process can move on to the choice of statistical techniques for analysis applicable to your study.

Finally, adequate interpretation of the results of statistical analysis enables you to answer important research questions: How is your research significant in its findings? How useful are the findings for any future studies, or for state policy? In short, what is the significance of the results of your research in terms of contribution to knowledge and/or policy?

Closing activities

You are asked to conceptualise a research problem, and go through any combination of steps, as defined earlier in this chapter.

Practical applications

1 Present a justification for using the quantitative approach in a study of inequalities in South Africa, with focus on education and its effect on poverty reduction.

2 List all the independent variables in relation to education performance in the two communities of the opening case study of this chapter.

3 Using the independent variables in the opening case study, why is education so important in any programme of poverty eradication?

4 The parliamentary portfolio on service provision in South Africa is concerned about the increasing discontent with the provision of social services as evidenced in public demonstrations in the country. How would you use the quantitative approach to study the delivery of social services (particularly education), and present your evidence to show the portfolio committee and the general public what the government has been doing to provide these services?

5 How would you present the need for an increased research budget (you can use your sample size) to justify quantitative research on, say, education in rural communities in South Africa?

6 Read the statement below carefully and then do the activity that follows:

> ### Reducing poverty and inequality
> The formulation of poverty measurement as set by the Millennium Development Goals (MDGs) is said to be too narrow in aspects of vision, scope and direction. Eradication of poverty should not simply be a numerical target to be achieved by a certain date. Poverty eradication, from a human rights-based approach, entails taking into account the non-quantifiable factors, such as active involvement of the poor and civil society, which enhances the implementation of any poverty reduction strategy. Getting people out of poverty should involve the elimination of their poverty status, as well as the process by which people are lifted out of poverty to a more comfortable level of living. It is a definition of poverty which encompasses the status of poverty itself as measured in the MDGs by income and hunger. It also includes the strategies employed by government embodying the social and political conditions that tend to promote pro-poor development, including education and skills development. Therefore, while level of income is effective in determining income poverty, it may not be as effective in measuring a country's progress in aspects such capacity building through education, freedom of expression and right to participate, which are also important factors to consider in any poverty reduction strategies.

Based on your understanding of the statement, design a research study to be presented to a funding agency, using the quantitative approach, to address the challenge of process measurement in the delivery of poverty reduction outcomes in South Africa.

Bibliography

Arowolo, O.O. 2000. Fertility in Namibia. In B. Fuller & I. Prommer (Eds). *Population-Development-Environment in Namibia*. International Institute for Applied Systems Analysis. Laxenburg, Austria (pp. 252–271).

Babbie, E.R. 2010. *The Practice of Social Research* (12th ed.). Belmont, CA: Wadsworth Cengage.

Barr, A.J., Goodknight, J.H., Sall, J.P. & Helwig, J.T. 1976. *A User's Guide to SAS 76*. Raleigh: North Carolina State University.

Bongaarts, J. 1984. A simple method for estimating the contraceptive prevalence required to reach a fertility target. *Studies in Family Planning*, 15(4):184–190.

Brians, C.L., Wilnat, L.B., Manheim, J.L. & Rich, R.C. 2011. *Empirical Political Analysis: Quantitative and Qualitative Research Methods* (8th ed.). Boston, MA: Longman.

Dietz, T. & Kalof, L. 2009. *Introduction to Social Statistics: The Logic of Statistical Reasoning*. London: Wiley-Blackwell.

Dixon, W.J. 1975. *BMDP: Biomedical Computer Programs*. Los Angeles: University of California Press.

George, D. & Mallery, P. 1999. *SPSS for Windows Step by Step*. Boston: Allyn & Bacon.

Ghiselli, E.E., Campbell, J.P. & Zedeck, S.1981. *Measurement Theory for the Behavioral Sciences*. San Francisco: W.H. Freeman & Company.

Guion, L.A., Diehl, D.C. & McDonald, D. 2002, 2011. Triangulation: Establishing the Validity of Qualitative Studies. Document FCS6014. Florida: Department of Family, Youth and Community Sciences, Florida Cooperative Extension Service, Institute of Food and Agricultural Sciences, University of Florida. Available at http://edis.ifas.ufl.edu. Accessed May 2014: 2http://edis.ifas.ufl.edu/pdffiles/FY/FY39400.pdf.

Kohler, H. 1994. *Statistics for Business and Economics* (3rd ed.). New York: HarperCollins College Publishers.

Namboodiri, N.K. (Ed). 1978. *Survey Sampling and Measurement*. New York: Academic Press.

Kish, L. 1965. *Survey Sampling*. New York: John Wiley & Sons.

Kish, L. 1987. *Statistical Design for Research*. New York: John Wiley & Sons.

McNabb, D.E. 2008. *Research Methods in Public Administration and Nonprofit Management: Quantitative and Qualitative Approaches* (2nd ed.). New York: Armonk.

Nie, N.H., Hull, H., Jenkins, J.G., Steinbrenner, K. & Bent, D.H. 1975. *SPSS: Statistical Package for the Social Sciences*. New York: McGraw-Hill.

Population Reference Bureau. 2007. Measuring Maternal Mortality – Challenges, Solutions, and Next Steps; http://www.prb.org/pdf07/MeasuringMaternalMortality.pdf. Accessed 12 December 2013.

Sharpe, M.E. & Singh, K. 2008. *Quantitative Social Research Methods*. Los Angeles, CA: Sage.

University of Southern California. Quantitative Research Reporting. Accessed December 2013: http://libguides. usc.edu/content.php?pid=83009&sid=615867 Also see: UKAid and United States Institute of Peace. Quantitative Research Module. Retrieved from: http://dmeforpeace.org/sites/default/files/1.3%20Quantitative%20Research. pdf; http://www.southalabama.edu/coe/bset/johnson/oh_master/Ch14/Tab14-01.pdf; AIU (2012). Qualitative vs. Quantitative Research. Retrieved from http://www.aiuniv.edu/Student-Life/Blog/October-2012/Qualitative-Vs-Quantitative-Research; Wordpress (2011). Advantages and Disadvantages of Quantitative Research. Retrieved from http://picardsflute.wordpress.com/2011/01/12/advantages-and-disadvantages-of-quantitative-research/ http://www.statssa.gov.za/publications/DiscussSamplingMeth/DiscussSamplingMeth.pdf.

CHAPTER 27

Bongani Bantwini and Oladele Arowolo

Presentation of qualitative research findings

KEY CONCEPTS

Qualitative research is a research method used for exploring issues, understanding phenomena and responding to questions. Qualitative research analyses and makes sense from unstructured data sets.

Research methodology refers to the process adopted in conducting research, consisting of identification of data sources, data collection [procedure, data consolidation and data analysis based on a framework.

Research reporting is the presentation of research findings emerging from the primary research that was conducted.

LEARNING OUTCOMES

By the end of this chapter, you should be able to:

▶ Understand and state the significance of presenting qualitative research findings.

▶ Apply various ways of reporting and disseminating qualitative research findings.

▶ Identify what to report and how to report it.

▶ Distinguish the key characteristics of a qualitative report.

▶ Understand and be able to apply the steps in preparing your dissemination of findings.

▶ Identify certain key elements to avoid in reporting your qualitative research findings.

▶ Understand how to present the various aspects of a completed research study that has used a qualitative approach.

Case study: Investigating poor learner performance in mathematics and science education

As you critically read this passage from a contextual case study, consider how you will present the qualitative data findings to the relevant audience.

The Floranda community in a large province in South Africa complains about the state and quality of mathematics and science learner performance. A social sciences research council therefore decides to conduct a qualitative study focusing on a group of schoolteachers to ascertain why the scores of learners in mathematics and science are so low compared with scores in other learning areas. Some of the teachers are interviewed, while others are observed during their teaching of both mathematics and science. The findings of the study reveal that there are various factors that could be attributed to the issue under investigation, including: there is a huge teacher shortage in these learning areas; the few teachers teaching these subjects struggle in their pedagogical and content knowledge; there is lack of the necessary resources for teaching and learning of these subjects; learners lack support from their home backgrounds in doing homework owing to high illiteracy rates; parents are not supportive of any school activities intended to help learners in these learning areas; and the school district is insufficiently involved in supporting teachers with their problems.

Introduction

Many publications and studies in the literature on qualitative research reports and dissemination are from Western countries. They tend to use examples, case studies and activities that originate from Western countries and worldviews. These examples and activities are mostly unfamiliar and uncommon to many African students and young scholars, especially those who have never been overseas. The students barely relate to the experiences they read about and thus have a gap in their research understanding.

This chapter presents you with contextual case studies, questions to reflect on, examples and activities intended to facilitate your understanding of reporting of qualitative research findings in an African context.

It is salient to mention upfront that the presentation of qualitative research findings is the most crucial and sensitive phase of every research project or undertaking. It is crucial because the generated research knowledge provides informative and perhaps transforming ideas, and viable solutions to the complex challenges that confront human beings on daily basis. Therefore, qualitative research plays a fundamental role in the lives of humans as it helps to unearth people's lived experiences, and the reasons for certain behaviours, attitudes and motivations. In Albert Einstein's wise words, we can't solve our problems by using the same kind of thinking we used when we created them. Qualitative research, with its deep and thorough investigative approach, facilitates the leap to the next phase in our thinking and actions. It offers empirical evidence useful to solve policy-related issues or perhaps provide sets of ideas essential in taking critical decisions.

Fundamental to writing up a qualitative research report is to present findings in a way that will be understandable and respond to the research questions and objectives, as well as allow the audience to comprehend them. Qualitative research is about asking simple questions and getting complex responses, which are essential to inform decision-making processes or policy development. The goal is to provide the missing knowledge, and should be geared towards change and development. However, a lack of report clarity, intelligibility, and relevance, can lead to underutilisation of the research findings by the audience. Suffice to say that there is nothing more uneconomical than having important findings lost in dull and disorderly text.

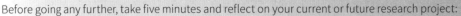
Before going any further, take five minutes and reflect on your current or future research project:
▶ Think about the reason why you want to conduct a qualitative research study.
▶ What would make you fail to clearly present your research findings?
▶ What do you envisage as potential challenges or hindrances in reporting qualitative studies?
▶ Write down all your points and keep them in mind as you navigate this chapter.

27.1 Importance of effective reporting of qualitative research findings

From the opening case study, it can be seen that the Floranda community views **qualitative research** as a viable approach in searching for evidence and solutions to their persistent problems. Nutley, Powell and Davies (2013) speak of research as strong evidence and that, in making good use of evidence, is essential if public services are to deliver more for less. Research evidence carries weight and is convincing about what developments should be pursued in future. However, the value of evidence depends more on what evidence is available, how to access that evidence, and how to critically appraise it. The significance of research reporting is that it is the crucial evidence useful for informing new reforms and policy development. Without clear and understandable research evidence reporting, it becomes difficult to identify and solve daily challenges, which most research is intended for.

Research reporting is critical to the success of research investigation. This also entails substantial challenges because there is an equal need not only to represent the social world that has been researched, but also to represent it in a way that both remains grounded in the accounts of research participants and explains its subtleties and its complexities (White, Woodfield & Ritchie, 2003). The reporting task therefore is not simply an act of recording the outcomes of the analysis but also an active construction and representation of the form and nature of the phenomena being explored (White, et al.). It requires and demands a complete engagement and the back-and-forth interaction of the researcher with the gathered data. In these respects, the reporting stage is the culmination of the analysis process. It provides an opportunity for further thought as the datasets are assembled into a coherent structure to convey the research evidence to the target audience. Reporting is then a continuation of the journey of interpretation and classification of patterns and associations, and more detailed interpretation and explanation. It is not the end in the research process, but is a step to another level of discussion and deliberations about the initial reason for the research.

The development of new policies that will help improve learner performance and outcomes in the mathematics and science learning areas depends mostly on the reporting of research findings. For instance, are the research findings reported in ways that will influence people and policymakers; in ways that reveal the quality of research findings in terms of accuracy and objectivity, credibility, relevance, *and* practicalities? It is no secret that most research findings end up not being utilised because of the poor quality of reporting or dissemination. Thus, the quality of qualitative reporting should aim to provide the reader/s with a sound understanding of the design, how the research was conducted, the analysis of data, the interpretation, and reporting of the research findings.

27.2 Steps to consider in preparing a qualitative report presentation

In considering ways to present qualitative research findings, it is important to remember that there is no single style or approach for reporting the findings from qualitative research. A qualitative researcher must choose not only what information or message they wish to relay, but also how this will be done. It is important to revisit and consider the objectives and purposes for which the research was undertaken as this will inform the basis for your reporting strategy or approach. This will also help in ensuring that there is coherence and rhythm in your reporting.

Also remember that ways of reporting may differ, based on the goal of the research. For example, what do you think was the goal or purpose of the research undertaken by the social sciences research council in the Floranda community? It is essential to ask yourself what the goal or purpose of your research is, and use this as part of your reporting guide. It is very easy to depart from your goal in the end, as you will be confronted by various datasets that sometimes hardly speak to your original research intent. Sometimes, your datasets may reveal new anomalies that you will want to pay more attention to, or put more emphasis on, in disregard of the key original issues.

More importantly, the structure of the report should be sure to include all voices meaningfully in the discourse, by using various formats for disseminating data. As a researcher, you need to establish mechanisms for speaking with the people for whom the research is conducted. Weiss (1979:428) notes that

> whether or not the best and most relevant research reaches the person with the problem depends on the efficiency of the communications links. Therefore, when this imagery of research utilisation prevails, the usual prescription for improving the use of research is to improve the means of communication […].

Qualitative research should respond to a variety of issues and challenges, which require various research designs and the presentation of results in several styles of research reporting.

There are several key steps to consider in preparing a qualitative research report. Some of the most important steps are discussed in the following sections, but please note that these steps are not necessarily in logical order.

27.2.1 Summary of the report

We advise you to develop a one-page summary of what the report is all about, at the outset. This will act like an executive summary in a business report, and help your target audience to develop an idea of what to expect. It will also prepare them to continuously engage with the report as they read through it. Depending on who your audience is, some audiences may not have the luxury of time to go through long reports, so report summaries become useful to them. Take note that your summary report may either engage and compel the reader to read more, or make the reader think that continuing with the report will be a waste of time. In the end, a well-written comprehensive summary report will increase the likelihood of your report being read and received with due attention.

27.2.2 Introduction and problem statement

Introducing and stating the research problem helps to situate the target audience. It gives the audience a global view of the area or field, the gaps and the existing challenges, and how they are all interlinked or intertwined. If an introduction is poorly written or constructed, or boring, if it does not communicate to the readers what they should know, if it does not help readers to situate themselves in your paper or report, then you can be sure that you have lost your readers' goodwill and interest right from the beginning. The introduction strengthens the case for why you undertook your research in the first place. Your introduction and problem statement should be brief and give relevant information, raise the readers' interest, while indicating the scope and direction of your report.

27.2.3 Objectives and purpose of the qualitative study

Thorough understanding the original research objectives and purpose will serve as a good guide in reporting your qualitative research findings. This knowledge will help you identify the appropriate ways to present your findings. Also, knowledge of why you are presenting your findings helps to keep you on your research path. Research objectives define what you intend to do, what will be achieved at the end of the project, and should also be linked to the research problem. They should, in the end, be a clear, concise statement that provides a guide and direction for the investigation.

The purpose in qualitative studies is sometimes reflected in the diversity of the final product. Knafl and Howard (1984) state that the end product of a grounded theory study will differ from that of a descriptive study. In this case, the reader should evaluate the quality and usefulness of a qualitative study within the context of the author's purpose. A clearly stated purpose will help the reader to formulate realistic expectations and explicitly structure the final report in terms of the original purpose.

27.2.4 Research questions

Research questions guide you and provide an opportunity to predict the approach to follow in your enquiry. They provide you with a starting point and allow you to locate the relevant information to support your assumptions. They influence the direction of your research. When confronted with huge datasets, it is easy to get distracted; however, the research questions will keep you organised in your writing.

27.2.5 Research methodology

Research methodology is a useful instrument for understanding the phenomenon under investigation; it is fundamental in any research and reporting. A research method provides us with deeper knowledge and understanding of the issue under investigation. Since it can become very complex and confusing if not appropriately reported, it is important to keep your research method simple. This is because in qualitative research the complexity is said to be in the data.

Toolbox What goes into a good qualitative research report?

A good qualitative research report comprises an explanation of how the results were obtained and analysed:

▶ The method that you select and use in your research will influence the research findings. So it is important that the target audience is made aware of the methodology process and the reasons why it was chosen. The audience needs to be informed about how the data were analysed and interpreted in order to derive the results or findings being reported.

▶ There are various research methods that you can choose from, depending on your research study. It is important to justify your selection from the range of methods. Always bear in mind that an untrustworthy method is likely to create unreliable findings.

▶ Provide a clear account of your data and how they were gathered. As a researcher, it is your responsibility to ensure that the reader knows that the data were gathered in a manner that is acceptable within the field of study.

▶ The objectives of the study should inform the method for appropriateness. For example, be sure you have a large enough sample size to be able to generalise and make recommendations, based on the findings.

▶ The role of the methodology is to address the predicted problems and the path you took to prevent these problems from recurring. Make sure that each problem that occurs is attended to so as to minimise its influence. The approach taken to minimise the problem should be presented in detail and highlighted if it influences the findings.

▶ Researchers should always be able to replicate a study. It is therefore crucial that the methodology used is described in full to provide other scholars with insight, and allow them to replicate your study. This is mostly the case when a new method has been developed.

27.2.6 Identifying your research audience/consumers/ stakeholders

Who will benefit most from your research; what purpose will they use it for; and what actions will result from it? are some of the key questions to ask when deciding about the target audience. Knowledge about your research audience is critical for the purpose of designing your report or findings communication plan: various stakeholders differ and prefer different communication modalities. This knowledge should be informed by the purpose, objectives and goals of your reporting strategy. For example, it is common knowledge that many politicians prefer shorter reports than long documents that they do not have enough time to read.

Also critical about identifying your audience is the accessibility of language used; it should be appropriate, common and acceptable among the target group. This knowledge also informs your reporting strategy and creates a link in the sequence of your reporting strategy. This knowledge helps to increase the readability of your research report, as one of the main goals of a research undertaking.

27.2.7 What do you know about the target stakeholders?

'Stakeholder' encompasses a number of varied groups and individuals with an interest or investment in a certain entity. Knowledge of your stakeholders helps you as the researcher to shape and devise appropriate modalities for your reporting and dissemination. For example, many policymakers barely find time to read long reports. That knowledge will help you develop reports that they will be able to read quickly, to grasp the intended message. Presenting research findings through policy briefs, which are a few pages in length, for instance, is likely to increase the successful dissemination of research findings. Background knowledge about your stakeholders will also help in selecting the most useful information to present to them.

27.2.8 What information do I disseminate?

One of the advantages of qualitative research is the ability to explain the collection, the range and variety of phenomena that occur. It possesses the power of inclusivity and speaks to the diversity of stakeholders. This is usually decided right at the beginning of the project. Identify the basic elements of the projected content you have to disseminate to each element of the potential audience. It is important to think through how to convey complexity without losing readability. It is also important to guard against getting bogged down in the details, but rather to focus on the main themes as they speak to your research questions.

Knafl and Howard (1984) contend that readers often find reports of qualitative research interesting, but unconvincing. Clearly, this calls for reporting that convinces the readers of validity and reliability of the research findings. It is imperative that you clarify what you are trying to accomplish through your reporting and dissemination activities. Furthermore, effective reporting considers new and compelling evidence or findings, which can be included in your reporting through the use of bullet points to draw attention.

27.2.9 Decide on the medium for report presentation/communication strategies

What will be the most effective and viable medium to reach the target audience and how accessible will the research report findings be? It is often said that the main problem in qualitative reporting is to find the best ways of presenting the research story in a clear and cogent way. It is so important that the sensitivity, richness and key aspects of the original material are displayed while keeping the right balance between narrative and interpretation. "A good report provides understandable and adequate description to allow the reader to comprehend the basis for an interpretation, and sufficient interpretation to allow the reader to appreciate the description" (White, Woodfield & Ritchie, 2003:289).

We suggest that you identify and select the appropriate modalities to reach your target audience. Decide on the medium or media through which the content of your message can best be delivered to your audience, the capabilities and resources that will be required of the audience to access the content for each medium to be used. In deciding on the reporting medium, cost should also be considered as it is fundamental to this process. Report presentation can be costly depending on your target group. Therefore it is advisable to exploit the existing resources in order to maximise your reporting outcomes.

It is imperative to identify those sources that your audience already respects as credible information sources, and to use them. Also, how will you know if your dissemination activities have been successful? This should also be carefully considered as you plan your project.

27.2.10 Research findings should be clearly and meaningfully communicated

Research findings that are not clearly and meaningfully communicated can result in the failure of your research project. From early on, it is useful to identify potential barriers that may interfere with the targeted audience's access and utilisation of your report, and to develop actions to reduce these barriers.

Findings should be clearly and meaningful articulated, and ambiguity avoided as much as possible. This will help prevent unnecessary confusion and guessing at what you are trying to say (you will find useful advice on this issue in Chapter 29). Also remember that your audience could be a busy group, or a group that does not read much, so making it easy for them will increase the accessibility of your report. This in turn will help relay the message of your findings to a wider community, making your research valuable and beneficial. The use of brief quotes where these illustrate a particular point really well, is recommended.

Your data should be arranged with the goal of telling a story. This makes it important that you arrange the data in a manner that will allow for transition from one example to another, just as storytellers arrange details in order to best relate the story. Critical to your findings is to ensure validity and reliability. The validity of research findings refers to the extent to which the findings are an accurate representation of the phenomena they are intended to represent. The reliability of a study refers to the reproducibility of the findings. More about reliability and validity in qualitative research is reported in earlier chapters.

27.2.11 Decide on the choice of words and visual aids for the intended audience

Some of the failure to comprehend qualitative research findings/results is mostly due to language use and the explanations provided. It is important to understand how the language used will help make your reporting understandable. Unclear or ambiguous reporting, as we have said, is likely to result in the target audience failing to understand the report.

You should identify strategies for promoting awareness of your research findings/information and the availability of alternate formats. Try to use common contextual concepts, terms and words, and avoid using anything that your audience will struggle to understand. Remember, it is not about the big confusing words that you can manipulate, but the message in your report. As pointed out earlier, what good is it to undertake cutting-edge research but fail to communicate its findings/results to your audience? Keep it simple and understandable and you will get satisfactory outcomes.

Visual aids are very important in qualitative research. However, the researcher should also carefully decide when they can be used, and what benefits they will yield. Qualitative findings can be more difficult and time consuming to characterise in a visual way (Anderson, 2010). Therefore, the use of visual aids should aim to clarify certain points and not used to show off. Visual aids play a critical role in reporting qualitative research findings as they can display the range and diversity of phenomena/factors involved. They can be used to show a relationship between different factors or phenomena, and their ongoing association with one another. They can provide clear understanding by explaining complex processes and dimensions and how they interact. They can provide an effective means for summarising information when a number of different elements is involved. The point is that they can help to reinforce the point or message being made.

What good is it?

It is important to ask yourself these questions: If qualitative research findings are not properly and coherently presented, clearly communicated, and disseminated in ways comprehensible to everyone, what good, then, is that research? What good is it to undertake cutting-edge research that makes no difference to people's lives because of vague and ambiguous reporting and dissemination strategies? What good is it to devise and employ innovative research methodologies when the final product will not make any significant difference to the lives of the end research beneficiaries?

27.3 Various ways of presenting qualitative research findings

There is no standard way to present qualitative research findings. However, this chapter tries to propose ways or modalities that will ensure that the beneficiaries of the research easily understand the findings.

27.3.1 Data from interviews

Data generated from interviews can be presented through quotations. The use of quotes should aim to support a proposed claim or depict a view that is representative of the research findings. Sometimes using quotes will make a point more clearly than any other mode. Consider the following two quotes: what message/s do they present?

Teachers speak

Teacher 1: I am not a trained science teacher but I have been teaching it for more than ten years. At the beginning, I did not enjoy teaching this subject but after some time I got used to it. However, I don't possess sufficient content knowledge and pedagogical approach knowledge and the department of education is not doing much to assist me in that area.

Teacher 2: In our school we have a problem of lack of resources to teach both mathematics and science. It is very difficult to theorise mathematics and science concepts to learners who already think that the subjects are difficult. I wish that the department of education would help us with more relevant resources.

Using these two quotes together is intended to emphasise the causes of poor learner performance and outcomes in mathematics and science subjects.

Sometimes quotes can be used to give the reader a sense of the conversation that took place. For example, from the following sequence you can clearly see the conversation between the researcher and the participant.

Teachers need support

Researcher: You mention that you are very unhappy in teaching mathematics and science. Why is that?

Teacher: Well, the reason is that I don't get sufficient support from the authorities in my school. My learners have a problem understanding these subjects and I have been requesting support with materials that can help me in explaining some of the difficult concepts and terms.

Researcher: When you request materials, what do they say?

Teacher: Mhmm, the principal will just tell you that there is no budget for resources as learners are no longer paying fees. It is really discouraging and I don't know what to do.

Researcher: Have you approached the local businesses and solicited their material support?

Teacher: Well, I am not sure if that is part of my job description.

From these examples, you can see that using quotes in presenting findings in qualitative research has a crucial value. Quotations serve as evidence for your interpretation and conclusions. Further, they are often easy to read, bring interest to the text, and can provide more insight than just the researcher's interpretation.

Stop and reflect

Consider your research study: In what other ways could you report findings from interview data?

27.3.2 Data from focus group interviews

One of the strengths of the focus group interview is its open and free discussion that generates diverse ideas and can provide a wealth of information that you are seeking from a group. So how do you present your focus group findings to your target audience? It is suggested that after your analysis, whatever method or approach you used, you list the key points, make summaries and comments. These help the reader to gain an understanding of how the research participants think about the question, or matter at hand.

In the next example, three teachers in focus group interviews were asked about the extent to which they are receiving support from the district office to facilitate the teaching and learning of science in their school.

Teachers speak out

Teacher 1: I would say we don't receive sufficient support from our district office. The only support that we get is maybe one workshop per year. Honestly, this is not enough for someone who does not have a strong background in mathematics and science.

Teacher 2: You know, I am the product of Bantu education, so the quality of training that I received did not prepare me for these new curriculum reforms. I need enough support, be it in content knowledge or teaching approaches. Honestly, I don't feel that I am getting it.

Teacher 3: My situation is different from theirs. I majored in mathematics and science and I think I don't have their problems. So I just don't care if the district office does not provide me with workshops, I'm good and have no complaints.

27.3.3. **Data from observations**

Findings from observations play a significant role in your research. To minimise any bias that comes with observation, a researcher needs to develop an observation plan that will guide you in your observation. After analysis, you can make summaries based on your observations.

Two obsevations

Example 1

The observed teachers' teaching approach raised many questions including how they are trained during their professional development. The use of question-and-answer and telling methods appear to be the prominent approaches at the intermediate phase level in teaching science education. The teachers seemed happy and satisfied with their teaching approach.

Example 2

Most of the observed teachers would begin their lesson by writing the topic on the chalkboard. Some would explain the goals but not the objectives of the lesson.

These two examples show how you can present your findings from observations.

27.3.4 **Data from literature review**

Sometimes it is not possible to collect data to answer all the questions that you are confronted with. Then the literature review can be helpful and provide concise and latest data on the issue. However, it is easy to write a bad literature review without even knowing it. A good literature review will focus on:

▸ What is already known about the question/s under investigation?
▸ What are the current theories in the field?
▸ What are the shortcomings in our understanding, or contradictions?
▸ What are the gaps and the information needed?
▸ Will the proposed study make any contribution in the field?
▸ What research method will increase the benefits of a new study?

These are just few of the questions that a literature review report should at least focus on.

27.4 **Key characteristics of a qualitative report presentation**

We now present a brief discussion of some of the key characteristics of a qualitative report presentation.

27.4.1 **Individuals or groups should be able to read and understand the report**

One of the primary characteristics of a qualitative report is its ability to be understandable by the target audience irrespective of their statistics background or mathematical understanding. It is critical to note that reporting to a certain extent relies on the richness and depth of the qualitative data as this helps to produce a cogent and intelligible story for the reader. It is said that human beings remember things best that are conveyed in the form of a compelling story (Mertens, 2010). Mertens also observes that no one remembers a deluge of facts that is like a shopping list.

According to Knafl and Howard (1984), qualitative findings are important in and of themselves since it is the richness and detail of the data that give the reader an understanding of the subject's social world. White, Woodfield and Ritchie (2003) mention that reporting involves ordering what is likely to be disorderly data, unravelling complexity, and providing sufficient directions for the reader to follow the story being unveiled. Thus it is imperative that you ensure coherence and flow in reporting of the various stages. Remember, in qualitative research everything can be data, even a disappointment, like that of going to an interview and in the middle of the interview the participant decides not to go any further because he or she is not willing to discuss certain questions. That, on its own, is data that require deep analysis of the situation, making connections with previous questions and the information discussed.

The role of language use becomes a critical issue as it is the mechanism for making individuals understand your research findings. One critique of quantitative research relates to its difficult language that is not understood by many people: this limits its scope and focuses only on those who speak the language of statistics and numbers. Though qualitative reporting does not subscribe totally to this critique of quantitative research, if not careful, reporting can also confuse and repel readers when the choice of language is not well considered. Critical to understand is that qualitative research is only useful if it can be accessed and understood by the target audience.

Critical thinking challenge

How can you ensure that your report is readable and understandable to your target audience? Present your answer as a set of guidelines to a qualitative researcher.

27.4.2 Ensure there is balance in the presentation of description, analysis and interpretation

A balanced research report has more weight and is more convincing than a slanted or biased report. To maintain the balance you need to ensure that the presentation of your description, analysis and interpretation somehow strikes the right proportions. Leaning more towards one of these components can discredit your research findings. In your description, which is more about storytelling, it is important to ensure that you carefully present the facts and details in an interesting manner, while still maintaining authenticity and accuracy. Ensure that the set of chosen facts for presentation is presented in a chronological order that will make sense to the reader.

Fossey, Harvey, McDermott and Davidson (2002) argue that a qualitative research report needs to include a detailed description of the methods used, explaining both the manner in which the study was conducted, and the researcher's reasoning, to address issues of congruence, appropriateness and adequacy. They say that reports should also include evidence of the evolving design of the study, making transparent the ways in which the data gathering and analysis processes informed each other and the study design, to address the issues of responsiveness and transparency.

Creswell (1998), in another view, sees the analysis of text and multiple forms of data as presenting a formidable task for a qualitative researcher. As a researcher, you have a challenge because you have to decide on how to represent the data, whether to put them in tables, narratives or matrices. We suggest that your analysis should include some of the common strategies: Reviewing the data and taking notes, sketching ideas, making summaries, displaying data, relating categories, and more. Then your data interpretation will draw meaning from the data.

Critical thinking challenge

How would you be able to tell that your qualitative research report is good? What are the key elements or components that you should look to consider in your report? Write your response as a set of criteria for evaluating a quantitative research report.

27.4.3 The report should be useful, contribute to existing knowledge and provide new insights

A qualitative researcher should ask him- or herself if the report is useful and what contribution it will make to existing knowledge. Will the report provide answers to questions or offer new, valuable insights? Philosophies of knowledge, as Polkinghorne (1997) contends, are quite different for those who understand knowledge as a certain product of logical operations, and those who understand it as a map or model of aspects of self, others, society, or the material world. These differences make reporting and dissemination of qualitative research a crucial component, as research functions to create knowledge and add to the discipline's body of knowledge. White, Woodfield and Ritchie (2003) note that integrity in reporting requires a demonstration that the explanations and conclusions presented are generated from, and grounded in, the data. They state that qualitative researchers should strike a balance between descriptive, explanatory and interpretive evidence; and also be transparent about the process of analysis so as to help the audience to comprehend the thinking processes that led to the drawn conclusions.

Critical thinking challenge

Based on the opening case study, how would you make qualitative research findings useful, so that they contribute to existing knowledge and provide new insights? What are the key elements that you should consider in your report?

27.4.4 The report should accommodate and cater for various individuals and groups

There are multiple formats for communicating and disseminating findings including conventional format, narrative, performance, or synchronic research report format. The format in which research is reported is not neutral and transparent, but should reflect a particular epistemological commitment (Polkinghorne, 1997). Polkinghorne asserts the importance of research reporting in a form that will communicate the complex and fluid unfolding of its undertaking, formats that can communicate the depth, complexity, and conceptuality of the knowledge generation. The structure of a qualitative report should therefore include an abstract, introduction, background to the problem, the researcher's role, theoretical perspective, methodology, ethical considerations, results, data analysis, limitations, discussion, conclusions and implications, references and appendix. Effective reporting should begin by identifying the purpose of the undertaken research.

Stop and reflect

What do you think the advantages and disadvantages of taking into consideration the beneficiaries of the qualitative research report are? Does it really matter if the report does not accommodate all the beneficiaries?

27.5 Suggestions on what to avoid

There is a number things that you need to be cautious about, and try to avoid in the process of reporting and presenting your qualitative research findings.

Critical thinking challenge

Now that you have gone through several chapters on qualitative research, reflect on what you think are some cautionary measures in reporting and presenting your qualitative findings. Write these as a set of pitfall warnings to a new researcher. Try to write from your own experience.

In the following pitfall warning, we bring to your attention some of the key research aspects that we believe you need to be aware of.

Pitfall warning

Avoid possible bias
▶ The quality and the acceptability of research are heavily dependent on your skills as a researcher as these can be easily influenced by your personal biases and idiosyncrasies. In fact, this is the limitation of most qualitative research. Above all, qualitative research should be designed to be inclusive in nature, irrespective of individual's background, gender, race, and ethnicity, and avoid as any possible bias. Since this does not come easily or naturally, it is important to bear in mind that validity is at stake here, and this is the most significant consideration.

Avoid sexist language
▶ A research report that is not aware of all the members of society – male and female – and inclusive of all, can offend individuals or groups. For instance, in some societies it is common to use a sexist language which can be offensive to individuals who are not part of that society. For example, it is common to hear people talking about 'manpower' as though work, its value and remuneration is associated only with men. In some cultures, this may be seen to exclude women as being unable to undertake real work. The use of sexist language can potentially distort the meaning and the intended message, thereby exposing your report to criticism and rejection of its research findings.

Avoid racist terms
▶ As a researcher you have an obligation to communicate with individuals from various racial groups without offending them. There are many sensitivities, known and unknown, making this a difficult path to tread. Above all, you need to exercise caution and be sensitive to changing trends. For example, sometimes it is better to identify individuals by nationality rather than ethnicity, unless you know the name they prefer to be called, or what is acceptable in referring to them as a group.

(continued)

Pitfall warning *(continued)*

Avoid including immaterial or insignificant details
▶ Include thorough and carefully chosen information that is relevant and to the point. Try to avoid providing any information that is unnecessary and that doesn't directly benefit the reader's understanding of why a particular method was chosen, how the data collection was conducted or coded, and analysed.

Avoid unnecessary explanation
▶ In every field or area of study there are basic guidelines or established procedures. Try to avoid unnecessary explanation as you are not writing a how-to guide about a particular method. Simply make the assumption that readers know enough and have a basic understanding. Focus on how you applied your chosen method, not on the technical aspects of carrying out a chosen method.

Challenges experienced during research
▶ When collecting or generating data, you are bound to come across problems or challenges. Do not shy away from or conceal these problems as they are also part of the methodology section. It is important to note how you dealt with the challenges as part of your methodology. The inclusion in the report of challenges and how you dealt with them will demonstrate to the reader the how you balanced your decision-making.

Avoid long, boring reports
▶ Quality is always better than quantity. Try to avoid producing a long and boring report as this may cause the target group to lose interest. A short, concise and straight-to-the-point report is more likely to be widely read.

Stop and reflect

Can you think of other possible pitfalls that researchers should be aware of in writing their qualitative research report?

Conclusion

From our discussion in this chapter, you will have noticed that presentation and reporting of research findings is the most challenging phase of the qualitative research project. This is because the reception and understanding of the research project relies so much on it. Every step of your research, be it conceptualising and developing a research problem, formulating research questions, identifying the objectives and purpose of the research, data collection or data analysis, is connected. Your reporting approach should be developed in the conceptual phase of your research to avoid adding it at the last minute. Knafl and Howard (1984) indicate that reporting of study results confronts qualitative researchers with a difficult problem. And, writing up qualitative research, as Mertens (2010) reveals, has emerged as an area of controversy partially reflected in the struggle of how to present qualitative data in terms of whose voice is represented in the written report, and how best to represent those voices. It is common to hear about the underutilisation of research findings when policymakers and other key stakeholders are developing social sciences policies. One of the most important barriers to the utilisation of research in typical research reports is its lack of clarity, intelligibility, and relevance, except to a very limited audience (Sandelowski, 1998). This means you can have good, rich data findings but still fail to properly communicate them to the target audience. Bear in mind that most of the readers of qualitative reports are not researchers, or versed in the processes that culminate in the reports they read. So it is your responsibility as a researcher to ensure that your qualitative research reporting makes sense to a wide audience.

In the past, qualitative research reporting has hindered the utilisation of qualitative findings. Knafl and Howard (1984) observe that reports of a qualitative study follow various formats, many of which may appear highly unorthodox and unacceptable to the reader who is accustomed to reading the results of surveys and experiments. These readers, they say, often find reports of qualitative research uninteresting and unconvincing. One of the biggest challenges is that there is no one style for reporting the findings from qualitative research. The researcher has a responsibility to choose not only what to tell, but how to tell it as well. Researchers have to choose, from an array of representational styles, formats and language, those that best fit their research purposes, method, and data, hence no one size fits all. We live in an era where everyone is busy, but at the same time flooded with information from various sources. This can make the audience very selective about what to read and not read, increasing the researcher's responsibility to ensure that choices in reporting draw the reader and achieve the goals of qualitative reporting.

Sandelowski (1998:379) has the final word in observing that qualitative research may put readers off with "turgid prose, seemingly endless lists of unlinked codes and categories, dangling participles, and dizzying arrays of multiply hyphenated and, sometimes, non-existent words that convey nothing more than the writer's willingness to destroy the English language." So, if inadequate reporting can lead to inappropriate application of qualitative research in decision-making, it is your responsibility to make sure this does not happen with your own research reporting.

Closing activities

Analysis and consolidation

1 Using the opening case study, present a justification for using a qualitative research in investigation of poor learner performance and achievement in the Floranda community.

2 Referring to the case study, how would you present the findings to a group of illiterate adults who are not familiar with educational matters?

3 What makes writing a qualitative research report so difficult?

4 Remember the list of 10 key components in preparing your qualitative research findings report, which you wrote down in one of the earlier *Stop and reflect* activities? With what you know from this chapter, how would you now order these components?

Practical applications

5 Here is a case scenario from a study: carefully read it and develop an account of the challenge Sipho faced in a qualitative research report for a group of stakeholders of your choice. This practical exercise will offer you first-hand experience in writing and disseminating a qualitative research report.

> ## Case study: Sipho deals with challenge
>
>
> Sipho is collecting data for a study on in-service teachers' professional development in their school district. Following the protocol, he plans to visit several schools and ask teachers to volunteer for his study. Sipho samples three schools in the Floranda school district. He visits the first school after receiving the necessary permission from the school authorities to distribute a questionnaire and interview the teachers. Arriving at the school, he finds the teachers are ignoring him. He quickly learns that the teachers
> *(continued)*

Case study *(continued)*

were not briefed about his visit as had been promised. He decides to call all the teachers concerned, brief them on his study, and then distribute the questionnaires. Together with the teachers, they all agree on a date and time for collecting the questionnaires and conducting the interviews.

6 Use the opening case study to design a qualitative research report to be presented to a funding agency. Ensure that you include the various key steps necessary in preparing a research report.

Bibliography

Anderson, C. 2010. Presenting and evaluating qualitative research. Available online: http://www.ncbi.nlm.nih.gov/pmc/articles/PMC2987281/.

Bantwini, B.D. 2009. District professional development model as a way to introduce primary school teachers' natural science curriculum reforms in one district in South Africa. *Journal of Education for Teaching*, 35(2):69–182.

Bantwini, B.D. 2009. A Researcher's Experience in Navigating the Murky Terrain of Doing Research in South Africa's Transforming Schools. *Perspectives in Education*, 27(1):30–39.

Chenail, R.J. 1995. Presenting qualitative data. *The Qualitative Report*, 2(3). Available online: http://www.nova.edu/ssss/QR/QR2-3/presenting.html.

Chilisa, B. 2012. *Indigenous Research Methodologies*. London: Zed Books.

Corden, A. & Sainsbury, R. 2006. *Using verbatim quotations in reporting qualitative social research: Researchers' views*. Social Policy Research Unit: University of York.

Creswell, J.W. 1998. *Qualitative inquiry and research design: Choosing among five traditions*. Thousand Oaks, CA: Sage.

Fossey, E., Harvey C., McDermott, F. & Davidson, L. 2002. Understanding and evaluating qualitative research. *Australian and New Zealand Journal of Psychiatry*, 36:717–732.

Knafl, K.A. & Howard, M.J. 1984. Interpreting and reporting qualitative research. *Research in Nursing and Health*, 7:17–24.

Mertens, D.M. 2010. *Research and evaluation in education and psychology: Integrating diversity with quantitative, qualitative, and mixed methods* (3rd ed.). Thousand Oaks, CA: Sage.

National Foundation for Educational Research. 2013. Developing young researchers. Available online: http://www.nfer.ac.uk/schools/developing-young-researchers/how-to-present-your-results.cfm

Perret, S., Anseeuw, W. & Mathebula, F. 2009. Poverty and livelihoods in rural South Africa. Investigating diversity and dynamics of livelihoods: Case study in Limpopo. Available online: http://ageconsearch.umn.edu/bitstream/60885/2/2005-01.pdf.

Polkinghorne, D.E. 1997. Reporting qualitative research as practice. In W.G. Tierney & Y.S. Lincoln (Eds). *Representation and the text: Re-framing the narrative voice*. Albany: State University of New York Press.

Sandelowski, M. 1998. Writing a good read: Strategies for re-presenting qualitative data. *Research in Nursing and Health*, 21:375–382.

Smith, L.T. 2012. *Decolonizing Methodologies Research and Indigenous Peoples*. London: Zed Books.

Sutcliffe, S. & Court, J. 2005. *Evidence-Based Policymaking: What is it? How does it work? What relevance for developing countries?* London: Overseas Development Institute.

White, C., Woodfield, K. & Ritchie, J. 2003. Reporting and presenting qualitative data. In J. Ritchie & J. Lewis (Eds). *Qualitative Research Practice: A guide for social science students and researchers*. London: Sage Publications.

Weiss, C.H. 1979. The many meanings of research utilization. *Public Administration Review*, 39(5):426–431.

USC Libraries. 2013. Organizing your social sciences research paper. Available online: http://libguides.usc.edu/content.php?pid=83009&sid=615865.

CHAPTER 28

Plagiarism: Causes, consequences and preventive strategies

KEY CONCEPTS

Bibliography is a list of all sources consulted, or read, but not necessarily directly quoted or cited in your text; it is placed at the end of your writing.

Citation is acknowledging other people's work that you have used in your own work, by means of referring to and indicating the source.

Direct quote is when you use the exact words of the author and/or source.

Paraphrase is when you use your own words to indicate your own understanding of the original source; it is normally the same length as the original source or passage.

Plagiarism put in simple terms, means a failure to acknowledge another person's work in your own work.

Reference list presents a list of sources cited in your text; it is placed at the end of your writing.

Summarise is when you present the overall or main ideas of the whole paragraph, passage or text in your own words. It is a shorter version of the paragraph or passage that it is derived from.

LEARNING OUTCOMES

By the end of this chapter, you should be able to:

▸ Demonstrate an understanding of what plagiarism is.

▸ Identify the causes of plagiarism and their consequences.

▸ Demonstrate skills to avoid plagiarism.

Case study: Is it plagiarism?

Matome is a first-year student at an institution of higher education. One of the prerequisites for one of his courses is to produce a well-researched assignment on a topic that has been covered in the course. Clear instructions are given that all the sources used in the assignment must be cited. Furthermore, students are instructed to make sure that their voice or argument is clear and their own. Matome has begun writing up his assignment after reading various articles on his topic. Matome has found interesting information, quotes, statistics, diagrams and models that explain what his topic is about, and he intends to use this information in his assignment. During the writing Matome in most cases indicates the source of his information. However, in some cases, he feels that he has indicated 'enough' sources already and so it will be 'okay' if he presents some sections as his own work, especially information from older books and the internet. Matome also thinks it is brilliant to substitute words and to paraphrase some sections from his reading, so that the work looks like his own arguments. In some work, Matome realises that he does not have dates and authors, so he thinks since there is no one claiming the work, he might as well claim it himself. In conversation with other students as he is finishing the assignment, Matome is told about plagiarism and that he needs to indicate all authors' work that he consulted in his assignment. Matome is now compiling a list of all the sources he used and is able to locate. He decides that he will just stay quiet about others that he cannot find.

Do you recognise any of Matome's thinking or actions? How typical do you think he is?

Introduction

There are different types, forms or styles of writings and each has its own conventions, guidelines and rules. There are numerous factors to be taken to consideration when writing, which might include the reason for writing and most importantly, the audience or people intended to read the article. There is writing for a popular magazine, a newspaper article, policy document, internet article, and so forth. This chapter speaks to academic writing skills. It is important to understand that in academic writing there are also rules, guidelines and conventions that need to be respected. Writing in academia demands recognition of work that came before yours. However, this is not done only to indicate the research or work that is in the public domain about your topic but more importantly, to link the current work with what is known to develop it further, and to contribute new findings or knowledge where possible. There are various challenges with academic writing and one of them is the issue of plagiarised work as this affects the originality of work presented when entering the academic community. In this chapter, we are going to deal with what **plagiarism** is; what are the causes and the consequences of plagiarising. We will also suggest a few steps for avoiding plagiarism.

28.1 What is plagiarism?

Plagiarism is the act or practice of taking someone else's work and passing it off as your own work. Plagiarism means "literary theft, stealing (by copying) the words or ideas of someone else and passing them off as one's own without crediting the source" (Park, 2003:472). It involves various spheres and happens when an author uses other people's ideas, words, artwork, music, images, and so forth, from any source (books, journal articles, newspapers, website, etc.) without giving them credit.

Barnhart (1988:801) in Park (2003:472) traces the etymology of the word plagiarism ('literary theft'), from the earlier English word plagiary ('one who wrongfully takes another's words or ideas'), derived from the Latin *plagiarius* ('kidnapper, seducer, plunderer, literary thief'), from *plagium* (kidnapping), from *plaga* (snare, net).

Now that we know what the definition of plagiarism is, it is important to address what the possible traps or mistaken beliefs that cause us to plagiarise are. In the next section we will deal with what might make us fall in the plagiarism trap.

28.2 Meaning of plagiarism, causes and consequences of plagiarism

Put in simple terms, plagiarism means a failure to acknowledge another person's work. It is considered a form of cheating in the academic world.

Plagiarism can take place in various ways:
▸ Buying, stealing or 'borrowing' someone's work and passing it off as your own.
▸ Copying a large section of text without using quotation marks and a citation.

Let us look at some of the common reasons for plagiarism.

28.2.1 Some reasons for plagiarism

The pressure to produce work and to achieve is the obvious reason why people, including authors, resort to plagiarism. There are various further reasons why students might fall in this trap:
▸ Pressure that comes with maintaining high academic standards.
▸ Fear of disappointing significant others, especially if they are academically inclined or when the student is seen as the hope of delivering the family out of poverty, through his or her academic success.
▸ Ignorance or misunderstanding of plagiarism because it is complicated and technical.
▸ Balancing one's academic life and social life can be challenging so students might procrastinate, and then look for quick fixes.
▸ With the increasing use of technology, the cut-and-paste function, for example, makes it easy to transport text from one source to your own without the need to rewrite or transcribe.
▸ Most often, students think that they will not get caught, or if they do, it is not very serious.

28.2.2 Types of plagiarism

There are various types of plagiarism. In this chapter, we focus on the most common types. WriteCheck (2014), identifies a number of types of plagiarism:

Aggregator The assignment or written work might have proper citation, but there is no original work cited. This might be a problem in using secondary sources, for instance.

Clone This is when you submit another person's work, word-for-word and pass it off as your own. This is also referred to as direct plagiarism.

CTRL – C The assignment or work handed in contains sections of the text from a single source where no alterations were made.

Find – Replace Here the student will change the keywords and phrases, but keep the essential content of the source.

Hybrid This is harder to detect because it is a combination of correctly cited sources with a few copied passages that are not cited.

Mashup This is like a stew, in which you find a blend of different material and/or sources.

Remix Paraphrased texts from multiple sources are made to fit together. So-called because it is like a remix of a music piece.

Recycle Like recycling, this is finding and using earlier submitted work and/or sources without citing them. A large part of existing work may also be recycled in the new assignment.

Re-tweet Just like tweeting, proper citation is done, however, it relies too closely on the text of the original wording and structure.

404 Error The student includes non-existent or inaccurate information about the source. The dates, for instance, might be inaccurate or even made up.

Bowdoin College (n.d.) further lists the following types plagiarism:

Accidental plagiarism When a student neglects to cite their source unintentionally. It can also take form of misquoting or paraphrasing without citation.

Direct plagiarism This is word-for-word copying of a section of another person's work without quotation marks. It is also referred to as cloning.

Mosaic plagiarism Using text from different sources without using quotation marks. It also occurs when original text is replaced with synonyms but maintaining the meaning and, to a greater extent, the general structure of the original work.

Redundancy/self-plagiarism This might happen in two ways:

▶ The student submits the entirety or sections of their previously submitted assignment without quotation or clear indication of their previous work; and

▶ The student submits several versions of the work that slightly differ from one another, to different but related courses without acknowledging this or receiving permission from all the lecturers concerned.

In this last section we discussed what might cause students to fall into the trap of handing in work that is plagiarised in some way or another. We also indicated the types of plagiarism that might occur. In the next sections we deal with the possible repercussions of plagiarised work.

28.2.3 Consequences of plagiarism

In academia, plagiarism is regarded as a serious offence because the academic community views it as author dishonesty. As in non-academic life, people are reluctant to engage, collaborate and work with a dishonest author or student.

According to iThenticate (n.d), there are six consequences of plagiarism:

▶ It destroys student reputations: Students can be suspended or expelled from an academic institution and their academic record will reflect this, possibly denying the student access in other institutions.

▶ It destroys professional reputations: A promising (in terms of a professional, political, business, etc.) figure's career might be negatively affected.

▶ It destroys academic reputations: Once a person has allegations of plagiarism against him or her, his/her academic career will be affected in the academic community.

▶ Legal repercussions: Copyright laws are absolute, saying you cannot use another person's material, including intellectual property, without permission. You could end up facing legal action.

▶ Monetary repercussions: The person who is caught plagiarising can be sued and this can lead to further loss of income through being fired, fined, paying legal costs, and so forth.

▶ Plagiarised research: This is possibly the most serious consequence because plagiarised work does not add new light in the field, or advance it.

(http://www.ithenticate.com/resources/6-consequences-of-plagiarism)

Now that we have addressed the possible consequences of plagiarism, let us look at ways to avoid plagiarism in academic writing.

28.2.4 Avoiding plagiarism in academic writing

The most effective way of avoiding plagiarism is to allow enough time for your work, take thorough notes, and go through your work more than once to ensure that all the work that is not yours is acknowledged. In academic writing it is important to *always* acknowledge the source where the information is from if it is not your original idea, work of art, presentation, and so forth.

▶ Always give recognition or credit to the original source.
▶ Always use quotation marks when you use another author's exact words and always include a citation.
▶ When paraphrasing text, always use your own words to show your own understanding.

The following flow chart designed by Harris (2001) will assist you in identifying and guiding you on what to do to establish whether work is original, that is, your own idea, or it possibly belongs to another author.

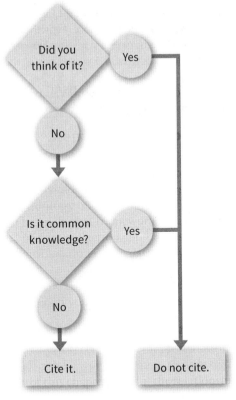

FIGURE 28.1: Quick guide to identifying original or another author's work
(**Source:** Harris 2001:155)

As a student in academia you will read many materials, ranging from magazines, journal articles, newspapers (including listening to the broadcast news), participating in various social media, the internet and all the various types of sources that might influence your thinking and the argument you are developing during your writing. The flow charts in Figure 28.1 above, and Figure 28.2 below are guidelines on establishing whether you should cite or not cite a source. However, it is on your shoulders to continually check whether the idea you have is original (that is, your own idea) or could have been influenced by sources that you came across and was exposed to.

28.2.4.1 Quick guide to know when to quote and cite to avoid plagiarism

The following flow chart as designed by Harris (2001) will assist you in deciding whether to quote, cite, reference, or not.

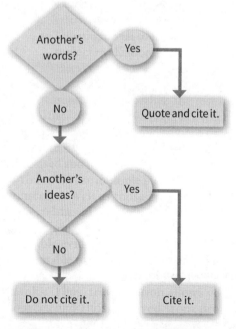

FIGURE 28.2: Quick guide to avoid plagiarism
(**Source:** Harris 2001:158)

28.2.5 Strategies for avoiding plagiarism

Here are three basic strategies for avoiding plagiarism:

- Always use quotations marks in everything that comes directly from the text.
- The sentence must make sense when you **paraphrase**. Do not just move words around.
- It is always important to check your paraphrased text against the original text to ensure that the information is correct and to highlight the meaning of the original text.

Toolbox Terms you need to know (or, What is common knowledge?)

Common knowledge is facts that can be found in different sources and are likely to be known by a lot of people.
Example: Nelson Mandela was elected the first democratic president of South Africa in 1994.
Information like this is general information. You do not need to document this fact.

However, you must document facts that are not generally known and ideas that interpret other facts.
Example: According to the American Family Leave Coalition's new book, *Family Issues and Congress*, President Bush's relationship with Congress has hindered family leave legislation.
The idea that 'Bush's relationship with Congress has hindered family leave legislation' is not a fact but an interpretation; consequently, you need to cite your source.

Quotation: this is using another person's words. Quotation marks must always be used at the beginning and end of the quoted text, and the source referenced accordingly.

Paraphrase: is used when referring to another person's ideas, but using your own words. It is, however, important to always acknowledge the source of the information.

(**Source:** Writing Tutorial Services, Indiana University, Bloomington, IN
http://www.indiana.edu/~wts/pamphlets/plagiarism.shtml#strategies)

Now that we have discussed what plagiarism is, let us look at some of the sources that can be plagiarised.

28.3 Sources that can be plagiarised

There are different sources that are used in academia for information, and information from these sources can be plagiarised if not cited correctly. In academia it is important for all sources used in your writing to be precisely located and referenced accurately. In this chapter, when we refer to sources that are cited in academia, they include sources like journal articles, newspaper articles, books, chapters in the books, government documents, periodicals, reviews, conference papers (both published or unpublished), posters, and so forth, that you are most likely to use when doing your assignments or academic writing. Furthermore, there are also movies, the internet, including social media, visual material such as pictures, and also audio material, that assist you in crafting an argument in your writing. It is important to always indicate the source of your information so that you do not plagiarise.

We describe a few of the sources you are most likely to use in your work:
- Books
  - These are published books that may be by a single author or have multiple authors.
- Edited books
  - These are published books that may be edited by a single author or multiple authors. Various other authors are invited to contribute a chapter or chapters.
- Chapters in books
  - This is a section in a published book, edited book, reports, and so forth.
- Government and official documents
  - These are writings that are referred to as command papers. They include sources such as acts, policies, white papers, green papers, government gazettes, commissioned reports, and so forth.
- Journal articles
  - In academia, a journal is made up by a collection of different articles on a specific topic (this type of journal is usually referred to as a special edition) or different topics, but of a common theme or subject matter, for instance social sciences, humanities, physical sciences, computer sciences, business, etc. Journals are peer reviewed so that they maintain the academic standard of the journal. A journal article is therefore a paper or work that is written and published in a journal.
- Internet
  - A digital platform and/or search engines of global interconnected computer networks, where sources of information can be downloaded and uploaded. Journal articles, books, social media, video and audio material, to name a few, can be downloaded. It is important to note that the authenticity of some of the information must be thoroughly verified.

We have looked at plagiarism, what it is, what the consequences are, and also how to avoid the pitfall of plagiarism in academic writing. We have identified a number of sources that can be plagiarised. Now let us look at ways of citing from these and other sources.

28.4 Plagiarism and citation

We have now addressed some of the common pitfalls that we can easily fall into, especially when unable to distinguish our own original thoughts and ideas from other authors'. In this section we look at proper citation and how doing it can assist us to avoid plagiarism. Plagiarism occurs mostly because of not citing the source of the work being used. It is thus important to know what and how to cite other authors' work.

28.4.1 What is citation?

Citation is acknowledging by means of referring to and indicating the source of other people's work used in your own work.

Before examining the specific citation style it is important to understand when to cite to prevent plagiarism.

28.4.1.1 Types of citations
To refer to other people's work one might use a:
- **Paraphrase**
  - This is when you use your own words to indicate your own understanding of the original source. It is normally the same length as the original source or passage

- **Summary**
  - › In a summary, you present the overall or main idea of the whole paragraph/passage in your own words. It is a shorter version of the whole paragraph or passage you have read.
- **Direct quote**
  - › This is when you use the exact words of the author and/or source.

Note: When you summarise a concept that is not common knowledge, you must cite your source. It is not necessary to cite information that is widely known by your audience – such as, "milk is a good source of calcium" or "good oral care prevents tooth decay" (Durham College & UOIT, 2011:1).

28.4.1.2 Information prominent in citation to avoid plagiarism

Another way of citing is when the author gives prominence to a certain idea or information. In this instance, the authors are required to write the information they want highlighted in parentheses at the end of the citation.

Using citation

The opinions of Zimbabwean entrepreneurs about the traditional methodologies of questionnaires and the more participatory-based approach were markedly different (Liamputtong, 2010:19)
or
Liamputtong (2010:19) asserts that "The opinions of Zimbabwean entrepreneurs about the traditional methodologies of questionnaires and the more participatory-based approach were markedly different".

There are various verbs that can be used to assist us with author-prominent referencing, and help us to avoid plagiarising.

TABLE 28.1: Author-prominent referencing verbs

state	point out	describe
remark	add	suggest
maintain	assert	affirm
agree	claim	clarify
disagree	contest	contend
highlight	find	show
imply	theorise	offer
predict	question	dispute
justify	confirm	reason

(**Source:** Central Queensland University, 2013:6)

Stop and reflect

Think of a piece of writing where you can use some of these verbs to assist you enrich your argument. Look at the work that you are writing now and try to use these verbs.

28.4.1.3 Citing and using Latin terms

The wrong usage of and disregard for the true meaning of Latin terms in academic writing might not only affect your written work, but might also change the meaning and open it to plagiarism as well. It is therefore important to know what the Latin terms mean.

TABLE 28.2: Meaning of Latin terms

Latin term	Meaning
et alii, or et al.	'and others' is used when more than three authors are cited. This is to shorten the in-text citation. It is important to note that in the reference list or bibliography, all the authors must be named in full. The term et al. is not italicised.
[sic]	'thus' or 'this is how it was written'. This is used when there is a spelling or grammatical error, or when sexist, discriminatory, inflammatory, derogatory or controversial language is used in the original source quoted. This term [sic] appears immediately after the original error or word. The word [sic] is not italicised and appears as indicated in square brackets.
ca.	This term denotes circa and means 'approximately'. It is used when only the approximate date of the work is known. It is not italicised and ends with a full stop.

(**Source:** Central Queensland University, 2013:9)

Use p. or colon?

Note that different lecturers might prefer a certain referencing style in terms of using a colon (:) or (p.) for indicating pagination within the parentheses or text. Ask your lecturer which referencing style to use and be consistent throughout your writing.

Example: 'Politics and university activism on gender representivity does not necessarily speak to diversity issues in post-apartheid South Africa' (Notshaya, 2013, p.49).

or

'Politics and university activism on gender representivity does not necessarily speak to diversity issues in post-apartheid South Africa' (Notshaya, 2013:49).

We have identified the information that needs to be addressed. Now let us look at citing protocols, that is, what citing looks like in the text of your written work.

28.5 Citing within text

28.5.1 Single and multiple authors

These are published sources that can be single authored or have multiple (more than one) authors. To cite a source in the text follow the following

Single author Surname (year of publication)
Example Ngobeni (2014) argues that…
Direct quote: Single author Surname (year of publication: page number) quotation mark
Example According to Ngobeni (2014:14), 'life in 2014 is not the same …'

Multiple authors (two authors) Surname and Surname, (year of publication) lament that ….
Example Kanyane and Mtsweni (2014) lament that …
Direct quote: Multiple authors (two to three authors) 'Security and safety are a priority …' (Kanyane & Mtsweni, 2014:79). However, …

Multiple authors (three or more authors) The first time of citing such sources, all the authors are named, then from the second, use et al.
Example **First citing in the written text** Surname, Surname and Surname (year of publication) are of the opinion that… Baloyi, Tlailane and Storm (2009) are of the opinion that… **Direct quote** According to Baloyi, Tlailane and Storm (2009:278), 'Tateni is …'
Example **Second citing within same text** Surname, et al. (year of publication) are of the opinion that … Baloyi, et al. (2009) are of the opinion that … **Direct quote** According to Baloyi, et al. (2009:278), 'Tateni is …'

28.5.2 Author with more than one publication in a particular year

Some authors may have written more than one publication in a particular year. Citing such authors becomes a challenge as you need to distinguish among different publications. You can differentiate the writings alphabetically (a, b, c, etc.).

> *Example*
> Surname, (year of publication, letters (a, b, c, etc.))
> Okeke (2005a) argues that… The road to democracy is …(Okeke, 2005b). However, according to Okeke (2005c), this does not indicate good….

28.6.3 Author is unknown

You might come across a source (either in print or on the internet) that you would like to cite in your work but unfortunately there is no information about the author. The fact that there is no author given does not mean that you can use that work and not indicate where or who the source is.

No excuse

The fact that you cannot locate the author of the work is no excuse for plagiarising it.

In cases where you cannot locate the source, Harvard Referencing Guide (Central Queensland University, 2013) suggests using 'Author unknown' in place of the author's name. This is used in the following circumstances:

- When the original source states 'Anonymous' or 'Anon' on the title page or on the web page.
- Information was found in a magazine, newspaper or journal and the author is unknown. However, please take note that if there organisation's name is there, the organisation's name can be used as the author.

All other examples of sources where there is no author's name use 'Author unknown' in place of the author, as follows:

Who is anonymous?

Please note that different lecturers or departments might prefer a certain referencing style. Ask your lecturer which referencing style to use and be consistent throughout your writing.
Example
Little is not small and small is not necessarily little (Author unknown, 2014).

28.5.4 Anonymous author

Finding that the author is anonymous is another pitfall that might easily lead to plagiarism. In situations where the material (either in print or internet) clearly says that it is produced by 'Anonymous' or 'Anon', you must still indicate in your text who the author is.

Anon doesn't mean it's yours

The fact that the author is said to be anonymous or 'Anon' you cannot locate the author of the work is not a reason to plagiarise it.

However, if there are no words such as 'Anonymous' or 'Anon' appearing on the material, you do not use 'Anonymous' or 'Anon' as the author, but Author unknown.

More about anonymous

Anonymous (2014)…
or
This was the peculiarity of the issue (Anon, 2014)…

28.5.5 Publication year unknown

At times you will come across material that you would like to use, especially on the internet or older printed material for which there is unfortunately no year of publication. You may be tempted to use the work as your own because you think it cannot be traced. If you cannot ascertain for a fact the date, do not make up the year for any reason. Rather indicate that there is no date.

When there is no date

The following information was found on a website on bullying:
Boys growing up in structureless homes might be easy victims to gangsterism as they search to belong.

Cite it in this manner
Boys growing up in structureless homes might be easy victims to gangsterism as they search to belong (Bullying website[give website], no date).

28.5.6 Quotes and quotation marks

The use of quotation marks is important to avoid plagiarism. They are your best friends when citing another author's work because they indicate clearly where your own voice is located within the text and where the cited work, that is, another author's voice, begins and ends.

Your argument, own voice or point of view is important, and while you might want to agree with another author, ensure that when you use quotations you do not over-use them. Always be mindful of your own voice.

But I quoted ...

The use of quotation marks does not mean you did not plagiarise. There are other important factors that must appear in the cited work: the author's name, year of publication, page number/s; and the entire source must also appear in the reference list.

28.5.6.1 Quotation marks

You can use either single: (' ') or double: (" ") quotation marks when using a quote.

A single (' ') quotation mark should be used with shorts quotes within the sentence while double (" ") quotations, that is, a quotation within a quotation are used inside single quotation marks.
Example
'The story opened on a depressing scene, when she opened the door and said "I want to die, I wish I was dead so as not to feel any of this" and this is clearly indicated' (Rapau 2012, p. 43).

Tip

Please note that different lecturers might prefer a certain referencing style. Ask your lecturer which referencing style to use and be consistent throughout your writing.

Quotation marks should only be used with short quotes and inserted into the sentence. They should be placed at the beginning and end of the quote to indicate to the reader the boundaries of the quote.

Tip

Generally, short quotes are less than 30 words and can be put in quotation marks, while longer quotes are more than 30 words and should be indented and placed in a separate paragraph.

The longer quotation should be introduced in your own words and should be on a new line. The quote should:
▶ be fully indented by default
▶ be in single line spacing
▶ change the font size to smaller than the normal text (this is optional).

Style of referencing also plays a major role in this section. Please ensure that you ask your lecturer or department which referencing style is preferred. It is also important that your referencing and citing is consistent throughout your work.

Indent a quotation to separate it from the lead-in statement with one blank line as indicated below. According to the Academic Learning Support (2007), the lead-in statement ends with a colon (:). Separate the quotation from the text that follows it with one blank line, as in the example:

Quote of more than 30 words

The conditions of education during apartheid were horrific and in some instance in the so called black universities. Thus black students in such universities took up activism.

> Politics of university activism however could not be navigated simply by issuing a consensus statement in opposition to education apartheid, as exceptional as that statement was. With the involvement in politically-charged township schools threatening 'the possibility of increased prescription from government (Dorn, 2013:49).

This was a defining moment in the South African struggle …

28.5.6.2 Using a direct quote

Tip

When using a quote, the words and punctuation should be *exactly* as in the source.

Information required when using a quote is:
Author's/organisation's name, the year of publication of the source: the page number of where the quote was taken from.

28.5.6.3 Errors in a quote

If you come across a quote that has an error and you would like to use it, do not correct it and make it appear as if it is your own work. That is still plagiarism. You must add the term [sic] next to where the error appears.

Reflecting errors in a quote

Matthew (2011, p. 16)
Nelson Mandela long walks to freedom book was launched
Cite as
Nelson Mandela long walks [sic] to freedom book was launched….(Matthew 2011, p. 16)

28.5.6.4 Adding or inserting a word in a quote and using square brackets in quotations

Plagiarism can easily happen when you think that because you have inserted or added a phrase or a word in another author's work, the sentence is your own argument. As indicated in the paraphrasing section, this should be done correctly and where necessary it should be cited.

Adding a word in a quote is allowed. However, this must be clearly indicated by placing square brackets [ ] around that word. Furthermore the author might want to insert a word that explains the meaning of another word in that quotation. The explanation must be placed in square brackets.

Using square brackets to show addition

Original text
As 'Nelson Mandela walked out the Victor Verster prison…'(Ngoasheng 1994:14)
With additions
As 'Nelson Mandela [and his then wife, Winnie Mandela] walked out the Victor Verster prison… (Ngoasheng 1994:14)…'
To explain a word
'The curriculum of the national schools in the 1870s included reading, writing, arithmetic, drill [physical exercises] and music' (Cowie et al. 1996:21).

28.5.6.5 Words omitted or not included from quotations

To leave out words from quotations, use an ellipsis (…). However the quotation must still maintain the same sense. This is also another import point to keep in mind in order to avoid plagiarism.

But I changed it …

The fact that you left out some words from original text, does not mean it is now your own work.

Using ellipsis 1

Original text
Barton (1994:7) describes literacy as a 'set of practices which people use in literacy events as they engage. Furthermore these literacy practices are situated in social relations'

With omission
Barton (1994:7) describes literacy as a 'set of practices which people use in literacy events […]' and that 'literacy practices are situated in social relations'

Please note that you must indicate to your readers when the quotation does not begin at the start of a sentence. Ellipses should be used to highlight the omitted word(s).

Using ellipsis 2

The emphasis [parents] place on literacy as a means of achieving '… equality of opportunity for their children and work opportunities to break cycle of poverty' (Mojapelo, 2011:4).

28.6 Page numbers

The last section addressed ways to cite and quote, and also where to extend or reduce a quotation. In this section we are going to deal with citing the page where a quotation used in your writing was found. Throughout the chapter, emphasis has been placed on the importance of pagination so as to avoid plagiarism. Page numbers are used when you directly quote material (word-for-word), use indirect quotes, and when paraphrasing specific pages from the original source.

Using page numbers

One page is referred to	Machaisa and Maphalala 1983:4
Pages that are not in sequence	Bangwa 1996, pp. 1–4 & 6 or Bangwa, 1996:1–4 & 6
Pages that are in sequence	Tabane, Mudau and McKay 2010:25–26
Pages from a website	Mabunda and Nkonyane 2013:1 of 2

(**Source:** Central Queensland University, 2013:8)

There are times where you will find that the source that you would like to cite does not have page numbers. In this instance it will be advisable to consult your librarian to conduct an advanced search for the latest version. If there is no new existing version and you want to use the source, do not physically count pages or develop your own pagination system. Rather, indicate all the relevant information and point out that there are no pages indicated in the document.

No page number indicated

The story opened on a depressing scene, when she opened the door and said "I want to die, I wish I was dead so as not to feel any of this" and this is clearly indicated' (Rapau 2012, page not indicated).

28.7 Importance of the reference list

In the previous section were dealt with pagination to indicate the precise source especially the page where the quote was taken from. In this section we are going to deal with referencing the sources consulted and used in your work or writing.

A **reference list** presents a list of sources cited in your text. It is placed at the end of your writing. It is presented alphabetically in terms of authors and where the same author is cited, publication is listed chronologically.

It is important to generate and keep a well-organised reference list because in academia, different readers might want to consult and go the original source that you have cited in your text. It will assist later readers to establish, for instance, whether the original source was cited properly, and whether the author has extended the understanding of the topic.

So why should you reference? References enrich your writing and make it more reliable. According to Academic Learning Support (2007:5), referencing assists your reader by:

▸ Showing the breadth of your research
▸ Strengthening your academic argument
▸ Showing the reader the source of your information.

References further, and most importantly:
▸ Allow the reader to consult your sources independently
▸ Allow the reader to verify your data.

28.8 Importance of the bibliography

In the last section the reference list was explained and the importance of such a list outlined. In this section we are going to address listing all sources that were consulted when writing up your work. A **bibliography** is a list of all sources consulted and read in the process of your research. It is placed at the end of your writing.

28.8.1 Differences between reference list and bibliography

There is often confusion between a reference list and a bibliography. Let us try to distinguish between the two. The difference between a reference list and a bibliography is in whether the source was cited in the main text or not. Remember with a reference list you list *only* the sources that are cited in your text, while with a bibliography you list *all* the sources that you have read on your topic but did not cite in your text. It is important to note these sources because they may have contributed to your thinking, argument and presentation of your topic. If not acknowledged, you may be guilty of plagiarism.

28.9 Computer software to check plagiarism

In this section we deal with computer software that assists us to check the originality of our work.

There are numerous cases of students found handing in other people's work and passing it off as their own original work. Institutions of learning are now employing various computer software that are able to detect whether the work students submit is their own original work. In cases where another author's work was used, the software is also able to indicate the original author and source of that work.

The use of this software is to deter students from plagiarising. Although the software might be prone to some errors, they are able to highlight work that might be suspicious. They can also be used as a supportive tool by the students to check their own work before handing it in so that they ensure that they do not inadvertently submit plagiarised work.

There are many different computer software packages that are designed to detect plagiarism. Some of the software are easily available on the internet and give a free trial of up to 30 days so that a student can see if he or she has plagiarised work and do necessary corrections. Table 28.3 shows some of the available software that the students can use as a support tool for their academic writing.

TABLE 28.3: Different plagiarism software package and applications*

Name	Features/techniques	Pros/cons	Costs
Copycatch http://www.copycatch.freeserve.co.uk/vocalyse.htm	A British (UK) system that compares text from emails using similar threshold to detect essays which are similar or not to others essays. It uses common words and phrases to detect similarity.	**PROS**: won an award for detection, clarity and value. It is hailed for its user-friendliness, speed and reliability. **CONS**: As it focuses on student work, unfortunately it cannot detect material downloaded from the internet.	Approx $700 AUD to purchase software.
Glatt Plagiarism Screening Program (GPSP) http://www.plagiarism.com/INDEX.HTM	It uses what is called the 'fingerprint' method by exploiting each work's fingerprint, looking at the uniqueness of each individual's linguistic patterns – 'cloze' technique. When students submit their work, it blanks every fifth word and the student must fill in the missing words. It is the number of correct answers that determines the originality of the work and the production of a final probability score.	**PROS**: It can be used to detect plagiarised work where the original source cannot be found. **CONS**: Time consuming because students have to physically sit down and be supervised when they fill in the blank spaces	Approx $580 AUD to purchase software. Plus additional subscription fee.
Turnitin.com is the user portal for Plagiarism.org. http://www.turnitin.com/	Uses the technology called 'document source analysis'. It makes digital fingerprint of any text document submitted. It then compares it against internet sources and against an in-house database. It gives results in a colour coded report and an underlined similarity text report to other sources; also gives the URLs of the sources.	**PROS**: It works on the internet so it covers a huge range of sources. Offers a digital portfolio service. in which students' work is archived. **CONS**: Unfortunately it makes extra work because it detects correctly-cited material as well as plagiarised material.	A free one-month trial is available. Costs are for subscription rather than purchase and vary according to extent of commitment (that is, number of academics, classes and/ or students using it).

All costs given are those at the time of writing (2014) and may have changed.

Name	Features/techniques	Pros/cons	Costs
iThenticate http://www. ithenticate.com	It is developed to detect plagiarism and originality of documents for educational institutions. It is used across the world by scholars, publishers and research institutions. iThenticate is developed by Turnitin.	**PROS**: Uses CrossCheck, a service offered by CrossRef and powered by iThenticate software **CONS**: N/A	N/A
EVE2 – Essay Verification Engine http://www. canexus.com/ eve/index.shtml	It searches internet sites with similarities to the submitted text. After the search, it produces a report underlining text passages possibly plagiarised.	**PROS**: It searches texts through the internet. **CONS**: Time consuming because the lecturer must individually load each work submitted by students.	15 days free download. Cost for purchasing is approx $40 AUD. However, it can be expensive because each user must purchase a separate copy and licence.
Plagiserve http://www. plagiserve.com/	It creates its own database and also uses the internet to check the originality of the student's work against its own created database and the internet. It produces an originality report that is colour-coded, indicating possible plagiarised work. It also provides a link to the original plagiarised source.	**PROS**: Comparison is done against the in-house database and this relevant as it can be discipline specific. This range of the search is complimented by internet search. **CONS**: It can also be time consuming because care should be taken when the material is handed in separately because formatting is lost during the checking process.	Free.
WordCHECK DP http://www. wordcheck systems.com/word check-dp.html	Users search manually for matching documents. WordCheck DP profiles documents by identifying keyword use and the frequency patterns of the word used. It uses an internally-generated database and produces reports with keyword profiles and a word frequency list.	**PROS**: It is a similar system to Copycatch. **CONS**: It only uses internally generated database. It is also time-consuming and tedious as a result of the manual matching.	Profiler Basic $185 ($115 academic price) Profiler Pro $570 ($345 academic price). Users can add "profile capacity" as they go: 2,000 profiles – $380; 5,000 profiles – $760;10,000 profiles – $1,540 (All dollars approximate AUD.)

Name	Features/techniques	Pros/cons	Costs
WordCHECK RA http://www. wordcheck systems.com/word check-ra.html	It is targeted at academic research rather than student assignments. Works on the same principles as the DP version.	**PROS**: As for the DP version. **CONS**: As for the DP version.	RA Individual Desktop $380 ($185 academic price) RA Department Desktop $1,925 ($1,347 academic price) plus profile expansion (All dollars approximate AUD.)
Measure of Software Similarity – an internal system (**Moss**) http://www. cs.berkeley.edu /~aikenn/moss/ html	Moss developed at University California (UC) Berkeley specifically for computer programming fields.	**PROS**: It is designed especially for computer programming code rather than text. **CONS**: Limited in scope.	Free but restricted to instructors and staff of computer programming courses. A request must be sent to use.
SIM http://www.cs.vu. nl /~dick/sim.html and http://www. cs.vu.nl /pub/dick/s imilarity_tester/	A computer code plagiarism detector developed at the Vrije Universiteit, Amsterdam. SIM tests lexical similarity in a number of computer languages including Java, Pascal, Lisp, and Miranda.	**PROS**: As for Moss **CONS**: As for Moss	Free through the website of the Vrije Universiteit, Amsterdam, where the software was developed.
JPlag http://wwwipd.ira. uk a.de:2222/	JPlag searches for similarities among multiple sets of source code files. It also detects plagiarism in computer programming. But it can also be used to support plain text.	**PROS**: Can be used and it can support both programming-type work as well as ordinary text. **CONS**: Limited, and not very satisfactory results with ordinary text.	Free, but an account must be applied for on the website.
Google http://www.google. com	It is primarily a search engine and not a plagiarism detector. However, Google is able to detect phrases and can rapidly identify source material from the internet	**PROS**: Quick and free. Google can access and use data from pdf files, which many search engines cannot. **CONS**: Time consuming. It is unsystematic, and involves manual entry.	Free.

Conclusion

In this chapter, we looked at plagiarism and the many possible reasons for it. The types of plagiarism and the consequences of plagiarism were outlined. The chapter also indicated the extent to which the research and academic community are likely to shun authors who are found to have plagiarised. Possible ways of avoiding plagiarism were also presented as well as flow charts for easy reference when you are not sure whether to cite or not. The chapter also covered the importance of citing, explained what it is, and suggested why it is necessary. We identified the different types of citing and highlighted how paraphrasing is an important skill to acquire. In order to assist students with paraphrasing as one of the skills in avoiding plagiarism, this chapter suggested different verbs that can be helpful when students paraphrase.

In this chapter we also covered the usage of quotations and also how to reference them. This chapter also went to the extent of indicating to you how and where to use quotation marks which is an important consideration in avoiding plagiarism especially when using direct quotes from other authors. The importance of the names or absence thereof (in terms of anonymity or unknown) of the author, precise year, precise quotation and pagination were highlighted. The importance of a reference list was discussed, as well as the difference between a reference list and bibliography and where they are used was highlighted. The chapter concluded by outlining different computer software used to detect whether work submitted is plagiarised, but most importantly, to suggest its use as a tool so that we can check the level of plagiarism in our own work before we submit it.

Matome, in the opening case study, should now be able to take advantage of the information before handing in his work. He will be able to cite the sources he used and those without authors and dates. He will be able to paraphrase sentences to craft his own arguments in his own voice, in relation to the literature that he has read. Matome will also be able to use the available computer software before he submits his work.

In conclusion, this chapter highlighted one important fact about plagiarism. When writing your assignment, research proposal, dissertation, or thesis, you are using other people's work to either enhance your argument or to disprove a point, so you both honour their work and enhance your own; but you must always indicate who said it, when was it said, and where you got that information.

Closing activities

Self-reflection questions

1 If you were Matome and you read this chapter, where would you start when you begin working on your assignment?
2 Have you ever submitted work that contains sections that are not yours and you did not cite the original source? How does this chapter affect your thinking about plagiarism now and what do you intend to change in your thinking from now on?

Practical applications

3 How would you quote the following extract while making information prominent by using parentheses?

Attention deficit-hyperactivity disorder (ADHD) is one of the most commonly diagnosed chronic childhood disorders. It is a neurocognitive behavioural developmental disorder that is characterised by a persistent pattern of inattention or hyperactivity-impulsivity.
(**Source:** Schellack, N. & Meyer, H. 2012. The management of attention deficit hyperactivity disorder in children. *South African Pharmaceutical Journal,* 79(10):12–20.)

4 Use the verbs on page 521 to quote the following extract while making information prominent by using parentheses?

Attention deficit-hyperactivity disorder (ADHD) is one of the most commonly diagnosed chronic childhood disorders. It is a neurocognitive behavioural developmental disorder that is characterised by a persistent pattern of inattention or hyperactivity-impulsivity.
(**Source:** Schellack, N. & Meyer, H. 2012. The management of attention deficit hyperactivity disorder in children. *South African Pharmaceutical Journal,* 79(10):12–20.)

5 How would you use the Latin term [sic] when quoting a text below:

Mudau contends that the of all the cultures in South Africa, VhaVenda culture is the most respecting culture.
(**Source:** Mudau A.V. 2014. VhaVenda culture. *Journal of Indigenous Studies,* 13(4):67–78.)

6 How would you extract a direct quotation from the following text in order to avoid plagiarism:
  a For less than 30 words?
  b For 30 words and more?

Human beings do not have any genes determining whether they are democrats or autocrats, therefore democratic or authoritarian values and behaviours must be learned. Formal education is inherently political as it involves values in relation to fundamental goals and purposes such as 'what kind of individual and society are we trying to shape?'
(**Source:** Harber, C. & Mncube, V. 2014. *Teachers and democracy.* Hatfield: Juta. (p. 263)

7 You want to use the following text, however, there are phrases and (in your opinion) errors that you would like to correct; you would also like to omit certain parts of the text, but add clarification. How would you do this?

Human beings do not have any genes determining whether they are democrats or autocrats, therefore democratic or authoritarian values and behaviours must be learned. Formal education is inherently political as it involves values in relation to fundamental goals and purposes such as 'what kind of individual and society are we trying to shape?'
(**Source:** Harber, C. & Mncube, V. 2014. *Teachers and democracy.* Hatfield: Juta. (p. 263)

Analysis and consolidation

8 You have an assignment on the topic of your interest. Draw a mind map or flow chart (as in Figures 28.1 and 28.2) on what information you will cite, which information regarding your topic you will not cite, and why?

9 Suggest one important practice in order not to become a victim of the pitfalls of plagiarism.

10 What do you think will happen to Matome in the future when he is a successful academic and it is then found that he has plagiarised his work?

Bibliography

American Psychological Association. 2005. *Concise rules of APA style*. Washington: APA.

Academic Learning Support. 2007. *Harvard (author-date) referencing guide*. Central Queensland University, Rockhampton, Queensland: Division of Teaching & Learning Services.

Birmingham University. n.d. *APA Referencing Guide for BSc (Hons) Psychology*. Birmingham: Birmingham University.

Bowdoin College. n.d. The common types of plagiarism. http://www.bowdoin.edu/studentaffairs/academic-honesty/common-types.shtml

Central Queensland University. 2013. *Abridged Harvard Referencing Guide*. CQUniversity, Australia: Academic Learning Unit.

Centre for the Study of Higher Education (CSHE). n.d. Overview of plagiarism detection software. http://www.cshe.unimelb.edu.au/assessinglearning/03/plagsoftsumm1.html.

Durham College & UOIT. 2011. *APA Citation Style. Guide to Bibliographic Citation*. Durham College & UOIT: The Library.

Harber, C. & Mncube, V. 2014. *Teachers and democracy*. Hatfield: Juta.

Harris, R. 2001. *The plagiarism handbook*. Los Angeles: Pyrczak Publishing.

Liamputtong, P. 2010. Cross-cultural research and qualitative inquiry. *Turkish Online Journal of Qualitative Inquiry*, 1(1):16–29.

iThenticate. n.d. Six consequences of plagiarism. http://www.ithenticate.com/resources/6-consequences-of-plagiarism.

Park. C. 2003. In Other (People's) Words: Plagiarism by university students – literature and lessons. *Assessment & Evaluation in Higher Education*, (28)5:471–488.

Patel, H. 2013. *Harvard Referencing* (2nd ed.). Manchester: Manchester Metropolitan University.

Schellack, N. & Meyer, H. 2012. The management of attention deficit hyperactivity disorder in children. *South African Pharmaceutical Journal*, 79(10):12–20.

University of Alberta. n.d. Preventing plagiarism. University of Alberta Libraries. http://www.library.ualberta.ca/guides/plagiarism/preventing/.

Indiana University. n.d. Plagiarism: What It Is and How to Recognize and Avoid It. Indiana University. http://www.indiana.edu/~wts/pamphlets/plagiarism.shtml#strategies.

University of Manchester. n.d. *JRUL: Essential Guide to the Harvard System of Referencing*. University of Manchester: The John Rylands University Library.

WriteCheck. 2014. Types of plagiarism. http://www.plagiarism.org/plagiarism-101/types-of-plagiarism/.

Additional sources

Gilmore, B. 2009. *Plagiarism: A How-Not-To Guide for Students*. Portsmouth, NH: Heinemann.

Latto, J. & Latto, R. 2009. *Study Skills for Psychology Students*. Maidenhead: Open University Press.

Neville, C. 2010. *The Complete Guide to Referencing and Avoiding Plagiarism*. Maidenhead: Open University Press/ McGraw-Hill – e-book.

Pennycook, A. 1996. Borrowing others' words: Text, ownership, memory and plagiarism. *Tesol Quarterly*, 30(2):201–230.

Weyers, J.D.B. 2013. *How to Cite, Reference and Avoid Plagiarism at University*. New York: Pearson.

University of Portsmouth. 2007. Bibliographic references Harvard format APA style. University of Portsmouth, University Library website: http://www.referencing.port.ac.uk.

CHAPTER 29

Connie Zulu

Essentials of academic writing

KEY CONCEPTS

Academic style is formal, scholarly, scientific writing, usually characterised by objectivity and an impersonal style.

Argument is a group of statements that are intended to affirm the truth or acceptability of a claim; also includes statements made to persuade or convince others of one's point of view.

Coherence is the relationships which link the meanings of sentences in a text; i.e. when sentences in a paragraph are related to one another and to the main idea.

Cohesion is the grammatical and/or lexical relationships between the different elements of a text; it is the meaningful connection of words and sentences to achieve smooth flow in the text.

Literary style is less formal, more creative way of writing, characterised by expressive language, generally used in short stories and novels.

LEARNING OUTCOMES

By the end of this chapter, you should be able to:

▶ Distinguish between formal and informal writing.

▶ Construct well-structured, coherent and cohesive paragraphs.

▶ Write an argumentative text using formal academic style.

▶ Revise, proofread and edit your work.

▶ Use concord, tense and the apostrophe appropriately.

Case study: What is wrong with Fikile's style?

Fikile is an African student doing her Master's dissertation at a university in South Africa. She has reasonably good spoken English language skills. However, she is puzzled by the comments she gets on her writing every time she receives feedback on her chapters. Not only does her supervisor complain about her grammar and choice of vocabulary, but she also makes comments about her writing style. Fikile wonders why her style of writing, which works well in her professional and other writing contexts, is no longer acceptable. She is quite frustrated by the numerous drafts she has to hand in, as she is not accustomed to writing and rewriting. Besides, as far as she is concerned, her language is very good, even quite impressive. She therefore believes her supervisor is unreasonable. Fikile's writing style shifts between informal, conversational and literary. Sometimes she uses a series of big words and long, run-on sentences. Her writing is extremely complex. She loves using metaphors and analogies that are often unsuitable. Her proofreading and editing skills are limited and she often submits work that is riddled with grammatical and technical problems.

What do you think Fikile's real problem is?

Introduction

The case study featuring Fikile – a postgraduate student – highlights the problems experienced by many students who are not familiar with academic writing discourse conventions. More importantly, it draws attention to the fact that everyday, conversational English and a literary writing style are not suitable in academic writing contexts. What is academic writing style? What distinguishes it from everyday, conversational English? Why is it necessary to write in an academic style? This chapter will provide you with explanations and practical examples of what academic writing is, and what it is not.

Academic writing, or scholarly writing, is a requirement for most university students in their various disciplines. As a research student you will conduct research, which includes: writing a literature review, citing and referencing sources, presenting and reporting research findings in the form of a project, dissertation, thesis or journal article. In order to do this successfully, you need to be familiar with the appropriate academic language, vocabulary, and style. This chapter will introduce you to academic writing and help you distinguish between formal and informal writing. It will also demonstrate the conventions of academic writing, such as constructing logically organised, coherent and cohesive paragraphs, as well as using grammar correctly, and avoiding plagiarism.

We will begin the chapter by looking at the distinction between formal academic style and informal (conversational/literary) style.

29.1 Writing styles

There are many different writing styles, but we are concerned here with describing and understanding what distinguishes academic writing in particular.

29.1.1 Formal versus informal style

You may have experienced some difficulty as a writer when faced with the requirement to change your style of writing from the one you normally use at work or when you write to friends and colleagues, to the style required in your assignments, projects, dissertations and theses. Changing from an informal to a formal style of writing is not an easy skill to master. Indeed, McMillan and Schumacher (1993:566) maintain that "perhaps the most difficult skill in writing research reports is making a transition from a literary style of writing to scientific and scholarly research writing, a style that reflects precise thinking. Effective writing of research requires an objective, clear, concise style of communicating an unambiguous description."

Let's take a look now at what we mean by informal (*conversational/literary*) style and formal (*scientific, scholarly*) writing. The style of writing most commonly used in literature is the literary style. This is the style we use when we write short stories, poems and novels. It is generally characterised by creative and expressive language. Creative and expressive language uses a lot of adjectives (describing/qualifying words), vivid expressions, metaphors and sometimes informal styles of communication to convey ideas, thoughts or feelings. Formal **academic style** is characterised by precision, and avoidance of excessive qualifiers, redundancy, ambiguity and colloquialisms.

Academic, scientific or scholarly writing is different and distinct from the literary style in its choice of formal language usage and avoidance of creative or expressive language. The formal academic style is normally used in writing academic textbooks, research reports and academic essays. Scientific or scholarly writing is the style university students are encouraged to use.

"Academic writing relies on logical argument, on the development and interconnection of ideas and on internal consistency and coherence. It depends on well-organised paragraphs with topic sentences, which are appropriately interconnected with each other." (Punch, 2006:72)

Let's first consider two examples of literary writing style: Example A and B. These examples contain creative and expressive language consisting of figurative language and many adjectives/ qualifying words.

A

I was busy reading an interesting paper in the early hours one morning a few years ago, when I heard a <u>howling</u> sound outside like that of a whirlwind. It seemed as if the wind was about to blow the roof off my house. As I was still wondering what that could be, there was a sudden <u>intensity</u> in the howling wind accompanied by a <u>strange shaking</u> of the room and <u>rattling</u> of the bed on which I was sitting. Seconds later, in the midst of the howling wind and shaking room, something like the <u>pattering</u> feet of a rat, moved across the ceiling from one end of the room to the other and fell to the ground outside with a <u>clearly audible</u> thud. Simultaneously with the thud, the howling and shaking suddenly stopped and there was complete silence – almost as if nothing had happened. All of this lasted less than a minute. To this day, I have no idea what it is that happened that morning. There were no reports of an earth tremor that day – so this will always be a mystery!

B

Taking a leisurely walk in a <u>crowded</u> city can be a <u>harrowing</u> experience. One afternoon, I decided to go shopping in downtown Johannesburg. As I was happily walking down one crowded street, I had an <u>unshakeable</u> feeling that I was being followed. I continued walking and tried to ignore the feeling, but it became so strong that I had to stop, turn around and look behind me. There indeed were four <u>guilty-looking</u> young men who were <u>unmistakeably</u> intent on 'repossessing' my crocodile handbag. As I deliberately looked each one of them in the eye, they looked away, and I heard one whispering to another, "*hhayi sonny, nguw'ofanele wenz'ikhuthuza*". It was then that I realised without a <u>shadow of doubt</u> that if I hadn't responded to that <u>nagging</u> feeling, I would have been in trouble that afternoon.

(Episodes are based on real-life experience of author)

As we said earlier, scientific or scholarly writing is different. It is distinct from the literary style that is used in examples A and B. Scholarly writing uses formal language and avoids expressive language and other forms of informal language, such as slang, jargon and clichés.

Let's now consider example C, which is a passage from a journal article. It is written in formal academic style.

C

The findings from this study of women academic HoDs' experiences of leadership and management of an academic department highlight the similarity of the ways in which these concepts are constructed by women of different countries and vast geographic distances. The findings illuminate the importance of the fact that academic leadership is supported by good verbal, listening, written, and collaborative skills, as well as decisiveness and the ability to empower others. These skills are considered critical to the work of the HoD.

(Excerpt from Zulu, 2011:848)

Stop and reflect

1 Reflect on examples A, B and C for a moment. Can you tell what exactly distinguishes example C from A and B?
2 Would you ever follow example A in writing your assignments and reports? Explain why or why not.

The following section demonstrates the style of writing we should avoid in formal academic writing. In order to write good paragraphs in good academic style, we should avoid long-winded sentences and *incomplete statements*.

29.1.2 Long-winded, rambling or run-on sentences

Take a look at the following sentences which are taken from students' writing:
A The case study was chosen over and above all the other research techniques (notwithstanding its shortfalls) because it is typically a strategy for doing research which involves an empirical enquiry that investigates a particular contemporary phenomenon within its real-life context using multiple sources of evidence. (46 words).
B Nevertheless, these barriers do not apply in the same way in all circumstances, e.g. they do not apply similarly to all women or at all levels of struggle for promotional posts for women in any education system in the world. (39 words)

Both sentences are longer than 30 words, and it is advisable in such cases to break the sentence up into two or more sentences. Try doing this now.

29.1.3 Incomplete statements

The statements in the following list have not completed the thought of the writer and are incomplete statements. Try your hand at completing them with appropriate words.
1 If only the business executive could slow down …
2 Although the preparation for the examination took many weeks …
3 As you know that learners are sometimes late to school …
4 Since the respondents were too many …

We can write good paragraphs (in formal academic style) by avoiding the following pitfalls.

To be avoided

Clichés – catchphrases we have read over and over again, that are now tired and overworked, such as: part and parcel; leave no stone unturned; to be honest, etc.

Repetition – using the same word or phrase many times in a single short paragraph

Contractions – such as don't, haven't, it's, you're

Abbreviations – such as Sat. for Saturday; awol for absent without leave, dept. for department

(continued)

To be avoided *(continued)*

Colloquialisms – informal words and phrases such as you use in the language of everyday conversation and familiar writing:

▶ Are you crazy?

▶ That guy is really touchy about his driving.

▶ It's crazy out here.

▶ I met some guys in the library.

▶ Can I crash at your possie tonight?

Slang – a type of popular language, considered to be below the level of standard educated speech, in which new words are created, or current words are used in a special way. Slang differs from colloquial language in that slang expressions are not as widely understood or used as are colloquial expressions. Slang tends to be 'in' for a few years then lost, as some new slang replaces the old, or comes into fashion.

Examples: 'hot and happening'; 'it's cool', 'I'm cool', 'pad' (house) 'dude' (person), 'split', 'scram' (go, leave), 'this is hip', 'I dig this song', 'it's hectic', 'he's up and coming', 'that's awesome'.

Ambiguity – double meaning, usually caused by using pronouns with no clear referents. In other words, when it is not clear what the pronouns refer to, ambiguity occurs.

Examples of referents which cause ambiguity: this, these, that, which, their, they.

Tautology and redundancy – tautology is saying the same thing twice over in different words. It is the repetition of the same idea or meaning in a phrase or sentence, which results in unnecessary or redundant words. Redundancy refers to unnecessary or superfluous words which can be omitted without loss of meaning.

Examples: In my opinion, I think the unemployment problem can be solved. (one of the italicised phrases is redundant – unnecessary).

A free gift (this is a tautology as a gift is always free)

Circumlocution and verbosity and long-winded sentences – when sentences go on in an unfocused way and contain unnecessary words, the writer is guilty of circumlocution or verbosity.

Example: At the present time, she has her abode in a rural environment.

Simple language: Now she lives in a rural area.

Pretentious or euphemistic language – using words that are long, showy (bombastic words) or evasive, such as using mild and indirect words to avoid saying something directly and explicitly. That is, words that 'attempt to impress'.

Example: To perpetuate our endeavour of providing funds for our elderly citizens as we do at the present moment, we will face the exigency of enhanced contributions from all our citizens.

Revised: Citizens cannot continue to fund social grants for the elderly unless taxes are raised.

Stop and reflect

Take a moment to reflect on what you have read about what to avoid in good academic writing by going through the following activities:

1 *At this point in time; repeat that word again; reverse back; a new innovation; to return again.*
   Can you explain the tautology in each of the above phrases, and also remove the redundant word?

2 *In developing the questionnaire, the researcher was, however, mindful of a few difficulties …*
   Restate and remove unnecessary words.

3 *Female teachers should prove people wrong by doing their duty.*
   To whom does '*their*' refer? Whose duty? The female teachers' duty, or the people's duty? How can this ambiguity be removed?

4 *The new teacher will be observing the experienced teacher while inducting her/him.*
   To whom does '*her/him*' refer? Who will be inducting whom? What makes this statement ambiguous? Can you rephrase this statement so that the meaning is not in doubt?

5 Here's another statement from a student's project: *This behaviour distracts the attention of other students and may laugh or join in and further disrupt teaching and learning process.*
   To whom does the phrase, '*may laugh or join in and further disrupt teaching and learning process*', refer? Try to rewrite this statement so that the meaning is clear.

We have now reflected on how we can write good paragraphs using appropriate academic style and avoiding several pitfalls. Let's now take a look at how a paragraph is structured.

29.2 Sentence and paragraph structure

A sentence is a statement usually of one complete idea, or proposition. A paragraph is made up of several sentences (although it can be just one sentence) that are linked by the idea or proposition they are supporting, describing, or qualifying. Punch (2006) maintains that academic writing depends on well-organised paragraphs consisting of topic sentences and supporting details, which are appropriately linked to one another to achieve consistency and coherence within the paragraph, and throughout the text.

In this section we shall look at sentence and paragraph structure which are the building blocks of an argument that is logical, consistent and coherent.

Writing well-structured paragraphs begins with the sentence. More sentences are added to the first sentence to build a paragraph, and more paragraphs are added to the first paragraph to build an argument until it fully developed, worked out, and concluded.

29.2.1 How is a sentence constructed?

The basic building blocks of a simple sentence are the subject, verb and object. However, in academic writing we do not write a sustained argument using a series of short simple sentences only. We often vary our sentence length and sentence type depending on the nature of the writing task.

29.2.2 What is a paragraph?

A paragraph consists of a number of sentences which revolve around one main idea expressed in a topic sentence. In other words, the subject or key point of the paragraph or the thesis statement is expressed in a sentence called the topic sentence. Sometimes, the main idea is not explicitly stated in a particular sentence, but may be inferred from the content of the paragraph. However, as a student writer, it is advisable to express the main point in the opening sentence, so that the reader can immediately understand what the paragraph is about. In a logically organised paragraph, the main idea is developed by means of a number of sentences which relate to it. In other words, the supporting details expand or elaborate on the main idea by way of exemplification, illustration, additional information, restatement, cause and effect, explanation, facts, comparison, contrast, and so on. These examples, additional information, explanations, restatements, and so, on are introduced by means of specific words, which perform a specific function and make it easy for the reader to understand the direction the argument is taking. It is therefore important for a writer to understand and use these words appropriately to convey intended meaning. These words are listed in Table 29.1 later.

Constructing an argument

Sentences and paragraphs are the basic building blocks of an argument. A simple sentence consists of a subject, verb and object. A paragraph consists of a number of sentences which revolve around one main idea expressed in a topic sentence. Sentences and paragraphs must be logically unified. Each sentence in a paragraph should relate logically to the next as well as follow each other in a meaningful sequence. Each paragraph should relate meaningfully to the rest of the paragraphs in a piece of writing.

The main point then is that all ideas in a paragraph should be logically related to one another. Each sentence should have logically connected ideas, and each paragraph should be controlled and pulled together by one identifiable idea which is developed in the paragraph by means of examples, explanations, illustrations, etc.

In section 29.2 we considered the structure of the sentence and the paragraph. We learned that sentences must be logically connected to one another to produce a meaningful paragraph which is controlled by one main idea. The next section considers how ideas in good paragraphs are not only coherent, but are also linked by means of specific words that make the text flow smoothly. When the text flows smoothly, it is cohesive.

29.3 Coherence and cohesion

Writing is unified through logical organisation of ideas and relevant linking words and statements. We say a paragraph is *coherent* when all the information in the paragraph relates to the main idea.

A piece of writing or text is coherent when ideas and sentences are organised in such a way that it is easy for the reader to move through the text without any interruption in the flow of thought. In other words, if sentences, ideas and concepts in a text are logically related, reading flows smoothly. This smooth flow or **coherence** should be evident at sentence level, paragraph level and section level. In other words, starting from the sentence, words should be arranged in a way that makes sense. Sentences should also be organised in meaningful relationship to one another. Paragraphs should follow each other in logical sequence. Whole sections must be arranged in meaningful relationship to one another, and be logically organised.

A piece of writing or text is *cohesive* when words in a sentence and sentences in a paragraph are linked together meaningfully by means of words which act as 'glue' to bind the words and sentences together into a meaningful whole. There are different types of words which act as 'glue', or cohesive devices. Pronouns are one such type of cohesive device which binds text together by substituting a noun with a pronoun.

The following sentence is an example of cohesion:

The participants were selected from a primary school. *They* were all Grade 3 female learners.

The pronoun, 'they' in the second sentence is related to the noun 'participants' in the first sentence. The pronoun acts as a cohesive device as it binds the second sentence to the first in a manner that indicates a relationship between the two sentences.

Other pronoun connectors are: he, she, and it; this, these and those.

In addition to pronoun connectors, there are other cohesive devices used to achieve text unity and flow, such as linking words and phrases, alternatively referred to as logical connectors or transition markers.

Table 29.1 gives a useful list of linking words and phrases which can help you improve your writing of academic texts. Try to make effective use of these examples in your writing tasks.

TABLE 29.1: Linking words and phrases

Function	Transitional/linking words and phrases
To add (information to what has already been said. Additive words may imply that new information is as important and significant as the preceding information)	In addition to; furthermore; moreover; and; again; equally important; similarly; also; further; likewise; too; at the same time; besides; as well as
To 'prove'	Because; for; since; then; for the same reason
To compare and contrast (used to introduce the other side of the story – to present alternative or contrasting information)	Yet; while; whereas; in contrast; however; on one hand … on the other hand; conversely; on the contrary; by comparison
To show exception	Yet; still; nevertheless; in spite of; despite; of course
To indicate time	Immediately; thereafter; soon; finally; then
To repeat (these words introduce a re-statement of an idea or concept. The writer may repeat something in different words in order to make the concept clearer, or to emphasise its importance.)	In brief; as I/you/we have noted; to reiterate; again; in other words; to repeat; that is
To emphasise (these words are used by a writer to highlight and underline important points)	Obviously; definitely; extremely; in fact; indeed; in any case; positively; naturally; surprisingly; undeniably; unquestionably; without reservation; more importantly; most importantly; above all
To give an example	For instance, for example; in another case; take the case of; to demonstrate; to illustrate; as an example
To summarise or conclude (to introduce a repetition of the data or information in a condensed or summarised form)	In brief; on the whole; summing up; in summary; to summarise; to sum up; in short; to conclude; in conclusion; as I have shown; hence; therefore; as a result; consequently
To show cause-and-effect relationships (used to introduce and link ideas of causality and consequence – to introduce the reasons or causes for something, or to list the results or effects)	Because; since; therefore; as a result; consequently; hence; thus; because of ; due to; as a result of

(continued)

(continued)

Function	Transitional/linking words and phrases
To show an adversarial or contrary position	Although; even though; despite the fact that; notwithstanding the fact that; nevertheless; in spite of
To clarify (to expand or enlarge upon the preceding ideas in the text by giving specific instances, these words are usually followed by examples, illustrations, or concrete instances of the ideas)	In other words; that is; as; for example; for instance; in fact; specifically; to illustrate such as;
To intensify	On the contrary; as a matter of fact; in fact
Sequencers (order words, these words are used to mark out a chronology of events, or to list data in a specific sequence[or to indicate stages in a process or procedure)	Afterwards, now, at the same time, before, first(ly) ...; second(ly)...; last(ly); finally; later; meanwhile; next; subsequently; then; ultimately; until; while;

(**Source:** Adapted from: Henning et al., 2005:75; Swales & Feak, 1994:22)

Making it flow

Take a look at the following passages from Swales and Freak (1994: 21). One of these passages exemplifies coherence, and the other, cohesion. Can you tell which of the two passages flows more smoothly and reads better than the other?

   (All the words used to achieve text unity and logical organisation in the text which flows smoothly have been highlighted (underlined or italicised). Note how these highlighted words function to make the text cohesive.)

Example 1

Lasers have found widespread application in medicine. Lasers play an important role in the treatment of eye disease and the prevention of blindness. The eye is ideally suited for laser surgery. Most of the eye tissue is transparent. The frequency and focus of the laser beam can be adjusted according to the absorption of the tissue. The beam 'cuts' inside the eye with minimal damage to the surrounding tissue – even the tissue between the laser and the incision. Lasers are effective in treating some causes of blindness. Other treatments are not. The interaction between laser light and eye tissue is not fully understood. (Swales & Feak, 1994:21)

Example 2

Lasers have found widespread application in medicine. <u>For example</u>, *they* play an important role in the treatment of eye disease and the prevention of blindness. The eye is ideally suited for laser surgery <u>because</u> most of the eye tissue is transparent. <u>Because of</u> *this* transparency, the frequency and focus of the laser beam can be adjusted according to the absorption of the tissue <u>so that</u> the beam 'cuts' inside the eye with minimal damage to the surrounding tissue – even the tissue between the laser and the incision. Lasers are <u>also</u> more effective than other methods in treating some causes of blindness. <u>However</u>, the interaction between laser light and eye tissue is not fully understood.

(Excerpts from Swales & Feak, 1994:21, adapted for use in Example 2.)

Example 1 showed you how a text can be coherent without being cohesive, and Example 2 showed you how a text can read smoothly with the addition of linking words and phrases (underlined) and pronoun connectors (*italicised*).

We can also achieve cohesion by using sequencers in the text. Sequencers are words such as: firstly, secondly, thirdly, etc., or first, second, third, finally. The function of these words is to indicate the logical progression of events or a sequence of actions, or stages in a process or procedure, essential in academic writing. (Refer to Table 29.1.)

Having looked at coherence and cohesion and how this is achieved in a text, we now move to the concepts of 'argument' and 'voice'. Coherence and cohesion are important tools in the construction of a clear and logical argument.

29.4 Argument and voice

An **argument** in the context of academic writing is not a quarrel or disagreement between two people, but it is the term we generally use to refer to the kind of academic writing at university in which we attempt to convince others of our standpoint about a particular issue. We might make a claim or state a position and then use a series of statements, examples and illustrations to convince the reader of the truth or acceptability of (our) claims. In other words, we use evidence, or supporting material to validate our claims. This is why it is useful to understand how to use logical connectors to indicate the direction an argument is taking.

Turning now to 'voice': in academic writing, you should strive to express your 'academic voice', that is, your viewpoint, feelings, opinions, values and choices should be apparent in your argument and not be drowned by the voices of other writers. In other words, be visible in your writing and do not let other writers speak for you. Use the views of other writers to substantiate your point. Avoid stringing together quotations from various authors without clearly indicating the relevance and importance of the ideas. What you must do is comment upon the ideas and interpret them and demonstrate the relevance and significance of the ideas to your argument.

Presenting a clear and logically organised argument involves the use of appropriate grammatical structures. The next section deals with specific grammar points that most students find troublesome.

29.5 Grammar in writing

In academic writing mastery of grammar is important. This section presents aspects of grammar that many students find troublesome, such as concord, tense, use of the apostrophe, spelling and punctuation. Examples are given to illustrate how these grammatical aspects function in academic writing.

29.5.1 Concord (subject and verb agreement)

The basic rule of concord is that if a subject is singular, the verb is also singular. If the subject is plural, the verb is also plural. Use a plural verb in subjects joined by *and*. Always make the verb agree with the subject closest to it if subjects are joined by *or*, *either – or*; *neither – nor*.

We use singular verbs with pronouns such as each, everyone, every one, everybody, anyone, anybody, someone, and somebody.

Making it agree

Singular subject, singular verb

Example   The **student writes** a paper. (subject – student; verb – writes)

He writes a report. (subject – he, verb – writes)

She manages a team. (subject – she, verb – manages)

Malaza (2014:5) **concurs** that …(subject – Malaza, verb – concurs)

Plural subject, plural verb

Example   The **students** write a paper. (subject – students, verb – write)

They write a report. (subject – they, verb – write)

We manage a team. (subject – we, verb – manage)

Malaza, Sibanda and Ndlovu (2015:1) **argue** that … (subject – Malaza, Sibanda and Ndlovu, verb – argue)

Subjects joined by *and* take a plural verb.

Example   The **student** *and* **her supervisor** write the article together.(subjects – student, her supervisor; verb – write)

Subjects joined by *or, either – or*; *neither – nor*: the verb agrees with the subject nearest to it.

Examples   The student or the **lecturer collects** the papers.

Either the lecturer or the **students collect** the papers

Neither the students nor the **lecturer collects** the papers

Each, everyone, every one, everybody, anyone, anybody, someone, and *somebody* are singular and require singular verbs.

Examples   *Each* respondent completes the questionnaire

Everyone is present

Every one (meaning each one) is welcome

29.5.1.1 Concord in citations

Dealing with concord in citations can be tricky, but here are some examples and rules to help you.

Miller and Goodnow (1995) state … (plural subject = plural verb). In this case, the subject consists of two authors, therefore the introducing verb should be plural, i.e state.

The same rule applies in the case of multiple authors:

Example: Ndlovu, Miller, Goodnow and Falika (2014:10) challenge the notion …

Or: Ndlovu, et al. (2014:10) challenge the notion… (the verb 'challenge' is plural because the subject 'Ndlovu, et al.' is plural since there is more than one author. This is denoted by the abbreviation et al., which stands for *et alii* – a Latin word meaning 'and others'.

29.5.1.2 Introducing verbs and phrases

Some examples of verbs and phrases commonly used by writers to introduce the direct words of an author, or information cited from other writers, are the following:

Assert:	Scott (2005:34) asserts that …
Suggest:	Mbigi (2005:219) suggests the following practice …
Regard:	Potgieter (2003:220) regards organisational management as …
Explain:	Miller and Goodnow (1995) explain that …
State:	Van der Westhuizen, et al. (2008) state that …
	Punch (2006:33) states that …
Concur:	Thom (1996:6) concurs, saying that …
Argue:	McMillan and Schumacher (2001:10) argue that …
Point out:	Sonjica (2014:10) points out that …

Further verbs that can be used include: mention, emphasise, recommend, note, write, comment, remark, maintain, observe, report, offer, aver, propose, holds, posit, add, advocate, contend, believe, conclude, identify.

And some useful phrases to use:
- According to …
- In the opinion of …
- … is of the opinion that …
- … refers to …

Mix it up – carefully

In your writing, try to vary the introducing verbs and phrases you use. This will make your writing less monotonous. However, be sure to use the appropriate verb or phrase which conveys the writer's intended meaning. For instance, if a writer is making a claim, then use the verb 'claims' or 'argues'.

Make a point of noting verbs and phrases when you read any book or article. Note particularly the context in which they are used. This will help you understand why a particular verb or phrase is used and not another.

Now let's consider another example, in the following passage. The first half contains errors of concord (agreement) and the second half exemplifies concord (agreement).

What went wrong here?

This aspect of grammar is quite problematic for many students who **is** speakers of English as a second language. You might be one of those **student** who find it difficult to master this aspect of grammar. However, as the **saying go, practice make** perfect and if at first you don't succeed, try, try, try again.

Does the above passage **sounds** familiar? Perhaps it **sound** familiar, but if it **don't** sound familiar, then you are not in trouble with this grammar point.

But, there are indeed many of us who **knows** what to say but find it difficult to write it in grammatically acceptable language. There are those who **is** experts in their fields, but not experts in grammar. They might, for instance, speak of **one of the pipe** which has burst **need** to be fixed, or complain of people who **drinks** and drive, or children who **doesn't** listen to their parents. They might comment on how **each of** their children **own** a cellphone, or how the **news are** so negative nowadays. You might have come across people discussing what the **criteria is** for selecting students, or how the mass **media influences** our children's behaviour. Students might be caught saying, "The **analyses reveals** that…" or "The **theses is** complete".

We are likely to cringe inwardly when we read this, but we do get the message all the same.

However, our understanding of subject and verb agreement **gets** a little complicated when more than one subject **is** involved. For instance, Lerato and Nosizwe are friends, but **neither** the students **nor** the lecturer **is** attending the seminar today. However, the lecturer and students **are** on a study trip. **Either** the interviewer or the interviewees **are** absent, and **neither** the interviewees **nor** the interviewer is present. **Each of** the interviewees **is** an experienced professional, but **each** of the interviewers is a novice researcher. **Neither** of us **is** an expert at soccer, but **each one** of us **is** a keen learner. We know, for instance, that **the number** of players in a soccer team is eleven and that **a number** of players **are** training for an upcoming match. **A list** of players **is** drawn up by the coach. **The number** of spectators **is** large, but **a number** of spectators are not wearing the club's colours and most of the **spectators are** rowdy. **One of** the coaches **is** excited during the game as his club is in the lead, but at the end of the game both **coaches are** excited as the **game ends** in a draw. Indeed, **this is** good **news**!

The mass **media are** having a field day reporting sports news. Who knows what **criteria are** used to select the best news items? Perhaps the first **criterion is** the newsworthiness of the item. A popular **mass medium is** radio. It is **one of** the most accessible of the **mass media** available today. I am not certain, however, which of the social **media is** the most popular. Perhaps Twitter, or Facebook **is** currently the favourite. Someone might want to write **a thesis** on the influence of social media on adolescents and then present **an analysis** of the findings.

Stop and reflect

Using basic rules of concord, can you correct the concord errors in the first half of the given passage?

29.5.2 **Tense**

The only correct tense to use in writing the proposal is the *future tense*. Future tense is marked by the verb *will*.

▶ Example: This study *will investigate* the prevalence of smoking among adolescent schoolboys in township schools.

There are two main tenses available for writing the report. The most commonly used is the *past tense*, because you are reporting a research study that has already been completed. The other is the *present perfect tense*.

▶ *Example 1*: This study *investigated* the prevalence of smoking amongst young adolescent boys in township schools. (past tense)
▶ *Example 2*: This study *has investigated* the prevalence of smoking amongst young adolescent boys in township schools. (present perfect tense)

Different tenses may be used throughout the manuscript but there are instances when certain verb tenses should be used, and these instances are:

▶ The literature review, use the past tense or present perfect tense.
▶ Description of procedures that have already taken place, use the past tense.
▶ Reporting the findings of a study, use the past tense.
▶ Discussing the results and presenting conclusions and interpretation, use the present tense.

What is important is to stay with the tense you have chosen and to avoid unnecessary shifts in tense.

29.5.3 **The apostrophe**

We use the apostrophe to indicate possession. This is referred to as the possessive case. The possessive case is generally used with reference to nouns. For example: 'The respondent's email address is required.' The apostrophe before 's' indicates possession. The email address belongs to the respondent. The same statement could be written differently as: 'The email address of the respondent is required.' But to avoid using too many words, the apostrophe is used to replace 'of the', and the word order is changed.

There are many instances where students use the possessive case incorrectly. This section will show you how to use the possessive case correctly.

Let us consider a few examples: Can you give an example of a word/name ending in 's' denoting singular that needs an 's' , s', e.g. boss's car?

▶ Lerato's paper is good. (the paper belongs to Lerato)
  It would be clumsy to say: The paper of Lerato is good.
▶ The learner's behaviour is not acceptable. (the behaviour of one learner)
▶ The learners' behaviour is not acceptable. (the behaviour of a number of learners)
▶ The teacher's strategy of learner discipline is effective. (the strategy of one teacher)
▶ The teachers' strategy of learner discipline is effective. (the strategy of a number of teachers)
▶ In Bongo's view …
▶ In Bongo's (2014:30) view – *not*: In Bongo (2014:30)'s view…

Its or it's?

The one exception to the rule that the apostrophe usually indicates possession is *its*, meaning something belong to it. *It's* is *not* the possessive form in this case, but is a contraction of *it is*. You can learn this by asking yourself:

Do I mean something belonging to it? = its (e.g. Its consequences were felt for a long time.)
Or, do I mean, it is? = it's (e.g. It's a lovely day.)

Stop and reflect

Note that the apostrophe is placed before 's' in singular nouns, but after 's' in plural nouns. Never use an apostrophe with a plural noun when you do not intend to show possession. For example, do not say: Teachers' are not happy with the current salary negotiations. What is wrong with the following sentences?

▶ The principal can initiate an activity where educators whose learner's did well in their respective learning area's are appreciated.

▶ Some of the student's enrolled for this course.

▶ Learner's feedback is duly acknowledged.

29.6 Revising, proofreading and editing

What is revising, proofreading and editing, and why do you need to revise, proofread and edit what you have written? Revising means making 'major changes in content, direction and meaning'. When you revise, you remove all passages that do not contribute necessary information to the point you want your academic paper to make. You cut out some text but may need to expand on some ideas. Ask yourself as you revise whether you have explained every concept clearly and added the information, illustrations and examples to make your academic paper convincing. Revise your paper so that it sounds objective and dispassionate, but still retains your 'voice'. Voice includes your tone and style as well as your values and choices, and your standpoint. It is important to be visible in your writing so that your work does not sound as if someone else, and not you, has written it.

Proofreading involves checking sentences for correctness of spelling, punctuation and capitalisation. Editing involves changing your language and not your ideas. You edit your work by checking if each word or phrase you have used is "necessary, accurate and correct and if it conveys your intended tone and style" (Halasek, et al. 1999:74).

Toolbox Do write

☑ **Write a straightforward introduction** which briefly addresses the issues to be discussed in the body of the paper.

☑ **Discuss one idea in each paragraph**, which is developed by means of supporting details, sentences, examples.

☑ **Use logical connectors** and cohesive devices to integrate information into one logical whole.

☑ **Always use a comma** after a logical connector (e.g. However, it was discovered that …).

☑ **Provide logical links** or 'bridges' between sentences, paragraphs and segments of text.

(continued)

Toolbox Do write *(continued)*

- ☑ **Distinguish,** in long pieces of writing, **topics to be discussed** in the body of the paper by means of sub-headings to enable the reader to follow the argument effortlessly.
- ☑ **However, avoid too many sub-headings** as these tend to fragment the writing and disrupt the flow of ideas.
- ☑ **Ensure that you use academic language** when writing academic texts. In other words, avoid informal and literary language.
- ☑ **Write in continuous prose** (i.e full sentences linked by means of appropriate connecting words which indicate the relationship between ideas expressed).
- ☑ **Vary the introducing verbs** you use.
- ☑ **Vary the length of sentences** and paragraphs.
- ☑ **Use the correct sequence** of tenses.
- ☑ **Use the apostrophe** before 's' in singular nouns and after 's' in plural nouns.
- ☑ **Remember the basic rules of concord**: singular subject – singular verb; plural subject – plural verb.
- ☑ **Use tentative language** such as 'might', 'perhaps', when presenting ideas that can be refuted or challenged by others.

Toolbox Do avoid

- ☑ **Using contractions** such as: he's, they're, you're, don't, can't, isn't, haven't, etc. Instead, write the full word: he is, it is, they are, you are, do not, cannot, is not, have not, etc.
- ☑ **Writing incomplete statements** and long-winded sentences.
- ☑ **Shifting tenses** within a paragraph.
- ☑ **Using definite or absolute language** (such as: definitely, certainly, assuredly) and qualifiers (such as: very, always) or words such as 'utmost', 'best', 'doubtless'
- ☑ **Passing an opinion off as fact.**
- ☑ **Fallacies in argumentation.**
- ☑ **Bulleted points** where ideas can be expressed in continuous prose.
- ☑ **However, there may be ideas** that are more clearly presented as bulleted or numbered points, such as lists like this one.
- ☑ **American spelling** (most common words – behavior, labor, honor, endeavor, etc.; these should be spelt with a 'u' after 'o' in behaviour, labour, honour, etc.).
- ☑ **Overusing the passive voice** (instead use the active voice as far as possible).
- ☑ **Excessive nominalisation** (i.e. turning a verb into a noun).
- ☑ **Excessive passivisation** (i.e. turning an active verb into a passive one) e.g. Active: The researcher collected data…; Passive: Data were collected by the researcher…

Conclusion

This chapter has highlighted the main features of academic writing. Writing generally must communicate what the writer intends the reader to understand. In academic writing, this is achieved through communication that is precise, clear, objective, unambiguous, and accurate.

Unlike informal and literary writing, formal academic writing is usually devoid of expressive and creative language, although it should not be uninteresting and uniform. Logically-ordered sentences and paragraphs, which are unified and are internally consistent, constitute the building blocks of an argument in academic writing – and your argument is what drives the writing and makes it interesting and engaging for the reader.

The argument follows an appropriate structure which consists of a claim, followed by supporting details. The argument is coherent and cohesive and for this purpose various logical connectors and cohesive devices are used to achieve coherence and cohesion in the argument. Flawed, unsound and misleading arguments are avoided by thinking logically through the sense of an argument.

Attention must be paid to style, grammar, punctuation and 'voice', as you will sink even the most thoughtful argument and interesting research findings if you lose your reader through your poor style of writing. Long-winded sentences are to be avoided and so are incomplete statements and unsubstantiated claims.

In academic writing, it is important to revise, edit and proofread your work to remove unnecessary information, improve language and style, and correct errors of spelling, grammar and punctuation.

Closing activities

The following exercises are intended to help you apply what you have learned in this chapter about the essentials of academic writing.

Reflection and consolidation

1 Test your understanding of academic writing and grammar:
   a What are the essential features of formal academic writing?
   b What characterises the style of writing normally used in novels and short stories?
   c Give examples of pitfalls to avoid when writing in a formal academic style.
   d What is coherence and cohesion?
   e How is coherence and cohesion achieved in a text?

2 Remove the tautologies in these sentences:
   a Reverse back into the alley.
   b You ought to return the book back to the owner.
   c There are many jobless graduates who are unemployed in South Africa.

3 The following sentences contain examples of circumlocution and verbosity. Rewrite in simple English:
   a The motorist was arrested by a law enforcement officer because he had partaken of too much liquid refreshment.
   b The listener found himself unable to believe his auditory faculties.

4 Correct the following errors of concord taken from students' writing:
   a … an analyses of the data shows…
   b … data collection methods was well explained.
   c One of the respondent are a school principal.
   d This rule apply in all cases.

5 Using your knowledge of grammar and spelling, correct the errors in the following sentences:

   a The need for self-actualisation means an individual being contend with who thier are, what they have achieved.

   b These barriers some of them are unavoidable.

   c The subordinate they do not respect them. More especially if they are men.

   d The childrens behaviour is poor.

   e They also stole lunch and money from their peers, and sometimes even their teachers.

   f The participants sited unemployment of teachers as a concern in their community.

   g Did you notice that the wording of the questions were all in the first person?

   h Change nevertheless is not easy and can be disturbing a comfortable situation.

   i Several questions will be asked to female principals.

   j Interviews were conducted from ten teachers'.

   k I ensured participants that confidentiality would be maintained.

   l The boundary is not penetrable to a large extend.

   m Learner indiscipline has been sighted as a major contributor to increased stress levels of teachers.

   n The lecturer gave me many advices on which to builded my argument.

   o The parents made their intensions clearly.

Practical application

6 Write a well-researched and well-organised argument on the topic: *Is water conservation important in South Africa?* Ensure that you construct a good, clear, coherent and cohesive argument using an acceptable academic writing style. Your argument should be about a two pages long, cite and list all sources consulted.

Bibliography

Halasek, K., Pauliny, T., Singleton, E., Taylor, R.G., Wallace, K.R. & Wanat, M. 1999. *A guide to first-year writing: The writer's companion* (2nd ed.). Needham Heights: Pearson Custom Publishing (p. 74).

Henning, E., Gravett, S. & Van Rensburg, W. 2005. *Finding your Way in Academic Writing* (2nd ed.). Pretoria: Van Schaik (p. 75).

Hofstee, E. 2006. *Constructing a Good Dissertation: A practical guide to finishing a Masters, MBA or PhD on schedule.* Sandton: EPE (p. 191).

McMillan, J.H. & Schumacher, S. 1993. *Research in Education: A Conceptual Introduction* (3rd ed.). New York: HarperCollins (pp. 566–568).

McMillan, J.H. & Schumacher, S. 2013. *Research in Education: Evidence-based Inquiry.* Harlow: Pearson Education Limited.

Pearsall, J. (Ed). 2001. *The Concise Oxford Dictionary* (10th ed.). Oxford: Oxford: University Press (p. 1705).

Punch, K.F. 2006. *Developing Effective Research Proposals* (2nd ed.). Los Angeles: Sage Publications (p. 72).

Richards, J.C., Platt, J. & Platt, H. 1992. *Longman Dictionary of Language Teaching and Applied Linguistics.* Singapore: Longman (pp. 61–62).

Swales, J.M & Feak, C.B. 1994. *Academic Writing for Graduate Students: A Course for Non-native Speakers of English.* Ann Arbor: The University of Michigan (pp. 21–22).

Sadler, R.K., Hayllar, T.A.S. & Powell, C.J. 1981. *Senior Language.* Brisbane: Chee Leong Press (pp. 54–55).

Van de Poel, K., Carstens, W.A.M. & Linnegar, J. 2012. *Text Editing: A handbook for students and practitioners.* Brussels: UPA (pp. 358–361).

Van den Berg, M.E.S. 2005. *Critical reasoning and the art of argumentation.* Pretoria: University of South Africa (pp. 37 & 126).

Zulu, C.B. 2011. Women leaders' construction of leadership and management of the academic department. *South African Journal of Higher Education,* 25(4):838–852.

CHAPTER 30

Micheal van Wyk

Writing for publication: Sharpening your academic writing skills

KEY CONCEPTS

Abstract is a concise summary of the purpose, research methodology, findings, conclusion and recommendations of a scholarly article.

Academic journal is an academic publication, usually on a specialised subject, which disseminates current research outputs and publishes on issues within the scope of the journal.

Argument is a form of scholarly or intellectual engagement which involves putting forward reasons to influence a reader by providing supporting evidence in the article.

Article is scholarly paper on a specific topic, published in an academic journal.

Manuscript is a complete written version of your proposed article, which can be offered for publication.

Paragraph is a logically sequenced string of grammatically complete sentences. These sentences express one idea or make one point in detail. All the sentences in a paragraph should contribute to this idea or point. They might potentially expand on it, but will not deviate from it.

Proofreading is a specific type of editing to make sure sentences are grammatically correct and punctuated properly, double checking the use of capital letters, spelling and language use, and ensuring that all referencing is formatted correctly.

Referencing is a systematic way of making clear that all words, ideas, quotations, concepts and theories from other sources used in your writing are acknowledged in the text, and in the bibliography of your written work.

Signposting language is not an official grammatical term but rather an academic writing tool to enhance and give a sense of direction in academic writing.

Systematic literature review is the clearly stated purpose, research question, defined research approach (stating inclusion and exclusion criteria), of critically described and appraised articles and other related publications.

LEARNING OUTCOMES

By the end of this chapter, you should be able to:

▶ Decide on the purpose, ideas and questions which reflect the background, issues and solutions to the phenomenon in your research study.

▶ Select and submit a paper to an appropriate academic journal.

▶ Think about your research questions and how to manage the research study.

▶ Decide on the approach, methodology and research design for the article.

▶ Write up the results and discuss the findings of the study.

▶ Formulate your conclusions and make clear recommendations for further research.

Case study: Scenario on writing for publication

James Doctoral is a full-time lecturer at a South African higher education institution. After successfully completing his doctoral thesis, Dr James Doctoral is called to the office of his mentor, Professor Established Researcher, to discuss writing an academic article for publication in the next six months. Dr Doctoral is excited about the prospect, but nervous and unsure about how to respond to this sudden request from his mentor, friend and supervisor. Postgraduate students, novice writers and emerging researchers fear the thought of having to compress three to five years of hard work that went into their dissertation or thesis, into an academic scholarly article. To write 20 to 30 pages, as most journals require, is sometimes a daunting task. Some new researchers believe that it is impossible to do because they do not yet have the knowledge, skills and competence to achieve it by writing between 5,000 to 9,000 words the first time. This is a typical response of postgraduate students' to writing for publication. As way forward, Dr James as a novice researcher, needs to consider the following components of successful academic writing:

▶ the purpose, ideas and questions related to the research study

▶ the research questions and how to manage the study

▶ the approach, methodology and research design for the article

▶ writing up the results and discussing the findings of the study

▶ formulating the conclusions and making clear recommendations for further research.

Some advice for Dr James may be from Kotze (2007), who argues that you should be organised, accurate, clear and concise in reporting your article writing. And you have to keep your eye on the details because, when writing an academic article, these can make or break the article.

Introduction

This chapter provides specific elements which you will find useful in preparing your scholarly **article**. Most postgraduate students baulk at the thought of having to condense their Master's or doctoral research work into an **academic journal** article of 20 to 25 pages. This is a huge challenge for those who do not have the academic writing skills. To sharpen your writing skills, a format, elements and examples are provided which will guide you in your academic writing process. Before you start with your writing project, this chapter provides specific guidelines on how to select and submit your paper to the right academic journal. Specific guidelines for writing an article are provided. The chapter focuses on sections such as the capturing of a concise title, how to summarise the abstract, identifying the keywords, formulating the introduction, critically reflecting a literature review, constructing the research methodology, capturing the main findings, discussing of findings. Finally, the chapter provides specific components to be included and formulates recommendations for practical implications for further research.

Before continuing to the next section on selecting the appropriate journal and submitting to it, try the following activity.

Stop and reflect

After reading and reflecting on the opening case study, it is clear that the introduction deals with the background of the study, the issue for investigating the phenomenon and possible solution to this problem. Reflect, in the following questions, on how you would advise Dr James from your own research experience:

▶ What led you to this particular research area?

▶ Was it a personal interest?

▶ Did your reading of the literature help you to realise that there were unanswered questions?

▶ Can you identify and write (in 200 words) the background, issues and solutions (BIS) of your research for your introduction to the article?

30.1 Selecting and submitting to the right academic journal

It is not enough just to decide that you want to publish an article in a scholarly journal. The question, of which specific journal to submit your work to arises? Most journals require author(s) to adhere to the specific format of the chosen journal. Here are some typical requirements that contributors must address or meet before an article is considered for peer review:

▶ The scope of the journal
▶ The types of article that have been published recently
▶ The research approaches and epistemological traditions the journal follows
▶ The academic style or format for preparing the article
▶ The length of the article
▶ A review of the reference section of the journal or current articles published
▶ Issues relating to plagiarism.

It is advisable to study the requirements and format of your specific chosen journal before you start writing the article. The following case study provides an example of what to look for before submitting to a journal.

Case study: Typical scope of an academic journal – Teaching in Higher Education

Teaching in Higher Education is an international journal concerned primarily with teachers, teaching, and teacher education, in an international context. *Teaching in Higher Education* is a multi-disciplinary journal, committed to no single approach, discipline, methodology or paradigm. It is concerned with teaching and teacher education in general, and devoted to all concerned with teaching. *Teaching in Higher Education* recognises that many disciplines have important contributions to make to teaching and teacher education, and the editors invite contributions from a range of disciplines related to education. In the absence of any dominant paradigm, the journal welcomes varied approaches to empirical research, theoretical and conceptual analyses, and reviews (both qualitative and quantitative syntheses) of high quality.

Teaching in Higher Education aims to enhance theory, research, and practice in teaching and teacher education through the publication of primary research and review papers.

Please see the Guide for Authors for information on article submission. If you require any further information or help, please visit the support pages: http://support.elsevier.com

Stop and reflect

Go to any academic journal website that covers issues within your specific field of research. Study the *Notes to authors or contributors*, of the journal. Look for the following elements in the journal:

▶ Name and scope of the journal

▶ Subject discipline covered in the journal

▶ The specific approaches (qualitative and quantitative design) and epistemology

▶ Theoretical approaches underpinning the articles

▶ Emphasis on original, conceptual or empirical research studies.

These days most journals articles submissions are online, using the Manuscript Central system.

Example of online login and submission to journal

Welcome to the *Teaching in Higher Education* manuscript submission site. To Log in, enter your User ID and Password into the boxes below, then click 'Log In'. If you are unsure about whether or not you have an account, or have forgotten your password, enter your email address into the "Password Help" section below.

If you do not have an account, please click here to create an account. http://mc.manuscriptcentral.com/cthe.

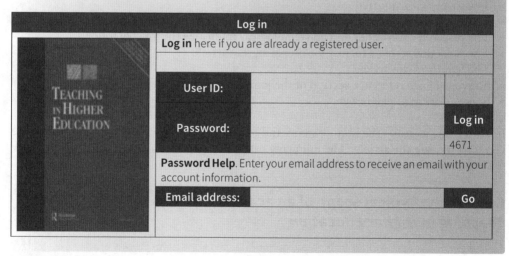

In the case study, the editor(s) of the academic journal make clear what they are looking for when you submit your article. You should also download any recently published article(s) from the website of the selected journal to understand more about what the journal is looking for in a manuscript.

30.1.1 Identifying an appropriate journal for your manuscript

Before deciding on the journal for your manuscript, there are different types to know about. It is important to differentiate between scholarly and non-scholarly journal articles.

▶ *Scholarly manuscripts* include academic or scientific manuscripts such as peer reviewed conference proceedings, monographs, peer reviewed articles. These manuscripts have usually undergone a rigorous or stringent peer review process.

- *Semi-scholarly manuscripts* include research reports, peer reviews, manuscripts, conference papers, and online journal submissions.
- *Non-scholarly manuscripts* include blogs, articles, blog postings, articles for subject or popular magazines.

30.1.2 Writing and publication for high impact journals

The following two elements will guide your writing. 'Publish or perish' holds true in most research environments, but a single publication in a high-impact journal can make a huge impact on one's academic career path. The first component is the *content of the manuscript*. Editors at high-impact journals seek exceptional qualities, especially in two components of a paper: the content and the scientific writing style. When it comes to content, editors of high-impact journals look for innovation and conceptual advancement. The findings must not have been published before; however, not all new concepts merit publication in high-impact journals, where the readership is broad. The work must provide a significant step forward for the field, and also take a new direction.

The second component, the *academic writing style*, can be achieved in the structure of your article with a strong title, abstract, literature review, research methodology, findings, conclusions and recommendations. It is essential to communicate key, self-contained points to the editor, and later to the peer reviewer. Abstracts are usually written in a standard, predetermined structure. The first few lines provide a basic introduction to the field, followed by background on the questions or problems within that field. Next, a specific question is addressed. In the results section of the abstract, some details on the methods used should be provided, but authors should seek to achieve a balance between too much and too little information. Avoid obscurity; you do not want an editor or reader to become frustrated with an abstract that requires multiple reads. Also, do not refer to figures or tables because readers at this stage won't have access to these. If a title catches their eye, they will proceed to the abstract to decide whether to go further with your article. Your work will attract increased exposure if it is featured in an editor's synopsis.

30.1.3 Some pitfalls in publishing in academic journals

Pay attention to the following issues when deciding on a journal for your manuscript. These are only a few drawbacks, and there are probably many more:
- Over-publishing in one peer review journal, which means you have submitted most of your manuscripts to one journal.
- Having more than one paper in a journal volume or in a special issue of a journal.
- Targeting only 'soft journals' to publish in.
- Publishing too much with co-authors.
- Not plotting a 'niche' area for yourself.
- Submitting the same manuscript to two or more journals at the same time, is both unprofessional and unethical.
- If the manuscript is rejected by the editor of one journal, you should not submit the same unrevised manuscript to another journal.
- Submitting an unrevised manuscript to another journal with a different format for manuscripts because you do not think it is worth changing it to conform to the new journal's requirements.

The next section focuses on specific layout or formatting of the article for the peer review journal.

30.2 The format of a scholarly article for a peer review

You may undertake research with the specific intention of submitting the outcome for publication in an academic journal. The acceptance and publication, or even rejection, of your peer review article is determined long before the idea of writing and publishing the article.

Kotze (2007) and Thomas (2013) highlight the following pitfalls or reasons why articles are rejected by leading academic journals:

- The article does not adhere to journal requirements.
- The article does not make an adequate scholarly contribution to the 'body of knowledge' in a specific discipline.
- The theoretical and/or conceptual framework is not well grounded in the research paper and therefore a critical reflection is missing from the article.
- The research methodology or design used is truly inconsistent, or the methods are questionable because of the reliability and validity of the measures used.
- The writing style of the author is poor and lacks coherence, and is not language edited (too many inconsistencies and poor sentence formulation).
- The abstract and article are badly formulated, vaguely written and lack coherence, and do not engage the reviewer's or reader's attention.

The length of most research papers in scholarly or academic journals is roughly 25 to 28 pages or 5,000 to 8,000 in words. The different components, title, keywords, abstract, introduction and discussion are possibly the most important part because these are the 'foundations' on which a reader would be most likely to access the article. It is therefore essential to use effective keywords, a title that grabs the reader's attention, and an engaging abstract, in order to encourage the reader to go further and deeper into the introduction and discussion.

The structural components of an article are discussed in more detail in the sections that follow.

30.3 The title of the article

Authors should always read and study the title requirements of scholarly journals before submitting their work for peer review. Formulate a 'catchy' title which will get the attention of the reader and raise interest in the topic under investigation. Thomas (2013) and Becker (2007) provide suggestions on how to re-align and construct the title of the article clearly, namely:

- ☑ The title should attract the reader's attention.
- ☑ The title should clearly reflect the main theme, issues or position discussed in the article.
- ☑ The title creates expectations about the content of the article.
- ☑ The title should exactly portray or capture the research focus of the study.
- ☑ The title should be explicitly stated in accordance with the required length, as set out in the journal's format specifications.
- ☑ Keywords listed after the abstract should appear in the title.

30.4 **The abstract**

Peer review journals set specific requirements for how the abstract is written. Abstracts must be written as stipulated within a word count of between 200 to 300 words. Peer reviewers first scan the abstract in order to decide whether reading the rest of the article would be meaningful and worthwhile. The **abstract** directs or guides the reviewer or reader as a starting point for the rest of the article. The abstract should provoke the reviewer's or reader's attention to the rest of the article (Arthur, Waring, Coe & Hedges, 2012; Feldman, 2003). Thomas (2013) and Becker (2007) recommend that an abstract should include the following aspects:

- ☑ The abstract should start with a brief theme sentence to orientate the reader to the overall issue addressed in the article. This sentence should grab the reader's attention.
- ☑ The abstract should then indicate the aim or purpose of the study.
- ☑ The academic and/or practical importance of the study should be explained.
- ☑ The research methodology used in the study should be briefly described.
- ☑ The main results/findings of the study should be summarised.
- ☑ A concise conclusion should indicate the contribution made by the study in filling gaps in the literature review.

There are different types of abstracts, namely
- ▶ empirical
- ▶ theoretical/conceptual
- ▶ case study.

30.4.1 **Example of issues in the abstract of an empirical study**

Abstract A **e.g.**

Cooperative learning, as an instructional methodology provides opportunities for students to develop skills in group interactions and in working with others that are needed in today's world. The purpose of this study was to determine the effects of the cooperative learning technique of Teams-Games-Tournaments (TGT) on the achievement, retention, and attitudes toward TGT as a teaching method. A pretest–post-test, quasi-experimental design was used. Data collection instruments, an achievement test (Test of Economic Literacy), an attitude towards TGT, and a retention test were used for the purpose of this study. Results indicated that the achievement test score for the TGT group was 52.99, while the Lecture control group was 50.13. This implies that the TGT group performed better in the achievement test compare to the control group. The retention test for both groups was very similar. The treatment group indicated positive attitude towards TGT as a teaching strategy for economics education (Van Wyk, 2011:183).

30.4.2 Example of issues in a conceptual paper/literature review

Abstract B

Scholars take the view that Afrocentricity is an educational, philosophical and theoretical paradigm. The purpose of this paper is to conceptualise and contextualise schooling in an inclusive education setting, towards an Afrocentric indigenous pedagogy. The Afrocentric canons necessitate a more comprehensive approach that goes beyond questions of what is learned, by whom, and how quickly it is learned, to a consideration of questions of how the knowledge being disseminated is structured and applied in diverse and inclusive classrooms. Indigenous knowledge is often perceived as a set of historical and ancient practices of African peoples, which is the problematic perception of a Westernised viewpoint. Furthermore, the underlying principles, educational value, teaching principles underpinning indigenous pedagogy and the benefits of an Afrocentric-indigenous pedagogy for an inclusive classroom context are explained (Van Wyk, 2014:292).

30.4.3 Example of issues in an abstract in a case study

Abstract C

From the outset, blogs served as personal social networking tools. More recently, blogs have facilitated the formation of online socially networked communities and have thus expanded to offer extensive uses in education. This paper explores the use of blogs to foster e-learning communities in empowering and supporting Postgraduate Certificate of Education (PGCE) students, who were learning to teach Economics education in open distance learning (ODL) environments. A blog for Economics education subject didactics students was created during their teaching practice period. Student teachers were encouraged to post their views on the 'Econblog' as a communicative platform to critically reflect on their learning processes, as well sharing teaching practice experiences to enhance professional growth. Data collected were qualitative in nature, consisting of student teachers' posted reflections and comments on the blog. Findings indicated that the blog as an e-learning tool promoted good relationships amongst student communities, support by exchanging ideas and information on teaching practice, opportunities to interact, and entry to dialogue and reflective practice. Students often talked of challenges faced during teaching practice placements (Van Wyk, 2013:525).

Before you continue with the next section, do the following activity.

Critical thinking challenge

1 After studying the examples of types of abstracts, draw a table of the types of abstracts and describe each one by answering the following questions:
   > What is the problem under investigation?
   > Who are the sample in the study/
   > What is the research method(s) employed?
   > What are the main findings?
   > What is the conclusion or practical implications or applications for theory, policy or practice?
2 After answering the questions, write an abstract for your own research paper of not more than 250 words using the guidelines provided for writing an abstract.

30.5 Keywords

Academic journals set specific requirements on how many keywords should be included in an article. This ranges from six to eight words.

Before continuing with the next section, complete the following task.

Stop and reflect

Download any academic peer reviewed article on your specific topic by using Google Scholar. Do the following with the article:

▶ Study the title of the article and count the words and underline the variables.
▶ Identify the keywords and count the words in the article.
▶ Summarise the components in the abstract of the article.
▶ Identify and briefly report on the background, issue and solution in the introduction to the article.

30.6 Introduction to the article

The introduction is a summary of what, why and how the research is done. The aim of the introduction is to:

▶ Set the tone or point of departure of the rest of the article.
▶ Motivate the reviewer to read, reflect on and provide constructive comments to the author(s) of the article.

Let us look at the main aspects or components when writing the introduction.

30.6.1 Aspects or components of an introduction

According to Kotze (2007), the introduction comprises specific aspects:

▶ Identifying the topic or problem under investigation in the study.
▶ The academic importance and relevance of the study. The introduction raises the reader's or reviewer's interest in the rest of the article. It should implicitly answer the question: 'What is the problem and why would anyone be interested in this article?'
▶ A well-structured literature review which encapsulates recent and previous studies that are relevant to the current research problem.
▶ The specific gaps, contradictions, inconsistencies and disagreements or controversies in the literature review that the current study will address, which explains the study's *main contribution* for undertaking this research.

The introduction then provides a summary of the research problem, the specific research objectives, the context and the units of analysis of the study. The introduction should always clearly indicate the following:

▶ There is *core research problem/question* to be addressed in the study.

An example of core research problem

Over the past two decades, researchers in the humanities and social sciences have shown a growing interest in exploring the concepts teacher autonomy and teaching for transformation (Palmer & Van Wyk, 2013:463).

▶ The *specific research objectives* that will guide your article process. To achieve your research objectives, the main research problem or answering the core research question. According to Kotze (2007), your specific objectives should be aligned to answering the research questions, while other objectives may relate to the gathering of descriptive data or developing a conceptual framework based on available literature.

An example of specific research objective

In this article, we locate our discussion on education within the broader framework of transformation. Autonomous teacher training imperatives for a transformative South African educational system will be discussed. In addition, the autonomy to teach for transformation, as reflected in teacher training practices in a faculty of education, will be analysed. In relation to this, we present the reflections of pre-service teachers in the faculty regarding their views and experiences of their autonomy to teach for transformation during teaching practice sessions (Palmer & Van Wyk, 2013:464).

▶ A description of the *context* in which the study will be located. Contextualise and conceptualise your introduction by writing a brief outline and provide a short explanation of the exact situation in which your study will be located and conducted.
▶ The *units of analysis* of the study refer to the objects under investigation and drawn conclusions (Kotze, 2007; Thomas, 2013; Cohen, Manion & Morrison, 2009). Examples of units of analysis might be teachers, learners, schools, family, community, families, teacher-learner relationships, etc.

An example of unit of analysis

This study advocates that pre-service teachers' emotional intelligence (EI) becomes an indispensible tool in their quest to teach for transformation in South African schools (Palmer & Van Wyk, 2013:463).

Before you move on to the next section, do the following activity.

Critical thinking challenge

After reading and reflecting on the components for writing the introduction, title and abstract of an academic article, do the following:
1 Write your own title (8–15 words), an abstract of 250 words, as well the introduction (800 words), as instructed earlier. Use the following questions to help you with writing the introduction.
  › Why is this problem important or worth researching?
  › How does this research relate to previous research which was reported earlier; how does the research differ from the previous studies; what is the 'gap'; and how will your study try to bring a different solution to the problem?

(continued)

Critical thinking challenge *(continued)*

> What is the objective or hypothesis of the study, and what is the link with theory?

> How does the research design relate to the objectives of the study?

> What are the theoretical and practical implications of the study?

2 Share your title, abstract and introduction with a colleague. Each critique the other's work.

30.6.2 The problem statement and research questions

The problem statement provides an enquiry into a specific problem that the researcher would like to investigate. A research problem is what you are interested in and want to provide a solution to. Usually, a research problem is the focus for the researcher. Kotze (2007) says, for example, that a researcher investigates issues relating to:

- teachers
- conditions they wish to improve
- difficulties they wish to eliminate, or
- questions that need to be answered.

There are specific research questions for:

- experimental research
- content analysis
- ethnographic research
- causal-comparative research
- correlational research
- survey research
- interview research.

What is a good research question?

Here are a few examples of the different types of research questions.

- Does student team achievement produce more satisfactory academic results than the direct instruction method in enhancing student academic performance? (experimental research)

- Are the report's findings of unemployment in rural communities in economics textbooks biased? (content analysis)

- What specific teacher–learner interactions happen in a Grade 6 history classroom during a lesson? (ethnographic research)

- Do male student teachers behave differently from female student teachers in mathematics education situations? (causal-comparative research)

- How can one determine whether a relationship exists between female students in terms of age and ability when learning specific-subject knowledge? (correlational research)

- How do teachers feel about the new school curriculum project for their subject? (survey research)

- How can the principal improve staff morale? (interview research)

In the next section, we focus on aspects or components when doing your literature review.

30.7 Compiling the literature review

Researchers mainly use a desktop-based research method for their literature reviews. This is a critical reviewing process of all literatures on the topic. The researcher critically appraises what is known about the topic and what gaps still exist for further enquiry. According to Fraenkel and Wallen (1990), a literature review is the most important part of writing an article.

It takes time to search and find the appropriate literature for your article. There are three stages for compiling a literature review. Kotze (2007) provides some questions which postgraduate students or novice researchers could use for doing a literature review:

▶ What, why and when is my literature review appropriate?
▶ How should I go about searching for information by using online searches, by identifying key words, and creating a search record?
▶ How should I read, critically, using research techniques by scanning, skimming and understanding my literature review?
▶ What writing style should I use when doing traditional or systematic compiling for a literature review?

There are four stages in compiling a literature review:

> ☑ *Getting information:* Searching and getting the appropriate sources of information.
> ☑ *Using information:* Reading skills, making notes and managing the writing.
> ☑ *Writing the review:* Writing up and critically reflecting on the review.
> ☑ *Proofreading effectively:* Editing your article before submitting to the journal.

30.7.1 Getting information

There is currently a range of information sources available for complex searches. In order to compile a literature review, you first have to register as a library user. You need to contact your institution's librarian for training in the use of their systems. Use the following options to search for the information on which to base your literature review. You can use www. Google scholar.com for your searches. You can start with keywords or with a topic of interest for your article. Your approach to searching for information may combine any number of the following resources:

▶ Library catalogue
▶ Digital library/electronic library
▶ Individual full-text journal databases
▶ Official websites
▶ Online repositories
▶ Bibliographic databases

To extend your search for relevant sources for your literature review, Chapter 8 on doing a literature review, provides a more detailed plan of how to get information.

30.7.2 Using information

After locating the relevant and appropriate sources for your literature review, now the hard part starts. A postgraduate student or novice researcher needs excellent skills in reading, making notes and writing, and in generally managing the literature review process. Some postgraduate and novice researchers may experience the management of the information gathered for a literature review as a challenging and daunting task. At some point in your reading you will need to make notes. There are three main reasons for recording and making notes:

▶ To identify and understand the main points of what you read.
▶ To help you recall what you have read.
▶ To make connections across texts and authors so that you can rearrange them for writing the review.

There are several excellent texts on critical writing skills which take you through the process of constructing good arguments. An **argument** in this section, means putting forward reasons that will influence the reader, supported by evidence. It is a form of scholarly or intellectual engagement with the reader of your article. Your argument should be clear, concise and constructive. It must convince or persuade your reader that your argument is soundly based on evidence which is provided in your article. An argument prompts you to make value judgements about a particular point of the literature. At some point in your writing, you should be critical of your own writing. Remember that to critique academically means to give both positive and negative points about an article, and to recognise the strengths and weaknesses of the article. Critical analysis, in the academic context of scholarly writing, is usually a positive constructive process involving reflection and evaluation of any text.

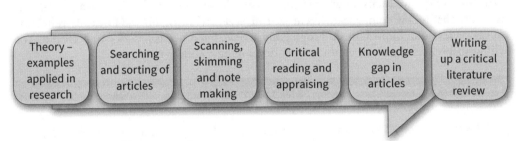

FIGURE 30.1: At typical literature review process

Figure 30.1, shows an overview of a typical process for a literature review. In this process, it is essential to be analytical in your reading. This means all the time you are evaluating what you read, reflecting on what is there in order to appraise the published work. Critical reading for review of an article requires you to apply critical thinking skills. Critical thinking is a process of assessing another author's position, arguments and conclusions about the topic. After scanning, skimming and critically reading the article, you start writing up your literature review.

30.7.3 Writing the review

Before you start writing up the literature review, you need to be able to write a **paragraph**. You will write several paragraphs in your literature review for your article. Osmond (2013:88) defines a paragraph as:

> ... a logical sequence of grammatically complete sentences. These sentences express one idea or make one point in considerable detail. All the sentences in a paragraph should contribute to this idea or point. They might potentially expand on it, but will not deviate from it.

There are general rules for putting sentences together which also apply when you are forming paragraphs; these must be clear, simple and to-the-point. It seems obvious and we assume that a paragraph is made up of clear and well-written sentences. But there is much more to constructing good academic paragraphs, than just writing sentence after sentence in a sequence of ideas and reflections. Most academic paragraphs on average use between 45 to 75 words. This means paragraphs will often consist of between three to seven well-structured sentences. Paragraphs should discuss one particular aspect, or make one point. You could support a point or reinforce it with relevant detail, references and good examples. Paragraphs should not ramble on a range of subjects but stick to the point of the topic.

We now turn to the different types of literature reviews. There is much literature on different types of reviews one can use. Chapter 8 of this book provides a more detailed discussion of each of the mentioned types of literature reviews, but here are the two most important ones:
▸ Traditional literature review
▸ Systematic literature review.

After employing either a traditional or **systematic literature review**, writing the paragraphs and putting paragraphs together is a serious and challenging exercise. We are now moving on to developing a good academic writing style.

In this section, we focus on what it takes to develop a good academic writing style. The examples that follow compare different writing styles. Writing up and critically reflecting on the review is an important skill for a good article, but it needs practice to perfect it. You will probably spend your academic career developing a good writing style.

Examples of good writing styles	Examples of poor writing styles
Previous research work conducted by Van Wyk (1997) shows that …	Van Wyk (1997) said …
Another study by Botha and James (2009) asserts that …	Botha and James said (2009) …
Current research (Spencer, 2013) indicates that …	Spencer (2013) wrote…

Chapter 29 of this book provides a more detailed explanation of good writing styles by using signposting language and logical connectors.

A key technique that comes into its own paragraphs is the use of **signposting language**. Signposting language is not an official grammatical term but only an academic writing tool to enhance your writing style. This means it refers to words and phrases that give your reader a sense of the direction your arguments is going in. While grammatical correct sentences and paragraphs can make effective points on their own, signposting language adds and extra level to an essay, providing the author with the change to tell the reader various things.

Using signposting language

Attitudes and beliefs about teaching in general are also largely derived from classroom experience. Teachers who have been consistently unsuccessful in helping students from educationally disadvantaged backgrounds to attain a high standard of learning, for example, are likely to believe these students are incapable of academic excellence. If, however, those teachers try a new instructional strategy and succeed

(continued)

in helping such students learn, their beliefs are likely to change. Again, the point is that evidence of improvement or positive change in the learning outcomes of students generally proceeds, and may be a pre-requisite for, significant change in the attitudes and beliefs of most teachers.

Learning outcomes are broadly construed in the model to include not only cognitive and achievement indices, but also the wide range of student behaviour and attitudes. They can include students' scores on teacher-made quizzes and examinations, as well as results from standardised assessments and achievement tests. But they can also include students' attendance, their involvement in class sessions, their classroom behaviour, their motivation for learning, and their attitudes toward school, the class, and themselves. In other words, learning outcomes include whatever kinds of evidence teachers use to judge the effectiveness of their teaching (Guskey, 2002:384).

Before you continue, one particular issue, **referencing**, is very important in academic writing. When you present your article with evidence from your reading, you must provide references in it. Referencing is a broad chronological system used to make clear to the reader when you are bringing other people's ideas, words, quotes, and concepts into your academic writing. It provides proof of sources used in your literature review process. There are different referencing styles to use. If you submit an article without proper referencing it could be interpreted as plagiarism. There are several software programs to detect where you copying another author's thoughts, ideas and writings in your own work. Remember, it is advisable to study academic journals' specific referencing style and plagiarism information before writing the in-text citations or bibliography of your article.

Chapter 28 of this book provides a more detailed discussion of different referencing styles and issues of plagiarism.

30.7.4 Proofreading and editing

While this section summarises some ideas in writing up information, it also focuses on the key part of academic writing, namely **proofreading**. A brief comment on effectively proofreading the article is necessary here because it can make the difference between whether the article is accepted or rejected for publication. Effective proofreading and quality editing have to be built into effective planning and time management of the article. Proofreading is a tool for 'tidying up' or double checking the article to make sure that it is correct and ready for publication in the journal. The purpose of proofreading and editing is to make sure your work is presented in the best way possible for publication, and is *absolutely necessary*.

In the next section, we focus on the research design and methods use in an article.

30.8 Research methodology

This part of the article describes or explains how the study will be designed, conducted and aligned for the purpose of researching the phenomenon in the study. Chapters 1 to 18 discuss in detail all that research entails, from research paradigms to questionnaires as data collection instruments.

In this chapter an overview, from research paradigm to the design of a questionnaire as a data collection instrument, is explained.

The research methodology consists of the following components:

▶ research paradigm
▶ research questions

- type and purpose a research design
- data collection instruments
- procedures to follow in the process.

In this section the research methodology typically includes the research paradigm, research questions, design, and sampling, research instruments for data collection and procedures, and procedures for reporting the results of the study.

30.8.1 Research paradigm

Leedy and Ormrod (2001:346) define methodology as both "the collection of methods or rules by which a particular piece of research is undertaken" and the "principles, theories and values that underpin a particular approach to research". Becker (2007:35) argues that methodology is the frame of reference for the research, which is influenced by the "paradigm in which our theoretical perspective is placed or developed". The most common definitions suggest that *methodology* is the overall approach to research, linked to the paradigm or theoretical framework, while the *method* refers to systematic modes, procedures or tools used to collect and analyse data.

Paradigm A

The researcher conducted an empirical investigation by employing quantitative and qualitative research approaches. A structured questionnaire and focus group interviews were used to investigate the impact of using social media as a teaching tool on student learning.

According to the literature, matching paradigms and methods implies that some paradigms have similarities and some of the research methods can thus be combined to gather the data.

Paradigm B

The researcher explores use social media as an e-learning tool on student learning by employing structured questionnaires and focus group interviews to collect data for the investigation.

30.8.2 Research design

The literature indicates that the research design is the plan of action which directs you in finding your way in executing your plan for the research methodology. This plan of action suggests the types and purpose of selecting the research design(s) for the article. There are different approaches in research design:
- Qualitative research design
- Quantitative research design
- Mixed methods research design.

Chapter 10 discusses in detail the types of approaches to research design.

30.8.3 Research questions

We further discuss and describe the steps followed in the execution of the study and also briefly justify the research methods used (Maxwell, 2013; Arthur, et al., 2012; Henning, et al., 2005). Once the research questions are formulated, researchers want to turn them into as good a question as possible. Jesson, Matheson and Lacey (2011) identify several characteristics of good research questions:

▶ The research question is *feasible* – it can be investigated within time and resources constraints.
▶ The research question is *clearly formulated* – most people would agree on what the key words in the question mean.
▶ The research question is *significant* – it is worth investigating because it will contribute important knowledge about the human condition.
▶ The question is *ethical* – no harm will result and confidentiality issues will be adhered to in the study.

In the next section, we are focus on sampling as very important component of the article.

30.8.4 Sampling

Sampling describes the target population(s) of and context(s) in which the study will be conducted. In this section, sampling is the units of analysis of the study. Chapter 13 describes in detail concepts such as population, sampling and sample size of the study. The purpose and motivation must be clearly stated when deciding on a specific sampling for your article. The sampling describes the following in detail:

▶ the rationale for the specific sampling method
▶ the description of the sampling frame
▶ a description of how sampling units will be selected
▶ the demographic profile of the respondents who will be participate in the study.

Sampling and sample size   e.g.

Only 108 PGCE students (n=108) at an institution of higher learning participated in this project. A purposive sampling of participating secondary schools was selected which teach Economics as a school subject. Of the 24 participating secondary schools (Grades 8–12) 10 were public high schools (Grades 8–12), four were private high schools (Grades 8–12) and 10 were combined schools (Grades R-12). There were 88 female and 20 male student teachers, ranging in age from 20 to 32 years (mean age = 21.23, SD = 3.2). This sample reported the following ethnicities: 40 per cent black, 9 per cent Coloured, 12 per cent Asian, and 39 per cent white. These students were enrolled in the PGCE programme sequence, and they were participated in the community engagement project for one year (Van Wyk, 2012:33).

30.8.5 Data collection and procedures

The purpose of selecting data collection instruments is very important for the research design of the article. From the outset describe the data collection instrument(s) which will be employed in your study and mention the specific pretesting method(s) used. Then describe how the data will be collected and analysed. In your description of data collection instruments, provide a clear description and motivation for the data collection method. Chapters 14 to 18 explain in detail what type of data collection instruments you can use. In these chapters, surveys, structured questionnaires, focus groups, face-to-face interviews and observations are all discussed.

Data collection procedure

A literature review of different research studies was done on the use of economics cartoons as a teaching strategy. The researcher designed a closed structured questionnaire for the purpose of collecting data. This 21-item questionnaire was employed as an instrument to collect information. Later, face-to-face interviews were conducted, recorded and transcribed into themes and sub-themes from the participants' responses to the different questions in the interview schedule (Van Wyk, 2011:117).

30.8.6 Ethical considerations

You already know that before you begin with the study, consent has to be obtained from the participants. The purpose of the study and confidentiality of the participants has to be explained. The researcher must obtain informed consent, assure participants of the confidentiality of all information, and that their participation is voluntary and they can still opt out at any point if they are no longer comfortable with answering any questions or participating in the study. Participants also need to be assured that in all data collection phases their information will be kept confidential and solely used for the purpose of conducting research, and will not be disclosed to any party for any reason.

30.9 The results

30.9.1 Presenting and reporting quantitative data

When presenting quantitative data resulting from analysis, they can include descriptive and inferential analysis. To do your statistical analysis of the captured data, the statistical package for the social sciences (SPSS) can be used. For descriptive statistical analysis, you can include frequency tables, histograms, and pie charts. Examples of descriptive statistical analysis are computed in the form of mean scores and standard deviations. For inferential statistical analysis, you can include t-test, chi-square, correlations and frequency tables with mean (Cohen, et al., 2009). Chapter 22 provides a detailed presentation and discussion of quantitative statistical analysis.

30.9.2 Presenting and reporting qualitative data

There are many different theoretical perspectives which are used to analyse qualitative data. These include action research, grounded theory, narrative enquiry-based research, phenomenology, life histories, observations, ethnography, case studies, and interviews. When conducting a qualitative study, the following four main components should be considered when reporting on the interviews (Henning, et al., 2005):
▶ The research relationship you establish with those you study
▶ The selection of settings or individuals you decide to observe or interview and what other sources of information you decide to use
▶ Data collection, which concerns the way in which you gather or collect the data/information you will use
▶ Data analysis, which relates to what you do with the information to make sense of it.

The qualitative data analysis is primarily an inductive process of organising the data into themes or categories and identifying patterns among or relationships between the categories. Chapter 25 provides a detailed presentation and discussion of qualitative statistical analysis.

30.10 Discussion

In the discussion section, using the data, you present answers to the research questions and/or hypotheses stated. In doing so, it is very important to refer back to the literature review process, so that you draw out clear comparisons and contrasts between what your research has found, what the literature review suggested, and what you might expect of not expected.

Kotze (2007) and Becker (2007) summarise the discussion section of an article as follows:
- The aim of purpose of the study is provided
- The importance and relevance of the study to the topic is emphasised
- The main findings relating to each stated research objective or hypothesis is provided
- Possible explanations for unexpected findings are suggested
- The practical implications of the study are discussed
- The limitations of the study are highlighted
- Insightful opportunities for future research on the topic are offered.

In the next section, we focus on the important component of the conclusion of the article.

Critical thinking challenge

1 With reference to the opening case study, Dr James Doctoral is busy writing the research methodology and main findings of his article. How would you advise him on the following questions:
   > What type of research paradigm can he choose and why?
   > What type of research design can he use for his article and why is it important for this particular study?
   > What are the features or components of the research methodology for the study?
2 Use and compare a downloaded article from Google Scholar to advise Dr James on the following components in the article:
   > research design
   > data collection methods
   > population and sampling
   > data analysis and procedures
   > ethical considerations.

30.11 Concluding remarks and writing up the research

Your concluding remarks are vital as a summary of the whole study. You should be able to reflect on your research and say what was good and/or bad about it, and suggest possible future research topics. The conclusion does not have to be long, and should include the following components:

- ☑ **Refer back to the introduction**, where you set out the purpose of your research study. The background on the area in which you are interested, the issue that you identified relating to that background and your undertaking to address the a solution (BIS).
- ☑ **Chart the progress of any change** in your questions as the research project progressed.
- ☑ **Briefly summarise the main findings** and outline in a page or two any dilemmas, questions and paradoxes that still exist.
- ☑ **Acknowledge your project's or research study's limitations** and weaknesses, which towards the end of the project you may have realised were fairly major.
- ☑ **Outline any recommendations** for those who have been participants in your research or policy implementation.
- ☑ **Outline topics** for possible further research.

Table 30.1 provides a list of issues to be included in your conclusion and suggests a number of phrases you could use when writing the conclusion of the article.

TABLE 30.1: Summary of main issues in concluding and some useful phrases

Issue	Possible phrases
Briefly summarising	▶ This project/paper/article investigated/explored …
Revisiting the background, issue and promised solution (BIS)	▶ The issue of … is of central importance to one's understanding of …
	▶ Despite this, little attention has been paid to …
	▶ In this research study, the researcher will endeavour to …
Evaluating the actual solution	▶ The findings of this study reveal that …
	▶ The findings support the idea that …
	▶ This study confirms earlier work by … and, further, suggests that …
	▶ It can be concluded that …
Limitations	▶ The research was restricted by …
	▶ The research focused only on …
	▶ Ethical considerations precluded the use of a control group …
	▶ The use of an interpretative approach promotes an understanding of specific … However, caution should be exercised in generalising these findings to the broader field of …
Recommendations for further research	▶ Further work needs to address …
	▶ A cohort study over three years, and involving …, would address the stability of the findings outlined here.
	▶ Research on the specific role of … would be of value in …
	▶ It would be interesting to assess the effects of …
	▶ It would be useful to compare the experiences of boys and girls.
Implications and recommendations for policy and practice	▶ Given the range of views around the issue of …, the evidence from this research suggests that …
	▶ My research implies that policy would tend to favour …

Conclusion

In this chapter, we have built on concepts discussed in all the other chapters in this book, where research philosophies, planning, designing and conducting educational research, analysing data collecting through fieldwork, reporting and disseminating research findings were explored. Most postgraduate students and some novice researchers remember how difficult it is if you do not have the academic writing skills to condense Master's or doctoral research work into an academic journal article. This is a huge challenge for those who have not aquired the academic writing skills or experience, to publish their research in a journal. Excellent academic writing is underpinned by good arguments which are a form of scholarly or intellectual engagement about a topic. This chapter provides guidelines for sharpening your academic writing skills towards publishing excellent articles. These guidelines provide a format, elements and examples which guide you in your academic writing process. Finally, the chapter provides sections on writing a concise title, writing the abstract, identifying the keywords, formulating the introduction, critically reflecting on the literature review, constructing the research methodology, capturing the main findings, discussing the findings, writing up the conclusions, and finally, proofreading the article.

Closing activities

Reflection questions

1 What is academic writing and how can this skill be sharpened to improve your writing for publication?
2 What are the elements pertaining to the introduction and why is an introduction so important in an article?
3 In relation to the structure of an academic article, briefly describe how you would plan each of the components of the article.

Practical applications

4 After further reading on writing for publication, you have been selected to make a postgraduate presentation to your colleagues on the structure of an academic article. What would be your main theme and points of departure? What applicable examples would you use to illustrate your ideas? How would you prepare yourself to answer specific concerns and uncertainties that would inevitably arise? Write up your detailed plan for this presentation.
5 Write an essay on the components to consider in writing the conclusion for your article.

Analysis and consolidation

6 Analyse and present your views on the scholarly value and relevance of writing an academic article for publication.

Bibliography

Arthur, J., Waring, M., Coe, R. & Hedges, L. 2012. *Research methods and methodologies in education.* London: Sage.

Becker, HS. 2007. *Writing for social scientists: how to start and finish your thesis, book and article* (2nd ed.). Chicago, IL: University of Chicago Press.

Cohen, L., Manion, L. & Morrison, K. 2009. *Research methods in education* (6th ed.). London: Routledge.

Elsevier Publishers. *Teaching and Teacher Education.* Elsevier Publishers: London, UK. http://mc.manuscriptcentral.com/cthe. Accessed 29 July 2014.

Feldman, D.C. 2003. The devil is in the details: Converting good research into publishable articles. *Journal of Management*, 30(3):1-6.

Fraenkel, J.R. & Wallen, N.E. 1990. *How to design and evaluate research in education*. New York: McGraw-Hill.

Guskey, T.R. 2002. Professional Development and Teacher Change. *Teachers and Teaching: Theory and practice*, 8(3/4):381-391.

Henning, E., Gravett, S. & Van Rensburg, W. 2005. *Finding your way in academic writing* (2nd ed.). Cape Town: Van Schaik.

Jesson, J.K., Matheson, L. & Lacey P.M. 2011. *Doing your literature review*. London: Sage.

Kotze, G. 2007. *Guidelines on writing a first academic quantitative article* (2nd ed.). Pretoria: Department of Marketing and Communication Management, University of Pretoria.

Leedy, P.D. & Ormrod, J.E. 2001. *Practical research: planning and design* (7th ed.). Upper Saddle River, NJ: Merrill Prentice-Hall.

Maxwell, J.A. 2013. *Qualitative Research Design: An interactive approach* (3rd ed.). London, UK: SAGE.

Osmond, A. 2013. *Academic Writing and Grammar for Students*. London, UK: SAGE.

Palmer, J.M. & Van Wyk, M.M. 2014. Exploring Pre-Service Teachers' Views Regarding Teaching for Transformation: A Proposed Autonomous-Transformative Framework for Higher Education Institutions. *Mediterranean Journal of Social Sciences*, 4(13):463-473.

Thomas, G. 2013. *How to do your research project: A guide for students in education and applied social sciences* (2nd ed.). London: Sage.

Van Wyk, M.M. 2011. The use of cartoons as a teaching technique in the Economics classroom. *Journal of Social Science*, 26(2):117-130.

Van Wyk, M.M. 2011. The Effects of Teams-Games-Tournaments on Achievement, Retention, and Attitudes of Economics Education Students. *Journal of Social Science*, 26(3):183-193.

Van Wyk, M.M. 2012. Measuring Student's Attitudes to Economics Education: A factorial analysis approach. *Journal Social Science*, 31(1):27-42.

Van Wyk, M.M. 2013. Exploring Students Perceptions of Blogs During Teaching Practice Placements. *Mediterranean Journal of Social Sciences*, 4(14):525-533.

Van Wyk, M.M. 2014. Conceptualizing an Afrocentric-Indigenous Pedagogy for an Inclusive Classroom Environment. *Mediterranean Journal of Social Sciences*, 5(2):292-299.

Index

Page numbers in italics refer to figures

communication strategies 502–503
comparative data analysis 420–424
complete observer 285, 286
complete participant 283
componential analysis 467–469
concepts
  defined 187–189
  dimensions 191
conceptual framework 305, 306
concluding remarks, writing 573–574
conducting surveys 252–254
confidence interval estimation 416–417
confidentiality 126, 306, 310
conscious sampling bias 237–238
consolidation of data analysed 489–490
constant comparison analysis 462–464
constructive alignment of major research designs 166
constructs see concepts
construct validity 204
consumers of research, identifying 501–502
content validity 203
context
  importance in conversing with women 89–91
  influence on findings from pilot studies 382–386
control variable 194
convergent parallel mixed methods design 182
correlation analyses with SPSS 444–445
correlative data analysis 424–430
covert observation 210
criteria for establishing Afrocentric research methods 16
criterion validity 204
critical analysis in literature reviews 137
critical approaches in social sciences 46–47
critical paradigm 60–61
critical research
  and Afrocentric paradigm 65–66
  aims 61–62
  defined 58–59
critical research and education research 64–65
critical theory and research 62–63

cultural interview 299
culturally sensitive research approach 305
cumulative frequency curves 410
cumulative frequency tables 409

D

DAFOR scale *198*
data
  from focus group interviews 505
  interpretation 158–159
  from interviews 504–505
  from literature reviews 506
  from observations 506
  obtained from measurement or counting variables 196–197
  presenting and reporting 572–573
  types, subdivisions *197*
data analysis 32, 35–36, 157–158
  in ethnographic design 178
  in narrative design 174
  in phenomenology 176
  statistical vs non-statistical methods 27
data collecting instruments 275–277
  surveys 276–277
data collection 35, 156–157
  and procedures 571, 572
  quantitative research reports 486–488
  subjectivity vs objectivity 26–27
data collection methods
  Delphi 378
  in phenomenology 175–176
  unique nature 209
data consolidation 479, 480, 489–490
data cooking 127
data triangulation 290, 292, 486
data trimming 127
deduction 32–33
deduction vs induction 25–26
Delphi data collection method 378
demands on researchers 107–108
dependent variable 194
descriptive research 155
  quantitative research reports 481
descriptive statistics, computing with Microsoft Excel 405–406
diaries 212–213
direct consent 118
disconfirmation 105
discussion sections of journal articles 573

dispersion or disparity, measures 399–405
documentary approach 213
domain analysis 465–466
double-barrelled questions 326
dual moderator focus groups 342
dueling moderator focus groups 342

E

edited topical life histories 213
editing articles for publication 569
electronic surveys, weaknesses 249
embedded design 182
emic perspective 283
empiricist research paradigm see positivist research paradigm
enquiry domain, locating Afrocentric research in 14–15
epistemological differences between positivism and interpretivism 23–24
epistemology 7, 60, 261
error, measurement of 200–201
estimation of population parameters 415–417
ethical issues
  in action research 74
  interview method 306–307
  questionnaires 330–332
  resolving 34–35
ethical procedures 572
ethics
  contexts 108–109
  defined 98
  demands on researchers 107–108
  ethically reflexive research, challenges 104–107
  objectivism and subjectivism in research 100–101
  potential issues in educational research *99–100*
  reflexivity 103–107
  studies that contributed to 101–103
  value freedom 103
ethics in human sciences research
  human participants 113–114
  (*see also* major ethical values and human participants)
ethnography in qualitative research design 177–179
ethnomethodology 46
etic perspective 283
evaluation of literature 137

O

objectives of qualitative study 500
objectivism and subjectivism in research 100–101
objectivity vs subjectivity, and data collection 26–27
observation 30
observation method
    application and suitability 290–291
    described 281–282
    field notes 286–287
    fieldwork setting, description 288–289
    strengths 291
    types of observation 282–286
    weaknesses 293
observations, quantitative 277
observer-as-participant 285, 286
ogives 410
one-group pretest–post-test design 266–267
online focus groups 342
ontological differences between positivism and interpretivism 23
ontology 7, 60
open-ended questions in questionnaires 319–320
operationalisation 191–193
ordinal level of measurement 392
ordinal scale of measurement 198, 199
ordinal scales 274
organisation and graphing of quantitative data 406
orientations, different 73
orphans and other vulnerable children (OVCs) 311
overt observation 210

P

paradigms in research, overview 59–61
participant-as-observer 283, 284
participant observation 209–211
participation observation 283–284
participatory action research (PAR) 71
Pearson's Chi-square test 429–430
Pearson's linear correlation coefficient test 424–428
Pearson's measure of skewness 404–405
peer review articles, formats 560

people, process for surveying 252
people with disabilities, ethical guidance for interview method 310–311
percentages calculations with SPSS 440–441
personal (structured) interview 299
personal response 253
phenomenological perspective 290
phenomenology 45–46, 175
phenomenon 216
philosophy of science 216–217
piggyback focus groups 343
pilot studies
    advantages 379
    challenges 381
    context, influence on findings 382–386
    defined 372
    Delphi data collection method 378
    disadvantages 379–380
    exclusions 382
    as feasibility studies 372–373
    findings 381–386
    instances where they are impossible 380–381
    internal validity, role in improving 377–378
    vs main study 373–374
    misconceptions 375–376
    qualitative pilot studies, findings 382
    reasons for conducting 376–377
    vs small sample study 373–374
    value of 374
pilot tests for questionnaires 330
plagiarism
    avoiding 517–519
    consequences of 516
    defined 514–515
    reasons for 515
    software for detecting 530–533
    sources that can be plagiarised 519–520
    strategies for avoiding 519
    types of 515–516
    (see also citation; citing within text)
point estimation 416
population 226
population and sampling frames 239–240
population size or number as basis for studies 167

positivism 216
positivist research methodology see hypothetical-deductive process
positivist research paradigm 21–22, 60
positivism vs interpretivism 22–25
positivist and interpretive research, criteria for choice between 28–29
postmodern feminism 82
post-test-only design with non-equivalent group 267
praxis 70–72
preliminary information gathering 30
pretest-only design 266
pretest–post-test control group design 267
pretests see pilot studies
primary data, collecting 246
probability sampling 234–235
problem conceptualisation 480
problem statement of qualitative research report 500
problem statements, in writing for publication 565
professional ethics 256
proofreading 569
pseudonyms 125
psychological attributes of researchers 29
purpose of qualitative study 500
purposive sample 235–236
purposive sampling 230

Q

qualitative data analysis
    ATLAS.ti 470–472
    constant comparison analysis 462–464
    domain analysis 465–466
    exponential analysis 467–469
    hermeneutic units 471
    keywords-in-context 468–470
    models 461–466
    qualitative research approach 460
    software packages 470–472
    thematic analysis 464–465
    validity 460
qualitative data collection methods
    diaries 212–213
    documentary approach 213
    edited topical life histories 213